HELLENIC STUDIES SERIES 88

LOVERS OF THE SOUL,
LOVERS OF THE BODY

Recent Titles in the Hellenic Studies Series

Audible Punctuation
Performative Pause in Homeric Prosody

Who Am I?
(Mis)Identity and the Polis in Oedipus Tyrannus

Demetrios of Scepsis and His Troikos Diakosmos
Ancient and Modern Readings of a Lost Contribution to Ancient Scholarship

Homer's Thebes
Epic Rivalries and the Appropriation of Mythical Pasts

The Cypria

Homeric Imagery and the Natural Environment

Achilles Unbound
Multiformity and Tradition in the Homeric Epics

In Her Own Words
The Life and Poetry of Aelia Eudocia

Particles in Ancient Greek Discourse
Exploring Particle Use across Genres

Agamemnon, the Pathetic Despot
Reading Characterization in Homer

Singer of Tales
Third Edition

The Tears of Achilles

Equine Poetics

The Art of Reading
From Homer to Paul Celan

Masterpieces of Metonymy
From the Ancient Greek World to Now

The Aethiopis
Neo-Neoanalysis Reanalyzed

Kinyras
The Divine Lyre

The Theban Epics

http://chs.harvard.edu/chs/publications

LOVERS OF THE SOUL, LOVERS OF THE BODY

PHILOSOPHICAL AND RELIGIOUS PERSPECTIVES IN LATE ANTIQUITY

Edited by
Svetla Slaveva-Griffin
and
Ilaria L. E. Ramelli

Center for Hellenic Studies

Trustees for Harvard University

Washington, D.C.

Distributed by Harvard University Press

Cambridge, Massachusetts, and London, England

2022

Lovers of the Soul, Lovers of the Body: Philosophical and Religious Perspectives in Late Antiquity

Edited by Svetla Slaveva-Griffin & Ilaria L. E. Ramelli

Copyright © 2022 Center for Hellenic Studies, Trustees for Harvard University

All Rights Reserved.

Published by Center for Hellenic Studies, Trustees for Harvard University, Washington, D.C.

Distributed by Harvard University Press, Cambridge, Massachusetts, and London, England

Production: Jen Jackowitz

Cover design: Joni Godlove

ISBN: 978-0-674-24132-9

Library of Congress Control Number: 2022933367

Contents

Contents

In memoriam
John D. Turner (1938–2019)

Acknowledgements

THE STUDY OF PHILOSOPHY and religion in late antiquity is more often than not considered mutually exclusive. We are grateful for the free spirit and intellectual generosity of our contributors who, although coming from the two sides of the divide we endeavor to bridge in this volume, and from ten different countries and diverse schools of thought, embraced our idea and made it a reality. The same spirit of sharedness brought Ilaria L. E. Ramelli and me together to foster this study, from inception to completion. I am in awe of her strength and endurance. We are also grateful to the anonymous reviewer for Harvard University Press for recognizing the merits of the book and for the enthusiastic suggestions as to how to enhance them. We warmly welcome the publication of *Christian Platonism: A History* (ed. A. J. B. Hampton and J. P. Kenney) Cambridge 2021, which appeared during the final production stage of this book. None of the above would be possible, of course, without the boundless energy and dedication of Casey Dué as the Executive Editor for the Center for Hellenic Studies, and Jill Curry Robbins and Angelia Hanhardt as the production team at the Center for Hellenic Studies and Harvard University Press. Mark Buzbee and Donald Griffin helped during the initial preparation of the manuscript, and Kathryn Gannon gave it her all, in both expertise and time, during the project's final stages. The book has also benefitted from sponsorship by the Alexander von Humboldt Foundation and the College of Arts and Sciences at Florida State University. Most of all, I, Svetla, am thankful to my husband for teaching me that love is life, and I, Ilaria, am thankful to all noble friends and colleagues, to those who help me at the University, at home, and in my scholarly travels, and above all to Heaven's awesome sustainment. We are also saddened by the passing away of John D. Turner whose piece on the *Platonizing Gnostic Views on Soul and Body* in this volume captures the spirit of his enormous scholarly contribution and his shining humanity. We dedicate this book to him.

Svetla Slaveva-Griffin and Ilaria L. E. Ramelli

List of Abbreviations

This list includes only the standard abbreviations of main reference sources.

ACO   Swartz, E. and J. Straub, eds. *Acta conciliorum oecumenicorum*. Berlin, 1914–.

BA   *Bibliothèque Augustinienne*. Paris, 1939–.

BG   Berolinensis Gnosticus 8502. Text and translation in: Schmidt, C. and J. C. Hinrichs, eds. *Alten Petrusakten Zusammenhang der apokryphen Apostellitteratur nebst einem neuentdeckten Fragment*. Leipzig, 1903.

CCSL   *Corpus Christianorum: series Latina*. Turnhout, 1953–.

CCSG   *Corpus Christianorum: series Graeca*. Turnhout, 1977–.

CH   Nock, A. D., ed. *Hermès Trismégiste. Corpus Hermeticum*, vols. 1–2. Translated by A.-J. Festugière. Paris, 1946.
        Festugière, A.-J., ed. and trans. *Hermès Trismégiste. Corpus Hermeticum*, vols. 3–4. Paris, 1954.

CPL   Dekkers, E. et al., eds. *Clavis patrum Latinorum*. 3rd ed. Turnhout, 1995.

CSEL   *Corpus scriptorum ecclesiasticorum Latinorum*. Vienna, 1864–.

CSCO   *Corpus scriptorum Christianorum orientalium*. Leuven, 1903–.

DK   Diels, H., and W. Kranz, eds. *Die Fragmente der Vorsokratiker*. 3 vols. 6th ed. Berlin, 1951–1952.

GNO   Jaeger, W., H. Langerbeck, H. Dörrie, et al., eds. *Gregorii Nysseni opera*. 10 vols. Leiden, 1960–1998.

GCS N.F. *Die griechischen christlichen Schriftsteller der ersten drei Jahrhunderte*. Leipzig and Berlin, 1897–.

IG   *Inscriptiones Graecae*. Berlin, 1924–.

LSJ   Liddell, H. G., R. Scott, and H. S. Jones, eds. *A Greek-English Lexicon*. Oxford, 1996.

NHC   Nag Hammadi Codex.

OC   Des Places, É., ed. and trans. *Oracles Chaldaïques*. Paris, 1971.

PG   Migne, J.-P., ed. *Patrologia Graeca*. Paris, 1844–1864.

SEG   Hondius, J., H. W. Pleket, R. S. Stroud, et al., eds. *Supplementum epigraphicum Graecum*. Amsterdam, 1923–.

SVF   von Arnim, H. F., ed. *Stoicorum Veterum Fragmenta*. 4 vols. Stuttgart, 1903–1905.

List of Figures

Practical Notes

THE DIVERSE NATURE OF *Lovers of the Soul, Lovers of the Body: Philosophical and Religious Perspectives in Late Antiquity* necessitates a few practical notes. We have strived to give the book the unifying feel of a monograph by applying the 'house style' of the Center for Hellenic Studies to the extent that the conventions of the particular field of a chapter allow. For this reason, we have also combined the bibliography of all chapters in one at the end, with the hope to provide another tool for further research of the subject. We followed the anonymous reviewer's suggestion to include the abstracts of the chapters in order to make their diversity more accessible. All dates not marked with the designation BCE are in the Common Era. In order to enhance the readership of the book, we have translated and transliterated all Greek and Latin phrases, in the main body of text and in the notes, which are less than three words long, unless the strictly philological nature of the discussion demands their appearance in the original. The orthography of Greek and Latin phrases is preserved throughout the book when the author has deemed it necessary to cite the original text in parentheses next to its translation. For the same purpose of facility, we have fully translated the titles of the ancient works throughout, and we have used their standard editions, unless otherwise noted. If there is more than one edition or another cause for confusion, the name of the editor or the location of a text in a large series is given after the numerical reference to the text, in a self-explanatory manner. The full bibliographical information of the primary sources can be found in the combined bibliography at the end. We did not separate the primary from the secondary sources in the bibliography in order to make the references user-friendly for the interdisciplinary audience, who may not be intimately familiar with specialized titles across the board. Critical editions, commentaries, and translations are ordered in the bibliography by the name of their modern authors. The references to Gerson's *The Cambridge History of Philosophy in Late Antiquity* include volume number before the page number. For example, Gerson 2010:1.1–10 refers to the first ten pages of the first volume of Gerson's edited work. The chronological number of Plotinus' *Enneads* is included in the notation only if it is germane to the discussion at hand.

Introduction

At the Crossroads of Two Pathways

SVETLA SLAVEVA-GRIFFIN

THE TITLE OF THIS BOOK, *Lovers of the Soul, Lovers of the Body*, is meant to place you, the reader, at the crossing of two pathways often traveled, to explore, and, ultimately, to reach an understanding of the relationship between the soul and the body, a point of contentious debate in late antiquity. The one, older path follows the well-known Platonic dichotomy between soul and body, while the other no-less-traveled path treads the scholarly division between the ancient philosophical and Christian views on the subject. We, the editors of this volume, met at these crossroads,[1] each coming from a different direction, each taught to heed the signposts that dictate which of the two distinct and time-worn paths we should travel separately to find the ostensibly different destinations we sought. But, instead of continuing our journeys alone, we stopped to consider whether or not banding together might be worthwhile. Were our goals so different? Could we not find understanding of this difficult and evasive subject together? This *aporia* fueled our curiosity. Deciding that the ground between the traditionally separate pathways appears to approach a place that unites our seemingly disparate objectives, we set out on a new path, one explored through this volume, and one on which we hope you will embark as well. As the subtitle of the book—*Philosophical and Religious Perspectives in Late Antiquity*—elucidates, our primary goal is to bridge the gap between the two most influential perspectives on the concepts of soul and body in the transformative times of the first six centuries of the Common Era, or in other words, from Philo to Olympiodorus.

1. Choosing a Path Forward

The two traditional pathways are presented diachronically in the allegory that begins this introduction, in order to emphasize the conceptual and historical

---

[1] We did so at the conference on "Neoplatonism and the East," organized by Menahem Luz at the University of Haifa in March 2011.

sequence between the two, but the order in which the two come to our attention, depends on the direction from which we start our journey. One can easily switch paths, as shown by the scholarship, uncovering new views from different directions. Readers have most likely arrived at the same crossroads at which we, the editors, met, but from the opposite direction to their familiar path, tracing the roots, as it were, instead of the branches of the most fundamental of themes in the ancient quest for knowledge; namely, seeking to understand the relationship between what is visible and impermanent, and what is invisible and permanent within us. These are the two principles, or as Socrates calls them in the *Gorgias*, the two pillars of human existence: body and soul, in this order.[2]

The relationship between these two pillars was argued over again and again, from many different perspectives in antiquity, as it is today. *Lovers of the Soul, Lovers of the Body* offers a new take on what may be seen now to be an old chestnut, not in the hopes of putting an end to an apparently endless debate, but in the hopes of showing that this old chestnut has in fact a complex, multi-disciplinary structure, albeit in need of a facelift, the essence of which cannot be found by any singular approach. In its place, we need a dynamic search, aided by many different and, perhaps new, approaches, along and between the pathways above. Our book offers an up-to-the-moment "instantiation" of this dynamic model. Our readers, presently at the crossroads between the two, are invited to follow the traffic in the direction of their interests, either by exploring new paths or by redirecting old ones.

2. Two Scholarly Perspectives, One Goal

The times have passed when the examination of the soul-body relation in ancient philosophy and theology was monochromatic and did not allow any gradations between black and white. *Lovers of the Soul, Lovers of the Body* is intended to bridge the current gap in the existent scholarship between the philosophical and religious perspectives on soul and body in late antiquity in a polychromatic scheme. Up-to-date there is one study that attempts to present the history of the soul-body relation in ancient philosophy somewhat comprehensively. In an edited volume, D. Frede and Reis (2009) trace the conceptual development of the subject from the Presocratics to Hellenistic philosophy. The collection skips altogether the Neoplatonic contribution to the subject to end with a limited three-chapter preview of its Christian permutations. Although not completely unexpected—considering the still compromised philosophical status of Neoplatonism in some academic circles today—the omission is nevertheless surprising in light of

---

[2] *Gorgias* 464a1–b8, especially *Gorgias* 464a1: σῶμά που καλεῖς τι καὶ ψυχήν. Cf. *Alcibiades* 130c1–3.

the resurgent interest in Neoplatonism as a philosophically respectable object of study in the last two decades, generously estimated. Our volume aims to fill in this omission by presenting the development of the subject in late antiquity. Instead of a strictly diachronic organization, however, we have opted for a more flexible thematic framework, which allows us to show that the polarity between the concepts of soul and body, as well as between the philosophical and religious schools of thought on these concepts, does not necessarily produce two disjoint universes (or two pathways that never cross).

The scholarship on late ancient philosophy, even when aimed comprehensively, tends to showcase the predominant Neoplatonic interest in the soul and its role in the soul-and-body compound at the expense of the body. The same predilection, but in the opposite direction, can be noted in the scholarship on early Christian theology and Patristic philosophy. The strong impetus of Christianity to redeem the ideological value of the body tends to sidestep the influence of the Platonic understanding of the soul.[3] Specialized studies of this nature bring to light the inner workings of each perspective.

Recently the publication of *Plato and the Divided Self* (Barney et al. 2012) has shown that even a central, divisive difference in perspective—in this case, one in which soul receives all the credit and the body all the blame for the virtuous ups and appetitive downs of the embodied life—is problematic even within Plato's own works. It is commonly agreed that the soul-body divide deepens in the Platonic tradition and becomes even more accentuated by the ideological rift between "pagan" philosophy and theology. This trend is recently invigorated by Karamanolis's summation of the early Christian views on the body as "an instrument of reason," which significantly differ from their (Neo)Platonic and Gnostic counterparts.[4] Most recently, Kukkonen and Remes, in a similar multiauthored venue, take a second, more penetrating look at "Neoplatonism's many ties with Western religious life," whereby the leading philosophical school of late antiquity weaves religion into its highly metaphysical structure while influencing, in its turn, the monotheistic religions of the Mediterranean.[5] Our book follows and extends this recent trend by comparing, contrasting, and at times polemicizing the plurality of pagan and Christian views on the soul-body relation in late antiquity in order to construct a broad, polychromatic image with which a reader may glimpse the "big picture" in real time, through diverse scholarly approaches. This thematic coherence, we hope, makes the book greater than the sum of its chapters.

---

[3] Karamanolis (2013:181–186) notes that there is no single Christian view on the soul–body relation.

[4] Karamanolis 2013:210.

[5] Kukkonen and Remes 2016:139.

We know that a single-author or coauthor venture cannot do justice to the rich territory of the soul-body relation in late antiquity because it could ultimately fall into the same constrained tracks we aspire to avoid. What we want, instead, is a polyphony of perspectives on the understanding of the soul-body relation, which revisits and probes the standard antithetical categorization of the two concepts, and the linear opposition between the philosophical, or "pagan," and religious, or "Christian," views of them.

We also understand all too well that this kind of thematic "hypermobility" comes only after—and thanks to—the valiant effort of the early scholarship to lay out the two traditional pathways. With gratitude to it, we build upon the separate treatments of the philosophical or religious perspectives on the concepts of soul and body in late antiquity in the pursuit of a full-bodied understanding of the two, as opposed to the microscopic examination of their specific natures, found in the authoritative histories of late ancient and early medieval philosophy by Armstrong (1970), Gerson (2010), and the *Cambridge History of Christianity* (2006 and 2007).

We have attempted to achieve our primary goal, as stated at the end of the opening paragraph of this introduction, with the following six contributions to the study of philosophy and religion in late antiquity and the field of Hellenic studies in general: (1) it fills a gap in the recent scholarship on the concepts of soul and body in antiquity; (2) it situates and reevaluates the question of the soul-body relation in the larger intellectual and religious milieu of late antiquity; (3) it offers a multidimensional representation of the dialogue between imperial, Neoplatonic, Hellenistic-Jewish, and Christian perspectives on soul and body;[6] (4) it relates the soul-body question to the issue of soteriology, which becomes prominent in late antique (Neo)Platonisms of all stripes—pagan, Jewish, and Christian; (5) it reaffirms the importance of the body in the intellectual discourse of late antiquity; and (6) it charts future directions of research on the interaction between philosophy and religion in late antiquity.

3. Two Concepts, One Explanation

In conceiving this volume, we took our cue from the consonance of two signature statements, defining the possible ways of life the two pillars of human existence respectively induce. The first derives from Plato's programmatic treatment of

---

[6] With this all-inclusive approach, we share the unifying spirit of Gerson's argument (2010:1.1–10) to view all shades of Platonisms, including Middle Platonism and Neoplatonism, as Platonisms in order to acknowledge their common ancestry. We do so only partially, however, because we do not want to strip these descendent schools of their distinctive character. For the latter, see Remes and Slaveva-Griffin 2014:3–5.

the soul-body relation in the *Phaedo*.[7] The other features Philo's propaedeutic exegesis of man's understanding of God in his allegorical commentary on the Genesis, entitled *On the Unchangeableness of God*.

In the *Phaedo*, Socrates describes the true philosopher's life as a form of purification preparing the soul's departure from the body as a liberation from the fetters of corporeality in pursuit of pure knowledge.[8] One who does philosophy correctly, he explains, is "a lover of wisdom" (*philosophos*) and does not fear death, while one who is distressed by the thought of dying is "a lover not of wisdom but of the body" (*philosômatos*).[9] When the time comes, Socrates continues, the soul of the true philosopher departs to "that place which is, like itself, invisible, divine, immortal, and wise," whereas the soul of the lover of the body "is weighed down and dragged back into the visible world, through fear, ... and hovers about tombs and graveyards" (*Phaedo* 81a4–d1). The lover of the body (*philosômatos*) Plato juxtaposes to the lover of wisdom (*philosophos* or *philomathês*) whom he implicitly portrays as a lover of the soul (*philopsukhos*). To drive his point home, he charts the main course of all Platonic psychology to come:

> But no soul which has not practiced philosophy (μὴ φιλοσοφήσαντι), and is not absolutely pure when it leaves the body, may attain to the divine nature; that is only for the lover of wisdom (τῷ φιλομαθεῖ). This is the reason, my dear Simmias and Cebes, why true philosophers (οἱ ὀρθῶς φιλόσοφοι) abstain from all bodily desires and withstand them and do not yield to them.
>
> Plato *Phaedo* 82b10–c5[10]

Plato is explicit that the philosophical way of life (and, to be precise, the Platonic way of doing philosophy) is the only way of obtaining pure knowledge about reality and our place in it. With this rationale, he conflates the lover of wisdom with the lover of the soul. The former is prerequisite for the latter and both states are stepping stones towards Plato's celebrated prescription that the ultimate goal of human existence is to become like a god or to be godlike as much as possible (ὁμοίωσις θεῷ κατὰ τὸ δυνατόν, *Theaetetus* 176b1). Consequently, the

---

7 Cf. *Phaedo* 62a1–84b7.

8 Not coincidentally, Plato's literal expression for a true philosopher is "one who does philosophy correctly" (οἱ ὀρθῶς φιλοσοφοῦντες) as repeatedly emphasized in the *Phaedo*. Cf. *Phaedo* 67d8, 67e5, 69d2–3.

9 *Phaedo* 68b9–10: οὐκ ἄρ᾽ ἦν φιλόσοφος ἀλλά τις φιλοσώματος;

10 *Phaedo* 82b10–c5: εἰς δέ γε θεῶν γένος μὴ φιλοσοφήσαντι καὶ παντελῶς καθαρῷ ἀπιόντι οὐ θέμις ἀφικνεῖσθαι ἀλλ᾽ ἢ τῷ φιλομαθεῖ. ἀλλὰ τούτων ἕνεκα, ὦ ἑταῖρε Σιμμία τε καὶ Κέβης, οἱ ὀρθῶς φιλόσοφοι ἀπέχονται τῶν κατὰ τὸ σῶμα ἐπιθυμιῶν ἁπασῶν καὶ καρτεροῦσι καὶ οὐ παραδιδόασιν αὐταῖς ἑαυτούς. Translation is by Tredennick 1989.

soul-body relation in Plato (and later in Platonism) outgrows the individual's parameters to express the macrocosmic relation between man and the divine. Plato's successors in late antiquity wholeheartedly embrace this idea and make it the foundation of their ethics, psychology, and cosmology.

From an anthropological perspective, the key notion in Plato's conceptualization of the relation between man and the divine is articulated in his qualification that we can attain the coveted godlike state only to the extent that is possible (κατὰ τὸ δυνατόν). The implication of this qualification is twofold: first, it generally restricts that we can attain this state only to the extent that our human nature allows us; and second, it further narrows it down to the specific restriction that each one of us can attain this state only to the extent that each one of us can. The latter also implies that not everyone can even minimally attain this state, without fully committing to the Platonic way of life. This implication portrays the nonpopulist character of Platonic aretology, which has nothing to offer to the lover of the body. This motif echoes throughout Platonic psychology with the resoluteness of a verdict.

In his exegesis on the Genesis, Philo, as a representative of Hellenistic Judaism—close to the so-called Middle Platonism—takes to heart the inclusive spirit of populist psychology. He suppresses, although does not completely erase, the Platonic valorization, embedded in the opposition between the lover of the soul and the lover of the body. In the principal postulate of Genesis 1:26 that man is created after the image of God, Philo discerns the deep roots of man's anthropocentric discursivity on which he elaborates in *On the Unchangeableness of God* 51–69.[11] He is comfortable to soften the contradiction between Numbers 23:19, which proselytizes that "God is as a man" (ὡς ἄνθρωπος), and Deuteronomy 8:5, which warns that "God is not as a man" (οὐχ ὡς ἄνθρωπος ὁ θεός).[12] Philo does so by looking back to the Platonic position in the *Phaedo*, and he does not de-ontologize the dichotomy between the lover of the soul and the lover of the body, but gives it an epistemological lift:

> Among men some are lovers (φίλοι) of soul, some of the body. The companions of the soul (ψυχῆς ἑταῖροι) who are able (δυνάμενοι) to associate with the intelligible and incorporeal natures, do not compare the Existent to any form of a created thing. ... But those who have concluded a treaty and a truce with the body (συμβάσεις καὶ σπονδὰς πρὸς σῶμα θέμενοι) are unable (ἀδυνατοῦντες) to doff the garment of

---

[11] Cf. Philo *On the Creation of the World* 69 and *Sacrifices of Abel and Cain* 94–96.
[12] *On the Unchangeableness of God* 51–69.

the flesh and see a nature uniquely simple and self-sufficient in itself, without admixture and composition.

Philo *On the Unchangeableness of God* 55–56[13]

The passage casts Plato's pronouncement in the *Phaedo* in a new light. Philo is aware of—and most likely fond of—the Platonic position. He accepts the ontological antithesis between the intelligible and the sensible, and supports the premise that some people are able, by nature, to grasp the highly abstract concepts pertinent to the intelligible and some are not. As a result, some people are simply unable to overcome their anthropocentric and anthropomorphic thinking to conceive of the divine in any other form than human. In comparison to Plato's tongue-in-cheek qualification that people can strive to attain a godlike state only "to the extent that is possible" to them, Philo spells out the qualitative division in the human ability to perceive the divine.[14] If we dig deeper into Philo's epistemic division between the two, we discover its ethical and soteriological roots. But we can also detect a note of tolerance in his categorization. At the turn of the first millennium, he stands in the beginning of the ongoing task of Christian philosophers to provide a conceptual mechanism for bringing the lover of the body to the same level of understanding of the divine as the lover of the soul. As Philo puts it, the anthroposomatic thinking about the divine is the elementary lesson (*isagôgê*) needed by those who cannot otherwise conceive of the divine.[15]

Regardless of its overarching intelligible framework, the corporeal nature of a human being has to be reckoned with. The late antique philosophical and Christian traditions go about this in what seem to be two separate ways, which we may dub as philosophical and religious psychology.[16] Upon closer inspection, however, the two do not appear to be entirely dissimilar. Despite their doctrinal difference on the question of whether the physical world is created metaphorically or literally, the physical world is still an expression of the divine for both ancient philosophers and Christian theologians.[17] The human body as a part of the natural world is also then a part of the divine script.

---

[13] *On the Unchangeableness of God* 55–56: τῶν γὰρ ἀνθρώπων οἱ μὲν ψυχῆς, οἱ δὲ σώματος γεγόνασι φίλοι· οἱ μὲν οὖν ψυχῆς ἑταῖροι νοηταῖς καὶ ἀσωμάτοις φύσεσιν ἐνομιλεῖν δυνάμενοι οὐδεμιᾷ τῶν γεγονότων ἰδέᾳ παραβάλλουσι τὸ ὄν, ... οἱ δὲ συμβάσεις καὶ σπονδὰς πρὸς σῶμα θέμενοι, ἀδυνατοῦντες ἀπαμφιάσασθαι τὸ σαρκῶν περίβλημα καὶ μόνην καὶ καθ᾽ ἑαυτὴν ἀπροσδεᾶ καὶ ἁπλῆν φύσιν ἰδεῖν ἀμιγῆ καὶ ἀσύγκριτον. Translation is by Winston 1981.

[14] Also treated by Ramelli 2014.

[15] Philo *On the Unchangeableness of God* 52–53.

[16] After Bréhier's original coinage of the term (1925:160). See Chapter 11 below.

[17] The latest trend in Neoplatonic studies focuses specifically on the contribution of natural philosophy, or as the ancients knew it, of physics to metaphysics; see Chiaradonna and Trabattoni 2009:1–8 and Linguiti 2014.

In fact, we can think of the human body as the Vitruvian man, inscribed in the cosmos. When ensouled, the living body becomes a centrifugal miniature model of the underlying principles of the universe, which brings them to the surface, so, to imagine, allowing examination. From this perspective, the living body is the final ontological outpost of the divine. It represents a self-enclosed and self-regulating system to the extent—I will repeat—"to which it is possible," considering its impermanent material nature. From a tomb of soul, to recall Plato's much-ploughed etymology in the *Cratylus*, the living body becomes a sign of soul as captured in Plotinus' analogy of ensoulment to a beautiful house and its architect, and even a proof of soul's divine nature as figuratively revealed by the resurrection of Christ's body from the tomb in which it was laid.[18]

Both philosophers and theologians in late antiquity grapple with the notion of the necessity of the body, but on their own terms, unifying or apologetic. They both understand that it is impossible to know the soul, as expressed in the human being, without knowing the body. To this, they offer their respective solutions with a varying degree of approving or disapproving emphasis on the place of the body in the embodied state of the soul. Even the most diehard critics of the body, such as Iamblichus or the Gnostics—to give an example from each side—accept the body, however imperfect or "dim" (*amudrôs*), as the lowest and yet necessary link in the ontological chain of cascading universal principles.[19]

About six hundred years after Plato and two hundred years after Philo, Plotinus defines the sole reason for the existence of the body as to provide a place (*topos*) for the soul in the physical world.[20] The body, he further conceives, is a product of soul, which is suspended in a balance between external ensoulment by the World Soul and internal ensoulment by the individual soul.[21] From this centripetal perspective, the living body turns out to be nothing else but a state of soul, as Labrune has pointedly observed.[22] This position is also shared by Origen, the Christian Platonist, as the treatment of Gregory of Nyssa's and Origen's views on the preexistence of souls in Chapter 14 elicits. The two pillars of human existence, as defined by Plato and his successors, presented in this volume, delimit the topography of human psychology from Plotinus to Olympiodorus, and from Philo to Nemesius of Emesa. If one of the pillars is overlooked, the other one loses its real-time foundation and becomes a fossilized museum specimen, conducive for detailed structural examination, but unable

---

[18] Respectively, Plato *Cratylus* 400b11–c10, Plotinus *Enneads* II 9.18.4–8, and Origen *Against Celsus* II 61–62. Cf. John 20:25. See Chapters 1 and 6 below.

[19] Cf. Plotinus *Enneads* II 4.10.28–31, 12.26–28; II 9.4.9–10; VI 6.18.22–24; and Iamblichus *On the Mysteries* II 10 [93] and III 28 [167]. For the Gnostics' views, see Chapter 5 below.

[20] *Enneads* IV 3.9.20–23.

[21] *Enneads* II 9.7 and IV 3.12.35–39.

[22] Labrune 1992:27–47. See p. 18 below.

to enact the holistic entity of the human being as a symbiotic multilayered compound of soul and body. This issue of perspective is examined in Chapter 13, which raises the question of where the soul stops and where the body begins. The fruitfulness of such a nondivisive and label-free approach is showcased in the last chapter of the book, dedicated to the philosophical and religious roots of sacred architecture.

4. Our Rationale

In order to give breadth and depth to the subject, we have commissioned three kinds of chapters, as permitted by the individual topics. To the first group belong the survey chapters, such as the treatments of Plato, Aristotle, and Augustine, offering a complete overview of the concepts of soul and body in these philosophers. The second group contains the chapters that offer a *status-quo* analysis of the soul-body relation, either in individual authors or across schools of thought, such as the discussions of Galen, Gnosticism, Gregory of Nyssa, Evagrius, Porphyry, Proclus, and Nemesius of Emesa. The chapters in the third group critically reevaluate well-established scholarly labels and positions, such as the examinations of Philo, the Middle Platonists, Plotinus, Origen, Athanasius, Gregory of Nyssa, Zosimos, and Olympiodorus.

Going back to the polyphonic and polychromatic rationale of the book, we would like to express our warm gratitude to our contributors, an international team of leading experts who enthusiastically accepted the challenge to participate in a volume that puts their names in company that is familiar and not at the same time. The stimulating and, at times, provocative treatments they have given us in return are gifts we will never be able to repay. The authors more than delivered what we could have only dreamed to receive, and we wholeheartedly acknowledge their individual contributions. In order to emphasize the multiplicity of shared perspectives on the unifying topic of soul and body, however, we identify in what follows, the individual chapters not by author, but by topic, and thereby perspective. This kind of presentation, we think, strengthens our call for an understanding of the soul-body relation in late antiquity outside of the traditional divide between scholars of ancient philosophy and scholars of Christian theology. It also presents the volume without borders, so to speak, as a unity of diverse perspectives. At the end, this method, we envision, turns an edited collection into a cohesive book, with an introduction and a conclusion.

The volume consists of nineteen chapters, organized in four parts: the first part introduces the concepts of soul and body in Plato and Aristotle, the second and third parts present the diversity of perspectives on the relation between the two entities respectively in imperial and late antique Platonism, and Hellenistic

Jewish and Christian Platonism. We use the above terms only descriptively—not taxonomically—as a road map of the existent scholarship. The last part offers points of conclusion and future lines of research.

The first part presents the foundation of the concepts of soul and body in Plato and Aristotle as the groundwork of the future developments of the two concepts in late antiquity. While using Plato's views on the subject as the starting point from which the book unfolds is self-explanatory, Aristotle's appearance warrants a brief explanation. In the history of late antique psychology, the Platonic position on the immortality of the soul wins the palm of victory across the board. Aristotle's view of the soul as the form and the active principle of the body that coexists and terminates with the body's destruction is, at wholesale, less appealing to the later generations of philosophers. His understanding of the soul as a network of different faculties, however, finds much fertile ground in them. The first two chapters systematically reconstruct the complexity of Plato's and Aristotle's views on the subject with a special emphasis on the living being as a phase of the psychic continuum that does not presuppose a radical separation between soul and body, and on soul as a noncomposite substantial being representing the principle of life.

The second part presents the polyphony of perspectives on the soul-body relation, in a roughly diachronic order, from Galen to Zosimos of Panopolis, with the Gnostics and prominent Middle Platonists and Neoplatonists in between. The chapters methodically examine different layers in the understanding of the human being as a compound of soul and body from Galen's cautious treatment (Chapter 3), to Plotinus' and Olympiodorus' ameliorative or "moderate" understanding of embodiment (Chapters 6 and 9), to the emphatic denial or elevation of the body, respectively, in the Gnostics (Chapter 5) and in Zosimos (Chapter 10). The conceptual interest in the body also culminates the continuously sharpened focus on the topic of the soul-body conjunction, from the more conceptual treatments in the Middle Platonists (Chapter 4) to the more technical treatments in Porphyry (Chapter 7) and Proclus (Chapter 8). The chapters demonstrate the wide-ranging understanding of the soul-body relation in imperial and late antique philosophy. While the opposing views of the lovers of the soul and the lovers of the body mark the two ends of the spectrum, the majority of views straddle a fine line in explicating the psycho-physical complex of the human individual. This line of thought emphasizes the paradigmatic significance of the soul, without excluding the body.

In a similar vein, the third part of the book directs its attention to the Hellenistic Jewish and Christian views on the soul-body relation, from Philo of Alexandria to Nemesius of Emesa. The growing interest in the body as philosophically redeemable concept in the beginning of the first millennium makes its debut in Philo's response to the Stoic corporealistic position on the soul in favor of the Platonic dualist psychology (Chapter 11). An even more poignant perspective on the soul-body relation addresses the pivotal role of the body in Christian psychology. The closer examination of Origen's and Athanasius' treatment of soul and body argues for a more nuanced sensitivity to the conceptual tension between the Christian and Platonic views on the soul (Chapter 12). The cautiously "Platonic" elements in the psychology of the early Christian thinkers gain more traction, with Plotinus' body-soul-mind model, in Gregory of Nyssa and Evagrius (Chapter 13). The complexity of the soul-body relation makes a new turn with Gregory of Nyssa's views on the preexistence of both soul and body (Chapter 14). An explicit illustration of the gradual, as opposed to the lapidary, fusion of Platonic and Christian tenets is best offered in Augustine's views on soul and body, as documented in his early works (Chapter 15). A later example of such transformative fusion, in which Christian thinkers make their mark on the long-standing philosophical debate about the method by which the soul relates to the body, is found in Nemesius' reception of Porphyry's view on the subject (Chapter 16). The continuous fusion of "pagan" and "Christian" perspectives, presented in the third part of the book, culminates in their figurative embodiment, from Porphyry's allegorical interpretation of Homer's Cave of the Nymphs to Nero's *Domus Aurea*, Hadrian's Pantheon, and early Christian architecture (Chapter 17).

The chapters in the second and the third part of the book follow the same trajectory, connecting and at times blurring the differences between lovers of the soul and lovers of the body. Both parts conclude with chapters on the heightened physical presence of the body in the long history of the soul-body relation in antiquity. The installments in both parts elicit parallel developments that make the traditional division between "philosophical" and "religious" views on soul and body less accurate and prepare the ground for questioning the viability of such a division in the conclusion.

One of the unifying themes, emerging in more than a half of the chapters, is—to quote the anonymous reviewer of the manuscript—"polemic or, perhaps better, apologetic which is centered either on the soul or the body, found in Christian and non-Christian authors alike." The theme is first detected in Aristotle's integrative understanding of the relation between soul and body in Chapter 2, offering an alternative to Plato's dualistic model, presented in Chapter 1. Chapter 3 introduces Galen's interest, as a philosopher, and his skepticism, as a physician, in the Platonic top-down understanding of the soul. Chapters 5 and 6 create a conceptual dialogue between the Gnostics' condemnation of the body and its ameliorative treatment in Plotinus and Origen. Following Plotinus' less extreme treatment of the body, the authors of both chapters urge scholars to pursue a more nuanced evaluation of views that may seem rhetorically or argumentatively augmented. Chapter 6 demonstrates that Plotinus' criticism of the Gnostics is a criticism—and a warning for those in his audience with similar aspirations—of taking a principal position such as Plato's less charitable attitude towards the body to an extreme. The same call for a balanced attitude towards the body is also issued by Origen, Plotinus' older contemporary. Chapter 7 zooms in on the stratigraphy of the relation between soul and body in Porphyry, revealing the robust attempts of one of the most prolific Neoplatonists at solving the difficulties of this relation from various angles and with differing emphases. It examines the epistemic and rhetorical limits of the Neoplatonic understanding of the soul's ontological relation to the body.

Chapter 11 presents the reverse of the apologetic perspective of Plotinus' treatment of the Gnostics in Chapter 6. It shows that, despite his undeniable debt to Stoicism and Platonism, in his views on the soul, Philo creates a hierarchy according to which Revelation presides over the other schools of thought among which Stoicism is at the bottom. Chapter 12 argues that a strict antithesis cannot be drawn between the philosopher Origen and the theologian Athanasius on the grounds of their use of Platonism. Instead, we need to adopt the label-free attitude, following the model of other fields of study. Platonism was, so to speak, in the air, and—in the author's words—"one who talks like a Platonist in order to think like a Christian is not, in the intellectual sense, a colleague of Plotinus."[23] Nor was he, I would add, an enemy to Plotinus. Chapter 13 employs this kind of sensitivity to show the multiperspectival views of Plotinus and the Cappadocians in constructing different but compelling models of the interaction between mind, soul, and body.

Chapter 16 illustrates the virtuosity with which later Christian writers, such as Nemesius of Emesa, navigate through the long philosophical legacy of examining the soul-body relation. They vet, with passion, the different explanatory models put forth by the ancient thinkers in search of the one that best fits their theological landscape. Not surprisingly, this is the model Porphyry sketches in the *Sentences* and *Miscellaneous Investigations*—namely, that the soul, as an intelligible and incorruptible entity, "is bound by the body in its relationship and inclination towards something," while it remains altogether uncompounded with it and thus impassible.[24] Placing himself at the crossing of the two pathways this book presents, Nemesius offers a paradigmatic model of how to navigate them without rejecting or getting stuck in the one or the other. With Porphyry's help, Nemesius ascribes the above position to Ammonius, "the teacher of Plotinus,"

---

[23] See p. 251 below.
[24] Nemesius *On the Nature of Man* 41 in Sharples and Van der Eijk 2008:83, cited on p. 355 below.

and conceptualizes on his theological terms that the relation between soul and body is reciprocal to the relation between a lover and a beloved woman in which the soul, as the lover, is bound to the body, as the beloved woman. This conclusion, implied in the title of Chapter 16, marks the crossing of the two pathways in the book. "The lovers of the soul" and "the lovers of the body," as identified in the title of the book, do not stand in opposition to each other. As the two peacocks on the front cover, they face each other in a constant dialogue that brings them together in order to move them forward. I will return to this point in the general conclusion of the book in Chapter 18.

Reflecting on the contribution of the present volume to the advancement of an integrative approach to the study of late ancient philosophy, Chapter 19 presses the strategic question of what imperial and late ancient (Neo)Platonism is. It highlights the importance of bridging the philosophy-theology divide and the ensuing specialized compartmentalization by offering one such unifying line of future research. In the chapter, as the last installment in the collection, my coeditor passionately argues that Hellenistic Jewish and patristic philosophy should be studied inseparably from imperial and late ancient philosophy.

The book presents the understanding of human psychology in late antiquity, with no labels and without borders. We invite the reader, both the expert and the enthusiast, to crisscross the two major pathways in the collection in pursuit of new crossroads and greater common grounds.

PART I

PLATO AND ARISTOTLE
ON SOUL AND BODY

1

Plato on Soul and Body

Luc Brisson

Abstract: When discussing the body, one situates Plato, by a kind of conditioned reflex, on the side of Christian asceticism and the separation established by Descartes between space and mind. It is true that for Plato, the body can be an obstacle to knowledge, but it is never condemned as such: the body is not opposed to the soul, although it is considered inferior to it. When the soul is incarnated, it needs the body, since it is by means of the senses that the soul knows. In addition, maintenance of the body in the individual and the city is necessary for its moral development, while once the body it inhabits is destroyed, the soul moves to another body that manifests the quality of that soul. One can therefore understand why, especially in the *Timaeus*, Plato takes an interest in the constitution of the body and its maintenance.

PLATO DEFINES HUMAN BEINGS by their soul (*Alcibiades* 130c1–3). This entails several paradoxical consequences, but not oblivion or even contempt for the body. Indeed, during its earthly existence, the soul must inhabit a body that is in the best possible state. This is why, in the *Timaeus*, the constitution of that body is described with a great deal of care, so as to avoid the illnesses that might handicap and destroy it. The soul cannot ignore the body, with which it interacts, and which, by means of sense perception, allows a living being to maintain constant relations with its environment. Moreover, the possibility for a soul to move from one body to another entails important consequences in a human being's relations with the animal world, and thereby a change in individual and social way of life. Thus, the body plays an important role in cosmology, biology, politics, and ethics: this is what the current chapter seeks to show.

In his work, Plato defends a philosophical doctrine, characterized by a twofold ontological revolution. First, the world of particulars perceived by the senses, in which we live, is a mere image of a world of intelligible realities (or

Forms), which, as models of sensible particulars, constitute genuine reality. Unlike sensible things, the Forms possess their principle of existence within themselves. Second, man cannot be reduced to his body, and his true identity coincides with what we designate by means of the term "soul"—whatever the proposed definition of the term may be—which accounts for all motion, both material (growth, locomotion, etc.) and immaterial (feelings, sense perception, intellectual knowledge, etc.), not only in man, but also within the universe. Throughout the history of philosophy, this twofold revolution has enabled the specificity of Platonism to be defined.

And yet, the definition of human beings by their soul has the greatest consequences from an ontological and a social viewpoint. From an ontological viewpoint, since the same type of soul is present in the gods and in human beings, the opposition between mortals and immortals no longer holds. The Platonists' goal of assimilation to divinity is the most obvious proof of this.[1] From a social viewpoint, the status of women undergoes a revolution. If human beings are defined by their body, a clear distinction must be drawn between women, whose role is to bear and raise children, and men, who must work to feed their wife and children, and who must fight to protect them. In Plato, the definition of human beings changes. Human beings are living beings—that is, the temporary conjunction of a soul and a body. The body, which is made up of the four elements (fire, air, water, and earth), and is dissolved after a certain number of years, is merely a temporary vehicle. Thus, it is the soul's excellence that defines the place and role of human beings in society, and no longer their body, endowed with male or female gender.

1. What Is a Living Being according to Plato?

Consequently, Plato calls "living beings" those that possess a body and a soul: "The combination of a soul and a body, is what is called a living being ..." (*Phaedrus* 246c5). This definition seems simple and clear, but upon closer inspection, things become more complicated, for in Ancient Greek, the term *zôion* is leaden with an insurmountable ambiguity: it does not allow a distinction to be made between "living being" in the broad sense, and "animal."[2]

By definition, all living beings possess a "body" (*sôma*), which is made up of the four elements: fire, air, water, and earth. Because all bodies have come into being, none is indestructible. The body of certain living beings, however, will not be destroyed, not because of their nature, but because of a decision of

[1] Sedley 1997, Mahoney 2005.
[2] Brisson 1997a.

the being who has fashioned them.[3] That decision enables a distinction to be drawn between living beings according to whether or not they have an indestructible body.

The four elements from which the body is composed are subject to mechanical motions, due to the fact that they differ in forms and size. Yet, if we go no further, the problems multiply: (1) we cannot assign an absolute origin to these motions, for we are then faced by an infinite regression; (2) nothing guarantees that this motion will not stop; and (3) above all, one would have to admit that everything is the result of chance.[4] To ensure that movement has genuine perpetuity—that is, to ensure it has neither beginning or end—and that it exhibits the genuine order necessary for life to appear and be maintained, one must, according to Plato, suppose that movement has a self-moving principle, the "soul" (*psukhê*), which is guided by a higher faculty, the "intellect" (*nous*). This principle must have two characteristics: (1) it has to be incorporeal; and (2) insofar as the soul belongs to another, separate type of reality, it can only come from outside to take up residence in the body, which it moves.

On a very general level, the "soul" (*psukhê*) is defined as the self-moving principle of all movement, psychic as well as physical. This has the following consequence: immortality must be accorded to the entire soul (*Phaedrus* 245d–246a). By definition, the soul has neither a beginning or an end, so that it can be concluded that it is immortal. This, however, applies to the soul as a principle, not to the individual embodied soul, which, as we shall see, seems to lose its identity at the end of each cycle of ten millennia, after which it falls back into anonymity, before finding a new identity within a new cycle.

2. The Soul as an Invisible Force Moving a Body

It is above all in the central myth of the *Phaedrus* (245c–247e) that the soul is described as a traveling entity. In this magnificent passage, Plato describes the ascent of human souls, which follow the procession of the gods and daemons in the sky to the outer rim of the sphere that constitutes the body of the world, in order to contemplate the intelligible realities above it. In this cosmic journey, the soul exhibits two sets of features:

1. As a "reality" (*ousia*), the soul can be considered, "by definition" (*logos*), a principle of motion and thus of life. It can therefore neither be born nor die. Indeed, if the soul did cease or die, all things in the world would cease or die.

---

[3] *Timaeus* 41a–c.
[4] *Timaeus* 52d–53b.

2. The soul is by nature a "composite power" (*sumphutos dunamis*). Both in gods and in men, it includes three elements. Plato does not give an analytically deduced description of the structure of the soul; he limits himself to comparing the soul to a chariot drawn by two horses that are led by a charioteer. In light of other Platonic dialogues, the charioteer can be identified with "intellect" (*nous*), and the two horses with "spirit" (*thumos*) and "desire" (*epithumia*). "Intellection" (*noêsis*) is the highest faculty of the soul, and intellect has the Forms as its objects. There can be no intellect without a soul (*Philebus* 30c), and soul must be guided by its own intellect (*Timaeus* 90a–e). In fact, the history of a soul is determined by the quality of the exercise of the activity of its intellect. On earth, this activity finds itself in competition with that of "spirit" (*thumos*) and of "desire" (*epithumia*); but by distracting the soul from its exercise of the intellect, these two parts of the soul have an influence on the activity of the intellect. The term "part" (*meros*) does not have a material meaning here, but indicates an aspect, or rather a capacity, of the soul.

Importantly, the *Timaeus* establishes a hierarchy among living beings, since, in the final analysis, any mythical construction whose purpose is to influence human behavior cannot do so without first establishing a hierarchical system.[5] The highest rank in this system is occupied by gods and daemons, followed, in order: by human beings (men and women); then by the animals that live in the air, on earth, and in the water; and, at the end, by plants. This hierarchy is based on two criteria: (1) the quantity and the quality of the relations between the soul and the intellect; and (2) the nature of the body that the soul enables to move or to change spontaneously. The first criterion establishes an impassable boundary between plants and the rest of living beings, whereas the second one establishes another barrier, just as impassable, between the gods and daemons on the one hand, and the rest of living beings on the other.

3. The Soul as a Permanent Inhabitant of a Divine Body

Plato gives the following definition of a god: "an immortal living being, which has a soul and a body, both naturally united forever" (*Phaedrus* 246d1). Yet there are several kinds of gods. First of all, there is the universe, a body shaped like a sphere; the celestial bodies, made up of fire; and the traditional divinities, also

---

[5] Brisson 2003.

endowed with a body, although we do not know what it is made of. In the middle, between human beings and the gods, one finds the daemons, who also possess a body. The bodies of the gods and the daemons are not in themselves indestructible, but they will not be destroyed, as a function of the will of the Demiurge who made them. What is more, the gods, whose body cannot be destroyed, cannot assume another appearance (see *Republic* 380d–382c); in other words, they cannot metamorphose themselves. The soul of gods and daemons is thus always associated with the same body.

The world, which is unique, has a body shaped like a vast sphere, without organs or members (*Timaeus* 33b–34a). This sphere contains within itself all the four elements so that nothing can come from outside to attack it, which makes it exempt from sickness and death (*Timaeus* 31b–33b). In addition, the Demiurge, who is benevolent, does not wish the universe to be subject to corruption. This body is inhabited by a soul, an incorporeal entity between the sensible and the intelligible, which possesses a mathematical structure (*Timaeus* 34a–40b).

The soul of the world is made up of circles, whose permanent motions are arranged according to mathematical ratios, and it is associated with an indestructible body over which it reigns. This soul has a twofold function: (1) a moving function, since it animates all bodies, including celestial bodies, and (2) a cognitive one (*Timaeus* 37a–c). The physical motion that animates the body of the universe is as simple as possible: that of a sphere rotating around its axis, from East to West, while remaining in place. In addition, the soul of the world possesses an intellect, which is perfect and perpetually active. This is what guarantees that the physical motions will be as orderly as possible.

The celestial bodies, made of fire, and the Earth, made primarily of earth, are qualified as "divine" since they meet the criterion stated above. They are indeed living immortals, consisting both of a body that cannot be destroyed, and of a soul that is proper to them, and endowed with an intellect. Celestial bodies are ranked according to their motion. The fixed stars follow the course imposed by the circle of Sameness, from East to West, with perfect uniformity, for the motion of their soul is not subject to any interference. The soul of the wandering stars introduces apparent anomalies with regard to the trajectory of the circle of Otherness, which transports them all. The Earth, for its part, remains at the center of the universe, simply because in its case the motion of Sameness and that of Otherness cancel each other out.[6]

---

[6]   Brisson 2010.

4. The Soul as a Temporary Inhabitant of a Mortal Body

Beneath the souls of gods and daemons in the hierarchy lie souls that possess an intellect like the gods, but are liable to be attached to a body, which, unlike that of the gods, is destructible. These inferior souls are subject to temporality; their existence is marked by cycles of ten thousand years, imposed by destiny, which involve a system of retribution based on reincarnation.[7]

4.1 The Human Body

As a sensible particular, the body of human beings can only have its origin in the two kinds of right-angled triangles, isosceles and scalene. As a function of their quality, however, these right-angled triangles give rise to the marrow and bones, on the one hand, or, on the other hand, to flesh.[8]

4.2 The Constitutive Elements of the Human Body

On the one hand, the Demiurge chooses smooth, regular triangles, which can produce fire, water, air, and earth, and which possess the most exact form (*Timaeus* 73b).[9] By mixing these triangles, he composes the marrow, with which he makes the brain, the spinal marrow, and even the sperm (*Timaeus* 73b–e). The primacy of marrow over flesh consists in the fact that the soul is anchored in the marrow (*Timaeus* 73c). Then, having watered and diluted pure earth, which had been sifted, with marrow, he fashions the substance of bone, which he uses to mold the skull, the spinal column, and all the other bones (*Timaeus* 73e–74a).[10]

Using elements made up of ordinary triangular surfaces, the Demiurge now composes flesh by a mixture of water, fire, and earth, to which he adds a ferment made of salt and acid (*Timaeus* 74a–d). As it dries, the flesh produces a film, which is called skin (*Timaeus* 75e–76a). On the skull, the moisture, exiting through the holes pierced in the skin by fire, and driven back under the skin by air, takes root there, giving rise to hair (*Timaeus* 76a–d). By this process, the Demiurge intends to protect the marrow, which was already protected by the bones.

Out of a mixture of bones and unfermented flesh, the Demiurge then fashions sinews, which he uses to attach the bones to each other (*Timaeus* 74d). Finally, out of a mixture of sinews, skin, and bone, he fashions nails with the

---

[7] Solmsen 1968:502–535, Brisson 2004.

[8] Hall 1991, Joubaud 1991, and S. A. Cleary 2000.

[9] The Greek reads: τῶν γὰρ τριγώνων ὅσα πρῶτα ἀστραβῆ καὶ λεῖα ὄντα. It is hard to imagine a distinction between the triangles. On the subject, see Brisson 2005c.

[10] Manuli and Vegetti 1977. For the gnostic views of the creation of the human body, see Chapter 5.

thought of men's future incarnation as women and as certain animals with claws (*Timaeus* 76d–e).

4.3 Various Systems of the Body

Unlike the body of the world, outside of which nothing subsists, and which is therefore indestructible (*Timaeus* 32c–33b), mankind's body is attacked by the surrounding elements, which bring about in it either "depletion" (*kenôsis*) or "fullness" (*plêrôsis*). Timaeus gives only the briefest description of this process of loss, in which the actions of fire (*Timaeus* 61d–62a) and of water (*Timaeus* 62a–b) are mentioned. In contrast, the process of filling is described very carefully with regard to the motion of the elements in the universe. Thanks to the mechanism of breathing, the fire within human beings never ceases to fashion the blood that it transports in the veins. Yet, since there is no void, the components of fire, air, water, and earth that make up blood are forced to fill the places left vacant as a result of the process of depletion.

The circulatory system (*Timaeus* 78b–79a), which is exclusively responsible for distributing nourishment to all parts of the body by means of the blood, is described as an irrigation system. Quite naturally, Timaeus makes no distinction between veins and arteries,[11] and above all, he is unable to discern any other function of the blood, which, in addition to serving the nutrition of tissues, provides oxygen to all the parts of the body, purifying them of carbon dioxide (*Timaeus* 77c–78e).[12] As we shall see, however, the blood will serve to transport the information given by the sense organs throughout the body as far as the soul.

The respiratory system,[13] which has the appearance of a funnel (*Timaeus* 78a–e), gives rise to a purely mechanical explanation (*Timaeus* 79a–e) that Timaeus very astutely uses to account for other phenomena. Respiration serves essentially for dissolving the food used for the fabrication of blood, and, on the basis of the blood, for the reconstitution of all the other components of the body (*Timaeus* 80d–81e, cf. also 78e–79a).

Finally, the reproductive system, necessarily different in men and women, does not appear until the second birth, when the distinction between the sexes becomes established—that is, in the course of the third millennium of a cycle of the soul, as we shall see.[14]

---

[11] Distinction discovered by William Harvey in the seventeenth century. For the ancient precursors of this distinction, see Nutton 2004:126.
[12] Esposito 1991.
[13] Solmsen 1968:583–587.
[14] See *Phaedrus* 248c–e.

In the course of a very difficult passage, Plato describes the mechanism of reproduction.[15] We are in the phase of the reincarnation cycle in which women appear—that is, in the third millennium. During the first millennium, the soul had no earthly body, while during the second millennium there was no sexual distinction.

> And this explains why at that time the gods[16] fashion the desire for sexual union, by constructing a living thing in us as well as an ensouled being in women.[17] This is how they made them in each case.

> There is a passage[18] by which fluids exit from the body. Where it receives the liquid that has passed between the lungs down into the kidneys and on into the bladder and expels it under the pressure of air. From this passage they bored a connecting one in to the compacted marrow that runs from the head along the neck through the spine.[19] This is in fact the marrow that we have previously called "seed."[20] Now because it has soul[21] in it through breathing,[22] it instilled a life-giving desire for emission right at the duct[23] for breathing,[24] and so fulfilled the want for procreation (ζωτικὴν ἐπιθυμίαν). This is why, of course, the male genitals are unruly and self-willed, like living being that will

---

[15] Turbayne 1976.

[16] The Demiurge's assistants; see *Timaeus* 69b8–c5.

[17] The male sexual organ is depicted as a "living being" (*zôion*) and the feminine sexual organ as an "animate being" (*empsukhon*)—that is, as a being possessing a "soul" (*psukhê*). We find the epithet applied to marrow at *Timaeus* 91b2.

[18] Here we have a description of the penis as containing the urethra, the channel that enables both the transportation of urine from the bladder to the external environment in the course of urination, and ejaculation, allowing the emergence of sperm, which contains the male gametes, the male reproductive cells, called spermatozoa.

[19] The marrow is the tissue in which the soul is anchored; see *Timaeus* 73b–c.

[20] The Greek reads *sperma*, which means "seed" in general, and in this case "sperm." See *Timaeus* 74a4, 77a6, 86c–d.

[21] The masculine relative pronoun *ho* can only have as its antecedent the term *muelos*, the corporeal tissue in which the soul is anchored, as we have seen above.

[22] The expression λαβὼν ἀναπνοήν corresponds to ἀναπνοὴν δὲ λαβοῦσα at *Phaedrus* 251e4. It seems that this strange formula must be associated with what Aristotle describes as an Orphic doctrine: "The same objection lies against the view expressed in the Orphic poems: there it is said that the soul comes in from the whole when breathing takes palace, being borne upon the winds" (τοῦτο δὲ πέπονθε καὶ ὁ ἐν τοῖς Ὀρφικοῖς καλουμένοις ἔπεσι λόγος· φησὶ γὰρ τὴν ψυχὴν ἐκ τοῦ ὅλου εἰσιέναι ἀναπνεόντων, φερομένην ὑπὸ τῶν ἀνέμων, *On the Soul* 410b27–30 = Kern, fr. 27 = 421F Bernabé), trans. M. A. Smith 1931. I must admit that this connection raises many problems because it assimilates the soul, which is incorporeal, to a material entity.

[23] We may supply *hêiper* to the feminine *diexodos* as an antecedent.

[24] It is hard to find an antecedent for this *touth'* [*touto*].

not be subject to reason[25] and driven crazy goaded by the sting of its desires, seeks to overpower everything else.[26] The very same causes operate in women. A woman's womb or "uterus" (μῆτραί τε καὶ ὑστέραι λεγόμεναι),[27] as it is called, is a living being within her with a desire of childbearing (ζῷον ἐπιθυμητικὸν ἐνὸν τῆς παιδοποιίας). Now when this remains unfruitful for an unseasonably long period of time, it is extremely frustrated and travels everywhere up and down her body. It blocks up her respiratory passages, and by not allowing her to breathe it throws her into extreme emergencies, and visits all sort of other illnesses[28] upon her, until finally the woman's desire and the man's passion[29] bring them together, and, like plucking the fruit from a tree,[30] they sow the seed into the ploughed field of her womb, living beings too small to be visible[31] and still without form. And when they have again given them distinct form, they nourish these living beings so that they can mature inside the womb. Afterward, they bring them to birth, introducing them into the light of day.

Plato *Timaeus* 91a1–d5[32]

One of the main difficulties in this passage comes from the fact that the sexual organs, both those of women and those of men, are considered to be living beings. This hypothesis allows one to understand why human beings have so much difficulty in mastering their sexual impulses; yet if one takes it literally, it introduces a number of difficulties. By what kind of soul are these living beings moved? By a soul as such, or by that part of an individual's soul that relates only to desire and is what moves plants, namely, *epithumia*?[33] This second option may be the right one, for in the contrary case, the notion of an individual in the most primitive sense becomes problematic: there would be a parasitical living being present within men and women. Plato seems to mean

---

[25] Because they are insolent.

[26] Because they are tyrannical.

[27] The term *hustera* "that which is right at the bottom" is probably a "modest" term or euphemism, like τὴν τῶν αἰδοίων φύσιν (*Timaeus* 91b5). See also Krell 1975.

[28] Fischer-Homberger 1969.

[29] Once again, ἡ ἐπιθυμία καὶ ὁ ἔρως. See Paganardi 1990.

[30] This is the sperm: "And if the seed of a man's marrow grows to overflowing abundance like a tree that bears an inordinately plentiful quantity of fruit, he is in for a long series of bursts of pain, or of pleasures, in the area of his desires and their fruition. These severe pleasures and pains drive him mad for the greater part of his life, and though his body has made his soul diseased and witless, people think of him not as sick, but as willfully evil" (*Timaeus* 86c–d).

[31] Ramirez Corria 1964, Rankin 1963.

[32] Hereafter the translation is according to Zeyl (2000), with my alterations.

[33] See *Timaeus* 69d.

that the male sexual organs, and the sperm of which they are the vehicle, are, like the female womb, animated by the desiring part of the soul of the men and women to whom the sexual organ and womb, respectively, belong.

The male sexual organ usually plays the part of a urinary system. In copulation, however, it is sperm that exits from it, for, as we saw above, the urinary tract is related to the marrow in the spinal column.[34] Yet the marrow is the most perfect tissue in the body, and it is therefore where the soul comes to anchor itself.

4.4 Illnesses of the Body

Generation has corruption as its counterpart.[35] For Plato, health consists in maintaining the order that has been just described (*Timaeus* 82b2–5). Illness makes its appearance as soon as this order is imbalanced (*Timaeus* 82b5–7). Timaeus' exposition on illness consists of three stages.[36]

Plato begins by taking into consideration the primary constituents of the human body: earth, fire, water, and air. Illnesses arise when the nature, quantity (excess or lack), or even the relative position of each of the elements is altered.

Plato then moves on to a second order of considerations. Since marrow, bones, flesh, sinews, and even blood are made up of the four elements, illnesses bring about excess or deficiency within them. More serious illnesses, however, are explained by a reversal of the natural order of the generation and nutrition of the tissues by the blood (*Timaeus* 82c–84c). When flesh dissolves and decomposes, it pours the decays that result from this decomposition into the blood. This leads to the formation of the humors, which bring about the corruption of the blood itself. As long as the "roots" of the flesh remain unaffected, an illness can be cured. However, when the substance that connects the flesh to the bones is attacked, the illness worsens. No longer receiving the air it needs, the bone heats up and decomposes. Finally, when the marrow concealed by the bones is attacked, death ensues, since the bonds that kept the soul attached to the body in man become loose.

A third class of illnesses (*Timaeus* 84d–86a) comes from three causes. The first class of illnesses is caused by the air (84d–85b). The second class is brought about by phlegm (85a–b). The final class comes from bile (85b–86a). The formation of these types of humors, bile (83b–c) and phlegm (83c–e), had been described earlier. Seeking to understand the causes of health and illness,

---

[34] See pp. 9–11
[35] Ayache 1997.
[36] Miller 1962 and Grams 2009.

Plato thus adopts the approach of a medicine that investigates the nature of the human body and of the universe (*Phaedrus* 270a–e).

Although, from a strictly biological viewpoint, one cannot doubt that Plato is under the strong influence of contemporary and previous medical doctrines, his approach in this area cannot be reduced to an eclectic, secondhand synthesis.[37] He certainly used several sources, but he thoroughly modified their orientation, and probably their content, as a function of his objectives. The most striking characteristic of Plato's exposition of the etiology of illnesses is the fact that it is in deep agreement with the principles of physics and physiology.

Nevertheless, Plato remains a philosopher who subordinates the body to the soul, and who sets assimilation to god incessantly contemplating the intelligible forms as the ultimate goal for this soul. One is thereby reminded of the principle that guides the *Timaeus*: necessity must be taken into account, which has always to be subordinated to the intellect gazing at the intelligible forms. Thus, Plato places the emphasis on purpose in this very important section of the *Timaeus*, which describes the constitution of the human body and its functioning. There is no organ or system that was not conceived by the Demiurge or his assistants (*Timaeus* 61c–81e, cf. also 45b–47e) with a view to a particular goal or the ultimate end of mankind. From this perspective, biology and medicine may be considered as the foundations of ethics. As early as in the *Gorgias* (464b–465e), one finds a parallel description of legislation and gymnastics as disciplines that train, respectively, the soul and the body, and of justice and medicine as disciplines that correct, respectively, the soul and the body.

5. The Union of the Soul and the Body

Human life is defined as the union of the soul and the human body (*Timaeus* 87e5–6). The primary point of contact between the soul and the body is the marrow (*Timaeus* 73b). The immortal part of the human soul is anchored in the cervical marrow (*Timaeus* 73c–d), while the mortal species are rooted in the spinal marrow (*Timaeus* 73d–e).

5.1 Localization of the Parts of the Soul

On the physical map of the body, the "intellect" (*nous*) is located in the head, which is considered as the acropolis of the human body (*Timaeus* 69d–70a). The mortal parts reside between the neck and the navel, a space that is divided into two by the diaphragm, resulting in a separation similar to that between the apartments of men and of women in an ancient Greek house (*Timaeus* 70a).

---

[37] Jouanna 2007 and Brisson 2013.

The aggressive part (*thumos*) is situated between the neck and the diaphragm, in the vicinity of the heart, which is compared to a guard's station (*Timaeus* 70a–b).[38] This location allows Timaeus to justify the existence, structure, and role of the lungs as cooling down the heart (*Timaeus* 70c–d).

For its part, the desiring part or "appetite" (*epithumia*), is tied up between the diaphragm and the navel, like a wild beast at its trough (*Timaeus* 70d–e). This localization allows Timaeus to justify the existence, structure, and role of the liver (*Timaeus* 71a–72c) and of the spleen (*Timaeus* 72c–d). Even the lower abdomen and the intestines (*Timaeus* 72e–73a) find their explanation in the insatiable nature of the mortal part of the human soul; the length of the intestines play a part in the well-being and survival of human beings.[39] The liver, a smooth surface cleaned by the spleen, plays the part of a mediator between the aggressive and the desiring species. It is used by the former for scarring the latter, by projecting terrifying images onto the liver, which plays the role of a screen.[40]

5.2 The Soul's Entry into the Body at Birth

Once they have listened to the Demiurge's speech, the younger gods borrow portions of fire, air, water, and earth from the universe to construct the human body to which they attach the revolutions of the rational part of the soul, and the "spirit" and the "appetite" as well (*Timaeus* 42e–43a). At first, the revolutions of the rational part of the soul are transported in every direction by the flux of material things, which, through the intermediaries of nutrition and sensation, agitate the human body in a twofold movement of (1) "filling" (*plêrôsis*) and "depletion" (*kenôsis*), and (2) "association" (*sunkrisis*) and "dissociation" (*diakrisis*).

For Timaeus, birth and childhood are periods when chaos reigns (*Timaeus* 43a–44a), insofar as the rational part of the soul is unable to exert domination, unlike the world as a whole, which begins a rational life, as soon as its soul is united with a body. The situation stabilizes over time (*Timaeus* 44b) and a temporary cooperation is able to be established. The key for this cooperation is sensation.

---

[38] Frère 1997.
[39] Romeri 2002 and 2005.
[40] Brisson 1974 and Struck 2003. On the tendency to link viscera with the divinatory practice of reading dreams, especially in the Hippocratic treatise *On Regimen* 1.14, 1.23–24, 2.40, 2.45, and 2.54, and Plato's *Timaeus* 44a–d, 69e–70e, and 71d, see Rotondaro 1997:275–280 and 307–316.

5.3 Cooperation between Soul and Body: Sensations

The cooperation between soul and body is the reason for which the *Timaeus* contains a detailed description of the mechanism of the various senses and the sensations they arise. This process constantly involves two complementary and opposing processes, "association" (*sunkrisis*), or union, and "dissociation" (*diakrisis*).

In general, one may say that the human body makes its presence known to the soul that is installed within it through this process, which can be described, very generally, as follows.[41] The impressions that strike the body as a whole (*Timaeus* 61c–64a) must, through a chain of movements transmitted by blood (*Timaeus* 64b–c, 77e), reach the soul and its rational part to become sensations of pleasure and pain (*Timaeus* 64a–65b). The same applies to the sensations associated with touch (*Timaeus* 61c–64a),[42] taste (*Timaeus* 65b–66c), smell (*Timaeus* 66c–67a),[43] hearing (*Timaeus* 67a–c, cf. 47c–e),[44] and sight (*Timaeus* 67c–68d, cf. also 45b–47c).[45] Sense perception not only enables us to connect with the world that surrounds the body, but triggers the process of reminiscence that gives access to the intelligible forms while we are on this earth.[46]

5.4 Reciprocal Action of the Body on the Soul and the Soul on the Body

Like the body that it moves, the human soul, however, can be subject to perturbations, which, for their part, are due to malfunctions of the body (*Timaeus* 86b–87a). There are two causes for this: one is due to the excess of seminal fluid[47] or humors; the other is due to poor institutions that entail a bad education (*Timaeus* 87a–b).[48] It should be noted, however, that the *Timaeus* warns against excessive ardor of the soul, which can bring about illnesses in the body (*Timaeus* 87e–88a). In short, soul and body interact within human beings.

To avoid or cure illnesses of the soul, one must avoid traditional medicine (*Timaeus* 89b–d) and systematically apply these principles: (1) maintaining a proper proportion between the body and the soul, which shall be exercised,

---

[41] See Brisson 1997b, 1999b, 2013 and Sisko 2006.
[42] Berger 1998 and Code 2010.
[43] Vlastos 1981.
[44] D. O'Brien 1997 and Lautner 2005.
[45] Brisson 1999b, Ierodiakonou 1997 and 2005, Speliopoulos 1997.
[46] See Brisson 1999a:23–61, 2007, 2008.
[47] As we have seen, there may even be an overabundance of marrow, see n30 above (*Timaeus* 86c–d). Note that the recourse to the image of the tree whose fruits are picked is also found in the passage cited above.
[48] Scolnicov 1997, Natali 2003, C. Gill 2000, Lautner 2011.

taking as one's model not only the motions of the soul led by the intellect, but also those of his or her body; and (2) within the soul, maintaining a proper proportion between its parts, by systematically granting preeminence to the intellect. In this context, responsibility remains a problem, insofar as the will does not have true autonomy with regard to reason. Nevertheless, a problem arises since the *Timaeus* ends with the description of a retributive system (*Timaeus* 90e–92c), which presupposes some kind of guilt. Some illnesses of the body can be induced by malfunctions of the soul, and some illnesses of the soul are induced by malfunctions of the body. As elsewhere, then, one cannot speak of a radical separation of soul and body, although it may seem surprising that a body and an incorporeal can interact with one another.

6. Death and Its Consequences for the Individual Soul

When it is in a body, the soul, by means of one of its activities—that is, the "intellect" (*nous*)—remains in contact with the intelligible, which, in fact, enables it to concern itself with the body to which it is attached. It must ensure first the survival of the body by means of ingestion of food and drink, and second its reproduction. It must also defend the body against aggressions that come from outside or even from within: this is why spirit and desire are necessary to ensure survival on this earth. What happens when this soul is separated from its terrestrial body, however? Its higher activity remains what it was, and it maintains the memory of its object, the intelligible, simply because this object is immutable. This contemplative activity, however, is qualified by the fact that when the soul was in a body, it paid greater or lesser attention to the sensible; thus, the application of a retributive system. When the soul becomes detached from the body for which it cared, its activities in this area cease to be exercised and it loses the memory of the objects and events associated with these activities. In Plato, a soul never recalls empirical events associated with a previous existence.

In this twofold sense one can, it seems to me, declare the functions known as the "spirit" (*thumos*) and "desire" (*epithumia*) to be "mortal" (*Timaeus* 69c–e). Insofar as they are the activities of a soul, these functions share the soul's immortality. But when the soul does separate from its body, spirit and desire cease to be exercised, and since no memory of what they have done in the past subsists, they can be qualified as mortal. From this perspective, the "death" that affects the functions of the human soul known as spirit and desire may be defined as a forgetting of the body, consequent on the soul's separation from the body it took care of.

After a certain period of time, the soul in question moves to another body. Its lower functions then adapt to the new body and stay in relation with it until they separate from it. The identity or individuality of the soul is thus attached to the series of its particular existences. However, this identity or individuality persists for a certain extent of time, but not for eternity, for it is linked to the history of a soul during a cycle of ten thousand years. At the end of this cycle, it may be assumed that the soul loses its identity before resuming its reascent to the intelligible with the gods and the daemons, and that it will acquire, for another period of ten thousand years, a new identity. In other words, it is the soul as a whole that is immortal, not any individual soul.

Therefore, there is no longer a contradiction in Plato's dialogues on the question of immortality. In the *Phaedrus*, as in the *Timaeus*, it is the soul in its totality that is, by definition, presented as immortal. Certain particular souls—the soul of the world, that of the gods, and those of the daemons—may be presented as immortal, because their body, although destructible in itself, will not be destroyed, in accordance with the Demiurge's promise. In the case of the human soul, immortality and mortality are a function of the soul's relations to a body. Because the body it animates is destructible, one may qualify certain functions of the soul as mortal. Nevertheless, the intellect of a soul is individualized, at least for a certain time, by the quality of its contemplation of the intelligible, which makes possible a system of retribution. In this context, individuality is associated with the body in a negative way, in the sense that the body reduces the quality of intellectual activity. Individuality is therefore defined by a deficit with regard to the intelligible. What is more, at the end of each ten-thousand-year cycle, this individuality disappears, since the soul must lose all its characteristics before being reintegrated within another cycle. In short, the human soul in Plato has only a relative immortality, limited in time.

6.1 Reincarnation and Retribution

Throughout nine thousand years, a human soul can be attached to an earthly body subject to destruction. In this way, the soul can be punished or rewarded for its previous lives (punished, for instance, by becoming attached to an inferior animal). Another period for this soul then begins, now deprived of its previous individuality. Here, Plato's thought on soul is not very different from Eastern doctrines of reincarnation. In this scheme, it is not the individual soul that persists, but, so to speak, the available pool of souls. Let us next consider the soul's wanderings in more detail.

In fact, Plato describes a psychic continuum, in which we find a hierarchical order of gods, daemons, human beings, and animals that live in the air, on the earth, and in the water, and even, as we shall soon see, plants. Intellectual activity, conceived as the intuition of Forms, constitutes the criterion that enables a distinction to be established between all these souls. Gods and daemons contemplate the intelligible reality, that is, the Forms, directly, and, as it were, incessantly. Human beings share this privilege from time to time only during a certain period of their existence when their souls are separated from all terrestrial bodies. Once human souls have been incarnated, their contemplation of the Forms is mediated since it must take place through the intermediary of sense perception; above all, it is more or less uncertain. As one goes down the scale of beings, animals use their intellect less and less.

Within the psychic scale mentioned above, we note two discontinuities: (1) a discontinuity between the souls of gods and of daemons, which never fall into a body subject to destruction; and the souls of human beings and of animals, which inhabit destructible bodies with diverse appearances; and (2) a discontinuity between the souls of human beings and of animals, which are endowed with a rational power, and the souls of plants, which are reduced to the desiring power.

Let us consider the consequences of these two discontinuities:

1. In this subordinated system, only souls possessing an intellect are subject to a retributive system that makes them ascend or descend on the scale of incarnate souls as a function of the quality of the exercise of their intellect. The gods and the daemons are situated beyond this class, and the plants beneath it. Thus, gods, daemons, and plants always remain at their level, at the upper or lower extremity.

2. Consequently, human beings situated at the upper limit of the class of incarnate souls must have the goal of assimilating themselves to the gods and daemons, seeking the most immediate and longest possible contemplation of the Forms, while ensuring the separation of soul and body. Thus, we have the theme of assimilation to the divinity by the philosopher who tends toward the knowledge that allows the contemplation of the Forms to be achieved. Those situated at the lower limit can stay at their level or go back up in the scale of living beings.

3. The hierarchy between human beings and animals, which is a function of the exercise of intellectual activity, is materialized by the body. The body in which a soul is present illustrates the quality of the intellectual activity of that soul. In short, the body is a "state of soul," to use the fine expression of Labrune.[49] Here we return to the famous

---

[49] Labrune 1992.

play on words *sôma-sêma* for which Plato offers three interpretations in the *Cratylus*:

> Thus some people say that the body (σῶμα) is the tomb (σῆμα) of the soul, on the ground that it is entombed in its present life, while others say that it is correctly called a sign (σῆμα), because the soul signifies whatever it wants to signify by means of the body. I think it is more likely the followers of Orpheus who gave the body its name, with the idea that the soul is being punished for something, and that the body is an enclosure or prison in which the soul is securely kept (σῴζεται)—as the name itself (σῶμα) suggests—until the penalty is paid; for in this view, not even a single letter of the word needs to be changed.
>
> Plato *Cratylus* 400c1–10[50]

To interpret *sôma* as a "tomb" is the result of an overdetermination that is easy to understand.[51] A tomb is a "sign" (*sêma*) indicating that a cadaver—or what is left of it—is present under the earth. The body is a "sign" indicating that it is animated by a certain type of soul, which, because it is situated within a body, is dead to a certain degree, in so far as it does not live totally by and for its intellect. As a function of the quality of its previous existence, the soul finds itself in such-and-such a body where, so to speak, it serves its sentence.

From this perspective, all human beings and animals that inhabit air, earth, and water thus constitute a vast system of signs—signs from the point of view of appearances, but also from the viewpoint of behavior, which justifies the recourse to a number of comparisons, images, and metaphors in which animals play a role. In the *Timaeus*, these signs refer to different types of souls whose moral quality is ultimately determined by their contemplation of the intelligible according to a number of details that may seem ironic or ridiculous, but that can be interpreted only in this sense: birds are naive astronomers who think that sight is the ultimate source of knowledge; quadrupeds need four feet in order to support their skull, which has been elongated by the deformations of the revolutions of the circles of its rational part; the stupidest terrestrial animals crawl; fish are even more stupid, and the lowest ignorance is that of shellfish.

Yet the reproduction and conservation of this material "sign" called "the body" must be ensured.

---

[50] The translation is according to Reeve 1997. See pp. 80n29, 113 and 172n4 below.
[51] Also p. 113 below.

6.2 Sexual Reproduction in the Context of *Metensômatôsis*

Beneath the gods in the hierarchy of living beings are souls that are endowed with an intellect like the gods, but liable to be attached to a body, which, unlike that of the gods, is destructible. These inferior souls are subject to temporality; their existence is marked by cycles of ten periods, each of one thousand years, imposed by destiny, which involve a system of retribution based on reincarnation, or metensomatosis, as we have seen.

During the first period (*Phaedrus* 245d–248c), the souls accompanying gods and daemons who contemplate the intelligible forms, are separated from all destructible bodies, whereas during the following nine periods (*Phaedrus* 248c–e), a soul passes from one body to another as a function of the moral value of its previous existence, which is determined by the quality of its intellectual activity. At the end of this first period, those souls are associated with the sensible body of a man—that is, a male, even though the sexual organs are still missing; this association remains valid for the following period. A man who loves knowledge or beauty—that is, the philosopher—and who has chosen an upright life for three consecutive periods, will be able to escape from the cycle of reincarnations and rise back up to the heavens. The others will travel from one body to another, beginning with the third period (*Timaeus* 90e–92c). The first category of bodies mentioned is that of women: whoever displays cowardice enters into a woman's body since virility is attributed to war in Ancient Greece. Only in the course of this millennium, the distinction between the sexes appears, thus allowing sexual reproduction. Then come incarnations in various kinds of what we call "animals," although there is no term in ancient Greek to designate this category of living beings. They are classified as a function of the elements (beginning with the air since fire is reserved for the gods) in a vertical order. At the top, birds fly through the air. Then come the living beings that inhabit the surface of the earth: the quadrupeds, insects, and reptiles. Finally, come the aquatic animals: fish, shellfish, and others; they are the most stupid.

In this context, reproduction raises significant problems for Plato—on the one hand, because souls can subsist independently of any earthly body, and, on the other, because human beings of the first earthly generation—that is, of the second period—do not make use of it. Although they are described as *andres*, they have no masculine sex organs since the two sexes do not make their appearance until the second generation, which cannot, therefore, come from sexual relations.[52]

---

[52] Scribano 2007, Fortuna 2007.

One must wait until the third period, and the appearance of women, for this to be possible. In addition, reproduction is to be the means, not only for creating a new body, but also for transmitting a soul that corresponds to such-and-such a body. To ensure the justice of this retribution, the souls that have not been able to remain in the heavens are first incarnated only in *andres* during the first period of one thousand years. Since, for the following eight periods of one thousand years, however, distinctions appear, particularly between those *andres* who have been courageous and those who have not, a division of the sexes becomes necessary on an ethical level. This division will nevertheless play an important biological role in the field of reproduction. Thus, there is ambiguity in Plato's position, which makes *Timaeus* (91a1–d5) particularly hard to translate and to understand.[53]

Part of the marrow mixed with earth serves for fashioning the bones that constitute the skull and the spinal column that serves to contain and to protect the rest of the marrow (*Timaeus* 73e–74a). The "generative marrow" (τὸν γόνιμον...μυελόν, *Timaeus* 77d3–4) that is in the spinal column is nourished by the blood, so as to provide it with maximum vigor. At the moment of sexual union, the male deposits his sperm in the womb. By so doing, he is said to sow into the womb living beings that are not yet formed, as one throws seeds into ploughed land. The remark concerning living beings is coherent with what precedes, for as we have seen, it is in the sperm that the soul is anchored. Note, however, the plural *zôia*. How, then, can one explain that in most cases a single child is conceived? In any case, Plato can be considered a preformationist, insofar as living beings are already formed within the sperm, even though they are invisible and unformed; in the womb, these living beings will merely grow and differentiate themselves. Finally, it should be noted that in the course of this process, the woman's role is merely to nourish the embryo. This, then, is a highly rudimentary explanation of the process of generation that has little to do with the explanation proposed centuries later by Porphyry in *To Gaurus on How Embryos are Ensouled.*[54]

Things become more complicated in Plato, for reproduction is not only a matter of biology, in that it involves ethical considerations. It is a soul's quality that explains why a given soul comes to establish itself in such-and-such a body, whether of a man, a woman, or an animal. Like human beings, either male or female, the soul of animals possesses a rational part, even if animals are what they are because they make little or no use of their intellect. In any case, nothing prevents an animal, whichever it may be, from climbing back up the chain to

[53] See pp. 10–11 above.
[54] Brisson et al. 2008 and 2012.

become a human being. Unfortunately, Plato provides no details concerning the process, and it is better not to put solutions into his mouth. However, these three consequences should be mentioned:

1. Animals are still, by a kind of axiom, intelligent beings. Plutarch, Porphyry, and several other authors insist on this point.[55]

2. Since they can rise or fall on the scale of living being, animals must have moral responsibility. They therefore have rights and are subject to duties. It must be admitted, however, that nothing on this point is to be found in Plato.

3. Human beings cannot kill animals in order to eat them, for the latter are endowed with a rational soul similar to our own. If they committed this crime, they would become cannibals. How, then, can one ensure the survival of human beings who need to feed themselves, without turning them automatically into cannibals? By giving them as food a species of living being that does not possess an intellect, namely, plants.

6.3 Vegetarianism: A Consequence of *Metensômatôsis*

Let us consider some of the consequences of *metensômatôsis*. First, the hierarchy of human beings and animals, which is a function of the exercise of intellectual activity, is rendered visible through the body. The body in which the soul is situated illustrates the quality of that soul's intellectual activity; in short, the body is a "state of the soul." Second, like that of human beings, either men or women, the soul of animals is endowed with a rational power and this is true even if animals are what they are because they make little or no use of their intellect.

After mentioning the four types of living beings that populate the universe, the gods associated with fire, human beings, men or women, the birds that inhabit the air, the animals walking or crawling on the earth, and the aquatic beasts, Timaeus briefly mentions the origin of vegetables, which he associates with the third, or "desiring power" (*epithumia*) of soul in the *Timaeus* (76e–77c).

Plato justifies the existence of vegetables by the human body's need to reconstitute itself in order to maintain itself in existence by consuming beings that possess soul like it, but a soul that is absolutely bereft of any intellect.[56] For man, to eat a human being endowed with an intellect, even if this living being did not make use of this higher faculty, would be an act of "cannibalism." This is no longer the case with plants, which possess a soul, but one that is bereft

---

[55] Porphyry *On Abstinence from Killing Animals.*
[56] Skemp 1947, Respici 2000, Brisson 2004, Carpenter 2008.

of intellect. The decomposition of plants within the human body enables the constitution of blood, which nourishes all the other tissues. In this way, plants enable the human body—which, unlike the world's body, may be destroyed by the external aggression of fire or of air—to reconstitute itself without consuming living beings animated by a soul endowed with an intellect. In short, Plato "invents" plants in order to be able to maintain his scale of living beings. We must insist on the following corollaries: since plants cannot possess an intellect, a human soul cannot be incarnated as a plant, as may be the case in Empedocles' doctrine (fr. 127).

The consequences Plato derives from this conception of the phenomenon of life are certainly not primarily biological, but ethical and political. The main purpose seems to be the establishment of a system of retribution that no living being—except gods, daemons, and vegetables—will be able to escape.

Defining human beings by their soul does not lead to contempt or even to oblivion of the body. The human body must be in an optimal state to enable human beings to live symbiotically with their environment. Thus, one must know its constitution in order to avoid illnesses and delay death. Nevertheless, defining human beings by their soul entails important consequences on a political level, where women are no longer reduced to remaining in the private sphere, and on an ethical level, where retribution requires reincarnation as a man, a woman, or even an animal, and *metensômatôsis*, moreover, implies vegetarianism. All this underscores the programmatic importance of the body in Plato's philosophy.

The systematic association of the soul with a body that makes its value manifest leads one to consider the world of living beings as a vast system of signs, and to wonder about the place and role of mankind in this whole. To know oneself is to remember, not one's past experiences in the sensible world, but the experience one has had of the intelligible; consequently, to know oneself is to dissolve the individual in the universal. And finally, as far as the soul's immortality is concerned, Plato was much closer to Eastern religious beliefs than to Christianity.

2

Aristotle on the Integrity of Life

DIMKA GICHEVA-GOCHEVA

Abstract: When writing about Aristotle's ideas of the divine and the material, the soul and the body of the living creatures, it is best to start with his overall cosmological picture: the cosmos-heaven is eternal, uncreated, and imperishable. By this definition, all living species in it are eternal, as well. Aristotle continues to a certain degree the endeavors of his teacher in the *Timaeus* and strives to explain the vitality and the perfection of the cosmos with no less passion than Plato, but he uses other concepts. His tools are not the world soul and the body of the world, but the five elements and the omnipresence of life-in-potency.

In what follows I argue that there is not only vitality but also admirable integrity in the discussion of the body and the soul in Aristotle's thought. I begin with his fundamental views as presented in *On the Generation of Animals* and *On the Heavens* and continue with an outline of his discussion of the soul in *On the Soul*. After directing my attention to his five different grades of spiritedness in the animated world, I conclude with an examination of the main problem of the immortality, not of the soul, but of the *nous thurathen*, which enters the human body and soul at birth and leaves at death.

IF WE WANT TO SKETCH the soul-body relation, and its puzzles, in Plato and Aristotle, it is perhaps best to be reminded first of their far-reaching considerations about the cosmos itself.

1. The Cosmos according to Aristotle: Perfect Body without Cosmic Soul

On the same principle the fulfillment of the whole heaven, the fulfillment which includes all time and infinity, is "duration"—a name based upon the fact, that it *is always*—duration immortal and divine.

Aristotle *On the Heavens* 279a25–29[1]

In the *Timaeus* we have the pleasure to follow step by step the creation of the perfect soul of the cosmos (*Timaeus* 34c–37c) and, immediately after it, the making of its perfect body (*Timaeus* 37d–40d).[2] The philosophy of nature in the *Timaeus* is founded on several axioms: the cosmos is created, but indestructible; generated, but eternal; initiated in a certain moment, but imperishable; endowed with the best spherical figure and rotating around its axis.[3] What is most important: it is ensouled and its immortal soul is older than its body. There is a perfect ontological symmetry between the cosmic body and the cosmic soul, and this proportion at the end of the dialogue turns out to be the paradigm to which every living creature would be better to adhere in order to be healthy, harmonious, and beautiful (*Timaeus* 87c–89d).

Aristotle shares some of these ideas, but not all of them. While he agrees with Plato that the cosmos is eternal, perfect, spherical, beautiful, and living, he disagrees with him about the rest. He argues at length with his teacher that the cosmos is not created and moreover that it is uncreatable, that it is ungenerated and unable to be generated.[4] For him, the following is more logical and therefore more convincing reasoning: the claim that the cosmos is eternal excludes the option of temporal generation—i.e. of a beginning in time. Eternity, according to him, means the absence of an initial and final moment in the existence of the cosmos in the duration of time.

Aristotle also agrees with Plato that the perfect body of the cosmos is composed of the four elements. However, he insists that his master is completely

---

[1] The translation is according to Stocks 1922, with his italics.

[2] See Brisson 1974 and 1989, Brisson and Meyerstein 1995, Scheffel 1976, Vlastos 1995, Burnyeat 2004, Karfík 2004, Sedley 2010.

[3] The opposite opinion has its champions in the scholarship; see Brisson 1992, Brisson and Meyerstein 1995, and Tarán 1975. They insist that Aristotle wrongly has attributed the axial rotation of the Earth to Plato.

[4] This speculative distinction between the actual un-createdness of the cosmos, supported by the exclusion of the probability of any future generation, and creation itself is developed at length in chapters 10, 11, and 12 of book 1 of *On the Heavens*. On Aristotle's cosmology, natural philosophy, and worldview, see Brentano 1977, J. J. Cleary 1995, Dick 1970, Duhem 1913, Düring 1966, Elders 1966, Rolfes 1923, Sorabji 1980, and Leunissen 2010.

wrong to envision the construction of the elemental bodies from the four solids. For Aristotle the four primary elements are earth, fire, air, and water, but they are not the stereometric beauties created by the Demiurge from the two initial triangles and their multiplications as Plato envisions. These four polyhedra, plus the fifth one, the dodecahedron—the body of the cosmos itself—despite all their proportional symmetries do not contribute at all to the explanation of the variety of qualities in the natural world. What matters for Aristotle is that the four elements are constituents of the cosmos, characterized mostly by their qualitative properties, combined in pairs of opposites. The most fundamental of them are comprised in the triad of: (1) wet and dry; (2) cold and hot; and (3) heavy and light. These three are most important for the composition of the entire cosmos, for its beauty and eternity. Among them the heaviness and the lightness appear to be the determinants of the spatial location of the elements in the sphere of the universe.

Since the physical bodies, by their nature, occupy physical places, they innately strive to remain in their physical places as in their physical homes. Aristotle's consistent use of the adjective "homey" (*oikeios*) in this context conveys the idea that in the perfect, beautiful, and "cozy" home of the cosmos everything is in its proper place.[5] The earth gathers around the center of the universe and is motionless; the water reposes on the earth, being a little lighter than it, but naturally moving towards the center of the cosmic sphere. The air and the fire, in their turn, naturally strive to move away from the center towards the periphery of the cosmos. And the periphery is the dwelling circle of the fifth body, the aether, which eternally runs within it, as the etymology of its name suggests.[6]

Aristotle inherits the idea of the fifth body from the late Platonic dialogue *Epinomis* and needs it more than anything else, since he strongly opposed Plato's proposition for the existence of the world soul. In it, the aether is one of the five primary bodies, together with fire, water, air, earth, and "each of the many and varied kinds of living things is brought to perfection with one of these playing the chief role" (*Epinomis* 981c),[7] whereas, in *On the Heavens*, the aether is the endlessly circulating outer sphere of the cosmos. In the place of Plato's concept of the world soul, Aristotle develops the theory that the cosmos is a perfect living being, enjoying perpetual, continuous, uniform, and uninterrupted circular movement. Thus, he solved three problems at once with the addition of aether to the original four primary elements: (1) time is boundless; (2) spatial

---

[5]   See *On the Heavens* 276b16: "homey cosmos;" also 270b17, 276b24, and 278b29: "homey places of the elements;" also 302b6 and 303b5: "homey movements of the elements."

[6]   *On the Heavens* 279a15–35.

[7]   The translation is according to McKirahan, included in Tarán 1975.

dimensions are not because of the spherical and limited form of the cosmos; and (3) the aether sustains the incessant movement of its outer circle. Whether this movement is self-generated and self-sustained eternal circulation of the uttermost sphere of the universe, rotating within itself, or it is a striving towards the transcendent Unmoved Mover, the alpha and the omega of the whole being, or the cosmos, is still a question of a heated debate today.

2. The Living Creatures and Their Perfect Bodies

In all natural creatures there is something amazing.

Aristotle *On the Parts of Animals* 645a17–19

Aristotle was a great admirer and a devoted researcher of the animal kingdom. It is not by chance that one third of his lectures, which we nowadays read as treatises, consist of biological writings (i.e. *On the Parts of Animals*, *On the Movement of Animals*, *On the Generation of Animals*, and *On the History of Animals*).[8] Neither is it surprising that, anytime he is unsatisfied with what the Greek language had to offer, he does not hesitate to coin a new word or an expression, however awkward, in order to capture and articulate precisely his thought on the matter. This is particularly true for the modal categories, which are indispensable in the analysis of the soul.[9] Still, the term "biology" is not found among his linguistic novelties because Aristotle did not conceive of his inquiries and lectures on the living world as a part of some compartmentalized scientific work.[10] The living beings provided for him an irrefutable proof and demonstration of the fundamental truths of his first philosophy, theology. He has convincingly presented them in a classification of the animals, which has emerged at the intersection of several criteria: the external image—"shape" (*eidos*)—of the animals, their habitats, and especially the ways of their propagation.

    Some of the genera of his classification, their labels and designations, may seem strange today, perhaps even ridiculous to some modern biologists. But Aristotle has conceived of them precisely as such, because one of the principles

---

[8]   Page 1942; Goold 1942, 1960, 1970, and 1973.

[9]   This is the kernel of my point of view, developed at length later in the chapter. See n25 below. For *entelekheia*, see *On the Soul* 413b16–20, 414a8–19, 414a25–27, 414b8–15, and the long passage at 417a21–b27, where the sense perceptions, thinking, and understanding are discussed, in general; also, the remarkable definition of light as *entelekheia* in *On the Soul* 418b29–419a11. For *energeia*, see *On the Soul* 417a13–17, 419b3–11, 422a17–19, 425b26–426a19.

[10]   For various approaches to his biology as a part of natural philosophy, see Balme 1962 and 1965, Bodnár 2005, Bodnár and Pellegrin 2006, Byl 1980, Furth 1988, Gotthelf 1985, Pellegrin 1986, Gotthelf and Lennox 1987, Gilson 1971, Krämer 1968, Schüssler 1982, and Tipton 2014.

of his worldview is the eternity of the cosmos and everything in it. All the genera of the animals are eternal—they have never changed and will never change in this eternal world, which likewise has never been created and will never perish. The ontological foundation of his all-inclusive classification of the animal world is doubtless. It has its philosophically positive but also ardent polemical motive: to expose the inapplicability of his master's method of dichotomy to explain the living.

His descriptions of the animal species in *On the History of Animals* are done with passion, care, and one would say even with love for all living beings. From the greatest mammals to the smallest bloodless insects and worms, from the horns and hooves of the largest animals to the tiniest legs of the flies, from the bones and the blood vessels to the stomach, from the heart and the brain to the residues of the bodies—everything has received Aristotle's most meticulous attention. Everything in the external appearances and the internal organs of all species and groups of living creatures is not only minutely described in *On the History of Animals*, but also causally explained in *On the Parts of Animals*. The dominance of the latter is beyond doubt. Hundreds of these descriptions and causal explanations are full of precise observations and subtleties, but there are also some astonishing mistakes in them, *made intentionally* and motivated by his metaphysical apriorism and teleological beliefs.[11] The metaphysical vocation is even more appealing in another treatise among his primers on the philosophy of life, *On the Generation of Animals*.

"God and nature do nothing in vain." This famous conclusion of a cosmological consideration in *On the Heavens* (271d35) may equally serve as the logo of his natural philosophy. It is also repeated twice with minor variations in the wording in the third book of *On the Soul* (432b21–23 and 434a31). Nothing happens as a deviation from the divine order of nature, which will eternally sustain and reproduce itself by the incessant propagation of all living species. His attention to the causes, responsible for the tissues, residues, generative stuff, the systems, and the organs in the *On the Parts of Animals* and *On the Generation of Animals* is driven by the desire to prove the basics of his ontology and to establish the supremacy of his teleology. This is the task of the tasks. In comparison to it, his attempt to oppose them to Plato's philosophy is only a minor ambition on his part.

His metaphysical credo is well known from the three core books of the *Metaphysics*, namely, seven, eight, and nine. All constitutive concepts of his *ousia*-philosophy also penetrate his three great treatises on the philosophy of

---

[11] Detailed analyses of his teleology can be found in Arnoldt 1960, Balme 1965 and 1975, Pellegrin 2003, Engels 1982, Gotthelf 1985, Gotthelf and Lennox 1987, Gilson 1971, Kullmann 1974 and 1998, Theiler 1965, Spaemann 1981, Leunissen 2010, and Tipton 2014.

life as well as in the smaller psychological and physiological writings, collected under the common title *Parva Naturalia*.

First and foremost among his metaphysical principles comes his concept of "substance" (*ousia*) the characteristics of which are as follows:[12]

1. The substantial being is the embodied *eidos*.[13]

2. The genus cannot exist independently from the species since the species exist as pertinent to the genus.[14]

3. The concept of species is defined as *logos*, derived from the *differentiae*.[15]

4. The final *differentia* (i.e. *specifica*) is the substance-being of the living thing.[16]

5. Substantial beings are the final species ("final" in the sense of not susceptible to any further division or the specification of a new *differentia*).[17]

6. It is impossible for any of the general predicaments, and *predicabilia*, to exist as self-substantial beings.[18]

7. The Platonic formula of the equation "if you add the *differentia* to the genus, you will receive the exact species" turns out to be absolutely futile.[19]

Second comes the principle of hylomorphism, which underlies Aristotle's philosophy of life and especially his understanding of propagation of all living creatures. One of the rare places in Plato in which he speaks about the sexual love between the male and the female is in the *Symposium* (206c1–e3). We find an echo of this in Aristotle's *On the Soul*:

> For any living thing that has reached its normal development and which is unmutilated, and whose mode of generation is not spontaneous, the

---

[12] For different interpretations of Aristotle's first philosophy, see Aquinas in Pasnau 1999, Aubenque 1962, Barnes 1995, Brentano 1975, Burnyeat et al. 1979 and 1984, Burnyeat 2001, Copleston 1976, Elders 1972, M. Frede and Patzig 1988, C. Gill 2006, Gilson 1974, Gomperz 1969, Graham 1987, Guthrie 1983, Happ 1971, Hartmann 1941, Heidegger 1967, E. Johnson 1906, G. E. R. Lloyd 1968, Maritain 1961, Owens 1978, Rapp 2012, Routila 1969, Schmitz 1985, Stenzel 1931, and Ross 1960.

[13] *Metaphysics* 1037a29: ἡ γὰρ οὐσία ἐστὶ τὸ εἶδος τὸ ἐνόν.

[14] *Metaphysics* 1038a5–9: τὸ γένος ἁπλῶς μὴ ἔστι παρὰ τὰ ὡς γένους εἴδη.

[15] *Metaphysics* 1038a8–10: ὁ ὁρισμός ἐστιν ὁ ἐκ τῶν διαφορῶν λόγος.

[16] *Metaphysics* 1038a19–20: φανερὸν ὅτι ἡ τελευταία διαφορὰ ἡ οὐσία τοῦ πράγματος ἔσται καὶ ὁ ὁρισμός.

[17] *On the Parts of Animals* 644a24: οὐσίαι μέν εἰσι τὰ ἔσχατα εἴδη.

[18] *Metaphysics* 1038b8–9: ἔοικε γὰρ ἀδύνατον εἶναι οὐσίαν εἶναι ὁτιοῦν τῶν καθόλου λεγομένων.

[19] *History of Animals* 490b15.

most natural act is the production of another like itself, an animal producing an animal, a plant a plant, in order that, as far as its nature allows, it may partake in the eternal and divine. That is the goal towards which all things strive, that for the sake of which they do whatsoever their nature renders possible. The phrase 'for the sake of which' is ambiguous; it may mean either (a) the end to achieve which, or (b) the being in whose interest, the act is done. Since then no living thing is able to partake in what is eternal and divine by uninterrupted continuance (for nothing perishable can forever remain one and the same), it tries to achieve that end in the only way possible to it, and success is possible in varying degrees; so it remains not indeed as the self-same individual but continues its existence in something like itself—not numerically but specifically one.

Aristotle *On the Soul* 415a26–b7[20]

In his biological works and in *On the Soul*, Aristotle goes even further. Not only the humans, but all living creatures, including plants, are striving to reach the eternal and the divine by creating their offspring, which are not identical with the parents or the organisms that have begotten them, but are from the same *eidos*. Consequently, the *eidos* of the living creatures remains eternal in the eternal cosmos. Aristotle explains how this occurs in all species of animals, group by group, in *On the Generation of Animals*, and leaves to Theophrastus the work on the explanation of plants—their *eidê*, habitations, and means of propagation. The radically ontological thinking of the hylomorphism in Aristotle is spread not only over all animals, insects, and bloodless creatures, but reaches to the barely perceptible small organisms, which appear in this world through self-generation. It is not difficult to explain and to attribute the form to the male, and the matter to the female, in all greater living beings and animals.

Aristotle postulates the above premise in the *Metaphysics* and traces this ontological heterosexuality in all species individually, without any omission, in *On the Generation of Animals*. But what about the most microscopic creatures, which appear in the mud, the water, the sand, and the cliffs? Aristotle has a resounding answer. In all these places, where some living creature appears, no matter how miniscule it is, no matter how difficult it is to determine what exactly it is as *eidos* or how to name it, he envisions the same principle of propagation to operate. The male typically is the active-and-acting agent, the female the passive recipient and patient. The female in these cases is the matter, the

---

[20] Hereafter the translation is according to M. A. Smith, available at http://classics.mit.edu/ Aristotle/soul.mb.txt (accessed on November 27, 2015).

nourishing milieu, in which the tiny living creatures are self-generated, and the male is the acting *pneuma*, which brings its vital heat, corresponding in these circumstances to the masculine principle-bearer of *eidos* or the form in the larger animals. He calls the vital principle that engenders life, immanent or connatural, *pneuma*, containing the vital or literally the psychic heat: "Animals and plants are formed in the earth and in the water because in earth water is present, and in water *pneuma* is present, and in *pneuma* soul-heat is present, so that in a way all things are full of Soul."[21]

At the end of this subsection, let us stress once again the importance of Aristotle's idea of the purposefulness and goal orientation of every bodily part in every living being. His passionate pursuit of teleology is not only all-pervasive, it is triumphalist. He is not simply delighted to find the final cause everywhere, even in places and in creatures repulsive in the eyes of others, but he praises it, with only one exception. In *On the Generation of Animals*, he concedes that sometimes, albeit rarely, things may go wrong and monstrous deformations can occur in the prenatal development of serpents and the hatching of birds.[22] This is the only failure he detects in the deeds of nature.

3. The Polemical Approach of *On the Soul*

The history of the soul reasonably is among our priorities.

Aristotle *On the Soul* 402a3–4

Aristotle begins his discussion of the concept of the soul in the eponymous treatise with the modest word *historia* (περὶ τῆς ψυχῆς ἱστορίαν), as if he warns the readers that what will be undertaken in the beginning is not a survey or a study, but rather a description or a narration—that is, a mere exposition.[23] In the first

---

[21] The translation is according to Peck 1942.

[22] This teratology occupies greater part of chapters three and four of book four of *On the Generation of Animals*.

[23] In the last fifty years, an enormous amount of secondary literature on Aristotle's *On the Soul* has been accumulated, especially on the problems concerning what today is conceived as epistemology, philosophy of mind, and cognitive psychology. There are at least three types of approaches in the scholarship, resulting in interpretations, meta-interpretations, and even meta-meta-interpretations. For the first kind, see Mansion 1961, G. E. R. Lloyd and Owen 1978, and Barnes, Schofield, and Sorabji 1975–1979. The second kind includes both polemical and expository meta-interpretative approaches that address the debates, ignited in the first group of interpreters rather than on the ancient and medieval approaches to the *Corpus Aristotelicum*, e. g. Schield's report on the recent literature, accompanying Hamlyn's translation 1968, and those collected in Nussbaum and Rorty 1995. The meta-meta-interpretations report the scholarly opinions in the previous decades, e.g. Matthews 2003. While working on this chapter, I found the greatest elucidation in the chapters on Plato and Aristotle in Blackwell's *Companion to*

book of the work he briefly presents and criticizes the views of nearly all his predecessors. This is a must in his philosophical style, which he never skips, but the critical and quite often biased history of philosophy is found in different places in his treatises. Sometimes it precedes the exposition of his own views, as it is in the *Metaphysics* and *On the Soul*. In other cases the critical survey follows immediately after the first book, as it is in *On the Heavens* and the *Politics*.

In *On the Soul*, he launches the polemical examination of his predecessors' theories as an introduction to the problem. His concise overview of the earlier misconceptions on the subject is intense, with an internal rhythm and pulse. The sentences are relatively short and with more compact syntactical structure than the exposition in the following two books. The counterarguments with which he confronts the conceptions of the earlier philosophers are clear. Moreover, if we compare the ratio between the polemical first part and the two other books, we see that *On the Soul* is maybe one of the treatises in which his critical approach to his predecessors' views and theories is most felt.

The first chapter begins with the importance of the history of the concept of soul for the attainment of universal truth and for the understanding of nature because the soul is the principle of all living beings. A few lines later, disappointed by his investigation of the earlier theories on the soul, he admits that the most difficult problem of all is to find something plausible about the soul, especially if one looks for its essence and formal cause. Next, he enlists the difficulties surrounding the method(s) of studying the soul to determine whether it is one method or many? The full list of these *aporiae* runs as follows:

1. Whether the soul is one genus of being or many (substance, quality, quantity).

2. Whether it is potentiality or *entelekheia*.

3. Whether it is divisible in parts or not.

4. Whether the soul is "homogenous-and-uniform" (*homoeidês*).

5. If it is not, what makes the difference: the genus or the species?

6. If there are not many souls, but the available ones are parts of only one (universal) soul, whether we should first look for the all-embracing (cosmic) soul or for its parts.

Ancient Philosophy 2006, the articles by Shields, Modrak, and Caston in Anagnostopoulos 2009, the analyses of Patzig and Shields offered in D. Frede and Reis 2009, and Johansen's lucid 2012 study. I also had the privilege to attend a seminar on Aristotle's *On the Soul*, organized by the South East European Association for Ancient Philosophy and UNCE in Prague, September 4–6, 2014.

7. Whether the "affections" (*pathê*) belong solely to the soul or they affect in some way the body as well. The examination of the latter leads to one of the pillars of Aristotle's psychology: the passions or the affections of the soul are inseparable from the physical matter of the living being (*On the Soul* 403a16–b19).

From here until the end of book one, Aristotle scrutinizes and rejects the views of almost all Greek Presocratic philosophers one by one, including his master and his fellow pupils in the Academy. He starts his historical survey with the general observation that ensouled beings (i.e. creatures) differ from ones deprived of soul by the two main characteristics of motion and perception. What follows is a detailed and well-grounded inventory list of his objections. According to him, his predecessors have failed to explain what the essence of the soul is, because all of them have overestimated the force of the soul to move itself and/or to move all the rest in the Whole. Instead, he continues, many of these thinkers have tried to reduce the soul to one of the material principles and causes. Democritus, for example, made two grave mistakes: first, he attempted to define soul as some kind of fire and as something hot; and second, he conceived it as aggregate of miniscule spherical atoms that are the seed-elements of all nature.

In a similar fashion, Aristotle exposes and rejects the opinions of almost all philosophers, one by one, because according to him:

1. The soul *cannot* either act or be acted upon, if it is separated or separable from the body.

2. The passions do *not* occur separately from the physical matter of the body and they are *not* conceivable without it, albeit not in the same manner, as the lines and the surfaces are actually present in the bodies and only virtually separable from them.

3. The soul should *not* be conceived as self-moving and its movement *should not* be counted as its most essential.

4. The soul *should not* be identified with the *nous.*

5. It *should not* be reduced to any of the initial elements and/or their transformations (as suggested by Democritus, Heraclitus, Thales, and Diogenes of Apollonia).

6. The soul should *not* be reckoned as the eternally self-moving principle, which by itself moves the Sun, the Moon, the stars, and the whole heaven (as suggested by Alcmaeon of Croton).

7. The soul should *not* be seated anywhere in the body of the sanguineous animals and men or reduced to some of the vital liquids in it (it is *not* engendered either by the blood or by the sperm).

8. The soul is *not* explicable as belonging either to one cause and element, or to several of them.

9. It is wrong to place it among the opposites, as thought by all of his predecessors who believe that the opposites are among the principles.

10. Even though it might be accepted that the soul is a moving principle, it is *not* necessary for it to be self-moving as well, because there are four types of movement.

11. The soul should *not* be conceived as magnitude, ratio, or proportion of a series of numbers because, if it is, the *nous* inevitably should be segmented and compartmentalized, whereas Aristotle holds it to be united and unique, and continuous, because the thinking of the thought is united and indivisible.

12. The soul is *not* harmony.

13. The dilemma of whether the soul is the only bodiless entity or whether it is the finest body, according to him, is false, because neither of the assumptions is correct.

14. The soul should *not* be divided into parts.

15. Those who have segmented the soul into parts, assign to each one of them some specific function in vain.

These objections demontrate Aristotle's disapproval of all existent theories about the soul. As it happens, in books one, thirteen, and fourteen of the *Metaphysics*, the most acerbic remarks are addressed to his classmates from the Academy according to whom the soul is a self-moving number. Unsurprisingly, Plato receives Aristotle's greatest attention in this critical introduction. Almost half of the refuted propositions are easily traced to his views on the soul, although not all of them are explicitly assigned to the exact dialogue. For example, the *Timaeus* is mentioned twice, but the titles of the other relevant dialogues, in which one or another view is presented, are omitted. In the following two books of *On the Soul*, he finds some other minor issues with the opinions of those before him, but they are just minor explanatory remarks on particular issues.

Based on his meticulous enumeration of what he considers to be conceptual mistakes about the soul, we can infer that he was not a materialist, dualist, idealist, spiritualist, or functionalist. His critical history of the concept of soul dismisses all views proposed by the earlier philosophers. The first book of *On the Soul* is not only the most expanded critical introduction, compared with the other two books and with other similar counterparts in the Aristotelian Corpus, but it is also the most critical one. There are many poetic and mythical images, abstract concepts, strange ideas, and curious views, which he disapproves of and sometimes distorts in his numerous polemic surveys of existent theories on the topics of the first and the second philosophy, political organization, or ethics.[24] Despite his critical approach, it is still indisputable how much he has inherited from his predecessors, and in particular from Plato. In the later books of *On the Soul*, it becomes clear that the initial impression of total negativity is not absolutely justified. Indeed, there are several solutions of some problems in the chapters, devoted to cognitive psychology or the philosophy of emotions, in which he is not an absolute beginner, but for the conceptual kernel of his theory he proposed something new: metaphysics of the soul. Having overthrown all previous views and opinions on the basics, he had to propose something new—and he did.

4. The Problem of the Body

Aristotle offers three different approaches to understanding the body. First, *On the Heavens* starts with the definition of the body as a three-dimensional entity. This approach relies on the geometrical postulate that the line has one dimension, the surface has two, and the solid has three. This quantitative or, even better, stereometric approach, at least on the spatial and cosmological level, remains separated from any notion of soul whatsoever. Yet, Aristotle is unsatisfied with the geometrical purity of Plato's explanations of the primary bodies and the elements in the *Timaeus* (53c–55d and 55e–56c). In *On the Heavens* 3.8 and 4.2, he lays out the arguments against it: the polyhedral approach is rigorous, exact, and neat, impeccable in all aspects, and fulfilling almost all demands, but fails with its inability to grasp the variety of qualities in the physical world, especially the ones, combined in the three pairs of opposites—heavy and light, cold and hot, and wet/moist and dry. He revisits the problem in several important places of *On the Soul*, and in particular in its second book. All the basic concepts of his first philosophy are here: substantial being or substance, principle, body, natural body, life, soul, matter, "form" (*eidos*), *hupokeimenon*, potentiality, being in potentiality, and perfection-in-actuality:

> Among substances are by general consent reckoned bodies and especially natural bodies; for they are the principles of all other bodies. Of natural bodies some have life in them, others not; by life we mean

---

[24] See Cherniss 1933, 1944, and 1971.

self-nutrition and growth (with its correlative decay). It follows that every natural body which has life in it is a substance in the sense of a composite. But since it is also a body of such and such a kind, viz. having life, the body cannot be soul; the body is the subject or matter, not what is attributed to it. Hence the soul must be a substance in the sense of the form of a natural body having life potentially within it. But substance is actuality, and thus soul is the actuality of a body as above characterized. Now the word actuality has two senses corresponding respectively to the possession of knowledge and the actual exercise of knowledge. It is obvious that the soul is actuality in the first sense, viz. that of knowledge as possessed ... That is why the soul is the first grade of actuality of a natural body having life potentially in it.

Aristotle *On the Soul* 412a11–28

We can summarize the main points of the above passage as:

1. The concept of life is the decisive criterion according to which there are natural bodies that possess life and others that are deprived of life.

2. Life is the disposition of the natural bodies to self-nourishment, growth, and decay.

3. The last three are the capacities through which life manifests itself and which lay the foundation of the two succeeding conclusions.

4. Every natural body, participating in life, is a composite substantial being.

5. From the above it follows that, in the living composite being, the soul is not a body.

6. The body is the subject or matter, not what is attributed to it (according to Smith's translation quoted above) or "the body is not something predicated of a subject, but exists rather as subject and matter" (translation by Hamlyn).

7. It is necessary for the soul to be a non-composite substantial being as the form (*eidos*) of a natural body that possesses life in potentiality.

8. The substantial being is *entelekheia*.

9. *Entelekheia* is twofold: one form is comparable to the knowledge that is already attained and possessed, but is not always or constantly used, as when we sleep, for instance; the other is the active practice of knowledge, as when we theorize.

10. For the above reason, the soul is the first *entelekheia* of the natural body that possesses life potentially.[25]

Of the above axioms, the fifth and the sixth are most crucial. The fifth denies the reduction of the soul to the body in some kind of general opposition to the majority of the Presocratics. The other is more puzzling. There are two viable translations of his statement that οὐ γάρ ἐστι τῶν καθ' ὑποκειμένου τὸ σῶμα, μᾶλλον δ' ὡς ὑποκείμενον καὶ ὕλη: (1) "the body is the subject or matter, not what is attributed to it," as rendered by M. A. Smith; (2) "for the body is not something predicated of a subject, but exists rather as subject and matter," as rendered by Hamlyn.

The first translation suggests that Aristotle's concept might be read and understood in the light of his *Metaphysics* and *Physics* (i.e. Aristotle's first and second philosophy), where ὑποκείμενον καὶ ὕλη is the passive substrate and the inactive material principle on which the active formal principle imposes its shape and structure, activates and energizes it, bringing what is acted upon to its ontological aim.

The second translation suggests another way of thinking about the body, without an explicit connection with the soul. Let us call this the "ontologico-linguistic" approach to the problem of the body. This phrase might be understood in relation to the optics in the *Categories*. The statement οὐ γάρ ἐστι τῶν καθ' ὑποκειμένου τὸ σῶμα, μᾶλλον δ' ὡς ὑποκείμενον καὶ ὕλη recalls his well-known postulate about substance in the *Categories*. The body is not among the predicates that are *predicated to a subject*, but rather it is comparable to the *subject in a sentence*.[26] This means that the body as a whole is more eligible for the ontological recognition of a substantial being than its parts, organs, systems, and functions. The living body, taken in its entirety is more substance than its parts, which cannot exist and be conceived of as substances, when detached from the whole to which they belong. (For example, the body as a whole is a more substantial being than the hair or the nails, the arms or the legs, which can exist only as parts of it. The body is indispensable for them, but they are not indispensable for the body.)

The third approach to the problem of the body is the elemental one. What is the composition of the ensouled body, which enables it to live and feel, to perceive and perform the functions, and which delineates the living bodies from the ones deprived of life? The three main peculiarities that characterize the living entities from the not-living ones are self-nourishment, growth, and decay

---

[25] *On the Soul* 412a27–28: διὸ ἡ ψυχή ἐστιν ἐντελέχεια σώματος φυσικοῦ δυνάμει ζωὴν ἔχοντος.

[26] This logical and linguistic reading, which has its ontological transposition, is found in Theiler's 1965 rendition of the passage.

(the second axiom above); and these aspects are common to everything alive (plants, animals, and humans). All living beings possess various sense perceptions, but the lowest one, which is also shared by plants and thereby is the most widely spread manifestation of life, is the sense of touch (*haphê*). Plants cannot hear and see, reason and recollect, dream and contemplate, but they are alive because they have *hê haphê*. Precisely, in the context of his discussion of the sense of touch (*On the Soul* 422b34–423a21, and again, at the very end of the treatise, 435b4–18), he reasons about the constitution of the ensouled body as follows: the body cannot be composed of air or water alone, because it has to be solid; thus, it has to be three-dimensional and it has to have some shape. Water and air are insufficient for the composition of any body, because they are instable and deprived of any shape. Instead, they are expanding and filling in the limits of the bodies embracing them. So, it remains for him to conclude that the flesh is a mixture of the three elements—earth, water, and air. More interesting is his next sentence: "Hence, the body must be the naturally adhering medium for that which can perceive by touch and its perceptions take place through it, manifold as they are."[27] To understand better what exactly he has in mind, we should look at a more literal rendition of the above statement: "So, it is necessary for the body to be the that-in-between (*to metaxu*) the adhering touching organism and its perceptions because of which the multitude of sensations is engendered."

The third book of *On the Soul* finishes with the same considerations (435b4–18): the ensouled bodies are compounds of the three elements—earth, air, and water—in different proportions because they cannot exist without the ability to touch. The sense of touch is the only indispensable of the five fundamental sense perceptions. The ensouled body is "that-in-between" the principal elements.

5. The Soul As Principle of Life

For the living creatures *to be* is *to live*; the soul is cause and principle of this.

Aristotle *On the Soul* 415b12–14

To some extent it is possible for Aristotle to articulate what the body is, without referring to the soul, as when he speaks of the cosmos and its eternally structured beauty and perfection (*On the Heavens* 1.9) or when he defines the bodies as three-dimensional entities (*On the Heavens* 1.1). He also offers, however, a

---

[27] *On the Soul* 423a15–17: ὥστε ἀναγκαῖον τὸ σῶμα εἶναι τὸ μεταξὺ τοῦ ἁπτικοῦ προσπεφυκός, δι' οὗ γίνονται αἱ αἰσθήσεις πλείους οὖσαι.

remarkable understanding of the essence of the soul, correlated to the body and leading it to its fulfillment and perfection. Yet, he does so without any inclination to reduce the one to the other, or to describe them as the parallel entities in the soul-body duality, or as independent universes, abiding in total remoteness and self-sufficiency, as found in contemporary String Theory. His solution is unique, in a way unprecedented by any other Greek philosopher and somehow marginalized by his successors, even by the ones who have tried to be as loyal to him as possible.

Aristotle starts with the exposition of his own views in the beginning of the second book of *On the Soul*: from this point on until the end of the text he defines the soul as the principle of life, nature, cause, and substantial being, but most often as the substantial agent in the substantial beings. To this end, he develops the conceptual triad of *dunamis–energeia–entelekheia*. No one has done so before him, because *energeia* and *entelekheia* have been purposefully coined by him, whereas *dunamis* has been around for awhile, but it does not have the specific ontological and modal meaning Aristotle assigns to it in the triad.

The noun *dunamis* and a number of cognate verbs appear in the most difficult mathematical puzzle in the *Theaetetus*. The three pages of text in *Theaetetus* 147c–148e cause a headache, but also inspire both the readers of the original and its translators.[28] In the *Epinomis* (986a5), the word occurs in the plural and designates the most divine celestial dwellers, the planets. At first glance, Aristotle almost completely neglects the geometrical and the astronomical meaning of the word and restores its initial etymological range, denoting "power" and "might." At a second glance, however, we may recognize the kernels of the future Aristotelian dynamic conceptualization of the term both in the mathematical task about the incommensurable lines and its solution by the seventeen triangles (proposed by the young Theaetetus); and also in the passage of the *Epinomis*, implying a dynamic self-movement of the planets, instead of the proposed static one as found in *On the Heavens*.

In the three core books on substance of the *Metaphysics*, and especially in book nine, we find the term fully fledged in an array of meanings from potentiality, potency, and possibility to the disposition-to-become-different and the readiness-to-become-other. The modal category has as its hylomorphic counterpart, the matter—the passive ontological ingredient—which co-opts *ousia* in the formation of the composite substantial entities, under the guidance of the active form (*eidos*).

---

[28] See Levett's translation and Burnyeat's commentary (1990:266).

In book four, among the vocabulary of the thirty most used philosophical terms by Aristotle, we find several entries on the meaning of *dunamis*:

1. The beginning of the movement or the principle of change that is in something else or is in the changed, but inasmuch as it *might* be different (*Metaphysics* 1019a15–16).

2. The beginning of the movement or the principle of change that is in something else or in the changed entity inasmuch as it *is* different. The important condition Aristotle raises here is that this passive-and-positive disposition to changes from outside occurs only in cases in which the changes lead to a better state (*Metaphysics* 1019a19–23).

3. The ability to reach a completion and to come to a successful end in a process of a change (*Metaphysics* 1019a23–24) that has been chosen or preferred by the entity itself.

4. With regard to the changes that are undergone by a passive entity, *dunameis* are the dispositions to remain unchanged, literally passionless; they are the passive powers of the entity to oppose a negative change; they are the resistance forces of the thing to deteriorate in a worse state (*Metaphysics* 1019a26–29); they are the ontological forces that preserve the things in a certain state, when their change entails worsening.

The first entry points to the capacity of an entity to be changed by something external or the power for something to change itself by itself. This meaning is embedded in the Latin *potentia* as one of the equivalents of *dunamis*. The second entry emphasizes the external origin of change. Compared to the former, the latter suggests that something might be changed more likely under external pressure, and only in a limited degree to its own disposition to the evolving change. This meaning is carried over to the Latin *possibilitas*. The third meaning of the noun is closer to the earlier Greek usages of the word in the literature and especially in the medical treatises: quality, capacity, skill, faculty, mastering, experience, power, and authority. These are the roots of the Latin renderings of *potestas* and *facultas*. The fourth entry is most striking: it says that a possibility must not be a possibility, that a power has to remain powerless, that an active force and a strength have to become, respectively, passivity and weakness. In other words, some possibilities to (self-)change have to be eliminated and some developments have to be impeded in order to preserve the entities in their present states, because at the end of the undesired processes they might deteriorate. These axiological accents on the third and the fourth entry in the vocabulary are due to the unquestionable ontological superiority of Aristotle's understanding of teleology.

The other two elements of the conceptual triad are the landmarks of Aristotle's metaphysics. Coined by him, they have become the bearers of the heaviest philosophical tasks in his ontology, natural philosophy, and psychology. In the realm of theology, *energeia* performs two crucial explanatory functions. First, in the most theological book of the *Metaphysics* (1072b27), the incessant activity and the perpetual actualization of the supreme first cause and final end, the *nous*, is life. Life is the phenomenon of "the active thinking of the thought" (*noêsis noêseôs noêsis, Metaphysics* 1074b34–35). The supreme *nous*, the first alpha and the last omega in the eternal cosmos, has been, continuously is, and will remain forever active. All over the eternal Whole, life is the manifestation of the activity of the supreme immaterial form in it, engaged in the endless act of pure thinking. Also, not less important is the other employment of the concept. Not only the highest being in the cosmos, but every single entity in it, alive or not, produced by art or naturally engendered, has come into existence because of the priority of the activity and its greater ontological importance, compared with passive matter or the potential changes and processes (*Metaphysics* 1049b24–25 and 1051a4–5).

The first of the two concepts has found its way through the centuries, although initially marginalized. Nowadays its meaning extends to a wide range of usages—starting from theology, philosophy, physics, and engineering through all the arts and sciences. The word "energy" (*energeia*) is everywhere. The other one is less lucky. The misunderstanding of *entelekheia* and its reduction and identification with *energeia* permeates the reception of Aristotle in the Latin West. In the translations and in the commentaries of his works done in the medieval European universities, slowly but irreversibly the difference between *actus primus* and *actus secundus* has been deleted.

The concept *energeia* is mostly used in the explanation of the cognitive activities and epistemic aspects of life of humans and animals. As explained above, all plants are endowed with the capacity of only one sense perception, i.e. touch. Through their roots, leaves, and trunks they receive water, nutritive stuff, and light. The animals share with humans four other more complex sense perceptions. They have the natural disposition not only to touch, but also to hear, to see, to smell, and to taste. All these powers, abilities, and faculties to perceive and to discern, to recollect and to remember, become active and actualized under certain circumstances and conditions. For the sake of clarity and conciseness, let us use the following demarcation here: *energeia* refers to the various aspects of the epistemological and the psychological activities of the living beings (in the animal kingdom and the human genus), whereas *entelekheia* is the more general metaphysical designation of the ensouled body, enjoying life, of "the entirety and the fulfilled perfection of the living monad."[29]

In the definition of the soul in the beginning of book two, as previously discussed, the ordinal number "first," attached to the concept *entelekheia*, might be understood as the ontological primacy and self-sufficiency of the living organism in its entirety and capability to perceive and/or think, and/or imagine, and/or consider, and/or move. *Entelekheia* is the first in respect of its ontological importance and significance. Especially elucidating is the example, given in *On the Soul* 413b16–20: there are activities performed by the parts of some dissected animals among the "insected" (*entoma*) creatures—which according to him comprise not only insects, but also worms and the like—which exhibit some functions and particularly some sensation long after their removal from the entire organism. If we look for a newer concept to identify these living beings in a less outdated manner, the most appropriate linguistic marker for me seems to be: the living monad. Aristotle is driven by the passion to explain the phenomenon of life, the magic of the living as a monad, in which the soul cannot be compartmentalized and cut off from the body, but it cannot be reduced to it either. No wonder that Leibnitz had borrowed so much from Aristotle, after the neglect of the concept of *entelekheia*, demontrated by so many scholastic authorities, who had failed to understand its richness. For Aristotle, the living beings—plants, animals, and humans—are ontologically fulfilled, perfect, and completed monads in which the corporeal and the spiritual ingredients are inseparable. A living creature cannot participate in life and be alive without a body and a soul, with all their aspects and activities, both psychic and cognitive.[30]

6. The Mystery of *Nous* in the Reign of Life

The problems surrounding Aristotle's teleological concept of the soul as *entelekheia*—form and principle of life—are many. Smallest among them is the difficulty to translate the term properly in many languages, including Latin.[31] The gravest problem of them all, however, is Aristotle's rejection of the predominant

---

[29] A proper map or an appendix is needed in order to vindicate such a delineation that might happen in a book, not in a short sketch such as the current chapter. For a list of relevant passages, see n9 above.

[30] The cognitive problems are extraneous to my focus here. For recent scholarly interpretations, see G. E. R. Lloyd and Owen 1978, Nussbaum and Rorty 1995, Gregorić 2007, Johansen 2012, Polansky 2007, and Wijsenbeek-Wijler 1978.

[31] Indeed, the best way is not to translate it at all, but just to transliterate it, as is done by Jannone and Barbotin's 1995 translation. There are so many Greek philosophical terms and concepts that have been adopted long ago in the Indo-European languages. *Entelekheia* might be finally added to them, instead of the desperate reductive translations "to act," "activity," or "actuality." Indispensable for the vindication of this insistence is Bos 2003.

(especially after Plato) view that the soul is immortal. It is the reason for which so many Aristotelians met their unfortunate end in the Middle Ages, despite the fact that their admiration for his philosophy did not force them to abandon their pious religious credo. For Aristotle, the soul does not outlive the body. It ensouls it because it is precisely the fulfillment-perfection-completion of the body. He could not find satisfaction in any materialistic or atheistic cosmological worldview. On the contrary, he firmly believed in immortality, but in the immortality of *Nous*, and not of soul.[32] We may search in vain through his texts for answers to the questions of whence this active *nous* comes and where it goes after the body dies. It is not clear either what its ontological status is before or after its cooperation with our ensouled body. Only the following places in *On the Soul* are unambiguous:

1. *Nous* is more divine and unaffected (by feelings, passions, and sense perceptions) than the joint entity of the soul-with-body; for this reason, the *Nous* neither recollects nor loves after the extinction of the soul-body compound (*On the Soul* 408b25–29).

2. *Nous* is unmixed with the soul-body (*On the Soul* 429a18).

3. *Nous* is defined as "that thanks to which the soul is reasoning and supposing" (*On the Soul* 429a23).

4. *Nous* is passionless or unaffected by anything, yet in a kind of deprivation, different from the absence of sensitivity (*On the Soul* 429a29–31).

5. *Nous* is completely detached from the soul, from all its sense perceptions, emotions, imagining, reasoning, understanding, memories, and recollections; yet because of it, the soul can reach the highest possible thinking and comprehending.

6. *Nous* is also intelligible as all other intelligibles; among the intelligibles that are without matter, to think and to be thought of are the same (*On the Soul* 430a2–4).

7. There is *an active*, or even *activating*, *nous*, i.e. *intellectus agens separatus*, comparable to the light that makes the colors-in-potency to become actual visible colors. Precisely this *nous* is detached, untouchable, and pure, with its essence being actuality (*On the Soul* 430a16–19).

---

[32] Aristotle did believe in the immortality of the soul in its entirety when he was a member of the Academy. The windings of his theories on the soul and the vicissitudes of his intellectual biography are variously evaluated by Nuyens 1948, Lefèvre 1971, 1972, and Pellegrin 2009; not to forget the completely opposite treatment of his theoretical life by Jaeger 1934 and Düring 1966.

8. Exactly this activating *nous* is always separated and solely this part of the human being is immortal and eternal, not remembering anything of the previous life (*On the Soul* 430a22–25).

9. Not the whole of the *nous*, but this one whose formal cause corresponds to the essence of its "being" (*nous*), attains the truth (*On the Soul* 430b28–30).

10. *Nous* is the *eidos* of all *eidê* (*On the Soul* 432a1–3).

In respect to the moral and theological consequences of this view, almost everything is unquestionable. It has been alluring for some heretical thinkers and distasteful to the Christian and Muslim philosophers and theologians alike. The questions of what happens with all these "impersonal reasons" (*intellecti*), where they retreat, whether they abide in the cosmos at all and if so, how they form the concentric subordinated cosmic spheres of the "divine celestial intelligences" (*intelligentiae*), have stirred the imagination of many bored intellectuals, starting in the late antiquity, with the authors with an exclusive taste (such as those of the *Stobaei Hermetica* and the *Corpus Hermeticum*), and also given quite poisonous food to some great, but self-indulgent, thinkers in Islamic philosophy.

This conceptual portrait of *nous* raises many questions, while it offers next to no answers. The ambiguousness concerning its ontological status enhances the highly sophisticated terminology through which the modal vision of the integrity of the living monads is expressed. Maybe these are the main reasons for their historical faith: the richness of Aristotle's view of the soul as an *entelekheia* of the body has been neglected, misunderstood, and oversimplified by many thinkers adhering to many of his other views.[33] The revival of his unique conceptual invention occurred centuries later in the anthropological texts of some of the Church Fathers in the fourth century, who, quite often implicitly, and strategically, remained silent about the source from which they have borrowed terms and conceptions. The real reintegration of his thinking on the soul occurred in Latin in the great scholastic writings of the university professors in philosophy from the thirteenth century onwards.

This overarching presentation of Aristotle's views on the soul and the body allows us to draw two conclusions with some certainty. First, Aristotle is more interested in the omnipresent omnipotence of life and the soul as its manifestation than in the narrower cognitive or psychic problems. He is also more concerned with thinking about the cosmos and the omnipresence of the vital principles in it rather than about the human soul, its cognitive capacities,

---

[33] Rather different and well-grounded views on the ancient reception of his ideas are collected in van Riel and Destrée 2009.

or even about man's immortality and the vocation. Second, Aristotle's understanding of spontaneous generation allows him to explain the everlasting and permeating potency of life. The principle of life permeates everything through the vital heat of the inborn *pneuma*. Everything in the cosmos, including inorganic material, is potentially ensouled.[34] Such is the inexhaustible power of the reign of life in Aristotle's view of the eternal cosmos. The three words that best summarize his teleological view of existence are: eternity, vitality, and cohesion. Not only in every living being is the soul the vital principle of the body, but also, in the cosmos as a whole, there is such vital congenial unifying bond because of the ontological analogy between the elements building the sublime stars and the powers in the generative foam, engendering the smallest imperceptible creatures everywhere—always and forever.

---

[34] On the inborn or connate *pneuma*, vital heat and spontaneous generation, see Balme 1962, Byl 1980, Furth 1988, Gotthelf 1985, Lennox 1985, Gilson 1971, Jaeger 1913, Peck 1953, Quinn 1964, Solmsen 1957, and Stavrianeas 2008.

PART II

SOUL-BODY PERSPECTIVES IN IMPERIAL AND LATE ANCIENT PLATONISM

3

Galen on Soul-Body Relations

John Dillon

Abstract: In the course of his treatise *That the Faculties of the Soul Follow the Mixtures of the Body* (QAM), the distinguished doctor Galen, who in general professes himself a philosopher with Platonist leanings, launches an attack on certain persons whom he terms "self-styled Platonists" (*QAM* 4.805 Kühn) for venturing to maintain "that the soul, though obstructed by the body in states of disease, performs its own functions without assistance or hindrance from the body provided the latter is healthy." These persons he proposes to confute by quoting against them a series of passages from Plato's *Timaeus*, which he feels argue for the contrary position. This chapter tries to work out, on the basis of what we know about doctrinal tendencies in the Middle Platonic period, and in particular, in the late second century, who these persons might be; and also, to explore, on the basis of this treatise and a number of other passages from his works, what was the position of Galen himself on the issue of the relation between the mind, or soul, and the body.

The view attributed to the Platonists here is very much that adopted by Plotinus in the middle of the next century, but that does not solve the problem. In surveying the known Platonists of the second century (Atticus, Numenius, Harpocration, Severus), the author is inclined to fix on the last of these, on admittedly very slim evidence. As for Galen's own views, the evidence is extensive, and most interesting, for one who considered himself a Platonist in philosophy.

IN THE COURSE OF HIS treatise *That the Faculties of the Soul Follow the Mixtures of the Body* (*QAM*), the distinguished doctor Galen, who in general professes himself a philosopher of the Platonist persuasion,[1] launches an attack on certain persons whom he terms "self-styled Platonists" (*QAM* 4.805 Kühn) for venturing to maintain that the soul, at least while the body is in a healthy state, performs its own functions without assistance or hindrance from the body.[2] These persons he proposes to confute by quoting against them a series of passages from Plato's *Timaeus*, which he feels argue for the contrary position.

My purpose in this chapter is, first of all, to set out, on the basis of this treatise and a number of other passages from his works, the position of Galen himself on the issue of the relation between the mind, or soul, and the body; and second, to try to discern, on the basis of what we know about doctrinal tendencies in the 'Middle Platonic' period, and more particularly, in the late second century, who these persons who call themselves Platonists might be.

1. Platonic Views on Soul-Body Relations

First of all, however, we need to go back, briefly, to remind ourselves of the position of Plato and the Old Academy. One notable feature of—or perhaps, rather, lacuna in—Plato's philosophy that only really comes into focus from the perspective of later developments is the virtual lack, in his published works, of any suggestion as to what influence, mechanism, or device the soul—which is presented as a substance of quite antithetical nature to the body (namely, eternal, immaterial, nonextended)—can employ to control and direct the body that it rules, sets in motion, and holds together.[3] In such works as the *Phaedo*, *Phaedrus*, *Republic*, or *Timaeus*, the soul just does this, in a remarkably nonproblematic way. In the *Phaedo*, after all, it is axiomatic that it is the role of the soul to rule, and that of the body to be ruled (80a), but how this takes place is never specified. The body, or love of the body, is said repeatedly to contaminate the soul, but we are never told how. Later, in the *Phaedrus*, in his most formal and

---

[1]   Never slavishly, it must be said, but if we consider carefully the assumptions behind such a work as that *On the Doctrines of Hippocrates and Plato*, we must grant that Galen takes Plato to be the greatest of philosophers, even as Hippocrates is the greatest of doctors, and that it is important for him that they are in agreement. On Galen's Platonism, see De Lacy 1972, and, more recently, Chiaradonna 2009, who presents a good conspectus of the negative argument.

[2]   Translation Singer 2013.

[3]   I think in particular of such a document as Plotinus' *Ennead* VI 4–5, a protracted enquiry as to how an immaterial being can be present to material things, beginning from the problem of how the soul can be present to the body. Plotinus seems to have composed this treatise at least partly in response to Porphyry's protracted queries as to how the soul can relate to the body (*Life of Plotinus* 13.11–12).

programmatic statement of the role and nature of the soul (245c–e), Plato presents it as self-moved, and the origin of all motion in other things;[4] but once again the mode by which this might be achieved is not perceived as a problem. Again, in the *Timaeus*, the various parts of the soul are distributed about the body[5] and interact with it in a way laying Plato open to criticism by Aristotle for making the soul an extended entity (*On the Soul* 404b16–18). However, there is still no suggestion as to how this works—although, in the later part of the dialogue (*Timaeus* 86b–89e), much is made of the mutual affection of soul and body in the generation of psychological and psycho-somatic illnesses. Lastly, in the *Laws* (894e–899c), the soul is once again identified as the source of all physical motion, but we never learn how it does this.

This is a legacy that Plato bequeaths to his followers, and they take it up in various ways. One possible strategy is to deny, or at least reinterpret, the immateriality of the soul. This appears to have been done, within the Old Academy, by the admittedly rather maverick figure of Heraclides of Pontus, who is reported as maintaining that, while the human soul is immortal, and subject to reincarnation (fr. 97 Wehrli), it is composed of at least a quasi-material substance, "light" (fr. 98), or "aether" (fr. 99). This latter testimony, from the proem of John Philoponus' *Commentary on Aristotle's On the Soul*, runs as follows:

> Of those who have declared the soul to be a simple body (ἁπλοῦν σῶμα), some have declared it to be an aetherial body (αἰθέριον σῶμα), which is the same as to say 'heavenly' (οὐράνιον), as for instance Heraclides of Pontus.

John Philoponus *Commentary on Aristotle's On the Soul*
9.5–7, my translation

This makes it sound as if Heraclides actually used the term *ouranion sôma*, but Philoponus plainly regards this as equivalent to *aitherion*, and he is probably right. He also seems to have declared that the Milky Way was the proper home of souls when they have left the body (*Commentary on Aristotle's On the Soul* 9.5–7), which would be consistent with their having an "aetherial" nature.

This, then, is one solution to the conundrum of interaction between the immaterial and the material, and it was one that could commend itself to a member of the Old Academy, albeit a notably independent-minded one. It also seems to go some way towards countering the criticisms of Aristotle. Aether and light are, admittedly, pretty rarefied forms of body, but at least they are not

---

[4] *Phaedrus* 245d6–7: οὕτω δὴ κινέσεως μὲν ἀρχὴ τὸ αὐτὸ αὑτὸ κινοῦν.

[5] Though in fact only the *epithumêtikon* is specifically assigned to its seat, namely, the liver—a vagueness that Galen is conscious of, and is concerned to remedy!

antithetical to the other substances of which bodies are made. We can see here, I think, the beginnings of a trend of thought that was to lead in the next genera-tion to the Stoic solution that the active principle in the universe was a certain sort of pure "intellectual fire" (*pur noeron*); but it was also a line of thought that seems to have reinserted itself into the Platonic tradition in interesting ways, as we shall see presently, and that was thus available as an option for Galen.

The other alternative is the postulation of an intermediary entity between (immaterial) soul and body, of the same substance proposed by Heraclides for the soul—that is to say, aether—which would necessarily have the property of, while being itself a kind of (very fine) matter, being able to mediate between the immaterial and the material. There is in fact some substantial evidence for this, if one brings Aristotle into the story, as I feel that one is quite entitled to do, as a quondam member of the Old Academy.

In fact, already from the period of Plato's old age, we have, I think, one little indication that such speculations had impinged upon his consciousness. At *Laws* 898e–899a, where the Athenian Stranger is discussing the way in which we may imagine the stars to be guided by their souls, he makes the suggestion that one possibility would be that a particular star might take to itself "a body of fire, or air of some sort." This, of course, does not explicitly address the problem of how a soul might relate to a terrestrial, mortal body, but it at least adumbrates it. It really sounds here as if Plato is taking account—rather grumpily (or perhaps, ironically?)—of problems about soul-body interaction being raised by various of the more troublesome of his followers.

Among the more outspoken of these would be Aristotle. His "deconstruc-tion" of the Pythagorean-Platonic soul in *On the Soul*, in which the soul becomes simply "the first actuality of a natural body with organs"[6] (ἐντελέχεια ἡ πρώτη σώματος φυσικοῦ ὀργανικοῦ, *On the Soul* 412b5–6)—a formulation that holds much attraction for Galen, especially as regards the two "lower" parts of the Platonic soul—certainly disposes of the problem of interaction between such an immaterial entity and the body, but it does not free him from the problem of how purposive action takes place. There is still the question of the nature of the "active intellect" at *On the Soul* 430a10–b6, and its action upon the "passive intellect" which is in some way inherent in the individual. This is mysterious enough, but on the whole less troublesome, and irrelevant to our concerns on this occasion, because both intellects are (presumably) equally immaterial.[7] The

---

[6] Or perhaps, as Bos 2003: especially 96–98 would maintain, with some plausibility, "a body which acts as an instrument for it." Aristotle, he points out, always elsewhere uses *organon* in this latter sense.

[7] The Active Intellect is indeed compared to the Sun, or to light (*On the Soul* 430a15), but that does not imply that it is itself fiery.

problem that Aristotle declines to address in *On the Soul* is how a decision arrived at in the passive, or immanent, human intellect is translated into the movement of bones and sinews to pursue some end that the human being has set for itself.

This problem, however, is addressed, as we know, elsewhere, and notably in the well-known passage of *On the Generation of Animals* 736b27–31. Here we are introduced to a special sort of "innate spirit" (*sumphuton pneuma*) residing especially in the blood around the heart, which constitutes the seat of the nutritive and sensitive soul, and which is responsible for the process of "image-making" (*phantasia*), as well as for purposive action. The substance of this, we are told, is "analogous to that element of which the stars are made" (*On the Generation of Animals* 736b37–737a1)—that is to say, of Aristotle's postulated "fifth substance," or *aithêr*. So at least we have now a bridge-entity, notionally capable of receiving immaterial impulses from the intellect, and transposing them, through the instrumentality of the blood, into movements of bones and sinews.[8]

This concept of the *sumphuton pneuma* is then related, by later Platonists, to the passage of the *Timaeus* (41e), where the Demiurge assigns each of the souls a star, and "embarking it onto it as a 'vehicle' (*okhêma*), exhibits to it the nature of the universe."[9] Whatever Plato really intended to convey by this, later Platonist speculation understood this astral vehicle to be a means for connecting the immaterial to the material through the mediation of an entity composed of a special sort of particularly refined matter, and it was accordingly linked up with Aristotle's *sumphuton pneuma* to produce an entity, the so-called "pneumatic vehicle," which can be pressed into service as an intermediary.

Wherever it began, we find the concept of a pneumatic vehicle as a conduit between soul and body well established in the Platonism of the second century. Galen, at any rate, seems to take it for granted in a passage of his *On the Doctrines of Hippocrates and Plato* (VII 7.25.3–26.1 De Lacy) where he is criticizing a theory of Posidonius that postulated a "light-like" (*phôtoeides*) pneuma as constituting the proper medium for the exercise of vision. Galen makes this the basis for a general comment about the nature of the soul, to the effect that we must accept either the Stoic and Aristotelian view of soul as a "luminous and aethereal body" (αὐγοειδές τε καὶ αἰθερῶδες σῶμα) or we may take the soul itself to be an "incorporeal essence" (*asômatos ousia*), and postulate that the above-mentioned body is its "primary vehicle" (*okhêma to prôton*) "through which as a medium it establishes communication with the rest of bodies."

It is not quite clear whether Galen is adopting this theory himself, but it does not on the other hand sound as if he has invented it off the top of his

---

[8]   Cf. also the intriguing passage in *On the Motion of Animals* III 10.703a4–22, where the *pneuma* is related to the whole process of *orexis* and its realization.

[9]   See pp. 74, 107, 149n76, 158–169, 284–289, 312–313 below.

head. There is further evidence, from (probably) the same period, in the pseudo-Plutarchan treatise *On the Life and Poetry of Homer*, the author of which is acquainted with philosophical trends, though without, it would seem, being a philosopher himself. In chapter 128 of the work, he reports it as the view of Plato and Aristotle that the soul at death takes with it "the pneumatic element" (*to pneumatikon*), which then serves as its "vehicle" (*okhêma*), implying that it already possessed this while it was in the body.[10]

There is other evidence that the theory was known to Galen's contemporary, the Pythagoreanizing Platonist Numenius (fr. 34 des Places, from Macrobius), and to the author(s) of the Chaldaean Oracles, which refer to the "rarefied vehicle of the soul" (*psukhês lepton okhêma*, fr. 120 des Places). On the whole, it seems most plausible that the theory of the *okhêma* was developed in Platonist circles of the early Roman Imperial period, in the generation or so after Antiochus of Ascalon (who was probably himself too much influenced by Stoicism to regard the soul as incorporeal), adapting Stoic theory of the soul as "intelligent fire" (*pur noeron*) or *pneuma* (SVF II 774, 885), and combining that with Aristotelian speculations about the *sumphuton pneuma*, to produce the concept of this substance as an indispensable medium for interaction with the body, after the doctrine of an immaterial, immortal soul had been reasserted within the Platonist tradition.

So this is another strand of influence emanating from earlier Platonism that has helped to form Galen's distinctive "Platonist" psychology. There is, however, a third strand that can help to explain Galen's firm distinction, in the *QAM*, between the "higher" rational soul and the two "lower" parts, the "spirited" (*thumoeides*) and the "desiderative" (*epithumêtikon*), the latter pair of which, at least, he takes, in a firmly Aristotelian way, to be no more than the development of the doctrine of the tripartite soul in the *Republic*. This does not explicitly involve the interaction between it and the body, except that now the passionate and irrational urges that were presented in the *Phaedo* as emanating from the body are attributed to the lowest, irrational part of the soul; but in the *Republic* 611b–612a, we have a remarkable passage, where the embodied soul is compared, memorably, to the sea-god Glaukos, encrusted by barnacles and deformed by the action of the waves, so that his real form can no longer be discerned. Our task is to discern the soul in its true form, "not deformed by its association with the body" (οὐ λελωβημένον δεῖ αὐτὸ θεάσασθαι ὑπό τε τῆς τοῦ

---

[10] Here I am ultimately indebted to the succinct but most useful survey undertaken by Dodds in an appendix to his edition of Proclus' *Elements of Theology* (1963:313–321), himself indebted to Kissling 1922. He is certainly sympathetic to Plato and Platonism, as well as to Pythagoras and Aristotle, but his stance is rather that of a well-educated member of the Second Sophistic than that of a professional philosopher. Cf. the whole passage §§122–130, on Homer's view of the soul.

σώματος κοινωνίας, *Republic* 611b10–c2). What is the implication of this image when transferred to the soul?

It seems to me that the "barnacles, seaweed and stones," so to speak, that encrust the soul (*Republic* 611d5), although presented here in a distinctively negative context, may be seen—grimly material though they are—as a sort of anticipation of the later concept of the "pneumatic vehicle," the *okhêma*, but it also serves to drive something of a wedge between the "higher" and "lower" souls. In this account of the soul in book ten, as has been frequently noted, the model of the tripartite soul, complete with its passionate element, has been abandoned in favor of a model of "true" soul, with accretions consequent on its association with the body, which it will then be divested of when it leaves the body. Later Platonists were certainly able to reconcile these two models by making appeal to the doctrine of the *Timaeus*, where a strong distinction is made between the "immortal" and "mortal" parts of the soul (*Timaeus* 69c–d), the latter of which is added to the "immortal" soul by the "Younger Gods" for the purpose of fitting it into the body—although by various later authorities a distinction was made even between the irrational part of the soul and the *okhêma*.[11]

Before we turn to the *Timaeus*, however, we should take at least a glance at the *Phaedrus*, where once again we have the situation of a soul—this time with a tripartite structure apparently antecedent to embodiment[12]—descending into a body and interacting with it. Once again, the fact of this happening is not problematic, while the mode of interaction with the body is systematically obscured. If we think, after all, of the titanic struggles of the charioteer with the unruly horse (*Phaedrus* 254a–e), where there is much leaping forward, vigorous reining in, falling back on the haunches, foaming at the mouth, bitter reproaches, and so forth, all this activity takes place *within the soul*. There must indeed be parallel movements performed by the body—the lover approaches his beloved, after all, and makes some overtures—but the connection between the two sets of activities is left in the air. Obviously, this struggle within the soul ultimately results in physical action, but Plato presents the process as quite unproblematic, though it would be here that the presence of some sort of vehicle for the soul would seem to be very much called for. Remarkably, though, in the midst of all this imagery involving a charioteer and pair of horses, Plato seems to have no use, in his

---

[11] In this passage of the *Timaeus*, it is rather the body that is spoken of as an *okhêma* for the soul (*Timaeus* 69c7), and the "mortal soul" is constructed to be a sort of "cushion" between immortal soul and body.

[12] Even the gods, indeed, appear to have tripartite souls—though very probably Plato himself did not intend this detail to be dwelt on (since the two horses of the divine pairs are both perfect, *Phaedrus* 246a7–8); but later Platonists plainly brooded somewhat on the possible identity of their three parts, as we can observe from Alcinous' *Handbook of Platonism* 178.40–45.

allegory, for the actual chariot (on which the charioteer must take his stand, and to which the horses are harnessed). It is almost as if this item was something of an embarrassment to him; it is mentioned initially, at *Phaedrus* 247b1-3, in conjunction with the chariots of the gods,[13] but it really plays very little part in the allegory after that.

The *Timaeus* also presents a strong correlation between each of the three "parts" of the soul and an area of the body—the rational part with the head, the spirited with the breast, and the passionate with the belly and "lower parts" (69d-71a); and indeed one particular organ, the liver, is portrayed as acting as a sort of "mirror" (71b4) that may receive impressions of the "rational thoughts" (*dianoêmata*) emanating from the intellect, based in the head. All this assumes that there is contact between soul and body, but it still does not address the question of *the mechanism* or *conduit* by which such contact might take place. To arrive at this, surely, we must postulate either a quasi-material element in the soul, or a quasi-immaterial element within the body, and this, despite the interesting introduction of the astral vehicle, Plato really shows no sign of doing.

2. Galen's Reasoning

What we can see from all this, I think, is that Galen is presented with no clear solution to his problem from the Platonic corpus, but yet with all the materials for arriving at a solution of his own.

And what, we may ask, is that solution? I will first essay a preliminary answer to that enigma, and then adduce a series of passages in support of my view. It seems to me, then, that Galen would seem to have begun his intellectual career with a more or less "orthodox" Platonist concept of the soul (insofar as such a term is permissible), as an immaterial, immortal substance, of tripartite structure, distinct from the body, derived from his period of study with the Platonist Albinus in Smyrna,[14] a doctrine with which, as his experience as a doctor, anatomist, and surgeon increased, he came progressively to be less satisfied. In such a work as *On the Utility of the Parts* (III 1-2), composed during his first stay in Rome from 162-166, he is content to speak of the body as an "instrument" (*organon*) of which the various faculties of the soul make use, which suggests at least an assumption of the *subordination* of the body to the soul, irrespective of the nature of the substance of the latter. On the other hand,

---

[13] They are "well-balanced and easily steered" (*euênia*), while "human" ones are steered "with difficulty" (*mogis*), because of the imbalance of the horses.

[14] *My Own Books* 16 Kühn. He also, it must be said, studied briefly with a Stoic teacher (*The Affections and Errors of the Soul* 412 Kühn), but the Stoic unitary model of the soul never attracted him—though he later came to value their concept of the soul as *pneuma*, as we shall see.

though, there is nowhere in these introductory chapters, which constitute a sort of Hymn to Man, and indeed an encomium of the demiurgic cause that fashioned both man's limbs and those of the other creatures, any mention of the immortality or incorporeality of the rational soul, and thus any suggestion of its separate existence.

In the later books of his great treatise *On the Doctrines of Hippocrates and Plato* (e.g. VII 3.19.3-5), composed somewhat later (in the period 169–175), we see him entertaining as alternatives: (1) that the soul itself is "immaterial" (*asômatos*), while residing in the cerebral *pneuma* as its "first home" (*prôton oikêtêrion*), or (2) that the soul is itself composed of *pneuma* (and thus itself corporeal).

By the time he is composing the treatise *That the Capacities of the Soul Depend on the Mixtures of the Body*, on the other hand, which dates to the period 193–210, a lifetime of experience has convinced him that at any rate the two "lower" parts of the soul are no more than "mixtures" (*kraseis*) of the four humors as operative in the two vital organs, heart and liver, respectively, while the rational part may or may not be something more than the particular mixture of those same humors as manifested in the brain. If the rational part of the soul is something more, however, Galen in his role as doctor is not prepared to say what that might be. Certainly, even if it is immaterial and immortal, it is not anything that, while in the body, can remain unaffected by the mixtures of the body. We must keep in mind, of course, that the *QAM* is a polemical work, and that Galen has in his sights a prominent contemporary Platonist, or group of Platonists, who hold what seems to him a profoundly "unscientific" view of the relation of the soul to the body. However, we may still postulate here, I think, a process of development in his view of the nature of the soul, leading from a straightforward acceptance of its immaterial and immortal nature in his youth, through a scientifically based *non liquet* in his mature years, to a pretty thorough skepticism in his more advanced years as to whether even the rational part of the soul is any more than a "mixture" of the bodily humors—with the proviso that we have yet to explore exactly what he means by "mixture."

First of all, however, let us consider one further passage from *The Doctrines of Hippocrates and Plato* (IX 9), where he has just been clarifying his position on the role of theory or reasoning, as opposed to empiricism, in medicine.[15] Reasoning, and philosophy in general (especially its logical part), is, in his view, absolutely necessary for the physician, but, for Galen, slavish adhesion to any dogmatic philosophical school is to be reprehended (e.g. *The Doctrines of Hippocrates and Plato* IX 7.9–19; *The Passions of the Soul* 8.5.43). The physician must be guided by

---

[15] M. Frede 1987 provides a fine analysis of Galen's attitude to "dogmatic" philosophy, which adopts positions not susceptible of proof on the basis of empirical evidence.

empirical observation, reinforced by logical rigor; he must refrain from making judgments about what is in principle unobservable. But Galen, basing himself primarily on the *Timaeus*, feels that he can claim Plato as an endorser of this position. In *The Doctrines of Hippocrates and Plato*, he states the situation as follows:

> But Plato declared that the cause that made us, the god who is the craftsman (δημιουργός) of the universe, commanded his children by speech (sc. *Timaeus* 41a–d) to fashion the human race, receiving from him the substance of the immortal soul and inserting in it the part that is generated. But we must recognize this fact that there is no similarity in kind between proving and positing that we were made in accordance with the providence of some god or gods, and knowing the substance of the maker, or even of our own soul. My earlier remarks make it clear that the fashioning of our bodies is a work of the highest wisdom and power; but the statements of the most divine Plato about the substance of the soul and of the gods who formed us, and still more all he says about our whole body, extend only to the point of being plausible and reasonable (ἄχρι τοῦ πιθανοῦ καὶ εἰκότος ἐκτείνεται), as he himself pointed out in the *Timaeus* (sc. 29c4–d3) when first he was about to enter upon an account of the natural world, and again when he inserted the statement in the middle of the account (*Timaeus* 72d4–8).
>
> Galen *The Doctrines of Hippocrates and Plato* IX 9.1–4[16]

What we can derive from this, I think, is Galen's view that, even if the divine Plato chooses to speak in terms of an immortal soul being inserted into the human body, and, most specifically, the human head, by the Demiurge, that may be viewed, on his own admission, as being expressed in a mythical, not to say whimsical, mode. We do not have to accept that Plato is claiming that the rational part of the soul is either incorporeal or immortal—simply that it is of a more exalted nature than the other two parts. This is, however, quite compatible, for Galen, with its being composed of some form of *pneuma*.

To turn now to the *QAM*, we can observe a new candidate being introduced for the *ousia* of the soul, namely, a "mixture" (*krasis*), albeit of a very distinctive sort, of the four humors, or elements, of the body. We may remind ourselves that Galen's purpose in this treatise is a polemical one, to argue, against certain Platonists, and supported by what seems to him a plethora of good evidence, that mental states are direct consequences of bodily conditions, or of external forces, such as alcohol or drugs, being brought to bear upon the body. This seems to him to leave no room for the postulation of an immortal, immaterial

---

[16] Hereafter the translation is according to De Lacy 1978–1984.

soul, though he recognizes now that Plato does in fact maintain that. In *That the Faculties of the Soul Follow the Mixtures of the Body*, we find the following:

> We have shown that the capacities (δυνάμεις) of the soul depend on its substance, since, indeed, the activities do so. Now if the reasoning form (εἶδος) of the soul is mortal, it too will be a particular mixture, [namely] of the brain; and thus all the forms and parts of the soul will have their capacities dependent on the mixture—that is, on the substance (οὐσία) of the soul; but if it is immortal, as is Plato's view, he would have done well, himself, to write an explanation as to why it is separated (sc. from the body) when the brain is greatly cooled, or excessively heated, dried or moistened—in the same way that he wrote the other matters relevant to it. For death takes place, according to Plato, when the soul is separated from the body. But why great voiding of blood, the drinking of hemlock, or a raging fever, causes this separation, I would have certainly wanted to learn from him, if he were himself alive. But since he no longer is, and none of the Platonist teachers taught me any cause, on account of which the soul is compelled by those things that I have mentioned to be separated, I dare to state myself that not every form of body is suitable to receive the rational soul. For I see this as consequent on the doctrine of Plato, but am not able to state any demontration of it, on account of the fact that I do not know what sort of thing the substance of the soul is (if we take as our assumption that it belongs to the class of *non*-bodily things).

Galen QAM 3.774–776 Kühn[17]

He continues at some length in this vein, emphasizing that, despite much thought and repeated enquiries, he has never been able to gain a satisfactory answer to the problem of how such a simple, immaterial entity could pervade and interact with the body, exhibiting its vulnerability to the effects of excesses in any of the four elements or humors, which can cause it at a certain stage to part company with the body. In any case, even if we grant Plato his postulate of an immortal soul (QAM 3.787–791 Kühn), we can conclude from his own description of the effects of bodily states on the condition of the soul in the latter part of the *Timaeus* (especially 86c–87a) that the capacities of the soul are indeed profoundly dependent on the mixtures of the body.[18]

[17] Hereafter the translation is according to Singer 2013.

[18] In this connection, G. E. R. Lloyd (1988:20–21) draws attention very pertinently to the tendentious nature of Galen's references to Plato, particularly in the matter of the interpretation of *trophê*, "nurture."

We have here, then, in this late treatise, Galen the hard-nosed scientific doctor, robustly dismissing dogmatic (Platonist) theories for which he can observe no evidence. As to the tripartite nature of the soul, he is entirely convinced (and therefore dismissive of the Stoic theory of a unitary soul based in the heart) by the results of his own experiments, involving ligatures of veins, arteries, or nerves of his tormented animal victims, to demontrate that the liver and heart are the seats of the two lower parts of the soul, and the brain of the higher, rational part, but he can see no need to postulate that these soul-parts are any more than special sorts of *krasis*, blends of the elements as present in those organs.

3. Galen and the Self-Styled Platonists

Lastly, I would like to address the problem of the identity of those "self-styled" Platonists who are his target in this treatise, and what exactly they believed, as Galen's polemical dismissal of them seems to betoken the existence, in some strand of Platonism already in the second century, a theory of the soul anticipating, to at least some extent, that of Plotinus in the third. Let us remind ourselves of what the "self-styled Platonists" are said to claim. It is that "the soul, though impeded (*empodizesthai*) by the body in sickness, performs its specific activities when the latter is healthy, and is neither assisted nor harmed by it" (*QAM* 9.805 Kühn). This position Galen proposes to challenge and refute, on the basis of passages taken from Plato himself.

Now, we might first of all question the plausibility of this being a true account of the position of these Platonists. After all, if their purpose is, as it seems to be, to assert the independence of the soul from the body, and its imperviousness to influences emanating from the body, then surely they will quite undercut their position if they grant that *the soul is impeded by the body in sickness*? What they may well have granted, however, as would Plotinus later, is that the distemper of the body may render it incapable of connecting properly with the soul, and receiving influences from it; only in this sense, then, would the soul's activity be impeded. Indeed, all that *empodizesthai* need mean is that the soul is hindered or blocked from exercising its influence over the body, not that it is itself disturbed or upset by influences emanating from the body.

So then, if that is accepted, we may survey the late second-century philosophical scene to see if any plausible Platonist candidate appears. There are few enough to choose from—Atticus? Numenius? Harpocration? Severus?—and a sad dearth of hard evidence, but, of all these, I would be inclined to settle on the last, as a reasonably plausible candidate. Severus' dates are unfortunately rather vague, but he is listed at one point by Proclus, in his *Commentary on Plato's*

Timaeus (III 212.8 Diehl), in what appears to be reverse chronological order, with Atticus and Plutarch (i.e. Severus-Atticus-Plutarch), so we may take him to belong to the latter part of the century, and thus largely contemporaneous with Galen.

His views on the soul are certainly interesting, and lend themselves to speculation along lines relevant to our quest. First of all, we know from the testimony of Iamblichus, in his *On the Soul* (364–365 Finamore-Dillon), and Proclus, in his *Commentary on Plato's Timaeus* (II 153.24 Diehl), that Severus saw the soul as an essentially *geometrical* entity,[19] interpreting the two elements of the soul as given in *Timaeus* 35a, the "indivisible and always identical essence" and that which is "divisible about bodies" as representing respectively "point" and "extension,"[20] in opposition to such dualistic predecessors as Atticus or Numenius, who would take the essence divisible about bodies as some sort of irrational, and thus "evil," world-soul. In an extant extract from (it would seem, the beginning, or near the beginning of) a treatise of Severus' *On the Soul*, preserved by Eusebius in his *Preparation for the Gospel* (XIII 17.1–7 = fr. 17 Gioé), Severus begins by arguing that the soul cannot be constructed out of a pair of opposites, like an intermediate color out of black and white, or a moderate temperature out of hot and cold, as all such compounds of opposites are liable to dissolution, and this is not true of the soul. The last section of the extract—Eusebius, frustratingly, breaks off his quotation just as Severus would seem to be working up to his own, distinctive solution of the problem he has presented—reads as follows:

> But since it is the common view of all that man is composed of soul and body, and that the affections that manifest themselves in us as voluntary or involuntary are said to be of the soul, the majority of people, taking this as evidence, declare that its essence is passible (παθητή), they assert that it is mortal and corporeal, not incorporeal.[21] Plato, on the other hand, was compelled to weave on (προσυφᾶναι)[22] to that which is impassible in its nature the passible essence.

---

[19] Probably inspired in this by Speusippus (with whom he is linked in Iamblichus' report), who defined it as "the form of the omni-dimensionally extended."

[20] Given by Proclus as *sêmeion* and *diastasis*, respectively. Iamblichus poses a slight problem by giving the first component as *skhêma*, "shape" rather than *sêmeion*, but we have suggested (Finamore and Dillon 2002:80) that this is either a scribal error for, perhaps, *stigmê*, or an error on Iamblichus' part.

[21] This could be taken to apply to both Stoic and Peripatetic philosophers.

[22] The verb is borrowed, rather pointedly, from *Timaeus* 41d1.

That neither of the scenarios set out by either of these two, Plato and the others, answers to reality,[23] we will try to demontrate, by presenting an account of the capacities which are operative within us.

Severus fr. 17 Gioé, my translation

Now, as I say, Eusebius chooses to cut off his quotation from Severus just as things are getting interesting. What we may gather from this, I would suggest, is that Severus is here declaring his dissatisfaction both with those who conclude that the soul is material and mortal, and with his master Plato (or at least the popular understanding of his doctrine), since Plato seems (e.g. in the *Timaeus* 41d and 69c–d) to wish to graft on two "mortal," passible soul-parts to the original, immortal rational one, and so create a functioning human soul. This, however, would result in the adulteration of the nature of the soul, by making it the combination of two "opposites," and this would render it destructible, for the reasons that Severus has just set out. So it would seem that some other solution must be found—to save Plato from himself, so to speak.

What, then, could this solution be? If we are to preserve the impassibility of the essential soul, the soul *in itself*, we must find some other repository of the multifarious passions and affects that plainly do not belong to the body alone, but to some form of consciousness. But if this is not the soul, then what is it? I would suggest that Severus' solution is in fact very similar to that of Plotinus a generation or so later, and that is to attribute these passions and affects, not to the soul itself, but rather to an intermediate entity between soul and body, namely that "pneumatic vehicle" (*pneumatikon okhêma*), the history of which I have discussed above (pp. 53–56).[24] We know, after all, that the concept was circulating in Platonist (and sub-Platonist) circles in the later second century, so there is no great difficulty about Severus adopting it.

Galen himself, as we have seen, knows of the theory, and is quite prepared, in various works, to accept that the soul, and specifically the rational soul, may be a type of *pneuma*, or use such *pneuma* as a "vehicle," but he is not prepared to pay more than lip service to the concept of an immortal soul over and above such *pneuma*. It is just not something for which he feels that any scientific evidence can be produced, and he is quite prepared to launch a vigorous attack

---

[23] This may be a slight over-translation of a rather elliptical, and possibly corrupt, Greek phrase: ὅτι δὲ μηδετέρως ἔχει, ἐξ ὧν ἑκάτεροι εἰρήκασι, Πλάτων τε καὶ οἱ ἄλλοι, but I think that it is needed to bring out what he means.

[24] It must be said, however, that Plotinus, although fully aware of the concept of the "vehicle," does not (for reasons that I have speculated about in Dillon 2013) approve it, preferring to postulate a sort of "shadow" (*skia*), or "trace" (*ikhnos*) of the soul in the body, as an immediate recipient of sense impressions, and a vehicle for passions.

on those who maintain such a doctrine. Those, therefore, who are not prepared to include him among the ranks of the so-called 'Middle Platonists' are doubtless justified in this. He is, however, in my view, albeit on his own terms, a willing member of the broader Platonic tradition, in that he regards Plato as on balance the greatest of philosophers, even as Hippocrates is the greatest of doctors—even if he is not prepared to go along with doctrines for which he can summon up no scientific proof.

The Middle Platonists on the Soul-Body Relation

HAROLD TARRANT

Abstract: This chapter presents the views among the so-called 'Middle Platonists' on the relation between soul and body. It begins with a fresh reassessment of the identity and the nature of thought of the Platonists who were active at the turn of the first millennium. By presenting their diversity, it prepares the ground for delving into their equally diverse views on the multifarious concept of soul. It addresses, in turn, the questions of what the soul is responsible for in Platonism and to what the Middle Platonists attribute souls. Central attention is given to the different kinds of soul (immortal and mortal), the mortal body, the soul's descent, the soul's point of entry into the body, the embodied soul, the soul as self, the salvation of the soul. On this last note, the chapter concludes with a characterization of the theoretical life as an expression and a goal of the Platonic way of life.

1. Who Were the Middle Platonists? A Working Definition

The term 'Middle Platonists' is generally given to those who worked primarily within the Platonic tradition in at least the first two centuries CE.[1] However, I do not use the corresponding term 'Middle Platonism' on the grounds that there was no single Platonist vision, distinct from that of Plato, no re-founder

---

[1] The term's place in the literature has been cemented by such works as Dillon 1977, the primary account of this period of Platonism in English; Deuse 1983, a significant study of Middle Platonist and Neoplatonist psychology; and Gioè 2002, which offers a collection of the fragments of several of them. While I have at times avoided it (Tarrant 2010), it is a moderately useful collective term, employed now by Boys-Stones 2017, the principal source-book for Platonism from 80 BCE to 250 CE, whose parameters are somewhat wider than those employed here.

of the school, and no distinctive type of Platonism that unites all Platonists of the period. Even so, there are some particular characteristics of the age that colored the work of these Platonists, and they preceded the highly influential work of Plotinus in the third century CE, who influenced others known as 'Neoplatonists' to varying degrees. They also had considerable influence over the intellectual environment in which early Christian theory took shape, so that many issues that arise here may resonate with those more familiar with the positions of the Church Fathers.

After Plato himself, one presumes that his successors in the Academy could be described as 'Platonists' until Arcesilaus took it more in the direction of skepticism, but the one to be called a *Platônikos* earliest in the literature is a certain Pamphilus who studied with Plato and taught Epicurus at Samos, so called by both Cicero (*On the Nature of the Gods* 1.72–73) and Diogenes Laertius (*Lives of the Philosophers* 10.14). That description was not used of the leaders of the Academy, and if Epicurus was himself responsible for it in this case then it is unlikely to have been honorific. From the third century to the first century BCE, various Hellenistic philosophies had dominated, and our evidence for people committed to something like a Platonic system of philosophy is thin indeed. Eudorus of Alexandria, perhaps late in the first century, is sometimes thought of as a Platonist, but he is known only as an 'Academic' and his extant fragments make a firm commitment to Plato no better than probable. What is not contentious is that an interest in details of Plato's works, demontrated by Cicero, by Posidonius the Stoic, and by Eudorus, was growing. Indeed, the origins of the reviving interest in Plato should undoubtedly be sought in the first century BCE.

The dominant philosophies of the Hellenistic period, including Epicureanism and Stoicism, had been materialist, and the so-called Skeptics, who then dominated in the Academy, had tended to work largely within these materialist systems. Plato's dialogues, with their emphasis on immaterial principles, immaterial intelligible entities, and an immaterial soul, had become something of a curiosity. Gerson (2013) has characterized Platonism in terms of its opposition to five other philosophical 'isms'—nominalism, mechanism, materialism, relativism, and skepticism—and while one might quibble about the details it would be fair to say that from Plato on those whom we should refer to as Platonists have been opposed at least to the extremes of such 'isms.' Above all, there was resistance to the idea that the world in which we find ourselves can be explained in purely materialistic terms. At a time when many ordinary individuals were searching for some kind of spiritual dimension in life, and perhaps some spiritual satisfaction in one or more of the many religions available in the early empire, several of those who were philosophically inclined sought for a philosophy that promised some kind of enlightenment, and allowed human beings to see themselves as much more than a machine, as something that somehow transcended the body, and as something with a goal that went beyond the confines of this life on earth. Platonism—and its close ally Pythagoreanism as it was now understood—could provide what they were seeking. It could also claim to be rooted in the ancient culture of Greece rather than in the Hellenistic age.

Many of those surviving authors who demontrated some kind of loyalty to Plato during the period concerned are known as much more than philosophers. These include Cicero, the politician and orator who is sometimes included, thanks to the many philosophical works written at the end of his life (46–44 BCE); Philo, the prominent Alexandrian Jew (fl. second quarter of the first century), who explained the books of Moses in terms of Greek philosophy, often but not exclusively Platonist; Plutarch (ca. 45–125), the prominent Greek intellectual and biographer, whose *Morals* contain many works influenced strongly by Plato both philosophically and in literary form; Apuleius, the all-around intellectual often considered a sophist rather than a philosopher, from Madaura in North Africa (fl. third quarter of the second century); Galen of Pergamum, the prolific medical writer and physician to Marcus Aurelius, who, though heterodox, admired Plato greatly, wrote a commentary on the medical parts of the *Timaeus*, and summaries of most if not all of Plato's dialogues; and Maximus of Tyre (fl. second half of the second century), the sophist-like author of several short prose works for rhetorical delivery, which generally have either a Platonist or a Cynic coloring.

Few Middle Platonist works that are not by such hybrid authors have survived intact, but among them may be mentioned first the *Exposition of Mathematics Useful for the Reading of Plato* of Theon of Smyrna, a contemporary of Plutarch and elsewhere attested as a Platonist. It is strongly reliant on the *Timaeus*, *Republic*, and (more surprisingly) the *Epinomis* usually ascribed to Philip of Opus. As the title would suggest it is of minimal use for the question of soul-body relations. Certain works were ascribed erroneously to Plutarch, but almost certainly were written by a teacher of Platonist philosophy in the same period, particularly the work *On Fate*. Most important, however, is *The Handbook of Platonism* or *Didaskalikos* ascribed to an Alcinous,[2] who cannot be dated but seems to belong between the middle and the end of the second century. This work sets out to express in rather different words the most important of the doctrines of Plato, arranging the material into sections on epistemology, logic, metaphysics, physics, psychology, and ethics (with politics). Because of its wide coverage and its attempt to convey a doctrinal system rather than to adjudicate

---

[2]   Once thought to be identical with Albinus, and treated as such by Dillon 1977, though he subsequently recants (1996:445–446); I have used the text of Whittaker (1980) and the prior translated title is that of Dillon (1993).

on more limited issues arising from Platonic texts, it features a great deal in the modern picture of Middle Platonism, and it is usually presumed to be a fairly typical example of a Middle Platonist handbook. The major difficulty in dealing with it is our inability to offer any account of its author, his date, or his environment. The very nature of the work is such that it does not offer direct information about the particular tradition in which it stood. Also important as an example of the Platonism of the time is the anonymous commentary on Plato's *Theaetetus*, of which over seventy papyrus columns survive more or less intact.[3]

There are other Middle Platonist authors about whom we can say much more, but they survive only as fragments in contemporary or later writers. Calvenus Taurus taught Platonic philosophy at Athens in the first half of the second century, and we receive glimpses of the workings of his classes from the *Attic Nights* of Aulus Gellius and quotations concerning his views on the *Timaeus* from Philoponus.[4] Others are known mainly from glimpses into their Platonic exegesis, usually of a commentary-like nature. Albinus, Severus, and Harpocration[5] are among the more important of these fragmentary authors to judge from their use by later Neoplatonists such as Proclus, and the literalist Atticus is quite interesting,[6] while there are a few fragmentary authors who may be regarded either as Platonists or as Pythagoreans. They include: Thrasyllus, court intellectual of the emperor Tiberius;[7] Moderatus of Gades, a Pythagorean contemporary of Plutarch; and Numenius of Apamea and his companion Cronius[8] from the middle of the second century. In his *Life of Plotinus* (20.71–76, cf. 21.1–9), Porphyry offers Longinus' view that these four were forerunners of Plotinus' inquiry into the first principles of Pythagoras, which they also took to be Plato's. Of these, it is usual to include Numenius, at least, in accounts of the Middle Platonists, and he is the one whose surviving fragments have the most to say about the soul.

While my own approach has ordinarily been to emphasize the diversity among the Middle Platonists (Tarrant 2010), other scholars, and now Boys-Stones (2017) in particular, have preferred to dwell on the important connecting threads between them. Indeed, in many ways this was a period of relearning the nature of Platonist philosophy, with the Platonic corpus itself exercising a

---

[3]   See Bastianini and Sedley 1995.
[4]   For the fragments, see Lakmann 1994 and Gioè 2002.
[5]   For the fragments, see Gioè 2002.
[6]   His views are often linked with those of Plutarch by Proclus; the fragments are collected in des Places 1977.
[7]   The fragments are collected in Tarrant 1993.
[8]   Both of the last two have their fragments included in Leemans 1937, but Numenius is now studied rather in des Places 1973; there is an English translation by Petty 2012.

controlling influence, contemporary debate giving further guidance, and the individual's own convictions, not only leading to the choice of Platonism, but also determining the stance to be taken where there was legitimate discussion of Platonism's proper stance. Fortunately, the number of times that Plato discussed soul-body relations, and the rather explicit nature of his position in dialogues like the *Phaedo* and *Alcibiades I*, which both featured widely in the Platonic curriculum, and were the very first two studied by Albinus' pupils (*Introduction to Plato's Dialogues* 5), meant that there was a considerable core of agreement on many relevant topics among the Platonists of the first and second centuries.

2. What Is Soul Responsible for in Platonism?

Different dialogues of Plato emphasize different roles for the soul, though this should not be taken so much as a reflection of his incoherence as of the different concerns that are important for him in different works and in different periods of his life. It is useful to begin with the *Republic*, for it probably occupied a central position in his creative life, and it clearly distinguishes three roles that the soul was held to play. All of them are in some sense motivating roles, leading normally to bodily, emotive, or intellectual activity. First, there is the role in responding to the basic appetites of the body, essential for ensuring that the natural organism continues to function and to thrive; second, there is the role of arousing the passions, including both angry and enthusiastic responses; finally, there is the reasoning role, which should come to dominate in the mature human being, ensuring that the other functions do not exceed what is best, and in general helping to bring about the traditional Greek virtues, which are most in evidence when all three functions work together under the control of reason. Ultimately, the reasoning faculty will also be responsible for the cognitive and philosophic successes of the individual.

The *Republic* (primarily book 4) appears to think in terms of "parts" of the soul, and this largely because they are to some degree separate and potentially in conflict with one another, resulting in internal tensions. The *Timaeus* (69c–72d) goes one step further in giving them different locations in the body, head, chest, and abdomen, but this may be part of the work's striving to depict pictorially the workings of unseen forces. Again, the famous "palinode" of the *Phaedrus* (246a–d and 253c–254a) depicts the three parts as a charioteer and two horses, one more cooperative than the other, but this mythlike material is again designed to offer a visual likeness of how the soul works, particularly when under the divisive influence of Eros. Clearly these "parts" had to be in contact with one another and to operate across the individual if they were to cooperate with one another: the *Phaedo* is keen to offer a picture that pertains to the well-integrated soul of the philosopher; and even book 10 of the *Republic* tends to present the soul as a more unitary construct.

All this must be pondered by the Platonists of the early empire, and in general they allowed themselves some flexibility in thinking about the alleged divisions within the soul, speaking of a unitary soul when they pleased, a tripartite one when they pleased, and often of a bipartite soul in which the reason is contrasted with the "affections" (*pathê*) generally. That is perhaps justified first by Plato's insistence (*Republic* 430e1–432b1) that it is the job of the rational part to rule and of the other two parts to be ruled; second, by the palinode of the *Phaedrus*, where the proper ruler of the chariot is depicted as a human charioteer while the *two* ruled faculties are horses; and third, by a common supposition that when the Craftsman creates the immortal ruling part and his deputies other mortal requirements (*Timaeus* 41c6–d3), the nonrational faculties were included among these latter.[9] It may have been in response to this last passage that Numenius (fr. 44 des Places) has developed a theory that could be interpreted as involving not simply two *parts* of the soul for each person, but more like *two separate souls*.

The freedom to think in terms of either three or two parts or faculties can be illustrated from Alcinous, who follows his discussion of the origins and three locations of the tripartite soul (*Handbook of Platonism* 176.8–34) with arguments for its having three powers (*dunameis*, 176.36), some of which are suggestive rather of bipartition as they primarily concern the separation of the rational from the affective soul (*pathêtikon*, 176.38–43 and 177.12–14). Nothing prevents them referring to further powers, particularly those of "nutrition and growth" (*threptikon*), "imagination" (*phantastikon*), and "sensation" (*aisthêtikon*), which one associates more with Aristotle's *On the Soul* than with Plato who uses such terminology sparingly. Plutarch, for instance, mentions the first only twice, the second about twenty times, and the third somewhere in between.[10] However, they tend not to give them official recognition as separate faculties.

One of the reasons for such a plurality of faculties is that the Platonic soul, particularly as presented in the *Phaedrus* (245c), is a self-moved entity responsible for movement in all else. Body is seen as inert in its own right, leading Plutarch (*On the Generation of the Soul in the Timaeus* 1016c; cf. also his *On Fate*) to regard the disorderly precosmic movement in the *Timaeus* (30a, cf. 52d–53a and 69b) as evidence of a precosmic soul, distinct from the *created* soul of the cosmos. Therefore, any of the powers within us that have the ability to set us in motion

---

[9] Cf. Atticus fr. 15 des Places = Albinus fr. 11T Gioé; Alcinous *Handbook of Platonism* 178.26–32.

[10] The imprecision results from the uncertainties of authorship in the corpus, as also from the difficulties of deciding which uses of the adjectives concerned have implications for psychology.

in any way are liable to be seen as faculties of soul. The connection between the soul and motion is also a result of its being seen as the bringer of life. When any animal dies, we think of what is left behind as inanimate (*apsukhos* "soul-less"). The final argument of the *Phaedo* was dependent on this very connection, since whatever soul comes to be present in will be alive (105c8–10). Indeed, Alcinous (*Handbook of Platonism* 178.21–23) affirms that: "He calls the soul self-moved because it has life embedded in its own nature, being always active in its own right."[11] The result is that anything that the animal does *only when it is alive* is done by the soul, while any involvement of the body is seen as akin to the part played by an instrument that facilitates the action. There was, in book ten of Plato's *Laws*, a passage of classic status for these Platonists, one that included a general list of such functions of soul:

> to want, to examine, to care, to deliberate, to opine rightly or mistakenly, rejoicing, grieving, being pleased or pained, cheerful or fearful, hating or loving, and every movement akin to these.

Plato Laws 897a1–4

3. To What Did These Platonists Attribute Souls?

It is natural to deduce from the connection between souls and life that anything with its own life also had a soul. There is much talk in Plato about the rebirth of a formerly human soul into some kind of animal (*Phaedo* 81e–82b, *Republic* 620a–d, *Timaeus* 42c), with bees, wasps, and ants among the tiniest, or even into a god (*Phaedo* 82b10–c1). This discourse, usually present in mythlike or visionary passages leading to ancient doubts about whether the Platonist was bound to accept it, does not extend to transformation into plants, even though some Greek myths refer to the transformation of Daphne into a laurel and Syrinx into a reed. Furthermore, the idea of transmigration into animals was useful to those who argued for vegetarianism, including a number of ancient Platonists,[12] while any further transformation into plants would invalidate that argument. Though Numenius regarded even the growth faculty (*hê phutikê* fr. 47) as part of the *immortal* soul, the context appears to be a debate about how much of the human

---

[11] All translations are my own, unless otherwise noted.

[12] They included Porphyry in *On Abstinence from Killing Animals*, just after our period, but also the youthful Plutarch who has left us two fragmentary attacks on the eating of meat (*On the Eating of Flesh*) and some interesting insights elsewhere (*Beasts are Rational* 991c–d). In *On the Eating of Flesh*, one may suspect the influence of the doctrine of animal *metempsukhôsis* when Empedocles is introduced at 996b–c, or again at 997e, while at 998d, Plutarch allows that the doctrine may be wrong but argues that it should at least cause us to hesitate.

soul is immortal (fr. 46a) rather than one over the status of plants, and he had made this claim on the basis of *Phaedrus* 246c5: "All soul is immortal."

Besides mortal creatures, various superhuman entities were seen as in possession of souls. While the *Phaedo* (82b10–c1) could allow that philosophers' souls might be reborn as gods, the palinode of the *Phaedrus* sets out to examine "the nature of soul, both divine and human" (245c2–3), and the psychical charioteer and horses that belong to the gods only differ from human ones in being all good and entirely of good stock. Thus, the gods discussed in the palinode, including Zeus (246e), are conceived of as superior ensouled entities. That did not necessarily mean that everything that could be conceived of as a Platonic god, the Idea of the Good for instance or the Demiurge of the *Timaeus*, would necessarily have a soul, but a certain class apparently belonging to the heavens would. An important passage in the *Laws* (896d10–899c1), taken by Plutarch as Plato's most explicit theological declaration (*On Isis and Osiris* 370e10–371a4), makes "soul or souls" (*Laws* 899b5) responsible for the movement of the heavenly bodies, whether or not this happens from within those bodies themselves; the theme is developed by the *Epinomis*, taken in antiquity either as genuinely Platonic or as the work of his follower Philip of Opus.

Alcinous (*Handbook of Platonism* 171.4–14) accordingly takes each of the planets, and it seems the power of the circuit of the fixed stars,[13] as "intellective living creatures" and gods. There is no question that the seven planets are gods with bodies (170.43), and that even the eighth power has shape (171.14). If the phrase "intellective living creatures" did not in itself imply the possession of soul, on the grounds that "intelligence can perhaps not be present without soul" (170.3–4),[14] then the ensuing discussion of *daimones* or "generated gods" (171.15–23) makes it plain that these have a place within every elemental zone, "so that no part of the cosmos should be without a share in soul or in some supernatural living being." So it seems that both the gods of the heavens and these additional supernatural powers within the elemental zones together

---

[13] I suspect, without proof, that this is the Milky Way, crucial in the thought of Numenius for instance (frr. 32, 34, and 35); thus, it would, like the planets, be a visible heavenly phenomenon, but move with the fixed stars.

[14] Note that this is a reworking of *Timaeus* 30b3, which includes no word for "perhaps"; Alcinous may suspect that his first god is the highest intellect (or intellect's cause) and inanimate as well as incorporeal, whereas Plato had also made it plain that intelligence (*qua, belonging to something*) needed soul. At *On the Face that Appears in the Orb of the Moon* 943a, Plutarch's speaker, Sulla, makes it quite explicit that intellect (our human intellect) is able to achieve a state where the soul as well as the body has been left behind, though there is no suggestion that it can *belong in anything* without soul as an intermediate. This passage seems atypical, and indeed it is represented as a departure from most people's views.

constitute the source of soul and of quasi-immortality for the individual parts of the universe.

It is unsurprising, given that the *Timaeus* treated the planets as gods, that it took the same view of the earth at its center (40b8–c3), for Earth (*Gê, Gaia*)[15] was one of the earliest gods in the preceding Greek tradition. She is here called "first and eldest of all gods born within the heaven," treated as our "nurse" (*trophos*) and given her own motion. Thus, she too can be assumed to be in possession of a soul. Accordingly, Alcinous (*Handbook of Platonism* 171.27–34) mentions her too as a divinity, actually calling her a "star" (*astron*, 171.31). But in addition to calling *Gaia* the eldest of the gods within the heaven, he adds "after the soul of the cosmos at least," indicating that this too is to be regarded as an immanent divinity. For regardless of these gods associated with the *parts* of the universe, the cosmos in its entirety was treated as a visible and tangible god, and as a single living creature embracing all others with it, in accordance with *Timaeus* 92c4–9. And this too had its own soul for these Platonists as it had done in that dialogue, and its construction and operation were largely as that dialogue had postulated (34b10–37c5), though there were inevitably disputes as to the interpretation of details of that account.

Therefore, a list of ensouled entities recognized by the Middle Platonists would include the souls of all animals, humans, *daimones*, astral divinities (including Earth), and the cosmos itself. The situation regarding gods of any other type, including the mythical gods mentioned at *Timaeus* 40d–41a, is much less clear; Plutarch, Apuleius, and Numenius have a considerable interest in gods of the Egyptians and some other non-Greek peoples, but their presumed relation to soul is seldom clear.

4. Immortal Soul, Mortal Soul, and Mortal Body

There is no doubt that the body of any normal animal species dies. But it is hard to comprehend one's own future nonexistence, as also to relate to the dead bodies of one's close friends and relatives as the people one had known. Platonists accordingly believed that the real person was not part of the biological organism that was supposedly constructed of earth, air, fire, and water, but something that somehow occupied that organism and directed it—something of an incorporeal nature. There was a "self" that did this directing, and that was actually involved in these personal relationships that involve speaking, thinking, and feeling. The *Alcibiades I*, always supposed to be a genuine work of

---

[15] Plato treats earth, the living cosmic body, as quite separate from Earth (*Gê*), the traditional god and consort of Heaven, who is named at *Timaeus* 40e5.

Plato in antiquity, actually went so far as to call it the "self," identifying this self with the soul (129a–131a), as we shall see. Since it was not supposed to be bodily, the soul did not have to share the body's mortality, though it did of course have to communicate with it and to be of such a kind that it was able to involve itself with bodily life.

When one examined what the soul was designed to do, it was natural to look first at the *Timaeus*, in which Plato offered teleological accounts of soul, body, and many parts of the composite human being, all in the instructive form of offering the actual reasons why the creator and his assistants made things in a certain way. Alcinous follows this path at the beginning of his account of psychological doctrine, and, basing himself mainly on *Timaeus* 42d–43a, informs us that the Demiurge provided an immortal human soul, while the younger gods with the task of creating mortal creatures added on two mortal parts, locating the immortal component at the highest point, i.e. the spherical head, to avoid its being infected by the trifling business of the mortal soul, and attached the rest of the body below like a vehicle for it, finding locations for the two mortal parts in the upper and lower part of the main body, respectively.[16]

Whether the Platonic text had really implied that *mortal parts of the soul* would be among the things that the younger gods added is open to debate, but it would seem that the majority of Platonists, including Atticus and Albinus, agreed with Alcinous' apparent position on this,[17] while Proclus would much later find their view naive.[18] But it is certain that the question of what exactly was being referred to as mortal parts here did exercise the Middle Platonists, for Alcinous goes on to allow that the extent of the human soul's immortality was disputed (*Handbook of Platonism* 178.25–26), and a passage from Damascius (*Commentary on the Phaedo* I 177) seems to show that Numenius could have drawn no such conclusion from the *Timaeus*, for he made us immortal "right from the reasoning soul to the animate condition" (= fr. 46b des Places). Furthermore, we are specifically told by Philoponus (*Commentary on Aristotle's On the Soul* 9.35–38 = fr. 47) that he took the claim at *Phaedrus* 245c5 that "All soul is immortal" to mean that not only the rational, but also the nonrational and vegetative soul was immortal.

---

[16] See p. 53n9 above.

[17] At *Handbook of Platonism* 178.21–32, after admitting that the issue is disputed, he lists plausible (*pithanon*) reasons why the nonrational soul, driven by "unsupported imagination" (*psilē phantasia*), failing to make use of judgment, observations, or their combinations, or universal comprehension, and totally unaware of the intelligible nature, should not even be of the same substance as the rational, but mortal and perishable.

[18] Atticus fr. 15 des Places = Albinus fr. 11T Gioé = Proclus *Commentary on the Timaeus* III 236.9–18. Proclus is now commenting on *Timaeus* 41d1–2, and referring to the "older interpreters" who thought they were following the letter of the text.

Numenius is an interesting interpreter here, for it would have been natural for anybody thinking that irrational soul was among the "mortal parts" added by the younger gods to suppose that this soul was first something of a very different kind from the rational soul supplied by the Demiurge, and second something truly mortal. Numenius subscribed to the first proposition postulating two souls with essentially different natures for each of us (fr. 44 des Places), but not the second. It is worth quoting the passage at greater length than des Places (1973) does:

> Others, among whom is Numenius too, think not that we have three parts of a single soul, nor indeed two, rational and non-rational, but two souls much as we have two of other things, the rational one and the non-rational one. Of these again some say both are immortal, while others say that the rational is immortal but the non-rational does not come to a stop merely in its activities by withdrawing from such and such a motion, but in its very substance by actually being dissolved.
>
> Stobaeus *Eclogues* 1.49.25a[19]

The discussion has so far concerned the number of *parts* of soul postulated by various schools. Now Porphyry has moved to those who postulate a more radical separation between rational and irrational (or nonrational) soul in humans. Note that Numenius is only an *example* of those who adopt this position, and not necessarily its author. While no indication is given here, one must surely heed the other evidence and allow that he was one of those who held that both souls are immortal, rather than one who adopted the more radical position that the nonrational did not merely fail to conform with a particular kind of motion,[20] but was subject to the dissolution of its very "substance" (*ousia*). The second alternative seems to be that favored by Alcinous at *Handbook of Platonism* 178.31–32, while one must surely assume that Numenius held the former of the two alternatives, allowing that the process undertaken by the younger gods somehow introduced an irrational (and vegetative) soul separate from the rational,[21] but not allowing that this was among the mortal parts on which the

---

[19] Stobaeus *Eclogues* 1.49, 25a: ἄλλοι δέ, ὧν καὶ Νουμήνιος, οὐ τρία μέρη ψυχῆς μιᾶς, ἢ δύο γε, τὸ λογικὸν καὶ ἄλογον, ἀλλὰ δύο ψυχὰς ἔχειν ἡμᾶς οἴονται, ὥσπερ καὶ ἄλλα, τὴν μὲν λογικήν, τὴν δὲ ἄλογον· ὧν πάλιν οἱ μὲν ἄμφω ἀθανάτους, οἱ δὲ τὴν λογικὴν ἀθάνατον, τὴν δὲ ἄλογον οὐ κατὰ τὰς ἐνεργείας μόνον ἀφίστασθαι τῆς ποιᾶς κινήσεως, ἀλλὰ καὶ κατ᾽ οὐσίαν διαλύεσθαι.

[20] I suspect that there is a reference to the way that sensation blocks the circuit of the Same and shakes up that of the Other, circuits central to the construction and function of the soul, at *Timaeus* 43c–44a.

[21] The words "somehow introduced" are chosen carefully, for Numenius might have seen it as a by-product of the process of constructing a living body, just as he regarded the imaginative faculty as a by-product of the faculty of assent (fr. 45 = Stobaeus *Eclogues* 1.49.25).

younger gods wove. So the passage shows two rather different two-soul theories among Porphyry's predecessors.

Clearly there were important issues here, and we have to take account of other factors impacting on how doctrine was formulated. The human being was widely considered to be a microcosm of the cosmos, likewise composed of a body and a soul. Therefore, we are entitled to ask what psychic forces were at work in the world itself, and Plutarch (*On Isis and Isiris* 370f10–371a4) had insisted on there being at least two soul-like entities at work in the world as postulated in book 10 of Plato's *Laws*, the stronger one participating in intelligence and acting beneficially, the other unintelligent and capable of the opposite (896e–897b). He also holds that Plato postulated a third entity, wrongly believed inanimate and unintelligent by some, that is caught between the two but always strives after what is better (*On Isis and Isiris* 370f6–371a). He makes these three the Platonic equivalents of the Egyptian powers Osiris, Typhon, and Isis, respectively, with the last subsequently spoken of (372e–f) in terms that make it plain that Plutarch is thinking of the Receptacle of the *Timaeus* (49a and 51a), and thus of an animate entity that serves as both space and primal matter. Would Plutarch's human being, perhaps, contain forces a little like this alleged cosmic triad?

Plutarch has a tendency to be rather opaque on issues where we should prefer clarity, but whereas his dualism always tends towards some kind of eventual harmony and reconciliation, this is not what we find in Numenius, who was equally willing to praise Plato's insistence on two opposing souls in *Laws* book 10 (fr. 52 des Places). The difference between Plutarch and Numenius is stressed in a passage from Iamblichus' *On the Soul*, also preserved for us by Stobaeus (*Eclogues* 1.49.37):

> There has been much controversy within the Platonic school itself, one group bringing together into one system and form the various types and parts of life and its activities, as for example Plotinus and Porphyry; another, exemplified by Numenius, setting them up in conflict with each other; and another again reconciling them from a posited original strife, as for instance Atticus and Plutarch. These last maintain that there supervene on pre-existing disorderly and irregular motions other later ones which organize and arrange them, and from both of them they thus weave together a web of harmony.
>
> Iamblichus *On the Soul* 374.17–375.15[22]

---

[22] Translated by Finamore and Dillon (2002:49).

Numenius here (fr. 43 des Places) preserves the struggle between two types of soul (or life) operating in the human being, and he sees even Plato's Atlantis story as symbolizing the struggle between two soul armies, the inferior one closely associated with the business of generation (fr. 37 des Places). Their key to Numenius' dualism, however, seems to be provided by Calcidius, talking initially of souls at the universal level:

> The same Numenius praises Plato for postulating two souls of the world, one extremely beneficent, the other malign—matter surely; this, while in a condition of unstable flux, must inevitably, given that it moves according to its own proper motion, be alive and receive a pulse from soul,[23] according to the rule of all those things that have inborn motion. This is also the originator and sponsor of the passive part of the soul,[24] in which there is something corporeal, mortal, and akin to the body, just as the rational soul enjoys reason and god as its originator. Hence that world came into being from god and from matter.
>
> Calcidius *On Plato's Timaeus* 29[25]

If Calcidius is presenting Numenius' outline of the "Pythagorean" position reasonably accurately, then it is clear from this that the psychic dualism in human beings mirrors the division between the cosmic soul derived from a rational creator-god and the power animating matter at the cosmic level. That power can never be eliminated, but, says Calcidius (*On Plato's Timaeus* 298) following the *Timaeus*[26] but presumably still giving Numenius' view, it can be rendered orderly with divine assistance. The other main point that I take from the passage is that Numenius does not deny that the passive faculties of soul have something mortal and corporeal about them, but does not call them such outright. The process of constructing bodies for human beings has inevitably

---

[23] *Convegetetur*, while translated rather tamely "[be] activated" by Petty (2012) and *"tenir sa vie"* by des Places (1973), strikes one as being a little more colorful; perhaps it represents some *sun-* compound in the Greek, and one might consider *sumphuton ekhei* (cf. frr. 15.9 and 16.10 des Places) or even *sumphuteuetai* (for *phuteuein* cf. fr. 13.2, 6 des Places). However, the most telling parallel may be that of the simple verb *vegetari* at Apuleius *Metamorphoses* 11.1, of the way that things on earth, including even inanimate things, are given a living presence by the light and power of the lunar goddess.

[24] The idea of parts of a single soul seems to have been rejected by Numenius, as Petty (2012:216) notes, but the Latin *patibilis animae partis* and *rationabilis animae pars* below probably reflect no more than the Greek *to pathêtikon* and *to logistikon*, so that Calcidius may be fleshing out the Latin rather than directly correcting problematic Numenian doctrine for a Christian readership.

[25] Corresponding to Numenius fr. 52 des Places.

[26] The language recalls *Timaeus* 30b4–5 and des Places (1977) mentions also 53b1–5. However, both passages concern only the cosmic ordering; for the human return to order; see rather 44b1–7 and 90c6–d7.

introduced the psychic power associated with matter, something from which matter can never be freed. Insofar as that power is still associated with bodies that are themselves dissolved and recycled, it does not have the look of an immortal entity, but if this is the self-moving principle of matter, and if all that is self-moving is immortal (*Phaedrus* 245c), that power is not perishable.

It seems, then, that Numenius' insistence on soul of whatever type being immortal may not always involve the personal kind of immortality that human beings envisage. Does that "soul of matter" within us have some personal identity anyway? Is not the division of psychical life by individual persons a feature of order and planning? And what would be the point of a personal immortality that did not retain the faculty of memory? Can a disembodied soul, leaving the corpse behind, ever retain a soul that is produced by the "soul of matter"? Even in Numenius, the notion of a soul that is eventually reabsorbed into the psychical totality to which it belongs, and of a thinking entity that moves on elsewhere, with a longer independent existence, seems not to be entirely new; Sulla's myth in Plutarch's essay *On the Face that Appears on the Orb of the Moon* (942f–945d) seems to postulate a soul that retains its individual existence much longer than the body, but a mind that has another journey before it even leaves the soul in the region of the moon. To what extent Plutarch recommends this view is quite unclear, and it ends with a suggestion that the auditors use the ideas as they please (*On the Face that Appears on the Orb of the Moon* 945d), but it does at least provide a partial parallel for there being two entities within us humans besides the body, one of which seems to enjoy a different level of existence after death from the other. It also confirms that the simple distinction between immortal soul and mortal body is not as simple as it seems.

5. Arguments for an Immortal Soul

The complications that we have experienced in examining the issue of whether the nonrational soul was or was not mortal are clearly related to the question of what the arguments for the immortality of the soul actually show. Did the Middle Platonist think that they showed that the human soul continued to exist after death as the same individual as before? Was it proven that memory of an earlier existence was retained? Did they show that that same individual continued to exist with all the functions of soul that were possessed before death? In short, what could I look forward to in the afterlife if "I" could really look forward to anything?

The primary text here is chapter 25 of Alcinous' *Handbook of Platonism*, which collects the arguments that are to be found in Plato, but with significant reworking. First comes an argument from the soul's always being the bearer of life at *Handbook of Platonism* 177.18–20, simplifying the final argument of the

Phaedo (105c–107a); next a version of that dialogue's argument from similarity (*Phaedo* 78b–84b) at *Handbook of Platonism* 177.21–35; next a version of its first argument (*Phaedo* 70c–72d) at *Handbook of Platonism* 177.36–44; then a version of the argument from recollection, the second argument in the *Phaedo* (72e–77a); then the argument from the inability of its special evil, vice, to destroy it, deriving rather from *Republic* 10 (609d–611a) at *Handbook of Platonism* 178.13–15; and finally an argument from the soul's being self-moved, derived from the *Phaedrus* (245c–246a) at *Handbook of Platonism* 178.15–23.

Alcinous begins with an emphasis on the idea that life is by its very nature built into the soul, and he concludes with that same idea employing the same word (*sumphutos, Handbook of Platonism* 177.19 and 178.22).[27] This must have been widely agreed among these Platonists. The argument from similarity maintains that the soul cannot lose its *coherence* or be scattered to the winds; so what belongs to the individual will not be broken up. None of these arguments, however, could be used to prove that a number of individual souls could lose their personal identity by the opposite process of reuniting with others of their kind or being reabsorbed within some much greater soul. The argument from recollection, however, does maintain that humans have some continuation of memory from an earlier discarnate existence, even if they are merely insubstantial glimmers of things forgotten at birth (*Handbook of Platonism* 178.12), so that there is reason to believe that some continuity of memory survives the passage between the incarnate and discarnate states. There is, however, nothing to suggest that the nonrational soul survives separation from the body unless it is directly implicated in the bringing of life. The argument from similarity in Plato does tend to be directly linked with the idea that traces of the life of the passions can endure beyond the death of the body (*Phaedo* 81b–82b), though the ideal is clearly to pass beyond this to what seems to be an intellectual life alone. Do we then even want the nonrational soul, which previously had to cater to our bodily needs, to continue into the world beyond? Alcinous seems far from certain that we do, and none of the arguments seem to imply that its existence as such should continue. It is noticeable too that in offering a version of the argument from self-motion, Alcinous refrains from referring to "all soul" as Plato had done (*Phaedrus* 245c).

An interesting consideration here involves the souls that gods are endowed with, for gods are necessarily immortal. Normally the human ideal is reflected in the concept of what a god actually is, but a divine soul too is supposed to have three parts so as to accord with the tripartition of the human soul. The difference is that the three faculties have different names in this case, reflecting the

---

[27] These are the only instances in the work as a whole.

needs of the gods to judge, to move, and to adjust to their surroundings;[28] and Alcinous affirms that we have these powers, but that they are transformed into the three familiar parts of the soul at birth (*Handbook of Platonism* 178.39–45). From this, one may deduce that Alcinous thinks that the powers that can result in the existence of a nonrational soul already exist in the disembodied mortal soul, while their nonrational functioning within the body has a different origin. The body, then, is what is responsible for actualizing the potentially nonrational powers, a factor that is compatible with, if not linked to, Plato's account of how the newly embodied soul is thrown into confusion by the various motions that detract from its natural circular motions.

6. The Descent of the Soul

Just before Alcinous brings in the souls of the gods, he speaks of the reasons for the descent of the soul into the body (*Handbook of Platonism* 178.36–39). He gives consideration to a wide range of reasons, arising from some fundamentally different attitudes towards bodily existence in Plato's dialogues. The *Phaedo* tends to be fairly pessimistic, particularly when drawing on what is (and was in antiquity) interpreted as the Orphic/Pythagorean background. Therefore, the image of the body as some kind of prison (or even tomb)[29] of the body will appeal to those who regard life in the body as something of a disaster, while the *Phaedrus* (246b6) can be taken as implying that the soul naturally has a role to play in the care of a body, and that the placement of souls in bodies is thus part of the providential governance of the world. Indeed, as the *Timaeus* (30b3) claims, soul must be in the world in order for intelligence also to be present. In any event, it was axiomatic that there was some rational purpose for the way in which the world worked, so that an explanation for the descent of souls was required.

There is evidence of a lively debate concerning the soul's embodiment in section 27 of Iamblichus' fragmentary *On the Soul*. Platonists following Taurus (34T) are said to adhere to the view that souls are sent here by the gods, a reason that one might detect in Socrates' discussion of suicide at *Phaedo* 62b–63a where the gods are the ones who should determine how long we stay here.[30] Some of these interpreters said that it is for the completion of the universe following *Timaeus* 41b–c, and the others that it is to offer a means by which the life of the gods will be made manifest. After this, Iamblichus then distinguishes the soul's

---

[28] The terms are *kritikon*, *hormêtikon*, and *oikeiôtikon*. The final term is rare enough for its meaning to be uncertain.

[29] The *sôma-sêma* doctrine is also found at *Cratylus* 400c and *Gorgias* 493a. See also pp. 19 above and 112–113, 172n4, 311n13 and n15 below.

[30] The plural occurs at *Phaedo* 62b7, b8, d6, and 63a10; the singular at 62c7 and d2.

willing descent, whether of its own choice or in obedience to the gods, from its unwilling propulsion into an inferior existence. There follows a section (*On the Soul* 379.10–20) on whether all souls (human, divine, cosmic) are embodied in the same way, in which the school of Plotinus favored various types of embodiments for various ranks of soul, while Atticus and others thought that they were the same. Iamblichus then contrasts his own preference for postulating different reasons for different embodiments with the stance taken by Numenius (fr. 48), Cronius (fr. 7), and Harpocration (17T), who take the same view of all embodiments and regard them all as evil. In Numenius' case, we also know that he took the description of our bodily environment as a *phroura* (*Phaedo* 62b) in the sense of "prison"[31] to refer to the hold that *pleasure* exercises upon us,[32] no doubt interpreting it in the light of a later passage where pleasures, desires, pains, and fears *bind* the soul into the body (*Phaedo* 83b7–e3), and perhaps also of the *Cratylus*' notion that desire is the strongest bond.[33]

Alcinous' brief treatment (*Handbook of Platonism* 178.36–38) packs four competing reasons for embodiment into two lines. The first explanation has something to do with waiting for numbers, but there may have been textual corruption;[34] the second is Taurus' view making it due to the will of the gods; the third blames the soul's own "lack of control" (*akolasia*), conceivably a reference to Numenius' "pleasure"; and the fourth attributes the soul's embodiment to its "love of body" (*philosômatia*). Either of the last two explanations might easily relate to Plato's *Phaedo*.[35] It is added that soul and body have a natural affinity for one another.

The very concept of a descent of the soul might be surprising to some readers of Plato. That is because the *Phaedo* seems comfortable with the traditional assumption that the disembodied soul goes to some kind of underworld capable of being called the house of Hades. Even so, it represents this earthly existence as hierarchically lower than its disembodied origin, so that we humans live deep in hollows "like frogs around a swamp" (*Phaedo* 109b), whereas the true philosophers will rise up to the surface of the true earth (114b–c). The

---

[31] This agrees with the work's pervasive theme of imprisonment and release.

[32] Cf. fr. 32.10, where pleasure is again given as a cause of the soul's descent.

[33] *Cratylus* 403b–c; on this fragment of Numenius and the Platonic interpretation that it implies, see Tarrant 2015:144–145.

[34] However, see Whittaker 1980:131; one may also note that Iamblichus' *On the Soul* 376.1–377.9 has the heading "Concerning the Measure of Soul," translated by Finamore and Dillon (2002:51) as "The Number of the Souls," and it contains the observation that Platonists require that souls should stand always in the same proportion, adding that Plotinus' school identified this with the perfect number.

[35] Pleasure and *akolasia* appear in close conjunction at *Phaedo* 68e2–7, just after the appearance of the concept of *philosômatia* (see the rare adjective *philosômatos* at 68c1).

Phaedrus, however, goes far beyond this in envisaging the world of disembodied souls as the heavens, where in a winged condition they each follow a god as high as possible, striving for their vision of the Ideas, which lie beyond the heavens (246d–248c). The *Timaeus* too has the souls, when first created, placed among the stars (41d8–e2) before they are implanted in bodies. These two dialogues are perhaps the most influential of all under the early empire, the former with the wider literary public and the latter with students of philosophy. As a result, the notion that the soul belongs on high appears in Plutarch, in the enigmatic myth of his *On the Face that Appears in the Orb of the Moon* (943a–945d), where a separable intellect is associated with the sun and soul proper with the moon (where Persephone and Hades are to be found), but Plutarch seems not to commit to the truth of this picture (945d). However, it is with Numenius (fragments 31, 34, and 35) and Cronius that we find a detailed, and presumably serious, attempt at mapping the path of the soul down to earth through the constellations, with the Milky Way playing an important part, as it had apparently done in the work of Plato's dissident pupil Heraclides of Pontus.[36]

7. The Soul's Point of Entry

There was clearly some debate already about exactly when the soul entered into the embryonic body, and so animating it. While important material on how this question had received many answers is found in Iamblichus, the passage names no Platonists prior to Plotinus. Yet we can mention at least two such Platonists. It is not an important topic for Alcinous, but he affords it one sentence and seems to believe that souls enter the embryo as it is developing (*Handbook of Platonism* 178.33–35). Numenius (fr. 36) was of the belief that it was at the moment of conception, since nothing could be conceived without soul. The relevant fragment is preserved in the second chapter of a work of Porphyry wrongly ascribed to Galen, *To Gaurus on how Embryos are Ensouled*. This work tackled the issue in detail, and its third chapter gives an account from a contemporary of Porphyry working in an earlier tradition, whereby the soul is drawn in from the surrounding air during the heavy breathing associated with intercourse; it seems from Iamblichus (*On the Soul* 381.12–24) that this had been one of three variations of the basic idea that the animating force is drawn in by the desires and exertions of one or both partners. Such ideas are not specifically related to Platonism, and following the Hippocratic writings (*On the Soul* 381.1–12), medical theorists would also have had ideas on animation.

---

[36] See Iamblichus *On the Soul* 377.11–23 and Finamore and Dillon 2002:153.

The emphasis on breathing no doubt reflects the observable connection between life and breath, by which the newborn baby takes its first breath and the dying animal takes its last. But what is breathed is also gaseous, or "airy," and this would have suggested a fine mobile substance rather than the structured entity that Platonists presumed the soul to be. The belief in individual souls that maintain their identity even in the disembodied state meant that Platonists would not normally have allowed that new souls could be constituted of whatever inhaled soul-stuff (or *pneuma*, as it was generally called in such circumstances) happened to be present in the vicinity of the site of conception. Animation required the new child to receive a single preexistent soul, not an unspecified quantity of animating stuff.

Before leaving this topic it would be well to make it clear that the issue of when the embryo becomes a living creature was one of medicine or natural philosophy as the opening of *To Gaurus* makes clear, a fascinating issue of how life begins but without any of the same ethical or religious issues that attach to it today. The number of ancient children who failed to survive birth and the first few months thereafter would have discouraged the view that any organism, once animated, had the right to live.

8. The Embodied Soul

The body is not the permanent home of an immortal soul, and thus it cannot be regarded as its true home either. The *Timaeus* (42b3–4) refers to its returning, after the right kind of life, to "the dwelling place of its lawful partner star," and Alcinous also speaks of a return to the "lawful partner star" (*sunnomon astron*) after a just life (*Handbook of Platonism* 172.14–15). This kind of life would involve embodied souls managing to control their sensations and the four principal affections, pleasure, pain, impulsiveness (*thumos*), and fear. These affections would be associated with life in the body, for which it would also receive its mortal parts. That the souls of the very young would be especially upset by their first encounters with the world of sensation received widespread assent. That many would continue to have such problems, and be unable to control the mortal parts was likewise accepted, and in a sense that assumption provided the basis for the ethical theory of these Platonists insofar as it was all about the minimization or even eradication of these affections, thus enabling us to achieve the greatest similarity possible to a god, in conformity with the theory of *Theaetetus* 176b–c.

But how was it that such passions were to be minimized? The *Timaeus* offered various hints that the restoration of the soul's cyclical motions was paramount and was effected by the study of the heavens (44b1–4, 47a1–c4, 90c6–d7), and there was also some emphasis on education more broadly (44b8–c1). With its emphasis on ethics rather than natural philosophy, as Eudorus of Alexandria had observed,[37] the *Theaetetus* (176b) attributes assimilation of god especially to our becoming as just as possible, mentioning also piety and wisdom as Alcinous notes (*Handbook of Platonism* 181.21–22). That dialogue had also characterized such assimilation as a flight from this world to the divine world, agreeing with the *Phaedo*'s characterization of philosophy as a practice of death (67e), and Platonists widely continued to represent philosophy as a flight of this kind.

Because the problems arising from the conjunction of soul and body in the *Timaeus* had been depicted in terms of the distortion of the cyclical motions and harmonic construction (43c7–44a5), while these in turn had been responsible for the perfect cognition of the universal soul (37a2–c5), it is inevitable that Platonists would attribute imperfections in our cognitive abilities as well as in our behavior to this conjunction. Some of these imperfections would potentially last for one's whole life. The anonymous commentator on the *Theaetetus* attributes our ability to know things in this world to our common or natural notions (*koinai ennoiai*, 23.7, 47.21; *phusikai ennoiai*, 46.43, 47.44), but the mere possession of such notions does not in itself bring us knowledge, for they require articulation (*diarthrôsis*, 46.43–46, 47.37–45, 53.45–46), something that Socrates' midwifery could facilitate. Human cognitive processes can be *influenced* by the common notions before they are articulated, but only brought to completion in knowledge once articulation is complete (46.43–49). Thus, when Plato seems to be saying that intellectual "conception" is something that everybody does in the *Symposium* (206c) but that not everybody can so conceive in *Theaetetus* (151b), it should be understood that not everybody can so conceive *in this life*, even though every soul will do so in the wider scheme of things. That Platonists were acutely conscious that the natural notions fell short of the direct "vision" of the Ideas in the other world is evidenced by a statement of Alcinous (*Handbook of Platonism* 155.24–28). He maintains that, whereas true intellection of the Ideas is only possible in our discarnate state, the corresponding cognition is called "natural notion" in our present bodily condition, "being a quasi-intellection stored away within the soul."[38] Therefore, the embodiment of the soul operates as a hindrance to it by producing an unacceptable level of affections with consequences for our moral well being, and by impeding our cognitive processes, not least by forcing us to approach the most important objects of knowledge, the Ideas, indirectly, if at all—thus, the need to flee this bodily life.

---

[37] See Eudorus as reported by Stobaeus in *Eclogues* 2.49.18–25, distinguishing the perspectives from which Plato's account of the goal was offered.

[38] *Handbook of Platonism* 155.27–28: νόησίς τις οὖσα ἐναποκειμένη τῇ ψυχῇ. The very distinction between cognition in and out of the body is of course primarily encouraged by the *Phaedo*.

9. Soul as Self

But how is it possible for us as agents to flee from our very own bodies and from the mortal parts of the soul that serve as the interface between the rational soul and the body's own needs? This implies a radical distinction between one's self as agent and the body with which it is associated. According to the *Alcibiades I* (130c–e), whose Platonic authorship was never in ancient times doubted, the soul, as opposed to either the body or the combination of body and soul, is the person's real self; it is intended to *control* the body, and employ it as a kind of tool. Control is a particularly important notion in this context, for many of the problems experienced by the infant according to the *Timaeus* are due to a *failure of control* at a time when the desires of the body are at their greatest. Furthermore, the virtue most prominent in the *Alcibiades I* and especially recommended to Alcibiades himself was *sôphrosunê* (133c–134d), which is that of both retaining self-control and knowing oneself. Moreover, the dialogue seems to look beyond the soul to a "self-itself," and to that very part of the soul that is concerned with knowledge, and that in turn would fit the general idea that it is the intellectual soul that needs to be in control, and that it must exercise control not merely over the body, but also of the various mortal "parts" of soul that deal with the body.

Whatever was intended by the fact that the *Alcibiades I* postulated the mind as a kind of self within the self, Plutarch, who certainly knew the dialogue,[39] was attracted to the idea of a mind that was still more able to be called the "self" than the soul and that the inferior parts of the soul were just as much its tools as was the body (*Against Colotes* 1119a). He twice introduces the idea of a separable intellect in his myths (*On the Face that Appears in the Orb of the Moon* 943a–945d; *On the Delays of Divine Vengeance* 564c), and the former myth also makes the following statement:

> For the 'self' of each of us is not our temper nor fear nor desire in the same way as it is neither flesh nor moisture, but it is that with which we are thoughtful and wise, ...

> Plutarch *On the Face that Appears in the Orb of the Moon*
> 944f–945a

So while this comes in the context of a myth and is therefore of ambiguous doctrinal status, it seems clearly to demontrate Plutarch's interest in seeing the "self" in its most restrictive sense as the rational faculty alone, or as that part

---

[39] See Renaud and Tarrant (2015:127–140) who should, however, have discussed *Against Colotes* 1119a in this context.

of the soul supplied by the Demiurge in the *Timaeus*, rather than by his young assistants.

The identity of the "self" had grown into a major issue of philosophy by the time of Plotinus, as recent literature demontrates,[40] and the trend was already to be observed in the previous century. In chapter 5 of Albinus' brief *Introduction to Plato's Dialogues*, the first two dialogues to be studied are the *Alcibiades I* and the *Phaedo*, the first because it encourages us to look within ourselves and recognize what we must take care of (i.e. our "self" or soul), and the second because it provides a paradigm of the philosopher's concerns—which are very much dependent on the soul being the true self, as is humorously demontrated when Crito asks Socrates how he wants to be buried (*Phaedo* 115c). Inscriptional evidence links a number of Middle Platonists with Delphi, and a connection between Platonism and the sanctuary would naturally increase the importance of the "self." A Delphic inscription invited its readers to "Know yourself," and any philosopher who accepted our obligation to know ourselves ought to be asking what this "self" really is. The *Phaedrus* (229e4–230a1) also has Socrates imply that Delphic self-knowledge is a knowledge that must take precedence over others.

In any case the identification of the soul, and particularly of the rational soul, with the "self" has two important consequences. First, it justifies our putting the health of the soul (through philosophy) ahead of the health of the body (through medicine), and makes the true philosopher a figure to be respected; and second, it enables one to contemplate leaving the body behind, whether by transcending it or by literally dying. This brings us close to a religious notion of the salvation of our souls.

10. The Salvation of the Soul

Between the first and fifth centuries, the probability that any given Platonist would be deeply involved in some religious movement increased considerably. Plutarch may have been a priest at Delphi, but holding office at a local religious site was no sign of fanaticism. That he was concerned that the shrine should continue to flourish is evident from his dialogues on Delphic themes, particularly *On the Obsolescence of Oracles*; his interest in religious stories from afar is also well documented; and that his detailed religious interests went far beyond those of Greece is evident from his *On Isis and Osiris* in particular. Philosophy and religion are seen as allies, but not yet as so deeply intertwined as they would be in Numenius, in Plotinus, and above all, in Iamblichus. Platonism did not yet

---

[40] See Remes 2007 and Mortley 2013.

entail religious practice. Yet the notion of a soul that was the real person, and could profitably be purified of the body and its associated passions, was one that both Platonic philosophy and a variety of religions could use. While philosophic methods of purification were different from the ritual means employed by religions, both might involve salvation by the purification and release of the soul from its worldly concerns.

The theme of purification and release is particularly evident in Plato's *Phaedo*, the dialogue widely known as *On Soul*. It seems that it had employed several traditional ideas, often Orphic, to purge away our fears concerning the impending death of Socrates, and, by extension, of anybody else who had practiced a philosophic life. It finds a use for some fairly sophisticated arguments, but also for enchantments (*Phaedo* 77e–78a, 114d6–7), prophetic swan songs (84e–85b), statements of belief about the true earth (108d–e), and myths with traditional elements (110b and 114d7–8). At the close, Socrates is gone, peacefully leaving a lifeless corpse behind, and destined to prosper even in the afterlife (58e5–59a1). So this dialogue provided Platonists with a kind of exemplar of deliverance, first by the minimization of bodily concerns while alive, and then from the body itself; and the deliverance is achieved partly by philosophic and partly by religious means.

The myth of Plutarch's *On the Face that Appears in the Orb of the Moon* (934a–b) postulated a double death: the first and more traumatic separation, leaving the body behind on the earth; and the second, gently leaving at least the good soul behind on the moon and allowing the intellect to rise further still. This accords perhaps with the fact that the *Phaedo* does not predict that death will bring any but intellectual activities for the philosopher, and indeed expects these activities to be unhindered in the next world. Our survival as intellects is something that the philosopher may well find attractive, though one doubts that it could ever have the widespread attraction that religious adherents will expect of salvation.

From the point of view of salvation, the most interesting text by a Middle Platonist is Apuleius' novel *The Golden Ass* (or *Metamorphoses*). Whether the author is really writing as a Platonist has certainly been disputed, for it functions well as entertainment without reading much philosophy into it, but various recent studies encourage one to accept the internal evidence that philosophy is part of the author's persona.[41] The novel tells of a young relative of Plutarch, led into a dangerous situation by excessive curiosity and libido, who is accidentally transformed into an ass after witnessing a witch transforming herself into an owl. Unable to find the fresh roses that will restore him to human form,

---

[41]   See M. O'Brien 2002 and Fletcher 2014.

he is subjected to immense hardships and dangers before his talents at human behavior are discovered. His moral indignation at the prospect of being made to copulate with a condemned woman causes him to bolt to a beach, where he receives a revelation associated with the full moon shortly before a festival of Isis. The goddess answers his prayers and he will soon be offered the roses he needs by a priest of Isis, and is ultimately dedicated to the service of the goddess. The most important part of the text for our purposes is the address by the priest to Lucius after his restoration to human form:

> Lucius, the troubles which you have endured have been many and diverse. You have been driven before the heavy storms and heaviest gales of Fortune, but you have finally reached the harbour of peace and the altar of mercy. ... you tumbled on the slippery slope into slavish pleasures, and gained the ill-omened reward for your unhappy curiosity.[42]
>
> Apuleius *Metamorphoses* 11.15[43]

The blind Fortune that has so far driven him at random has somehow managed to deliver him into the hands of a Fortune with eyes that now protects him, and he will hereafter serve the goddess in happiness. The story is one of fall and redemption, with the fall symbolized by the bestial form in which a human soul has somehow become imprisoned.

While the worship of Isis had been the subject of an essay by Plutarch and Egyptian religion is used as a quasi-philosophic source by Numenius (fr. 1a), nothing in the extant remains of the Middle Platonists prepares us for this kind of story. This is not philosophic redemption, but a religious redemption that may be intended to parallel philosophic redemption in a colorful and humorous way. Interestingly, it fails to paint the kind of picture of Lucius the initiate that really makes his life one that we want to emulate, and this has been largely where Platonism had failed too: life as a disembodied soul in a community of disembodied souls, especially if it is eternal life, just does not sound interesting. We may be anxious to escape from our life of troubles in this world, but we should perhaps take care that we do not find the higher life unsatisfying.

Others took up the challenge. We see the development of hybrid movements that fuse elements of Platonism and religion into a seamless whole that will prove more attractive to us. The Chaldaean Oracles, Hermetic Writings, and Platonist Gnostic treatises all seem to fall into this pattern, and some at least held out the prospect of an ascent of the soul through the heavenly spheres

---

[42] Not simply an inquiring mind, but a dangerous inquisitiveness that causes one to meddle in things that one should have nothing to do with—in Greek *polupragmosunê*.

[43] The translation is according to Walsh 1995.

that would mirror its descent into earthly existence. The Middle Platonists have brought us only to the threshold of redemption.

11. Conclusion

Regardless of any position on religious redemption, the Middle Platonist view of soul had considerable implications for human life here on earth and within our bodies. That we are souls, and that our souls are above all the cognitive faculty, or intellect, had the inevitable consequence that taking care of our selves involved first and foremost taking care of our souls, and taking care of them in such a way as to privilege the exercise of their intellect over their pleasures and passions. Acceptance of *our* assimilation to the divine as the ultimate human goal entailed that our souls and intellects should become as divine as possible within our present lives. As for the body, it was not only a tool, but a tool that could be replaced in a subsequent life, so that there was a limit to the extent to which we should be concerned for it.

While the priority of the soul over the body was something of a commonplace in Greek philosophy, the reasons for this priority were important. The extension of that priority to the intellect, together with the exemplar offered by the *Phaedo*, led to a greater emphasis on the theoretical life than in many philosophies. Though Aristotelianism also highlighted the theoretical life, the Platonic insistence on an immortal soul transformed the very concept of *theôria*, by transferring the ultimate theoretical experience to a discarnate world and making our theoretical activity in this world aim at the recreation of a vision. While this did not result in downplaying the virtues of justice, temperance, and courage, it did tend to result in the separation of the virtuous behavior of the ordinary person, produced either by good breeding or persistent habituation as in Alcinous (*Handbook of Platonism* 30), from the divine virtues of the accomplished philosopher, all produced together by the perfect disposition of the soul (*Handbook of Platonism* 29). It also turned contemplative activity into an act of religious piety, as also into an act of inspiration and love for the divine. Therefore, theology begins to transcend ethics, and it would continue on this path for some time to come.[44]

---

[44] For an example in Porphyry, see pp. 144–152 below.

5

Platonizing Gnostic Views on Soul and Body

John D. Turner[†]

Abstract: After a general introduction, this chapter discusses gnostic views of the soul and then of the body, consequently subdividing each of these two sections into Hermetic, Valentinian, and Sethian literature (in order of the reader's probable familiarity). In presenting the above views, the chapter addresses the common charge that Gnosticism is consistently anticosmic and antisomatic.

W HILE ALL GNOSTIC AND many Platonic thinkers of the first three centuries are agreed that the presence of the soul in the body is a misfortune from which it must be extricated, some attribute its enforced presence in the body to a specific cause antecedent to the creation of individual human souls, while others do not.[1] Those who propose a specific primordial cause usually do so by means of an elaborate myth that combines a theogony, cosmogony, and anthropogony based on the two dominant protologies of their time: Plato's *Timaeus* and the initial chapters of the book of Genesis, often read in the light of the *Timaeus*. In these myths, the creation of this world is attributed to the fall of a creative principle from the aboriginal perfection of the higher world at some point subsequent to its initial deployment. In general, it is a cosmic soul or some equivalent being to whom this failure is attributed.

---

[1] By 'Platonists,' I mean to designate late antique authors who explicitly recognize Plato as the basic authority behind their metaphysical doctrines, and by 'Gnostics,' I restrict myself to the exponents of those doctrines Irenaeus attributes to the school of Valentinus in chapters 1–8, 11, 13, and other *gnostici* (later identified as Sethians and Ophites) discussed in chapters 29–30 of his *Against Heresies*, as well as the Coptic texts from the *Nag Hammadi* and related codices, whose doctrines are indisputably similar to those described by Irenaeus. By dint of their clear affinity with Platonic teaching and these Gnostic sources, I also briefly discuss certain treatises from the *Corpus Hermeticum*. Throughout this chapter, citations of Gnostic literature are taken from Foerster 1972, Meyer 2007, and Robinson 1988.

As Jonas argued many years ago,[2] the link between later Platonism and Gnosticism lies in the mutual transformability between metaphysical dynamic emanationism and the narrative sequence of the gnostic myths. In the gnostic myths, the sequence of the unfolding of the higher to the lower world proceeds in terms of dramatic episodes, personified aeonic beings, sexual procreation, and the praising of the parent by the offspring; in Platonist metaphysics, it proceeds in terms of arithmetical progression from unity to plurality, hypostatic universal principles, the shift from potentiality to actuality, and the contemplative reversion of the product on its source. Although the number of such myths is substantial, I will here discuss only those associated with Hermetic, Thomasine, Valentinian, and Sethian Gnostic thought. There are, however, a number of documents associated with Gnosticism that do not use elaborate mythical narratives to explain the soul's origin, experience, and destiny, but merely describe the soul's plight as a given, and proceed from there to present the means of its extrication and salvation. Thus among the Nag Hammadi Codices, the *Exegesis on the Soul* (NHC II 6) represents the soul as an exile falling among robbers who rape her repeatedly, and then repent and call upon her father, but it does not make clear what leads to the original transgression. This situation is reversed by the inward turning of the soul, regarded as a cleansing baptism, which leads to the soul's restoration to her former self, a resurrection and spiritual marriage to her undescended heavenly counterpart.[3] *Thomas the Contender* (NHC II 7), properly an Encratite rather than Gnostic treatise, merely starts from the bitter condition of the soul being burned alive by the fiery passions of the body, but assigns no cause for the origin of this condition. The reversal of this condition is accomplished by leading a severely ascetic life among like-minded persons, a mortification of the flesh which will free the soul from its prison.[4] The *Authoritative Teaching* (NHC VI 3), although similarly characterizing the situation of the embodied soul in terms of rape, lust, ignorance, and drunkenness, attributes this to a cause, namely an "Adversary" and certain "hostile forces" responsible for casting the soul into the body. This situation is to be reversed by stripping away the passions, attending to the teaching of the evangelists, and entering into a spiritual marriage with the divine mind above.[5]

Gnostic literature featuring the grand myths of origin typical of Valentinianism and Sethianism devotes comparatively less space to the description of the soul's incarnate experience, and comparatively more to the explanation of its original cause. This cause is to be found in the transcendent world-soul,

---

[2]   Jonas 1954 passim.
[3]   *Exegesis on the Soul* (NHC II 6) 127.19–31, 131.13–132.2, 133.1–133.9, 133.34–134.15.
[4]   *Book of Thomas* (NHC II 7) 138.39–139.12, 140.1–5, 140.18–37, 141.5–18, 141.33–38, 142.12–18.
[5]   *Authoritative Teaching* (NHC VI 3) 23.12–24.23, 28.10–25, 31.9–32.27, 34.32–35.10.

subordinate to the divine mind, whose direct knowledge of the supreme deity it attempts to reproduce, but with disastrous consequences. The quintessential personification of this psychic principle is Sophia, the divine wisdom, who becomes guilty of a transgression in seeking an independent direct knowledge and imitation of the creative power of the supreme deity. This attempt leads to the creation of the material world, and ultimately to the imprisonment of human souls within it as lost fragments of the originally divine substance. Platonism and Gnosticism both postulate a female principle, either generated from or coeval with the ultimate principle of all, usually male or androgynous.[6] The female principle is characterized as negative, boundless, and lacking in form, but possessed of an independent desire to generate multiplicity. In order to account for the imperfect and disorderly nature of the world as it now exists, one may characterize the generative act of the female principle (including human souls) in terms of a fall, an act of disobedience, or lack of harmony with the divine world (as did most Gnostics, and as did many Platonists, like Plotinus). Such a notion is grounded on the idea that the rise of anything different from or other than the original unitary principle must be ontologically worse than it and must proceed through all possible stages of inferiority to the ultimate point of nonbeing, called Matter.

1. Hermetica

Although much of the body of Hermetic literature can hardly be classified as Gnostic, for our purposes it presents a combination of Platonic notions concerning the plight of the fallen human soul with a means of its salvation through revelation and self-knowledge instructively close to that found in the classical gnostic theologies to be commented on next.

According to the first Hermetic tractate, *Poimandres*, the Mind of the supreme power (*authentia*), either the highest or next-to-highest principle, emits a dark, wet substance upon which leaps a *logos* from his light. He then generates a demiurgic Mind who creates the realm of nature beginning with the planetary spheres, after which the *logos* and demiurgic mind unite, perhaps as a kind of rational world-soul. The Demiurge creates irrational animals, while Mind creates mankind in his image, who sees his image in Nature below and unites with it to produce mortal men. From nature, human bodily nature is governed by Fate; but from the light and life of the archetypal human, mankind also acquires mind and soul. As Mind, Poimandres frees good humans from bodily

---

[6] See Dillon 1980.

passions, but to the evil, he is present as an avenging daemon who punishes the soul by exciting these passions.

Aristotle's doctrine of the separateness and immortality of *Nous* (*On the Soul* 430a10–b6) is frequently reflected in the *Corpus Hermeticum*: in CH I and X, there is a clear separation of *nous* and *psukhê*. In CH IV, man is invited to be baptized in a *kratêr* god has filled with intelligence, consubstantial with god himself. In CH XII, the human intellect has emanated into us as the very substance of god, like as a ray of light from the sun; our intellect is the very soul and self of god. In CH X, *nous* becomes the *daimôn* sent to reward and punish human souls. In the *Corpus Hermeticum*, incarnation is not necessarily an evil. In fact, the Latin *Asclepius* views the soul as a psychic mixture that includes an element or form made directly by god (*Korê Kosmou*, a crater full of mathematical entities, as in Plato's *Timaeus*), but which needs a corporeal envelope to survive on earth, provided by God in the form of the body.

On the other hand, in the *Korê Kosmou*, god creates souls from his own breath to overcome the inertness of the celestial realm, although when the souls descend to earth, they are mixed with qualities of the various levels of the atmosphere. After exercising an audacious curiosity about the stuff of which earthly animals are to be made, humans are commanded by god to model the animals out of it. Those obedient to this demiurgical task stay in heaven, while the disobedient are punished by falling into human bodies. If they live well, they return to heaven; if badly, they are incarnated into beasts. But even here, the possibility of an ascent to heaven is revealed by Isis and Osiris, who disclose to humans, despite being ignored by them, the true knowledge of civilization and the nature of the soul formerly deposited by Hermes on steles. Thus, while in CH I and XIII salvation is through the regeneration caused by self-knowledge, in *Korê Kosmou* it is made available by two saviors.

2. Thomasine Christianity

Among the major exponents of Thomasine Christianity are the texts the *Gospel of Thomas* and the *Book of Thomas* (the Contender or *athlêtês*) from *Nag Hammadi Codex* II, which contain traditions closely related to the Syriac and Greek versions of the *Acts of Thomas*. All of these likely derive from the ascetic, pre-Manichaean Christianity of the Syrian Osrhoëne, between Edessa (modern Urfa) and Messene, which is probably the original home of the early traditions regarding the life and teaching of Judas Thomas, the twin brother of Jesus, and the apostle and missionary to Syria, Parthia, and India. It is in Eastern Syria and eastward into Mesopotamia rather than in Egypt that the ascetic Christianity of the third and fourth centuries assumed its most radical form, with the universal requirement of post-baptismal chastity, and a reversion to a life deprived of all civilized luxury.

Of these texts—with the exception of the *Hymn of the Pearl* portraying the soul's descent from the spiritual realm into this world of ignorance from which it must be awakened and restored to its true self (*Acts of Thomas* 108–113)—the dichotomy between body and soul is most pronounced in the *Book of Thomas*. Apart from its Platonic-Gnostic-Hermetic doctrine of salvation by self-knowledge, familiar from the *Gospel of Thomas*, the basic and original theme of the text is an unbending asceticism that condemns anything to do with the flesh and sexuality. The dominant catchword is "fire": the fiery and lustful sexual passions of the bestial body that inflame the soul condemn one to an eternal fiery punishment in hell, thus implementing a Dantean *contrapasso*—one is punished by that by which one sins. Although it attributes to Jesus' sayings formulae typical of the Jesus of the synoptic gospels ("Woe to you," "Blessed are you," and "Watch and pray"), the underlying conceptuality of the dialogue between Jesus and Thomas that occupies its first half is Platonic, inspired by prominent passages from four of Plato's principal dialogues, the *Phaedo*, *Phaedrus*, *Republic*, and *Timaeus*.[7]

According to the Savior's initial revelation (*The Book of Thomas* 138.39–139.31), the bodies of men and animals alike are devoid of reason, which is the property of the soul alone. The souls in the invisible realm above are nourished by their own root; they are self-sufficient and eternal, but the bodies of the visible realm must be nourished by other bodies, whether that of other animals or plants, and never produce anything else other than more bodies. The language of this section is drawn from *Phaedo* 78e–79a and *Phaedrus* 250e.

In *The Book of Thomas*, we read:

> Then the Savior continued and said, "O unsearchable love of the light! O bitterness of the fire that blazes in the bodies of men and in their marrow, kindling in them night and day, and burning the limbs of men and [making] their minds become drunk and their souls become deranged. [And the fire which is imprisoned] in them [dominates] males and females [by day and] night—and moves them [and arouses them] secretly and visibly. For the males [move; they move upon the females] and the females upon [the males]."
>
> *The Book of Thomas* 139.31–42

---

7 A detailed analysis of explicit passages from these dialogues placed upon the lips of Jesus is offered in Turner 2007.

Ancient medical and philosophical lore held the element of fire to constitute the male and female generative principle leading to birth.[8] Much of the language of this passage seems to be drawn from the *Timaeus'* interpretation (86b–e) of the human sex drive as due to a physical cause: the leakage of the liquid "universal seed" (*panspermia*) stuff comprising the marrow ("whenever a man's seed grows to abundant volume in his marrow") through the porosity of the bones (*Timaeus* 73b–c).[9] While *The Book of Thomas* assigns the motivating element of sexual overindulgence to the fire of passion, it agrees with Plato's *Timaeus* that this motivating element is a kind of disease or madness.

The use of language drawn from the *Phaedo* (81a–83e) could not be more obvious than in the following passage from the *Book of Thomas* (140.18–37):

> There are some who, although having wings, rush upon the visible things, things that are far from the truth. For that which guides them, the fire, will give them an illusion of truth, [and] will shine on them with a [perishable] beauty, and it will imprison them in a dark sweetness and captivate them with fragrant pleasure. And it will blind them with insatiable lust and burn their souls and become for them like a stake stuck in their heart which they can never dislodge. And like a bit in the mouth, it leads them according to its own desire. And it has fettered them with its chains and bound all their limbs with the bitterness of the bondage of lust for those visible things that will decay and change and swerve by impulse. They have always been attracted

---

[8] For example, Cicero *On the Nature of the Gods* 2.10.28: "It follows that, since all parts of the universe are sustained by fire, so also the universe itself in like measure is born and preserves its eternal nature, and all the more so because it must be understood that this heat and burning is extended in every nature, such that it contains the power of procreation and the cause of generation, since it is that by which all living things including those whose roots are sustained by the earth, must both be born and grow" (my translation); and Empedocles (fr. 262 Fairbanks) found in Simplicius *Commentary on Aristotle's Physics* 381.31–382.3: "But come now, hear of these things; how fire separating caused the hidden offspring of men and weeping women to arise, for it is no tale apart from our subject, or witless. In the first place there sprang up out of the earth forms grown into one whole, having a share of both, of water and of fire. These in truth fire caused to grow up, desiring to reach its like; but they showed as yet no lovely body formed out of the members, nor voice nor limb such as is natural to men" (Fairbanks' translation 1898). "Cyprian" *On Chastity* 9–10 refers to the flame of lust, wherein the blood grows hot and stimulates the natural fires stirring in the marrow to seek a remedy: "Thus the flame of resuscitated lust recalled them into the glowing heats of their bygone youth ... the blood, still inexperienced, grows hot, and stimulates the natural fires, and the blind flames that stir in the marrow, to seek a remedy" (Wallis' translation 1869).

[9] For a discussion of Plato's account, see pp. 8–11.

downwards; as they are killed, they are assimilated to all the beasts of the perishable realm.

The Book of Thomas 140.18–37

In many ways, *The Book of Thomas* is an interesting example of the Christianizing of Platonic teaching, or, better still, of the Platonizing of Jesus. Its diatribe against the lusts and passions of the body, traditionally ascribed to the power of *eros*, constitutes an ironic parody of Socrates' encomium on *eros* in the *Symposium* (210a–212a). There, Socrates recounts the path to the vision of absolute beauty into which he had been initiated by the wise Diotima as a redirection of *eros*, the moving force of the soul, away from the lower visible realm to the higher invisible and intelligible realm. Similarly, in *The Book of Thomas*, the Savior acts to convert the interlocutor Thomas' *eros* and, by extension, the readers' *eros* away from seeking gratification in the visible, tangible realm toward seeking a higher union with a more suitable lover—the divine King of all:

> For when you come forth from the sufferings and passions of the body, you will receive rest from the good one, and you will reign with the king, you joined with him and he with you, from now on, for ever and ever, Amen.

The Book of Thomas 145.12–16

3. Valentinian Christianity

One of the most successful Christian Gnostic movements was founded by Valentinus around 140. Near the end of the second century, the school of thought inaugurated by him was considered by Irenaeus, bishop of Lyons, as the most dangerous of all the Gnostic "heretics," but Valentinian writings continued to circulate among churches across the Eastern Empire through the fourth century.

According to Valentinian theology,[10] a single first principle called the Father, or "Depth," produces his Son, the divine Intellect, through an act of self-knowledge. The Father and Son are paradoxically one and two at the same time, thus enabling the generation of a plurality of spiritual beings called Aeons, who collectively comprise the divine realm, the *Plêrôma*. The last and youngest of these Aeons, usually called Mother Wisdom (Sophia, or in the *Tripartite Tractate*, the *Logos*), attempts to grasp the spiritual totality of the Father, but fails and is split apart into a spiritual part that returns to the *Plêrôma*, and a lower,

---

[10] See the masterful exposition of Thomassen 2006 to which I am here indebted.

imperfect remainder, often named Achamoth, of irrational and negative passions, which initially give rise to "matter" (*hulê*). This "fall" can be viewed either as an act of presumption, as in the Ptolemaic system summarized by Irenaeus in *Against Heresies* 1.2.1–5, or as a positive act in accordance with the supreme deity's will, as in the case of the *Logos* in *Tripartite Tractate* (NHC I 5 76.23–30). On repenting from this failure (cf. the Neoplatonic idea of "reversion" [*epistrophê*]), she produces the "psychic" (*psukhikos*) substance of souls, whereupon the *Plêrôma* sends down upon her the Savior together with a host of angels, the vision of whom heals her of her passions and causes her to experience joy, thus enabling her to bring forth a third kind of offspring: "spiritual beings" (*hoi pneumatikoi*) as images of the Pleromatic Aeons.

This succession of emotions, from passions—such as grief, sorrow, and perplexity—through repentance to joy, are the respective origins of the "material" (*hulikos*), "animate" (*psukhikos*), and the "spiritual" (*pneumatikos*) substances from which the cosmos is fashioned by the powers that arise from and rule as "Archons" over the psychic substance, whose chief is called the "Demiurge" (craftsman). Of course, the true creators are the Savior and the repentant Sophia or *Logos*, while the Demiurge is merely a tool used by them to make the earth and the planetary spheres above it out of the matter and psychical substance over which he thinks he presides.

These powers fashion the first human being, Adam, into whom Sophia secretly inserts a spiritual "seed"—the preexistent heavenly Church—derived from her vision of and restoration by the Savior.[11] All subsequent humans thus possess a spiritual element imprisoned in their souls and material bodies that must be liberated by the savior Jesus, who descends to earth from the *Plêrôma* to awaken humans to the identity of their true Father and of their essential spiritual nature, and conquer the powers of materiality and death that presently enslave them. After Jesus' return to the *Plêrôma*, the earthly Church continues his mission by conferring the baptismal rite of "Redemption" that serves to reunite one's spiritual essence with the *Plêrôma* (the "bridal chamber"), thus undoing the separation of the spiritual element from the *Plêrôma* that began with Sophia's passion.

Meanwhile, at the appearance of the Savior, humans are divided into three essential types, the spiritual (the "elect," "those of the right"), the psychic (the "called," "those of the middle"), and the material (the "hylic," "those of the left"). The spiritual kind is saved immediately; the psychic kind, which, although it is not naturally inclined to evil, must strive for salvation through knowledge

---

[11] See *Tripartite Tractate* (NHC I 5) 105.10–35; Irenaeus *Against Heresies* 1.5.6; *Excerpts from Theodotus* 53.2–5; and Hippolytus *Refutation of All Heresies* 6.34.6.

of and confession of the Son; and the material kind is lost through its ignorance and inclination of evil.[12]

Nevertheless, all humanity shares the common plight, namely, that the Demiurge made bodies for human souls out of matter and a devilish essence; it is a dead thing by means of which the soul is enslaved.[13] Hippolytus (*Refutation of All Heresies* 6.34.4–5) tells us that some Valentinians conceived the material human body as an inn, inhabited by either the soul alone, or by the soul and daemons, or, if the body has been cleansed of all daemons, as a place in which the soul can share its accommodations with rational principles (*logoi*) that have been sown from above. There is a certain variability in this view, in that the body can be viewed, not only as a dangerous and dirty public facility, but also a place that can be cleansed and made habitable, even if not a true home.[14] Given that the salvation of the soul was the primary object of the Valentinian church, it appears that this could be accomplished, not only by its separation from the body, but also by improving its life within the body, not to mention the possibility of the salvation of the body itself.

---

[12] See *Tripartite Tractate* (NHC I 5) 118.14–119.2: the three types "conform to the triple disposition of the *logos* from which the material ones and the psychic ones and the spiritual ones were brought forth. Each of the three essential types is known by its fruit. The spiritual race, being like light from light and like spirit from spirit, when its head appeared, it ran toward him immediately ... It suddenly received knowledge in the revelation. The psychic race is like light from a fire since it hesitated to accept knowledge of him who appeared to it"; cf. *Tripartite Tractate* 119.20–34: "The psychic race, since it is in the middle when it is brought forth and also when it is created, is double according to its determination for both good and evil. It take its appointed departure suddenly and its complete escape to those who are good." One finds a similar division of classes in Plotinus *Enneads* V 9.1 (cf. *Enneads* I 6.8) between earthbound persons, those who try to ascend upwards but without sufficient energy, and a third class of persons who succeed in finding their true selves after long wandering (*planê*).

[13] *Excerpts from Theodotus* 72–73: the evil one and adversaries attack the soul through the body and bind it to slavery; cf. *Interpretation of Knowledge* (NHC XI 1) 12.37, where the body is "the disgrace of the carcass ['skin']." Concerning the creation of the first human, cf. also *Tripartite Tractate* (NHC I 5) 105.30–106.25.

[14] Cf. *Interpretation of Knowledge* (NHC XI 1) 6.26–38: "the entire defect restrains them until the final reality that is their portion, since he brought us down, having bound us in nets of flesh. Since the body is an inn [*pandokheion,* cf. Luke 10:34] which the rulers and authorities have as an abode, the human within, being imprisoned in the fabrication [*plasis*] fell into suffering" (probably a simile based on the parable of the Good Samaritan, where the man who is beaten and robbed represents the suffering soul within, and the thieves are the archons). A comparable simile occurs in one of the fragments of Valentinus (Clement of Alexandria *Stromata* 2.114.3–6), in which the human heart is compared to an inn (*pandokheion*) inhabited by *daimones* who abuse it and leave it in a filthy condition; yet when it is visited by the Father, the heart will be sanctified and will see God. For a similar view in Plotinus, cf. *Enneads* II 9.18.1–20.

Nevertheless, the dominant view seems to be that the fleshly body is a fetter whose tendency is to be ignored; indeed to flee the body is to be resurrected.[15] The resurrection is the process by which one's fleshly body and soul, which were received at birth, are transformed into a spiritual body.[16] Insofar as salvation is achieved either by transcending the body altogether or by some kind of transformation of the body, the Valentinians as Christians had to deal with the fact that their Savior, Christ, was acknowledged to have taken on bodily form.

Just how this was done was a matter of dispute, the solutions ranging from the Eastern Valentinian assertion that Christ's body was entirely spiritual through the claim of Western Valentinian thinkers that it was a psychic entity upon which the spirit descended at his baptism, or perhaps was a kind of spiritual flesh similar to the resurrection body.[17] Whether his death was actual[18] or only apparent, most Valentinian sources agree that Christ the Savior was somehow embodied.[19] At the point of the Savior's bodily manifestation, the spiritual class recognizes and responds to the Savior immediately and the material class entirely rejects him to their own final condemnation, while the psychics at first hesitate to receive him, but eventually most of them finally join the Savior.[20] This salvific reunion with the savior is usually

---

15 *Treatise on the Resurrection* 49.11–16: "do not live in conformity with the flesh for the sake of unanimity, but flee from the division and the fetters, and already you have the resurrection."

16 According to Epiphanius (*Panarion* 31.7.6), the Valentinians "deny the resurrection of the dead, saying that it is a spiritual body that rises" (cf. 31.7.10–11: "their own class, the spiritual, is saved with another body, one that is within, which they call a spiritual body"). According to *Treatise on the Resurrection* (NHC I 4) 45.38–46.2, "the spiritual resurrection swallows up the psychic in the same way as the fleshly." Cf. *Treatise on the Resurrection* 47.1–24, 47.38–48.3, 48.13–19; and *On Baptism B* (NHC XI) 2b42.28–29: "We were brought from seminal [bodies] into [bodies] with a perfect form."

17 On the distinction between the (probably earlier) Eastern and Western branches of Valentinianism, see Tertullian *Against the Valentinians* 11.2; Clement of Alexandria *Excerpts from Theodotus* 1.1; Hippolytus *Refutation of All Heresies* 6.35.5–7; and Thomassen 2006:Chapter 4.

18 *Gospel of Truth* (NHC I 3) 20, 25; *Tripartite Tractate* (NHC I 5) 114.30–115.23.

19 *Tripartite Tractate* 113.34–114.16: "Concerning that which he [the savior] previously was and that which he is eternally, an unbegotten, impassible one from the *logos*" (cf. 116.28–30: the savior was an "image of the unitary one, he who is the totality in bodily form," [i.e. the Son], and *Gospel of Truth* [NHC I 3] 66.14: "the Son is the body of the bodiless", who came into being in the flesh [cf. *Gospel of Truth* 26.8 and 31.4–6]...They say that it is a production from all of them, but that before all things it is from the spiritual *logos* who is the cause of the things that have come into being, from whom the savior received his flesh [cf. 26.8: the *Logos* became a body]). In *Tripartite Tractate* 115.8–116.2, the Savior as well as his companions (the angels) took on body and soul in their incarnations. According to 122.12–17, "the election shares body and essence with the savior because of its unity and agreement with him," "while the bodies remain on earth" (135.12).

20 The nature of the Savior's appearance was a matter of dispute according to Hippolytus (*Refutation of All Heresies* 6.35.5): "Italian Valentinians like Heracleon and Ptolemy say that the body of Jesus was psychic, and the spirit came on him at baptism. Eastern Valentinians such as Axionicus and Ardesianes say that the Savior's body was pneumatic, since the Spirit came upon Mary already";

portrayed as a reunion between the heavenly, male, and angelic component of each person which accompanies the Savior on his descent; just as the Savior can be united with Sophia as his permanent consort, so also each of these "elect" are reunited with his or her female, spermatic and psychic counterpart or component (the "called").[21] The pneumatic element of the elect soul cannot perish; its salvation is preordained by virtue of its origin from and consubstantiality with the *Plêrôma*.[22] Interestingly, in the next century, Plotinus too develops a similar doctrine according to which a part of *every* human soul is always resident in the higher hypostases, while only a portion of it undergoes earthly incarnation;[23] similarly, during this life, the

---

on this passage and the identity of Ardesianes, see Ramelli 2009:47–52. The essential immateriality of the Valentinian Savior is clear: "They say that his body was brought down from above, and passed through Mary's womb like water through a pipe, without receiving anything from her" (Epiphanius *Panarion* 31.7.4); Irenaeus *Against Heresies* 1.7.2: the pleromatic Savior descends on the psychic Christ, which alone suffered, at baptism. According to the *Excerpts from Theodotus* 59–61, the purpose of his body was to serve as a vehicle of communication: "At death, the Spirit departed a bit, otherwise the body would never have died. So Death seized only the body. Once Death had seized it, the Savior sent forth a ray of power, and destroyed Death." In several Valentinian sources, the Savior is a compound being appearing in three aspects (pneumatic, psychic, and sensible): Irenaeus *Against Heresies* 1.7.1–2; *Excerpts from Theodotus* 59; Hippolytus *Refutation of All Heresies* 6.36.3–4. There are many such triadic schemes, generally representing modes adopted by the Savior, which correspond to the character and condition of those he comes to save in the various levels of the cosmos: cf. the Christ of the three natures, bodies, and powers of the Peratae (Hippolytus *Refutation of All Heresies* 5.17.1); the triple Sonships of Basilides (5.7.22); and the intellectual, or psychic, and earthly Christs of the Naasenes (5.6.5–7).

21 Cf. *Valentinian Exposition* (NHC XI 2) 39.25–26; *Excerpts from Theodotus* 2.1, 21.1–3, and 39–40; Irenaeus *Against Heresies* 1.7.1.

22 See Irenaeus *Against Heresies* 2.14.4: "Those who hold the same infidelity have ascribed to spiritual beings that which is within the *Plêrôma*, but to animate beings the intermediate space, while to corporeal beings they assign that which is material. And they assert that God Himself can do no otherwise, but that each of the [three substances] mentioned passes away to those things which are of the same substance (*homoousios*)." The salvation of the pneumatic element of the soul, which never loses its link to the divine *Plêrôma*, is thus guaranteed: for the *Tripartite Tractate* (NHC I 5) 119.19–20: "the spiritual race will receive complete salvation in every way." Cf. 122.14–15.

23 As Narbonne 2011 points out, Plotinus' thesis of the partly undescended soul is the reformulation of the Gnostic notion of the consubstantiality between the core human self and its divine ground. For Plotinus, a portion of every human soul is not only akin to the divine, as Plato had already taught, but in fact never descends and remains consubstantial to it (*Enneads* IV 7.10.18–19: θείων μετὸν αὐτῷ διὰ συγγένειαν καὶ τὸ ὁμοούσιον), thus granting to *every* human what the Gnostics reserved for all but a few, an uninterrupted and indissoluble link with the highest realities: "every soul is a child of That Father" (*Enneads* II 9.16.9). The audacity of this approach, recognized by Plotinus (*Enneads* IV 8.8.1–3), consists in challenging Platonizing Gnostics who attend his school and who claim for themselves *alone* the power to reach the Intelligible (*Enneads* II 9.9.79).

inward withdrawal of the contemplative is thus a rejoining with one's true self, an anticipatory escape from the wheel of rebirth. [24]

4. Sethian Gnosticism

Another set of myths relating the pretemporal fall and primordial incarnation of the soul into the world of matter is that associated with Sethian or "Classical" Gnosticism.[25] Sethian metaphysics generally reflect a hierarchy of divine principles: the Father/Invisible Spirit; the Mother/Barbelo; and their Child Autogenes, supplemented by the Child's four Luminaries or Aeons (Harmozel, Oroiael, Daveithe, and Eleleth), who contain a total of twelve ideal beings, the lowest of which is Sophia in the Aeon of Eleleth at the very periphery of the divine world. The Barbeloite cosmology takes its start with the appearance of the creator and governor of the lower world, Saklas/Yaldabaoth, either at the behest of Eleleth or from the illicitly creative act of Sophia, acting either alone or at Eleleth's behest.

The Sethian equivalent for the cosmic soul is not immediately obvious until one considers the possibility that the Sethian metaphysics may have been constructed on a Middle Platonic model (as in Plutarch's metaphysics) which envisions two souls, one rational and the other irrational—that is, a higher and lower cosmic soul.[26] The obvious candidates for this role are the two mother

---

[24] Cf. the *Tripartite Tractate* (NHC I 124) 13–25: "The redemption is also an ascent <to> {and} those levels [*bathmos*] that exist in the *Plêrôma* and with all those who have been given names and who comprehend them [themselves?] according to the capacity of each individual aeon, and it is an entry into that which is silent, where there is no need of voice, nor of knowing, comprehending, or illumination, but all things are luminous and have no need of illumination."

[25] Schenke 1981 established a typology that purported to define a religio-philosophical movement of the first four centuries that he called "Sethian Gnosticism": (1) the Gnostic self-understanding as the pneumatic seed of Seth; (2) Seth as heavenly-earthly savior of his seed, sometimes appearing in the guise of Jesus; (3) the heavenly trinity of Father, Mother, and Child (identified with the preexistent Christ); (4) the Child's four Luminaries who are the dwelling-places of the heavenly Adam, Seth, and his seed; (5) the evil creator-god Yaldabaoth/Saklas/Samael who tries to destroy the seed of Seth; (6) the division of history into three ages defined by the appearance of the savior at the times of the flood, the conflagration of Sodom and Gomorrah, and finally in the present time; and (7) the practice of a cultic ritual of baptismal ascent, the "Five Seals." These motifs are present in patristic sources (Irenaeus *Against Heresies* 1.29–30; Theodoret *Compendium of Heretical Accounts* 1.13–14; Epiphanius *Panarion* 26, 39, 40; and "Tertullian" *Against All Heresies* 2), in the Nag Hammadi treatises (*Apocryphon of John, Gospel of the Egyptians, Apocalypse of Adam, Three Steles of Seth, Zostrianos, Allogenes, Marsanes, Melchizedek, Thought of Norea, Trimorphic Protennoia,* perhaps the *Hypostasis of the Archons*), and in Codex Tchacos (*Gospel of Judas* and perhaps a short work featuring Jesus as Allogenes).

[26] In his *On Isis and Osiris*, Plutarch offers the first clear example of an irrational and hostile cosmic principle (Seth/Typhon) inimical to the divine principle of rationality (Osiris). Yet the world (Horos) that results from the interaction of form (Osiris) and irrational yet receptive matter (Isis) is an authentic image of the intelligible world. A proactive cause of evil (Seth/Typhon) is there,

figures in the *Apocryphon of John*, namely, Barbelo and Sophia.[27] If it is granted that these two mother figures exhibit some of the features of Plato's Receptacle, then it appears that this entity too has been split into two levels: a higher, stable one (Barbelo) in whom the Autogenes Son is begotten from a spark of the Father's light; and a lower, agitated one (Sophia), in whom is begotten the formless Yaldabaoth, born from Sophia without a male partner to contribute a form for him. Such a division of the Mother figure into two levels reminds one of a bipartitioning of the cosmic soul, or *logos*, into a higher, stable, and intelligible level, and a lower level in motion, as in the case of Plutarch's Isis, who as the material principle is the honored consort of God, and as mother of Horus, is also the irrational aspect of the cosmic soul. Such also seems to be true not only of the Valentinian figures of Sophia and Achamoth, but also of the Chaldaean figure of Hecate, who seem to function at two levels in their theology: first, as the processing power of the paternal Monad (the "center" and "membrane" between the Paternal Monad and the divine Intellect, OC fragments 6 and 50); and at a lower level, as the source of the World Soul, from whose "right side abundantly flows the ineffable liquid" of the primordial soul (OC fr. 51).

---

but can never overcome the *logos* (Osiris). According to the analysis of Dillon (1977:202–208), Plutarch, as well as Atticus, derived these sources of irrationality from a conflation of Plato's introduction of an irrational soul in book ten of the *Laws* and the precosmic chaos of the second part of the *Timaeus* together with the characteristics of necessity and disorder associated with the Receptacle of becoming in the third part of the *Timaeus*.

27 Called the Father's Pronoia, the merciful Mother of the All, Barbelo is an androgynous Mother-Father, the second member of the Sethian supreme Father-Mother-Child trinity, also called Ennoia ("unuttered thought") and Pronoia ("providence"). As a kind of rational cosmic soul or maternal principle resembling Isis, the mother of Horus, in the metaphysics of Plutarch, Barbelo is the mother, not only of the self-begotten Christ, but also ultimately of all those who possess within themselves a spark of the divine, which *Trimorphic Protennoia* refers to as her "seed" or "members." As the recipient of sparks of light as formal principles from the Invisible Spirit, she gives rise to her offspring, the only-begotten Son, Christ, a process rather like that which Plato ascribes to the paternal forms, maternal recipient, and generated images in *Timaeus* 48e–52d. In the version of the *Apocryphon of John* found in the Berlin Codex, the figure of Sophia is likewise called "Mother," and gives likewise birth to an offspring, only in this case, the ignorant archon Yaldabaoth. However, instead of being receptive to the formative powers of her consort, she tries to imitate the highest deity's production of the higher mother Barbelo by attempting to produce an offspring alone without the cooperation of a male consort, which results in the production of the archon Yaldabaoth. As the source of such disorder and evil, Sophia is, like Plutarch's Isis, a feminine principle eager for offspring, but unfortunately unmastered by the masculine principle of order. Upon the appearance of Yaldabaoth, unlike Barbelo's rejoicing at the appearance of the Autogenes, Sophia becomes "agitated," a notable characteristic of Plato's Receptacle and Nurse of becoming, caused by a disequilibrium of certain unbalanced powers (hot, cold, moist, dry) and passions that enter into it. Since motion can only be caused by soul, it thus appears that the disorderly Receptacle could be regarded as a lower irrational soul, which indeed Sophia appears to be.

The Sethian conception of individual human souls is complicated by its supposition of their existence at two levels, those souls which exist above in the Aeons of the Four Luminaries, and those souls of earthly persons.[28] At the transcendent level, one finds the souls of the saints, that is, of the "seed of Seth," of "the immovable race," located in the third Luminary Daveithai, while the souls of those who, though of good conduct (probable ascetics), are ignorant of the *Plêrôma*, but who eventually "repent," are located in the fourth Luminary Eleleth. In addition, there are other, lower, yet still nonearthly, levels at which various souls are located, such as those called the Exile and the Repentance in the treatise *Zostrianos*, perhaps to be associated with the respective aeonic places of those mentioned in the *Apocryphon of John* 9.14–23, who "persisted for awhile" and those who "repented afterwards."[29]

Evidently, just as in the case of the Valentinian notion that the Savior descends with the transcendent male angels, the "elect," in order to unite them in Pleromatic fashion with their earthly counterparts, the female seed, the "called,"[30] so too in Sethianism there is the notion of ideal beings who reside in the divine world in anticipation of the salvation of their earthly counterparts. It seems that this notion is a gnostic equivalent of Plotinus' later doctrine of the undescended soul, according to which a part of the human soul is always resident in the higher hypostases, while only a portion of it undergoes earthly incarnation.[31] Of course, the main preoccupation is with those souls who live on earth, whose origin can be traced to Sophia's creative attempt; they are to be the object of the higher mother's attempts to rescue the fragments of her substance captured by the creator Yaldabaoth and incarnated into human beings.[32]

---

[28] *Marsanes* (NHC X 1) 41.18: "the embodied souls do not understand them (the noetic matters?), namely, the embodied souls upon earth, as well as those outside of the body, who are in heaven, more than the angels." Cf. *Zostrianos* (NHC VIII 1) 8.27.9–11: "Other immortal souls associate with all these souls because of Sophia who looked down."

[29] *Apocryphon of John* (NHC II 7) 9.14–23: "And in the third aeon the seed of Seth was placed over the third light Daveithai. And the souls of the saints were placed there. And in the fourth aeon were placed of those who do not know the *plêrôma* and who did not repent at once, but who persisted awhile and repented afterwards; they are by the fourth light Eleleth." For these additional levels, see *Zostrianos* (NHC VIII 1) 27.9–28.17 and 42.20–44.22. Cf. also Philo *Confusion of Languages* 77–78.

[30] Cf. *Valentinian Exposition* (NHC XI 2) 39.25–26; *Excerpts from Theodotus* 2.1, 21.1–3, 39–40.

[31] Thus, the Four Lights, at least in the *Apocryphon of John*, serve not merely as ideal periodization of the primordial salvation history of Adam, Seth, the seed of Seth, and other repentant souls who will be saved after the time of Noah. They are heavenly residences (cf. *Trimorphic Protennoia* [NHC XIII 1] 50.14–15) where there reside not only the souls of those who have been saved, such as Adam, Seth, his antediluvian seed, and those Sethians who have died up until the present time, but also the spiritual counterpart of the race of Seth and certain souls destined, in advance of their earthly life and death, to repent and be elevated to join their counterparts in the Four Lights.

[32] *Trimorphic Protennoia* (NHC XIII 1) 35.12–22: "I am the life of my Epinoia that dwells within every power and every eternal movement and in invisible lights and within the archons and angels

The actual incarnation of souls is spelled out in terms of the attempt of Yaldabaoth and his archontic assistants to trap the image of the divine first human being, Adamas, in the material body of Adam, in which act they produce a "psychic human being." The details of this process are taken both from Plato's *Timaeus* (73e–77d), which describes the shaping of the mortal soul as a kind of "marrow" enclosed in bone, sinew, flesh, blood, skin, and hair,[33] and from Genesis 2:4, regarded as describing the capture of the divine image in a body that remains inert until the archon unwittingly inspires it with the divine breath stolen from his mother Sophia. The excerpt from "the Book of Zoroaster," which relates the contributions of the 365 angels to the psychic and material body of Adam, surely has to do with certain astrological doctrines concerning the powers of the thirty-six decans and their subdivisions characteristic of the celestial world, perhaps the one called the "aeonic copies" (*antitupoi*) in *Zostrianos*. In any case, the sheer multiplicity of these powers and the parts of the body they represent may convey something of the endless multiplicity inherent in matter and the disorderliness and irrationality of the ignorance and psychic passions arising from Sophia's deficiency.[34] The protoplast eventually gains enlightenment when

---

and daemons and every soul dwelling in Tartaros and in every material soul. I dwell in those who came to be. I move in everyone and I delve into them all. I walk uprightly, and those who sleep I awaken"; and 41.20–24: "I am the first one who descended on account of my portion which remains, that is the spirit that dwells in the soul but which originated from the water of life and out of the immersion of the mysteries." In Hippolytus' account (*Refutation of All Heresies* 19.15–16) of the Sethians, bodily incarnation is like drowning in water: the mind is put into human nature like a perfect god in a temple, which is begotten of water; it is intermingled with bodies, but struggles to free itself from them, and cannot find its release or escape; the whole thought and concern of the light from above is, how and by what means the mind may be freed from the death of the wicked and benighted body. Cf. *Refutation of All Heresies* 19.19.20, where the perfect word of the Light took on the likeness of the serpent/beast, entered into the unclean womb, deceiving it by his likeness to the beast, in order to undo the bonds that constrain the perfect mind; taking "form of a servant," he came down into the virgin's womb.

33   *Apocryphon of John* 15.13–23: "And the powers began: the first, goodness created a bone-soul; and the second, foreknowledge, created a sinew-soul; the third, divinity, created a flesh-soul; and the fourth, the lordship, created a marrow-soul; the fifth, kingdom, created a blood-soul; the sixth, envy, created a skin-soul; the seventh, understanding, created a hair-soul." For Plato's account of the human body in the *Timaeus*, see Chapter 1.

34   According to *Hypostasis of the Archons* 87.11–31, the human is modeled after the body of the archons and after the image of God that appeared in water. They initially produce a material man, and then infuse him with soul (88.3–10). Adam, initially inert, then receives "spirit" from the Adamantine land, making him a living soul (88.10–15), but then becomes endowed merely with soul when Eve is extracted from his side (89.3–11), at which the spirit is transferred first to Eve, and thence to a tree, and thence to the snake-instructor, leaving Adam and Eve altogether denuded of the spirit even after eating from the tree of knowledge (89.11–90.20)—unless one assumes it may have returned in their production of Seth and Norea. For the inspiration of the divine spirit into psychic Adam, see *Apocryphon of John* 19.10–33 and *Apocalypse of Adam* 66.19–21: "Do you not know that I am the god who created you? And I breathed into you a spirit of life as a living soul."

the Mother on high sends him a helper, the spiritual Eve, who causes his merely psychic status to be replaced by a spiritual one.[35] A more typically Platonic view of the origin of souls and bodies is found in *Zostrianos*, according to which souls, bodies, and matter exist, not because of the work of an inferior creator, but because of the high deity himself.[36] In general, the Platonizing Sethian treatises *Zostrianos*, *Allogenes*, *Three Steles of Seth*, and *Marsanes* exhibit a notably positive view of the physical world, which is regarded, not as evil, but as merely defective and capable of rectification.[37]

Sethian texts frequently distinguish between the various conditions of human souls, according to the degree to which they are aware of the higher world from which they originated. The *Apocryphon of John* distinguishes between two varieties of incarnated souls, those upon whom the Spirit of Life descends, and those upon whom the counterfeit spirit descends. The former variety is comprised of both those who did and did not lead a pure life, while the latter variety is comprised of three types: those in which the power of the counterfeit spirit is overcome by the Spirit of Life during their first incarnation, those in which the counterfeit spirit has gained the upper hand and are condemned to another round of incarnation and purgation in which they succeed in remembering their origin, and those souls which utterly turn away from the Spirit of Life. The first three types will certainly be saved; the fourth, if, after undergoing another reincarnation, it succeeds in acquiring knowledge, will also be saved. Only the fifth type, the souls which utterly turn away from the Spirit of Life, will be eternally punished.[38] So also *Zostrianos* makes a distinction in classes of

---

[35] Cf. *Hypostasis of the Archons* 89.7–19 and 90.13–14.

[36] *Zostrianos* (NHC VIII 1) 73.18–25: "Because of him (the Triple-Powered One?) there exist those with souls and those without souls; because of him exist those who will be saved; because of him exist those who will perish because they have not received of him; because of him matter and bodies (exist)."

[37] In *Allogenes* (NHC XI 3) 51.28–32, Autogenes works "successively and individually" so as to rectify nature's flaws or defects; in *Marsanes* (NHC X 1) 4.24–5.16 and 5.24–26, the perceptible world "is worthy to be saved entirely." For *Zostrianos* (NHC VIII 1) 31.10–14, one must separate oneself from the physical world in order that it might be saved: "Release yourselves, and that which has bound you will be dissolved. Save yourselves, in order that it may be saved." For the gnostic negative view on the body and Plotinus' criticism of it, see the next chapter.

[38] Interestingly, in this section of the *Apocryphon of John* (NHC II 1) 25.17–27.30, which bears the marks of a redactional insertion, those upon whom the spirit of life descends and who led a pure life will be taken into the Aeon of the Four Lights, while those of the same category who did not lead a pure life will change for the better and their souls will be taken up to the "rest of the aeons," perhaps such as the Repentance, Exile, and the Antitypes mentioned in *Zostrianos* (and chided by Plotinus in *Enneads* II 9.6.2!). Both the Berlin Codex (BG 65.2–7) and (NHC III) 33.4–7 of this "*de anima*" have the first group becoming worthy of "these great lights," and being visited by the "receivers" (*paralêmpores*), who in the *Gospel of the Egyptians* (NHC III 2) 64.22–25 are identified as Gabriel, Samblo, and Abrasax, the receivers and ministers of the four Lights. *Apocryphon of John* (NHC II 1) 25.17–27.30 [in part]: "I said, 'Lord, will all the souls then be brought safely into

souls located at the levels of the Self-begotten ones, the Repentance and the Exile—namely, souls who innately know the truth, souls which at first sinned but then repented and sought the truth, and those who stumble as they "follow the ways of others."[39]

In the matter of the salvation of souls, Sethianism offers two distinctive methods by which the divine substance is released from its psychic and somatic residence. One group of treatises considers salvation to be conveyed by means of a horizontal, temporally ordered history of divine salvific visitations by successive descents of separate figures or repeated descents of the same figure in different modalities. According to the *Trimorphic Protennoia* ([NHC XIII 1] 47.21–28.14; 49.21–20.12) and the Pronoia hymn concluding the longer version of the *Apocryphon of John* ([NHC II 1] 30.11–31.27), the final saving descent of Barbelo confers the Five Seals, a baptismal rite of visionary ascent that releases the recipient from the somatic prison, stripping away the somatic and psychic thought (ignorance), replacing it with radiant enlightenment.[40] On the other hand, in the treatises *Allogenes*, *Three Steles of Seth*, *Zostrianos*, and *Marsanes*, one finds a more vertically oriented, nontemporal, nonhistorical scheme in which salvation is not brought from above to below by divine visitations, but rather occurs through a graded series of visionary ascents by the gnostic himself. Here one finds an exemplary visionary utilizing a self-performable technique of successive stages of mental detachment from the world of multiplicity, and a corresponding assimilation of the self to the ever more refined levels of being to which one's contemplation ascends, until one achieves the absolute unitary stasis of self-unification, mental abstraction, and utter solitariness, characteristic of deification. Needless to say, both body and soul are left behind during the ascent, yet when the ascent is completed, the visionary descends and again dons his psychic and corporeal garment, which is somehow renewed and purified, no longer a burden, but a vehicle by which to share the revelation with other embodied souls.[41]

---

the pure light?' He answered and said to me ... those on whom the spirit of life will descend and with whom he will be with the power, they will be saved and become perfect and be worthy of the greatness [or: "of these great lights"] and be purified in that place from all wickedness and the involvements in evil ... They are not affected by anything except the state of being in the flesh alone, which they bear while looking expectantly for the time when they will be met by the receivers." Cf. also the plea of Norea in *Hypostasis of the Archons* (NHC II 4) 96.17–28.

[39] *Zostrianos* (NHC VIII 1) 27.9–28.17 and 42.20–44.22.

[40] See Turner 1980:324–351, esp. 341–351.

[41] While not entirely clear in *Zostrianos* and *Marsanes*, owing to their fragmentary condition, according to *Allogenes* this ascent occurs in three stages: through the three levels of the Aeon of Barbelo, through the three levels of the Triple Powered One, and culminates in a "primary" or "originary manifestation," which amounts to a "non-knowing" reabsorption of the aspirant into its aboriginal prefiguration in the supreme Unknowable One. In *Zostrianos*, the aspirant ascends

5. Conclusion

In conclusion, I would like to draw attention to the general lines of debate concerning the relation of Platonism and Gnosticism. It seems clear that Jonas's attempt in the belated (1954) second volume of his *Gnosis und Spätantiker Geist*, to associate figures such as Philo and Plotinus with a Gnostic view of the cosmos and of the situation of the soul within it has more or less set the terms of a debate, and has provoked a vigorous reaction, especially from scholars of Platonism, concerning the similarities and differences between the two movements.[42] Most scholars seem anxious to separate Platonic thinkers from Gnosticism as much as possible, yet at many points they must and do admit certain similarities. Ultimately, the difference between the two bodies of thought comes down to a question of world rejection versus affirmation of the body and even the cosmos, or a pessimistic versus optimistic worldview. It seems to me that these categorical distinctions, except only in very general terms, fail to have much explanatory value, since one can find many exceptions to them within individual thinkers and texts. Both Gnostics and Platonists agree that there is something deficient about the human situation in the world and are optimistic that the divine principle behind all things has already provided for its solution, and that this solution can be discovered and taught to whomever will listen to it and work in a rigorous and disciplined way to realize it for themselves. Both groups tend also

---

only into the Barbelo Aeon. There, Zostrianos begins his ascent by "parting from the somatic darkness within me" (1.10) and "casting his body upon the earth to be guarded by glories" (*Zostrianos* 4.24–25); upon his return, Zostrianos shares his vision with the successively lower realms through which he passes (129.16–22) and at its terminus says: "then I came down to the perceptible world and put on my image. Because it was ignorant, I strengthened it, and went about preaching the truth to everyone. Neither the angelic beings of the world nor the archons saw me, for I negated a multitude of judgments which brought me near death" (130.5–13).

42 Jonas 1934:1.253: "Indem Platon die Philosophie als Scheinreligion stilisierte, ermöglichte er einer späteren Religion die Stilisierung als Schein-philosophie"; Nock 1964:xvi: "One can see why Simone Pétrement once called Gnosticism 'un platonisme romantique', for which we might be tempted to substitute 'Platonism run wild'"; Theiler 1966:113: "Gnosticism is a product of a generally anticosmic *"Proletarier-platonismus"* which is concerned to offer a soteriology dressed up in pseudo-scientific terminology"; Drijvers 1968:342: "However strongly Gnosticism may make the impression of being a philosophy, in essence it is not so, but an attempt to render all philosophy superfluous—it is first and foremost a 'secret revelation'"; Dillon 1977:384: "One ... large field [of Middle Platonism] is what one might term the 'underworld' of Platonism, in which category may be included such sub-philosophical phenomena as the Gnostic and Hermetic writings and the *Chaldaean Oracles*"; Armstrong 1978:101: "Any influence which may have been exerted by any kind of Greek philosophy on Gnosticism was not genuine but extraneous and, for the most part superficial. We are dealing with the use of Greek ideas, often distorted or strangely developed, in a context which is not their own, to commend a different way of faith and feeling, not with a genuine growth of any variety of Gnosticism out of philosophy, whatever some ancient heresiologists may have thought." For Philo, see Chapter 11 below; for Plotinus, see the next chapter.

to be pessimistic about the prospects for the general mass of human kind, who do not possess sufficient reflective or cognitive powers to take this teaching seriously.[43] On the whole, Gnostics tend to stress the hidden but revealed character of the solution, yet Platonists also tend to see it as apparent only to a very few elite individuals. Both groups tend to see the human being situated in a struggle for the self-knowledge that leads to salvation. By virtue of their reliance upon myth, most Gnostics, but few Platonists, tend to see the antagonist in this struggle as anterior and exterior to the psycho-physical complex of the human individual. But both groups also exteriorize and "anteriorize" the human psycho-physical complex itself into a cosmic structure that has its own soul and body. Gnostic hostility toward the world and the body in reality reflects the Gnostic perception of the hostility of the latter toward the former. Gnostics generally have in mind proactive spiritual forces that govern world and body, rather than its materiality as such. Platonists, on the other hand, tend to have in mind a certain inherent and necessary intractability of the material substrate of physical world or certain passions of the soul which refuse complete submission to rational formation, rather than the proactive hostility of the Gnostic archons. In the final analysis, it seems to me that the basic difference between the two lies in a preference either for myth and dramatic personification, or for conceptual analysis and distinction as a vehicle for rendering an account of basically the same human problematic.[44] Rather than accounting for their common pessimism and optimism in terms of a theory of social crisis, however, it seems more promising to view both groups engaging in a common enterprise to apply—and where necessary to reinterpret—ancient traditional wisdom to the even more age-old problem of the situation of the self in the ever-changing world.

---

[43] Compare the Valentinian distinction between spiritual and material persons with Plotinus' distinction between "philosophers" (the *spoudaioi*) and the "common rabble" (the *phaulos okhlos*) in *Enneads* II 9.9.7–12.

[44] Although both Plato and Plutarch make notable use of both methods of exposition!

6

Reconsidering the Body
From Tomb to Sign of the Soul

SVETLA SLAVEVA-GRIFFIN

Abstract: This chapter questions the linear interpretation of Plato's pronouncement in the *Cratylus* 400b11–c10 that the "body" (*sôma*) is a "tomb" (*sêma*) of the soul, based on Plotinus' tolerant—in comparison to the Gnostics—view of the body as a "beautiful house" in *Enneads* II 9.6–9 and as "a sign" of soul in *Enneads* IV 4.18–19. The latter discussion offers an opportunity to examine the congruent views of Plotinus and Origen on the experience of medically related pain in the *Enneads* (I 1, III 6, and IV 4) and *Against Celsus* (2.23–25). The scholarship on philosophy and religion in late antiquity has been readily inclined to pit Plotinus and Origen against each other. The hypothetically conceived rivalry between them can be considered an expression of their irreconcilable ideological differences. A closer examination, however, of the role of physical pain in Plotinus' and Origen's understanding of the relation between soul and body shows that, at least when it comes to the role of the body in the psycho-somatic compound known as "living being" (*empsukhon*), the two thinkers are in agreement. The Neoplatonist critical attitude towards the body and the Christian redemptive view of it make this conceptual agreement between them worth noting. They both consider the body, regardless whether a house or a tomb, a sign and thus a proof of soul's immortal nature.

F EWER EXPRESSIONS HAVE become signature pillars of Platonism than Socrates' equation of "body" (*sôma*) with "tomb" (*sêma*) in the *Cratylus* 400b10–c11. It has shaped the subsequent development of Platonic psychology into *Weltanschauung*. The dichotomy between soul and body expresses the greater ontological antithesis between *what is* and what is *here and now*. In due course, the scholarship has copiously explored every nook and cranny of the idea that the body, with its density, spatiality, and self-insufficiency, is nothing but a hindrance weighing the soul down in appetitive squalor and material alienation.[1] The above determination is time and again promoted by the Platonic schools of all shades, from Speusippus to Olympiodorus.[2] With the finality of a verdict, ancient and modern interpretations alike have *prima facie* left no room for something new, by which I mean something different, to be added to Socrates' equation. Yet, as the first Platonic lesson teaches us, every copy—and every interpretation for that matter—is a step away from its original. The growing interest in the body on both sides of the divide between philosophy and religion in late antiquity offers an opportunity to reexamine the standard interpretation of Socrates' *sôma-sêma* analogy in the *Cratylus* and its later permutations, found in Plotinus and the Gnostics, discussed below.[3]

In particular, this chapter examines Plotinus' ameliorative or 'soft' understanding of the body in the psychosomatic compound, presented in *Enneads* II 9.6–9 and IV 4.18–19, in relation to the Gnostics' denigrating or 'hard' understanding and Origen's theological explication. Plotinus' view stands between the two latter interpretations, orienting the soul-body compass on the vertical axis of Neoplatonic cosmology. His view does not reject—nor does it absolve—the body in its ontologically decompensated position, but uses it as an empirical tool for understanding the ensouled state of our true self.

1. The *Sôma–Sêma* Analogy in the *Cratylus*

The *Cratylus* examines the question of the relation between words (nouns or names) and their meaning, that is, the true *logos* behind their phonetic orthography.[4] Crombie's skepticism about the date of its composition does not jeopardize the contextualization of the tension between soul and body in the broader framework of Plato's psychology.[5] The following passage presents Plato's layered etymology of *sôma*:[6]

---

[1]   The bibliography is abundant. A few guiding references include Guthrie 1978, Gosling and Taylor 1982, Kraut 1992, Irwin 1995, Annas 1999; recently Russell 2005, Barney and Brennan 2012.

[2]   Dillon 1977 and 2003, Gerson 1996 and 2010, Blumenthal 1971, Emilsson 1988, Chiaradonna 2009, Chlup 2012, Remes 2007, Remes and Slaveva-Griffin 2014, Caluori 2015, Griffin 2015.

[3]   Scarry 1985, Perkins 1995, A. Smith 2004, Boudon-Millot and Pouderon 2005, Edwards 2006, Gerson 2010, Chiaradonna 2012.

[4]   On etymology in Plato, see Rosenmeyer 1998, Sedley 1998, Barney 1998; on its reception, see van den Berg 2008. The question is still found in the beginning of modern textbooks on the philosophy of language, e.g. Martinich 1996.

[5]   Crombie 1963:323, Guthrie 1978:5.2. For its latest dating, see Riley 2005:9–10.

[6]   By definition, etymology as a product of man's linguistic activity bears the notion of multiplicity. It indicates man's knowledge of his physical environment which is by nature multiple

I think this [the name σῶμα] admits of many explanations, if a little, even very little, change is made; for some say it [the body] is the "tomb" (σῆμα) of the soul which may be thought to be buried in our present life; or again, because by means of it the soul indicates (σημαίνει) anything it would indicate (ἂν σημαίνῃ). And it is for this reason also properly called "sign" (σῆμα), because the soul gives signs to the body. But I think it most likely that the Orphic poets gave this name, with the idea that the soul is undergoing punishment for something; they think it has the body as an enclosure to keep it safe (ἵνα σῴζηται), like a prison (δεσμωτηρίου εἰκόνα), and this is, as the name itself denotes, the safe (σῶμα) for the soul, until the penalty is paid. According to this view, not even a letter of the word need be changed.

Plato *Cratylus* 400b11–c10[7]

The concluding thought of the passage is a good starting point. To acknowledge the import of the explanation he has just offered, Socrates admires the perfect match between the content and the form in the word *sôma*. According to Plato's principal position in the dialogue that nouns denote the true realities behind them, the etymology of *sôma* does not simply visualize the idea that the soul is in the body "like a prison" (*desmôtêriou eikona*, *Cratylus* 400c7), but elicits the nature of the relation between soul and body. It further explicates that the soul is in the body "in order to be kept safe" (*hina sôizêtai*, *Cratylus* 400c7), or—if we want to capture the passive voice of *sôizô*—"in order to come to a safe place."[8] The parsing of the syntax, however, yields an unexpected, if not paradoxical, conceptual results: the "prison" of the body is for the safety of the soul.

Following Socrates' interest in the semantic nature of language in the dialogue, we too can be faithful to the text and note that Plato chooses to cast the true meaning of the soul-body relation in the syntactical organization of the final clause above. I do not think we can bypass this as insignificant for two reasons. First, because the final clause, according to its proper definition, serves to express the goal of the involved action. Second, because, in the above instance,

---

and divisible. The etymologies of the nouns Socrates offer in the *Cratylus* reflect, perhaps indirectly, the principal Platonic understanding that everything which pertains to the higher echelons of reality is unified and indivisible, while everything below them has different degrees of multiplicity and divisibility. For example, at *Cratylus* 397c4–400c10, Socrates offers only one interpretation for the etymology of *theos*, two for *daimôn* and *hêrôs*, a more complex explanation of *anthrôpos*, a revolving explanation of *psukhê*, and three meanings of *sôma*. There is a palpable downward semantic proliferation of god–daemon–hero–man–soul–body.

[7] The translation follows the rendering of H. N. Fowler 1926, in consideration of Jowett's interpretation 1989 and with my alterations. See also pp. 19 and 80n29 above and 172n4 below.

[8] See LSJ; Smyth 1984:493.

the action is positive, in the sense that the action is done for the benefit of the subject. Since the subject of the final clause is the soul, this suggests that, on purely syntactical grounds, the action is done for the benefit of the soul. If we zoom out from the grammatical details, we face the notion, unsettling for any ancient and modern reader of Platonic texts, that the body is in a position to do not just any good for the soul but to keep it safe.[9]

Yet, we need something more than a single purpose clause and a passive-voice verb to reconsider the 'hard' Platonic tenet of the body as an impediment to the soul on a completely new ground. The constraints of this ameliorative notion, implied by the final clause, are already present in the text. The conditions under which the soul undergoes the "safety watch" of the body are not ameliorative but punitive: (1) the soul is in the body as a punishment for its wrongdoings and (2) the soul is in the body temporarily, only for the duration of its punishment. The first condition depends on the comparison of the body to a prison; the second relates to the principal Platonic tenet of the immortality of soul. After its atoning sojourn in the body, the soul returns to, and thus restores, its original disembodied state. If the implications of the soul's embodiment are so incriminating, then what are we to make of Plato's choice to use an affirmative final clause to elicit the safety feature of the soul's dwelling in the body?

I suggest that the answer to this is given in Socrates' concluding thought at the end of the passage, cited above. The hypermobility of the word *sôma* bifurcates its semantic field into: (1) the standard 'hard' line of interpretation of the body as a "tomb" and a "prison" of the soul and (2) the traditionally overlooked 'soft' line of interpretation of the body as a "safe" place and "a sign"—but not necessarily a tomb-sign—of the soul.[10]

The second line of interpretation does not have the moralistic challenge of the former and for this reason it has been left largely unnoted in the scholarship.[11] Its philosophical significance is eclipsed by the dominant presence of the former in the Platonic corpus and its later tradition. But if we are to understand all conceptual nuances of *sôma*, embodied—pun intended—in the

---

[9] It is not clear from what the body saves the soul—presumably from complete dissipation in matter.

[10] The idea of the body as a "sign" is also present in the notion of the body as a "tomb" itself. The precise meaning of *sêma* in regard to burial practices denotes a "sign" by which a grave is known, henceforth the metonymic meaning of "tomb." See LSJ. Even this meaning, however, is secondary to the primary denotation of *sêma* as a "marker" or an "indicator" of something, including the elevated meaning of "a sign from heaven."

[11] Riley (2005:59) does not comment on it. In antiquity, the physical nature of the body falls in the domain of natural philosophy, including psychology as proved by the organization of the Aristotelian corpus in which the treatise *On the Soul* is placed after the *Physics*. A more redeeming approach to the study of the physical world in later Platonism is found in Chiaradonna and Trabattoni 2009, and Linguiti 2014.

polysemantics of Socrates' explanation in the *Cratylus*, we have to put on our Platonic psycho-somatic shades to discern the subtle second line of interpretation. If Plato's interpretation of the body as that by means of which "the soul indicates (*semainei*) anything it would indicate (*an semainei*)," formulated in *Cratylus* 400c3, lacks a philosophical meaning for Plato, why does he mention it or why does he not make his disapproval of it somehow known?

The principal meaning of *sêma* as "a sign," I argue, supports both lines of interpretation, offered by Socrates in the *Cratylus*. If the body is indeed a *sêma* of the embodied, physical state of the soul and not only a torture chamber for its ethical shortcomings, then the Platonic *topos* of the body as "a tomb" requires a philosophically meaningful upgrade. This upgrade would not be lost on a nuanced interpreter as Plotinus.

2. From a Tomb to a House

Enneads II 9[33] and IV 4[28] belong to the middle group of treatises according to Porphyry's chronological arrangement, when he was already in residence at Plotinus' school.[12]

Enneads II 9 or *Against the Gnostics* contains—as adumbrated by its full title— Plotinus' opposition *Against Those Who Say That The Creator Of The Cosmos And The Cosmos Are Evil*. Gertz has recently noted—and I support his position—that Plotinus does not direct his objection against any particular Gnostic sect, but against anyone, including students in his circle, who are or may be receptive to the idea of absolutely rejecting any value of the physical world.[13] Rejecting this 'hard' view, the treatise culminates in Plotinus' analogy of the human body to a "beautiful house" in which our true self dwells and to which it tends for the duration of its embodiment.[14] While still treading the Platonic party line about the ontological inferiority of the body, Plotinus' view—I argue below—gives a layered perspective on his understanding of the body that does not easily fit the standard Platonic interpretation found on the pages of handbooks and textbooks today.

Ennead IV 4 is one of the classic texts of Neoplatonic psychology addressing problems concerning the concept of soul. The question of the relation between soul and body pushes both Plotinus and Porphyry, as is demonstrated in the next chapter, to their analytical limits. Porphyry self-reports that once he stopped Plotinus from the course of his lectures for three days in order to explicate "how

---

[12] Helleman-Elgersma 1980:37.

[13] On this, see p. 101n23 above and Gertz 2017:19.

[14] For Plotinus' definition of a living being (*to zôion*) as a compound of soul and body (*to sunamphoteron*), see *Enneads* I 1.3–7, IV 3.26–27, IV 4.14.

the soul is with the body" (πῶς ἡ ψυχὴ σύνεστι τῷ σώματι, *Life of Plotinus* 13.11). Plotinus begins his explication—supposedly behind the sequence of the treatises known to us as *Difficulties about the Soul* to which *Ennead* IV 4 belongs—with an enthusiastic gesture towards Porphyry's inquisitiveness, by exclaiming: "For what could one more reasonably spend time in discussing and investigating extensively than this?" (*Enneads* IV 3.1.5–7). In *Ennead* IV 4.18–19, he addresses the last of the five major *aporiae*, raised by Porphyry's question, which examines the "affections" (*pathê*) of the "ensouled body" (*to toionde sôma*) and its contribution to understanding the state of being "ensouled" (*empsukhon*). Plotinus' treatment of the body in the two treatises casts doubt that he has a monolithic interpretation of the body as "a tomb" of soul.[15]

One of the difficulties at hand is how to understand the union between the two ontologically opposite entities that come together in the composition of a living being (*to zôion*, *Enneads* I 1.3.2–3), be it an animal, a plant, or a man. In Platonic psychology, soul and body, as the two entities from which a living being is composed, are qualitatively different (soul is immortal; body is mortal). Because of their ontological opposition, the compound of the two cannot be homogenous as when each one of them is within their own natures, but only heterogeneous as each one of them enters the temporary union of a living being, while retaining their individual natures.

In *Enneads* II 9, Plotinus conceives of this kind of qualified union as a "partnership" (*koinônia*) in which the soul and the body play separate roles in accordance with their heterogeneous natures (*Enneads* II 9.7.3–4). We can dynamically visualize this relation, if we think of the soul-body partnership as a bird-in-a-cage model, with two scenarios.[16]

The first scenario supposes that the bird in the cage constantly flies against the cage ribs in order to escape from it. The other supposes that there is a cat in the room in which the cage is, and the bird is in the cage in order to be kept safe from the cat. The first scenario enacts the 'hard' interpretation of *sôma* as the place in which the soul is retained if in a prison (*desmôtêriou eikona*, *Cratylus* 400c7) or as in a tomb. This is the line of interpretation Plotinus ascribes to the composite portrait of the Gnostics in *Enneads* II 9, and vehemently, as will

---

[15] In his seminal *Plotinus' Psychology* (1971:vii), Blumenthal observed: "students of Plotinus have tended to concentrate on the higher regions of his world, and there is still no satisfactory treatment of his doctrines of the embodied soul." Almost half a century later, major steps have been made to fill in this gap by Emilsson 1988, Remes 2007, and most recently Caluori 2015. But there is still plenty of room left. Up to date, there is no specific study of Plotinus' concept of the body.

[16] This model is inspired by Porphyry's reference to the presence of the incorporeal in the body as an animal in a cage, see *Sentences* 28, discussed p. 138 below. For Augustine's interpretation of it, see p. 312 below.

be discussed next, rejects.[17] This interpretation also reinforces Plato's definition of the body as an "obstacle" (*empodion*) to the soul in the *Phaedo* with which Plotinus begins his criticism of the Gnostics' view in *Enneads* II 9.17.1–6. The second scenario enacts the 'soft' interpretation of the soul-body relation implied by the affirmative final clause in Socrates' view that the soul enters the body in order to be safe until the time for its natural release.[18]

In *Enneads* II 9, Plotinus rejects the first scenario found in the Gnostic cosmological negativism towards the physical world:[19]

> And yet, even if it occurred to them to hate the nature of body because they have heard Plato often reproaching the body for the kind of 'hindrances' (ἐμπόδια) it puts in the way of soul—and he said that all bodily nature was inferior—they should have stripped off this bodily nature in their thought and seen what remained, an intelligible sphere embracing the form imposed upon the universe ...
>
> Plotinus *Enneads* II 9.17.1–6[20]

The Platonic origin of the Gnostic view does not stop Plotinus from pronouncing his verdict in the opening statement of his closing argument: "those arguments of theirs make men 'flee' from the body since they 'hate' it from a distance" (*Enneads* II 9.18.1–2).[21] His criticism suggests that he is not in favor of any view that takes the bird-in-the-cage model to the extreme, as envisioned by the first scenario. Instead, he argues for a 'softer' interpretation of the original Platonic position, which he summarizes at the end of his verdict

---

[17] Kalligas (2014:408) recognizes the Gnostic origin of Plotinus' analogy. To make his case, Plotinus draws, as is common for him, ammunition from his opponents' repertoire. His disagreement with the Gnostics has been recently discussed in the context of Early Christian philosophy by Karamanolis 2014:210–211.

[18] *Cratylus* 400c7; see p. 113 above.

[19] Cf. *The Tripartite Tractate* 115.23–117.8, *The Second Book of John* 20.28–30.11, *On the Origin of the World* 123.2–31. On this view, see the previous chapter.

[20] *Enneads* II 9.17.1–6: καίτοι, εἰ καὶ μισεῖν αὐτοῖς ἐπῄει τὴν τοῦ σώματος φύσιν, διότι ἀκηκόασι Πλάτωνος πολλὰ μεμψαμένου τῷ σώματι οἷα ἐμπόδια παρέχει τῇ ψυχῇ–καὶ πᾶσαν τὴν σωματικὴν φύσιν εἶπε χείρονα–ἐχρῆν ταύτην περιελόντας τῇ διανοίᾳ ἰδεῖν τὸ λοιπόν, σφαῖραν νοητὴν τὸ ἐπὶ τῷ κόσμῳ εἶδος ἐμπεριέχουσαν ... The Dative of σώματι in the second line is peculiar because the verb μέμφομαι takes Dative specifically to indicate a person and not a thing to be blamed. Plotinus transfers this specialized semantic aspect of the verb to the body itself as if the body stands in place of the person. This move is Platonically controversial. One possible interpretation is that for an ignorant, or at least not fully Platonically informed, person, the body indeed does all the work in the psycho-somatic compound and its desires represent and thereby can stand in the place of the person. The translation of the *Enneads* is according to Armstrong 1966–1988 unless otherwise noted and with my alterations.

[21] *Enneads* II 9.18.1–2: ἀλλ᾽ ἴσως φήσουσιν ἐκείνους μὲν τοὺς λόγους φεύγειν τὸ σῶμα ποιεῖν πόρρωθεν μισοῦντας.

above—namely, that "our views hold the soul down to [the body]" (κατέχειν τὴν ψύχην πρὸς αὐτῷ, *Enneads* II 9.18.3). This move on Plotinus' part does not only project the correct way of understanding the soul-body relation but also the value of pursuing it. Instead of promoting the idea of an immediate escape from the body, he promotes the idea of learning how to "live in" the body and use it as "a stepping stone" for understanding its underlying principle, the soul, and the intelligible entourage behind it.

To explain his position, he compares the proponents of each view to two people who live in the same house. The first tenant, Plotinus elaborates, despises the structure of the house; the other does not. Instead, the second tenant appreciates its craftsmanship and waits for the time "when he will not need a house any longer" (*Enneads* II 9.18.4–8). Plotinus' distinction between the two tenants enacts the two bird-in-the-cage scenarios hypothesized above. The first tenant subscribes to the Gnostic view and the first scenario in which the bird constantly tries to escape from the cage. The second tenant illustrates Plotinus' own interpretation of the Platonic position, promoting the second scenario in which the bird tends to its cage because it knows that the cage provides a safe place for it while the cat is on the outside. Plotinus' disagreement with the first scenario is not as surprising as it may initially seem. The Gnostic view treats the living body as a tomb rather than a house. A tomb implies that something dead is enclosed in it, whereas a house implies that someone alive occupies it. If the soul is immortal, as both the Gnostics and the Platonists agree, then the soul is not dead, but alive and therefore cannot live in a tomb, but only in a house.[22]

The body-house analogy in *Ennead* II 9 is a step away from the body-prison analogy in the *Cratylus* to propose a more valorized view of the soul-body relation. It allows us to add two more observations about the etymology of *sôma* in Plato's dialogue: (1) since the soul is the agent that arranges the body as the house of its temporary abode, the house, however imperfect, is the only sign that indicates that its tenant is in; (2) since its tenant is immortal, then the sign the house indicates must somehow express the higher ontological nature of its tenant. Plotinus is emphatic about the latter. The body is not just a house or any house, but a beautiful one (*oikos kalos*, *Enneads* II 9.18.4): "While we have bodies," he concludes, "we must stay in our houses, which have been built for us by a good sister soul which has great power to work without any toil or trouble" (*Enneads* II 9.18.14–17).[23]

---

[22] On soul's embodiment, see p. 19 above. On soul's moderate embodiment, see below p. 172n4.

[23] *Enneads* II 9.18.14–17: δεῖ δὲ μένειν μὲν ἐν οἴκοις σῶμα ἔχοντας κατασκευασθεῖσιν ὑπὸ ψυχῆς ἀδελφῆς ἀγαθῆς πολλὴν δύναμιν εἰς τὸ δημιουργεῖν ἀπόνως ἐχούσης. See Helleman-Elgersma 1980.

By criticizing the Gnostics, Plotinus checks his own Platonic view—or that of his students—from falling on the Gnostic track and opens the door for the 'soft' interpretation of the *sôma-sêma* analogy in the *Cratylus*. Although he accepts the confining role of the body as a "prison" (*desmôtêrion*) of the soul, he concentrates on the "binding" nature (*desmos*) of the soul-body relation:[24]

> ... we are bound (δεδέμεθα) by a body which has already become a bond (δεσμοῦ γεγενημένου). For the nature of the body is already bound (φύσις δεδεμένη) in the universal soul and binds (συνδεῖ) whatever it grasps.
>
> Plotinus *Enneads* II 9.7.10–13[25]

The passage elicits Plotinus' take on the 'hard' interpretation of the body. The body is not a place which binds (*desmôtêrion*), as the *Cratylus* suggests, but a bond (*desmos*). Its binding nature is not, however, determined by the fact that it binds the individual soul to itself, but by the fact that it is already bound in the World Soul as its creator. This new line of interpretation offers a different perspective on the soul-body relation in the psycho-somatic compound of a human being. Namely, that the body is the *desmos* that binds together the internal ensoulment of the individual soul and the external ensoulment of the World Soul. The body is the bond itself that hangs in the balance between internal and external ensoulment. Its beauty as a house then derives from its binding nature participating in these two kinds of ensoulment. This interpretation of the binding nature of the body supports the second scenario of the bird-in-the-cage model in which the bird tends to its cage for the duration of its safe-keeping.[26]

According to Plotinus, the extreme denial of any value of the body shows nothing else than the inability to recognize the beauty of the house in which the soul temporarily resides. The problem with such an extreme denial is not so much that it prematurely brings the birdcage to ruin, but that it disables us from ultimately recognizing the beauty of its architect (the World Soul) and its

---

[24] Both notions are interplayed in the *Phaedo* 60c6, 67d1, 114c1.

[25] *Enneads* II 9.7.10–13: ἡμεῖς μὲν ὑπὸ τοῦ σώματος δεδέμεθα ἤδη δεσμοῦ γεγενημένου. ἐν γὰρ τῇ πάσῃ ψυχῇ ἡ τοῦ σώματος φύσις δεδεμένη ἤδη συνδεῖ ὃ ἂν περιλάβῃ. The body is bound to the World Soul for the duration allowed by its nature. Sometimes, it can wither as a shoot that is grafted on a stock which lives its own life (*Enneads* II 9.7.20–22) or it can be trampled like a tortoise that is caught in the middle of "the ordered movement of dancers" (*Enneads* II 9.7.36–39). These scenarios happen when the body is either incapable, for whatever accidental reason, to maintain its bond with the World Soul, or when the body, for whatever less fatal reason, is prevented from smoothly maintaining its bond with the soul. For a synthesis of Plotinus' position, see Porphyry *Sentences* 8.

[26] Cf. *Enneads* IV 3.9.29–34 and IV 4.18.10–13.

house-keeper (the individual soul). If we are not able to discern the beauty of the house we live in, how can we discern the beauty of our true self, with or without the homey enclosure of the body? Even more, if we cannot discern the beauty of the physical world around us in the first place, how can we discern, in the long run, the beauty of the underlying principles of what is around us?[27]

So what conclusions can we draw from the above analysis? Plotinus' refutation of the Gnostic miso-somatic attitude should not be misunderstood as an attempt to exonerate the body as the moralistic obstacle to the well being of the psycho-somatic compound. Plotinus is Platonist at heart and his soul-body dualism is unquestionable.[28] We can think of his criticism, however, as a criticism of taking the Platonic ontologically discriminating view of the body too far, to the extreme that denies its constitutive, biological value as an expression—a living sign and not a tomb—of the soul. This kind of 'hard' extremism, even if it came from close Platonic quarters and not necessarily from the Gnostics, would run against Plotinus' signature view of the universe as a holistic network no part of which is superfluous or ugly.[29]

His 'soft' understanding of the *sôma-sêma* analogy, I further conclude, crumbles the walls of the standard interpretation of the body as a tomb in the *Cratylus* by proposing a more appealing, and still Platonically designed, dwelling place for our true self. For Plotinus, as for Plato, this understanding penetrates the life-giving responsibility of the soul to tend to its safe-house for the duration of its embodiment. The living being is a body which, like a beautiful house and its binding nature, indicates the craftsmanship of the World Soul and the stewardship of the individual soul.

3. From a House to a Sign

Plotinus' rejection of the Gnostic denial of the body and his body-house analogy are not simply products of his rhetorical acumen. They come in the wake of his long discussion of the soul-body relation Porphyry, as mentioned above, reports

---

[27] In Narbonne's words (2011:87), "the message that Plotinus repeatedly expounds against his adversaries is that one cannot condemn the sensible world without also incriminating that from which it arises."

[28] His attitude is not linear regardless of how strict a guideline we use *pace* Remes 2007:185–191. In *Enneads* IV 8[6]3.4-5, an early treatise dealing specifically with the descent of the soul in the body, he hits all the high Platonic notes referring to the body as a "chain" (*desmos*) and a "tomb" (*taphos*), echoing Plato's *tethammenês* from Socrates' *sôma-sêma* analogy in the *Cratylus* 400c2 (but not *desmôtêrion*), and the world as a "cave" (*spêlaion*) and a "den" (*antron*). Even in the famous painting episode with which Porphyry opens his teacher's biography, the body is treated as an "image" (*eidôlon*), not a tomb or a prison (*Life of Plotinus* 1.7).

[29] As conceptualized in the recent treatment of Plotinian metaphysics by D. O'Meara 2010 and Remes and Slaveva-Griffin 2014:4–7.

in the *Life of Plotinus* 13.11.[30] The last of the five main *aporiae* in the discussion, addressed in *Enneads* IV 3-4, concerns the question of whether the body in the psycho-somatic compound can express anything either of its own or of the soul.[31] The question allows Plotinus to articulate his understanding of the body as a *sêma*:

> ... the body itself, in which there is soul and nature, must not be the same kind of thing as what is soulless (ἄψυχον) or that air is when it has been lit, but rather like air that has been warmed; the body of an animal, or indeed of a plant, has something like a shadow of soul (οἷον σκιὰν ψυχῆς), and pain (τὸ ἀλγεῖν) and taking pleasure (τὸ ἥδεσθαι) in the pleasures of the body is the business of the body so qualified (τὸ τοιόνδε σῶμά ἐστιν); but the pain of this body (ἡ τούτου ἀλγηδών) and this sort of pleasure (ἡ τοιαύτη ἡδονή) come to the notice of our self for dispassionate cognition (εἰς γνῶσιν ἀπαθῆ).
>
> Plotinus *Enneads* IV 4.18.4-10[32]

In the passage, Plotinus defines the principal characteristic of the body to be warmth. According to him, warmth indicates the soul's presence in the body and the change of state of the body from "un-ensouled" (*apsukhon*) to "ensouled" (*psukhon*). Because this change of state depends on the heterogeneous natures

---

[30] See pp. 115-116 above.

[31] The five *aporiae* tackle the different aspects of Plotinus' understanding of the individual soul: (1) its relation to the World Soul; (2) the manner in which it descends in the body; (3) the manner of its embodiment; (4) its departure from the body; (5) the joined activities of body and soul. This list follows the thematic outline of *Enneads* IV 3 in Dillon and Blumenthal 2015:41-52. On the problems, inherent in Plotinus' layered concept of soul, Blumenthal 1971 remains unsurpassed. The latest installment on the subject is Caluori 2015.

[32] *Enneads* IV 4.18.4-10: ἢ καὶ αὐτὸ τὸ σῶμα, ἐν ᾧ καὶ ψυχὴ καὶ φύσις, οὐ τοιοῦτον εἶναι δεῖ, οἷον τὸ ἄψυχον καὶ οἷον ὁ ἀὴρ ὁ πεφωτισμένος, ἀλλ' οἷον ὁ τεθερμασμένος, καὶ ἔστι τὸ σῶμα τοῦ ζῴου καὶ τοῦ φυτοῦ δὲ οἷον σκιὰν ψυχῆς ἔχοντα, καὶ τὸ ἀλγεῖν καὶ τὸ ἥδεσθαι δὲ τὰς τοῦ σώματος ἡδονὰς περὶ τὸ τοιόνδε σῶμά ἐστιν· ἡμῖν δὲ ἡ τούτου ἀλγηδὼν καὶ ἡ τοιαύτη ἡδονὴ εἰς γνῶσιν ἀπαθῆ ἔρχεται. The translation is according to Dillon and Blumenthal 2015, with my alterations. Armstrong's translation of τὸ ἀλγεῖν καὶ τὸ ἥδεσθαι as "pain and bodily pleasure," repeated in the following sentence, as "the pain of this and pleasure such as this," captures Plotinus' shift of attention from soul to body. His substitution of *lupê* in the standard treatments of pain and pleasure in Plato, Aristotle, and the Stoics, with cognates of *algêdôn*, suggests his distinction between "physical pain" (*algêdôn*) and "emotional pain" (*lupê*). The former does not appear on the Stoic list of kinds of "pain" (see SVF III.100), but in the medical literature, whereas the latter is a hallmark of the standard discussion of pain and pleasure in ancient psychology. The final result of Plotinus' long-term project in including the former in the list of affections appears in the opening question of the second to last treatise he wrote, *Enneads* I 1[53]1.1-2. For the classical version of the list, see Aristotle *On the Soul* 408b1-3. Somatic and psychic pleasures are not distinguished in the semantic register of *hêdonê* and *hêdesthai*.

of the soul and the body, before he characterizes the nature of the psychoso-matic compound, he determines the individual nature of its elements.

In order for the body to express its own nature, it has to be outside of the compound and thus "un-ensouled" (*apsukhon*). In this state, he explains, the body would not experience anything: "if the body is divided, the division would not affect the body itself but its unity" (*Enneads* IV 4.18.23–24).[33] Dillon and Blumenthal (2015:377) find this explanation unclear. I suggest that the key for understanding it lies in the divisible nature of the un-ensouled body. Plotinus argues that the divisibility affects the body only quantitatively, not qualita-tively. For instance, if a corpse is missing one arm, the corpse is still a corpse. Its nature remains unchanged and in this sense homogeneous. The only differ-ence is that now, since one of its arms is missing, it is an incomplete or one-arm corpse. As outside observers of the corpse, we are in a position to tell the quan-titative change in the corpse. But the corpse itself cannot tell that one of its arms is missing because it does not have something other than itself to tell this to it. The corpse and that which can tell this to it, Plotinus concludes, must be heterogeneous.

The situation with the soul is just the opposite. The soul does not allow division and evades everything (*Enneads* IV 4.18.23–25). When it is by itself, the soul is present in itself holistically. When it is embodied, he clarifies, the soul is present everywhere in the body. To use the hypothesized example above, it is impossible for any part of the body to be un-ensouled, if the rest of the body is ensouled. Unlike with the corpse, we cannot cut off the part of the soul that is in the arm from the rest of the soul in a living body. When we cut off the arm, the state of the soul that is present in the rest of the body is not affected, qualitatively or quantitatively, because the nature of the soul is indivisible.

Plotinus does not gear his discussion of the opposite natures of the soul and the body so much towards explaining their polarity as towards demonstrating that the nature of the psycho-somatic compound itself is different from the individual nature of its elements. In the compound, the body and the soul are always in relation to each other and never by themselves. The first *sêma* of this relation is the presence of the soul in the body, which changes its state from un-ensouled to ensouled. In his words, the body's first possession is "something like a shadow of soul" (οῖον σκιὰν ψυχῆς, *Enneads* IV 4.18.7), which qualita-tively transforms the body from being *apsukhon* to *empsukhon*.[34] This qualitative change is not induced through an external source, such as light, but through

---

[33] The divisibility of the body is a direct result of its extension in space; see Emilsson 1988:146–147.

[34] He also refers to this shadow of soul as "a trace" (ἴχνος and τὸ ἴχνος τὸ ψυχικόν, *Enneads* IV 4.28) or an "image of intelligence, the lowest of the soul" (ἴνδαλμα φρονήσεως ἡ φύσις καὶ ψυχῆς ἔσχατον, *Enneads* IV 4.13.3–4). This lowest layer of soul is identified with nature as the vegetative

an internal source, such as vital heat, which transforms the corpse from a cold mass into a warm, living being.[35] He identifies the warmth of the living body as the first and thus principal sign, indicating the soul's presence in it.[36]

The passage above also identifies the second sign of ensoulment. It pertains to the affections of "pain" and "pleasure," as elaborated next:[37]

> We are concerned with its [the body's] pleasures and its pains in propor-
> tion as we are weaker and do not separate ourselves, but consider the
> body the most honourable part of ourselves and the real human being
> (τὸν ἄνθρωπον τιθέμεθα), and, so to speak, sink ourselves in it (οἶον
> εἰσδυόμεθα εἰς αὐτό).
>
> Plotinus *Enneads* IV 4.18.15-19[38]

Here Plotinus treads the standard Platonic line of understanding the body as an impediment to the soul and cautions against the common misperception of the body as the most valued part of a human being. The view of ensoulment as a process of sinking—and its dangerous implications for the soul—is not far removed from the Gnostics' disparaging attitude towards the body in *Enneads* II 9 discussed in the previous section of the chapter. There, he even issues a formal warning "not to love the body" (*mê philosômatein*) in order to prevent the soul from sinking as deeply as possible in it.[39]

---

power of growth (*to phutikon*), inherent in every living being. Cf. *phutikê psukhê*, *Enneads* IV 4.22.14 and *gennêtikê psukhê*, *Enneads* IV 4.27.1-2. See Blumenthal 1971:44-46, 62-63.

[35] "Hot" and "cold," together with "dry" and "wet," are considered in most ancient medical circles the primary causes of disease. The author of the Hippocratic *On Ancient Medicine* critically responds to this view by arguing for a more empirically based understanding of the constitution of the human body as "complete coction and rest, with no particular powers displayed" (*On Ancient Medicine* 19.54-57). Plotinus appears to follow the dominant medical opinion.

[36] Heat is the most characteristic feature of the ensouled body. In Aristotle as in Galen, it is the physical symptom that indicates that a body is alive. On the brain as the warmest of the body parts, see Aristotle's *On Sense and Sensibles* 439a2-4. On man as the warmest by nature, see Aristotle *Problems* 897b21. Cf. Galen, *On Mixtures* I 538.4 Kühn: εἰ γάρ τι τέθνηκεν, οὐ θερμόν. On the importance of physical symptoms for shaping the understanding of the body in the fifth and fourth centuries BCE, see Holmes 2010, especially her discussion of physical symptoms as making invisible powers and properties of the body appear (2010:121-191).

[37] Pain and pleasure are fundamental for the philosophical project on ethics and psychology ever since their treatment in the *Philebus* 31b-58a. See D. Frede 1992.

[38] *Enneads* IV 4.18.15-19: διὸ καὶ ἡδομένου καὶ ἀλγοῦντος μέλει, καὶ ὅσῳ ἀσθενέστεροι μᾶλλον, καὶ ὅσῳ ἑαυτοὺς μὴ χωρίζομεν, ἀλλὰ τοῦτο ἡμῶν τὸ τιμιώτατον καὶ τὸν ἄνθρωπον τιθέμεθα καὶ οἶον εἰσδυόμεθα εἰς αὐτό. On the "weaker" human nature, see *Theaetetus* 149b9. On ensoulment as weakness in the soul, see *Enneads* I 8.14.21-22. See also Narbonne 2011:79-88.

[39] *Enneads* II 9.18.41, echoing Socrates' definition of "a lover of the body" (*philosômatos*) in *Phaedo* 68c1 and, as pointed to me by Ramelli, Sextus' *Sentences* 76.1.

Clearly, Plotinus does not support either extreme. The love of the body, just as the Gnostics' distaste of the body, destroys the 'binding' balance of ensoulment. The above passage recognizes the danger of "loving the body" as the extreme of the soul's sinking in the body. The caution he issues against "loving the body" in *Ennead* IV 4 chronologically precedes his refutation of the Gnostics' 'hard' view of "hating the body" in *Enneads* II 9. As we learned, there he understands the nature of the relation between soul and body as a meeting point of "binding" (*dedemetha*) between external and internal ensoulment, between the World Soul and the individual soul, respectively.[40] In light of the binding nature of the compound in *Enneads* II 9, we can understand his view of the "sinking" nature of the process of ensoulment in *Enneads* IV 4 as tightening and thus straining the body as the bond of the two kinds of ensoulment.[41]

He uses the affections of pain and pleasure to measure how deeply the soul has sunk in the body: "so it [the body] swings up and down, and as it comes down it proclaims its 'pain', and as it goes up its 'longing for partnership'" (*Enneads* IV 4.18.34–36).[42] The two affections form a vertical measuring scale of ensoulment, with pleasure—that is the lack of pain—at the top and pain at the bottom.[43] Unlike the first sign of ensoulment, pain and the lack of pain do not indicate the soul's presence in the body, but measure how far the soul has sunk in the body.

The origin of pain, he further identifies, is in the partnership of the heterogeneous natures of the soul and the body in the compound (*Enneads* IV 4.18.25–27).[44] Pain indicates that the relation between the two elements is off balance, leaning towards the body. The lack of pain indicates that their relation leans towards the soul.[45] According to this model, the *modus vivendi* of the compound oscillates between pain and pleasure. Pain, he explains, is "'knowledge' (*gnôsis*) of the withdrawal of the body [from the composite] which is being deprived of the image of soul," while pleasure is "'knowledge' (*gnôsis*) of the living thing that the image of soul is again fitting back in the body" (*Enneads* IV 4.19.1–4).[46] He

---

[40] *Enneads* II 9.7.11.

[41] In the first part of the sequence (*Enneads* IV 3.3.151–154), Plotinus refers to the soul's descent as spatial stretching. See Caluori 2015:138.

[42] *Enneads* IV 4.18.34–36: κάτω τε οὖν καὶ ἄνω αἰωρούμενον φερόμενον μὲν κάτω ἀπήγγειλε τὴν αὐτοῦ ἀλγηδόνα, πρὸς δὲ τὸν ἄνω τὴν ἔφεσιν τῆς κοινωνίας.

[43] On the uniqueness of Plotinus' vertical theory of pain and pleasure, see Dillon and Blumenthal 2015:377.

[44] *Enneads* IV 4.18.25–27: ὅταν δὲ δύο ἐθέλῃ ἓν εἶναι, ἐπακτῷ χρησάμενα τῷ ἓν ἐν τῷ οὐκ ἐᾶσθαι εἶναι ἓν τὴν γένεσιν εἰκότως τοῦ ἀλγεῖν ἔχει.

[45] On health as a "lack of pain" (*anôdunia*), see *Enneads* I 4.6.24–25.

[46] *Enneads* IV 4.19.1–4: τοῦτο δὴ τὸ λεγόμενον ἡδονήν τε εἶναι καὶ ἀλγηδόνα, εἶναι μὲν ἀλγηδόνα γνῶσιν ἀπαγωγῆς σώματος ἰνδάλματος ψυχῆς στερισκομένου, ἡδονὴν δὲ γνῶσιν ζῴου ἰνδάλματος ψυχῆς ἐν σώματι ἐναρμοζομένου πάλιν αὖ. Cf. Clement *Prophetic Eclogues* 35.2: ὡς γὰρ ἡδονὴ τὴν τῆς ἀλγηδόνος ἀπαλλαγὴν οὐσίαν ἔχει, οὕτως ἡ γνῶσις τῆς ἀγνοίας τὴν ὑπεξαίρεσιν.

defines both affections as knowledge, gathered by the soul through the experience of the body. But this knowledge, he maintains, is unaffected (εἰς γνῶσιν ἀπαθῆ, *Enneads* IV 4.18.11) by the affections themselves.[47] Plotinus understands the body as an instrument which does not only indicate whether the soul is present or not, but also affects the degree to which the relation between their heterogeneous natures is balanced. The affections of the body act as a gravitational force on the balance between the two.[48]

Plotinus' understanding of the two affections also shifts Plato's ethical definition of pain and pleasure, found in the *Philebus*, on ontological terms.[49] He views their presence or lack thereof as a physical "sign" (*sêma*) of the ontological truth that the soul and body are heterogeneous in nature. The biological foundation of his understanding is further supported by his elaborate reference to "a surgical procedure" (*tomê*) as a medical experiment, proving the heterogeneous natures of the soul and the body in the psycho-somatic compound (*Enneads* IV 4.19.8–29).[50] His hypothesis is that the experience of "pain" (*êlgunthê*) during the procedure indicates that the body is affected and not the soul:

> ... as in a surgical operation (ἐν τῇ τομῇ) when the body is cut the division (διαίρεσις) is in its material mass, but the distress is felt in the mass because it is not only a mass (ὄγκον), but a mass qualified in a particular way (τοιόνδε ὄγκον); it is there too that inflammation occurs.
>
> Plotinus *Enneads* IV 4.19.8–11[51]

He uses the surgical procedure as an experimental proof of his argument about the divisible and indivisible nature, respectively, of the body and the soul he has just discussed.[52] According to it, in order for the body to experience pain from the cut, something else, not the body, has to 'tell' the body that it is experiencing pain. The body sends a sign to the sense-perceptive kind of

---

[47] For discussion of the meaning of *apathês* as resistant to affections, see Blumenthal 1971:55.

[48] Cf. *Enneads* IV 3.1.34–36: τὸ ψυχὴ δὲ πᾶσα παντὸς ἐπιμελεῖται τοῦ ἀψύχου.

[49] Plato's definition identifies pain and pleasure, respectively, as disrupting and restoring the natural state of the body (*Philebus* 31d4–9 and 32a8–b4).

[50] Since the Hellenistic times, medicine uses anatomical dissections, predominantly of animals, to prove different epistemological points. Galen's works provide lavish evidence for the culture of surgical spectacles at the turn of the new millennium. Plotinus shows that he is not unfamiliar with it.

[51] *Enneads* IV 4.19.8–11: οἷον ἐν τῇ τομῇ τεμνομένου τοῦ σώματος ἡ μὲν διαίρεσις κατὰ τὸν ὄγκον, ἡ δ' ἀγανάκτησις κατὰ τὸν ὄγκον τῷ μὴ μόνον ὄγκον, ἀλλὰ καὶ τοιόνδε ὄγκον εἶναι· ἐκεῖ δὲ καὶ ἡ φλεγμονή. Here I follow Armstrong's translation (1984:187) who takes *tomê* to refer to a proper surgical operation rather than an accidental cut. This reading is supported by Boyadjiev (2005: 402–403), *pace* Dillon and Blumenthal 2015:378–379.

[52] See pp. 121–123 above.

soul, which he understands to be closest to the body and thus "in the neighbourhood of affection" (*Enneads* IV 4.19.6).[53] This kind of soul identifies "where the wound and the pain are" and converts this information into "unaffected knowledge" (*gnôsis apathês*, *Enneads* IV 4.19.27). If the soul were to feel the pain, he further argues, since the soul is everywhere in the body, the soul would not be able to identify the location of the pain in the body but would feel the pain all over the body. When "the finger hurts" (ὁ δάκτυλος ἀλγεῖ), he concludes, "the man hurts" (ὁ ἄνθρωπος ἀλγεῖ) because the finger belongs to the man (*Enneads* IV 4.19.19–20). The "pain" (*odunê*) in the finger "indicates" (*sêmainei*) that the finger withdraws from the trace of soul in it to sink towards its state of un-ensouled matter (*Enneads* IV 4.19.24).[54] Presumably, the deeper the cut, the greater the dissolution of the finger's bond with the soul is. The severance of the finger from the body reduces the finger, like the arm of the hypothetical corpse I previously described, back to its original state of being un-ensouled.[55]

In this staged surgical procedure, Plotinus uses medically informed concepts and vocabulary to describe technical details and physiological symptoms: "wound" (*plêgê*), "inflammation" (*phlegmonê*), and physical "pain" as both *algêdôn* and *odunê*.[56] His dependence on the medical art is not for rhetorical purposes. His argument for the heterogeneous nature of the psycho-somatic compound follows the logic of the leading Hippocratic argument, espoused in *On the Nature of Man*, that the composition of man is not homogeneous, consisting of one substance, but heterogeneous, consisting of substances of different natures.[57] The author of the treatise—who might have been Hippocrates' son-in-law, Polybus, or not—states the premise of the Hippocratic position up front in the work: "if man were basically of one substance, he would never feel pain

---

[53] This kind of soul is situated "next" to the body (*ephexês*, *Enneads* IV 4.19.12) and thus lowest in the internal stratification of the soul. It is elsewhere called "affective" (*pathêtikon*, *Enneads* III 6.1). On the difficulty of his terminology of the lowest part of soul, see Blumenthal 1971:45–58.

[54] Plotinus warns us against identifying the pain itself with the neurological receptor of pain. The latter is only the messenger of pain because if the messenger could be affected by the pain, he would not be a "reliable messenger" (*hugiês angelos*, *Enneads* IV 4.19.29).

[55] See p. 122.

[56] Socrates uses both terms. The latter appears in his description of philosophy as a snakebite in his heart (*Symposium* 217e7–218a6). For his reference to the pain of philosophy, see *Theaetetus* 148e6.

[57] This is the most conceptually important treatise in the Hippocratic Corpus from a philosophical perspective. It was highly regarded by Galen. Based on the rare factual remarks in the text, Craik (2015:212) dates it to the last decades of the fifth century. Its organization has been a subject of a long debate whether the work derives from more than one source or not. The details of the debate are irrelevant for us here, but for the sake of full disclosure, I accept Craik's argument (2015:210–211) for a single authorship and thematical coherence. For an early assessment of the problem, see W. D. Smith 1979:201–202. For the reception of the treatise in Nemesius of Emesa, see Beatrice 2005.

(*êlgeen*), since, being one, there would be nothing to hurt (*algêseien*)."[58] He places this premise in the foundation of the Hippocratic theory according to which the four humors (blood, phlegm, yellow bile, and black bile) build the constitution of the human body (*On the Nature of Man* 4.1–2) and thus establish its heterogeneous nature.

The above parallel demonstrates that Plato's legacy of using medical knowledge in philosophical discussion is not foreign to Plotinus. Although he is often described as "otherworldly," he is nevertheless comfortable to use the art of medicine in matters pertinent to the biological body.[59] The two principal signs of ensoulment that he identifies—innate heat and the presence and absence of pain—are paradigmatically medical.[60] They suggest that his use of the surgical procedure is not a simple rhetorical device, but a staged experimental proof, albeit theoretical, of his argument.[61] My discussion of Plotinus' use of medicine here aims at demonstrating his reliance on the art that specializes in treating the body, as a source of informed and thus reliable knowledge about the body. It shows his understanding of the body as a philosophically sophisticated concept that extends beyond its moralistic label of a "prison" or a "tomb," affixed to it by the 'hard' line of interpretation of Plato's etymology of the *sôma* in the *Cratylus*.[62]

4. Tomb as a Sign of Immortality

Plotinus' understanding of physical pain as a sign of the degree of ensoulment of the body is not conceptually isolated.[63] By the third century, the early Christian theologians have also been working, for some time, on the question of

[58] *On the Nature of Man* 2.13–15: εἰ ἓν ἦν ὁ ἄνθρωπος, οὐδέποτ' ἂν ἤλγει· οὐδὲ γὰρ ἂν ἦν ὑφ' ὅτευ ἀλγήσειεν ἓν ἐόν Jouanna. The translation is according to J. Chadwick and Mann 1978.
[59] The technical overtones of his explanation strengthen the medical motif in his previous answer comparing the task of the Demiurge who orders and governs the universe, to the physician's job in administrating and regulating the proper function of man's body (*Enneads* IV 4.11.1–7). If he finds the medical profession useful in constructing the portrait of the Demiurge, it can be most suitable for discussing the role of the body in *Enneads* IV 4.
[60] For the Hippocratic Corpus as a resource for the understanding of ancient semiotics, see Manetti 1993:49–50.
[61] By Plotinus' time, the medical curriculum in Alexandria is well established. See Iskandar 1976, W. D. Smith 1979, Marrou 1982, Watts 2006, Pormann 2010, Craik 2015. From the *Life of Plotinus* (2 and 7), we know that Plotinus' inner circle of disciples included at least three physicians: Paulinus from Scythopolis, Zethus of Arabia, and Eustochius of Alexandria, see Slaveva-Griffin 2010:93–95.
[62] See pp. 112–120 above.
[63] Scarry 1985 and Perkins 1995 have demonstrated the growing cultural interest in the body in the first centuries of the new millennium. For the early Christian theologians' robust interest in the medical knowledge of the body, see Boudon-Millot and Pouderon 2005. It would be prudent not to dismiss the similar development on the Neoplatonic side as coincidental.

the soul-body relation.[64] They reformulate the question, however, in the specific terms of Christ's two natures.[65] As the Son of God, his immortality is above any doubt. His humanity, though, and how it relates to his immortality are subject of much contention inside and outside the theological milieu. It reflects the conceptual debate in their contemporary philosophical quarters, as my discussion in the preceding sections of the chapter reveals.

Contemporaries and *alumni* of the educational circle of Ammonius Saccas in Alexandria, Plotinus and Origen show conceptual confluence on the topic of the body worthy of further investigation.[66] Here I will briefly introduce two cases from Origen's *Against Celsus* in order to show that, in his views on the body, Plotinus works within a broader ideological context which has been already established by his engagement with the Gnostics, discussed in the second section of this chapter.

The first case relates to Celsus' objection to the supposition that Christ, although a god who voluntarily incarnated in the human body, experienced pain and grief in his embodied life (*Against Celsus* 2.23–25). Origen retorts by emphasizing Christ's own willingness to experience death for the benefit of humankind, and refers to Christ's experience of pain as a proof of his mortality:

> ... once he had assumed his body by birth (τὸ διὰ γενέσεως σῶμα) he had assumed that which in its nature is capable of feeling pain (πόνων ... τῶν τοῖς σώμασι) and the grievous agonies (ἀνιαρῶν) which befall those who live in bodies, understanding the word 'grievous' as not including what is under the control of the will. Accordingly, just as he *intentionally* assumed a body whose nature was not at all different from

---

[64] Karamanolis (2014:210–211) notes the conceptual agreement between Plotinus and the early Christian thinkers such as Lactantius and Gregory of Nyssa. The medico-theological treatise *On the Nature of Man* by Nemesius of Emesa, the subject of Chapter 16 below, brings to fruition a long gestational process, beginning with Clement and Origen. For traces of medical authors in Origen, see Ramelli 2012:321–322.

[65] Young 2006:452–469, Bertrand 2005, and Karamanolis 2013:181–213.

[66] The scholarship on philosophy and religion in late antiquity has more often than not pitted Plotinus and Origen against each other. This channeled view is originally fostered by Porphyry's hostile treatment of Origen, documented in Eusebius (*Ecclesiastical History* 6.19.6) but absent from Porphyry's own description of Plotinus' circle in his biography of the master. The personal rivalry between Plotinus and Origen, in fact, is, in the eyes of ancients and moderns alike, an expression of the fundamental rift of their ideological differences. The jury is still out on this, however. For the latest assessment in favor of identifying the Origen mentioned in Porphyry's *Life of Plotinus* with the Christian Origen, see Prinzivalli 2010:284 and Chapter 14 below.

human flesh, so he assumed with the body also its pains (τὰ ἀλγεινά) and griefs (ἀνιαρά).

Origen *Against Celsus* 2.23.11–16[67]

Origen understands pain—and grief—as the telling sign of human embodiment.[68] Similarly to Plotinus, he considers physical pain a defining characteristic of the living body. To emphasize it, he draws his own parallel to a surgical operation:

> It is rather like what is said by a physician who has cut open bodies and inflicted painful wounds in order to cut out of them the things which are harmful and hinder good health; he does not leave off with the pains and the incision, but by his cure he restores the body to the health that is intended for it.

Origen *Against Celsus* 2.24.31–36[69]

Unlike Plotinus who uses medicine as a logical proof for the dispassionate knowledge the soul gains about the body, Origen uses medicine as an ethical proof for Christ's passionate knowledge about the body.[70] Although pursing opposite ideological goals, the rationale of Origen's and Plotinus' arguments follow the same line of reasoning. Plotinus uses pain to prove the heterogeneous natures of the soul and the body in the psycho-somatic compound, while Origen uses pain to prove the union of the heterogeneous—divine and human—nature of Christ.

The fact that they use the same reasoning from their separate ideological perspectives is momentous, when it comes to the study of the body in late antiquity. The living body, of Christ or us, experiences pain as a telling sign of the body withdrawing from its union with the immortal soul that has ensouled it. While in Plotinus, pain measures the weakening of the bond between the body

---

[67] *Against Celsus* 2.23.11–16: ἅπαξ ἀναλαβὼν τὸ διὰ γενέσεως σῶμα ἀνείληφεν αὐτὸ καὶ πόνων δεκτικὸν τυγχάνον καὶ τῶν τοῖς σώμασι συμβαινόντων ἀνιαρῶν, εἰ τοῦ ἀνιαροῦ μὴ ὡς προαιρετικοῦ ἀκούοιμεν. Ὥσπερ οὖν βουληθεὶς ἀνείληφε σῶμα οὐ πάντη ἄλλης φύσεως παρὰ τὴν ἀνθρωπίνην σάρκα, οὕτως συνανείληφε τῷ σώματι καὶ τὰ ἀλγεινὰ αὐτοῦ καὶ τὰ ἀνιαρά. Hereafter the translation is according to H. Chadwick 1953.

[68] The two form a pair which distinguishes between "physical pain" (*ta algeina*) and "psychological pain" (*aniara*). The former is consistent with Plotinus' use of the medically correct cognate of the word (*algêdôn*); the source of *aniara* is less certain.

[69] *Against Celsus* 2.24.31–36: ὅ τι ὅμοιόν ἐστι <τῷ> λεγομένῳ ὑπὸ ἰατροῦ, διελόντος σώματα καὶ τραύματα χαλεπὰ ποιήσαντος ἐπὶ τῷ ἐξελεῖν αὐτῶν τὰ βλάπτοντα καὶ ἐμποδίζοντα τῇ ὑγιείᾳ, καὶ οὐ καταλήξαντος εἰς τοὺς πόνους καὶ τὴν διαίρεσιν ἀλλ' ἀποκαθιστῶντος τῇ θεραπείᾳ τὸ σῶμα ἐπὶ τὴν προκειμένην αὐτῷ ὑγιείαν.

[70] On the medical motifs in Early Christian authors, see Boudon-Millot and Pouderon (2005).

and the soul in the living being, in Origen, it measures the strengthening of the bond between the divine and the human nature of Christ. This is the same rationale which reaches two ideologically opposite conclusions.[71]

The second case involves Origen's apologetic treatment of Thomas' famous line "Unless I thrust my hand into the print of the nails and touch his side, I will not believe" (*Against Celsus* 2.61–62; cf. John 20:25). Thomas' incredulity as a testimony that Christ's corporeality is a matter of doubt among the believers is outside of my current scope. My attention is directed at Thomas' use of the senses of touch and sight to gather empirical data for the two natures of Christ. He touches Christ's body to gain a proof of his human nature. The consequence of this experimental act is that it provides "the telling sign" of Christ's divine nature. In Thomas' case, the body serves as a *sêma*, expressing the union between Christ's mortal and immortal nature.

To my knowledge, there is no textual evidence which addresses the question of whether Christ experiences pain from Thomas' act of touching. Origen is also silent on the issue. Considering the apologetic spirit of his exegesis, it would be surprising if he did not clarify that Christ experienced pain, if he thought that it was so indeed. His silence and the silence of the other sources suggest that the Christian theologians were at least unsure about it. Ultimately, upon his resurrection, Christ's empty tomb, understood literally, and his missing body reveal his divine nature to the senses.[72] The emptiness of the tomb provides empirical evidence, as Thomas' sense of touch, about that which cannot be seen or touched. Origen considers the tomb and the body "signs" (*sêma*) of Christ's immortality.[73] To go back to my hypothetical model in the beginning, in the case of Christ, the cage has been opened and the bird has safely left it.

For Plotinus as for Origen, Christ's tomb would be empty. But it would be empty for different conceptual reasons. For Plotinus, it would be empty, first because in internal ensoulment (*Enneads* IV 4.18.7), the soul does not descend in the body, but only its shadow[74] and second because the body is not a tomb but a beautiful house (*Enneads* II 9.18.4) and thus expressing the divine nature of the World Soul as its creator and the individual soul as its attendant. Unlike his refutation of the Gnostic disparaging view of the body, Plotinus is, however, in

---

[71] While Origen uses the above example to defend the idea of the resurrection of the body, Plotinus plainly rejects it: "the true wakening is a true getting up from the body, not with the body" (ἀπὸ σώματος, οὐ μετὰ σώματος, ἀνάστασις, *Enneads* III 6.6.71–72).

[72] Origen explains Christ's state at the time of resurrection as "transitory" (*en methoriôi*) "between the solidity of the body as it was before his passion and the condition of a soul uncovered by any body" (*Against Celsus* 2.62.8–10).

[73] For the idea that Christ resurrected in a light immortal body as opposed to a heavy mortal one, see Ramelli's discussion in Chapter 14 below.

[74] See p. 122n34 above.

conceptual agreement with Origen about the significance of the body. Despite their ideological differences, they pursue to understand the heterogeneous partnership between soul and body respectively in the psycho-somatic compound or in Christ's human nature. Both the empty tomb in Origen and the beautiful house in Plotinus define the body as "a state of soul."[75] In this, its true value lies for Platonists of all persuasions.

---

[75] Labrune 1992 and Brisson's treatment of Plato's understanding of the soul-body relation in Chapter 1 above.

7

Bodily Images
Some Difficulties in Porphyry's Psychology[1]

AARON P. JOHNSON

Abstract: Porphyry of Tyre was a central figure in conversations about the relationship of soul and body in Late Antiquity. This chapter addresses a significant problem that arises in attempting to delineate Porphyry's precise understanding of the soul-body relationship: how does the notion of soul as being "everywhere and nowhere" and having no spatial extension (as illumining bodies without contamination, in the *Sentences*) and his critique of corporeal notions of the soul fit with the notion of "ensoulment" of bodies, of souls being enveloped by *okhêmata* and picking up corporeal clumps, and the notion of limitations to free will due to the "condition" (*kataskeuê*) of bodies? Are such latter expressions declarations of ontological realities or merely metaphors for understanding an incorporeal nature? Avoiding any attempt to explain apparent inconsistencies by an alleged shift in Porphyry's thinking based on a hypothetical chronology of his fragmentary writings, the chapter offers a flexible yet coherent account of Porphyry's position. Significant weight is given to patterns of expression that align with different contexts of literary genre or rhetorical aim.

PORPHYRY OF TYRE was a central figure in conversations about the relationship of soul and body in Late Antiquity. Within the corpus of his varied writings is a rich fund of material that grapples with the nature of the soul

---

[1] The title is taken from *similitudines corporum* at Porphyry *On the Return of the Soul* fr. 290 Smith. The research and writing of this chapter were generously funded through a Lindsey Young Fellowship at the Marco Institute for Medieval and Renaissance Studies at the University of Tennessee at Knoxville and a President's Research Award from Lee University. I am particularly grateful to Heidi Johnson and Tina Shepardson for unstinting encouragement and discussion.

and its relation to bodies in a number of different ways, several of which may seem mutually contradictory. Porphyry engaged with a greater range of ancient cultural manifestations of the body's significance for the well being of the soul than Plotinus (in works such as his *Philosophy from Oracles* or *On the Inscription 'Know Thyself'*), and explored the ramifications of Plato's diverse expressions on the relationship of soul to body (whether in commentaries or polemical treatises, such as his *Against Boethus on the Soul*). He may have even provided later Christians with concepts applicable to understanding the *Incarnation of the Logos* in a human body (in the *Miscellaneous Questions*).

The following discussion seeks to highlight a significant tension in Porphyry's thought: while he presents us with a notion of soul as being "everywhere and nowhere" and having no spatial extension (as illumining bodies without contamination, in the *Sentences*)[2] and criticizes corporeal notions of the soul (in the *Against Boethus on the Soul*), he also composed other works that articulate a notion of "ensoulment" of bodies (in the *To Gaurus Concerning the Way in Which Embryos Are Animated*), of souls being enveloped by "soul-vehicles" (*okhêmata*) while picking up corporeal clumps (in the *Commentary on the Timaeus*), and the notion of limitations to free will due to the "condition" (*kataskeuê*) of bodies (in *On Free Will*).[3] Are such latter expressions declarations of ontological realities or merely metaphors for understanding an incorporeal nature? How should we account for the extent to which bodily images shape Porphyry's discussions about the soul? It would seem that there is a certain inescapability from such images in his writings.

The following discussion seeks to address this tension in Porphyry's thought by reading three salient sections of his *Sentences* in conversation with several relevant discussions in other works that might provide us with a more precise account of the relation of souls and bodies. In so doing, we may discover a complex attempt to grapple with the particular dynamics of the soul-body connection that protects the incorporeal integrity of the soul while providing a rich description of the ensoulment of bodies in ontological, ethical, and mythical terms.

1. The Soul as Incorporeal

In an influential study, Dörrie noted that the union of soul and body was a problem of unique magnitude for Neoplatonism.[4] For Stoics the union of soul and body was relatively unproblematic: since Stoic psychology posited the materiality of

---

[2] *Sentences* 27.11–13. Here and after the text of the *Sentences* is according to Brisson 2005b. cf. Porphyry *Commentary on Plato's Timaeus* fr. 61 Sodano.

[3] See A. P. Johnson 2015:186–201; also pp. 53–59 and 107 above and 149n76, 158–169, 284–289, 312–313 below.

[4] Dörrie 1959:12.

soul itself, the union was explained through their doctrine of the mixture of two material things (namely, the soul and the body). For Peripatetics also it was not a problem: since they held soul to be a form and *entelekheia*, it was easily conceived as immanent in the body. While earlier Platonists had partly resolved the problem by interpreting the relevant passages in Plato's dialogues[5] as representing the soul as a mean binding intellect to the bodily world, one of the most important innovations of Plotinus, followed by Porphyry, was the rejection of this middling notion of the soul and an emphasis instead on its transcendence.

Yet, in spite of this emphasis on the transcendence of the soul, a serious and careful investigation was given in different ways by both thinkers to the precise way in which the soul could be said to be present to the body—and, indeed, Porphyry already problematizes the characterization above when he says that the soul is "some median thing between the indivisible and the divisible being [which] surrounds bodies."[6] Porphyry may not have fallen as deeply into Platonism's problem of overemphasizing the soul's transcendence as Dörrie's account alleges.[7] A particularly pertinent discussion is found in Porphyry's *Sentences* 27–29, where both less and more is stated than in its sister passages in Plotinus (*Enneads* IV 3.20–23). Whereas the *Sentences* is often characterized as little more than a paraphrased synopsis of what Porphyry took to be the highlights of Plotinus' thought as "starting points" (*aphormai*) to a schooling in the master's philosophy, what strikes the reader about these three sections is the rather tenuous textual connection to Plotinus' treatise.[8] The question of whether soul can be in a place (introduced by Plotinus at *Enneads* IV 3.20), as well as the problems with other ways of formulating the soul's "being present in" (*parestin*) a body (*Enneads* IV 3.21) and the conclusion that the relationship must be characterized in terms of the soul's powers (*Enneads* IV 3.22–23), provided Porphyry with the opportunity to articulate the relationship of a "bodiless entity" (*to asômaton*) to body, without mentioning the soul at all in *Sentences* 27–28, and then in *Sentences* 29 to raise a particularly problematic way of speaking of the soul found in Plato.[9]

---

[5]   *Phaedo* 81b, *Phaedrus* 246d, *Republic* 617d, and the entirety of the *Timaeus*, esp. 30b and 36e. See Dörrie 1959:12n1.

[6]   *Sentences* 5. See Goulet-Cazé 2005a:1.95.

[7]   See also, Dörrie 1966:165–187.

[8]   Even after an extensive analysis of parallels between Plotinus' thought and Porphyry's *Sentences* in which he identifies a number of areas where the latter contradicted the former, Schwyzer (1974:251) concluded that although Plotinus is nowhere named in the treatise, every chapter could begin with "he said"; cf. Zambon 2002:19–20. For a highly useful enumeration of Plotinian passages parallel to each section of the *Sentences*, see D'Ancona 2005:1.198–250, with discussion at 139–197.

[9]   Not mentioned in Plotinus, though it may have been suggested to Porphyry by *Enneads* IV 3.15 and 24; cf. *Enneads* IV 4.45 and VI 4.16 (cited by Lamberz 1975:17); see also, Schwyzer 1974:247–248.

His exposition in section 27 of the *Sentences* makes the following claims. A body cannot impede an incorporeal entity "in itself" (*to kath' hauto*, 27.1–3 Brisson) from being where it wants and how it wishes. Just as that which is without mass cannot be grasped by the body and is nothing in relation to it, so that which has mass cannot be something tacked on, "an additional supplement" (*anepiprosthêton*),[10] to the incorporeal entity—it is present to the incorporeal as if it did not exist at all.[11] The incorporeal does not move in place; it is "in place, being everywhere and nowhere," because it is present through its "disposition" (*diathesis*, *Sentences* 27.11–13).[12] This already shifts the discussion to a different level than that of Plotinus' treatise. The relation of the incorporeal to the corporeal is a key motif of the *Sentences* and was the focus of its first several sections. The only incorporeal thing mentioned by Plotinus, on the other hand, was place.[13] In contrast, Porphyry asserts that place "subsists together with mass" and thus one is precluded from speaking of an incorporeal entity going anywhere in terms of "place" (*topikôs*, *Sentences* 27.5–7). The first declaration of the *Sentences* had claimed that, "All body is in place, but none of the incorporeals 'in themselves' (*kath' hauta*) is such as to be in place" (*Sentences* 1).[14] Incorporeals in themselves cannot be "place" or "in place" because they are "greater than all place," and thus are everywhere, though not in terms of divisions or parts (*Sentences* 2).

By speaking more generally of incorporeals, rather than souls as such, Porphyry is able to alleviate confusion about the relationship of souls to bodies in a much more definite way than if he had maintained his investigation at the specific level of souls. The ontological category of incorporeals (more strictly speaking, of transcendent incorporeals[15]) set limitations on what could properly be said of a soul.[16] While it could be described as being "in relation" or "in

---

[10] *Sentences* 27.5. This seems to be the first occurrence of this compound in Greek (it is listed among the neologisms of the *Sentences* by Schwyzer 1974:251). It no doubt derives ultimately from the *locus classicus* at *Republic* 611d7–612a5, mediated through *Enneads* I 1.12.9–22, where the body is like "encrustations" (*ta prostethenta*) on the sea god Glaucus.

[11] See Goulet-Cazé 2005a:1.90.

[12] On the different significations of being "everywhere and nowhere" relative to different ontological levels, see *Sentences* 31. For discussion, see Goulet-Cazé 2005a:1.101–102. The term *diathesis* here seems to carry the same semantic weight as *skhesis* in related statements (see *Sentences* 3, *Commentary on the Timaeus* fr. 10.9–10, *Miscellaneous Questions* fr. 261.43 Smith) and possibly even *epistrophê* (see *Sentences* 7); cf. Goulet-Cazé 2005b:2.583. The degree to which any of these terms might be equivalent to Plotinus' *hexis* deserves further investigation (e.g., *Enneads* VI 1.6–7); see *Miscellaneous Questions* 88 Dörrie.

[13] *Enneads* IV 3.20.19.

[14] Cf. *To Gaurus on How Embryos are Ensouled* 13.7.

[15] See *Sentences* 42 on the distinction between proper and improper (or immanent and transcendent) incorporeals, with the illuminating discussion in Chiaradonna 2007:35–49.

[16] Cf. *Enneads* I 6.6.13–14.

disposition" to bodies, in itself it was everywhere and nowhere.[17] This distinction between soul in itself and soul in relation to bodies is central to Porphyry's psychology.[18] In a lengthy fragment of his *On the Powers of the Soul*, Porphyry utilizes the distinction to provide a charitable means of embracing a broad range of theories on the parts of the soul within a Middle Platonist and Neoplatonist psychology—or rather, to ameliorate the problem within Platonism itself of speaking of parts of an otherwise indivisible soul.[19] The soul "in itself" was indeed indivisible, while "in relation" to bodies it could be said to be divided into parts. Throughout the fragment Porphyry seems to waffle on the issue by using the language of parts but offering the repeated reminder that ontologically the soul always maintained its integrity and, strictly speaking, was indivisible.[20]

This fragment from *On the Powers of the Soul* seems to elucidate well Porphyry's position in *Sentences* 27, and together they provide a context for understanding a fragment from another understudied treatise. In Fragment 244 of his *Against Boethus on the Soul*, Porphyry refers to the soul's embodied state as "being supplemented and impeded by the destructive formation lying before it" (fr. 244.12–13). Such a formulation seems to contradict the *Sentences*' assertion that an incorporeal could not be impeded by a body or receive it as an "additional supplement." Because the fragments of the *Against Boethus on the Soul* contain a number of features that are somewhat opaque and some fragments have been deemed sufficiently problematic to doubt their attribution to Porphyry,[21] we may be tempted to withhold judgment on the tension seen here. Yet, a solution arises from the fact that the language of the fragment appears to be a tissue of allusions to Platonic models. While much of the immediate context is dominated by language redolent of the *Phaedo* (especially 80a10–b5), there seems to be an echo of the *Republic* that had prompted Porphyry's articulation of the soul-body relation in this fragment. The clause describing the soul as impeded and supplemented by a body is introduced by a concessive "although" (*kaiper*), which is the successor to an earlier concession that the soul was "buried" in the mortal body. Together with the subsequent simile of gold surrounded by mud, these lines recall the assertion in the *Republic* that the eyes of the soul had been "buried in barbaric mud" when it had fallen into a body.[22] The fragment thus appears to posit that even with the adoption of Platonic similes the soul's

---

[17] Cf. *Enneads* I 1.11.11.
[18] See Dörrie 1966:165–187.
[19] *On the Powers of the Soul* fr. 253 Smith. See Goulet-Cazé 2005a:1.94–95.
[20] *On the Powers of the Soul* fr. 253.77–87, 107–122.
[21] See variously, Gottschalk 1986:243–257; Karamanolis 2007:91–109.
[22] *Republic* 533d1–2; for an echo of the Platonic passage just after this one elsewhere in Porphyry, see A. P. Johnson 2012:67–68.

divinity would be manifest, not that the Platonic language provides a precise ontological articulation of the body's relationship to a soul.

To turn to *Sentences* 28: even if one were to say that the incorporeal could be "held down in a body," it would not be locked up like an animal in a cage[23] or like liquid or wind in a wineskin (*Sentences* 28.1–4).[24] Instead, the incorporeal sends down powers[25] that "incline[26] towards the external away from unity with it; descending through these, [the incorporeal] is interwoven with the body" (*Sentences* 28.4–6).[27] The notion that it is the powers that are "in" bodies again recalls the discussion in *On the Powers of the Soul*. The soul may remain integrally indivisible and incorporeal in itself, while it may be in relation to bodies or in bodies by means of powers that are active in the parts of the body and thereby allows one to speak of "parts" of the soul.[28]

The vivid interpretive essay, *On the Cave of the Nymphs*, provides confirmation of Porphyry's concern to emphasize the role of powers in mediating the soul's relation to body and thereby maintaining the soul's separation from body. "Souls," he writes (in a manner conceding a broad range of views, in particular the Stoics' whom he had just mentioned), "whether corporeal or incorporeal yet dragging along a body, and especially those about to be bound down to blood and moist bodies, necessarily "incline" (*rhepein*) toward moisture and are associated

---

[23] I have been unable to find this particular metaphor in a philosophical context before this occurrence in Porphyry; it is certainly not Plotinian, as noted by Schwyzer 1974:243 (who notes the parallel usage at Porphyry *To Gaurus or How Embryos are Ensouled* 14.4 and 54.23); cf. Goulet-Cazé 2005c:2.587. On Augustine's use of it, see p. 312 below.

[24] The reference to wind in a wineskin may be an allusion to the bag of winds given by Aeolus to Odysseus at *Odyssey* 10.19–22; cf. Iamblichus *On the Soul* in Stobaeus *Eclogues* 1.49.43 = p. 384.12–14 Wachsmuth, cited by Goulet-Cazé 2005c:2.587. The use of the wineskin metaphor is paralleled in the material at Nemesius *On the Nature of Man* 41.9–10 Morani. For its ascription to Porphyry, see von Arnim 1887:276–285; *Miscellaneous Questions* Dörrie; Goulet-Cazé 2005c:2.587 and 573–578 *passim*. Smith, prints it as fr. 261 (the metaphor is at 261.29–31). Vigorous resistance to attributing this material to Porphyry has been raised by Rist 1988:402–415. Pending a closer study, I must admit that I find the Nemesian material often resonant of Porphyry's language and thought; my most serious reservation is due to the fact that I cannot find Porphyry anywhere speaking of soul's "union" (*henôsis*) with body (see the passages enumerated in the index of Brisson 2005b for *henizesthai*, *henôsis*, etc., where such language designates the oneness or unification of a body or of soul with its principal, never with what it informs or ensouls). At the same time, *henôsis* is precisely the terminology Nemesius needs to build up to his Christological claims at the end of the chapter. On the soul-body relation in Nemesius, see Chapter 16 below.

[25] See Goulet-Cazé 2005a:1.102–103 and 2005c:2.587–588. On Porphyry's positive reception of Longinus in this regard, see Männlein-Robert 2001:620–623.

[26] See Goulet-Cazé 2005b:2.577–578 and 2005c:588.

[27] See A. Smith 1974:1–5. All translations are my own, unless otherwise noted.

[28] *On the Powers of the Soul* fr. 253; see Goulet-Cazé 2005b:2.575–576. A comprehensive account of Porphyry's doctrine of powers has yet to be made; see, however, the important discussions of A. Smith 1996:63–77; Viltanioti 2017.

with "body" (*sômatousthai*)[29] by having become dampened" (*On the Cave of the Nymphs* 11.64.9–13 Nauck). The cave, which was the abode of sea nymphs in Homer's poetry, signified the material world and was "proper to the nymphs presiding over water," namely, "those with 'individual powers' (*merikôterais dunamesi*)."[30] Earlier, he had asserted that "we claim that the nymphs are Naiads (i.e., sea nymphs) and in particular the powers presiding over the water, but others say that they are also the souls descending into generation altogether in general" (*On the Cave of the Nymphs* 10.63.7–10).[31] The treatise is recognized as allowing for multiple positions and interpretations to remain in play. So, later, the poet's description of the cave can be said to convey "different symbols, some referring to souls, others referring to the watery powers" (*On the Cave of the Nymphs* 13.65.16–18). Though Porphyry's essay offered a complex layering of interpretive levels, the water always carried a negative valuation as a site of ontological instability and flux. Furthermore, it seems clear that the treatise maintained a notion of powers that ever reside with bodies and seem to function as a buffer between the souls inclining toward bodies and the watery bodies themselves.[32]

The discussions of *On the Cave of the Nymphs*, *On the Powers of the Soul*, and *Sentences* 28 thus provide complementary pictures of the soul that simultaneously protect its status as an incorporeal and account for its work in bodies. Of course, the concern in the *Sentences* passage is primarily on the former issue, as is manifested in his remarks about the nature of the departure of soul from body, to which we must now turn.

One cannot say that the body, once it dies, releases the incorporeal; on the contrary the incorporeal releases itself when "it has turned to itself, away from the passionate 'attachment' (προσπάθεια) [to the body]" (*Sentences* 28.8–10).[33] Though here it is presented only in the general terms of an incorporeal entity's turning away from body, the mechanisms of the soul's separation from body mark a special point of concern for Porphyry in a number of his works. Already in an earlier section of the *Sentences*, the philosopher states in a line that appears programmatic: "Soul is bound to body in its turning toward external passions

---

[29] Cf. *Enneads* I 6.5.57.

[30] *On the Cave of the Nymphs* 12.65.11–12, 14.

[31] Porphyry then cites Numenius' allusion to Genesis 1:2.

[32] This seems to be the inference to be drawn from his reference to "soul-guiding powers" (*hai psukhopompoi dunameis*) when introducing a line of Empedocles (*On the Cave of the Nymphs* 8.61.19–20).

[33] See Schwyzer 1974:248. In translating *prospatheia* as "passionate attachment," I follow O'Brien Wicker's (1987) translation of an important parallel passage at Porphyry *Letter to Marcella* 32.496; see also *Sentences* 29.10 and 12, 32.107; *On Abstinence from Killing Animals* 1.30.4 =108.12 Nauck, 1.31.5 =110.2 Nauck. Festugière (cited by Goulet-Cazé 2005c:2.589–590) does not emphasize this negative valence.

and it is released again by an absence of 'passion' (*apatheia*)" (*Sentences* 7).[34] That the soul is both its own binder and looser in relation to bodies is made quite explicit in the next section of the work, where we are told that the "soul releases itself from body" (*Sentences* 8).[35] If the body's release from the soul is one kind of death, this releasing of the body by the soul is a second kind of death that belongs to philosophers and presumably can be performed in the course of a human life.[36] The report of the *Life of Plotinus* that the master achieved union with the One is well-known and is surely the sort of release from a body that is spoken of here in the *Sentences*.[37]

In a probably earlier work, *On Abstinence from Killing Animals*, Porphyry elaborated the manner of release. It involves a twofold process—or "two exercises" (*duo meletai*)—of putting off the things that stimulate sense perception and the imagination, which means in this work primarily the avoidance of meat, and then of recollecting the things of the intellect.[38] Put another way:

> The first will involve things that are plain to see, the second things that are less apparent. For instance, not eating [meat], or not taking bribes, is obvious and public, but not even wanting to is less apparent. So we should become detached from doing things, and then from the attraction (προσπάθεια) to do them and from passion. For what is the use of detaching oneself from actions, but being riveted to the causes of the actions?
>
> Porphyry *On Abstinence from Killing Animals* 1.31.4–5[39]

Removing the causes of attachment to corporeal life can be designated as the "forgetting and death" of these causes.[40] Thus, the second sort of death in the *Sentences*' "two-fold death" is the removal of the soul's desire for bodies and for the things encountered through bodies. It involves a simultaneous recollection of the intelligibles in the soul's true "homeland," which it had forgotten

---

[34] On the non-Plotinian elements in this claim, see Schwyzer 1974; D'Ancona 2005:1.203.

[35] On the compatibility of Porphyry's claim here with Plotinus' thought, see variously Schwyzer 1974:246, Kühn 2005:2.396–397, and D'Ancona 2005:204. On *Sentences* 8, see also pp. 314–315 below.

[36] *Sentences* 9; Brisson 2005b:2.397 notes that this is the only occurrence of the term "philosopher" in the *Sentences*; cf. *Phaedo* 64–67.

[37] *Life of Plotinus* 23.12–14. Dörrie 1966:184 makes the intriguing suggestion (which I do not find entirely persuasive) that Porphyry relates Plotinus' four experiences of unification in contrast to his own single experience in order to highlight the distance of his own psychological conceptions from those of the master.

[38] *On Abstinence* 1.30.4–5.

[39] The translation is according to Gillian H. Clark 2000.

[40] *On Abstinence* 1.32.1: λήθης αὐτῶν καὶ θανάτου.

while in its bodily sojourn (*On Abstinence* 1.30.3), and a forgetting of the corporeal things towards which one's soul had initially turned or inclined. Indeed, as he would remark in his letter to Marcella, the philosopher was the one who sought "to remember the return home from their foreign travel here" (*Letter to Marcella* 6, cf. 8).

Two points deserve further consideration: the approach to the divine and the role of memory. The former recalls another passage later in *On Abstinence*; the latter will lead us to material from his treatise *On the Styx*. Both treatises should prove illuminating for our inquiry into the soul and body in the *Sentences*.

2. Psychology and Ritual

As with nearly all philosophers of Late Antiquity, Porphyry's thought is marked by a recurrent concern to delineate the proper approach to the divine. The emphasis on separating oneself from one's body articulated in book one of *On Abstinence from Killing Animals* would raise issues for how one might properly conceive of that approach. Significantly, there were crucial ramifications of the turning back toward intelligibles in the area of religious performance, in particular sacrifice. In the second book of his defense of vegetarianism, Porphyry expounds a hierarchy of sacrificial procedures deemed appropriate for each of the levels of a Platonic ontological–theological hierarchy. Traditional animal sacrifices were directed towards wicked daemons (even if the performers of such sacrifices did not recognize this fact); vegetal sacrifices were directed to the heavenly gods; hymns and prayers were directed to the intelligible gods; and finally thoughts of the intellect were directed to the "god who rules over all" (whether this be understood as the divine Mind or the One who was beyond being).[41] Entities that were more highly incorporeal or more removed from the world of bodies deserved sacrificial offerings of greater incorporeality. The understanding of a soul's relation to bodies as formulated in the *Sentences* was not a mere academic exercise, but had social, religious, and moral implications, as drawn out in *On Abstinence*, since a rejection of the traditional animal sacrifices of Greek and Roman political communities was prescribed by such a psychology.

In spite of recent suggestions that Porphyry was possessed of a broader concern to protect or legitimize popular forms of religion for the non-philosopher,[42] a delineation of the soul's relation to the body in such a way as to carry a moral obligation to turn away from the embodied world (as we see formulated in the *Sentences* and applied in *On Abstinence*) could not allow for

---

[41]   *On Abstinence* 2.34–36 (cf. 37–40); for discussion, see variously Tanaseanu-Döbler 2009:113–116, A. P. Johnson 2013:84–85, 123–126, and Proctor 2014:416–449.

[42]   Simmons 2009:169–192, Addey 2014b:152–157, TeSelle 1974:131–133; earlier, see Bidez 1913:91–95.

such a democratizing move. Even in a work that was accused by Augustine of exhibiting Porphyry's lack of courage in explicitly stating his rejection of traditional religion, we find the philosopher marking out a distance between what he considered to be philosophically acceptable forms of piety and corporeal ritual of any kind, popular or unpopular. His treatise *On the Return of the Soul*, which survives in only the polemical paraphrase of Augustine, declares emphatically: "We must flee from all body."[43] Even theurgic procedures, which purported to offer humans a powerful connectedness with higher divinities, were averred in several fragments of this treatise to fail in profound ways.[44] Such ritual work could not aid the rational soul in return to the incorporeal realm at best,[45] and might even bring harm to the human performer of the ritual at worst.[46] Because of the incapacity of material ritual to effect salvation of the soul Porphyry declared in a passage, quoted with smug satisfaction by his fifth century Christian opponent, that he had been unable to discover a ritual means of salvation for all people, philosophers and non-philosophers alike, namely, a *via universalis*.[47]

Virtue was a surer means of salvation than embodied ritual, for it could purify the "spiritual soul" (i.e. the part below the intellect; we shall have occasion to consider this below in the examination of memory).[48] But, even virtue, if we may invoke an oft-studied section of the *Sentences* here, must be understood in terms of a hierarchy similar to the sacrificial hierarchy expressed in *On Abstinence*.[49] In an extension of Plotinus' own development of Plato's representation of the four virtues in the *Republic* and the *Phaedo*,[50] ever higher grades of virtue were to be cultivated as the soul purified itself of corporeal taint and practiced releasing itself from the body. The "civil virtues" (*politikai aretai*) promoted moderation of "passion" (*metriopatheia*)[51] and released the soul from one kind of evil, the excess in passions.[52] The "purifying virtues" (*kathartikai aretai*) promoted a "'withdrawal' (*apostasis*) from the things here" for the person advancing towards contemplation and were displayed "in abstinence from the activities of the body and fellow-feeling toward it" (*Sentences* 32.15–18). The

---

43 *On the Return of the Soul* frr. 297.21–22, 297a–d, 300a, 301; cf. *Letter to Marcella* 10.175–176.
44 See P. Hadot 1995: 211, *passim*; Tanaseanu-Döbler 2009:139–143.
45 *On the Return of the Soul* frr. 288, 288a, 290, 290b, 292, 293a.
46 *On the Return of the Soul* frr. 289, 289a, 294.
47 *On the Return of the Soul* fr. 302. In spite of a recent argument that Porphyry made it his primary goal to develop a universal soteriology, open for all classes and backgrounds of people, there is little evidence to support such a view.
48 *On the Return of the Soul* fr. 291.
49 *Sentences* 32; for discussion, see Brisson 2006:89–105 and 2005b:1.131–136; Brisson and Flamand 2005:2.628–642; D. O'Meara 2003:40–49; A. P. Johnson 2013:292–296.
50 See Schwyzer 1974:224–228.
51 *Sentences* 32.6, 30; on the introduction of this non-Plotinian word, see Schwyzer 1974:225.
52 *Sentences* 32.45–47.

contemplative virtues—or literally, "those belonging to the soul acting intellectually" (νοερῶς τῆς ψυχῆς ἐνεργούσης, *Sentences* 32.55–57)—have as object the performance of intellectual activity and of not even having in mind the withdrawal from passions.[53] Finally, the "paradigmatic virtues" (*paradeigmatikai aretai*) are in the intellect and provide models for the lower virtues of the soul, which are their likenesses.[54] Since purification is possible in this life, Porphyry commends the pursuit of the purifying virtues to the reader: "For this is the withdrawal from the body and from the irrational movement of passion ... The foundation and support of this purification is to know oneself, that one is a soul bound together with a 'foreign object of another substance'" (ἐν ἀλλοτρίῳ πράγματι καὶ ἑτεροουσίῳ, *Sentences* 32.95–103).

More could be said about this important section of the *Sentences*, but it is sufficient here to note the emphatic denial of the body and its desires and the fundamental role played by an ascending series of virtues at levels of progressively greater incorporeality, from control of bodily passions to complete withdrawal from those passions, and then to the absence of even noticing them.[55] The assumptions about the morally problematic space of embodied experience for a soul with the consequent prescription to eschew bodily concerns and desires in an ascent or a turning back towards the intelligible realm is equally expressed in the fragments of *On the Return of the Soul*. This common moral-ontological framework is evident in spite of the fact that we entirely lack verbatim quotations of the latter work and must attempt to catch sight of its original tenor and purpose(s) through the dark glass of Augustine's rhetorical maneuvers.[56] We can state that the treatise *On the Return of the Soul* denied that theurgic ritual provided anyone with salvation[57] but instead presented it with bodily images (frr. 290 and 290a); that true purification of the soul came not through ritual but through virtue (in particular, continence) and through the paternal intellect (fr. 291), or first principles (fr. 284); and that perfection in wisdom may only come after separation from the body (fr. 297).[58]

---

[53] *Sentences* 32.87–89.

[54] *Sentences* 32.63–65.

[55] See Dörrie 1966:185 on the importance in Porphyry's psychology of continual progress in turning back towards unity.

[56] On Augustine's rhetorical maneuvers, see Gillian H. Clark 2007:127–140 and 2011:395–406. On the soul-body relation in Augustine, see Chapter 15 below.

[57] *On the Return of the Soul* frr. 288 and 288a. Attempts to find Porphyry here developing differing grades of salvation for different categories of people employ an overly wide notion of "salvation" that Porphyry probably would have denied. It is doubtful that he would have considered a soul's remaining within the physical world, even if among the stars, to be properly named salvation. See A. P. Johnson 2013:141–144.

[58] This is a point consonant with the *Sentences*' remark that at least the political and purificatory virtues were available to those in this life, which implies that the intellectual grade of virtues

We may usefully round out our discussion of the implications of Porphyry's understanding of the soul-body relationship to ritual practice by briefly recognizing a rich passage from his *Letter to Marcella*, which is frequently assigned (on thin evidence) to a date late in the philosopher's life.[59] Elaborating an allusion to Plato's recommended aim of "likeness to God,"[60] he tells his wife that she will honor God best if she likens her "thinking" (*dianoia*) to God, but that this likeness is through virtue alone. "For virtue alone draws the soul upward and toward what is kindred" (*Letter to Marcella* 16.267–268). In words that recall the sacrificial hierarchy of *On Abstinence*, Porphyry continues: "A wise man in his silence honors god, but the foolish man, even when he is praying and offering sacrifice, defiles the divine" (*Letter to Marcella* 16.279–280). It is "by likeness in his own 'disposition' (*diathesis*)" that the wise man pleases God and becomes God (*Letter to Marcella* 17.286–287). This notion, which often receives the label of spiritual or intellectual sacrifice, receives exquisite expression at the climax of his discussion of piety: "This is the supreme fruit of piety: to honor the divine in the ways of 'our forefathers' (τὰ πάτρια), not as though he needs it but as though he invites us towards reverence out of the venerable seriousness of his blessedness" (*Letter to Marcella* 18.294–293). The ways of the forefathers here refers to the ancient simplicity and restraint of an earlier era of holy philosophers.[61] Later in the letter, Porphyry reminds us of the direct connection between rejection of corporeal matters and piety, declaring: "The more [the wise person] holds aloof from passionate 'attachment' (προσπάθεια) to the body, the more he draws near to the divine" (*Letter to Marcella* 32.496–497).

3. Psychology, Memory, and Corporeality

In addition to the consequences of Porphyry's psychology for religious matters, the area of memory became a particularly important conceptual space to work out the soul-body relation.[62] As already noted, *On Abstinence* had observed that the recollection of intelligibles (which was required because of the previous forgetting of such realities in the embodied state) entailed a forgetting of corporeal things, even while in a body.[63] The *Letter to Marcella* would reiterate the importance of memory in the soul's turning from body.

---

might be accessible only after death.
[59] See A. P. Johnson 2013:20–21.
[60] *Theaetetus* 176b1–2.
[61] See Gillian H. Clark 2007:140; see also, Tanaseanu-Döbler 2009:117–119 and Alt 1996:205–206.
[62] Memory was likewise important in Plotinus' psychology; see variously Blumenthal 1971:80–99; Mortley 2013:14–39.
[63] *On Abstinence* 1.30.4–5.

You could gather together and unite the concepts implanted within you by attempting to distinguish those which are confused (συγκεχυμένας) and drawing into the light those which are shadowy ... Furthermore, if you would remember, you would distinguish what you have heard, recounting it in your memory and deeming it right to hold to such counsels from words as were good and for the rest exercising through deeds what you have learned, and through hard work (τοῦ πονεῖν) itself keeping it safe.

Porphyry Letter to Marcella 10.183–190

These remarks evince a positive valuation of memory, even when what is remembered are merely the verbal refractions of intelligibles in a previous conversation.

A much richer conception of memory comes to us in the fascinating fragments of Porphyry's exegesis of underworld depictions in the Homeric poems in his treatise *On the Styx*.[64] The account of memory in two fragments in particular is arresting. Homer, Porphyry informs us, supposed that there were three places for souls: in the inhabited world on the "earth" (*epigeios*) where humans and animals live; in the Elysian Plain where the souls of the blessed went; and in Hades.[65] Souls remained embodied in the first two places, but Hades "belonged to souls who had been released from this body" (*On the Styx* fr. 377.24–26). The geography of Hades was sharply divided by the River Acheron beyond which only the souls of the properly buried could proceed. Ironically, those who had not received burial (i.e. a memorial) nonetheless "have a share of the memory of those who lived with them" (*On the Styx* fr. 377.32–33). Unjust souls received their punishments on this side of the river,

> ... through their thoughts and memory of those who lived. For they receive appearances (φαντασίας) of as many terrifying things as they have done in life and are punished, the sin being present to them in their thinking and punishing them through the punishments which are assigned for their sins. For this reason some souls seem to carry stones and be punished by being squeezed, while others receive appearances of thirst and eternal hunger, and others [are punished] by some other thing that made them shudder in their mortal life.

Porphyry On the Styx fr. 377.35–45

---

[64] For introduction and commentary, see Castelletti 2006; see also, A. P. Johnson 2013:31–37.

[65] Porphyry *On the Styx* fr. 377.9–26 Smith; the translations used here are (sometimes significantly) revised from the preliminary translations in A. P. Johnson 2013:333–338.

On the other hand, those who were allowed to enter Hades (those who had received a proper burial and who were not judged to need punishment for sins in this life) "are forgotten and have ceased from thoughts about human things" (*On the Styx* fr. 377.33–35). In Odysseus' visit to the Underworld, the shades of the dead only remembered Odysseus when they had drunk the blood of the sacrifice. This point allowed Porphyry a moment to consider the biological relationship between one's own blood and thinking. Drawing on lines of Empedocles that claimed that "blood is thought,"[66] Porphyry notes that blood is "like a tool for understanding" (*On the Styx* fr. 377.73–74). It seems significant that he avoids Empedocles' term *noêma*, most likely because of its more recent (Neo-)Platonic valences that posited a higher hypostatic place for it within *Nous*, and instead employs a range of terms for thinking, especially λογισμὸν τῶν ἀνθρωπίνων (but also, *gnôrisis*, *sunesis*, and *phronêsis*). While those on this side of the Acheron do not need to drink blood to "think human things" (τὰ ἀνθρώπινα ... φρονοῦσι), of those properly within Hades only Tiresias retained human thought. The other souls have a different form of thought, "a particular 'way of thinking' (ἰδιότητα φρονήσεως), which they have obtained in Hades," and thereby are able to recognize each other. It is unclear if this latter assertion is merely an attempt to explain how the souls of Agamemnon, Ajax, and the others are able to recognize each other in the account of the *Odyssey*, or if it is a serious epistemological claim about postmortem individual thought.

For our purposes, what is abundantly clear is Porphyry's attempt to highlight, through Homeric exegesis, the comforting absence of memory on the part of the departed souls and the sharp presence of memory for punishment of souls who cannot yet fully depart. Bodily memories are a source of punishment and a soul cannot be happy while retaining them. Forgetting is bliss. But how does remembering or forgetting take place for a soul that has been released from the body? What are the ontological mechanisms of memory? How can a φαντασία from a soul's time in a body continue to haunt it after death? Porphyry has already mentioned the continuation of human reasonings, the possession of "thoughts about human things." The dead Patroclus' ghostly appearance to Achilles in the twenty-third book of the *Iliad* provided the philosopher with a descriptive and verbal fund to draw on. First, souls were named the "'images' (*eidôla*) of the weary."[67] But, second, Porphyry shifts the *eidôlon* to designate something carried by the soul, not the soul itself: "The unburied spend time

---

[66] Fr. 105, quoted at *On the Styx* fr. 377.77.

[67] *Iliad* 23.72; admittedly this line is omitted from the original text of fr. 377, which only has line 73 (at fr. 377.124). It is inserted in the text of Stobaeus (our source for all the fragments of *On the Styx*) by Heeren, cited by A. Smith 1993:456. The line is included in fr. 378.8.

outside of the river, bearing an 'image' (*eidôlon*) of their body and their body's clothes" (*On the Styx* fr. 377.109–111).[68]

The next fragment from *On the Styx* gives more attention to the intersection of memory and appearance in a soul's experiences after death. After citing Patroclus' appearance to Achilles, looking the same as himself when alive in stature, eyes, and clothing, the philosopher notes the close association of memory to bodily features of recognition.

> Together with the memory, tokens of familiar bodily things have also been laid out with them; it is also clear that it shows the bodily features by means of appearance (φαντασία). For the appearance [occurs] through memory, as Plato says in the *Philebus*;[69] when memory is taken away, the thing imagined (φαντασιούμενον) is also taken, and when it joins in leaving, the soul's bodily experiences (πάθη) are also taken away. When they have left these behind, the soul's punishment also has ceased, since there is around it only an intellectual condition and it passes its time with the wise god.

> Porphyry *On the Styx* fr. 377.9–18 Smith

One should note that the term *phantasia* occurs in Homer not at all and in Plato not in the *Philebus* (where *aisthêseis* is used instead).[70] Porphyry has thus wedded Plato's conception of memory as the inscribing of perceptions on the soul (with his own late Platonic metaphysical lessening of these perceptions' ontological status through the language of *phantasia*[71]) with Homer's vivid description of the ability of the living to recognize the shade of the dead. Oddly it is the souls' forgetting of bodily things that seems to grant them the status of "shades" to the living. References in both the *Iliad* and *Odyssey* to the shades of the dead prompt Porphyry to offer the (somewhat confusing) line of interpretation that, on the one hand, "shades flit about beside them [the souls in Hades]" of things that they no longer remember; on the other hand, in relation to corporeal things, they are shades "because of their being incorporeal and lacking memory, so that perhaps the soul is like smoke in comparison to

---

[68] Cf. the Plotinian use of *eidôlon*, with Schwyzer 1974:243; Pépin 2005:2.592 and passim.

[69] *Philebus* 39a. Alternatively, Porphyry will elsewhere assert that children have better memories because their faculty of 'imagination' (*to phantastikon*) is more easily impressed; see *Commentary on the Timaeus* fr. 25.

[70] One may consult Cunliffe 1963. In the *Philebus* passage, Socrates does say that "they seem to me" (*phainontai moi*), which, while cognate to *phantasia* can scarcely be Porphyry's stimulus to cite the *Philebus* passage; instead, it is Socrates' connecting of memory and perceptions, which "'fall together' (*sumpiptousa*) at the same time" (*Philebus* 39a1–2).

[71] See Sheppard 2007:71–76.

the thickness of the body" (*On the Styx* fr. 378.22–26). Anticleia did not recognize or remember her son, Odysseus, until she drank from the blood of bodily remembrance. Heracles is the other Homeric hero who comes to mind in this context.[72] Odysseus meets his *eidôlon* in the Underworld and Plotinus does not miss the opportunity to address the relation between his shade and his "real self" above.[73] Also, Socrates' account of the posthumous fate of the soul at the end of the *Gorgias* comes to mind where the soul is said to be naked and bearing the scars of its embodied life on itself so that the judges can base their judgment on them.

So far, this discussion only hints at the mechanisms of forgetting (while being much clearer about those of remembering). It is the lines about Anticleia that prompt a signal observation: "Homer," Porphyry states,

> considers the blood capable of drawing the imagining and remembering soul (φανταστικῆς καὶ μνημονικῆς ψυχῆς), whose reasoning (λογισμός) also is a gatherer of memory through appearances (φαντασιῶν), when [the soul] summarily categorizes [them] into universal (καθόλου) judgments. But the reasoning [part] (τὸ διανοητικόν), towards which <the> soul being inside the Acheron runs, is different.

Porphyry On the Styx fr. 378.35–40 Smith

Though Porphyry does not make this point explicitly, probably the best way to understand the earlier references to the soul as (bearing) an *eidôlon* is to take them in the light of this claim about the "imagining and remembering soul."

Ultimately though, the statement here, as well as most of this fragment, raises more questions than it answers and leaves one with a somewhat opaque understanding of the soul. We must return (as promised earlier) to the *Sentences* for help in determining the assumptions at play in his Homeric exegesis. *Sentences* 29 directly addresses itself to what is meant when one states that the soul is "in Hades"—that is, when it presides over a shade that is limited by place and resides in the realm of becoming.[74] Although he is probably not thinking (primarily) about the poetic representations of the souls of the dead but rather of Plato's discussion in the *Phaedo*, this section of the *Sentences* is, I believe, quite resonant of many claims made in his *On the Styx*. At the outset, some tension between the two texts can be alleviated if we take the *Sentences'* considerations of being "in Hades" to designate only that area referred to in *On the Styx* as "outside of the Acheron" (where souls experienced punishments

---

[72] See Slaveva-Griffin 2018.
[73] *Enneads* I 1.12.31–35.
[74] On this section, see generally Pépin 2005:2.590–606.

through appearances)—that is, on this side of the dividing river and not in the inner parts of Hades.[75]

Porphyry's account of the soul "in Hades" continues his discussion of the relation of soul to bodies in terms of place in sections 27–28 of the *Sentences* already considered above. He reiterates his claim that the soul is not properly speaking in a place. "It is for the soul to be in Hades when it presides over an 'image' (*eidôlon*) that possesses a nature of being in place, but has obtained its 'subsistence' (*hupostasis*) in darkness" (*Sentences* 29.3–5). It is through this image that a soul can be said to be "in Hades," and thus at the same time is "not drawn away from its existence" (*Sentences* 29.6–7). Furthermore, the same "spirit" (*to pneuma*), which the soul gathered together from the spheres on its descent into the corporeal world, "attends on it when it departs from the body" (*Sentences* 29.8–9).[76] The difficulty in fully escaping the body, of entering fully into the blissful forgetfulness of Hades described in *On the Styx*, is that, when the soul during life had a "relationship" (*skhesis*) with a particular body in accordance with its "individual rational 'principle' (*logos*)[77] projected" from its passionate "attachment" (*prospatheia*)[78] to the body, an "impression of the appearance" (τύπος τῆς φαντασίας) was "wiped off" onto the spirit that surrounded the soul. Thus, "it is said to be in Hades because its spirit obtained an 'invisible' (αἰδοῦς) and darkened nature" (*Sentences* 29.9–15).[79]

Here, we finally discover the precise means by which memory keeps bodily appearances present to the soul even after death. Even when it has left its body the corporeal *pneuma* remains attached to it, strengthened from a lifetime of "passionate attachment" to the bodily experiences. These experiences are thus able to torture the soul even after death because of the impressions left on the enshrouding *pneuma*. The implication, which arises if we recall the admonitions of *On Abstinence*, is that one ought to begin in this life to train oneself in lessening the exposure to such impressions so as to alleviate one's suffering after death. The less an embodied soul allows impressions to be wiped off on its enveloping

---

[75] I think this localization of the "in Hades" designation of the *Sentences* is important if we are not to conclude that the latter text is only speaking metaphorically of Hades as this human life in bodies (as Pépin 2005 does at 2.590–591). While there is certainly a metaphoric element, such an interpretation of this passage neglects the fact that Porphyry speaks of experiences "under earth" that occur after a person's death. Also, the assertion about a hierarchy of bodies is an ontological statement. See A. Smith 1974:79.

[76] On the un-Plotinian elements in this statement, see Schwyzer 1974. For discussion of the role of *pneuma* as a "vehicle" (*okhêma*) for the soul in Platonist thought, see Finamore 1985, Dodds 1992:313–321, Deuse 1983:218–227, Pépin 2005:2.593–596, A. P. Johnson 2013:120–121, and p. 134n3 above.

[77] On the "individual *logos*," see Pépin 2005:2.596–597.

[78] For *prospatheia* here, see Pépin 2005:2.598.

[79] Cf. *Enneads* VI 4.16.37, cited by Schwyzer 1974:248.

spirit the quicker will be its release to the felicity of forgetfulness following its departure from the body.

In a foreshadowing of his elaboration of "purifying virtues" in *Sentences* 32, Porphyry turns to a brief exposition of a corporeal hierarchy dependent upon varying levels of a soul's purification of its *pneuma*. The fitness of higher or lower types of bodies was dependent on the "sort of disposition" (*diathesis*) that the soul had practiced towards bodies in the first place. The top of the corporeal hierarchy, which was a place "closest to the immaterial," was the aethereal region; below was that of the sun (as the soul sent "a projection toward appearance" in its descent); then came the region of the moon (as the soul became enamored of [physical] "form" [*eidos*][80] "like a woman[81] and full of passion");[82] and finally was the region of (human) bodies (where a "complete ignorance of reality, darkness, and infantile nature" attended on the soul, whenever it should stop in accordance with "its shapeless form,"[83] having fallen into bodies which were composed of moist vapors, *Sentences* 29.24–31).[84]

This corporeal hierarchy corresponds somewhat unevenly to the hierarchy of virtues that Porphyry develops later in the same work since these three levels of purified embodiment map onto only the first two levels of virtue, the political and purifying.[85] What it highlights, however, is the personal ontology that provides a proper context for appreciating the levels of virtue and furnishes a metaphysical impetus for pushing beyond the political to the purifying virtues. If one does not make serious progress in purification of the soul even while in one's body, the consequences are disheartening, to say the least: Porphyry concludes his outline of the corporeal hierarchy with an account of the postmortem experiences of a soul that had inadequately practiced separation from the body.

> And still even during its departure [from the body], when a soul has its spirit muddied by the moist vapor, it casts a shadow and is weighed down, since this sort of spirit is naturally eager to go into a corner of the earth, unless some other cause attends to it in a contrary manner. Therefore, just as it is necessary for a soul having round itself an

80 See Christensen 2005:2.600–601.
81 On this reference to being womanish, see Pépin 2005:2.601; cf. *Letter to Marcella* 33, *On the Styx* fr. 377.78–80.
82 Cf. *Commentary on the Timaeus* frr. 16 and 22.
83 Alternatively, "when the form stops in accordance with [the soul's] formlessness;" for different attempts to make sense of this clause, see the translations of Brisson 2005b:1.329 and 331, and Dillon 2005:2.806–807, with remarks of Pépin 2005:2.602–603 and Dillon 2005:2.807n82.
84 On the negative significance of wetness, see *On the Cave of the Nymphs* 11.64.9–25, discussed below.
85 For an earlier development of this notion, see pp. 137–139 above.

oyster-shell of earth, so to speak, to be constrained on earth, so also it is necessary for a soul drawing a moist spirit to have round itself an image (εἴδωλον). It draws a wet [spirit] whenever it continually practices at being conversant with nature, [since] the effect of nature is to be in a moist [condition] and rather to be under-worldly.

Porphyry *Sentences* 29.32–40

This passage, so evocative of Platonic descriptions of the soul, provides us with a sense of how Porphyry may have developed his interpretation of the *eidôla* of Homer's poetry in his *On the Styx* in philosophical terms. Through its perpetual engagement with bodies, the pneumatic attendant of a soul received impressions that formed an *eidôlon*. This image marked by wetness and confusion added weight to the *pneuma*. Like wet clothing heavily hanging on a person's limbs, this sodden spirit weighed down the soul.

Much in this description resonates with the better known statements offered in his *On the Cave of the Nymphs*. There Porphyry remarks that souls descending into generation are signified by Homer's references to wetness: "The poet called them moist since blood and moist seed are dear to them" (*On the Cave of the Nymphs* 10.63.21–23). The inclusion of blood as a wet substance may be meant as a slight allusion to the attraction to blood of the souls of the dead in Odysseus' visit to the Underworld (the *Nekuia*) as expounded in his *On the Styx*, since he later asserts that the souls of the dead are "invited by the outflow of bile and blood" (*On the Cave of the Nymphs* 11.64.13–15). At this point, his exposition of Homer's deeper meanings provides a briefer yet close parallel to his account in *On the Styx*. If a soul is a "lover of bodies" (*philosômatos*),[86] it will drag its moistened *pneuma* so that it "thickens like a cloud." This *pneuma*, being thickened and moistened by "greediness" (*pleonasmôi*) becomes visible: "from such souls arise the manifestation of 'images' (εἰδώλων), because their *pneuma* has become tainted, which appear to some people through their *phantasia*" (*On the Cave of the Nymphs* 11.64.17–20).[87] "The soul," he adds, "becomes wet and rather damp in accordance with its desires for mixture [with bodies], while the soul, because of its 'inclination' (νεύσεως) toward generation, drags along a wet 'vapor' (ἀτμόν)" (*On the Cave of the Nymphs* 11.64.22–25). The vapor here seems identifiable with the visible *pneuma* mentioned in the previous sentence. Porphyry has thus developed an ontological account not only of how a soul can relate to bodies through a spiritual mediator (the *pneuma*) but also provided a legitimation of ghost sightings. Like a watery cloud or steam, the spirit has

---

[86] Cf. *Phaedo* 68c1.
[87] Souls are again said to drag a *pneuma* later at *On the Cave of the Nymphs* 25.73.11–15.

become so engrossed with things of the body, being the soul's means of activity in the material world, that its greedy attraction to bodies has rendered it visible even after the soul's separation from the body at death. In other words, the separation from a body at death was not a clean break with the corporeal; the soaked spirit had become a weight upon the otherwise incorporeal soul.

Within the broader context of Porphyry's understanding of the soul's relation to bodies through a *pneuma*, which is afforded by *On the Styx* and *On the Cave of the Nymphs*, the picture presented in *Sentences* 29 seems to be at some distance from that with which we started in *Sentences* 27 and 28. In fact, there may seem to be a rather severe tension between the incorporeality of soul and the soul as heavy and damp from its pneumatic clothing or, in an alternative image, encased in an earthen oyster-shell. The tension is resolved when we recognize (as noted above) that Porphyry was considering the soul "in itself" (i.e. as incorporeal) or the soul "in relation" (i.e. as having round itself a spirit) at different times.[88] What becomes evident in all this, however, is the great interest in formulating a robust account of the latter in a number of different contexts, whether as anagogic starting points in the *Sentences* or Homeric exegesis in *On the Styx*. Far from demythologizing the Underworld myths of Plato's dialogues or Homer's epic poetry, throughout his corpus Porphyry assures the features of these myths an ontological space within his own post-Plotinian metaphysical vision. For Plato, the soul in its relation to bodies was like Glaucus, the god of the sea, encrusted with barnacles.[89] Like Glaucus, too, Porphyry's various articulations of the soul-body relation remained encrusted with bodily images, weighed down with the heavy wetness of bodies. Porphyry's soul was not merely like a light shining without contamination on material bodies, as in Plotinus, but, like Plato's Glaucus, remained covered with pneumatic encrustations in the sea of embodied life.

4. Conclusion

The *Life of Plotinus* records an episode in which Porphyry pressed his teacher for three days on the issue of the precise relationship of the soul to the body.[90] It has been suggested that such unrelenting pressure by the student may have prompted the composition of Plotinus' treatise(s) on the difficulties pertaining

---

[88] Dörrie (1966:182–187) interprets what I see here to be a resolution of tension as instead a discrepancy motivated by Porphyry's own divided personality (his theory at odds with his experience). The discussion above of the ontological mechanisms of memory in terms of images imprinted on the soul's *pneuma* should allow a glimpse of the sort of serious theoretical elaboration Porphyry could employ in accounting for the soul "in relation," which Dörrie missed.

[89] *Republic* 611c7–612a6. See Slaveva-Griffin 2018.

[90] *Life of Plotinus* 18.

to the soul (*Enneads* IV 3–5).[91] The issue was one to which Porphyry returned, as we have seen, following various angles and with differing emphases within different rhetorical projects. While remaining firmly within a Plotinian-Platonic framework, he was possessed of vibrant exploratory inclinations in his psychological and metaphysical thought. Such inclinations allowed him to contribute to late antique psychological understanding on philosophical, literary, and religious levels, thus making a deep impact upon both the Christian and pagan intellectuals who came after him.

91 Goulet-Cazé 2005b:2.574.

8

Proclus and the Conjunction of Soul and Body

JOHN F. FINAMORE

Abstract: Plato, in the *Timaeus*, has the Demiurge generate the rational soul and then hand on the rest of the construction of the human being to the younger gods (*Timaeus* 41c–d). The gods go about their work, taking the rational soul from the Demiurge and fashioning composite human beings, joining their rational souls to the lower souls and to the body (*Timaeus* 42e–44c). This process involves borrowing amounts of the four elements to make the human body and forming them into a unity by welding the parts "with numerous rivets, invisible because of their smallness" (*Timaeus* 43a) and placing the circuits of the same and the different (that make up the rational soul) into this newly hobbled-together body. The rational soul is at birth thrown into confusion by the body but can—in time—bring the compound subject into harmony and can lead a good, moral life (*Timaeus* 44a–c).

Proclus, in his *Commentary on the Timaeus*, investigates this compound of soul and body. His discussion is complicated by the Neoplatonic proliferation of psychic entities: the vehicle housing the rational and irrational souls, along with the inclusion of the Aristotelian nutritive, perceptive, imaginative, and desiderative faculties of the soul. Nonetheless, Proclus argues that the compound of soul and body can lead with proper care to a unified human being, just as Plato would have wished (*Commentary on the Timaeus* III 320.10–356.28). This chapter examines what Proclus says about the soul-body complex in his *Commentary on the Timaeus*, with an eye to discovering if his view of the body is positive here. Proclus' discussion proceeds along with the soul's descent, and so we watch as the soul and body become progressively more corporeal. Although the commentary ends in our manuscripts before the crucial passage about the body, a fragment from the

Arabic translation (toward the end of the *Timaeus*) indicates Proclus' view. The Arabic translation complements the surviving Greek section. Proclus' theory thereby follows Plato's doctrine in the *Timaeus* of the body's positive value.

PLATO, IN THE *TIMAEUS*, has the Demiurge generate the rational soul and then hand on the rest of construction of the human being to the younger gods (*Timaeus* 41c–d). The gods go about their work, taking the rational soul from the Demiurge and fashioning composite human beings, joining their rational souls to the lower souls and to the body (*Timaeus* 42e–44c). This process involves borrowing amounts of the four elements to make the human body and forming them into a unity by welding the parts "with numerous bolts, invisible because of their smallness" (*Timaeus* 43a) and placing the circuits of the same and the different (that make up the rational soul) into this newly hobbled-together body. The rational soul is at birth thrown into confusion by the body, but can—in time—bring the compound subject into harmony and can lead a good, moral life (*Timaeus* 44a–c).

Proclus, in his *Commentary on the Timaeus*, investigates this compound of soul and body. His discussion is complicated by the Neoplatonic proliferation of psychic entities: the vehicles housing the rational and irrational souls, along with the inclusion of the Aristotelian nutritive, perceptive, imaginative, and desiderative faculties of the soul. Nonetheless, Proclus argues that the compound of soul and body can lead with proper care to a unified human being, just as Plato would have wished (*Commentary on the Timaeus* III 320.10–356.28).

In this chapter I will examine Proclus' doctrine of the soul-body relationship as it is expressed through his exegesis of Plato's *Timaeus*. Little has been written on this topic, and much of what Proclus writes in the final pages of his *Commentary on the Timaeus* that remains to us depends on his own doctrines of demiurgy and the soul. It will be necessary therefore to look at several texts in detail and use them to work out what Proclus' precise doctrine may be. Of Proclus' doctrine on the soul-body connection there is no better indicator than his understanding of how the soul came to be connected to its body and of how the soul in each of us must work together with its body to cultivate and advance our philosophical nature.

1. Plato

In the *Phaedo*, Plato discusses the soul-body relationship. It is marked by stark contrasts. After a discussion of the distinct qualities of souls and bodies (*Phaedo* 78b–80a), Plato sums up the differences in this way:

The soul is most similar to what is divine, deathless, intelligible, uniform, indestructible, and always unchanging and invariable with respect to itself, while the body is most similar to what is human, mortal, multiform, without intelligibility, destructible, and never unchanging with respect to itself.

Plato *Phaedo* 80b1–5[1]

The soul then is more akin to the invisible Forms and so it should rule the body and not *vice versa*. The body, in fact, impedes the soul in its pursuit of knowledge of the Forms. Although Plato never changes his view of the soul itself, in the *Republic* (435e1–441c3) he contrasts the soul not only with the body but also internally within the three parts of itself.

When Plato discusses the conjunction of body and soul in the *Timaeus*, he does so by means of myth. The Demiurge, having created the immortal rational soul, turns over the job of creation to the younger gods (*Timaeus* 42d2–e5). The younger gods then fashion human bodies from the four elements, "fusing them with close-packed bolts invisible because they were small" (διὰ σμικρότητα ἀοράτοις πυκνοῖς γόμφοις συντήκοντες, *Timaeus* 43a3). The gods placed the immortal soul into this body. The soul, imagined as a smaller "wave" (*kuma*, *Timaeus* 43b6) within the Circles of the Same and of the Different, was engulfed by the currents caused by the material elements, and so the newborn child moved haphazardly and only later in life did the adult come to control motion and thought (*Timaeus* 42e5–44c4). Plato does not explain how the incorporeal soul and the material body can affect each other, and the image actually seems to give corporeal substance to the human soul. Nonetheless, the soul and body are imagined as completely separate entities, and the body still has its characteristic negative effect on intellection.[2]

---

[1] *Phaedo* 80b1–5: τῷ μὲν θείῳ καὶ ἀθανάτῳ καὶ νοητῷ καὶ μονοειδεῖ καὶ ἀδιαλύτῳ καὶ ἀεὶ ὡσαύτως κατὰ ταὐτὰ ἔχοντι ἑαυτῷ ὁμοιότατον εἶναι ψυχή, τῷ δὲ ἀνθρωπίνῳ καὶ θνητῷ καὶ ἀνοήτῳ καὶ πολυειδεῖ καὶ διαλυτῷ καὶ μηδέποτε κατὰ ταὐτὰ ἔχοντι ἑαυτῷ ὁμοιότατον αὖ εἶναι σῶμα. All translations are my own.

[2] Plato never solved the problem of the soul's ability to interact with the body. Late in his life in the *Laws*, he tried to imagine how the soul of the Sun moved its body. He gave three possible ways in which the soul moved its fiery body: the soul is in the Sun's body and moves it from there (and this, Plato adds, is how our souls move our bodies), or the soul takes over a second body of fire or air and externally moves the Sun's body, or bodiless it moves it with some other astonishing powers (*Laws* 898e8–899a4: ὡς ἢ ἐνοῦσα ἐντὸς τῷ περιφερεῖ τούτῳ φαινομένῳ σώματι πάντη διακομίζει τὸ τοιοῦτον, καθάπερ ἡμᾶς ἡ παρ' ἡμῖν ψυχὴ πάντη περιφέρει· ἢ πόθεν ἔξωθεν σῶμα αὐτῇ πορισαμένη πυρὸς ἤ τινος ἀέρος, ὡς λόγος ἐστί τινων, ὠθεῖ βίᾳ σώματι σῶμα· ἢ τρίτον αὐτὴ ψιλὴ σώματος οὖσα, ἔχουσα δὲ δυνάμεις ἄλλας τινὰς ὑπερβαλλούσας θαύματι, ποδηγεῖ. Here, as in the *Timaeus*, the human soul moves its body internally, but again it is not clear how an incorporeal soul can do so. Plato seems to take for granted that it can.

2. Proclus

It was left to later Platonists to explain the conjunction of soul and body. Proclus tackles the problem in his *Commentary on the Timaeus*. Before we turn to those passages, let us look first to a fragment of Iamblichus' *Commentary on the Timaeus* that is preserved by Proclus (Iamblichus fr. 88), and which Proclus himself supports. Iamblichus wrote that one cannot conclude how the gods produce the body or the soul or how they weave them together because such explanations are beyond human comprehension.[3] Thus, precise, complete answers are impossible—and Plato knew as much.[4] Answers to some issues will be forthcoming, but we cannot expect Iamblichus or Proclus to know the secrets of the gods.

With that prelude, let us turn to Proclus' interpretation of the younger gods' formation of the body. He begins by setting the creation in context. There are, it turns out, not just the rational soul and body involved but also an irrational soul and two vehicles, an immortal and a mortal one. The Demiurge fashioned the immortal rational soul and its immortal aethereal vehicle. In the soul's descent through the cosmos, this vehicle picks up vestments of the four elements, which form its mortal vehicle. The human body, although made up of the four elements as well, is not the same as this second mortal vehicle.[5] We have, then, an immortal rational soul, which is enclosed in an immortal ethereal vehicle; as this complex descends, it is encased along with the irrational soul in a second mortal vehicle; the whole is placed in the human body.[6]

---

[3] Iamblichus fr. 88: ὅθεν δή φησιν ὀρθῶς ὁ Ἰάμβλιχος, <ὡς> οὐδὲ ταῦτα συλλογίζεσθαι δυνατόν, πῶς μὲν τὸ σῶμα παράγουσιν οἱ θεοί, πῶς δὲ τὴν ἐν αὐτῷ ζωήν, πῶς δὲ συμπλέκουσιν ἀμφότερα ἀλλήλοις· ταῦτα γὰρ ἄγνωστα ἡμῖν ὑπάρχει. καὶ ὅτι μὲν ἀπὸ θεῶν ὑφέστηκε πάντα, εἰς τὴν ἀγαθότητα αὐτῶν ἀποβλέποντες καὶ τὴν δύναμιν διατεινόμεθα, πῶς δὲ ἐκεῖθεν πρόεισιν, ἡμεῖς γιγνώσκειν οὐχ οἷοί τέ ἐσμεν.

[4] Compare *Phaedrus* 246a3-6, where Plato states that describing precisely the soul's form is a task for the gods, but to express what it resembles is humanly possible.

[5] Proclus refers to an earlier section of the *Timaeus* (42c-d), where he had found evidence for this second vehicle and its attached irrational soul (*Commentary on the Timaeus* III 330.7-331.20). The context is the Demiurge's actions after his speech to the younger gods in *Timaeus* 41a-d. After the Demiurge fashions the human rational soul and (for Proclus) the first immortal vehicle, the speaker (Timaeus) discusses transmigration, first into a woman and then (if the human being persists in evil) into animals. Then comes the passage in question: "And he will not cease from his toils in the transformations until he draws together the large mass and later accretion (turbulent and irrational) from fire, water, air, and earth to the circuit of the same in him" (*Timaeus* 42c4-d1: ἀλλάττων τε οὐ πρότερον πόνων λήξοι, πρὶν τῇ ταὐτοῦ καὶ ὁμοίου περιόδῳ τῇ ἐν αὐτῷ συνεπισπώμενος τὸν πολὺν ὄχλον καὶ ὕστερον προσφύντα ἐκ πυρὸς καὶ ὕδατος καὶ ἀέρος καὶ γῆς, θορυβώδη καὶ ἄλογον ὄντα). This "later accretion" of the elements is for Proclus the second vehicle.

[6] See pp. 53-56 and 134n3 above. On the history of the vehicle of the soul in Neoplatonism, see Dodds 1963:318-321. For the differences between the doctrines of Porphyry, Iamblichus,

The proper life of souls is to rise to the Intellect, but when they descend to their earthly body they first pass through a median realm:

> For souls as they descend to earth take from the elements garments of different types (airy, watery, earthy), and in this way finally enter into this thick mass. For how would it pass immediately from immaterial *pneuma* to this body? For before they enter into this [body], they possess the irrational life and the vehicle of that life, which was prepared from the simple elements, and they put on the conglomerate [i.e., the second vehicle] from these [elements], so called because it is different from the connate vehicle of the souls [i.e., the first, immortal vehicle], since it [the second vehicle] is made from different sorts of garments and weighs the soul down.
>
> Proclus *Commentary on the Timaeus* III 297.21–298.2[7]

There are then three "bodies" that carry the soul, and each of these adapts the rational and irrational soul that it contains to live in a different part of the cosmos. The immortal aethereal vehicle makes the soul a citizen of the cosmos (i.e. the aethereal zone of the stars and planets), the second vehicle (composed of the four elements) part of the realm of generation (i.e. the area between the Moon and the earth), and the third (the human body) a specific living person on earth:

> For it [i.e. the soul] does not immediately project the life of some specific human but before this [it projects] the human life; and before some specific generated life, [it projects] the generated life. And in this same way, the descent is from the incorporeal into body and into a life with a body in such a descent that the soul lives together with the heavenly vehicle, and then in this way from this body into a body that belongs to generation, through which it is in generation, and from

---

and Proclus on the vehicles, see Finamore 1985:11–27 and 165–169. For Proclus' doctrine, see Siorvanes 1996:131–133 and Chlup 2012:104–105. Cf. *Elements of Theology* Propositions 208–211.

[7] *Commentary on the Timaeus* III 297.21–298.2: εἰς γῆν κατιοῦσαι γὰρ αἱ ψυχαὶ προσλαμβάνουσιν ἀπὸ τῶν στοιχείων ἄλλους καὶ ἄλλους χιτῶνας, ἀερίους ἐνυδρίους χθονίους, ἔπειθ᾽ οὕτω τελευταῖον εἰς τὸν ὄγκον τὸν παχὺν τοῦτον εἰσκρίνονται· καὶ πῶς γὰρ ἔμελλον ἀμέσως ἀπὸ τῶν ἀύλων πνευμάτων εἰς τόδε τὸ σῶμα χωρεῖν; καὶ πρὶν οὖν εἰς τοῦτο κατέλθωσιν, ἔχουσι τὴν ἄλογον ζωὴν καὶ τὸ ἐκείνης ὄχημα κατεσκευασμένον ἀπὸ τῶν ἁπλῶν στοιχείων, καὶ ἐνεδύσαντο ἀπὸ τούτων ὄχλον, οὑτωσὶ καλούμενον ὡς ἀλλότριον μὲν τοῦ συμφύτου τῶν ψυχῶν ὀχήματος, ἐκ παντοδαπῶν δὲ χιτώνων συγκείμενον, βαρύνοντα δὲ τὰς ψυχάς.

this body into the earthly one in accordance with which it lives with its oyster body.

Proclus Commentary on the Timaeus III 298.10–16[8]

Thus, the human soul associates itself with the three bodies (aethereal vehicle, mortal vehicle, and earthly body) and thereby creates its different lives. In the second vehicle, it becomes not the specific person it will become on earth but rather an entity with an irrational nature. It does not yet have the body fitted with the appropriate organs to be a human being.[9]

The second vehicle, like the human body, consists of the four elements, but there is a difference. The vehicle has a simpler union of simpler elements, while the corporeal body has a more complex internal union because it is more composite.[10] The second vehicle was constructed from the four simple elements, as we have seen.[11] The organic body is not from simple elements but from compounds made up of all four elements together:

> Therefore there [296.7–300.20] we were saying that the irrational mass of fire, water, air, and earth was clearly the second vehicle and the life in it. But here (for Plato is not content with simple [elements] but he has added what is appropriate to the organic body) we say that the account concerns this [earthly body]. For it is not possible to say only that this [body] is only from simple [elements] but also from similar-parted (ὁμοιομέρων) entities.

Proclus Commentary on the Timaeus III 320.20–26[12]

---

8 *Commentary on the Timaeus* III 298.10–16: οὐδὲ γὰρ εὐθὺς τὸν τοῦ τινὸς ἀνθρώπου προβάλλει βίον, ἀλλὰ τὸν ἀνθρώπου πρὸ τούτου καὶ πρὸ τῆς τινὸς γενέσεως τὸν γενέσεως, καὶ ὡς ἀπὸ τοῦ ἀσωμάτου εἰς σῶμα ἡ πτῶσις καὶ τὴν μετὰ σώματος ζωήν, καθ' ἣν συζῇ τῷ οὐρανίῳ ὀχήματι, οὕτως ἀπὸ τούτου εἰς σῶμα γενεσιουργόν, καθ' ὃ ἐν γενέσει ἐστί, καὶ ἀπὸ τούτου εἰς τὸ χθόνιον, καθ' ὃ ζῇ μετὰ τοῦ ὀστρεώδους σώματος. Cf. *Commentary on the Timaeus* III 298.27–29: "The connate vehicle makes the soul encosmic; the second makes it a citizen of generation; and the oyster body makes it earthly" (τὸ μὲν οὖν συμφυὲς ὄχημα ποιεῖ αὐτὴν ἐγκόσμιον, τὸ δὲ δεύτερον γενέσεως πολίτιν, τὸ δὲ ὀστρεῶδες χθονίαν). See also *Commentary on the Timaeus* III 297.2–3. For ὀστρεῶδες applied to the human body, see Plato *Phaedrus* 250c6.

9 Proclus further differentiates the three (interpreting the Platonic lemma), *Commentary on the Timaeus* III 299.9–300.20.

10 *Commentary on the Timaeus* III 320.18–20: ἀλλ' ἐκεῖνο μὲν ἕνωσιν ἁπλουστέραν ἔχει τῶν ἁπλῶν χιτώνων, τοῦτο δὲ ποικιλωτέραν, ἅτε συνθετώτερον ὄν.

11 See especially *Commentary on the Timaeus* III 297.26–28: ἔχουσι τὴν ἄλογον ζωὴν καὶ τὸ ἐκείνης ὄχημα κατεσκευασμένον ἀπὸ τῶν ἁπλῶν στοιχείων.

12 *Commentary on the Timaeus* III 320.20–26: διὸ ἐκεῖ μὲν τὸν ἐκ πυρὸς καὶ ὕδατος καὶ ἀέρος καὶ γῆς ὄχλον ἄλογον ὄντα τὸ δεύτερον ὄχημα δηλοῦν ἐλέγομεν καὶ τὴν ἐν αὐτῷ ζωήν, ἐνταῦθα δέ (οὐ γὰρ ἠρκέσθη τοῖς ἁπλοῖς, ἀλλὰ προσέθηκε τὰ οἰκεῖα τοῦ ὀργανικοῦ σώματος) περὶ τούτου

The younger gods produced these complex parts from combining the simple elements.[13] Thus, the compounds are constructed from similar parts (that is, the four elements) but they exist in compounded, not simple, form.[14]

Proclus goes on to interpret Plato's statement that the gods fused the bodies together with bolts that were thickset and invisible because of their smallness:[15]

> This is what has need, so to say, of all the small, invisible bolts because the compound is from dissimilars, and it has need of many, thick-set bolts because the composite is easily dissolved.
>
> Proclus *Commentary on the Timaeus* III 321.9–11[16]

Thus, the organic body is an assemblage of compounds of the four elements. These compounds of elements, unlike the pure elements themselves, are sufficiently dissimilar from each other that they do not naturally adhere to one another and so have need of bolts to hold them together.

What these bolts were was a matter of debate in the Platonic school. Proclus cites two interpretations from earlier thinkers:

> As to 'the thick-set bolts', some interpreted them to be the fitting of the triangular elements together; Iamblichus the community of the natural reason principles, just as 'fusion' is the demiurgic cohesiveness and union.
>
> Proclus *Commentary on the Timaeus* III 323.7–10[17]

The first interpretation from an unnamed philosopher connects the bolts with the two basic right-angled triangles (half-equilateral isosceles and scalene) out of which the four primary bodies (tetrahedron, octahedron, icosahedron,

---

φαμὲν εἶναι τὸν λόγον· τοῦτο γὰρ οὐ δυνατὸν φάναι μόνον ἐκ τῶν ἁπλῶν εἶναι, ἀλλὰ καὶ ἐκ τῶν ὁμοιομερῶν.

[13] *Commentary on the Timaeus* III 321.6–7: ταῦτα δὲ κολλῶντες τὰ ὁμοιομερῆ γεννῶσιν, οἷς ἐκ τῶν τεττάρων στοιχείων ἡ σύνθεσις ("Having combined these [four elements], they produce the compounds of similar-parted forms, whose composition consists of the four elements").

[14] Proclus uses the term *homoiomerês* elsewhere to mean "having the same constituents." Thus, in *Commentary on the Timaeus* II 253.24–29 and III 321.6–7, he uses the term in reference to souls in the mixing bowl, which are *homoiomereis*, since made up of Being, Sameness, and Difference. Cf. *Commentary on the Timaeus* II 163.5, where the soul is again *homoiomerês*.

[15] *Timaeus* 43a3, cited on p. 157 above.

[16] *Commentary on the Timaeus* III 321.9–11: τοῦτο γάρ ἐστι τὸ δεόμενον πάντων ὡς εἰπεῖν τῶν σμικρῶν καὶ ἀοράτων γόμφων διὰ τὴν ἐξ ἀνομοίων σύστασιν, καὶ πολλῶν τούτων καὶ πυκνῶν διὰ τὸ εὔλυτον τῆς συνθέσεως.

[17] *Commentary on the Timaeus* III 323.7–10: τοὺς δὲ 'πυκνοὺς γόμφους' οἳ μὲν τὴν τῶν τριγώνων στοιχείων συνάρμοσιν ἤκουσαν, ὁ δὲ Ἰάμβλιχος τὴν τῶν φυσικῶν λόγων κοινωνίαν, ὥσπερ τὴν σύντηξιν αὐτῶν τὴν δημιουργικὴν συνοχὴν καὶ ἕνωσιν.

and cube) are constructed (*Timaeus* 53a–55c). This would make each triangle a "bolt," probably in the sense that each triangle connects with another to form the compounded figure.[18]

Iamblichus interprets the bolts more imaginatively, making them not the binding object but the metaphysical force behind the binding. The *logoi* are the forces at work through the younger gods in nature. The fusion is caused again through the gods' act of creation. Thus, the bolts and the fusing are demiurgic operations enacted by the gods in the realm of generation.

Proclus takes a more practical view of the bolts:

> We say that these thick and invisible bolts are the insertions (παρενθέσεις) of small and innumerable elements into the larger-parted (μεγαλομερεστέροις) and the infusion is appropriate to Hephaestean works, since fire accomplishes through rarefaction in the fusion the passing of all things through one another, just as occurs in the case of melting metals down, and in fusion the smaller-parted [elements] (τῶν σμικρομερῶν) enter the larger-parted [compounds] (εἰς τὰ μεγαλομερέστερα) and thus the blending occurs. It follows that they glued together what they had received, not making bodies by means of indestructible bonds but fusing them with small and innumerable bolts. For there is need of fusion and gluing in the generation of similar-parted things. Moisture provides the latter, and heat the former. For everything is fused by fire and is glued by water.

> Proclus *Commentary on the Timaeus* III 321.12–25[19]

The bolts then are the simple elements themselves (fire, air, water, earth) that serve to link and bind together the larger compounds (combinations of all four simple elements). The compounds are again "similar-parted" because

---

[18] Dillon 2009:381–382 compares chapter 203 of Calcidius' commentary. Calcidius says that Plato calls the bolts "points of junction" (*coniunctiones*) and again says that each is "a bond or link in small, solid bodies" (*Inuisibiles porro coniunctiones gomphos adpellat ... Quorum omnium quendam nodum concatenationemque dicit esse in minutis solidisque corpusculis, quae gomphos cognominat*). This explanation is not quite the same as the first given by Proclus, which is more precise: the constituent triangles. Triangles are a kind of bond, but there are other sorts, some of which Calcidius lists.

[19] *Commentary on the Timaeus* III 321.12–25: τοὺς μὲν οὖν πυκνοὺς καὶ ἀοράτους γόμφους λέγομεν τὰς τῶν σμικρῶν καὶ ἀοράτων στοιχείων παρενθέσεις τοῖς μεγαλομερεστέροις, τὴν δὲ σύντηξιν οἰκείαν εἶναι τοῖς Ἡφαιστείοις ἔργοις, τοῦ πυρὸς ἐργαζομένου διὰ τῆς ἀραιώσεως ἐν τῇ συντήξει τὴν πάντων δι' ἀλλήλων χώρησιν, ὡς ἐπὶ τῶν συγχωνευομένων γίνεται μετάλλων, εἰσδυομένων ἐν τῷ τήκεσθαι τῶν σμικρομερῶν εἰς τὰ μεγαλομερέστερα καὶ οὕτω τῆς συγκράσεως γινομένης. ἔστιν οὖν τὸ ἀκόλουθον, ὅτι τὰ λαμβανόμενα συνεκόλλων, οὐκ ἀλύτοις δεσμοῖς ἀπεργαζόμενοι σῶμα, ἀλλὰ πυκνοῖς γόμφοις συντήκοντες αὐτὰ τοῖς σμικροῖς καὶ ἀοράτοις· δεῖ γὰρ καὶ τήξεως καὶ κολλήσεως εἰς τὴν γένεσιν τῶν ὁμοιομερῶν, ὧν τὴν μὲν <ἡ> ὑγρότης παρέχεται, τὴν δὲ ἡ θερμότης· ἐτήκεται γὰρ τὸ πᾶν ὑπὸ πυρός, κολλᾶται δὲ ὑπὸ ὕδατος.

they are all compounded from the four elements. Proclus includes an analogy to metallurgy, whereby Hephaestean fire softens and makes the metal porous so that the bolts can enter the larger compounds. This process is followed by cooling, which embeds the bolts in the compounds, thereby binding two compounds together. This is not permanent, as Proclus points out, but enduring, and is similar to the bond that metalworking produces.[20]

Now that the gods have fashioned a durable body, the soul can enter into it. As we have seen before, this is not simply the rational soul, but the whole complex of rational and irrational souls plus the two vehicles:

> After the union of many dissimilar [parts], the soul is added: first the altogether mortal [soul] (for through this [soul] things flow out of the body, through the nutritive, perceptive, and desiderative life); and second the immortal soul (for this does not enter simply into a body but into a body that is subject to influx and efflux). The former [soul] is born with the body, and the latter is bound to the body.
>
> Proclus *Commentary on the Timaeus* III 321.25–32[21]

Plato writes that the younger gods "insert the orbits of the immortal soul into the body into which and out of which things flow" (*Timaeus* 43a4–6).[22] Proclus interprets the inward and outward flow as occurring in a specific kind of body, much as Aristotle states that the body in which the soul is present is a natural one endowed with organs (*On the Soul* 412b4–6). For Proclus, however, it is not simply such a body but also the irrational soul (the soul that acquired the simple garments from the elements on its descent, the garments that formed the second vehicle). The body must be functioning already with the powers of the lower soul: nutritive, perceptive,[23] and desiderative. That is to say, the lower soul casts its powers outwards (and indeed inwards) from the body—taking nourishment in and sending waste out, taking in sense perceptions, and acquiring and creating desires. These, Proclus thinks, must be in place and functioning

---

[20] Festugière (1965:203n1) thinks that the *homoiomereis, megalomereis*, and *smikromereis* all refer to organic tissue. If my interpretation is correct, however, the compounds (*homoiomereis, megalomereis*) are indeed organic tissue (constructed from the four elements) but the smaller-parted natures are the elements themselves, not compounds, and therefore not flesh. Being simple and small, they make stronger "bolts," and so would be more durable.

[21] *Commentary on the Timaeus* III 321.25–32: μετὰ δ' οὖν τὴν ἕνωσιν τῶν πολλῶν καὶ ἀνομοίων ἡ ψυχὴ παραγίγνεται, πρώτη μὲν ἡ θνητὴ πάντως (διὰ γὰρ ταύτης ἀπόρρυτον διά τε τῆς φυτικῆς καὶ τῆς αἰσθητικῆς καὶ ὀρεκτικῆς ζωῆς), δευτέρα δὲ ἡ ἀθάνατος (αὕτη γὰρ οὐκ εἰς σῶμα ἁπλῶς, ἀλλ' εἰς ἐπίρρυτον σῶμα καὶ ἀπόρρυτον ἐνδύεται)· καὶ ἡ μὲν ἀπογεννᾶται μετὰ τοῦ σώματος, ἡ δὲ ἐνδεῖται εἰς τὸ σῶμα.

[22] *Timaeus* 43a4–6: τὰς τῆς ἀθανάτου ψυχῆς περιόδους ἐνέδουν εἰς ἐπίρρυτον σῶμα καὶ ἀπόρρυτον.

[23] Diehl 1906 prints the reading of Codex Q αἰσθητῆς, but Codex D and the *recensio vulgata* σ have αἰσθητικῆς, which seems the better reading.

before the rational soul is added. Proclus is most probably drawing on Aristotle's framework in *On the Generation of Animals*, where the heart of the fetus is formed first, and so the nutritive soul is in place before birth. Touch becomes possible in the womb afterwards, but thought requires birth. Thus, Proclus states that the entry of the rational soul takes place at the moment of birth.[24]

The immortal rational soul enters into this body that possesses irrational soul and that therefore has nourishment and sense data coming in and waste and sensation going out. Whereas the irrational life is in the baby before birth and so can be said to be born in it, the rational soul is separate and becomes bound to the body/irrational soul complex. Later (*Commentary on the Timaeus* III 322.31–323.5) Proclus notes that Plato identifies the immortal soul as the two circles, those of the same and the other (*Timaeus* 43a4–6). Thus, the whole rational soul descends and enters the body.[25]

Later, at *Commentary on the Timaeus* III 329.13–330.9, Proclus considers how the placement of the rational soul into this body and this world of generation affects the rational soul in the newborn child. The problem arises, as we have seen already, from the nutritive and perceptive powers. The nutritive faculty because of the moisture it encounters emits a material outflow, but because of its life-producing heat has need of inflow of other things (III 329.21–24). The perceptive faculty, bombarded by external sensations from material bodies, disturbs the rational soul (III 329.24–27). These "passions" (*pathê*, III 329.27) cause "disturbance" (*thorubon*, III 329.27) in the rational soul, and the disturbance is especially acute in children (III 329.27–330.9).[26]

There is, however, hope for us as we grow older. Plato explains the problem and its solution in terms of the two circles:

> When the stream of growth and nourishment becomes less, and the circles have again grasped calm and continue on their own proper road and with time passing are more established, then the orbits of each of the circles that are going correctly according to their nature have been set straight, they name the different and the same correctly, and they bring it about that the one who possesses them becomes prudent.
>
> Plato *Timaeus* 44b1–7[27]

---

[24] *Commentary on the Timaeus* III 322.17–20: ἐκ δὴ τούτων κἀκεῖνο δῆλον, ὅτι τὴν εἴσκρισιν τῆς ψυχῆς κατὰ Πλάτωνα γίγνεσθαι ῥητέον ἅμα τῇ προόδῳ τοῦ βρέφους· τότε γὰρ τέλειόν ἐστι τὸ κύημα καὶ οὐ πρότερον. ("From these things it is clear that it must be said that the entry of the soul occurs according to Plato at the same time as the newborn leaves [the womb]. For then the fetus is perfect and not before.")

[25] This offers Proclus an opportunity to criticize Plotinus for his theory that the highest part of the soul does not descend (*Commentary on the Timaeus* III 323.5–7).

[26] Cf. Festugière 1968:211n2.

[27] *Timaeus* 44b1–7: ὅταν δὲ τὸ τῆς αὔξης καὶ τροφῆς ἔλαττον ἐπίῃ ῥεῦμα, πάλιν δὲ αἱ περίοδοι λαμβανόμεναι γαλήνης τὴν ἑαυτῶν ὁδὸν ἴωσι καὶ καθιστῶνται μᾶλλον ἐπιόντος τοῦ χρόνου,

In his commentary on this passage (*Commentary on the Timaeus* III 348.29–349.21), Proclus contrasts the descent of the soul in the *Phaedrus* myth with the soul's return to its proper state here in the *Timaeus*. After a summary of some of the features of the *Phaedrus* descent, Proclus writes:

> Inversely, in these words [Plato], having dramatically described the passions of the soul that has fallen into the realm of generation—its turnings, fractures, flowings—wishes little by little to lead it back to its intellectual life, one that is in accord with its nature.

Proclus Commentary on the Timaeus III 349.9–12[28]

Thus, as the individual matures, there is the possibility of bringing the circles of the same and different, which make up the rational soul, back into their appropriate harmonious motions, which were disturbed by the irrational powers of the lower soul not being able to process correctly the material bodies assaulting their nutritive and perceptive natures.

Proclus takes up Plato's words and offers his readers the possibility of recovering from the irrationality of childhood and of becoming rationally thinking individuals:

> But here [in the *Timaeus* passage] as the worse [revolutions in the soul][29] and the impediments from matter were ceasing, the soul in accordance with [its] nature rouses itself,[30] and better natures make themselves known: order, reason, and a rational and prudent condition. For as we ourselves proceed into the prime of life, we also become more prudent

---

τότε ἤδη πρὸς τὸ κατὰ φύσιν ἰόντων σχῆμα ἑκάστων τῶν κύκλων αἱ περιφοραὶ κατευθυνόμεναι, τό τε θάτερον καὶ τὸ ταὐτὸν προσαγορεύουσαι κατ' ὀρθόν, ἔμφρονα τὸν ἔχοντα αὐτὰς γιγνόμενον ἀποτελοῦσιν.

28 *Commentary on the Timaeus* III 349.9–12: ἐν δὲ τούτοις ἔμπαλιν τὰ πάθη τῆς εἰς γένεσιν πεσούσης ψυχῆς καὶ τὰς στροφὰς καὶ τὰς κλάσεις καὶ τοὺς ὀχετοὺς ἐκτραγῳδήσας ἐθέλει κατὰ μικρὸν ἐπαναγαγεῖν αὐτὴν εἰς τὴν νοερὰν καὶ τὴν κατὰ φύσιν ζωήν.

29 Proclus writes: "the worse ceasing" (ἀπoληγόντων τῶν χειρόνων, *Commentary on the Timaeus* III 349.16). There is no noun for the adjective to describe. Festugière (1968:230) translates "cessation de l'etat pire" which catches the ambiguity nicely. The worse state of the rational soul, however, would refer to the distortion in its two circles, and Proclus is contrasting that internal psychic state with external problems caused by matter on the irrational powers of the lower soul (τῶν ἐκ τῆς ὕλης ἐμποδίων, *Commentary on the Timaeus* III 349.16–17). Thus, increasing age brings on two concomitant results: the rational soul itself begins to assume its correct patterns and so the external bombardment of matter causes fewer problems.

30 The *recensio vulgata* σ has *anaireitai* ("takes up for itself," "undertakes"). Codex D omits approximately five lines of text, from *anaireitai* through to *Galênos* in line 22. Codex Q has αναι and some missing letters (Festugière 1968 estimates seven). Kroll conjectured *anazôpureitai* ("is rekindled," "is excited"). Diehl (1906:3.349) writes *"expectaveris anegeiretai sim,"* which would mean "rouses itself." Festugière conjectures *anagetai* ("is raised up," "ascends"). I follow Diehl; the exact verb is irretrievably lost, but the general meaning is not at issue.

and rational and seek after[31] an equable and orderly life, with nature as our guide.

Proclus Commentary on the Timaeus III 349.15–21[32]

There is no guarantee that we will all reestablish the appropriate motions in the two circles of the rational soul. Indeed, Proclus goes on to argue that proper education is also necessary. The disruption of rational thought, however, need only be temporary. Age brings a calm, and it is up to us to make use of the rational soul to control the irrational.

Thus far Proclus has agued that the rational soul is trapped in a body that causes it problems. Plato later in the *Timaeus* (87c–89e) makes his strongest case in any of his dialogues for the importance of caring for the body as well as the soul. If care of the body asserts greater control, then the soul becomes weak, but if care of the soul becomes paramount at the expense of the body, weakness and diseases result. Thus, the intellectual must take up exercise of the body, just as the athlete must care for the soul. We should model ourselves on the workings of the heavens (*Timaeus* 88c7–d), bringing the motions of our own circles of the Same and Different into harmony with those of the heavens.

Although Proclus' commentary runs out long before this part of the dialogue, there are two passages that shed some light on his interpretation of this positive view of the human body. The first comes in the midst of an argument against Galen.[33] Proclus begins by asserting what Galen or any physician might aver about the relationship between the soul and the body:

Galen might say: 'The powers of the soul follow the mixtures of the body'. If [the body] is watery, unstable, and completely in flux, the soul is foolish and unstable. When [the body] re-establishes itself into harmony, [the soul] sets itself right and becomes wise.

Proclus Commentary on the Timaeus III 349.21–25[34]

---

[31] Codex Q has *poioumetha*. I have adopted Kroll's conjecture *antipoioumetha*, which Festugière also accepted. Diehl also suggested adding *tên proodon* ("follow the path of") or using the verb *promethoumetha* ("show regard for"), and these bear good sense as well.

[32] *Commentary on the Timaeus* III 349.15–21: ἐνταῦθα δὲ ἀποληγόντων τῶν χειρόνων καὶ τῶν ἐκ τῆς ὕλης ἐμποδίων κατὰ φύσιν εὐθὺς †ἀναιρεῖται καὶ ἀναφαίνεται τὰ κρείττονα, τάξις καὶ λόγος καὶ ἡ λελογισμένη καὶ ἔμφρων κατάστασις· εἰς γὰρ ἡλικίαν ἰόντες αὐτοὶ ἐμφρονέστεροι γιγνόμεθα καὶ μᾶλλον λελογισμένοι τῆς τε ὁμαλοῦς καὶ εὐτάκτου ζωῆς †ποιούμεθα, τῆς φύσεως ἀγούσης.

[33] Festugière (1968:231n2) says that the allusion is general (about the doctrine of the four humors which Galen and others accept) and also raises the possibility that Proclus had made use of Galen's treatise on the *Timaeus*. For Galen's commentary, see Daremberg 1848 and Schröder 1934.

[34] *Commentary on the Timaeus* III 349.21–25: φαίη ἂν ὁ Γαληνός· ταῖς τοῦ σώματος κράσεσιν ἔπονται τῆς ψυχῆς αἱ δυνάμεις, καὶ ὑγροῦ μὲν ὄντος καὶ ἀστάτου καὶ παντοίως ῥέοντος ἄνους καὶ ἄστατος ἡ ψυχή, καθισταμένου δὲ εἰς συμμετρίαν κατευθύνεται καὶ ἔμφρων γίνεται.

The problem as Proclus sees it is that this medical theory makes the body and its material mixtures responsible for the proper or improper functioning of the rational soul. For him it is the soul (not the body) that takes the lead in such matters:

> For it is not right that he makes the immortal soul that exists before the body intellectual because of the body, but rather one must say that the body itself sometimes becomes for the soul an impediment to a well-ordered life and that sometimes it burdens it less.

Proclus *Commentary on the Timaeus* III 349.26–30[35]

This is not ringing praise for the body. It is still an obstacle to the soul, sometimes a greater one and sometimes a lesser one, but an obstacle nonetheless. It is keeping with Plato's view in the *Republic* that the rational soul should be in charge of the other parts of the soul and the body. Indeed, Proclus will take up the role of education in training the soul in the next section (III 351.19–352.9). The proper education provides to the irrational soul (which is, of course, more closely connected to the body and its needs) "the habituation of good actions and life in accordance with correct opinion"[36] and this occurs through "character training" (*êthesi*, III 351.26). Education of the rational soul, on the other hand, proceeds from scientific training and dialectic[37] through the learning of "doctrines" (*dogmasi*, III 351.26). In this way the irrational soul obeys the rational, and the rational ascends to Intellect and contemplates true being (III 351.27–28). The body can help or hinder this education, but it does not determine it. If we return to the Galen section, we can see the effect that the body has on education and the soul:

> The conjunction with the body sometimes disturbs the soul and sometimes stops the tumult, and the soul becomes calm. It [the calm soul] is more in accord with nature than the troubled soul, but it is not yet

---

[35] *Commentary on the Timaeus* III 349.26–30: τὴν γὰρ ἀθάνατον ψυχὴν καὶ πρὸ τοῦ σώματος οὖσαν οὐ θέμις διὰ τὸ σῶμα νοερὰν ποιεῖν, ἀλλ᾽ ἐκεῖνο μᾶλλον τὸ σῶμα ποτὲ μὲν ἐμπόδιον γίγνεσθαι τῇ ψυχῇ ῥητέον πρὸς τὴν εὔτακτον ζωήν, ποτὲ δὲ ἧττον ἐνοχλεῖν.

[36] *Commentary on the Timaeus* III 351.22–24: συνεθισμὸν τῷ ἀλόγῳ τῶν ἀγαθῶν πράξεων παρεχομένην καὶ τὴν κατὰ ὀρθὴν δόξαν ζωήν.

[37] *Commentary on the Timaeus* III 351.25–26: διὰ δὲ τῆς παιδεύσεως μαθήμασι καὶ τῇ διαλεκτικῇ τὴν λογικὴν οὐσίαν τρέφουσαν.

[calm] until education is present. Thus the body hinders the wise life but it by no means creates it.

Proclus *Commentary on the Timaeus* III 350.3–8[38]

The body presents a threat to the proper life of the rational soul, agitating and impeding it. If we imagine a painful disease in the body, then we can understand how the body could prevent the soul from being tranquil. The normal body pains and aches, however, although a minor hindrance, would not necessarily inhibit tranquility in the soul. How much the body's influence affects the soul depends very much on the soul's training. Since training one's soul to be calm involves training one's body not to be an impediment, it does seem that Proclus is tacitly accepting Plato's arguments in *Timaeus* 86e–89e. The philosopher must train both equally.

There is corroboration for Proclus' approval of Plato's upgrading of the body to be found in the Arabic translation of Proclus' commentary.[39] The Arabic version picks up at *Timaeus* 89e3 just after the Platonic passage dealing with need for treating body and soul equally (*Timaeus* 86e–89e), and it continues to *Timaeus* 90c7. This section from the dialogue covers the three parts of the soul, and the need for a balance among them.

The Arabic commentary begins with Proclus summarizing what Plato had been doing in the earlier passage and looking ahead to the next. The earlier section, he says, dealt with remedies for caring for the soul-body complex and for the body, and what will follow will concern treatment of the soul (*Arabic Commentary on the Timaeus* 28–29). He reiterates the Platonic doctrine that the rational soul is to take the role of the leader of the other parts and of body. The body "is the attendant and servant of the [soul's] activity" (*Arabic Commentary on the Timaeus* 29).[40] Thus, the soul is most worthy of care and treatment.

In his commentary on *Timaeus* 89e3–90a2, Proclus argues that all three parts of the soul must be exercised and strengthened. He specifically notes that the motions of all three parts should be "in due proportion to each other" so that none prevails, and he adds that the rational part "should not stultify and diminish the activities of the irascible and the appetitive" (*Arabic Commentary on the Timaeus* 30). He continues:

---

[38] *Commentary on the Timaeus* III 350.3–8: ἡ τοῦ σώματος συνάρτησις ὁτὲ μὲν ἐκταράττει τὴν ψυχήν, ὁτὲ δὲ ἀνίησι τὸν θόρυβον, ἢ δὲ ἐν γαλήνῃ γίγνεται· καὶ μᾶλλον μὲν αὐτὴ τῆς ταραττομένης ἔχει κατὰ φύσιν, οὔπω δὲ οὐδὲ αὕτη, πρὶν αὐτῇ καὶ παιδεία προσγένηται. τὸ ἄρα σῶμα κωλυτικὸν μὲν ἦν τῆς ἔμφρονος ζωῆς, ποιητικὸν δὲ οὐδαμῶς.

[39] Arnzen (2013:1–45).

[40] All translations of the Arabic text are by Arnzen.

The activity of these [parts of the soul] is preserved in the following way: I say that any motionless and inactive thing is very weak, while anything trained is very strong. Therefore, it is necessary that the motions of the soul are in due proportion, in order that each [part] can perform its activity. Proportionality of these motions consists in that the rational [soul] is the regulator and the origin, from which motion starts, while the irascible and the appetitive [parts of the soul] pay attention and are submissive and obedient to the rational [soul] and move and act only to such an extent which is in accordance with the rational [soul] and gives to it what it demands. For, when the motions of these [parts of the soul] are in this state, there is stability, appropriateness, proportionality and order for the whole soul.

Proclus *Arabic Commentary on the Timaeus* 30

As in the earlier passage in the commentary we have examined, Proclus is creating a balance between the superiority of the rational soul and the need for the parts to cooperate. There is still stress on the greater importance of the rational soul, but there is also a concomitant concern for the irrational parts. Just as the body cannot be neglected, so too these parts may not be ignored without causing disruption to the human being. When they work in harmony, they all benefit, as does the entire individual.

3. Conclusion

In his *Commentary on the Timaeus*, Proclus examines the soul's entry into the body. The soul becomes progressively more corporeal in its descent, picking up the second vehicle and irrational soul first and the body afterwards. The body is made from compounds of the four elements bound together with "bolts" of fire and water. The rational soul is at first thrown into confusion by the force of the irrational soul in the body, but eventually, by carefully balancing all three parts of the soul so that the rational soul is in control but no one part wrongly dominates the others, the rational soul's two circles resume their correct revolutions. Proclus' theory thereby follows Plato's doctrine in the *Timaeus* of the body's positive value.

9

Olympiodorus on the Human Being
A Case of Moderate Embodiment

PAULIINA REMES

Abstract: In the *First Alcibiades*, the author makes an influential distinction between the soul as a user, and the body as that which is used, the instrument. This distinction begins the whole historical tradition of the instrumental understanding of the body, much criticized in later and contemporary philosophy. Olympiodorus provides a less crude and more insightful interpretation. While confirming that a human being is a rational soul using a body as an instrument, his discussion shows that the true import of "user" and "instrument" terminology lies in the way that it captures an embodied agent. Human being is neither her automatic vegetative-living functions, nor the perfect, disembodied intellect, but a rational being capable of goal-directed acting in material-political circumstances. For such a conception of human being, embodiment is moderate: the body has repercussions for how her goals of action get shaped.

ONE OF THE LEGACIES—and perhaps its only long-lasting legacy—of *Alcibiades I* which is sometimes considered spurious, is a conjunction of two related ideas: that the human being is the soul rather than the body, and that the body should be understood as an instrument of the soul rather than a true part of human nature. The instrument idea is, arguably, one source for the antithetical categorization of soul and body observed and problematized by the editors of this volume.[1] It suggests a radically asymmetric relation, evicting the body from humanity *in toto*, and demoting it to the level of shovels, pencils, screwdrivers, etc. Embodiment is here often understood as a weak relationship: body is a tool that implements practical solutions arrived at by reason that is

---

[1] See pp. 52n6, 56, 71, and 125 above.

in its essence disembodied.[2] The user of the instrument is independent from the existence and availability of the instrument, whereas the instrument, *qua* instrument, depends upon its user for being what it is, and for fulfilling the function given to it. This, however, is not the way the Neoplatonic commentator, Olympiodorus of Alexandria (ca. 500–570 AD), understands the dialogue. Olympiodorus, it will be argued here, interprets embodiment as moderate. In *moderate embodiment*, body is seen as having a functional role: embodied activities structure perception and shape our understanding.[3] Practical solutions are essentially embodied, and not mere executions of abstract decisions done by a disembodied rational ability. Accompanied with Olympiodorus' view on embodiment as moderate is his definition of the human being as an embodied agent, a being that is neither the vegetative-animal nor the exclusively purified and intellectual. A close study of Olympiodorus' view dismantles any simplistic assumptions of the Neoplatonists as capable of only either neglecting or abhorring the body.

The identification of our nature with the soul rather than the composite arises from the controversial argument of the *Alcibiades* (129–130) in which Socrates identifies our selfhood with soul. The position of the body can be understood through the relationship of "using an instrument." Even useful tools or devices are not indispensable for the existence and properties of their users. The view propounded seems to differ radically, then, from a hylomorphic account that underlines the unity the two parts, soul and body, form. What is suggested looks like a special, "lopsided" kind of dualism, with two profoundly different things of which one is not, however, independent of the other: the body fulfills its functions only through being moved and activated, i.e. "used," by the soul.[4] There are some general considerations, however, that already qualify an exclusively intellectualist-dualist reading.

As regards the original work, we may first point out that the human body is not an instrument like any other instruments—in the value-hierarchy of things

---

[2] A. Clark 2008:43 and Lo Presti 2015:34.

[3] A. Clark 2008:203 and Lo Presti 2015:35.

[4] *Alcibiades I* is not, of course, the only source of such a view. We have, among other things, the rhetorically strong view originating especially in the *Phaedo* according to which the body is not a part of the thing whose survival we are interested in, but, rather, its prison or tomb (*Phaedo* 82d–e and 83d; see also *Cratylus* 400b–c, *Gorgias* 493, and pp. 19, 80n29, 113 above and 311n13 and n15 below). Second, there is the ontological view related, namely, that the soul can both exist and actualize itself in the best possible way separated from the shackles of the body. Being embodied is seen, at best, as a necessary evil, or, if to practice philosophy is to practice dying, not necessary at all. In Neoplatonism, this asymmetric relation becomes even more radical as the body comes to be understood to come *to be* through the soul. Without the hypostasis Soul, and the World-Soul, there would be no bodies, whose being, unity, and organization are an appearance of the higher principles: One, Intellect, and the Soul.

of which to take care, the body enjoys a privileged position right below the soul, before and above ordinary instruments.[5] Without its mediation, we could use no other instruments. It is our access to the world. Some of the Neoplatonic commentators, Olympiodorus among them, take further very seriously the level of the discussion of the dialogue. Since the emphasis of the dialogue is on the level of political life and virtue, body, while being a tool, is not a dispensable one. It is a necessary part of a human being understood as a whole, as that agent who operates in the realm of politics. As Renaud and Tarrant point out, this aspect is part of a general interpretative strategy of a Socratic dialogue: a Socratic discourse is one that takes place on two simultaneous planes, that of life and that of knowledge.[6] A Socratic dialogue with Alcibiades, then, must take its start from Alcibiades and his motivations. This methodological point provides the context for central concepts in the dialogue. For Olympiodorus, body, as we shall see, forms part of the definition of human being. In this context, human being is a specific conception, crucial for the *telos* of the dialogue: a grasp of what a human being is, is necessary for the acts of persuasion and care of self which are fundamental to politics, and thus, necessary for the life and knowledge of the politically active person, Alcibiades.

Finally, there is an aspect that is perhaps not very predominant in the dialogue itself, but that is highlighted and further developed by the Neoplatonic commentators. The distinction between users, their belongings, and the belongings of belongings is not only an ontological-normative hierarchy; it also suggests activities directed to different levels of goodness. Socratic care of the self relies, according to the *Alcibiades*, on the idea that to be able to care for shoes, feet, and the soul in an appropriate way, the appropriate level of the hierarchy must be recognized. The Neoplatonists explicitly separate different levels of goodness. The appropriate care of each level follows the nature and qualities of the kind of object involved. But the current state of the object cannot be an exhaustive source of information for the kind of care chosen. Caring in the Platonic sense is a form of essentialist perfectionism: it involves the normative-teleological idea of enabling and supporting the actualization of the kind of goodness possible for the kind of object in question; that is, actualization of its proper natural constitution as fully as possible. This idea, explicit in both

---

[5]   I discuss the original text in Remes 2013, with fuller references to previous research on *Alcibiades I*, and some remarks on the question of whether the dialogue is spurious or authentic. For relevant literature note especially the commentary of Denyer 2001, as well as Taylor 1979. After the publication of my article, at least one important volume has come out: Renaud and Tarrant 2015.

[6]   Olympiodorus *Commentary on Plato's Gorgias* 8.1; Renaud and Tarrant 2015:193.

Proclus' and Olympiodorus' commentaries, leads to a more inclusive picture of the good life appropriate for the human being, understood as embodied agent.[7]

The view propounded, although perhaps unplatonic in tone, arises in the end from some very orthodox Neoplatonic concerns about the ways in which body affects soul's activities. It is good to emphasize, one more time, the level of the discussion chosen. The topic of the chapter is embodiment as a part, or a way of existing, of the human being, and human being understood as the civic-political agent. Olympiodorus is a good Neoplatonist—and indeed, Aristotelian—in thinking that there is an aspect of our nature, perhaps pure theoretical reason, that is not essentially embodied at all. This aspect, however, is not the primary topic of the dialogue he comments on, nor the primary focus of the comments themselves. Moreover, we ought not to be misled into thinking that a moderate embodiment is the same as a classic hylomorphic picture, in the sense of body being a combination of matter and form. According to both views, the body itself is not the most basic level, since it is already an organization of something material. Olympiodorus' view of this lower, ontologically more basic level of material organization is that body is "enmattered form" (εἶδος ἐν ὕλῃ). Form is in matter as human being is in a space/place (ἐν τῷ τόπῳ),[8] not made out of or composed of form and matter (οὐδὲ τὸ σῶμα ἐξ ὕλης καὶ εἴδους). At the more basic level of the formation of bodies, only a weak sense of being enmattered holds. Neither the form nor matter ontologically undergoes anything in the coexistence (*On the Alcibiades* 211.9–212.3), and the two elements are not of equal worth in the combination. We should perhaps not speak of elements at all, but simply of form and the necessary condition for its actualization. What is important is that on this basic level, formal power is not affected by the matter in which it is actualized. This does not mean, however, that soul's activities would not be affected by embodiment: on the higher level of embodiment, as we shall see, being in a body conditions the kind of activities the soul can actualize.

---

[7]   This emphasis is very natural, given the place of the dialogue in the late Neoplatonic curriculum. Together with the propaedeutic Aristotelian readings, it was considered appropriate for beginners. For curricula, see e.g. Festugière 1969 and Tarrant 2014.

[8]   Note that this idea is not the same as the idea of the intelligible not being in matter spatially (as in the adjective *topikos*), an idea common in Neoplatonism. The Neoplatonists deny that universal or formal power would be something divisible in space (see e.g. Sorabji 2005:6.4). Olympiodorus here seems to make a different point: namely, that as human being is necessarily in some space, but no specific space is necessary for his existence, nor part of his definition, in the same manner, the form (in the sensible) must be in some matter, but not necessarily in this or that matter. And likewise the essence of the human being is unaffected by that place, so does matter not have power to affect form.

1. Using an Instrument

Olympiodorus spends some time, in a couple of passages, spelling out the anthropology of the *Alcibiades*. His definition of the human being is driven by the overall methodology and approach of the dialogue, as interpreted by him. The *skopos* of the dialogue, all Neoplatonic commentators seem to agree, is self-knowledge (*On the Alcibiades* 3.3–4). There is a difference, however, in how Olympiodorus' predecessors understand this. Damascius, he reports, understands the object of self-knowledge as solely the civic or political self. Proclus, however, puts emphasis on the ideal and ultimately more real, cathartic level of selfhood. Olympiodorus steers in the middle, and endorses Damascius' view, with the qualification that the dialogue is not exclusively about the civic selfhood, but that the author establishes, towards the end of the dialogue, the need to attend to—and the reality of—the higher aspects of our nature (*On the Alcibiades* 4.15–6.4). As a commentator, Olympiodorus is especially perceptive as regards the contextual personal method of Socrates: Alcibiades' person, his political desires and ambitions, form the basis of Socrates's chosen approach, the *psukhagôgia* of the dialogue (*On the Alcibiades* 6.1–7.11).[9] On the ontological level, this is accompanied with a view that the target of self-knowledge in the dialogue has to take into account also the individual (*atomon*, *On the Alcibiades* 210.4–16),[10] not only general features of souls and human beings. It is the flesh-and-blood individual, Alcibiades, with his particular characteristics and life situation, living an individual life (*On the Alcibiades* 210.5), that must form the basis of the discussion, even though the *telos* lies in higher, impersonal, and not essentially embodied activities and existence. Given this down-to-earth, "civic" or political background of the discussion, there is a need to know what or who the individual human being is. Moreover, a philosophical grasp must reveal *the general features pertinent to that level* of discussion (*On the Alcibiades* 210.13–15)—therefore, the metaphysical theory of the individual, and the need to define human being in a manner relevant for the civic inquiry.

The basic definition of human being repeated a few times is "*a rational soul using a body as an instrument.*"[11] The purified soul does not use the body as an

---

[9]   See Addey 2014a:66 on Proclus' view on the importance of receptivity and suitability of the receiver of the argument and Renaud 2014 on the way in which Socrates elicits particular or contingent premises from interlocutors, because they are drawn from their personal experience. I discuss methodological issues in more detail in a current project, entitled "Medicines Drenched in Honey: Olympiodorus on the Superiority of Platonic Philosophy."

[10]   Cf. Griffin 2016:41. Unless otherwise stated, I will use Griffin's translations of the commentary and the Greek edition of the commentary by Westerink 1956.

[11]   *On the Alcibiades* 177.14–15: ὁρίζεται γὰρ ἐφεξῆς τὸν ἄνθρωπον ‛ψυχὴν λογικὴν ὀργάνῳ χρωμένην τῷ σώματι;' again at 208.7–8; and at 205.5–6 where it is introduced as Proclus' opinion also. Hereinafter italics in quotations are mine for emphasis.

instrument (rather, it becomes its impediment), and so the discussion is located on the civic level (*On the Alcibiades* 177.15–17). But without further qualifications the extension of this definition is too wide. Olympiodorus apparently has two concerns: to exclude other normal, ensouled beings, like plants and animals, and to make sure that heavenly bodies do not fall under the same definition. These two groups are barred with different moves, moves that explicate also the exact meaning of the definition. Let us inspect here first the relationship of "use as an instrument," and then, in the next subsection, take these moves of exclusion in turn.

The expression "using as an instrument" (e.g. χρωμένην ὀργάνῳ, *On the Alcibiades* 209.22) is the key to understand the definition, and indeed, much of the dialogue. As the original text has it, the same notion of use governs the relationship between the body and its instruments (feet and shoes, fingers and rings, body and cloak, etc.) and the soul and its body-instrument (*Alcibiades*, throughout 128–130). It is this equation that causes the troubling view of the human body as a mere instrument. But at the same time, the notion of use involved is rarely subjected to proper scrutiny.[12] According to Olympiodorus, possible instruments are many: carpenter's hammer and smith's anvil, as well as philosophers' practice of rational discourse (*On the Alcibiades* 210.17–19). The difference between the first two, lies, I take it, in the way that they act as instruments. The first, the hammer, is, as it were, a continuation of the hand of the carpenter, playing an active part in the act of hammering. The second, the anvil, is not in active motion in the act of forging, nor does it improve the qualities and powers of the hand itself, yet it is an instrument nonetheless: without it, forging would be impossible, and of course it has been previously designed, made, and adapted to play a role in the production of metal things.

The philosopher's use of arguments, is no less a use of a tool (*Alcibiades* 129b1–c4 and *On the Alcibiades* 205.14–19 and 210.17–21): there is a *telos*—the moral and cognitive development of the pupil/interlocutor—for which Socrates strives through a skillful use of the tools we have available; namely, words that comprise rhetorical *psukhagôgia* and philosophical argumentation (ἡ λογικὴ πραγματεία, *On the Alcibiades* 210.19). Now, none of these tools are, of course, indispensable for the existence of their users: even when not hammering, the carpenter exists, and the sleeping philosopher remains a philosopher. But note that the tools may be indispensable for reaching the goals that these agents have. Moreover, one might claim that some such tools (although not exactly *this* particular hammer, with *this* particular set of characteristics) are indispensable for the activities *typical* of these skilled people. If a person never used any

---

[12] An exception is provided by Taylor 1979.

hammer and similar instruments, but say, only designed wooden products, it is questionable whether he would be a carpenter—his activity would be something rather different, and we would perhaps not call him a carpenter, but an industrial designer. Similarly, a woman who never used arguments but who would somehow miraculously have reached cognitive identity with being and cosmos, might merit a name other than a lover of wisdom.

The instrument idea, then, does not demote the object that functions as an instrument to a status of something that has no significance whatsoever. Particular kinds of instruments are best suited to help in striving for goals of particular type. Nonetheless, the purpose of this terminology is to make it absolutely clear what in the combination of user and instrument is the proper agent: the origin of activities. Hammers, anvils, and arguments are not instruments on their own—that is, without someone putting them to the kind of use appropriate for them. Similarly, body is seen as a necessary tool for the kind of activities that only it can actualize, but not the ultimate cause of those activities themselves.

2. Defining the Human Being

The way that the user-instrument relation differs from some other alternatives receives further illumination when Olympiodorus distinguishes stars, plants, and nonrational animals from human beings. He starts with the perhaps less intuitive case of stars: "That the human being, according to Plato, is a soul using a body that moves in straight lines (εὐθυπόρῳ); for this ought to be added [to the definition] to account for the souls of the heavenly [bodies]" (*On the Alcibiades* 212.10–12; see also 208.10). Heavenly bodies are ensouled, and the soul in them originates a movement that is circular. Human beings do not exhibit such a perfect circular motion: their motions do not repeat the kind of perfect circle, always returning to where they started from, making it actually impossible to mark a beginning and an end of their movements. They move in a more straight line—perhaps not straight literally, but starting from point A and ending in point B—and may do additional kinds of motion, with other starting and ending points; and, at least ultimately, there is a clear starting point and an end point, in birth and death (see Plato *Phaedrus* 245d1–5; Aristotle *Physics* 261b28–29).

The second exclusion that comes immediately afterwards is directed to beings nearer to us in the cosmos: "But the vegetative and non-rational [souls] will not be captured [in the definition 'a soul that uses the body as an instrument'], as we have pointed out, because they use the body not only as an instrument, but also as a subject, *hupokeimenon*" (*On the Alcibiades* 212.12–14). There are various considerations that might be connected to the use of this term. Olympiodorus might mean that for plants and animals, the body is a substratum, that which persists in change (see Aristotle *On Generation and Corruption* I 4.319b8–12). But by this he cannot simply mean that the bodies of animals and plants acquire and lose properties, since it is clear that the human body also undergoes similar changes. One perhaps banal difference between the animals and plants and human beings could lie in the idea of immortality already introduced in the case of stars: when the body of a plant or an animal perishes, they will die. There are no activities entirely separate from the body, or activities that could continue after the perishing of the body.

If *hupokeimenon* is taken with roughly the meaning it has in Aristotle's *Categories* and *Metaphysics* (e.g. *Categories* 2; *Metaphysics* 1028a20–25 and 1029a10–27), it would signify the ultimate subject of predication. According to a peripatetic scheme—also followed by Neoplatonic commentators—there are two kinds of predication, the accidental and the essential or substantial; of these, what is accidentally predicated cannot exist without its subject.[13] Olympiodorus' point may be, accordingly, that for plants and animals, it makes sense to predicate properties to the body, and that this body is the *hupokeimenon* also in the sense of being necessary for the existence of the qualities predicated. The yellow of the daffodil is a property of its body, as is, at least in some sense, the growing of red hair of an Australian terrier, and neither exists without a body as their subject. Perhaps it is the soul that gives rise to bodily changes, but the qualities involved are predicated of and actualized in the body of an animal or a plant, and not of any disembodied, rational soul.

One possible interpretation that suggests itself here is that the relationship of a rational human to her body is profoundly different from that of plants and animals, whose being is tied to and, as it were, exhausted by the activities that always actualize in the body—the body acting as their subject. If a human being enjoys a very different, more distanced relationship to her body, the idea would then be that the properties of human beings, unlike those of plants and animals, are not predicated of the body, but of the soul forming the body. But the reading of this sort raises the question of the vegetative and living functions of a human being: are we to understand that they are only partly similar to those same activities in other living things? The explanation of the content of the activity, of, say, using nutrition or perceiving, would be the same, but the structural way in which these actualize and are predicated within the body-soul combination would differ. Why would not Madeleine's blond hair, or its growth, be in the very same sense predicated of her body as the terrier's red fur, and dependent upon there being a body in the first place? One may wonder what motivation, furthermore, would Olympiodorus have to insist that human

---

[13] See also Porphyry *Commentary on Aristotle's Categories* 73.22–30.

nutrition, or, say, bodily growth, would be activities in which the relationship to the body is in some special way instrumental, that of "using" in the same sense as a carpenter uses an hammer, and how fitting that metaphor would be for this relationship. It does not seem adequate to dismiss these problems as resulting from the well-known Neoplatonic strategies to save the soul from any contamination of the body, since the solution is neither the most simple explanation, nor does it save the phenomena. In which sense can automatic, nonvoluntary, and nonintentional activities we share with other living beings be understood as distinct from them, and grouped, rather, with the use of instruments such as anvil or hammer?

There is a possibility, however, of a different reading according to which Olympiodorus is not interested in saying much about plants and animals, or comparing them with human beings, but talks of activities of and within human beings. Earlier in the commentary, he states:

> Now since the target of the dialogue is knowledge of ourselves—not as our body, nor as external things (for it's been entitled 'Alcibiades, Or Concerning the Nature of Human Being') but as the soul, and not as the vegetative soul, nor as the non-rational, but as rational; and since it's certainly not about knowing ourselves as [the rational soul] when it acts to purify itself, or in its contemplative or theological or theurgic aspects, but as a civic person ...

> Olympiodorus *On the Alcibiades* 177.1–8

Given this interest in finding the rational human being, I interpret the ruling out of vegetative and irrational souls (φυτικὴ δὲ καὶ ἄλογος, *On the Alcibiades* 212.11–12) from the human being as a move of excluding vegetative and nonrational layers of soul, within the human being, from the definition of human being more narrowly understood. Within the tradition stemming from the *Timaeus*, through Plotinus, the vegetative and other living functions are seen as so different from rational activities that Platonists more than toy with the idea that they are the result of a soul that is distinct from the higher, intellectual soul, and even has another origin (e.g. *Timaeus* 41d–43a; Plotinus *Enneads*, e.g. IV 3.25–31).[14] Our evidence in Olympiodorus' commentary is too insufficient to determine anything about the locus of origin of the lower soul. I merely mention this line of interpretation to show that the main division that these authors are preoccupied with is not one between other living beings and human beings, but a potential gap within our own nature. Our nature as rational

---

[14] Against this view in Plotinus, see Caluori 2015:171–179.

individuals capable of rational and theoretical activities is seen as *sui generis*: this is distinctive of human beings, and differs from anything else in nature, human vegetative and animal activities included.

Following this line of thinking, the definition of the human being as a soul that uses the body as an instrument is not designed to differentiate human embodied souls on the basis of a special, distanced relationship that they have to their bodies but, rather, to highlight a very special way in which a human being *can* relate to its body. Of the activities that human beings exhibit, some are radically different from the activities that we share with other living beings. Remembering Plato's *Phaedo* (97–99), to explicate the functioning of Socrates' bones and sinews is not false, but it does not answer the interesting question of why he does not, after the unfair death sentence, flee from Athens. Our living functions demand some explanations, but the really interesting aspect of humanity, for these philosophers, is the way that a human being can orient herself in accordance with different, more and less weighty (intentional), and potentially good, virtuous goals. To rule out, from the definition, vegetative and nonrational activities would, according to this interpretation, be a move to rule out from the extension of "human being" those of her activities she shares with other living things. Rather, a human being is definable through the particular way she is able to use the body as an instrument for goal-directed activities. According to this reading, vegetative and nonrational activities can function in the same way in the human being as they do in animals.[15] The particularity of the embodied human being lies in those activities it originates that use the body not only for living functions, but also for rational goal-directed behavior. In these activities, the body cannot function as the ultimate subject of predication, since the goals are set and have to be understood through the soul that initiates them.

If this reading is correct, the picture presented is a kind of amalgamation of Platonic and Aristotelian commitments about the soul. As in Aristotle, there are different kinds or levels of souls, explaining a range of activities from vegetative to rational. The human soul is not distinguished from the soul of an animal or plant because the nonrational nature of these souls is somehow different in kind, nor is the nonrational nature of the human soul committed to its body less than the soul of an animal or plant to its body; the human soul is distinguished from these others by the presence of an additional aspect to its nature that is rational.

---

[15] This does not need to mean that all the activities that are shared function entirely similarly. The case of perception, for example, is one in which the rational soul may pereive things in a way different from a nonrational animal.

What is Platonic about this picture is the fact that the lower, irrational activities are mentioned only in passing (in excluding them from the definition of human being), whereas the main discussion elaborates and highlights the kind of embodied and civic activities of which only human beings are capable. With this understanding, the human being is actually something rather narrow: it is the embodied ability to effect goal-directed actions, both practical and theoretical. While the first interpretation created a gap between the way in which one and the same activity is structurally understood in the plant or animal case and in the human case, the latter interpretation creates another kind of gap, a gap between human nature as a living being and human as a rational-intentional being.

If this, indeed, was Olympiodorus' view, and if he grasped the dialogue correctly or even if only correctly in part, then the entire posterity that blames Plato for originating a view according to which the body is only an instrument of the soul would have been misguided. In defining the human being in the way that Olympiodorus does, it would not have been Plato's (or whoever wrote *Alcibiades I*) intention to explicate the general relationship of the soul to its body in the case of human beings, but, rather, to narrow down humanity to the aspect that is neither the vegetative-animal, nor the disembodied-intellectual, but the level in which we exhibit, in this world, goal-directed rational behavior, using the body as our instrument. This interpretation takes the agent, the locus of also political activities, as that which is most properly a human being, in a narrow sense of the term.

There is a further difficulty, however, of a straightforward identification of instrumental use of the body with intentional, goal-directed behavior. Animal and vegetative souls were said, in the above quote, to use the body *not only* instrumentally but also as a *hupokeimenon* (*On the Alcibiades* 212.12–14); that is, it seems that even some of the vegetative or animal activities are related to the body in an instrumental way. The idea of goal-directed activities affected in and through the body is not as exclusive to rational-intentional human beings as my suggestion would have it. The capacity of instrumental usage seems to be a feature of the vegetative-animal souls—at least in the human case and maybe even in the case of plants and animals themselves. As a response to this, one might appeal to the general understanding of natural changes as teleologically structured in antiquity. While natural changes have the body as their subject, they are also themselves goal-directed, towards the actualization of the nature of the thing in question. Therefore, the line between natural changes and intentional behavior is not as sharp as one might think. Moreover, as the philosophers of biology would quickly point out, there are species—like otters, birds, apes, and the like—the specimens of which use what are widely agreed to be instruments.[16] The break in between the human and the animal-vegetative is empirically also not sharp but gradual. There may, then, exist a similar teleological structure between a plant turning towards the sun and a sleeping human wrapping herself more tightly in a duvet. Yet the human case is nonetheless special, and will exemplify, in addition to this kind of behavior, much more complex and intentional teleological directedness. There are differences in both extension of and level at which intentional "tool-using behavior" is detected: it is not typical for species, with a few rare exceptions, other than human beings, and in most cases it does not involve nonintuitive creating or forging of an instrument. Moreover, the goal-purposiveness in the animal-vegetative case is not longsighted, planned, nor connected to any higher-level goals. In the animal examples, what we see is simple usage of tools available (afterwards to be abandoned) for the immediate urges of the animal in question.

Olympiodorus' emphasis on use of instruments becomes especially pregnant, and revealing of the kind of activities in which he is mainly interested, when situated in the overall context of the dialogue. His definition of the human being is not merely "the soul using the body as an instrument," but "the *rational soul*" doing that. Of the instrumental kinds of relationship he narrows down to the way in which human beings orient themselves in the world, seeing it, at any given moment, as full of availabilities, not only making *ad hoc* use of what is on offer, but evaluating those abilities and working out long-term plans, and doing all this in a context of a political community. The instrumental relationship of human beings to their bodies, then, not only reveals the necessary medium through which humans can exist and operate in the world. In the human case, this instrument opens up possibilities that are closed for animals and plants, because of their lack of a rational soul.

Finally, it is a little interesting that the heavenly bodies are not disqualified from the extension of the definition by this second move, by being related to the body in some other way than instrumental. If they were, it would seem superfluous to add the straight movement to the definition. Olympiodorus must think that heavenly bodies are similar to human souls in being related to their bodies in the way that the user uses an instrument. Famously, in the creation myth of the *Timaeus*, inspiring for many Neoplatonic commentators, the bodies of stars are inhabited by gods who carry the two motions typical for these entities: rotation around their axes and circular orbits (*Timaeus* 40a–b). It seems that the relationship of these divinities to their bodies is not, if we take them as being captured by the definition without the exclusion of things

---

[16] New Caledonian crows fashion "hooks" from twigs and wires and then use these to "fish" insects from inside tree bark. See Hunt 1996.

that engage in circular movement, necessary for their existence, but one step distanced, and something to which the metaphor of using is suitable. This does not seem to work very neatly in Plato's text, since the motions of the heavenly bodies affect the thoughts of these gods, which suggests a closer bond to the moving body than what theoretical rational souls have. Yet it is also true that these motions are endowed to the gods, rather than to the bodies, and thereby perhaps tell little of the depth of the embodiment in question.[17] Be that as it may, Olympiodorus seems to think that the relationship of a god presiding over a star-body is potentially of the same sort as that of a human soul's relationship to its body in its goal-directed action. But if this is the case, the definition of what is proper for *human beings* is in danger of including heavenly bodies; thus, the addition of straight movement to the definition.

At the outset, the move to exclude heavenly bodies might be seen as favoring the first reading presented above, for the reasons that have to do with symmetry. The two restrictions would, in that reading, embody a double exclusion of other kinds of living beings from the definition. If we allow a little bit of asymmetry into the interpretation, we may note that this narrowing down to beings with straight motions rather than circular suits the latter idea, the definition of human being as a thing that actualizes its goals in and through the body, rather than as the more extended being with immortal and embodied parts. By ruling out beings with eternal motion, the exclusion makes human beings mortal: only circular motion is perpetual, while straight motion of which we are capable has a beginning and an end. Through different alleys, then, we get to the human being as an embodied, goal-directed agent in the civic and political life, rather than to the wider conception inclusive of immortal-theoretical parts. In purified as well as ascended states, goal-directed embodied activities are no longer actual, and ourselves no longer primarily human beings.

3. Instruments Contributing to the Goals

The above steps of exclusion explicate and justify the programmatic statements in the beginning of the part treating the question of self-knowledge. As we remember, the topic of the dialogue was explicated as knowledge of ourselves "not as our body, nor as external things (for it is been entitled *Alcibiades, Or Concerning the Nature of Human Being*) but as the soul, and not as the vegetative

---

[17] What is clearer is that Plotinus thought that if there is some affection between star-souls and human beings, it is from the former to the latter, and not *vice versa*. While stars may either govern or serve as signs of providential government, human prayers cannot move or affect them (*Enneads* IV 4.6.4–7 and 35.37–39). Perhaps they are seen, thus, similarly distinct and beyond anything bodily as the rational individual soul.

soul, nor as the non-rational, but as rational" (*On the Alcibiades* 177.16). The proper level of the dialogue is the civic person, the human being. And human being, in turn, is neither the body, nor the aspects of the soul we share with other living beings. Yet the human being is not equated, thereby, with pure rational soul or intellect. Remember that Olympiodorus continued: "Besides ruling; and since it's certainly not about knowing ourselves as [the rational soul] when it acts to purify itself, or in its contemplative or theological or theurgic aspects, but as a civic person ..." (*On the Alcibiades* 177.18). A few lines below, he repeats the idea and gives one possible motivation for excluding the purified soul and self from the definition:

> [Socrates] defines the human being as 'a rational soul using the body as an instrument': and only the civic person is like this; for the purificatory person does not use the body as an instrument, if *instruments one associates with contribute to the goal of the user* (τὰ ὄργανα παραλαμβόμενα συντελεῖ τῷ χρωμένῳ); rather, the body becomes more of an impediment to the purificatory person ...
>
> Olympiodorus *On the Alcibiades* 177.14–18

Olympiodorus refers, though rather obliquely, to the Neoplatonic doctrine of grades of virtue. The goal of the dialogue is especially in leading an embodied person, Alcibiades or the reader, to the level of civic virtue, combined with the idea that this is a level below the true goal, that of purification. Civic virtue, famously, resembles *metriopatheia*: this is virtue that does not rely on getting rid of the bodily inclinations altogether, but on a precarious control over them.[18] But why is a purified, apathetic soul that still lives in and through the body not identified as a "human being"? After all, "instrument" is a technical term here that distinguishes a relationship with the used thing that retains the ontological difference between the user and the used. By using the body, the rational soul does not become immersed in any union; it does not participate in creating some one thing that would then act as the proper subject for predication for everything initiated by that person. Moreover, in Plotinus we have an explicit view by a Neoplatonic predecessor arguing that the soul, in using the body as an instrument, need not be affected by that instrument, just as the craftsmen are not affected by their instruments (χρωμένη μὲν οὖν σώματι οἷα ὀργάνῳ οὐκ ἀναγκάζεται δέξασθαι τὰ διὰ τοῦ σώματος παθήματα, *Enneads* I 1.3.35). Olympiodorus presents a view that is different, although perhaps not conflicting. The reason for the exclusion of the rational soul from the definition

---

[18]   For the grades of virtue, see e.g. Dillon 1983.

of "human being" lies for him in what role embodiment in his view has for setting goals. To use body as an instrument does compromise the purity of the rational soul in another way: instruments, their qualities and the possibilities they open for action, *contribute to the goals of their users.*[19] A person left in an empty room with only, alternatively, a ball, or a pencil and paper, will engage in different activities accordingly. The human body is suited for walking and running, but not for flying. In setting our goals for action, we take into account what is possible for us through the instruments available. As an instrument, the human body is, of course, amazing, opening up a wide number of possible courses of action. But it does impose certain constraints, and these constraints are, moreover, inescapable. There is no other room, so to speak, to walk in, no other instrument to try. The only real possibility of widening our options may be to get rid of that instrument altogether.

The Neoplatonic ultimate goal of purification, then, is motivated by a perceptive realization of what the human embodiment brings with itself. This concern may reveal itself through different doctrinal emphases. Plotinus' concern is in nonphilosophical people who let the soul get mixed with the body, and do not recognize the separateness of the rational soul. Embodiment is a threat to vulnerable or weak people, people who allow themselves to be guided by emotions triggered by the body and its deeds. His point is twofold: on the one hand, people wanting to acquire virtue and become philosophers should recognize the soul as not mixed with but using the body (this is "separating the soul by philosophy," χωρίζειν διὰ φιλοσοφίας); and, on the other hand, the fact that a philosophical soul is capable of refraining from, for some moments or periods, even a controlled or virtuous use of the body (*Enneads* I 3.3.15–27). For both Plotinus and Olympiodorus, the "use" of the body, then, does not signify the way in which soul as a whole, lower parts included, is related to the body. Using the body is a more conscious way of acting, actively rather than passively, in and through the body, and of not being "mixed" with it. But while Plotinus highlights the possibility of contemplative moments when the philosophical separation reaches its summit and is not directed to the world at all, Olympiodorus' interest is in explaining, descriptively, the way in which "using," a relationship that may not entail any proper passive affection, is nonetheless constrained by the world. Even though form is metaphysically independent from and unaffected by

---

[19] In *Cratylus* 386d–387b, Socrates introduces the idea of "nature of cutting" and "the natural tool for cutting." The idea is that the agent cannot succeed in acting by doing whatever she likes, but must abide by the nature of the activity and the tools available for it. Besides making action teleological in a radical normative sense (some actions are right by nature), the view does imply that the goals of actions are not entirely independent from the kind of activities there are and the tools we use for them.

matter, the body nonetheless enables and shapes the goals that a person (or her soul) has. This is depicted, in the above quote, as a positive thing for the civic person, but it is, of course, also the very reason why the civic life can never be the highest, most purely virtuous state of a human soul. If embodiment were a *weak* relationship, a relationship where the user remains entirely untouched by the body, it would not pose the kind of danger to our existence as it does. It would not be a proper fall. Olympiodorus' interpretation, however, suggests *a moderate embodiment*: embodied understanding is affected in and by the body. The body contributes to the goals of action of an embodied rational soul. It does not constitute the understanding of that soul (that would be equivalent to *a strong embodiment*), but it does affect the shape its goals take. This contributing or shaping of the goals can be seen as a good or a bad thing, depending upon what kind of goodness we are interested in.

We have seen that for vegetative and nonrational souls the body is not merely an instrument, but the proper subject of predication without which the predicated qualities could not exist. We have further seen that Olympiodorus recognizes that this may well be the case even for human beings, but that he thinks the concept that is a human being is not exhausted or perhaps not even truly captured by tracking activities of this kind. The idea might be good to understand against the background of Alexander of Aphrodisias and his naturalism. Alexander was much used and read, and Olympiodorus' relationship with his teachings seems to have been close, given that he refers to him explicitly in other works.[20] As regards main points of divergence between Aristotelianism and Platonism, Alexander functioned as an opponent. He is keen on distinguishing higher from lower activities, but he thinks of the former as necessarily built upon the latter.[21] A Neoplatonist might or might not buy into the idea that, say, vegetative activities necessitate the existence of a body, but they would want to see the highest cognitive abilities as independent from bodies, indeed sometimes hindered rather than enabled by them. Olympiodorus and other Neoplatonists want to make it very clear that, *pace* Alexander, the embodiment of higher rational souls is of a specific kind, something that does not function as a necessary foundation for the rational soul, and something the affections of which the rational soul can learn to dismiss or even avoid.[22] This kind of separation, however, is not an available option for an embodied individual working mainly in the ordinary world. In so far as the individual has goals that lie in the material-temporal realm, or at the very least necessitate functioning in

---

[20] Wildberg 2008 mentions, for example, references in the commentary on Aristotle's *Meteorology*.

[21] *On the Soul* 28.22–26.

[22] For philosophical practice of dying as something entirely different—learned and voluntary—from ordinary death, see Mouzala 2014.

that realm, that person has to strive for those goals with the help of the special "instrument" through which she is in that realm—the body.

4. Grades of Goodness, Grades of Perfections

Aristotle's function argument establishes that the good of each kind of thing is connected to its particular kind of function, the fulfillment of which is desirable to the thing in question, and in at least the human case brings it well-being or happiness (*Nicomachean Ethics* 1097b22–1098a20). The Neoplatonists appropriate this idea to their hierarchical cosmos, and combine it with their commitment that this hierarchy is a descending system of grades of reality and goodness. In his commentary to *Alcibiades* (a source well-known to Olympiodorus), Proclus states:

> But the same good is not supremely proportioned to primary and secondary beings, nor perfection, varied according to being, to similar beings; but, as the Athenian stranger observes, the equality that assigns the unequal to the unequal, a greater portion to the greater, and a lesser to the less, is the most harmonious and best of all. Now according to this equality the good varies in different beings, and the natural good therein doubtless corresponds to the nature of each. Therefore the perfection of intellect is in eternity, but of soul in time; *the soul's good is according to the intellect, but the body's according to nature; again the perfection of gods differs from that of angels and spirits, which in turn differs from that of individual souls.*

Proclus On the Alcibiades 3.5–13[23]

Given that the commentary starts with these thoughts, it seems that Proclus understands what happens in the dialogue's search for the self to be cared of as a method of establishing, first, the kind of thing in question (its *ousia*), in order to be able to determine, then, its natural, appropriate kind of good. This differs already from the unsophisticated, non-scholarly view of the dialogue, since the purport of the distinction between soul and body-instrument and other instruments is not in the way in which we try to locate the one and only aspect of us the well-being of which matters for human being. Yes, the soul and its well-being is the highest and most valuable locus in this hierarchy, but from that does not follow that the other levels would not feature any goodness. And more importantly, the goodness they exhibit is not only quantitatively different: they

---

[23] The translation is according to O'Neill 2011.

do not merely exhibit less goodness; they exhibit their particular kinds of goodness, kinds that are not typical for the highest level.

This idea of the connection of kinds of goodness is adopted by Olympiodorus, who repeats the idea that "in relation to different [kinds of] being, care and perfection are different" (*On the Alcibiades* 198.67). He applies it in two different ways. On the one hand, as regards the big question of what we care for when we care for ourselves, he establishes different kinds of goals. If the self to be cared for was (or in his words echoing Plotinus usage of *hêmeis*, "if 'we' would be") simply the body, then the goal would be strength and beauty. If the self to be cared for was spirit, then the goal would be victory; but if the self was the Platonic tripartite soul, then the goal would be the moderation of emotion. But since, he states, "we" are our reason (*logos*), the goal is freedom from affection. This picture in itself suggests an exclusive view: we are none of the things listed, nothing other than *logos*, and our perfection is its perfection. This, indeed, is the ultimate truth about selfhood, of what kind of beings we ought to strive to be.

But as becomes clear later on, the reality of other aspects of our nature and lives is not ignored. He later confirms:

> And the entities are not confounded with one another, nor is their care, nor their modes of perfection, but in fact none of the [particular] skills are productive of fulfillment. For our own perfection comes about through philosophy, but [the perfection] of our belonging through [the skills of] exercise and medicine, and [the perfection] of our belonging's belongings through [the skill of] money-making.

> Olympiodorus *On the Alcibiades* 200.6–10

The way to perfection, then, is not finding one *tekhnê*, even if it was as marvelous as philosophy, that ultimately makes people happy, but, rather, disentangling the kinds of things that there are, and finding the proper kind of perfection for each. Having done that, one is able to provide the kind of care, through a use of the relevant *tekhnê*, of the thing in question. For care of self, who we actually are, users of arguments, philosophy provides the kind of care needed. But for the whole human being, the thing that also uses the body as its instrument, a care of the instrument cannot be neglected. This care is different: exercise, medicine, things that keep us healthy and strong. According to this model, one who has set one's main goal in strength, or, say, victory, is misconceiving the truth about our selves, missing our real and most valuable nature. But it also follows from this system that a person who, say, tries to use philosophy, or commerce, for improvement of the condition of the body is ludicrous, and violates the order of the three columns (*sustoikhiai*): the user, the belonging, and the belonging of the belonging. Each column has its proper end, care, and perfection distinct from those featuring in the other columns.

Although this general idea of proper kinds of goodness also applies, of course, to everything else in nature, the concern in commenting this particular dialogue seems to be in human beings. Again, then, the efforts of the commentators seem to be directed at understanding different aspects and activities within human nature, and the goals that they have.

The view defended here is that Olympiodorus defines the human being rather narrowly, as that side of the rational soul that uses the body as an instrument in its goal-directed activities. This aspect of our nature has a particular kind of good of its own: a sociopolitical activity which is as effective and virtuous as possible (that is, living the life that human beings live situated within their family, social position, and city, to the fullest). Importantly, human beings also do that in order to manage complex entities like households and entire cities, spreading well-being both outside their immediate surroundings as well as planning for it in the long term, diachronically. Ultimately, of course, this involves understanding something about the columns of goodness: of being able to determine the kinds of perfections and best possible activities for different kinds of things.

This brings us to a problem concerning the repercussions of this picture for the kind of (good) life chosen, and one that echoes classical challenges originating already in Plato. Is the political life only a preparation for something better, say, for pure contemplation? If this is the case, just how much attention should we pay to it? What we can say about the way in which the perfections, or Proclus' goods in three different columns, are related? And, worryingly, given that our nature encompasses both the political human nature as well as potentialities for higher, cathartic, and purely theoretical states of the soul, can they conflict with one another? And, since this seems even likely, how are we to determine the conflict situations? Remember the philosopher-guardians of the Kallipolis, drawn to contemplation but being forced to manage the city (e.g. *Republic* 520e–521b). Within the Neoplatonic hierarchy of goodness, we might think that in problem situations the safest course of action is always to choose the higher good. Why go for a lower, less perfect good if you can go after more valuable perfection? But is it enough merely to say that we in those cases always, ultimately, must choose the good of the higher, rational soul? If the philosopher-kings withdraw from the city, what happens to its development? Olympiodorus does not confront these issues directly in this context. What he does is to argue for the usefulness of the kind of self-knowledge propounded even for the statesman. Having the power or authority to do what one likes, as a statesman, is not going to make cities better places to be, if the statesman knows no justice or self-control himself. He quotes (*On the Alcibiades* 229.7–11) Plato's original work: "So it's not walls or war-ships or shipyards that cities need, Alcibiades, if they are to prosper, nor is it numbers or size, without virtue" (*Alcibiades* 134b5–6). The individual attempt at the acquisition of virtue is not, then, in itself in conflict with ruling a city—rather, it is the very thing that promotes good statesmanship.

But this ancient wisdom, neglected in present-day politics, is no answer to the conflict that the philosopher-guardians of the Kallipolis find themselves in, given that they have concluded the self-improvement needed, and thus already make good statesmen, but would nonetheless prefer, from the individual point of view, the activity of theoretical contemplation. What grounds, if any, are there for assuming that the acquisition of purificatory virtue and the life connected to it never clashes with the demands of political virtue? Quite likely a Neoplatonist will advocate the preservation of the first at the expense of the latter.[24] Moreover, there has to be something more interesting to say on how the possession of the highest, theoretical good also makes us understand the good of the lower columns, and in what circumstances and proportion attention should be given to each.[25] But this, and the wider question of the relationship of the individual and the city in late Neoplatonism, we must leave for another occasion and context.[26]

5. Conclusion

Above, I have argued for three main things. First, Olympiodorus' definition of the human being is "the soul using the body as an instrument," or more fully, "the rational soul using as an instrument the body that moves in straight lines." This definition captures the aspect of the rational soul capable of effecting, actively and consciously, goal-directed action in the world. It rules out not merely plants, animals, and heavenly bodies, but also automatic life-activities we share with other living beings. (According to Plotinus, the relationship of such use seems, further, to rule out passive affections.) The human being is separated not only from its surrounding nature, but also from those perfect,

---

[24] See e.g. Plotinus *Enneads* VI 8.6.1–23.

[25] I have elsewhere argued (Remes 2006) that Plotinian good man understands the good overall, inclusive of different places and tasks that things have in the cosmic order and is thereby equipped to answer at least some questions that pertain to normal, embodied and political life.

[26] See D. O'Meara 2003. For example at 77–78, O'Meara suggests, plausibly, that the providential care that a philosopher-king shows towards the world is not in conflict of the theoretical good, a good that actually informs it. One reason to think in this way that he argues for is the idea of god-likeness, and its interpretation in late antiquity. Assimilation with the divine will consist of imitation of both the inner and the outer activities of God.

intellectual, and divine souls that are not related to bodies in any way. With the notion of "human being" an embodied and political agent and object of self-knowledge is targeted. Second, this definition is grounded in the locution of "use as an instrument," a notion that is not meant to signify, according to the way Olympiodorus uses it, the way in which the soul, generally, is related to the body. It captures the kind of relationship typical for human beings in which the body is used to enable different goal-directed activities in the world. Third, such a relationship entails moderate embodiment. The soul is metaphysically separate from the body, and a philosophically enlightened soul may even recognize this separation and thus not be enslaved to bodily inclinations. But by using any instrument, the user's goals are shaped by the kind of instruments used. Embodiment, then, is moderate rather than weak: in and within embodied activities the body contributes to the goals enabled by it. Moderate embodiment also fits together well with the late Neoplatonic idea of the kinds of goodness particular to different entities. The soul's good is according to intellect, while the body has its own kind of good, a good according to nature. Being in the body is a way of actualizing this particular kind of good.

The embodied, politically and socially active life strives for the kind of good goals made possible by the body-instrument. Even a wise person cannot be merely weakly embodied. Insofar as she engages in something else than fully abstract, theoretical thinking, the body will shape her activities, and contribute to those goals that motivate the activities in the world.[27]

---

[27] I wish to express my gratitude to the editors of this volume and Holger Thesleff, as well as Lorenzo Casini, Olof Pettersson, and Hallvard Stette.

10

Lessons from the Body

Alchemy and Spiritual Exercises in the First
Lesson on Excellence of Zosimos of Panopolis

OLIVIER DUFAULT[1]

Abstract: This chapter first demonstrates that Zosimos of Panopolis, the first identifiable writer of Greek alchemical commentaries, was most likely writing in the function of a client scholar. It then points to striking parallels between the images found in the first *Lesson On Excellence* and those found in eschatological narratives, thus providing evidence for seeing in the *Lesson* more than the allegorical transcription of metallurgical recipes. Read together with other passages from his work, the *Lesson* shows that Zosimos also saw alchemy as a soteriological practice by which one could extract his or her soul (considered as immaterial) from its body and the material world. It concludes by noting that Zosimos' description of alchemy is close to what Pierre Hadot called spiritual exercises and that his philosophical outlook was not different from that of many other late antique scholars.

***

The ears of corn nodding down to the ground, the lion's puckered brow, the foam gushing from the boar's mouth, and much else besides—looked at in isolation these things are far from lovely, but their consequence on the processes of nature enhances them and gives them attraction. So any man with a feeling and deeper insight for the workings of the whole will find some pleasure in almost every aspect of their disposition, including the incidental consequences. Such a man will take no

---

[1] Research for this paper was funded by the Graduate School Distant Worlds, Ludwig-Maximilians-Universität Munich and the Fonds Québécois de la Recherche–Société et Culture.

less delight in the living snarl of wild animals than in all the imitative representations of painters and sculptors; he will see a kind of bloom and fresh beauty in an old woman or an old man; and he will be able to look with sober eyes on the seductive charm of his own slave boys. Not all can share this conviction—only one who has developed a genuine affinity for nature and her works.

Marcus Aurelius Meditations 3.2[2]

A RE THESE THE MUSINGS of a "cuddly and wandering little soul," as Marcus Aurelius' spiritual father might have said,[3] or are they the incoherent thoughts of a morbid pessimist who only saw corpses in the most refined dishes and for whom sex was a mere rubbing of flesh and an excretion of humors?[4] As P. Hadot argued, what scholars perceived as the contradictory valuation of the cosmos in the *Meditations* was not the intimate expression of a sick or confused man. Marcus Aurelius' cold, "scientific" descriptions were school exercises; reminders that these natural scenes—however beautiful or terrible they might have seemed—had to be considered as indifferent as far as the good and one's will were concerned. They were occasions in which one could rehearse a certain type of spiritual exercise, the type that exploited the persuasive effects of natural science.[5]

A similar argument can be made with the works attributed to Zosimos of Panopolis, one of the most revered authors of Greek, Arabic, Syriac, and Latin alchemy.[6] Zosimos was probably active between the late third century and the beginning of the fourth century.[7] Unlike Marcus Aurelius, Zosimos sought to

---

[2] The translation is according to Hammond 2006. All other translations in the chapter are mine.
[3] *Hadrianus* in *Augustan History* 25.3.
[4] Marcus Aurelius *Meditations* 6.13.
[5] P. Hadot 1987:119–133.
[6] These traditions are still untapped. The Greek texts among them are currently edited by the Belles Lettres. For a recent edition of a Syriac text of Zosimos not represented by the Greek tradition, see Camplani 2000. For a recent study of the Arabic tradition of Zosimos, see Hallum 2008.
[7] Zosimos quoted Julius Africanus (Berthelot-Ruelle 1888:2.169.7), who was active ca. 200 and who died before 240 CE. As *terminus ante quem*, Mertens 1995:xvi argued that Zosimos wrote before 391 since his mention of the "libraries" (*bibliothêkais*) of the Ptolemies imply that they were still standing (see Zosimos *Authentic Memoirs* I 8.82–85). This suggests that Zosimos wrote before the destruction of the Serapeum and of its library in 391. Proposing to shorten the dating bracket further, Mertens argued that the negative mention of Mani (alluded to by Zosimos *Authentic Memoirs* I 14) suggests that Zosimos probably wrote shortly after 302, when a rescript sent to the governor of the province of Africa in 302 forbade Manichaeanism (this rescript is only found in the *Comparison of Mosaic and Roman Laws* 15.3 and was not included in the Theodosian code). Unfortunately, anti-Manichean polemics and legislation were repeatedly published after the rescript (see e.g. *Justinian Code* 1.5.11; Photius *Against the Manicheans*). It is also possible that

prepare the self for its immaterial life after the destruction of the body. As in the *Meditations,* however, his depiction of embodied life was sometimes particularly negative. He enjoined his addressee Theosebeia to transform herself back into the primordial and immaterial human, perhaps describing this process as that of "spitting over matter."[8] By looking into oneself, Zosimos wrote, one could "contemplate the son of God, who becomes everything for the love of the holy souls, in order to extract the soul from the world of destiny toward the incorporeal."[9]

In the following, I argue that Zosimos' understanding of alchemical practice as described in the first *Lesson on Excellence* can be characterized as a form of late antique spiritual exercise the goal of which is to bring the soul back to its prefallen state. It is also important to point out that this argument does not imply that Zosimos considered alchemy exclusively as a soteriological practice.[10] The first section introduces Zosimos and suggests one possible social environment for his work. The next two sections look at external and internal references in Zosimos' first *Lesson on Excellence* in an attempt to explain the soteriology he advocated. To anticipate on my findings: (1) Zosimos was most likely a "client scholar;" and (2) he referred to eschatological narratives describing the world of the afterlife in his first *Lesson on Excellence*; (3) I will conclude that Zosimos saw the solution to the soul's embodiment in the study of physical transformations.

1. Zosimos and Alchemy in Late Antique Egypt

The use of the term "alchemy" to discuss Greek texts from late antiquity is worth an explanation. The history of alchemy and chemistry sometimes separates texts into two exclusive categories, those of "practical" proto-chemistry and those of "spiritual" alchemy. Considering that the output attributed to Zosimos concerns the production of luxury goods as well as the liberation of spirit from matter, I see no point in keeping with this distinction here. In the following, "alchemy" (close to ancient Greek *khêmeia* or *khumeia*) refers to a group of "dyeing techniques" (*baphai*) aimed at the production of imitation luxury goods whether their practice was motivated by soteriological concerns or not.

Zosimos' name itself could have been used by later pseudepigraphs. The very fact that some of his writings were called "authentic" cast doubt on their authenticity.

[8]   See Festugière 1949:367–368.

[9]   Zosimos *Authentic Memoirs* I 64–67.

[10] That is not according to the definition given in P. Hadot 1987:60 but according to the one given in P. Hadot 1995:22: "des pratiques, qui pouvaient être d'ordre physique, comme le régime alimentaire, ou discursif, comme le dialogue et la méditation, ou intuitif, comme la contemplation, mais qui étaient toutes destinées à opérer une modification et une transformation dans le sujet qui les pratiquait."

The two oldest extant Greek alchemical manuscripts, dated ca. 300, were found in Egypt, perhaps together with some of the recipe books edited by K. Preisendanz in the *Greek Magical Papyri*. Some of the papyri were probably written by the same person who wrote the two alchemical manuscripts.[11] Works attributed to Zosimos would be roughly contemporary to these texts, if we can trust that it was not also the object of pseudo-epigraphy. Complicating the issue of identifying the date and milieu where Zosimos worked, there is almost no late antique evidence showing individuals practicing anything close to alchemy. Even the term *kheimeutês* (and other spellings), a close equivalent to the modern "alchemist," is only attested for the first time in the *Chronicle* of Malalas (sixth century).[12]

There are, however, a few sources external to the corpus mentioning counterfeiters and people who compared theological or physical ideas with metallurgical procedures. Proclus, who shared with alchemical writers the notion that each celestial sphere is associated with a different metal,[13] also argued against "those who attempt to make gold" on the basis that "nature creates the unified [or one-of-a-kind] species of gold before the mixture of species they [i.e. the "alchemists"] speak about."[14] Almost all of these sources appear to have rhetorically amalgamated the "corrupt" ideas of their targets with the "debased" metals they dealt in.[15] Aëtius of Antioch, a theologian accused of counterfeiting gold, was nonetheless described as a goldsmith by an ecclesiastical historian sympathetic to his doctrinal position.[16] One wonders if some of these theologians were not actually involved in preparing and selling precious metals in order to survive, or, as several alchemical authors wrote, in order to

---

[11] See Brashear 1995:3401. Note that the "Theban magical library" hypothesis is based on short description found in an auction catalogue. Considering how the business of archaeology was conducted in the nineteenth century, these indications are unfortunately unreliable. For a different point of view, see Zago 2010.

[12] Malalas *Chronicle* 16.5.2.

[13] See Proclus *Commentary on the Timaeus* I 43.1–20 and *Commentary on the Republic* III 94.10–20. The same idea is attributed to a Mithraic doctrine in Origen *Against Celsus* 6.22.

[14] Proclus *Commentary on the Republic* II 234.16–19: οἱ χρυσὸν ποιεῖν φάσκοντες ἐκ μίξεώς τινων εἰδῶν, τῆς φύσεως πρὸ μίξεως ὧν οὗτοι λέγουσιν τὸ εἶδος ἐν τοῦ χρυσοῦ ποιούσης. The word *hen* here could be possibly read as the equivalent of *monoeides*, with which Plato described gold (*Timaeus* 59b2) and which meant there "monospecific," i.e. of a kind with only one species.

[15] See Martelli 2014a. For similar mentions in early heresiology, see Irenaeus *Against the Heresies* 1.21.3–5 and "Hippolytus" *Refutation of all Heresies* 5.19–21, with Charron 2005 and Burns 2015. It is also likely that polemical (and anti-Paulinian) distortions of performative allegories can be found in a peculiar passage from the *Pseudo-Clementines Homilies* (2.26), where Simon the Samaritan is accused of a human sacrifice of sorts: having created a fetus inside a glass vessel out from *pneuma*, Simon is said to have made a drawing of his "*homunculus*" and to have returned it back into the air.

[16] See Philostorgius *Ecclesiastical History* III 14–20, with Prieur 2005.

"vanquish poverty, this incurable ill."[17] It seems, in any case, that the modern term alchemist—i.e. somebody recognized in his own social milieu for his or her professional practice and study of alchemical recipes—does not apply to late antique evidence.

Like the other authors of alchemical texts in the alchemical corpus, Zosimos was called a *philosophos*.[18] Jung called him a Gnostic. This is a decent etic label considering the close similarities between his writings and some of the Nag Hammadi treatises as well as the alchemical allegories used by the Sethians of Irenaeus.[19] Still, calling him a Gnostic in the restricted sense of the word would be missing the fact that his ideas were more widely diffused than this label often implies. His mention of Christ, as the one "who becomes everything," recalls the saying attributed to the Valentinians, according to whom the Savior "is the All."[20] These, moreover, are similar to the "son of God" equated with the cosmos in Hermetic texts[21] and to the idea of Christ-Logos as "all things as one" found in Clement of Alexandria and later in Origen and Gregory of Nyssa.[22]

Zosimos was also influenced by Hermetic literature.[23] As with Greek alchemical literature, the social environment of "Hermetism" is mostly unknown. Even though the *Corpus Hermeticum* suggests that Hermetic literature was not just a personal "literary mystery," it is still unclear if some of those who read and copied this literature were recognized as part of a distinct sect and if the modern term "hermetist" refers to any ancient social reality.[24] Like ancient "alchemists," "hermetists" in the fourth century were probably not recognized as such.

Zosimos does not appear to have been part of an exclusivist sect or a group that favored a certain tradition over others. He cited and interpreted many different authors or pseudo-epigraphs, including Hesiod, Hermes, Nicotheos "the Hidden,"[25] and Pseudo-Democritus.[26] He also gave Christ an important role in his

---

[17] See Zosimos *Authentic Memoirs* I 188 and Berthelot-Ruelle 1887–1888:2.212.21. The alchemical treatise entitled *Dioscorus to Synesius* attributes this saying to Democritus; see *The Philosopher Synesius to Dioscorus* 5. See also Berthelot-Ruelle 1887–1888:2.211.10-11, 285.3, 414.9.

[18] See Mertens 1995:ix.

[19] For a systematic overview of the evidence, see Mertens 2002. See also Stolzenberg 1999, Charron and Painchaud 2001, Fraser 2004, Charron 2005, Fraser 2007, and Burns 2015.

[20] Irenaeus *Against Heresies* 1.3.4.

[21] *Corpus Hermeticum* IX 8, X 14.

[22] See Ramelli forthcoming (a).

[23] See Mertens 2002, Fraser 2007, Camplani 2000, and Van Den Kerchove 2012:281–282, 314–315.

[24] See Van Den Kerchove 2012. For a different interpretation, see Bull (2018).

[25] See Jackson 1990.

[26] In all of his literary output, Zosimos quotes Maria (76 instances), Democritus (74 instances, excluding those where he might have been referred to by the expression "the philosopher"), Hermes (60), Agathodaimon (37), Ostanes (19), Plato (10), Aristotle (9), Pebichios (9), Moses (6), Apollo (6), Chu-, Che-, Chimes (5), Isis (3), Hesiod (3), Nicotheos (2), Pammenes (2), Aratos (1), Poimenandres (1), Bitos (1), Salomon (1), and Membres (1).

soteriology but named him only once.[27] His description of an alchemical drug as a Mithraic mystery might also show that he had specialized knowledge of Mithraic symbols.[28] Intellectually speaking, however, it would not be entirely accurate to describe Zosimos as a universalist. He rejected traditions implying commerce with demons, which, as he claimed, presided over Egyptian temples (see below).

Leaving ethnic/linguistic, religious, and intellectual categories asides, I find it more interesting to situate Zosimos socioeconomically as a scholar working in close association with a richer (or more influential) patron. Lucian of Samosata provides an extensive description of these "client scholars", who, through relatively informal (or at least noncontractual) means, came to "live with" status-conscious patrons in order to teach them or their family, entertain them, and to grant them access to all that *paideia* had to provide, "magic" and "divination" included.[29] Lucian's satire obviously contains exaggerations, but it could not have been entertaining if it did not dramatize and distort real experiences. Zosimos appears to have written his alchemical treatises in a similar context.

2. Theosebeia's Household

In his treatise *On the Vaporization of the Divine Water that Fixes Mercury*,[30] Zosimos described a reception organized by Theosebeia (his addressee) in which a retainer called Paxamos and identified as a *strouktôros* cooked a fowl in a sort of *couscoussier*. To Zosimos' amazement, the steam not only cooked the bird but also conveyed its color to it. He saw in this process a parallel with alchemical "tinctures" (*baphai*), and this reminded him of the design of an apparatus he had earlier seen in a book from Theosebeia's library. In the rest of this short treatise, Zosimos dealt with the process of vaporization and fixation in alchemical processes.[31]

The Greek *strouktôros* transliterates the Latin *structor*, meaning a servant or slave responsible for setting the dinner table.[32] In some cases, however, the role implied more sophistication. The first course of Trimalchio's dinner in Petronius' *Satyricon* (35–36 and 39) provides us with some idea of the kind of literary/philosophical games played by *structores*. Trimalchio's *structor* designed

---

[27] Zosimos *Authentic Memoirs* I 13.121–126. Festugière (1949:270n10) and Reitzenstein (1904:105n4) considered this passage as a Christian interpolation. See however Mertens 1995:6n80.

[28] *Authentic Memoirs* XIII. As Mertens pointed out, the "encephalic alabaster stone" mentioned by Zosimos was most probably a code name for the egg (see Berthelot-Ruelle 1888:2.18.2–3, 20.19–21). There is a Mithraic monument from Housesteads (UK) depicting the birth of Mithras coming out of an egg instead of the traditional stone. See Vermaseren 1956, catalogue number 860.

[29] See Lucian *The Dependent Scholar* 27.14–17 and 40.12–18.

[30] *Authentic Memoirs* VIII.

[31] See *Authentic Memoirs* VIII 1–10.

[32] See Mertens 1995:26n2.

a meal course hidden in a spherical vessel inscribed with the twelve zodiacal signs. He set an appropriate piece of food on top of each sign (e.g. two fishes over Pisces), placed a piece of turf in the middle of the vessel, and laid a honeycomb on the turf. Finishing the scene, he ordered an Egyptian slave to serve bread out of a silver oven while circumambulating the spherical vessel. The vessel and its "sorry morsels" (*viles cibos*), however, were only meant as an intellectual appetizer. Once opened, the vessel revealed the udders of fattened sows, a hare with wings ("to look like Pegasus"), and fishes splashed by peppered *garum* flowing out of wineskins held by four Marsyas. As Trimalchio made clear (*Satyricon* 39), the entire meal represented life and death and was meant for lovers of literature: the spherical dish, as shown by the piece of turf, represented the earth, "round like an egg," and the honeycomb represented the goods that can be found in it; "the world turns like a mill," Trimalchio concluded, "and always cause[s] some evil, causing humans to be born or to die." While Trimalchio did not interpret the meaning of the Egyptian slave carrying bread "around" (*circumferebat*) the hosts with a silver oven, it was most likely meant as a representation of the moon. Trimalchio's *structor* perhaps also wanted to complete the flattering *tableau vivant* with the hosts themselves, who stood for the planets—that is to say, gods surrounding this Dionysian grotto.[33]

Theosebeia's use of an unusual and specialized servant suggests that she was relatively wealthy. Zosimos' surprise at the work of the *structor* and the fact that he noted his title as a novelty also suggests that Theosebeia might have come to Egypt from the Latin-speaking world, or, at least, from a social environment alien to that of Zosimos.[34] The mention that Theosebeia owned a library, a fact noted *en passant* by Zosimos, also supports the hypothesis that she came from a wealthy family.[35]

Zosimos, however, did not describe Theosebeia like a Greco-Egyptian Trimalchio or as the "uneducated book-collector" of Lucian of Samosata. Theosebia held alchemical initiations[36] and it is perhaps in preparation for these initiations that she consulted with Zosimos together with Neilos the "priest" and Paphnutia the "virgin," who are known only through Zosimos' criticism.[37]

---

[33] See also Plutarch *On the Delays in Divine Vengeance* 565f–566b. On the image of the "crater of Dionysios" standing for the Earth, see Edwards 1992:56.

[34] *Authentic Memoirs* VIII 2–3: ἐθαύμαζον μὲν πᾶσαν τὴν τοῦ παρὰ σοὶ καλουμένου στρούκτωρος ἐργασίαν.

[35] That this mention would be another piece of flattery is suggested by the fact that Lucian of Samosata was particularly annoyed by what he called "uneducated book collectors," the title of one of his satires. This *topos* is rehashed in *The Dependent Scholar*.

[36] This is known only through a Syriac manuscript. See the recent edition and translation of the passage in Martelli 2014b:11–13.

[37] On Neilos and Paphnutia the "virgin/girl" (*parthenos*), see Berthelot-Ruelle 1887–1888:2.190–191.

Zosimos' positioning with regard to Neilos (at least) is related to the polemics of his treatise *On the Letter Omega*.[38] This work is striking for its use of embedded dichotomies dividing Zosimos and his rivals over different alchemical techniques, their attitude toward fate, and their understanding of the nature of humanity. Zosimos' rivals, whom he called the "many" and who ridiculed his (lost) book *On Furnaces and Apparatus*, are said to be "without intellect" (*anoas*)[39] because of their reliance on "timely tinctures" (*karikai katabaphai*). These "tinctures" are alchemical processes dependent on the will of the "demons" (*daimones*, *On the Letter Omega* 2). These rivals ignore the "lessons of the body" (*sômatika paideutêria*), know nothing of "immaterial things" and hopelessly try to circumvent fate (4–5) with "the magic of the corporeal language" (7). Zosimos' rivals are like Epimetheus (6), who stands for the "external human" (*exô anthrôpos*; 12) also called Thoth and Adam, contrasting with the "pneumatic" and "inner human" (*esô … anthrôpos*) called *Phôs* (8-10). In contrast, philosophers are comparable to Prometheus and *Phôs* (12), and refuse to rejoice in the gifts of fate. The "timely tinctures" of Zosimos' rivals are also comparable to the "demon-fearing practices" (*deisidaimonias*) of "bonesetter priests" (*hiereus ostodetês*), which are opposed to the practices of physicians. Through this last opposition, Zosimos associated his own practice with the way by which physicians apply bandages with braces to fractured limbs after having consulted "books with diagrams" (18). Zosimos did not claim that his rivals' techniques or those of the bonesetter priests were superstitious or inherently ineffective. He rather argued that the timely tinctures were unreliable and immoral because they implied reliance on demons, which Zosimos wished to avoid.

The treatise entitled the *First Book of the teleutaias apokhês by the Theban Zosimos* (which I will call the "Final Abstinence")[40] explicitly associates users of timely tinctures, and thus Zosimos' rivals in the treatise *On the Letter Omega*, with the priesthood of the Egyptian temples. The book narrates how the "divine techniques of the 'minerals' (*psammôn*)" (i.e. the different kinds of *baphai*) of Egypt were originally taken over by "local overseers" (*hoi kata topon ephoroi*) who instigated a racket over their practice. These overseers hid the original techniques and replaced them with "non-natural ones" (*aphusika*), which they delivered to "their priests" (*tois heautôn hiereusi*) to make sure that "their sacrifices" (*hai thusiai autôn*) would be perpetuated in exchange for success in these

---

[38] *Authentic Memoirs* I.

[39] Most likely related to those described as having not received Intellect in the *Corpus Hermeticum* IV.

[40] This book is usually called "The Final Count" or "Quittance," but it is unclear how the content of the work relates to a "count" or "quittance." My choice comes from the parallels between the content and title of this work and Porphyry's *On Abstinence from Killing Animals*. See Knipe 2011, Camplani and Zambon 2002.

techniques.[41] The nonnatural and (unreliable) "timely tinctures,"[42] are a part of the traditions of the Egyptian temples, while the natural and reliable "timely tinctures" are an independent set of recipes found in written documents.

Since Zosimos also criticized the rivals of *On the Letter Omega* for their "timely tinctures" (also associated with demons), it is likely that Zosimos' rivals were Egyptian temple priests or that the cults they practiced were identified as Egyptian.[43] As recently argued, the reputation of the Egyptian priests for their expertise in *mageia*, broadly conceived, combined with the dwindling rights and revenues of the Egyptian priesthood under Roman rule probably convinced some priests to offer their services to rich or influential patrons.[44] Zosimos' place among Theosebeia's entourage and his polemics against the traditional Egyptian priesthood suggest that he could have been in competition with them for patronage. He could consequently be considered to have occupied a similar socioeconomic position.

3. A Heavenly Ascent into the Alembic

To show how Zosimos sought to escape embodiment and how this did not lead him to reject the body and materiality, I will present here a translation of a portion of Zosimos' first *Lesson on Excellence* followed by an analysis of its links with eschatological narratives.[45]

The portion of the *Lesson on Excellence* analyzed here can be separated into five sections: (1) a seemingly disjointed list of ideas beginning with the "rest of the waters," which is presented as the content of the first allegorical vision; (2) the first allegorical vision; (3) the (abridged) second vision; (4) an interpretation of the visions, which involves a comparison between human and cosmic processes of exchange; and (5) a concluding allegorical recipe explicitly described as a summary of the preceding text.[46]

> [(1)] Rest of the waters, movement, increase, disembodiment, embodiment, extraction of *pneuma* from a body, binding of *pneuma* to a body; these are not (coming) from natures that are foreign or brought from

---

[41] See Festugière 1949:366.6–26.

[42] On the terminological problems surrounding the timely tinctures in this treatise, see Stolzenberg 1999. On the opposition nature/culture in Zosimos and in modern scholarship, see Grimes 2010.

[43] Martelli 2017.

[44] See Frankfurter 2000 and Moyer 2011:208–273.

[45] I use this term to describe both what is called a "*katabasis*" narrative and a common feature of apocalyptic literature, the "heavenly ascent" or "voyage to hell" narrative (on these, see Segal 1980, Himmelfarb 1983 and 1993). All these narratives take place in the world of the afterlife and generally involve some form of punishment and some form of guide presenting these to the visitor.

[46] The text is according to Mertens' 1995.

outside. Rather, uniform nature possesses the hard shells of the minerals as well as the soft pulp of the plants itself and only in respect to itself.

Zosimos *Lesson on Excellence* I 1–6

The two manuscript traditions give two different lessons for the following part:

[Version A] The rich variety of the universe, consisting of many materials, and the research takes shape (σχηματίζεται) in this uniform and multicolor species. Hence the fact that it lays (ὑποβάλλει) the abatement (λῆξιν) and the increase (αὔξησιν) by which nature flees (ὑποφεύγει), nature being under the temporal influence of the moon.

Zosimos *Lesson on Excellence* I 7–16

[Version B] The rich and diverse research of all things is preserved in this uniform and multicolor shape (σχήματι). Hence the fact that it lays (ὑποβάλλεται) the cessation and the increase by which nature rushes (ἱππεύει), nature being under the temporal influence of the moon.

Zosimos *Lesson on Excellence* I 7–16

[(2)] As I was saying these things, I fell asleep; I see a sacrificer (ἱερουργόν) standing before me above an altar in the shape of a libation bowl (βωμοῦ φιαλοειδοῦς). The altar was at the top of fifteen steps and a priest stood there (ἱερεύς). I heard a voice coming from above saying:

'I have accomplished the action consisting in going down the fifteen steps of shining darkness and going up these steps of illuminating light. The sacrificer is now changing me (καινουργῶν) by shedding away the consistency of my body. Consecrated by force I accomplish myself as *pneuma*.'

After I had heard the voice of the one who stood in the bowl-altar, I asked to know from him who he was. He answered saying with a weak voice:

'I am *Iôn*, the priest of the shrines and I undergo an intolerable violence. At sunrise, someone came running and mastered me, dividing me with a blade, pulling me apart according to the structure of the assemblage and skinning my head with the sword he held. He intertwined the bones with the flesh and burned (them) with the fire from his hand until I learned to become *pneuma* by changing (my) body. This is the intolerable violence I endure.'

As he was talking to me and that I was urging him to speak, his eyes became like blood and he vomited all his flesh. And I saw him as a small, mutilated human, kneading himself with his own teeth and falling down (συμπίπτοντα). Frightened, I woke up and I wondered: 'Would not that be, perhaps, the rest of the waters?' And I was resolved to believe that I had truly understood.

Zosimos Lesson on Excellence I 17–43

[(3)] And I fell asleep again. I saw the same bowl-altar and boiling water above and an infinitely large population in it. There was nobody I could interrogate outside of the altar. I climb to look at the sight inside the altar and I see a small razor-wielding[47] and grey-haired human (πεπολιώμενον ξυρουργὸν ἀνθρωπάριον) saying to me: 'What are you looking at?' I answered that I was amazed by the agitation of the water and of the humans who burned together and yet lived. He responded to me saying: 'The sight which you see is the entrance, the exit and the transformation (μεταβολή).' I interrogated him further: 'What trans-formation?' He replied, saying: '(This is) the place of the exercise which is called maceration (ταριχείας, also "embalming"), for the humans who wish to reach excellence enter here and become spirits (πνεύματα) after having escaped their body.' I said then to him: 'And are you a spirit?' And he answered, saying: 'Both spirit and guardian of spirits.'

Zosimos Lesson on Excellence I 44–59

[Jumping over I 59–73]

[(4)] And after I had these visions, I woke up again and I said to myself: 'What is the cause of such a vision? Is this not the water which is white and which is yellow, the boiling, the divine?' And I found that I under-stood well (καλῶς ἐνόησα) and I said that it was good to speak and good to hear, good to give and good to take, good to be poor and good to be rich. How does nature learn to give and to take? The copper-human gives and the liquid-stone takes. The metal gives and the plant takes. The celestial bodies give and the flowers take. The sky gives and the earth takes. Thunder gives of the revolving fire.

---

[47] Or "tonsorial," as suggested by the LSJ.

Everything is woven together and everything is unwoven. Everything is mixed and everything is put together (again). Everything is blended and everything is separated. Everything is inundated and everything is dried, everything blooms and everything loses its bloom in the bowl-altar; for everything (exists) according to method, according to a measure and according to the minute measurement of the four elements. The weaving and unweaving of all things and the interconnection of the universe do not occur without method. Method is natural; it breathes in and out and it takes care of the orders [i.e. the "order of things"], increasing (αὔξουσα) and abating (λήγουσα) them. And, to summarize, if method is not left behind, all things that are harmonized through separation and union transform nature (ἐκστρέφει, also: "turn nature inside out"). Transformed (στρεφομένη [i.e. "turned"]), nature turns into itself (εἰς ἑαυτὴν στρέφεται). This is the nature and the interconnection of the excellence of the entire cosmos.

Zosimos *Lesson on Excellence* I 74–99

[(5)] In short, my friend, build a monolithic shrine (ναόν) for yourself that is like white lead, like alabaster, like (marble) of Proconnesus, and which has neither beginning nor end in its construction.[48] Inside, it has a source of the most pure water and a light shining like the sun. Seek diligently for the entrance of the shrine (ἡ εἴσοδος τοῦ ναοῦ), take a sword in your hand and search for the entrance. For the place where is the opening of the way is narrow and there is a snake lying next to the entrance and guarding the shrine. Once you have mastered it, first sacrifice it and having skinned it, divide its flesh and its bones part by part. After you have put back its parts one by one with the bones, make yourself a base next to the entrance of the shrine. Climb, enter and you will find there the thing sought for. For the priest, the copper-human, the one you see seated in the source and collecting the thing—you do not see him a copper-human (anymore). He changed of color (and) of nature and has become a silver-human. If you wish, in a short time you will have a gold-human.

Zosimos *Lesson on Excellence* I 100–118

We might start picking this text apart by looking at *Iôn*, one of the most striking and most crudely corporeal elements of the text. Who is he? Why must

---

48   Most likely an alchemical metaphor for the egg, see Mertens 1995:223n39.

he suffer? And why in that particular way? *Iôn* was methodically separated, reunited, and then burned; he turned his body inside out and then outside in, which finally caused him to "collapse." As *Iôn* himself explains, these processes led him to learn how to transform his body into *pneuma*.[49]

All exchanges between Zosimos and the inhabitants of his imaginary world involve "violence" (*bia*) or "punishments" (*kolaseis*), leading to the "transformation" (*metabolê*) or "bodily change" (*metasômatoumenos*) of a body into *pneuma* and taking place in a bowl-shaped altar found in the first vision at the top of fifteen steps of "illuminating light" and "shining darkness." The climbing up and down of the fifteen steps of light and darkness is a reference to Egyptian representations of the moon cycle, consisting in fourteen steps leading to a platform, on which the moon is symbolized.[50] The association of *Iôn*'s travel up and down the staircase with the moon's cycle suggests more specifically that the thirty steps should be associated with some form of voyage through the sky. As such, it also probably referred to an eschatological journey.

Eschatological narratives, especially those of the Platonic or Apocalyptic traditions, generally take place after a voyage through the heavenly spheres and often involve a divine guide explaining the punishments found in the afterlife.[51] Punishments and guides are also found in Zosimos' two visions, and both visions are separated by a linking formula similar to the one found at the beginning of the eschatological narratives of the *Zostrianos* from Nag Hammadi and the Hermetic *Poimander*.[52] The most striking analogies with Zosimos' *Lesson on Excellence*, however, do not come from these texts but from Plutarch's *On the Delays of the Divine Vengeance*.[53]

---

[49] *Authentic Memoirs* X 2.34–35: ἔμαθον μετασωματούμενος πνεῦμα γενέσθαι.

[50] As Mertens (1995:35n7) noted, since the introductory text of the visions (section 1 in my translation) referred to the moon, it is likely that the fifteen steps refer to the moon cycle. The fourteen-step staircase leading to the moon is a common representation in Egyptian temples and must have inspired Zosimos. In Edfu and Dendara, for example, the moon phases are represented by a staircase of fourteen steps leading to a platform, the fifteenth step, on which rests an eye (= the moon). See von Lieven 2000:127–132; I would like to thank Joachim Quack for the reference. Even considering that Zosimos was unaware of Egyptian moon-symbolism, he could have reached it through Greek texts. Plutarch mentions that some associated Osiris with the lunar world and that the dismemberment of Osiris in fourteen parts was associated with the waning phases of the moon (*On Isis and Osiris* 367c–368b). See also Derchain 1962:25–26.

[51] For angelic guides in Apocalypticism, see Himmelfarb 1983:50–60 and 1993:38–40, 55–57, 67–69.

[52] *Authentic Memoirs* X 2.17: καὶ ταῦτα λαλῶν ἀπεκοιμήθην. See *Nag Hammadi Codices* VIII 1.3.14–1.4.1 and *Corpus Hermeticum* I 1.

[53] I would like to take the occasion to thank the organizers and participants of the *Katabasis* colloquium, which took place in Montreal and Quebec City in 2014 (www.katabasis.ca), and more particularly Renaud Gagné who brought the "upward *katabasis*" of Plutarch's *On the Delays of the Divine Vengeance* to my attention.

The closing myth of *On the Delays of the Divine Vengeance* narrates the visions of a certain Thespesios, who found himself in heaven after having violently fallen on his neck and lost consciousness. Looking down through the airy depths of heaven, Thespesios could see flamelike bubbles coming up (from the Earth) and letting go "compact human shapes" as they reached the surface where he was standing.[54] On this "calm sea" situated between the Earth and the Moon,[55] Thespesios met a "kinsman" (*sungenês*), who gave him a tour of the heavenly sphere where souls are punished and purified from past errors.

Thespesios saw that souls in heaven faced punishments tailored to the nature of the crimes they committed. The souls of hypocrites who pretended to be virtuous were "forced to turn themselves 'inside out' (*ektrepesthai*) ... like sea-centipedes that have swallowed a hook and that turn upon 'themselves' (*ektrepousin*)."[56] It is likely that Zosimos had a similar image in mind when he described the transformation of Iôn. In any case, the image of self-regurgitation and redigestion seen in the light of eschatological narratives appears as an apt allegory of moral self-examination. Moreover, as showed in the anthropological and eschatological narrative of the treatise *On the Letter Omega*, Zosimos explicitly described his eschatological goal as the extraction of the "inside human."[57] The same process appears to have been transposed in his vision as self-regurgitation.

Next to the bowl-altar, Zosimos found a "small human" (*anthrôparion*) who answered his questions and played a role analogous to that of Thespesios' kindred spirit, the divine guide found in most eschatological narratives. In the eschatological myth of *On the Face that Appears in the Moon*, the role of the guide was played by a human who had previously shed its fleshy body and who was on its way toward a "second death" (943a–944c). Like the souls reaching the space between the moon and the earth, Thespesios' divine relative and guide was a "compact human form." The image of the "small human" (*anthrôparion*) appears analogous to that of the inhabitants of heaven in Plutarch's eschatological myths, and to that of Thespesios' guide as well.

---

54 *On the Delays of the Divine Vengeance* 564a.
55 This is also the case in Plutarch's *On the Face that Appears in the Moon* 943c.
56 *On the Delays of the Divine Vengeance* 567b: τούτους (sc. the souls) ἐπιπόνως καὶ ὀδυνηρῶς ἠνάγκαζον ἕτεροι περιεστῶτες ἐκτρέπεσθαι τὰ ἐντὸς ἔξω τῆς ψυχῆς ... ὥσπερ αἱ θαλάττιαι σκολόπενδραι καταπιοῦσαι τὸ ἄγκιστρον ἐκτρέπουσιν ἑαυτάς. The *Apocalypse of Paul* (Hilhorst and Silvertsein 1996:140) similarly depicts the punishment of a presbyter who attended to his ritual duties while being impure as an evisceration operated through the mouth with an iron implement.
57 *Authentic Memoirs* I 10–15.

Like Thespesios' heaven, the bowl-altar of Zosimos' second vision is the sight of tortures involving boiling substances scorching metal-like souls.[58] The place was also described by the guide of Zosimos' vision as an "exercise" (*askêsis*) and "a maceration" (*tarikheia*). *Tarikheia* can also refer specifically to the Egyptian art of embalming[59] and this would also make the bowl-altar a place for death-exercises. The last explanation of the guide, who described the altar-bowl as the site of a transformation into *pneuma*, confirms this reading.

The eschatological narrative of Thespesios in Plutarch's *On the Delays of the Divine Vengeance* includes a similar vision. During his visit of heaven, Thespesios observed the work of a team of demonic goldsmiths in a sort of perverted version of the scenes of industrious cupids in Pompeii's house of the Vettii:

> There were also pools placed one next to the other, one of boiling gold, one of icy lead and another of turbulent iron. Daemons attended these and, like blacksmiths, they were lowering and pulling back each of the souls of those who erred because of cupidity and greediness. Indeed, after the heat had started to make them glow and had made them translucent, they threw them into the lead and immersed them (βάπτοντες). Solidifying on the spot and becoming hard like hailstones, they moved them to the (pool) of iron. They became terribly black in there and, breaking down because of their extreme hardness, they were ground down and changed shape. They were then brought back to the gold, agonizing, as he said, from the painful changes to which they were submitted.

Plutarch *On the Delays of the Divine Vengeance* 567c[60]

The general idea is similar to that of Zosimos' vision: color change and metallurgical processes, i.e. a "quenching" (*baphê*)—the hardening of a metal through rapid cooling—all taking place in an imaginary space where humans learn to forget the passions of the soul and to abandon the body that produced them. The problem of greed is obviously related to the production of ersatz luxury goods, and, as I will point out below, the question of giving and taking—simultaneously conceived on a human and a cosmic scale—was a central concern of Zosimos' first *Lesson on Excellence*.

Zosimos' visions as well as the last allegorical explanation involve cultic imagery. This feature is also found in eschatological narratives in which heaven is represented as a temple.[61] The main place in which the two visions occur is an

---

[58] This is made clear in I 59–73 (not translated above).
[59] See Ritner 1993:56.
[60] The text is according to Pohlenz (1929).
[61] See Himmelfarb 1993:14–16.

"altar" (*bômos*) shaped in the form of a *phialê*. In an alchemical context, this word does not primarily refer to a libation vessel but to the top part of the alembic or to the distillate receptacle.[62] As Mertens noted throughout her edition, Zosimos' visions are replete with allusions to alchemical processes. It is also certain that the *phialobômos* was meant to represent an alchemical apparatus.

The similarities between the *Lesson on Excellence* and eschatological narratives show that Zosimos had some awareness of eschatological narratives or of their images.[63] The similarities between the *Lesson on Excellence* and Hermetic symbolism, which will be examined in the next section, suggest that he depicted the "altar/alchemical apparatus" as the site of a self-reforming, bodily sacrifice.

4. Running Down into the Crater, Running Up toward Poimenandres

In the first vision, then, we have an alchemical apparatus/sacrificial altar upon which *Iôn* the "priest" (*hiereus*) is transformed into *pneuma*/"a small human" (*anthrôparion*). In the second vision, Zosimos learns that *Iôn* is both "sacrificer" (*hierourgôn*)—i.e. the one whom he saw standing outside of the bowl-altar—and the sacrifice itself. This was indicated by Zosimos in the passage omitted from the translation above: "and he ['house-master' (*oikodespotês*)] said to me 'the one which you have seen as a copper-human vomiting his own flesh is the sacrificer and the one who is being sacrificed.'"[64] The second vision consequently makes clear that *Iôn* stands for both object and subject of the sacrifice/alchemical operation. The perspective taken by Zosimos has also changed. The bowl-altar now takes gigantic proportions and includes "an infinite" (*apeiron*) number of people boiling and moaning in its waters.

The introductory and concluding sections of the first *Lesson on Excellence* are key to our understanding of these images since they contain explicit interpretations of the visions. Both sections make clear that the topic of the *Lesson on Excellence* is nature. The first six lines describe nature as "uniform," or made "of one species" (*monoeidês*), as well as delineating its activities and the species it contains. The activities include "movement," "increase" (as well as other phenomena that could be said to be more human-specific), "disembodiment," "separation of a spirit from a body," "embodiment," and "binding of a spirit to a

---

[62] See Mertens 1995:cxxi–cxxiii.

[63] To cite another parallel, the ascent narrative of the *Passion of Perpetua and Felicity*, mentions that Perpetua reached the heavenly staircase by stepping on the head of a guardian snake as if it were the first step of her ascent (4.7).

[64] *Authentic Memoirs* X 3.69–72: λέγει μοι ὅτι τοῦτον ὃν εἶδες χαλκάνθρωπον καὶ τὰς ἰδίας σάρκας ἐξεμοῦντα, οὗτός ἐστιν ὁ ἱερουργῶν καὶ ἱερουργούμενος.

body." A first apparent contradiction can be noted: if nature is *monoeidês*, i.e "of one species" or "uniform," it should not contain multiple species such as plants and minerals.

The self-contradictory observation that nature is uniform and multiple at the same time appears in the second part of the introduction and is repeated throughout *The Lesson on Excellence*. In fact, the movement from unity to multiplicity is what Zosimos calls "the excellence" (*aretê*) of the cosmos.[65] The mention of "the hard shells of the minerals" and "the soft pulp of the plants" was thus probably meant to contrast with the statement that nature was uniform. At the end of the treatise (not translated above), Zosimos gave a final exhortation, which he described as excellence (*aretê*): "pay attention to the nature as you turn it inside out [i.e. transform it], and conceive as made of a single material that which is made of multiple materials."[66] Awakening from the second vision, Zosimos declared having "well understood" and listed opposite notions beginning with moral terms and finishing with amoral ones: some humans speak, other listen and some give and some take; it is good to be rich and good to be poor just as the sky gives and the earth takes (*Lesson on Excellence* I 77–85). The identification of moral and cosmic exchange processes dissolves the subjective point of view. In other words, social oppositions and imbalances must also be considered to be part of the "order of things" (*Lesson on Excellence* I 93–95). Method—considered from a human point of view as the correct use of tools, "books with diagrams," or of "demonstrative reasoning"[67]—is also found in nature (*Lesson on Excellence* I 93). It guarantees the "weaving" and "unweaving" of all things, that is to say, the sympathetic and antipathetic network of influences through which reciprocal processes occur (*Lesson on Excellence* I 90–99). Zosimos expresses this process of natural self-perfection by punning on the verb (*ek*)*strephein*: "turned inside out, nature turns into/transforms itself."[68] The expression is more complicated to understand than to translate. Indeed, the idea that a transformation only reveals what was there before is already contained in the English expression "to turn into" something else. This universal process of cyclical changes, which includes intrahuman reciprocal exchanges as well, is what Zosimos calls the *aretê* ("excellence") of the cosmos.[69]

The visions' guides—the two *anthrôparia* and the house-master—show how this *aretê*, i.e. the circularity of natural processes, also relates to human events

---

[65] See Mertens 1995:213–214.
[66] *Authentic Memoirs* X 7.133–135: ἐκστρέψας τὴν φύσιν ἐπίστηθι, καὶ τὴν πολύϋλον ὡς μονόϋλον λογίζου.
[67] See *Authentic Memoirs* I 2.18.
[68] *Authentic Memoirs* X 4.98–99: ἡ γὰρ φύσις στρεφομένη εἰς ἑαυτὴν στρέφεται.
[69] *Authentic Memoirs* X 7.

taking place in Zosimos' eschatological narratives. Whether we understand the house-master as an estate manager or as a star ruling over its celestial house, the name of this character is appropriate to his external point of view since his discourse unites the process-oriented interpretations of Zosimos and *Iôn*'s description of his torments. By revealing that the copper-human "who was seen vomiting his own flesh" (i.e. *Iôn*) is "the one to whom was given the rule over the water and over those who are punished," the house-master is putting *Iôn* in the position of the user of the alchemical apparatus. *Iôn* the copper-human, which we can now also associate with the generic user of alchemical apparatus, was also said by the house-master to be both sacrificing and sacrificed. Since sacrifice stands for operations made within the alchemical apparatus, this would mean that Zosimos alluded to the user of alchemical apparatus both as object and subject of his alchemical work. We once again find the idea of a circular process and a double identity: nature transforms itself "through itself" and *Iôn* "turns himself out" and chews himself "with his own teeth" until he "learns to become *pneuma*." That is to say that as nature changes itself and is the object of its own theodicy, so does the alchemist, who meets his own transformative punishments and who is the object of his own justice.

The final allegory of the treatise (section 5 of the text translated above) brings these ideas together. The flesh of the snake must be sacrificed, flayed, its flesh separated from the bones "limb by limb," and its body recomposed bit by bit.[70] Placed in front of the opening of the shrine, the reassembled corpse is then used to find "the thing sought for," represented by the final transformation of the copper-human into a gold-human. Similarly, it is through the methodical dismembering of *Iôn* that transformation is achieved. *Iôn* says that his torturer first "separated" (*dielôn*) him apart methodically and then "weaved" (*suneplexen*) his flesh and bones together. This process transformed *Iôn* into an *anthrôparion*, that is to say, into *pneuma*. When describing the virtuous transformations of nature, Zosimos used the same textile metaphor seen in the case of the weaving of flesh and bone of *Iôn* and also referred to an autonomous self-inversion: "Turned inside out, nature turns into itself;" all things "are woven together" (*sumplekontai*) and "unwoven" (*apoplekontai*) by nature (*Lesson on Excellence* I 85–90), in this way, nature ensures its union and "excellence."[71]

The separation and recombination of *Iôn* and the snake stand here for the most universal process of all, world-transformation. The bowl-altar is an

---

[70] *Authentic Memoirs* X 5.108–113. In describing the separation and unification of bodies, Zosimos must have borrowed language from Ezekiel 37 (ὀστᾶ τὰ ξηρά ἑκάτερον πρὸς τὴν ἁρμονίαν αὐτοῦ), which was interpreted by Origen (among others) as the reconstruction of the body of Christ. See Ramelli forthcoming (a).

[71] See p. 270n52 below.

alchemical apparatus and it also stands for the universe.[72] Processes found inside it are just like processes found throughout nature: they work transformation through separation and unification of parts, i.e. through a coming and going from unity to multiplicity.

This reading is supported by Hermetic texts, which Zosimos knew.[73] The most telling passage figures at the end of the narrative portion of the *Final Abstinence*, which justifies the abstinence from temple sacrifices.[74] Enjoining Theosebeia to "perfect" herself by obtaining the "timely, genuine and natural tinctures," Zosimos finished his exhortation writing that she should "run down to *Poimenandra*" and that "having been immersed in the crater" she would "run up to [her] own kind."[75]

The name of *Poimenandra* (i.e. *Poimandrês*) and the image of the "baptism" or immersion in the crater are specific to *Corpus Hermeticum* I and IV. Poimander in *Corpus Hermeticum* I is the "Intellect of the authority" (*nous authentias*) and "Father-God" of the second Intellect.[76] In the light of the *Corpus Hermeticum* I and IV, "running down toward Poimander" means acquiring the knowledge that brings "a return to life,"[77] and which is acquired by recognizing oneself as being made of light and life, that is, as being the same as the "Father-God."[78] This process involves "leaving the body to alteration" as well as its dissolution.[79] The final stage of the "return to life," or what is also called a "rebirth" (*palingenesia*), is the heavenly ascent through the seven spheres up to the "Ogdoadic nature" (i.e. the eighth sphere). There, the "Father-God" is praised with hymns and is finally integrated. This divinization is "the goal for those who possess 'knowledge'" (*gnôsis*)[80] and it corresponds relatively well with Zosimos' anthropology and soteriology.[81] It does not explain, however, why acquiring the correct alchemical techniques should help Theosebeia becoming "perfect" and whether

---

[72] The metaphor is explicitly found in the seventh century work of Stephanus of Alexandria *On the Great and Sacred Art* 9.245.3 Ideler.

[73] Compare Festugière 1949:367.18 with *Corpus Hermeticum* XIII 11.7-8. See also Festugière 1949:365.15, 366.12, *Authentic Memoirs* I 4, 5, 7, 8, 15; Berthelot-Ruelle 1888:2.150.13, 156.8, 156.14–17, 157.2, 162.3, 169.9, 175.14–15, 188.19, 189.4, 198.3.

[74] Festugière 1949:367.24–25.

[75] Festugière 1949:368.1–4: ὅταν δὲ ἐπιγνῷς σαυτὴν τελειωθεῖσαν, τότε καὶ <ἐπιτύχουσα> τῶν φυσικῶν τῆς ὕλης κατάπτυσον, καὶ καταδραμοῦσα ἐπὶ τὸν Ποιμένανδρα καὶ βαπτισθεῖσα τῷ κρατῆρι, ἀνάδραμε ἐπὶ τὸ γένος τὸ σόν.

[76] *Corpus Hermeticum* I 1.1.9–10, 1.9.

[77] *Corpus Hermeticum* I 1.1.21.

[78] *Corpus Hermeticum* I 1.1.19.

[79] *Corpus Hermeticum* I 1.1.24.

[80] *Corpus Hermeticum* I 1.1.25–26.

[81] See *Authentic Memoirs* I 11–15.

the "immersion in the crater" was meant to be more than a reference to the *Hermetica*.

In *Corpus Hermeticum* IV, entitled *Hermes to Tat: the Crater or Monad*, it is said that God filled a crater with intellect and that he sent it down with a herald and the following message: "you [feminine pronoun] who can immerse yourself in this crater, you who believe that you will go back to him who sent the crater: you who know why you were born."[82] Being filled with "intellect" (*nous*), the immersion in the crater was meant to "give intellect" to the soul (a word of feminine gender in ancient Greek and most probably referred to in this quote). The intellect acquired in the cup brought knowledge of all things in the world, which led one to relinquish it and to acquire immortality.[83]

The two other "baptismal" images found in the *Corpus Hermeticum* have generally been contrasted with that of *Hermes to Tat* since they are negatively connoted. In the treatise *To Tat On the Common Intellect*, the soul that enters the body is said to step into and be immersed in pleasure and pain, which are compared to boiling humors.[84] The other text appears to strike an even more dissonant note: souls are "immersed" (*bebaptismenai*) in flesh and blood, not *nous*, and immersion is described as "a punishment" (*baptismou kai kolaseôs*).[85] In both cases, however, immersion in the cup allegorizes embodiment.

The positive uses of the image of the immersion in the cup found in *Corpus Hermeticum* IV and in Zosimos' *Final Abstinence*[86] are neither unrelated to the three so-called negative uses of the same image nor are they in contradiction with them.[87] The tension perceived in the *Hermetica* between worldly concerns and "technical" treatises on one side and rejection of the world and "philosophical" treatises on the other can be explained by the existence of a Hermetic curriculum by which knowledge of the world was considered as the preliminary step in order to "acquire intellect."[88] That "rebirth" must first go through a contemplation of materiality, "the visible god," is the topic of *Corpus Hermeticum* V, entitled *That the Invisible God is the Most Visible*. Since the source of the world is invisible, Hermes states, its contemplation should start with the visible

---

[82] *Corpus Hermeticum* IV 4.

[83] *Corpus Hermeticum* IV 5.

[84] *Corpus Hermeticum* XII 2: σώματος γὰρ συνθέτου ὥπερ χυμοὶ ζέουσιν ἥ τε λύπη καὶ ἡ ἡδονή, εἰς ἃς ἐμβᾶσα ἡ ψυχὴ βαπτίζεται.

[85] *Hermetic Fragments from Stobaeus* XXV 8.

[86] *Corpus Hermeticum* XII 2 and *Hermetic Fragments from Stobaeus* XXV 8. Ephraim the Syrian (fourth century) also mentioned a Hermetic teaching according to which a cup attracted souls into it and made them forget where they came from. According to Ephraim's reading, the cup represented the body (see testimony 22 in Festugière and Nock 1954:vol.4; edition and English translation in Mitchell 1921:210). See Van Den Kerchove 2012:301–302.

[87] Edwards 1992.

[88] Fowden 1986.

creation. But since it is not possible to climb to heaven to study the most orderly part of creation (and, consequently, the closest representation of the creator of the universe), the contemplation of God must be made by the study of the created world. Human parturition stands as an especially apt means to achieve this contemplation since it is the visible paradigm of universal creation.[89] The four references to immersion in the cup refer to the same reality: the visible world, and more specifically the human body, is the first means by which one can access knowledge of the divine. The "immersion into flesh and blood," i.e. embodiment, is a punishment and this punishment in matter is exactly what leads toward rebirth, the "return to life."

Since Hermetic immersion could symbolize embodiment as well as salvation and that the alchemical apparatus stood for the universe as well as that by which salvation was procured, Zosimos could have associated both crater and apparatus with the universe, and the act of entering these structures as embodiment. Zosimos' comparison between the formation of the embryo in the uterus and alchemical tincture further suggests that he saw a similarity between alchemical transformation and embodiment.[90] From the Hermetic perspective one must first study the creation to perceive the invisible creator, the alchemical apparatus must have seemed as the fruitful site where one could reflect upon the "lessons of the body"[91] through the study of analogical changes in matter, get rid of passions, and consequently reach rebirth after the death of the body.

5. The Alchemy of Zosimos As Spiritual Exercise

Unlike the typical eschatological narrative, the visionary journeys of the first *Lesson on Excellence* are set neither above nor below the earth. By "climbing and entering" inside the tool of his trade in order to "find the coveted thing," Zosimos not only decided to "lean down toward the dark-gleaming cosmos"[92] but also considered the study of the cosmos and its transformations as a soteriological enterprise. This enterprise was characterized by the double movement

---

[89] *Asclepius* 20–21. For similar examples, see *Asclepius* 8, *Corpus Hermeticum* V 1, IX 6–7, IX 21–22, XII 21, *Hermetic Fragments from Stobaeus* XXIII 3. Jean-Pierre Mahé (2009) also showed how an astronomical Hermetic treatise (*Hermetic Fragments from Stobaeus* VI) could have been conceived as a spiritual exercise in preparation for the flight of the "perfect" through the seven spheres. This is also similar to the comparison of the travel to the altar-bowl with the travel of the moon across the sky. On the study of heaven as a didactic travel going through several *gradus*, see Manilius *Astronomica* II 750–787, IV 119–121 (here not only "steps" but also zodiacal "degrees") with Volk 2004.

[90] Berthelot and Ruelle 1888:2.216.4–9.

[91] *Authentic Memoirs* I 4.

[92] *Chaldean Oracles* fr. 163 des Places.

of humanity initiated by the fall of *Phôs* into matter and concluded by the voyage "up" toward rebirth. This is the "virtuous cycle" of life, which Zosimos described to Theosebeia: "'running down' (*katadramousa*) to Poimander to get baptized into the crater, 'run up' (*anadrame*) toward your race."[93]

Parallels found with the Hermetica suggests that Zosimos expected to gain greater clarity about the universe through the practice of alchemy and that it was this knowledge—brought by alchemical practice—that could produce a radical transformation of the self. That this soteriological process was mixed with the creation of fake luxury goods might sound paradoxical. He was well aware of this tension and I would even go as far as to say that it played a fundamental role in his combination of metallurgical and soteriological techniques. Thanks to the powers of analogical thinking, he exploited the persuasive effects that physical science exerted on imaginations to bring the observation of natural principles to bear on the perception of one's self. In other words, he conceived alchemy as a spiritual exercise derived through persuasion from the efficacy of metallurgical processes. Conversely, Zosimos also transformed the practice of a particular trade into a spiritual exercise.

If Zosimos recommended Theosebeia to "spit on matter" it was not because of a radical anticosmism. The human body (and matter in general) was not simply a hurdle for him. Paradoxically, matter was also the key to the afterlife. From this perspective, his work is not entirely atypical for late antiquity. If what we know of Zosimos' social context can be used to help us reconstruct the social context of works found in similar corpora (such as the Nag Hammadi codices), exploring early Greek alchemy might be particularly useful in understanding what brought late antique scholars to work with or against each other, irrespective of their theological persuasions and cultic affiliations.

---

[93] Festugière 1949:368.3–4.

PART III

SOUL-BODY PERSPECTIVES IN HELLENISTIC JEWISH AND CHRISTIAN PLATONISM

11

Philo and the Stoic Conception of Soul

CARLOS LÉVY

Abstract: This chapter examines the relation between body and soul in Philo of Alexandria and its philosophical (Platonic) and Biblical roots. Even though Philo has no real eschatology, his soteriology is robust and concerns the soul alone, and not the body.

IN HIS EXTENSIVE DOXOGRAPHY in *On Dreams*, which shows many parallels with Cicero's one in the *Tusculan Disputations*, Philo reaches the conclusion that we know more about our body than about our intellect/soul.[1] The fourth element, he says, is unintelligible by us and this is true about heaven in the world as well as about the intellect in the human being.[2] About the essence of the sky and the intellect, it can be said only that they are holy. For this reason, Bréhier says that Philo's purpose was not to present a philosophical psychology, but a religious one.[3]

But what is a religious psychology? One in which it is not important to determine the exact nature and function of the soul but its relation to God. In the lines following his declaration of negative dogmatism about the intellect/soul, Philo defines soul as a divine emanation. He adds that the real human prerogative is to be able to worship the One Being.[4] However, Philo's thought is

---

[1] *On Dreams* 1.14–57. About the comparison between this passage and Cicero *Tusculan Disputations* 1.18–23, see Lévy 2008:118–120.

[2] *On Dreams* 1.33: οἱ δ' ὑπὸ καρδίας αὐτὸν ἀγαλματοφορεῖσθαι διανοηθέντες γνωσιμαχοῦσιν. ἀεὶ δὴ τὸ τέταρτον ἀκατάληπτον, οὐρανὸς μὲν ἐν κόσμῳ παρὰ τὴν ἀέρος καὶ γῆς καὶ ὕδατος φύσιν, νοῦς δὲ ἐν ἀνθρώπῳ παρὰ σῶμα καὶ αἴσθησιν καὶ τὸν ἑρμηνέα λόγον. The "fourth element" here replaces "fiery air" (*pneuma*), which was for the Stoics the nature of the soul. On this point, see Long 1982.

[3] Bréhier 1925:160: "Au milieu de toutes ces banalités, une idée importante se fait jour cependant, c'est celle de l'unité morale et intérieure de l'âme; mais l'affirmation de cette unité dépend beaucoup plus de la psychologie religieuse que de la physique."

[4] *On Dreams* 1.35.

quite rarely linear and monolithic. Although the relation to God is for him absolutely essential, there is another aspect of his work on the subject that cannot be neglected: Philo's relation to the different philosophical theories about the soul and especially to the Stoics' views.

Of course, we should ask why we find Stoicism, and not Platonism, in this position. The answer to this question is rather simple: because Stoicism is the system with which Philo has the most complex relationship. Obviously enough, he could not accept the Stoic doctrine of immanence, but at the same time it was difficult for him not to use the Stoic concepts that in many ways, by Philo's time, had become a *lingua franca* of philosophy. In this chapter, we will direct our attention to the Stoic texts that are most influential to Philo's understanding of the soul. We are going to analyze some texts that we consider most important in order to understand why Stoicism is so present in Philo's discussion of the soul. Our main purpose will be to check whether the Stoic terms, concepts, and metaphors—or at least those that look so—testify only to the Stoic influence on Philo or whether his use of them is also a means for him to dismiss Stoic naturalistic immanentism.

1. The Puppets and Their Master: *On the Creation of the World* 117[5]

Our first text is generally interpreted as a testimony to the presence of the Stoic concept of soul in Philo's psychology:[6]

> Since things on earth are dependent on the heavenly realm through a natural affinity, the principle of the seven, which began on high, has also come down to us and made its presence felt among the mortal kinds. To start with, the part of our soul separate from the directive part is divided sevenfold, into the five senses, the organ of speech, and finally the reproductive part. Just like in puppet shows, all these are manipulated by the ruling element through the nerves. Sometimes

---

[5] The same metaphor appears in *On Abraham* 73 and *On Flight and Finding* 46. In *Who is the Heir of Divine Things* 232, the metaphor is developed within the dichotomy between the indivisibility of the intellect and the divisibility of the senses.

[6] About this passage, Runia (2001:288) writes: "Philo's psychology here draws on Stoic doctrine (this text is referred to at SVF II 833)." On Philo as the user of the Stoic conception of the soul, see also Reydams-Schils 1999:157–165, who, however, as remarked by Runia (2001:288), does not pay special attention to this particular text.

they are at rest, at other times they move, each producing its own appropriate disposition and movement.

Philo *On the Creation of the World* 117[7]

One cannot deny that all the elements of the Stoic topography of soul are present,[8] but despite these similarities the difference between the two is even greater. The Stoic main metaphor, representing the soul, was that of the octopus. There is a big difference between the octopus and the puppets. As is brilliantly put by Ildefonse about the former:

> Contre un cloisonnement des facultés distinctes, la métaphore du poulpe engage l'âme dans un modèle continu, communicant et simultané de déformations multiples, singulières et ramifies, qui lui assure une mobilité plastique de configurations et reconfigurations par tension et détente continues.

Ildefonse 1992:37

From this point of view, the Platonic metaphor of the puppet master is opposite to the living dynamic of the octopus. The octopus is a living unity, an organism, while the puppet master is essentially different from his puppets. The Stoic metaphor of the octopus is a monist one; the Philonic image, inspired by Plato,[9] is strongly dualistic. What is even more significant: the puppets are not even irrational beings; they are mere objects. Aristotle had transformed the Platonic metaphor in order to adapt it to his own conception of reality.[10] The Stoics seem to have avoided it, most probably because of its strongly dualistic nature. What does it mean to use a Stoic metaphor in a Platonic way? In my opinion, Philo does not use it in order to give a syncretistic view of the faculties of soul. There is a hierarchy in his use of the puppet metaphor. Plato is the philosopher whom he considered as being right about the principles of

---

[7] *On the Creation of the World* 117: ὁ τῆς ἑβδομάδος λόγος ἄνωθεν ἀρξάμενος κατέβη καὶ πρὸς ἡμᾶς τοῖς θνητοῖς γένεσιν ἐπιφοιτήσας. αὐτίκα τῆς ἡμετέρας ψυχῆς τὸ δίχα τοῦ ἡγεμονικοῦ μέρος ἑπταχῆ σχίζεται, εἰς πέντε αἰσθήσεις καὶ τὸ φωνητήριον ὄργανον καὶ ἐπὶ πᾶσι τὸ γόνιμον· ἃ δὴ πάντα καθάπερ ἐν τοῖς θαύμασιν ὑπὸ τοῦ ἡγεμονικοῦ νευροσπαστούμενα τοτὲ μὲν ἠρεμεῖ τοτὲ δὲ κινεῖται τὰς ἁρμοττούσας σχέσεις καὶ κινήσεις ἕκαστον. ὁμοίως δὲ καὶ τοῦ σώματος εἴ τις ἐξετάζειν ἐπιχειρήσειε τά τ᾽ ἐκτὸς καὶ ἐντὸς μέρη, καθ᾽ ἑκάτερον ἑπτὰ εὑρήσει. The translation of this passage is the one given by Runia (2001:77–78). In the rest of this chapter, I have adopted, with some modifications, the translation of Colson and Whitaker 1929.

[8] *Allegorical Interpretation* 3.115 shows that Philo had a clear perception of the debates inside the Stoa and between Stoics and Platonists about the structure of the soul as regards to real partition or powers.

[9] Plato *Laws* 644d.

[10] Aristotle *On the Generation of Animals* 734b: ἐνδέχεται δὲ τόδε μὲν τόδε κινῆσαι, τόδε δὲ τόδε, καὶ εἶναι οἷον τὰ αὐτόματα τῶν θαυμάτων.

metaphysics and psychology. However, the Stoics were more precise about the functioning of soul. This kind of hierarchy was not Philo's invention. *Mutatis mutandis*, the same process is found in Cicero, when, in *Tusculan Disputations* 4, he announces that he will use the Stoic language and divisions about the passions, but without abandoning the Platonic dualism: *Sit Plato fons*.[11] The *tamen* that follows is quite important. It means that even if there is a contradiction between Plato's doctrine about passions and the Stoic one, both can coexist, if and only if one takes into account the difference of level between them. To adopt the Stoic technical language of psychology was Philo's way to affirm that Stoicism had its place in philosophy, but only if it was already inserted in a philosophy of transcendence. Was this his usual and permanent attitude?

It seems that what we said about the puppet metaphor is contradicted by *Allegorical Interpretation* 1.28, when, in the commentary on Genesis 2:6, he writes:

> 'And a spring went up out of the earth and watered all the face of the earth.' He calls the mind a 'spring' of the earth, and senses its 'face,' because Nature, exercising forethought in all things, assigned this place to them out of all the body as most suitable for their special activities: and the mind like a spring waters the senses, sending to each of them the streams suitable to it.

Then he adds:

> See then, how, like links in a chain, the powers of the living creature hold on to each other; for mind and 'sense-perception' and object of sense being three, 'sense-perception,' is in the middle, while mind and object of sense occupy each extreme. But neither has the mind power to work, that is, to put forth its energies by way of 'sense-perception,' unless God send the object of sense as rain upon it; nor is any benefit derived from the object of sense when so rained down, unless, like a spring, the mind, extending itself to reach the 'sense-perception' stir it out of its repose to grasp the object presented to it. Thus the mind and the object of sense are always practising a reciprocity of giving, the one lying ready for sense-perception as its material, the other, like a craftsman, moving sense-perception in the direction of the external object, to produce an impulse towards it.

> Philo *Allegorical Interpretation* 1.28

---

[11] *Tusculan Disputations* 4.11: *sit igitur hic fons; utamur tamen in his perturbationibus describendis Stoicorum definitionibus et partitionibus, qui mihi videntur in hac quaestione versari acutissime.* On this passage, see Lévy 1992:474.

In the passage, Philo seems to emphasize the monistic functioning of the soul, especially in relation to the interconnection between its different powers. When he says about the intellect that he pushes the senses outside "like a craftsman" (*tekhnitês*), we are not far from the figure of the puppet in the hands of the master, even if he is not explicitly mentioned. But despite this, we can still say that between this passage and the former one, the difference is more apparent than real. Above all, while in Stoic psychology generally there is no explicit mention of God's acting, Philo says that the human mind cannot act if God does not. Actually, it is one of the strangest aspects of Stoicism, to associate the affirmation of the perfect unity of the system with the autonomous presentation of each of its parts.[12] Stoic gnoseology seems to be "secular," especially when it is exposed in doxographic presentations,[13] while it is underpinned by a strongly immanentist theology. To give but one example, how could we have understood that almost all representations are true without the assertion that Providence created the best world possible for humankind? It is Providence that gives the human being the possibility of becoming a god, and if one follows Seneca, more than a god,[14] an idea that Philo would have considered simply monstrous. Instead, he envisions a double continuity, which involves the process of knowledge, compared to a stream, and that flows between human mind and God. This understanding rejects the central dogma of Stoic gnoseology, i.e. that human mind is autonomous in the process that leads from the representation to the assent.[15] This is the reason why, in *On Flight and Finding* 46, he mentions again the puppet metaphor and raises a provocative question: "Know thyself, and the parts of which thou dost consist, what each is and for what it was made, and how it is meant to work, and who it is that, all invisible, invisibly sets the puppets in motion and pulls their strings, whether it be the Mind that is in thee or the Mind of the Universe."[16] There is little doubt that for him only the latter is right. We can confirm this by the comparison with *Allegorical Interpretation* 2.68, where he writes: "By the only true God I deem nothing so shameful as supposing that I exert my mind and senses."[17]

---

12   On the systematic form of the Stoic doctrine, see Gourinat-Barnes 2009.
13   On the general problem of the doxography of soul, see Mansfeld 1990.
14   Seneca *Moral Letters to Lucilius* 53.11: *Est aliquid quo sapiens antecedat deum: ille naturae beneficio non timet, suo sapiens.*
15   Cicero *On Academic Skepticism* I 40: *Sed ad haec quae uisa sunt et quasi accepta sensibus, assensionem adiungit animorum, quam esse vult in nobis positam et voluntariam.*
16   *On Flight and Finding* 46: γνῶθι σαυτὸν καὶ τὰ σαυτοῦ μέρη, τί τε ἕκαστον καὶ πρὸς τί γέγονε καὶ πῶς ἐνεργεῖν πέφυκε καὶ τίς ὁ τὰ θαύματα κινῶν καὶ νευροσπαστῶν ἀόρατος ἀοράτως εἴτε ὁ ἐν σοὶ νοῦς εἴτε ὁ τῶν συμπάντων.
17   *Allegorical Interpretation* 2.68: μὰ τὸν ἀληθῆ μόνον θεὸν οὐδὲν οὕτως αἰσχρὸν ἡγοῦμαι ὡς τὸ ὑπολαμβάνειν ὅτι νοῶ ἢ ὅτι αἰσθάνομαι.

Of course, in the Stoic doctrine, thanks to an elaborate manipulation of a complex causality, the individual soul is inserted in the network of the universal rationality. This insertion, however, does not forbid the Stoics to claim the autonomy of the mind in its confrontation with the world of sensations. It is true that in Philo the puppet metaphor is somewhat incomplete. It expresses the subordination of the senses to the mind, but it does not describe what for Philo is still more important: the subordination of the human mind to God.

2. Assent Absent: The Meaning of a Specificity

Our first passage occurs in *On the Change of Names*. The general theme of the context is that of the acknowledgements and gratitude we owe to God. Philo says that to Him everyone must offer something in proportion to his ability. But beyond the social situation of everyone lies the simple fact of being a man or a woman which must be considered as the first and essential gift for which everybody must express his gratitude: "Vast is the number of such gifts, birth, life, nurture, soul, sense-perception, mental picturing, impulse, reasoning" (*On the Change of Names* 223).[18] The structure of the sentence itself is quite interesting. The three first terms have physical and biological meanings. Then occurs *psukhê*, which is not just a term in the enumeration but a word that is further developed by the last four terms on the list. These four terms are not organized without a specific significance in mind. The first three (sense-perception, mental imaging, and impulse) are those by which the living beings are distinguished from the nonliving. The philosophical explanation of this structure is extensively presented in the following section:

> For the living creature surpasses the non-living in two respects, in the power of receiving impressions and in the active impulse towards the object producing them. The impression is produced by the drawing nigh of the external object, as it stamps the mind through sense-perception; while the active impulse, close of kin to the power aforementioned, comes about by way of the mind's power of self-extension, which it exercises through sense-perception, and so comes in touch with the object presented to it, and goes towards it, striving to reach and seize it.
>
> Philo *Allegorical Interpretation* 1.30

---

[18] *On the Change of Names* 223: μυρίων δ' ἔλαχε, γενέσεως, ζωῆς, τροφῆς, ψυχῆς, αἰσθήσεως, φαντασίας, ὁρμῆς, λογισμοῦ.

The description of the psychological process of knowledge and action is clearly Stoic, as a comparison with many other sources confirms.[19] There is a difference, however. In the Stoic understanding of the soul, "assent" (*sunkatathesis*) plays a great role as it is emphasized, among others, by Iamblichus who clearly states that for the Stoics, the *hêgêmonikon* is the place of representation, assent, impulse, and *logos*.[20] But Philo replaces it with the term *logismos*. Why?

1. The first explanation could be that, in this context of dichotomy, *logismos* introduces a new distinction. After having distinguished living beings from non-living, Philo, through the use of *logismos*, expresses the difference between rational and not non-rational beings: the former possess *logismos*, the latter lack it. And since the main idea of the passage is that the human being is privileged in the Creation—an idea that, in entirely different contexts, was common to both Stoicism and Judaism—Philo's inclusion of *logismos* in his enumeration seems normal.

2. This explanation would be fully convincing if Philo frequently used the term "assent" (*sunkatathesis*). But the term is almost absent from his large corpus.[21] It must be added that not only does Philo rarely use the term *sunkatathesis*, even the verb *sunkatatithesthai* is absent from his work. It is always, however, difficult to base our interpretation of a text on an *argumentum ex silentio*, as it is generally considered weak. At the same time, it would be an equally serious mistake to pretend that the silence does not exist.

3. It is also tempting to invoke a stylistic reason. Philo's style is known for avoiding neologisms and technical terms. *Sunkatathesis* was a specifically Stoic word, created by Zeno to describe the functioning of

---

[19] See SVF II 52–121. Philo gives an extensive description of the process in *On the Unchangeableness of God* 41–44: ψυχὴν δὲ φύσεως τρισὶ διαλλάττουσαν ὁ ποιῶν ἐποίει, αἰσθήσει, φαντασίᾳ, ὁρμῇ· τὰ μὲν γὰρ φυτὰ ἀόρμητα, ἀφάνταστα, αἰσθήσεως ἀμέτοχα, τῶν δὲ ζῴων ἕκαστον ἀθρόων μετέχει τῶν εἰρημένων. αἴσθησις μὲν οὖν, ὡς αὐτόπου δηλοῖ τοὔνομα, εἴσθεσίς τις οὖσα τὰ φανέντα ἐπεισφέρει τῷ νῷ· τούτῳ γάρ, ἐπειδὴ μέγιστόν ἐστι ταμεῖον καὶ πανδεχές, πάνθ' ὅσα δι' ὁράσεως καὶ ἀκοῆς καὶ τῶν ἄλλων αἰσθητικῶν ὀργάνων ἐντίθεται καὶ ἐναποθησαυρίζεται. φαντασία δέ ἐστι τύπωσις | ἐν ψυχῇ ὧν γὰρ εἰσήγαγεν ἑκάστη τῶν αἰσθήσεων, ὥσπερ δακτύλιός τις ἢ σφραγὶς ἐναπεμάξατο τὸν οἰκεῖον χαρακτῆρα· κηρῷ δὲ ἐοικὼς ὁ νοῦς τὸ ἐκμαγεῖον δεξάμενος ἄκρως παρ' ἑαυτῷ φυλάττει, μέχρις ἂν ἡ ἀντίπαλος μνήμης τὸν τύπον λεάνασα λήθη ἀμυδρὸν ἐργάσηται ἢ παντελῶς ἀφανίσῃ. τὸ δὲ φανὲν καὶ τυπῶσαν τοτὲ μὲν οἰκείως τοτὲ δὲ ὡς ἑτέρως διέθηκε τὴν ψυχήν. τοῦτο δὲ αὐτῆς τὸ πάθος ὁρμὴ καλεῖται, ἣν ὁριζόμενοι πρώτην ἔφασαν εἶναι ψυχῆς κίνησιν. τοσούτοις μὲν δὴ ζῷα προὔχει φυτῶν.

[20] Iamblichus *On the Soul* ap. Stobaeus *Eclogue* 1.369.5 = SVF II 831. On the relation between representation and assent in Stoicism, see the clear and useful synthesis in Ioppolo 1990.

[21] On this point, see Lévy 2010.

the human soul, both free and inserted in the universal causality. But at the same time Philo uses frequently *katalêpsis*, to which the Stoics had given a new meaning by defining the word as the assent given to a *phantasia katalêptikê*.

What does *logismos* mean exactly? Before trying to give an answer to this question let us summarize Whittaker's conclusions in the rather interesting article he devoted to "The Terminology of the Rational Soul in the Writings of Philo of Alexandria."[22] His main purpose was to analyze the presence of the doublets *nous kai logos/nous kai logismos*. He rightly takes as starting point that these "have their individual identities and associations." About the relation between *logismos* and *nous*, he admits that there can be no satisfactory answer. In the context of a comparison between Philo and Plutarch, he emphasizes that Plato, their common source, characterizes as "deliberation" (*logismos*) the Demiurge's mental activity—a choice that was attacked by Aristotle with his idea of the immobility of God.[23] He simply remarks that in "some Philonic instances of the couplet of *logismos* is clearly subordinate to, or a faculty of *nous*, while in other contexts Philo gives the impression of exploiting the two terms interchangeably."[24] In his opinion, the term *logismos*, which was also utilized by the Stoics to designate the *hêgêmonikon*, the directive part of the soul, represented "a convenient meeting ground" for Platonists and Stoics. Let us dwell longer on this in the following lines. About the expression *nous kai logos*, which designates the rational element of the soul, he says that the use of the doublet was already a Stoic practice, as illustrated in Cicero's *On the Nature of the Gods*.[25] Strictly speaking, *mens atque ratio* could be a Ciceronian term, i.e. a Platonizing equivalent of the word he found in a Stoic text, but we should still recognize that it is more probable to suppose that the doublet was present in the Stoic text itself from which Cicero was working. Whittaker underlines the "terminological fluidity" of the expression *nous kai logos*. Since he found very few relevant instances of the doublet in Plato, he believes that the origin of this doublet must

---

[22] Whittaker 1996. Here we will not linger to discuss the philological problem he raised about κέκληται, that he considers as corrupt and he replaces with κεκλήρωται in the Philonic passages (*The Worse Attack the Better* 83, *On Rewards and Punishments* 26) about the higher part of the soul.

[23] Whittaker (1996:4) writes: "The mental deliberation posited by Plato was attacked already by Aristotle and was out of step with Middle Platonic and later notions of the immobility of god and of the absence of progression from his mental life." He also quotes Plotinus' *Enneads* IV 8.8.13–16, where it is said that the world soul does not deliberate but maintains without effort the beauty and order of the whole, by intelligence.

[24] Whittaker 1996:7n22 quotes Galen who says in *On the Doctrines of Hippocrates and Plato* IX 1.15 that it makes no difference whether you say *dianoia, nous,* or *logismos* as long as the meaning is clear.

[25] Cicero *On the Nature of the Gods* 1.4: *Sunt autem alii philosophi, et hi quidem magni et nobiles, qui deorum mente atque ratione omnem mundum administrari et regi censeant.*

be found in the Stoic tradition. This leads him to focus on the addition of *aisthêsis* to the doublet in many Philonic passages. This triad, in which sometimes *nous* and *aisthêsis* collaborate and at other times are at variance with each other, is also found in Cicero, Plutarch, and Plotinus, among others.

Our purpose here is a bit different from Whittaker's. We will try to demonstrate that, for Philo, *logismos* was primarily the means that would allow him to avoid the systematic framework of Stoicism.

In the passage of *On the Change of Names* we quoted above, we find quite an interesting perspective on the meaning of the term *logismos*. Its role seems to be much more philosophical and theological than psychological: "*Reasoning as a name is but a little word, but as a fact it is something most perfect and most divine, a piece torn off from the soul of the universe, or, as it might be put more reverently following the philosophy of Moses, a faithful impression of the divine image.*"[26] The two words *apospasma* and *ekmageion* deserve comment also. They are used by Philo many times and especially in *On the Creation of the World* 146, a text that has provoked many commentaries.[27] *Apospasma* has an old philosophical pedigree reaching as far back as Empedocles,[28] but Plato uses it only once,[29] and Aristotle seems to have ignored it. Actually, the Stoics are frequent users of the concept, as attested in numerous references of Zeno, Chrysippus, and Posidonius.[30] By contrast, Plato uses *ekmageion* many times, especially in the *Theaetetus*.[31] The two words aim to give an idea of the link between God and the human being. *Apospasma* conveys the idea that the human soul is only a piece of the universal soul, an idea that Cicero captures in his expression *animus decerptus ex mente divina*,[32] while *ekmageion* is the philosophical expression of the Biblical idea that man was created in God's image. *Logismos* is not a technical Stoic term, but a rather general one, expressing the capacity of reflection and deliberation, as we can see, among many examples, in this passage of the *Allegory of the Law*:

---

[26] *On the Change of Names* 223: λογισμὸς δὲ βραχὺ μὲν ὄνομα, τελειότατον δὲ καὶ θειότατον ἔργον, τῆς τοῦ παντὸς ψυχῆς ἀπόσπασμα ἤ, ὅπερ ὁσιώτερον εἰπεῖν τοῖς κατὰ Μωυσῆν φιλοσοφοῦσιν, εἰκόνος θείας ἐκμαγεῖον ἐμφερές.

[27] On this point, see Runia 2001:345.

[28] Empedocles fr. 55, where it is said that moon is an *apospasma* from sun.

[29] Plato *Phaedo* 113b.

[30] See especially the references given in SVF I 128 = Eusebius *Preparation for the Gospel* I 128 and Posidonius in Diogenes Laertius 7.143 = fr. 99 Kidd-Edelstein: ὅτι δὲ καὶ ζῷον ὁ κόσμος καὶ λογικὸν καὶ ἔμψυχον καὶ νοερὸν καὶ Χρύσιππος ἐν πρώτῳ φησὶν Περὶ προνοίας καὶ Ἀπολλόδωρος [φησιν] ἐν τῇ Φυσικῇ καὶ Ποσειδώνιος· ζῷον μὲν οὕτως ὄντα, οὐσίαν ἔμψυχον αἰσθητικήν. τὸ γὰρ ζῷον τοῦ μὴ ζῴου κρεῖττον· οὐδὲν δὲ τοῦ κόσμου κρεῖττον· ζῷον ἄρ' ὁ κόσμος. ἔμψυχον δέ, ὡς δῆλον ἐκ τῆς ἡμετέρας ψυχῆς ἐκεῖθεν οὔσης ἀποσπάσματος.

[31] Plato *Theaetetus* 191c, 194d–e, 196a–b.

[32] Cicero *Tusculan Disputations* 5.38.

Look at a doctor's reasoning: I will feed him up, I will prescribe medicines and put him on a diet that will make him well, I will operate, I will cauterize. But many a time has nature either brought recovery without these means being used, or brought death when these have been resorted to, proving all of the doctor's calculations to be vain dreams, nothing but guesswork in the dark.

Philo Allegorical Interpretation 3.226[33]

On the surface the passage seems to bear no interest for our examination when in fact it contains the main characteristics of *logismos* in Philo's works:

1. It is a human characteristic. Animals have no *logismos*,[34] and the word is never used about nature, for which Philo prefers always the word *logos*. As it is said in *The Worse Attack the Better*, the body perishes if the soul quits it, and the soul if reason quits it, and reason if it be deprived of virtue.[35] The *logismos* is the essence of human soul, but at the same time, it expresses its imperfection. The lack of virtue, common to most human beings, makes its functioning highly problematic. The concept of *logismos* is used in regards to angels in *On the Special Laws* 1.6. They are said to be disembodied souls, without any irrationality, similar to monads through their pure *logismoi*. Ontologically the fact that the human being is embodied makes this kind of perfection impossible, except perhaps in most exceptional circumstances, like Moses on Mount Sinai.[36] To deify *logismos* is in Philo's opinion a major error.

2. It is the means by which the human mind tries to find a solution to a problem. For Philo the main error is to imagine that *logismos* is entirely ours, while it is only a kind of divine loan; it is often fallible since it is instable.[37] Only the mind of the sage can be stable, an idea that Philo shares with the Stoics. Consequently, it is necessary to remind a

---

[33] *Allegorical Interpretation* 3.226: ἴδε λογισμὸν ἰατροῦ· κενώσω τὸν κάμνοντα, θρέψω, φαρμάκοις ἰάσομαι <καὶ> διαίτῃ, τεμῶ, καύσω· ἀλλὰ πολλάκις ἡ φύσις καὶ ἄνευ τούτων ἰάσατο καὶ μετὰ τούτων ἀπώλεσεν, ὡς τοὺς ἰατροῦ πάντας ἐπιλογισμοὺς ἐνύπνια εὑρεθῆναι ἀσαφείας καὶ αἰνιγμάτων πλήρη.

[34] *Allegorical Interpretation* 2.89.

[35] *The Worse Attack the Better* 141.

[36] On this aspect of Moses, see Sterling 1993 and Litwa 2014.

[37] *On Dreams* 1.192: ἀνίδρυτοι μὲν γὰρ οἱ λογισμοί, φαντασίας ἀπὸ τῶν αὐτῶν πραγμάτων οὐχὶ τὰς αὐτὰς ἀλλ᾽ ἐναντίας ἔχοντες, ἀνίδρυτον δὲ καὶ τὸ σῶμα, ὡς μηνύουσιν αἱ ἐκ βρέφους ἄχρι γήρως τῶν ἡλικιῶν ἁπασῶν τροπαί, ἀνίδρυτα δὲ καὶ τὰ ἐκτὸς ἐπηωρημένα φορᾷ τύχης ἀεὶ σαλευούσης.

fragile rationality of its limits, since it has a strong tendency to forget them.

Let us explore this third aspect. In *On the Cherubim* 69, Philo stresses the idea that to think that we have *logismoi* is a kind of insanity. Not only does he invoke all the pathologies that can affect reason, but he clearly asserts that its functioning is highly erratic, with vain conjectures, illusions, omissions, and oversights. His conclusion is that all these dysfunctions sap the control one imagines to have over one's mind. His deepest reflection on the fragility of the *logismos*, however, is found in *On Rewards and Punishments* 29. There he bases the waywardness of *doxa* on likelihoods and possibilities, but above all on the self-affirmation of "reasoning" (*logismos*) and "sense-perception" (*aisthêsis*). They are most of the time unable to perceive their mistake in understanding the difference of who "takes God for his sole stay and support with a reasonableness whose resolution flatters not, and a faith unswerving and securely founded" (*On Rewards and Punishments* 29). At the same time, Philo seems to say the contrary in *On the Preliminary Studies* 155, a very complex passage, where in the context of the comparison between the culture of the schools, embodied by Agar, and philosophy, by Sarah, he says: "while what is implied by the mistress reaches to the soul, for wisdom and knowledge and their implications are referred to the reasoning faculties."[38] Here the meaning of *logismos* is certainly positive, since "mind is more powerful, more active (δυνατώτερον καὶ δραστικώτερον) and altogether better than the hand" (*On the Preliminary Studies* 155). In *The Life of Moses* 2.185, *logismos* is described as "the highest authority within us," most relevant in the case of those who are virtuous and devote themselves to a life of austerity and hardship. And in a very popular Philonic allegory, it is said that: "the rational which belongs to mind and reasoning is of the masculine gender, the irrational, the province of senses is other feminine."[39] We can also add *On the Virtues* 151, where he evokes "the keen-sighted vision" (ὀξυôpia) of the *logismos*. What exactly is his position about this faculty?

There is a skeptic perception of *logismos* in Philo, as exemplified in *On Joseph* 142. There he admits that those who imagine that they can perceive without any risk of error the nature of things by their own reasoning are wrong. It is important to note the following ambiguity, however. Reasoning is unstable since it has its source in sense-perceptions and is engaged in a permanent fight against desire.[40] But it is not said, at least explicitly, that *logismoi* themselves are unstable

---

[38] *On the Preliminary Studies* 155: τὰ δὲ τῆς κυρίας εἰς ψυχὴν ἔρχεται· λογισμοῖς γὰρ τὰ κατά τε φρόνησιν καὶ ἐπιστήμην ἀνατίθεται. On Sarah in Philo's thought, see Niehoff 2004:413–444.

[39] *On the Special Laws* 1.201: τὸ μὲν λογικὸν τῆς ἄρρενος γενεᾶς ἐστιν, ὅπερ νοῦς καὶ λογισμὸς κεκλήρωται, τὸ δ' ἄλογον τῆς πρὸς γυναικῶν, ὅπερ ἔλαχεν αἴσθησις.

[40] See *On the Virtues* 113.

if they originated from another source than sense-perceptions. Actually, in *On the Special Laws* 1.20, Philo affirms clearly the possibility of the *logismos* to go beyond the visible world in order to give honor to the Immaterial, the Invisible, the Apprehended by the understanding alone.[41] In *On the Special Laws* 1.37, in a passage that is not without similarity to a passage in Cicero,[42] the reasonings and conclusions of philosophy are described as the means for the reason "to soar away from earth into the heights" and to accompany the revolutions of the sun and moon. And a little further in the same treatise, the explanation of the process of prophecy allows Philo to suggest that *logismos* is the tenant of soul, not its real owner.[43]

3. The Four Legs of the Horse[44]

The metaphor of the horse used to explain the nature of the soul is generally considered an element of Platonic philosophy, because of the myth of the chariot in the *Phaedrus*. But in *Allegorical Interpretation* 2.99, we find a sign of evolution in the understanding of the metaphor, for which Philo certainly is not responsible. The text deserves to be analyzed with some precision:

> Let then the principle of self mastery become a serpent upon the soul whose road lies through all the circumstances of life and let it seat itself upon the well worn track. What is this? The path of virtue is unworn, for few tread it while that of vice is well worn. He calls upon him to beset with his ambush and to lie in wait upon the beaten road of passion and vice, on which reasoning powers that flee from virtue wear out their life. 'Biting the horse's heel.' It is quite in keeping that the character which upsets the stability of created and perishable life attacks the heel. The passions are likened to a horse. For passion, like a horse, is a four-legged creature, impulsive, full of willfulness.

> Philo *Allegorical Interpretation* 2.98-99[45]

---

[41] *On the Special Laws* 1.20.

[42] *Allegory of the Law* 1.60–61.

[43] *On the Special Laws* 4.49. See also *On the Special Laws* 1.293 and *On the Decalogue* 177.

[44] A first version of this section was given in Lévy 2005.

[45] *Allegory of the Law* 2.98–99: γενέσθω οὖν ὁ σωφροσύνης λόγος ὄφις ἐπὶ τῆς ψυχῆς τῆς ὁδευούσης διὰ πάντων τῶν ἐν τῷ βίῳ πραγμάτων καὶ ἐγκαθισάτω ἐπὶ τρίβου. τί δὲ τοῦτ' ἐστίν; ἄτριπτος μὲν ὁ ἀρετῆς χῶρος, ὀλίγοι γὰρ βαίνουσιν αὐτόν, τέτριπται δὲ ὁ κακίας· ἐγκαθίσαι δὴ καὶ ἐνεδρεῦσαι καὶ λοχῆσαι παραινεῖ τὴν τετριμμένην ὁδόν, τὸ πάθος καὶ τὴν κακίαν, ἐν οἷς κατατρίβονται τὸν βίον οἱ φυγάδες ἀρετῆς λογισμοί. "δάκνων πτέρναν ἵππου." ἐχομένως πτερνιστής ἐστιν ὁ τὴν στάσιν τοῦ γενητοῦ καὶ φθαρτοῦ διασείων τρόπος. τὰ πάθη δὲ ἵππῳ ἀπεικάσθη· τετρασκελὲς | γὰρ καὶ τὸ πάθος ὡς ἵππος καὶ ὁρμητικὸν καὶ αὐθαδείας γέμον καὶ σκιρτητικὸν φύσει.

The passage is a commentary on Genesis 49:16, 18, where it is said: "Let Dan be a serpent on the road." For Philo, this road is the symbol of the soul, an over-crowded place, full of thousands of negative items, but also of holy, virtuous, and authentic realities. Strangely, however, the serpent, traditional allegory of pleasure in his thought, is here the symbol of temperance. The commentator asks what the text means. His answer is that temperance must bite the pastern of the horse.

In addition, the number four has importance in Philo's work, through the metaphysical symbolism of the tetrad (*On the Creation of the World* 53.62). We also find it in many passages, as an allusion to the Stoic doctrine of the four negative passions. For example, in the last book of *On the Special Laws*, we read:[46]

> By the four legged and many footed he means the base slaves not of one passion only, desire, but of all. For the passions fall under four main heads but have a multitude of species, and while the tyranny of one is cruel, the tyranny of many cannot but be most harsh and intolerable.

> Philo *On the Special Laws* 4.113[47]

Tetraskeles is a word with no philosophical pedigree before Philo. It pertains to the lexical register of tragedy and medicine. It seems hopeless to try to identify with precision where Philo found it. However, there are some elements that seem to direct us towards Stoicism. The verb *apeikazô* is used many times by Philo to express metaphors and allegories. But in two treatises, *On the Change of Names* and *On Husbandry*,[48] he explicitly mentions the creators of a metaphorical interpretation, those who compared philosophy to a field with three elements—trees, fruits, and the fence representing, respectively, physics, ethics, and logic—as "philosophers of the old time." Evidently it is an allusion to the Ancient Stoics who created a doctrine they wanted to be an absolutely perfect system.[49] Philo's use of the passive form of the verb (*apeikasthê*) refers to a tradition that certainly enjoyed some notoriety in his time. We can also note the clear Stoic echo detected in his use of the adjective *hormêtikon*.

The coherence of the metaphor is problematic, however, and Philo works hard on smoothing it out. If a serpent bites a horse that runs fast, the bite entails the risk of bringing down the rider. Philo does not deny this risk, but he makes a distinction between two kinds of falls. If the rider falls forward, that means that

---

[46] For the most recent bibliography on passions in Stoicism, see C. Gill 2006 and C. Gill and Morton 2007.

[47] The translation is according to Colson 1939.

[48] *On Husbandry* 14 and *On the Change of Names* 74.

[49] On metaphors in Stoicism, see Rolke 1975.

he will meet passions; if he falls behind, he will avoid this kind of disaster. This distinction allows him to give some unity to his interpretation of two important Biblical passages:[50] (1) about Pharaoh and his army, "He cast horse and rider into the sea;"[51] (2) but in his blessings to his son Dan, Jacob says, "The horseman shall fall backwards."[52] Things are clear for Philo. Egyptians, allegory of a dishonest way of life, will perish, while the rider evoked by Jacob symbolizes the possibility to escape the destruction.

The exegetic process is somewhat laborious, as though Philo absolutely wanted to harmonize a philosophical pattern with texts that did not fit this structure. What seems more interesting is the transformation of the Platonic image of the chariot, by a process of integration. The rider on his horse is a more unified figure that the one used by Plato in the *Phaedrus*, where the driver is separated from the horses by the chariot. It can be added that the metaphor of the chariot is in itself a kind of *scala naturae* associating objects, animals, and human being. The rider on his horse symbolizes the Stoic distinction between the rational and irrational elements in the physical world.

Anyway, the presence of the four legs of the horse is a clear allusion to the Stoic theory of passions. Philo himself acknowledges that he is not the first to associate this theory with the metaphor of the horse. To the best of our knowledge there is no mention of this metaphor before Posidonius, who uses it twice. In a first passage, he takes over the Platonic metaphor, evoking the charioteer and the two horses, *epithumia* and *thumos*. In the second one, he tries to understand how passions tend to calm down. His answer is that the passionate part of the soul eventually satisfies its own desires. Then the charioteer can master his horse. This could be an element of Philo's source. As a confirmation, we can mention *On the Preliminary Studies* 81, where Philo exposes his view about the genetics of passion. He says that passion is the natural status of soul at the beginning of life. The list of passions is close to that of the Stoic doctrine of passions.[53] At the same time, he affirms that passions are present in human being since the beginning of the life, a somewhat strange affirmation, since passions are a disease of reason, and reason does not appear before the child becomes seven years old. The ingenious solution found by Philo is that reason is present, but it sleeps. But Galen says that according to Posidonius passions are also present in childhood.[54] There is a probable supplementary argument

---

[50] *Allegory of the Law* 2.102.
[51] Exodus 15:1.
[52] Genesis 49:17.
[53] In this text, Philo replaces fear (*phobos*) by *ptoia*. On his variations about the orthodox Stoic list of passions, see Lévy 2006.
[54] See frr. 31, 159, and 169 Kidd.

in favor of the dependence of Philo on a Posidonian source. For him the four negative Stoic passions are not equivalent. There is a hierarchy, since pleasure is considered as the source of the other three. This is perhaps a consequence of the Posidonian affirmation that, from birth, a child grows accustomed to pleasure. But the presence of a strong influence does not imply that there is no Philonic originality. The fact that he introduces hope among the Stoic "good passions" (*eupatheiai*) reveals his main purpose to be exegetic in nature.

4. Conclusion

To interpret Philo's concept of soul as syncretic is an understandable, but somewhat dangerous, attitude. It is *undeniable* that Stoic elements are common in his description of the soul. He omits, however, perhaps the most important one among them: assent. It is the most visible sign of human freedom and responsibility, despite the Stoa deterministic conception of the world. Philo and Cicero were very different thinkers, but both believed that Stoicism had a place in their thought, only at the condition to admit the supremacy of Platonism, and more generally of transcendence. Despite Panaetius' and Posidonius' efforts to shorten the distance between the doctrines, the gap between transcendental and immanentist psychology remained deep. Philo certainly appreciated the high precision of the Stoic psychology, but the many variations on his presentation of soul were mainly a means to establish a hierarchy at the bottom of which lies Stoicism, above it, Platonism, and, at the top, Revelation. Bréhier (1925) was not wrong, when he mentioned *une psychologie religieuse*.

Origen, Athanasius, and Plato

MARK EDWARDS

Abstract: In recent years most scholars have refrained from peremptory attributions of Platonism either to Athanasius or to his arch-opponents, the so-called Arians. Nevertheless, while the biblical matrix of arguments on both sides is sufficiently manifest and uncontested by serious students, Athanasius wrote at least one two-volume work (*Against the Heathen/On the Incarnation*) as a reply to Platonic impeachments of Christianity, while one of his critics, Eusebius of Caesarea, is our principal witness to the lost works of Numenius and Porphyry, which he cited in vindication of the gospel. Since every ecclesiastical controversialist of the early fourth century was also an apologist, no controversy could be purely internal. Questions like the following still await solutions, and the solutions may throw light on the development of doctrine:

1. Which is more Platonic—threefold unity in the Godhead or the "second god" of Eusebius? (Revisiting the arguments of Cudworth 1820).

2. How far, and for whom, is the debate about the eternity of the Son comparable to the debate among the Platonists as to whether the world was sempiternal or temporally finite? (Revisiting the arguments of Stead 1964).

3. Is it likely that Christians could have found warrant for the use of the term *homoousios* either in Plotinus or in Hermetic literature, as Beatrice 2002 had maintained?

4. Should the failure of Athanasius to posit a human soul in Christ be regarded as a defect, or as an indication that he had abandoned the

Platonic anthropology of *De Incarnatione*, and therefore no longer had to answer questions framed on Plato's dualistic presuppositions?

5. Would a Platonic ontology of the noetic realm supply the missing premises in Athanasius' argument that we cannot be gods by participation in the Word unless he is God by nature? (Revisiting the arguments of Wiles 1962).

IN REVIEWING THE history of doctrine, it is hard to say why one man becomes a saint and another a heretic, while others seem to escape the bar of history altogether. Augustine condemned Pelagius while the Greeks condemned Celestius; the status of Eusebius was as contestable in his own day as in ours; no monograph on Marcellus of Ancyra has proved as durable as the enigmatic smile of Athanasius. The origins of heresy are also a puzzle, at least for those who can still hold that the voice of the church is the voice of the Holy Spirit, or that all legitimate questions can be foreclosed by a body of occasional writings put together without design in the course of the first there Christian centuries. In ancient heresiology, errors in doctrine are generally attributed to a conspiracy between Satan and the philosophers; modern historiography claims no acquaintance with the devil and is divided as to the salience of philosophy. Many Catholics have been glad to believe that the truths revealed to the church had been reinforced by the best in pagan ratiocination; Protestants, on the other hand, have often seen philosophy as a cancer to faith, not least to the faith that passes for orthodoxy. From Harnack to Grillmeier, however, it has generally been agreed that where there is heresy there is always a pagan scholarch at the back of it, most commonly Plato or one of his successors. Thus, Origen is the first name that comes to mind when one speaks of Christian Platonism, whereas only a friend of Plato or a critic of orthodoxy would apply this term to the thought of Athanasius, master builder of the faith that we now call Nicene. The present chapter is not so much an attempt to redress the balance as a plea to refrain from the use of loaded scales.

I shall not maintain that Origen learned nothing from Plato, any more than I should feel bound to maintain this of Marcus Aurelius. The mere mention of Marcus Aurelius should prepare the reader for my attempt to demonstrate in the first section of this chapter that to call an author a Platonist ought to signify something more than the anecdotal presence of Platonic matter in his writings. My subsequent discussion of Athanasius is divided into three sections, illustrating three distinct goals that an author may be pursuing when he makes use of such matter. His usage is *eristic* or *strategic* when his purpose is to outflank or reconcile his interlocutors. Even strategic borrowings may acquire a *subsidiary* value when they enhance the logical cogency of his argument in the eyes of a particular group of readers. His usage becomes *fiduciary* when it is no longer calculated to quicken the interest or secure the consent of others, but enables him to express his own convictions in the form that he himself finds most persuasive.

1. The Question of Platonism

For over a century it has been an unexamined commonplace of scholarship that Origen was a Platonist. In recent years, some scholars have contested this assumption: they have pointed out that Origen seldom mentions Plato except to criticize him, that his extant writings (still voluminous) seldom confirm and sometimes contradict what was said against him in antiquity, and that many of the heterodox positions that are eagerly traced to Plato in modern scholarship are derived by him, quite plausibly, from the scriptures. Tzamalikos has gone so far as to style him an "anti-Platonist,"[1] and some scholars seem to think that they can explode this claim, without any further perusal of his three books, by showing that Origen held some beliefs that were also held by Plato or that, like intelligent Christians in all ages, he carried on philosophical disputations in the current language of philosophy. These, however, are philological short-cuts, and in philosophy every shortcut is a *cul-de sac*. The longer way that Plato would commend is also a slower one, which requires us to surrender one piece of inadmissible evidence after another at a series of logical tollgates. It is simply begging the question to cite any proposition in a Christian author as evidence of his Platonic sympathies unless: (1) it is undeniably Platonic; (2) it is so distinctively Platonic that it could not be attached to any other school or reckoned among the eclectic doctrines; and (3) it was still a doctrine on probation, which had not already been grafted onto a common stock of Christian beliefs. When these three criteria are observed, it will be clear that we need a subtle fan to winnow the truly Platonic elements in a Christian author from the residue of a general training in philosophy.

For instance, a strong assertion of the unity of God will not satisfy the first condition, since monotheism is not universally ascribed to Plato by the best scholars.[2] It will not satisfy the second, since it is Aristotle, not Plato, who habitually uses "god" (*theos*) as his name for that which is highest in the scale of being.[3] And it will not satisfy the third, as there was no sect in antiquity so intractable

---

[1] See Tzamalikos 1991, 2006, 2007.

[2] For a succinct discussion of the question, see the much-cited article by Hackforth 1936.

[3] See e.g. *Eudemian Ethics* 1248a24–29, *Magna Moralia* 1212b34–38, *Metaphysics* 1072b24–31. For some apposite qualifications, see Brunschwig 2000.

as the church in its refusal to worship any God but its own; even among the Jews we hear of no rabbi who anticipated Christ by reciting the Shema—"Hear, O Israel, the Lord our God is one Lord" (Deuteronomy 6:4)—as an epitome of the *Torah*. To identify the highest deity with the highest Goodness and to derive all other existents from the divine will may be salient, if not ubiquitous, tenets of Platonism, but at most they distinguish it from Aristotelianism, not from Christianity. There was certainly no Aristotelian precedent for the use of *monas* in Origen and Arius as a designation for God the Father; to them, however, this was already a Christian term, baptized by Athenagoras and sanctified (for Arius) by the authority of the unimpeachable Bishop Dionysius of Alexandria. Nor did one have to look beyond the Christian lexicon of the third century to find such adjectives as "incorporeal" (*asômatos*), "unoriginate" (*anarkhos*), or "immutable" (*analloiôtos*), none of which (whatever its provenance) retained the odor of the pagan schools in Origen's time.

By contrast, the locution "second god" (*deuteros theos*) was never associated with any school but Plato's, and could still be denounced as a watchword of that school after its adoption for apologetic purposes by Origen and Eusebius. In Origen it occurs only when he is answering, and appears to be echoing, Celsus;[4] it is probable, however, that like Eusebius he had encountered it as one name for the demiurgic intellect in Numenius of Apamea.[5] Others ascribed this usage to Plato—Constantine with qualified praise, and Marcellus of Ancyra with reprobation.[6] While Philo's use of "second god" as an honorific sobriquet for the *Logos* escaped these authors, Lactantius made a collection of testimonies from the *Hermetica*, ignoring the fact that Hermes had equated his second god with the visible cosmos.[7] This last example illustrates the duplicity of language as a witness to the history of thought. "Second god" as a formula satisfies all three conditions—it is (1) Platonic, (2) distinctively so, and (3) unassimilable to the majority of Christians—yet it was never employed by Christians either to justify the deification of the created order or to disparage it, with Numenius, as the product of a tragic estrangement of the divine intelligence from the Godhead in repose.

---

[4] At *Against Celsus* 6.61, he argues that what cannot be predicated of the First god is not predicable of the second; at 6.64, he proposes that the only begotten of god may be the substance of substances even though the Father remains superior; at 6.47, he concludes that the two are so conjoined that they are no longer two but one. Since he appears to be speaking of the incarnate Word in both these passages, it is clear that we are far from Aranism.

[5] See fr. 16 des Places.

[6] Constantine *Oration to the Saints* 9; "Anthimus" (Marcellus of Ancyra) in Mercati 1901. It does not follow that the use of this term is a proof of Arian sympathies; see Edwards 2006.

[7] See *Epitome* 37.1.5 and, for all Hermetic citations in Lactantius, W. B. Scott 1936:9–27.

What of the soul? Many biblical scholars assure us that the Hebrews knew nothing of it as a thing distinct from the body, and that the Fathers who uncoupled the two were putting a false construction on Paul's antithesis between the inner and the outer man. Certainly no Greek schools denied the existence of a soul (although its status in Aristotle is uncertain), but Platonists from Atticus to Marsilio Ficino have regarded the doctrine of immortality as a defining tenet of their tradition, notwithstanding a few camp followers among the Stoics who opined that nobler souls may outlive the dissolution of the body. The *New Testament* in fact opposes body to soul and flesh to mind, but only the body—the spiritual body—is declared to be incorruptible. Did the early Christians therefore fall into Platonism when they embraced the immortality of the soul as a concomitant to the promised resurrection of the body? We should remember that the same doctrine is attributed to the Pharisees and the Essenes by Josephus; if this is true, and not merely a concession to pagan ignorance, the reason will be not that these Jewish sects had been seduced by the ambient culture, but that in order to make sense of the final judgment they were forced to posit some survival of consciousness to maintain the identity of the one who was buried with the one who rose again. For Christians of antiquity, a Platonist was one who holds not merely that the soul will live again but that it has passed through a series of lives before the present one, expiating the sins committed in previous embodiments or in a disembodied state before its sojourn in this world. All Christians whose works survive anathematize this doctrine; some held more attenuated theories of preexistence, which they fortified by arguments that no Platonist would have employed. Thus, Origen infers that two creations of humanity are recorded in the scriptures because the first is the creation of the inner man; Nemesius of Emesa contends that the work of the first six days was unrepeatable, and therefore there can be no new creation of souls. Origen himself denounced belief in transmigration as a heresy;[8] if, as his detractors said, he held that souls on earth are being punished for sins in heaven, it was not his metaphysics but his theodicy that required this explanation for the inequality of human fortunes. The notion of a fall of souls through error (as opposed to a descent by the will of God) is: (1) Platonic, (2) distinctively so, and (3) unassimilable to the majority of Christians; the evidence that Origen taught it, however, is more easily elicited from the writings of his enemies than from his own. It seems likely that he was condemned in 553 not only for doctrines that he endorsed but for those that he entertained as temporary hypotheses, and for those that were taught in his name by aberrant thinkers to whom he was still a venerable authority.

---

[8]   See Edwards 2002:98–99 and 2012.

No doubt there are historians for whom words are not ductile media of thought but party-labels, and for whom therefore expressions like "second god" or "preexistence of the soul" mean one thing always and one thing only. For such historians, bishops in the church are like bishops in chess, moving only on squares of a single color. The meagerness of our knowledge makes it possible for us to reduce the political and intellectual ferment of the early Christian era to a binary play of forces, though we would never accept such caricatures in a modern account of the Reformation or the French Revolution. The hairs that I have split in the foregoing discussion of Origen and other Christian writers are no more tenuous than those that are split every day by students of Plato and Plotinus; when I wrote a book called *Origen against Plato*, I was not denying that any Platonic sentiments can be attributed to Origen, but inviting theologians and historians of the church to weigh the term "Platonist" on the same delicate scales that are now used by historians of philosophy. To illustrate what is still to be done I shall end this section with a brief reply to a recent contribution to *Origeniana Decima*, in which Hengstermann undertakes to show that Origen held what he styles a "soteriontology based upon the twin pillars of divine procession and creative contemplation."[9] This he declares to be "truly Neoplatonic," notwithstanding the chronological priority of Origen to Plotinus; and although he notes that many of Origen's fundamental tenets contradict those of every known Platonist, he concludes that he was not only *Christianus* but *vere Platonicus*.

No word that denotes "procession" occurs in any of the passages quoted from Origen in this article; one is produced in which Origen concedes that the eructation of the word from the heart at Psalm 44:1 represents the Father's expression of himself in Christ. The phrase "creative contemplation" appears to comprehend two distinct activities: the contemplation of the Father by the Son as Wisdom and the creation of the world by the Son as *Logos*. On the mere authority of Cadiou, we are assured that for Origen contemplation implies participation in the object. I suspect that one could improve on this elliptical presentation of Hengstermann's thesis, but an argument so free of dates and definitions can be of little use to the historian. Will anyone venture to maintain that Origen, a prodigy before the birth of Plotinus, could have fallen under the influence of the younger man in his later years as Plato fell under the influence of Isocrates? Can we securely identify a precursor of Plotinus who held the same theories of emanation and participation? Hengstermann will reply that he has employed the term "Neoplatonist" in a taxonomic rather than a chronological sense; but even if it could be shown that Plotinus and Origen both affirmed a "divine procession," it would also need to be shown that they attached the same

---

9   Hengstermann 2011.

meaning to the word "procession" (and indeed to the word "divine"). Origen asserts that the Son and Father are of the same nature; drawing expressly on Wisdom 7:25–26 and not on any Platonic notion of "emanation" (*aporroia*), he likens the Son to the vapor exhaled by an ointment, which remains consubstantial (*homoousios*) with its source.[10] Of course no such community of essence between the first and the second hypostases can be maintained by a philosophy which asserts that the One is superior to essence and denies it every positive attribute. It is equally misleading to flourish the term "participation" as a badge of Platonic sympathies; if it were, we could all be Platonists by participating in a gameshow, a sponsored walk, or a karaoke. The usage becomes Platonic only when the participation to which it refers is that of a concrete entity in the transcendent form, which Plato calls the idea (*eidos*). When Origen alludes to this world of separable forms, he declares it chimerical (*On Principles* 2.3.6); when he suggests that the genera and species, and perhaps the individual forms, of all things have existed forever in the divine intellect (*On Principles* 1.4.5), he is ascribing to God a knowledge of entities not yet created, and therefore incapable of participation in any higher realm of being. Once created, rational agents participate in the *Logos*; if there is any equivalent to the *Logos* in Plotinus, it is *nous* (the unincarnate, suprapersonal intellect), and he may be the first to speak of our participation in it. But he also speaks, as Origen does not, of participation in the Forms and in the One.

We see that Platonism is not so easily detected, even where it is supposed to be pervasive. It has not been common even to suppose this of Athanasius, who seldom refers to Plato and harbors no opinions that an orthodox critic might have been unwilling to derive from canonical sources. "Platonist," like "Origenist," is an epithet more commonly applied to his opponents, though no attempt to unearth the pagan roots of Arius' thought has proved more credible than his own claim to be a literal interpreter of the scriptures. In the modern age—where partisan churchmanship does not preclude the admission that a heretic may have something to teach the orthodox—it is generally acknowledged that Athanasius subscribed to Origen's view on certain questions that divided the church of his day. He himself says as much when he cites Origen as a witness to the coeternity of the Son and the Father, and in histories of the doctrine of original sin he figures as the next Alexandrian teacher after Origen who spoke of a fall from a state of initial perfection.[11] It is to his understanding of the fall that we shall now turn to illustrate his eristic or strategic use of the Platonic repertory.

---

[10] See Pamphilus *Apology for Origen* 99, with Edwards 1998.
[11] See N. P. Williams 1927.

2. Platonism and the Fall

If we believe the most hostile witnesses,[12] Origen taught that souls were first created as pure intellects, not for embodiment but for the unceasing contemplation of God. All but the soul of Christ, however, have fallen away as a consequence of "satiety" (*koros*),[13] and have been punished, in proportion to the grossness of their transgression, by confinement to angelic, human, or demonic bodies. We have each received the lot that we deserve, with the freedom of will to make the best or the worst of it. This is clearly a modification of the great myth in the *Phaedrus* of Plato, according to which souls shed their wings and fall to earth from the supercelestial heaven after failing in the struggle to reach the highest plane of vision (*Phaedrus* 246a–254e). *Koros* is the cause of the soul's apostasy in Philo and Plotinus,[14] though in Origen's extant writings it is predicated only of the embodied intellect, not of the soul or intellect in heaven. Neither in his own writings nor in later reports do we hear how Origen met the obvious criticism that human bodies are perishable whereas those of angels and daemons are immortal; we know enough at least to be sure that he never embraced the doctrine of transmigration that is indispensable to Plato's teaching. Again, we do not hear how daemons come to inhabit lighter bodies than ours when they are weighed down by greater sins, or how Origen could be certain that every soul but that of Christ will fall (*On Principles* 2.6.3–4) so long as there are humans yet to be born and therefore souls not yet embodied. In short, we have every reason to doubt that so able a theologian could have held the positions ascribed to him, and these doubts are hardly allayed by his own assertion at *On Principles* 1.6.4 that no creature could maintain a discrete existence without a body. Undoubtedly, he posits a creation of the soul before the body, if only to explain how the making of both male and female in the image of God at Genesis 1:26–28 could precede the fashioning of Adam's body and the subsequent creation of Eve from his rib. At *On Principles* 3.6.1, he concludes that the first creation was imperfect, as the likeness of God was still to be earned as the reward of virtue; he says nothing of any merit that has been lost in the descent from a higher realm. In *Against Celsus*, the fall of Adam and Eve is described as an opening of the eyes of sense that blinds those of the intellect—a Pauline notion[15] expressed (for Celsus' sake) in the philosophical vernacular, but without implying, any more than Paul implies, that the darkening of the mind increases the thickness of its carnal envelope.

---

[12] See e.g. the matter inserted at *On Principles* 1.9.1 in Koetschau 1913.
[13] Koetschau 1913:159, citing the anathemas attributed to the Fifth Ecumenical Council in 553.
[14] Philo *Life of Moses* 2.239 and Plotinus *Enneads* III 5.10.
[15] Cf. 1 Corinthians 1:15, 2 Corinthians 4:18, and Romans 7:25 and 8:7.

No doctrine of a preexistent, yet alone a fallen, soul is countenanced in the writings of Athanasius. In his *Against the Heathen*,[16] he does not say so clearly as Origen that the fall occurred in Eden, but speaks of the race collectively as Plato does when he speculates on the origins of society in the *Statesman* and the *Protagoras*. He also applies to God the Platonic title *dêmiourgos*,[17] whereas previous apologists show a preference for maker (*poiêtês*), Father (*patêr*), or the more biblical Creator (*ktistês*). No doubt this choice enables him to contrast the omnipotence of God, the true Craftsman, with the misspent labor of the human sculptor who worships the products of his own workshop; but how are we to account for his description of the fall on two occasions by the word *tolma*, a usage redolent of the Gnostic myth in which Sophia's temerity leads to her banishment from the *Plêrôma*, and also of *Enneads* V 1 where the same term characterizes the necessary but painful alienation of intellect from the One?[18] Athanasius shows enough knowledge of Plotinus to imitate him when he likens the soul's desertion of God to the submersion of a body in a watery abyss (*Against the Heathen* 8.3–4). The treatise in which Plotinus employs a similar conceit was the first of the *Enneads* to be written,[19] perhaps the only one that Plotinus himself gave to the world, and certainly the one best known to Christians of the fourth century. If Athanasius read it in full, he will have seen that Plotinus completes his argument by an exhortation to polish the statue within us. Any Christian theologian would construe this as an allusion to the tarnished image of God, which Athanasius, following Origen against Irenaeus,[20] identifies with the soul; in contrast to Origen also,[21] though in common with the other great theologians of his century, he acknowledges no distinction between the image already given and the likeness still to come. In the West it was Augustine who resurrected this distinction;[22] the scholars who portray him and Irenaeus as antipodal figures

---

[16] The first part of an apologetic diptych that, to judge by its triumphant tone, was written when the pagans had lost their ascendancy in the Empire. On its date, see Anatolios 1988:26–27 and Kannengiesser 2006.

[17] *Against the Heathen* 7.1, 8.3, 11.1, 27, 29.5, 30.4, 35.2, 39.1, 39.6. Slaveva-Griffin reminds me of Numenius fr. 21 des Places.

[18] See *Against the Heathen* 5.1 and 9.3 on the "temerity" (*tolma*) of the first humans; Irenaeus *Against Heresies* 1.2.2 on the *tolma* of Wisdom in the Valentinian cosmogony. Notwithstanding its inevitability, the separation of *nous* from the One is described as a *tolma* by Plotinus at *Enneads* V 1.1. Cf. Quispel 2008:197–298.

[19] *Enneads* I 6.8.

[20] *Against Heresies* 5.6.1.

[21] See e.g. *On Principles* 3.6.1, where Genesis 1:26 is reconciled with Genesis 1:28 by the hypothesis that God vouchsafed the image to Adam immediately, but withheld the likeness to be the reward of virtue.

[22] See *Diverse Questions* 51; also *On Free Will* 3.72, where Adam is said to have been endowed with reason but not yet with the *sapientia* which he would have attained had he not eaten from the tree of knowledge.

forget that it was only in the Latin world that a full text of the latter's *Against Heresies* survived.

Athanasius, like Augustine, holds that a tendency to fall into nothing is natural to beings who were created out of nothing. Both philosophers, against those who personify evil, insist that evil has no being of its own but is a deficit of being. For Athanasius, however, the class of "things which are not" includes not only that which is absolutely nonexistent but anything that falls short of the dignity of God. Plato's equation of evil with nonbeing had been endorsed by Origen, at least for the purpose of exegesis;[23] but Origen had distinguished between the icon that is a copy of some real creature and the idol that, as Paul avers at 1 Corinthians 8:4, represents "nothing in the world" (*Homilies on Exodus* 8.3). Athanasius employs the term "idol" without discrimination, and regards the portrayal of fantastic creatures as the most heinous case of a universal propensity to worship "things which are not."[24] The fullness of being promised to the righteous soul is described in the *Against the Heathen* as the contemplation and intuition of God by the emancipated mind, the consummate vision of "things above the earth," which the embodied soul perceives in imagination, an inward knowledge and apprehension of the Word of God.[25] A similar trope—it is widely attested in philosophical literature—had commended itself to Justin before his conversion from Platonism to Christianity.[26] For Origen the climax of the soul's ascent through the spheres after death is union first with Christ, then with the Father who will be its all in all (*On Principles* 3.6.6): here again his idiom is biblical, and that of Athanasius more Platonic. It is Origen, not Athanasius, who robs the soul of the fanciful wings in which Plato draped her,[27] deriding the efforts of all the schools to demonstrate her natural immortality (*On Principles* 3.80). Christ comes into his own in the sequel to the *Against the Heathen/On the Incarnation*; yet even here the terms in which Athanasius speaks of God's condescension are colored by his recollection of Plato. "Taking pity upon (*eleêsas*) our race, compassionate to our weakness," he writes, "he took for himself a body" (*On the Incarnation* 8.2). In Plato's *Symposium*, Aristophanes the comic poet recounts that Zeus, having bisected the globular creatures who had threatened to oust the gods from heaven, "took pity" (*eleêsas*) and bound up the parts, which became the genital organs (191b). Plotinus had given his own turn

---

[23] On John 1:3, see *Commentary on John* 2.96, with M. S. M. Scott 2012:29–30.

[24] *Against the Heathen* 34.2, 45.4, 47.2; *On the Incarnation* 11.2, etc.

[25] *Against the Heathen* 30.3, 31.5, 32.3.

[26] Justin *Trypho* 4.2; Courcelle 1972. In *Against Heresies* 33, Athanasius seems to allude more than once to the celebrated trance of Aristeas of Proconnesus, recounted at length by Origen (*Against Celsus* 3.26) in response to Celsus and following Herodotus *Histories* 4.14–15.

[27] *Against Celsus* 4.40. It is barely credible that this text should be adduced as evidence of Origen's subscription to the Platonic theory by Beatrice 2009:507n13–14.

to the phrase at *Enneads* IV 3.12.8, and the echo will not have been lost upon a knowledgeable reader.

Should this then be our conclusion—that Athanasius is more of a Platonist than Origen? Why not, when the philosophers were now as dumb as the oracles, and their works as ripe for appropriation as the idolatrous temples that were being transformed into churches? We should hesitate, nonetheless, to make such a judgment in the light of a single work, composed with an apologetic motive; it is, after all, a common device of apologists to return the enemy's missiles dipped with poison. The word *dêmiourgos*, for example, first occurs in a passage that is plainly (for all its reticence)[28] a refutation of Marcion (*Against the Heathen* 6.1). Since the *Against the Heathen* is addressed by turns to an anonymous Christian and to the Greeks at large, one purpose in writing it may have been to arm the faithful against heretical subtleties, and it may be that the use of *tolma* in a novel sense is calculated to forestall its abuse by Gnostics.[29] When he laments that humans have found no "satiety" (*koros*) in sinning (*Against the Heathen* 8.4), it may be his purpose to illustrate the correct use of this term against the Origenists, who attributed the Fall itself to "satiety" (*koros*) in the contemplation of God.[30] His own view that the fall is rendered possible by the natural lability of the soul is expressly grounded on Plato's argument that the soul never ceases to move because it contains in itself the principle of motion.[31] When he likens its aberration to that of a wayward charioteer (*Against the Heathen* 5.2) he is amplifying the famous simile in the *Phaedrus* (246a–254e). This, we may assume, he would know at first hand, but it is likely enough, as Thomson suggests,[32] that he had also studied the works of recent Platonists, or at least the extracts from Porphyry that Eusebius had compiled in his *Preparation for the Gospel*. Porphyry is the silent interlocutor in the one passage that is not simply formulaic in its representation of the opposing party:

> Those who are more philosophical than these [the more shallow apologists] and profess to speak more profoundly say that the purpose for which statues are wrought and moulded is the invocation and

---

[28] Cf. Meijering 2010:177.

[29] See *Against the Heathen* 5.1 and 9.3 on the "temerity" (*tolma*) of the first humans. Notwithstanding its inevitability, the separation of *nous* from the One is described as a *tolma* by Plotinus at *Enneads* V 1.1.

[30] *Against the Heathen* 8.4. Cf. Origen *On Principles* 1.4.1, though here it is not certain that he is speaking of a fall before embodiment. For Plotinus (*Enneads* III 5.9–10), *koros* is the plenitude of the unfallen intellect, in contrast to the "affluence" (*poros*) that causes it to descend and thus enrich lower realms of being. Cf. *Symposium* 203a.

[31] See *Against the Heathen* 4.2 and *Phaedrus* 245c.

[32] Thomson 1973:91n1, citing Porphyry *On the Soul* from Eusebius *Preparation for the Gospel* XI 28.7–12.

manifestation of divine angels and powers, so that becoming manifest through these [the powers] may instruct them about the knowledge of God. And [statues] are as it were letters for human beings, by acquaintance with which they can know about the apprehension of God[33] from the manifestation of the divine angels which takes place through them.

Athanasius Against the Heathen 19.4

Eusebius' *Preparation for the Gospel* includes long excerpts from a treatise by Porphyry that rebukes the critics of images as "unlearned men" for whom letters of the alphabet would be mere ciphers. The treatise commenced with the declaration that God is "luminous" (*phôtoeidês*) in aspect, which a Christian would be apt to read as a philosophical rendering of the dictum "God is light." Porphyry knew as well as any Christian that the first apostles, by Luke's confession, were "unlettered men" (Acts 4:13); Celsus had said as much in the second century, and even Origen found some matter for boasting in the fact.[34] Porphyry was the Goliath at whom every Christian champion took aim at some time in the early fourth century: his fame ensured that those who were not Platonists already would become temporary Platonists for the purpose of answering him.

3. The Soul of Christ

The *subsidiary* use of alien resources in Athanasius is exemplified by his striking but anomalous references to the human soul in *Against the Heathen*. One of the commonest strictures on the Church Fathers is that, under the influence of Greek philosophy, they treated as a dogma of theology the existence of an entity called the soul, the status of which is undetermined in the scriptures. Another, and apparently contradictory, charge is that in their eagerness to vindicate Christ's divinity they lost sight of his humanity, reducing it to the mere fact of embodiment without reference to the soul as the seat of feeling and volition.[35] It is obvious that this second charge cannot hold unless we waive the first— that is, unless we take it as an axiom that the possession of a soul is a condition of being human. If it is true that the bible says otherwise, it would seem that those who chose to speak with biblical simplicity of the flesh of Christ, without discrimination of soul and body, deserve congratulation rather than censure. If it has never been usual to congratulate Athanasius on his failure to credit Christ with a human soul, the reason must be that those who upbraid and

---

[33] I take this to mean that the direct apprehension of God is vouchsafed to the angels alone and received by us as secondhand knowledge.

[34] *Against Celsus* 3.39; but cf. 3.49–75.

[35] Against this judgment, see Anatolios 1988:70–73.

those who defend him both assume that he shared the Greek, if not the Platonic, concept of the soul. A thinker who held this concept yet denied a rational soul to Christ—as Apollinarius certainly did, for example—could be justly charged with mulcting his humanity. But how strong is the evidence that Athanasius did regard belief in a soul, whether rational or irrational, as a *sine qua non* of Christian anthropology?

It is often said that this is implied in one of his last pronouncements, a letter from Alexandria to Antioch, in which he declares, as the verdict of a council, that it would be blasphemous to suppose that the Savior was either *anous* or *apsukhos*.[36] But this is as vapid a proclamation as ever escaped a council, for these words need not be taken to mean that either the *nous* or the *psukhê* is a thing, a substantial element, without which the person would be incomplete. In the *Against the Heathen*, Athanasius ascribes to certain pagans the false opinion that the stars are neither *aloga* nor *apsukha* (*Against the Heathen* 27.2); he does not accuse them of endowing the stars with *human* souls. To be *anous* is simply to lack the capacity for deliberation and reasoning, and to be *apsukhos* is simply to lack an animating principle, and no one who believed that the body of Christ was inhabited by the Word of God would argue that he suffered from either of these privations. If Athanasius ever imagined Christ as God in a "space-suit" (to adapt Hanson's celebrated quip),[37] he would have had no cause to change his opinion after transcribing this conciliar resolution, which excludes not the "space-suit" theory, but only the theory that Christ was a mere automaton: this, of course, was never held by anyone, as is almost sure to be true of any form of words unanimously proscribed by a committee.

There is one work in which Athanasius argues that the soul is not merely an element but the most precious element in our composition. Having urged in the *Against the Heathen* that the one true image of God is his human creation, having mocked and bewailed by turns the practice of sacrificing humans to the effigies of which both captor and victim are living archetypes, he goes on to asseverate that the soul is the organ within which sets us apart from beasts (*Against the Heathen* 31), enabling us to contemplate our Maker (*Against the Heathen* 30), curbing the instincts of the body and sustaining the harmonious operation of its members (*Against the Heathen* 32). Its natural immortality is proved (as any Platonist would contend) by its unlikeness to the body, by its unique capacity to originate motion, and by its ability to transcend the body in thought and

---

[36] PG 26.804. Grillmeier 1975:318–327 puts questions to this text that I do not believe it was designed to answer; thus, he draws the inevitable conclusion that it neither affirms nor denies the "theological value" of Christ's human soul. On the circumstances in which the letter was written, see also Pettersen 1990.

[37] Hanson 1988:448.

imagination (*Against the Heathen* 33). Defiled as it is, it awaits the re-creation, which has been rendered possible in these latter days by the incarnation of the Word in a human body (*Against the Heathen* 34). It is by assimilation to his inalienable perfection that the soul will be purged of the stains that have occluded its likeness to God since the first transgression.

Only a heretic, it appears, would doubt that the soul is the essence of our humanity, though pagans fall into an analogous error when they refuse to admit that a God is necessary to sustain the equilibrium of the cosmos (*Against the Heathen* 30). The resurrection of Christ is proof that other embodied beings may rise from the dead; since, however, the body itself is perishable by nature, immortality must be predicated on that which possesses all the human attributes that cannot pertain to the body (*Against the Heathen* 33). Even in the present life then it is possible for the image within, when it takes the incarnate Image as its paradigm, to become a polished mirror to the Father (*Against the Heathen* 34). Thus, the soul becomes worthy of the simile that was applied at Wisdom 7:25–26 to the Word before incarnation in his character as Wisdom. In a similar vein, Athanasius proclaims at *On the Incarnation* 29 that in the hope of the Resurrection even the weak no longer fear the descent to Hades, but have courted it "with eager souls"—a palpable allusion to Psalm 16:8, "thou wilt not leave my soul in Hades," which had been understood since the first Pentecost (and by Origen among others) as a prophecy of Christ's rising from the tomb.

It is all the more surprising, therefore, that Athanasius not only omits to quote this verse but refrains throughout *On the Incarnation* from any mention of the soul of Christ. It is not that biblical warrant was lacking, for Origen and Tertullian had already drawn the obvious conclusion from Christ's own words, "My soul is troubled unto death."[38] Again, it is not that the question had been put beyond controversy, for Eustathius of Antioch, whom Athanasius reckoned among his allies, regarded the substitution of the *Logos* for the human soul of Christ as one of the heresies of Arius. Yet, a reader of *Against the Heathen* and *On the Incarnation* would be hard-pressed to find an antidote to this error, for while we are told repeatedly that the body of the Word was the instrument of our salvation, nothing is said of his assuming a human soul. At one point, where he protests that the infinite power of the Word is not curtailed by his occupation of a finite body, it might almost be inferred that the Word is to Christ what the soul is to everyman:

> It is the proper activity of soul to contemplate by reasoning that which
> is external to its own body, yet not to be at work outside its own body or

---

[38] Matthew 26:38; cf. John 12:27, Origen *On Principles* 2.8.4, and Tertullian *On the Flesh of Christ* 9.

to move things that are distant from it by being present ... It was not so, however, with the Word of God in the man, for he was not bound to the body, but was rather the one who himself had dominion over it, so that being within it he was also in all things, yet external to all that exists, reposing in the Father alone.

Athanasius *On the Incarnation* 17

One could reply that Athanasius no more denies the presence of a human soul in Christ than he affirms it,[39] and that what would be a culpable omission in a dogmatic work could be excused or even praised as a deft economy in an apologetic text addressed simultaneously to unbelievers and to fellow Christians. Athanasius must speak in Greek to the Greeks, for whom the immortality of the soul was a more familiar concept than the resurrection of the body. At the same time, he could not afford to say anything unpalatable to Christians whom he wished to retain as allies. He could assert the full divinity of Christ as an article of mere Christianity because Arians, in his view, were no longer his coreligionists; to take a view on the soul of Christ, however, would be to obtrude his own convictions on an undecided church in which there were some who would tolerate nothing less than the affirmation of a rational or hegemonic soul, while others could stomach nothing more than the biblical evidence for a human susceptibility to anger, grief, and fear.

No such explanation can be offered for his silence in the third of his orations against the Arians, where once again we find ubiquitous reference to the body of Christ as a vehicle of disclosure and an instrument of redemption, but with no allusion to his human soul. We are told that in assuming flesh he became lord of all flesh (*Against the Arians* 3.30) but did not remain alien to its suffering (*Against the Arians* 3.32); that he assumed a body of the same nature as ours in order to expiate our sins (*Against the Arians* 3.31); and that it was for the sake of the flesh that he dissembled his omniscience, manifesting a human ignorance of the date of his own second coming (*Against the Arians* 3.39). We are not told, however, that he assumed a soul with the human body: the verse "My soul is troubled" receives no gloss and is cited only to illustrate the abuse of scripture by his unnamed interlocutors. The presence in humans of an invisible counterpart to the body is recognized only when Athanasius contends that Christ asked "humanly" where the body of Lazarus lay in order to reveal "divinely" that he knew the location of his soul (*Against the Arians* 3.46).

One notable difference, however, between this treatise and *On the Incarnation* is that nothing is said here to indicate that the soul is a *desideratum* of our being

---

[39] Grillmeier 1975:326.

human. The passage quoted above on the soul of Lazarus suggests, if anything, that for Athanasius (as for Homer) the soul is not so much the animating principle in the living person as that which remains when the body succumbs to death. We are therefore free to assume that Athanasius uses the term "flesh" in its biblical sense, subsuming the full ensemble of psychic and corporeal functions that are opposed not to "mind" or "soul," but to "God" and "spirit." Indeed, it may be urged that we are bound to do so, as grief and trepidation cannot be affections of an inanimate body. The Arians have no need of a soul in Christ because they predicate these infirmities of a *Logos* who is something less than God; since Athanasius cannot allow any suffering to the *Logos* in his own nature, he must make some provision not only for a human body but also for human sentience. For most Greeks this would entail the postulation of a soul in contradistinction to the body, and it may be that Athanasius was merely accommodating this assumption in his eulogy of the soul in the *Against the Heathen*. He had no reason to practize such diplomacy when writing for the instruction of Christians or professing Christians, and, since his principal adversaries based their position on a literal reading of the scriptures, he had in fact every reason to prefer the less dichotomous anthropology of Paul.

4. Participation in God

What has been said so far, if true, would suggest that the Platonism of Athanasius is never more than *eristic* or *subsidiary*—that he grants to Plato only so much, and only for as long, as is necessary to secure a tactical victory over the pagans. It can be maintained, however, that in adopting the concept of participation he also made it his own—that it was for him *fiduciary*, and all the more so when he seems to be barely conscious of adopting it. In Plato's metaphysics, as Plotinus reminds us,[40] there can be no community of essence between the participant and that in which it participates: the former is always inferior to the latter, whose transcendence makes the relation possible. When, therefore, the opponents of Athanasius speak of Christ's participation in the Father, they seem to him to be insinuating that he receives by grace those properties which are in fact essential to him by virtue of his sonship. The inference to be drawn is not that good theology will eschew the term,[41] but that it will modify its usage to allow the participant a share in the essence of the thing participated:[42]

---

[40] *Enneads* VI 6.13.

[41] Cf., however, *Against the Heathen* 46, where Athanasius denies that Christ, as the image and Word of the Father, can be said to participate in him. Perhaps a distinction is to be drawn between participation in the Father and participation in the divine essence.

[42] See further Boulos 2001:479.

Such reasonings having been proved absurd and contrary to truth, it necessarily follows that [the Nicene formula] 'from the essence of the Father' means that the Son is in his entirety proper [idiom] to him. For if God is participated in his wholeness, that is as much as to say that he also begets. And what does begetting signify but a son? Now all things participate in the Son according to the grace of the Spirit which he causes to be in them; and from this it is manifest that the Son himself participates in nothing, but the one participated who is from the Father—this is the Son.

Athanasius *Against the Arians* 1.16.1

Plato is thus dethroned as a theologian; if, however, participation in his sense corresponds to grace in Christian parlance, might it not be legitimate to speak of our participation in God? "God became man in order that man might be god": the celebrated maxim of Athanasius is anticipated in Irenaeus, while Origen had alluded more than once to the "deification" (*theopoiêsis*), which is promised to the elect at John 10:35 (i.e. "Is it not written in your law, *I have said ye are gods*?"). Athanasius, however, would appear to have been the first to adduce the power of deification as evidence for the full divinity of Christ:

And just as we would not have been set free from sin and the curse if the flesh which the Word assumed had not been human by nature (for we had nothing in common with flesh of a different origin), thus humanity would not have been divinised if he who became flesh were not by nature from the Father, his true and proper Word. For the reason why such a conjunction occurred was in order to join him who was a human being by nature to the One who was by nature of the Godhead, rendering his salvation and divinization secure.

Athanasius *Against the Arians* 2.70.1

Wiles no doubt speaks for many readers when he wonders why it would have been any less possible for Christ to impart divinity to others if his divinity were acquired and not essential.[43] It is certainly true in common life that power and gifts may be transmitted by an intermediary who does not possess them either by right or by nature. A magnetized needle may attract other needles; as the agent of a billionaire, I might pass on a fortune to someone else without having a penny to my name. Plato himself would grant that this objection is unanswerable so long as by "participation" we mean something analogous to the division

---

[43] Wiles 1962.

of a sailcloth;[44] in that case, it would be possible for the recipient of one portion to divide it again and distribute the products to a new class of recipients. This, however, is not what Plato intended when he spoke of the participation of the individual in the form, for it is the purpose of the theory of forms to explain how we can attach one predicate, truly and univocally, to a whole class of particulars that are not identical in all respects. It would not suffice to say, of things exhibiting the predicate *p*, that some are *p* by virtue of participation in the form *P*, and others by virtue of participation in some member of their own class. In that case, predication would not be univocal, for univocal predication, *ex hypothesi*, is the consequence of participation in a single form. It follows that the saints cannot all be gods in a uniform sense unless they participate in that which is essentially and eminently divine.

This is not to say that the argument succeeds. Athanasius purports to have shown in *Against the Arians* that there can be only one God because a God by definition is eternal, uncircumscribed by other beings, and the self-sufficient cause of his own existence. We ourselves do not possess these attributes of eternity, infinity, and aseity; how then, but by some trick of homonymity, can we be said to be divine? One might reply that eternity at least is an attribute of every form, but not of the individuals who participate in them: if a thing may be beautiful or just without partaking in the eternity of the form of beauty or justice, why should it be unthinkable for that which is not eternal to be divine? To say this is to forget that the eternity of the forms of justice and beauty pertains to them only in respect of their being forms and not in respect of the beauty and justice that they exemplify. According to Athanasius, on the other hand, eternity, infinity, and aseity are logically implied in the very notion of the divine, and it would therefore be impossible for anything to possess divinity, even by participation, without these attributes. It might be argued, therefore, that the divinity implied in such a verse as "I have said ye are gods and children of the Most High" is an imputed one, homonymous with that of God in the sense that the humanity of a statue is homonymous with the humanity of its living original. If that is so, an Arian could maintain that the imputation of divinity does not require participation in one who is fully divine, and that it would suffice for Christ to be God in a weaker sense than we give to that term when we apply it to the Father.

Strict Platonism accommodates such gradations of divinity; Athanasius assumes them to be impossible when he argues—in the teeth of the distinctions made by Origen, which would have been endorsed by Arius—that since the

---

[44] See Plato *Parmenides* 130a–131e, with Fine 1986:71–97. On participation in Athanasius, see Meijering 1968:144 and Leithard 2011:66.

church worships Christ, it recognizes him as God. In this respect he is evidently no Platonist, and it was pointed out above that the notion of participation in God is a deviation from the theory of Forms, to which Athanasius never adhered. Thus, it cannot be said without qualification that he invokes Platonic premises when he argues that only one who is fully divine can impart divinity; it would be truer to say that, so long as these premises function surreptitiously, they lend a specious color to his argument. Once they are exposed, however, they prove to be unequal to his purpose and his reasoning will appear cogent only to those who already maintain the full divinity of the *Logos*. The lacuna that Wiles detects in the reasoning of Athanasius cannot be bridged by crediting him with a clandestine or occasional Platonism.

5. Conclusion

No strict antithesis therefore can be drawn between the philosopher Origen and the theologian Athanasius. It would be rare piece of prose from late antiquity that did not contain a tincture of Platonism; but an author does not become a disciple merely by alluding to Plato, not even by wholesale plagiarism when the purpose of it is to consolidate a system that is hostile or antithetical to that of the great Athenian. In any case, it is not plagiarism to use a term that happens to have been coined by Plato before it entered the common parlance of philosophers. Too many scholars are satisfied to catch a Christian talking like a Platonist; but one who talks like a Platonist in order to think like a Christian is not, in the intellectual sense, a colleague of Plotinus. On should add, to avoid misunderstanding, that the label Origenist also can be given only polemically—eristically, as one might say—to Athanasius, who cites Origen only as an early patron, not as the author, of the doctrine that prevailed in Alexandria. There are other fields of intellectual history in which scholars dispense with labels altogether, writing the history of persons rather than parties. We may hope that one day this will not be true only of other fields.

Plotinus, Gregory of Nyssa, and Evagrius of Pontus

Where Does the Soul Stop and Where Does the Body Begin?

KEVIN CORRIGAN

Abstract: This chapter compares the thought of Plotinus and the Cappadocians (primarily Gregory of Nyssa) on what might be termed the mind/soul-body relation. In Plotinus' case, it examines the range of his writings from the early to the later treatises, focusing upon: (1) typical common misunderstandings of Platonism and Neoplatonism; (2) the role of the soul's illumination or image that is roughly the psycho-somatic compound; and (3) the fully developed, revolutionary articulation of this relation (*Enneads* VI 7.1–11 and I 1.1–7). In the Cappadocians' case, the chapter analyzes: (1) the often misunderstood mind-and-passions relation in Gregory of Nyssa's *On the Soul and Resurrection*; (2) the even more revolutionary (than Plotinus) development of this theme in Gregory's *On the Making of Man*, the sequel to Basil's *Hexaëmeron*; and (3) some important corollaries to what is, in fact, a multiperspectival theory in Basil, Gregory of Nyssa, and Gregory Nazianzus, especially the all important, though unrecognized, attempt, as far as the author can see, to rethink the subject-attribute model in the light of Trinitarian theology, an attempt that anticipates, and grounds, significant work in the twentieth and twenty-first centuries to rethink our habits of grammar and syntax in the context of Einstein's theories of relativity, among other things.

HOW ARE WE TO THINK about the mind/soul-body relation in the third and fourth centuries? Here I shall concentrate on the thought of Plotinus, an Egyptian living in Rome and writing in Greek in the third century, and on that of two Christian thinkers in the next century, Gregory of Nyssa and Evagrius of Pontus, who knew each other well, both earlier and during their time at the Council of Constantinople—especially after the untimely death of Gregory's brother, Basil the Great, in 379.

Some typical modern views of Plotinus emphasize his extreme otherworldliness; he was, for instance, famously ashamed of life in the body, according to Porphyry's testimony at the beginning of the *Life of Plotinus* (1.1–2);[1] and throughout the *Enneads* Plotinus is often concerned to deprecate bodily existence, in language borrowed from Plato's *Phaedo*, among other dialogues, and to argue that real human freedom is only internal to Intellect, involving complete disentanglement of our will from any bodily attachment or action at all—a position that looks decidedly Stoic.[2]

In the case of Gregory and Evagrius, similar assessments tend to prevail. Gregory is either an eclectic who adopts different mind/soul-body scenarios from Plato, Aristotle, the Stoics, and others, somewhat uncritically and haphazardly; or again, he is a Platonist thinker who often assumes an anti-body scenario or who takes soul, not body, to be our real identity; these are views that may be thought typical of dialogues such as Plato's *Phaedo* or *Alcibiades I*, respectively, but they cannot be representative of the new positive evaluation of the body that Christianity surely requires.[3] Evagrius' asceticism, even more so, has been thought to be so extreme as to be more Buddhist than Christian and to involve the extirpation of any authentic subjectivity or compassionate concern for others.[4]

Even if such impressions cannot be altogether denied, these views are nonetheless misguided, as some recent scholarly works have tended to emphasize.[5] So here I shall not attempt to confront the larger questions of the overall character of Plotinus' thought or of the relation between Platonism/Neoplatonism and Christianity. Instead, I shall focus, first, upon the multiperspectival character of Plotinus' thinking on this question and then go on to argue for three important formulations of the mind/soul-body question in Plotinus, Gregory, and Evagrius that have been for the most part overlooked in historical treatments of the philosophy of mind and body.

---

[1] For a different view of this question based upon a more positive (and surely correct) evaluation of the body in Plotinus' works (especially in relation to the refutation of a Gnostic pejorative view of body) and in later Neoplatonism, see Song 2013:96–108.

[2] See, for example, *Enneads* VI 8.5.34–37; and see Lavaud 2007:6.264n93–94.

[3] Generally, see Cherniss 1930:133 and Zachhuber 2000:173.

[4] von Balthasar 1939b:31–47, von Balthasar 1939a:181–206, Bamberger 1981:53n7, and R. Williams 2003:76–77.

[5] See, among others, Dysinger 2005, Corrigan 2009, and Ramelli 2015.

1. Plotinus

Plotinus' thinking on the mind/soul-body question is intrinsically multiper-spectival, though here I shall only concentrate only on those perspectives that are immediately relevant to our topic.[6] From one perspective, body is the substrate of soul and form, that is, body provides a seat or place for soul and takes on different qualities or shapes; from another perspective, soul is not "in body" or "in" matter as in a substrate (*Enneads* I 8.14.33)—as the Peripatetic commentator, Alexander of Aphrodisias, had also argued (*On the Soul* 13-17; *Problems and Solutions* 1.8, 2.17, 2.26).[7] Rather soul is a quality inherent in matter as in its subject; but if soul is the actuality or energy of what it means to be body—that is, if soul is the reality that *makes* body what it is—then soul cannot be a simple quality "in" something else. We tend to think of soul, if we think of it at all, as somehow being *in* body. But Plotinus sees bodily organization and matter, from a much broader perspective still, as merely the tip of a much vaster iceberg: soul is not in body so much as body is *in* soul[8] (as Plato states, in *Timaeus* 36d–37c and 34b–c). Bodies, nature, and the entire physical world are rooted in

---

[6] The notion of matter is a case in point. From the perspective of intelligible form—from the top down, that is, from the perspective of the unified whole, all things are substantial, not just substance as form and compound, but even matter as "a last form" (*Enneads* V 8.7). This is in line with Aristotle's view of matter, compound, and form, respectively, as different forms of *ousia* in *Metaphysics* 1028a1–1029b12 and it makes very good sense, since in Alexander and Plotinus, matter from this perspective is not privation or nonbeing but something that is made by the shaping form into a definite nature—a *tode ti*, "characteristic of substance." Thus, for Alexander and Plotinus, there is also, from a slightly different perspective, a *logos* or definition of matter (see Alexander *On the Soul* 26.28; cf. Plotinus *Enneads* III 8.2.23–25 and III 3.4.37–40). But from yet another perspective, anything that can be connected with or expressed through *logos* is, in principle, intelligible; see, for example, *Enneads* VI 2.21-22, where Plotinus argues, first, that anything that can be fitted to a *logos* belongs in the intelligible world and, ultimately, that this includes "bodies and matter" (*Enneads* VI 2.21.52–53). From a further perspective, however, corporeality, that is, a compound of form and matter, can be understood from two different perspectives: either as "body ... composed from all the qualities with matter" or as "a formative principle ... which makes body" (*Enneads* II 7.3). In this latter case, Plotinus says that the formative principle does not include the matter but enters matter and brings the body to perfection so that the body is matter and indwelling *logos*. Here the matter remains as substrate for the indwelling *logos* and yet is perfected in the bodily compound. At the same time, apart from these perspectives expressed in different ways in *Enneads* V 8, II 7, and VI 2, there are at least three other perspectives to be found in the *Enneads*. From the bottom up, by contrast with the top-down perspective, sensible reality can be traced back to the intelligible through *logoi* (as in *Enneads* III 8 and V 8); or again, sensible substance precisely as sensible is only an imitation and not "true substance" (as in *Enneads* VI 3.8.19–36). This last perspective itself can also be analyzed in different privative ways (as occurs in *Enneads* III 6, II 4, II 5, and I 8). For commentary on these works, see Corrigan 1996:32–246; on *Enneads* II 4, see Narbonne 1993.

[7] See also *Enneads* IV 3.20-21.

[8] See *Enneads* III 8.3.3, IV 3.22-23.

three much larger originative principles: they are "in" all Soul, which, in turn, is "in" all Intellect, and everything is ultimately rooted in the principle of all things that Plotinus calls simply the One or the Good (see, for example, *Enneads* VI 7.42.21–24). Since Intellect includes everything in a more intensified unity than Soul—Plotinus calls Soul a one-and-many and Intellect a one-in-many—and since our intellects derive through Soul ultimately from Intellect, we shall simply assume in what follows that the soul-body relation is really a mind or intellect/soul-body relation.

All of the above makes sense if we ask how soul moves the body. Plato had posed three possibilities in *Laws* 898e–899a: (1) soul directs from inside body as our souls carry us around; (2) soul direct body from outside by propulsion; or (3) as incorporeal entirely, soul guides body. For Socrates-Diotima in the *Symposium*, everything is moved by the power of *eros*; and in Socrates' palinode in the *Phaedrus*, soul is a self-mover that moves and is moved by love. For Aristotle, bodily compounds are moved by love, immediately through individual unmoved movers or souls;[9] and the hierarchy of forms is moved ultimately by love for the Unmoved Intellects and for the First Unmoved Mover itself (*Metaphysics* 1072a19–1076a4). God moves the Sphere of the fixed stars immediately by nonreciprocal contact (just as a person who grieves us "touches" us, but we do not "touch" him, Aristotle observes in *Physics* 201b16–202a12 and *On Generation and Corruption* II 6.323a25). None of this prevents physiological explanations in their own sphere, as long as one retains the broader picture. Equally for Plotinus, motive agency comes from above: love and desire move everything (including Soul and Intellect), but proximate movers are mind/soul agents. The intellectual-soul agent moves the body directly, but she could not do so if the appropriate psycho-physical structures did not permit. So, the central point I want to make here is that, in the light of the Good, Intellect, and Soul, we too are real agents.[10]

What then is body? Body is composed of form and matter; and in bodies, form or *logos*, as motive power entering into the matter (as Plotinus puts it dynamically in *Enneads* II 7.3), comprises all the qualities, quantities, relations, etc. that make up the whole. So, while body is composite, but dynamic, soul is simple in the sense that it is not composed of sensible or visible qualities, but multiple in that it comprises many spiritual or nonbodily powers and capacities—nutritive, perceptive, intellectual powers:

---

9   Cf. *Physics* 258b19–20 and Ross's note (1936) on 258b16–22. They must be unmoved, of course, in relation to bodies, but moved by love for what is above them. For similar unmoved movers in nature and the whole, see *Enneads* III 8.30.2–3.

10   On this further, see below.

... The soul is many and one, even if it is not composed of parts; for there are a great many powers in her, reasoning, desiring, apprehending, which are held together by the one as by a bond. The soul then brings the one to others being herself also one by virtue of something else.

Plotinus Enneads VI 9.1.39–44[11]

Everything in the physical world, composed of form and matter, is a reflection or outflow of the motive power of Soul/Intellect, organized by soul's generative power, ranging from more complex organisms such as the heavenly bodies—or visible gods, as Plotinus calls them, and other living creatures, including all animals and plants, all the way down to rocks and the elements that look inanimate, but are saturated by the power of soul from different perspectives: all Soul from the top, as it were, including every soul-perspective; World Soul as responsible for the world's physical structure (that includes our human organic structures); the soul of the earth, and so on.[12] In *Enneads* VI 7.11, Plotinus maintains that before the individual soul takes up its place in the human body, the World Soul provides a "preliminary outline" (*proüpographê*) "like illuminations running on before into matter, and the soul which carries out the work [follows] traces of this kind and [makes] by articulating the traces part by part, and each individual soul [becomes] this to which it came in shaping itself ..." (*Enneads* VI 7.7.8–15). Individual ensoulment, then, is a collaborative productive work in which different perspectives come into dynamic focus. Plotinus says body is like:

a beautiful and richly various house ... ensouled in such a way. It has a soul that does not belong to it, but is present to it; it is mastered, not the master, possessed, not possessor. The universe lies in soul that bears it up, and nothing is without a share of soul. It is as if a net immersed in the waters was alive, but unable to make its own that in which it is. The sea is already spread out and the net spreads with it, as far as it can; for no one of its parts can be anywhere else than where it lies.

Enneads IV 3.9.34–42; cf. Enneads II 9.18.14–17

How then does Plotinus see the mind/soul-body relation in concrete individual circumstances—if the soul is "present to," without "belonging to" body?[13]

---

[11] Hereafter the translation is according to Armstrong 1966–1988, with my alterations.

[12] For the soul of the earth, see *Enneads* IV 4.22; for plants and the elements, see *Enneads* VI 7.11.

[13] For presence without "belonging," see *Enneads* IV 3.9.35–36 where it is ensouled in the following way: "it has soul not of itself, but [present] to itself, mastered, not mastering, possessed but not having" (ἔχων ψυχὴν οὐχ αὐτοῦ, ἀλλ' αὐτῷ, κρατούμενος οὐ κρατῶν, καὶ ἐχόμενος ἀλλ' οὐκ ἔχων).

Does this mean that soul does not form a unity with body—that the soul is not the actuality or energy of the body, as in Aristotle?[14] Is the self or the "we," as Plotinus puts it, only soul, not body? At first glance, it might seem so. While Plotinus presents us, as Dillon and D. O'Meara have shown,[15] with many acute analyses of the processes by which an impulse from the body or physical world, reaches the soul (on this, see below), nonetheless in his mature thought he came to adopt a rather extreme version, in Dillon's words, of the traditional Platonist distinction between rational and irrational soul. According to this view:

> the soul in itself is regarded as *apathês*, not subject, despite appearances, to passions or affections as such, but rather an emanation or irradiation (*ellampsis*), or trace (*ikhnos*) of soul, which is what immediately animates the body, and which constitutes the animate body, which he likes to term the 'combination' (*sunamphoteron*) or the 'commonality' (*koinon*).
>
> Dillon 2013:75

A good example of this model can be found in the late work *On What is the Living Being and What is the Human Being* I 1.1–7.[16] After arguing in the early chapters against a physical mixing or interweaving of soul-body, in favor of a view of soul as touching upon matter, as the steersman steers the ship, and, therefore, as nonseparate in one sense (i.e. really present), but separate from body in another sense as not being a part or function of body, he defines their relation, in terms of perception, in a single sentence as follows in chapter seven:

> Let it be the compound then that perceives, and the soul by her presence does not give herself in this qualified way either to the compound or to the other element in the compound but makes out of the body qualified in this way and a kind of light that is given from herself the nature of the living creature, something different, to which perceiving and all the other affections of the living creature are said to belong.
>
> Plotinus *Enneads* I 1.7.1–6[17]

---

14 Cf. Bréhier 1928:200.
15 Dillon 2013:73–84 and D. O'Meara 1985:247–262.
16 Here I focus predominantly upon *Enneads* I 1[53], although there are many earlier significant works, such as *Enneads* VI 7[38]1–7, VI 8[39]14—and earlier still *Enneads* IV 7[2]; IV 3[27]–4[28], especially *Enneads* IV 3[27]20–23 and 20–25; IV 4[28]18–29. For the definition of the human being in Aristotle and Plotinus in the context of the question of substance, see Corrigan 1996:341–390.
17 *Enneads* I 1.7.1–6: ἢ τὸ συναμφότερον ἔστω τῆς ψυχῆς τῷ παρεῖναι οὐχ αὑτὴν δούσης τῆς τοιαύτης εἰς τὸ συναμφότερον ἢ εἰς θάτερον, ἀλλὰ ποιούσης ἐκ τοῦ σώματος τοῦ τοιούτου καί τινος οἷον

In other words, human existence is layered but unified. We are not simply soul, for the extension of soul goes far beyond us, but we exist as real historical individuals by virtue of soul's animating power.[18] And it is "we" who perceive, Plotinus adds, because we are linked to the composite, even if perception does not always have to be of sensible objects and even if there are things of more value in the substance of what it means to be human (*Enneads* I 1.7.6–12). Does this mean that the soul-body relation is only instrumental, with soul prosthetically moving the body so that there is no real union of the two? This cannot be the case, for while the union of this color or this characteristic in body or matter is an accidental union (that is, the union of a quality in a subject), and while the unity of the psycho-somatic compound is a much more complex and layered business, ranging from thoughts and feelings to perceptions and foods, the functioning of the whole being requires a more comprehensive, indeed, substantial unity to account for the real motive force in its traces.

There is then a three-tiered structure in the above passage: (1) the body; (2) the productive compound of qualified body and a kind of light from soul; and (3) the motive/making soul that does not give herself in a qualified way. Let us briefly take each in turn. First, body is not an abstract "body" somehow separated from soul. It is instead an organic body in a relation of potentiality: it is "the other element" in the compound, Plotinus says, but it is in dynamic relation within the compound that is being made. Second, compound existence is not a union of form and qualified matter as of two different things or items, but rather, as Aristotle also argues in book seven of the *Metaphysics*, not an aggregate-unity of letters A+B, but "something different," namely, a syllable: AB.[19] The gift of a kind of light and the qualified body is actively transformed into "something different" by the making power of soul. And this, Plotinus adds, is what "we call" both the *active* perceiving subject and the *passive* subject of affections. As a compound subject or psycho-physical organism, a lot of my experience is analogous to qualities characterizing a subject: my thoughts, feelings, moods, colorings have to be "in" a compound subject. But that does not exhaust my capacity for still higher order activities or eliminate the need for the substantial animating principle that makes activity possible and that is necessary to, indeed, the fully comprehensive feature of, the whole description.

In an earlier work, Plotinus had criticized the famous Aristotelian definition of soul as "the first actuality/'entelechy' of an organic body that is potentially

---

φωτὸς τοῦ παρ' αὐτὴν δοθέντος τὴν τοῦ ζῴου φύσιν ἕτερόν τι, οὗ τὸ αἰσθάνεσθαι καὶ τὰ ἄλλα ὅσα ζῴου πάθη εἴρηται.

18 As Plotinus puts in *Enneads* I 1.13.1–3, "who has carried out this investigation? We or the soul? No, we, but by virtue of the soul. By having soul? No, but in so far as we are soul.

19 *Metaphysics* 1041b12–19.

alive" (*On the Soul* 412a27), primarily on the grounds that this makes soul something bodily or something that belongs to body; consequently, he argues, the Peripatetics had to introduce a second "entelechy" (namely, intellect) to explain the first (*Enneads* IV 7.8[5]).[20] Why not therefore posit a single, economical "entelechy" that can account for everything at the qualitative and substantial levels? We should note that in *Enneads* I 1.7, the "kind of light" Plotinus points to in substantial generation and subsequent historical experience is analogous to Aristotle's claim that the active mind is a *hexis* "like light" (*On the Soul* 430a16–17). Implicitly, here, this is the unified light of mind/soul that makes body and psycho-somatic existence possible—the warmth of the ensouled body.[21] Nonetheless, this cannot be the mind/soul simply—or else you and I would simply be soul or mind.

The third level of explanation is therefore necessary. Activity and intensity of unity come from above. Without this there would only be an accidental union. And the highest, substantial level in the mind/soul-body complex *is* impassible in relation to lower-order functions: *we* blush, shiver, and hope, but *the soul*, as Aristotle points out, does not.[22] At the same time, as Socrates argues in *Republic* 580d, the higher soul in us possesses its own desires and its own pleasures; or, as Plotinus puts it, very much in tune with Gregory of Nyssa, "... the real drive of desire of our soul is towards that which is greater than itself" (*Enneads* I 4.6). Impassibility is compatible with the soul's own desire, just as to be unmoved in relation to body and the compound is to awaken a new trajectory of desire that finds its *telos* in Intellect and the One.[23]

Where, then, does the mind/soul stop and the body begin? If we look from below, there seems to be only body, and the soul may hardly appear at all; but if we ascend to a different level, as if we were to climb up Plato's divided line (*Republic* 509d–511e) from *eikasia*, *doxa*, and *dianoia*, into *noêsis* or "understanding," then a different picture emerges: not by "guesswork" (*eikasia*) or "syllogistic reasoning" (*sullogismos*), Plotinus argues, but "as if one went up to some high viewpoint and raising one's eyes saw what no one saw who had not come up with one" (*Enneads* IV 4.5). From this perspective, the soul and mind constitute another dimension of experience that one might miss altogether at

---

[20] In *Enneads* IV 7, there are *five* chapters 8. These chapters were preserved in Eusebius, but do not appear in the Latin translation of Marsilio Ficino from which our chapter numbers derive—hence *Enneads* IV 7.8[5].

[21] For light, see also *Enneads* IV 3.27.22–23 for warmed air, see *Enneads* IV 4.28.18. For the history of Plotinus' understanding of the warmth of the body, see p. 123n36 above.

[22] Aristotle *On the Soul* 408b11.

[23] This was also apparently the view of Plotinus' teacher Ammonius, according to Porphyry's *Miscellaneous Questions* (frr. 259 and 261 Smith) and compare Nemesius *On Human Nature* 38.12–42.9 Morani.

the levels of *eikasia* or even calculative reasoning, but a dimension that is crucial for being able to read the larger significance of everything in the full range of our experience.

So, from the bottom up, there seems to be nothing except body, but from the top down the body is woven into soul in such a way that soul's spiritual or intelligible significance transforms what was merely material into *logos*, however attenuated or enmattered that *logos* might be. At the same time, in the very experience of coming down from understanding and in the fluctuating chances of everyday life, we forget and thus come to distrust the bigger picture of soul and mind;[24] and, psychic beings though we are, we can become progressively materialized so that nothing of soul's value seems to be retained or even to exist. In something of this way, the soul and body dimensions run into each other; sometimes the soul seems to perish in the body; sometimes the body seems to rise into the soul, to be at first discarded or left behind, and then to be retained and transformed, since body too is a window into the soul.[25]

Where then precisely is the "relation," we might still ask, between the immaterial and the physical? Given the above picture, a "relational" account in an aggregative sense is certainly the wrong way to frame the question since it implies a connection from one thing to another and the immaterial is not a thing. Indeed, too, there can be no "between"—since there is nothing in between.[26] Moreover, if the physical is ultimately the outward appearance or the extension of the spiritual into different material modalities, there is equally no connection between two things, for in looking only at a physical object we are, in fact, seeing the spiritual from a single perspective, not everything that it actually is. From a more comprehensive perspective still, mind/soul-body is at root a single activity seen from two different points of view; what is an *energeia* from one viewpoint is a *kinêsis* from another. This allows what is psychic activity from one perspective to be physical motion from another; the movement and the activity may be distinguished ontologically, just as teacher and pupil are different beings, and guitar player, melody, and string obviously distinct, but in operation a single activity. Analogically, in Aristotle's *Physics* 3.3, teaching and learning constitute a single activity in two different subjects: "teaching is the activity of the teacher, but in some patient and it is not cut off, but of this on this" (*Physics* 202b6–8); or, to put this more plainly, the operation or activity of

---

[24] See *Republic* 450d8–451a1 for the contrast between the one who speaks with knowledge, security, and confidence, and knows the truth, on the one hand, and the other, like Socrates himself at this point of the argument, who, on the other hand, is distrustful of himself and in search of the truth; cf. *Enneads* V 8.11.33–40 and V 5.1–2.

[25] See *Enneads* VI 2.21 where anything that can be linked to a *logos* is in principle intelligible (1–36) and where "there are bodies there too since there is matter and quality" (52–53).

[26] Cf. Aristotle *Physics* 202b7–8 and Plotinus *Enneads* I 1.2.9–14 and V 9.9.8–15.

teaching is not some abstract isolated project but a single, shared, and symbiotic activity of, and from, the teacher, but immediately in, and upon, the student.[27]

There is, therefore, no soul-body "relation" in this sense, but rather the deeper activity of the body *in* soul, that is, in a much wider universe of reference that cannot be understood without the holistic and local, but thoroughly holographic presence of Intellect. Intellect too makes us what we are, but without belonging exclusively to us. Therefore, any attempt to conceive of any body-soul microconnection must in some way map physiological or psycho-somatic activities onto the whole structure of the compound organism without losing sight of this much broader but *immediate* universe of reference, that is, soul-mind.

And this is what Plotinus does in some of his other treatments of the soul-body connection—in the light of the discovery of the nerves by Herophilus and Erasistratus in the third century BCE and the later mapping of the soul-powers onto the bodily systems of the head, heart, and liver. Galen, for example, maps the Platonic tripartite division of reasoning, spirited, and desiring parts or powers onto the three bodily systems noted above, something that seems to fit the physiology of the *Timaeus*, although he freely adapts other psychological schemata too.[28] Plotinus seems uneasy with the tripartite division,[29] probably because he sees the soul not in terms of strict allocated functions but as a unitary source of energy.[30] The soul, he argues, is not seated in any part of body and is not present in the same way to all the body; rather, the parts participate in the soul in different ways (*Enneads* IV 3.22–23) and the different organs produce different kinds of sense-perceptions (*Enneads* IV 3.3.17–31).[31] The organs of touch, for instance, "are situated in the first nerves," which can communicate motive impulse because these nerves "begin in the brain," thus allowing doctors to establish the beginning of perception and impulse in the brain—or rather, Plotinus says, "it would be better to say the beginning of the actualization of the power/potency is there ..." The power, of course, is everywhere, Plotinus emphasizes, but the "beginning" (*archê*) of its actualization is the point where the organ begins (*Enneads* IV 3.23.15–21). Similarly, the reasoning part is "there" with the perceptive part since the latter draws on it; the growth and nutritive

---

[27] On this and double act theory, see Rutten 1956:100–106, A. C. Lloyd 1990:98–106, and Emilsson 2007:22–68.

[28] For Galen, see especially his *On the Doctrines of Hippocrates and Plato* in De Lacy 1978:84 and chapter 3 above.

[29] Cf. Blumenthal 1971:21–25.

[30] To be fair to Plato, Socrates calls the tripartite structure *dunameis* (443b), *eidê* (435c–439e; 440e), *genê* (435b; 441a–d; 443d) more often than *merê* (442b–c) in book four of the *Republic*, and in the famous definition of inner and outer justice Socrates recognizes the possibility of other kinds in between the ones for which he has argued.

[31] On this, see Blumenthal 1971:74–75.

power, as appetitive, is present throughout the body nourishing it by means of the blood in the veins and liver (*Enneads* IV 3.23.34–40); and the "thin, light, sharp, pure blood is the appropriate organ for the spirited power whose fountain-head (*pêgê*) is the heart" (*Enneads* IV 3.23.42–44).

According to the above account, then, the qualified body or the broader composite is like a multipurpose antenna, each part of which has a natural sympathetic resonance with every other part[32] and different capacities for attunement on many different frequencies—reasoning, perception, imagination, growth, nutrition, appetition, and spiritedness. A faulty organ may mean that a capacity cannot be actualized, but healthy physiological functioning provides a path to psycho-somatic integrity and the proper alignment of body with soul and mind. What this means, in practice, for Plotinus is that the source of motive agency for either good moral action or psycho-somatic and physiological functioning comes from above, *from the mind/soul as agent*, but it still needs *the appropriate moral and physiological structure for the activity to be actualized* in action and function. As Plotinus puts it, the human being here is "a compound, a soul in a particular kind of forming principle ... a particular kind of activity, and the activity not being able to exist *without the active subject*" (*Enneads* VI 7.5.1–5). Similarly, in *Enneads* VI 8, his definition of free human agency is an actualization of the intelligible dimension of agency in empirical life. It unites the inner and the outer forms of agency and extends intelligible motive power to everything that was hitherto merely external: "Everything ... that comes from ... this will is in our power, *both everything external and everything self-dependent*" (*Enneads* VI 8.6.29–30).

2. Gregory of Nyssa

Gregory of Nyssa, like Plotinus, takes a multiperspectival view of this issue, but he goes beyond Plotinus in many ways, not least because he insists on an equal beginning for *both* body and soul, and because he discovers the orchestra and the conductor (and, to some extent, the computer) some thousand years before their official invention, as a model for understanding the mind/soul-body complex.

First, let me sketch the broad picture and then focus upon one fascinating, quite revolutionary text. Gregory's interest in medicine, an interest shared by his brother, Basil, is pronounced, much more so than in Plotinus—as we might expect of such a brilliant Christian thinker. Medicine is the art of determining psychophysical processes within the body, just as philosophy is the medical

---

[32] For sympathy, see *Enneads* IV 4.24–45.

art of the soul "through which we learn the therapy of every passion affecting the soul" (*On Virginity* [GNO VIII i.335–336; PG 46.408b]). The two arts therefore necessarily complement each other. Gregory adopts different perspectives on the mind/soul-body structure, depending upon how that structure is lived—somewhat along the broad lines we find in Plotinus. From one perspective, the whole human being is made in the image of God; from another related perspective, the same body we possess now will be reunited integrally with soul in the resurrection.[33] Both perspectives put a decidedly new emphasis upon the nature and structure of body. From yet another perspective, inherited from Plato, among others, even soul—no less than body—must suffer a kind of death because of attachment to sin and material pleasures.[34] We therefore have to purify soul from body as an ascetic practice to purify ourselves of the passions.[35] Yet even our passions—"motions"—when turned to the good can contribute to our real being (*On the Soul and Resurrection* 65d–68a). And so, the desire for the good and the beautiful is "equally consubstantial" and free in *both* body and soul (*On the Lord's Prayer* 4 [GNO VII ii.49.15–20]). It is not necessary to suppose that Gregory is uncritical in borrowing motifs from different traditions, since, by the fourth century, he shares the language and thought of these traditions and evidently has the pastoral and, indeed, human wish to speak to people of different persuasions.

In line with his innovative approach to understanding the role and destiny of the soul, he adopts different psychic structures: the Platonic tripartite structure (which he maps onto a system of virtues and vices in the *Canonical Letter* [PG 45.224a–225a], as does Evagrius in a different way); an Aristotelian bipartite structure of rational and irrational powers and an Aristotelian sequence of powers (rational, sensitive, nutritive); a Pauline triad of body, soul, and *pneuma* or "spirit" (*On the Soul and Resurrection* 145c–d), or heart, soul, and mind/*dianoia* (*On the Soul and Resurrection* 145d–148a); and an interesting system of life-powers in the body, providing heat, moisture, and, finally, directive impulse transmitted via the nerves to the various bodily parts and extending through the joints and organs. The "root of all these powers" and the "beginning" of the motions of the nerves is situated in the nervous tissue surrounding the brain (*On the Making*

---

[33] *Catechetical Oration* 37.93c–d (GNO III iv); *On the Soul and Resurrection* (PG 46.157a–b); see also Corrigan 2009:149–155.

[34] *Life of Moses* 2.187 (PG 44.385d; GNO VII i.4–5). For this theme of soul sinking into, and being unable to escape from, the (Orphic) mud of Hades in Plato, see *Phaedo* 69c–d and 81c–e; and also Plotinus *Enneads* I 8.13.14–26, where in sinking into the mud, "the soul dies, as far as a soul may die, and its death ... is to sink in matter and be filled with it" (I 8.13.21–23). Compare Plato *Statesman* 273d–e and *Republic* 534c–d with *Phaedo* 69c6 and Plotinus *Enneads* I 8.13.16–26.

[35] *Commentary on the Canticle of Canticles* (PG 44 1093d–1096b; GNO VI 440). Cf. Evagrius *Praktikos* 52; *Eulogios* 15.1–4 Sinkewicz 2003.

of Man PG 44.244c); the heart provides the warmth that gets distributed via the arteries and veins, and the liver is where the blood is prepared from ingested food. In other words, because Gregory is careful to preserve the nonlocal activity and primacy of mind/soul as a whole, these interrelated systems of nerves/brain/reason, arteries/heart/spirit, and veins/liver/desire provide a complex physiological infrastructure for psychological functions and a nonreductive localization of different psycho-somatic functions.

The revolutionary passage that I want to examine in a little more detail here sets out Gregory's remarkable view that the human being is constituted equally of both soul and body and that both have a single beginning in historical existence just as they do in the foreknowledge of God. The body is therefore not an afterthought, inferior to soul, but its proper expression. This view Gregory works out in *On the Making of Man*, written as a conclusion to his brother Basil's unfinished *Hexaëmeron*.[36]

Gregory argues as follows:

> Since mind (νοῦς) ... is an intellectual and incorporeal thing, its peculiar grace would have been incommunicable and unmixed, if its motion were not manifested through some reflection. That is why there was need of this organic structure so that it might, like a plectrum, touch the vocal organs and indicate through the particular impression of the sounds the motion from within. And as some skilled musician, who may from circumstance not have his own voice, yet wish to make his skill manifest, might make his melody through the voices of others, displaying his skill through flutes or a lyre; so also the human mind, as a discoverer of all kinds of notions, because it is unable to show the impulses of its thinking (τὰς τῆς διανοίας ὁρμὰς) to the soul that perceives through bodily senses, touches like some skillful conductor (καθάπερ τις ἁρμοστὴς ἔντεχνος) these ensouled organs and makes clear through the resonance in them its hidden notions (τὰ κεκρυμμένα νοήματα).

> Gregory of Nyssa *On the Making of Man* 149.24–152.6[37]

In this passage, there appears the idea of the conductor, crucial to the later development of the orchestra.[38] The mind is like a skilled and experienced musician who, without his own voice, makes music through the instruments of others and conducts the ensouled organs in order to express its thoughts.

---

[36] In what follows on Gregory, I rely on Corrigan 2010:147–162.

[37] Translations of *On the Making of Man* are either my own or adapted from Schaff and Wallace 2007.

[38] Cf. *Enneads* III 6.4.30–52 and my comments in Corrigan 2010:147–162.

This might seem to be an extravagant instrumentalist view according to which the mind functions like a ghost-in-the-machine, in Ryle's terms,[39] rather than a genuinely unified agent; but this does not fit Gregory's time or viewpoint, for while he holds that an incorporeal mind is not to be reduced to any single organ and that it should be viewed holistically, this does not mean that mental "epiphenomena" cannot be given psycho-somatic or physiological explanations or that the root and pathways of thought should not in a derivative sense be traced to the brain and the nerves or the heart and the arteries.

Gregory goes on to develop the orchestral (or at least "chamber") simile in the text that follows, and on this occasion he gives it a symphonic physiological organization that the reader might not at all anticipate:

> Now the music of the human instrument is a sort of compound of the flute and lyre, sounding together in unison with one another as in some concerted piece of music (ἐν συνῳδίᾳ τινί). For the breath, as it is pushed up from the air-receiving vessels through the windpipe, whenever the impulse of the speaker attunes the part with the tension for speech, and as it strikes the internal projections which divide this flute-like passage in a circular way, imitates in a way the sound produced through the flute, driven around in a circle by the projecting membranes. But the palate receives the sound from below in its own hollow and dividing the sound by the twin flutes that lead to the nostrils and by the cartilages around the perforated bone (colander) like scaly projections, makes its resonance stronger. Whereas cheek and tongue and the organization of the pharynx by which the chin is relaxed when drawn in and extended out as it tightens—all these answer to the movement of the plectrum on the strings in complex and diverse ways, transposing with great speed as the moment requires the arrangement of the tones. And the opening and closing of lips produces the same effect as players who stop the breath of the flute with their fingers, according to the harmony of the melody.
>
> Gregory of Nyssa *On the Making of Man* 149.40–152.7

What exactly is Gregory referring to in this passage? Is the music of the human instrument simply the compound of two bodily senses (roughly equivalent to flute and lyre)[40] or of the ensouled body as a whole? Or does it include soul in the broader sense as a soul-body compound in which soul answers to

---

[39] Ryle 1949.
[40] *On the Making of Man* 152.10–12: οὕτω τοίνυν τοῦ νοῦ διὰ τῆς ὀργανικῆς ταύτης κατασκευῆς ἐν ἡμῖν μουσουργοῦντος τὸν λόγον, λογικοὶ γεγόναμεν ...

the flute and body to the lyre? The image is still more complex. First, soul is certainly included since the soul explicitly perceives through the sense organs (διὰ σωματικῶν αἰσθήσεων ἐπαϊούσῃ τῇ ψυχῇ). Second, the beauty of the analogy is that flute and lyre answer to either or both of soul and body. Third, mind is not excluded from the picture since the "impulse" of the speaker/musician answers to the "impulse of the *dianoia*" and thus incarnates the agency of mind in the symphony. Mind makes the music possible, from one perspective, and body organized into mind, from another perspective, actualizes music. In fact, this is more an image of mind than it is of body—an interpretation necessitated by the very next words in the text at the beginning of 10: "In this way then since the mind makes the music of *logos* by means of this organic structure in us, we are born *logikoi*." (*On the Making of Man* 152.10–12).

What is striking is that from the perspective of mind, everything—every physiological and even mechanical detail—is brought into cognitive focus without losing sight of its own physical level of significance. So, a mechanistic-physiological description confirms the hypothesis that, not only hands (ἴδιον τῆς λογικῆς φύσεως αἱ χεῖρες, *On the Making of Man* 149.12–13), but also lips, bone, and breath are *propria* of our rational nature. Gregory then goes on to provide a psycho-somatic two-way application of his thesis in *On the Making of Man*: "the operation of the instrument is two-fold, involving the production of sound and the reception of concepts from outside that do not meddle in each other's business but abide in unison, each in its own proper activity."[41] Note the emphasis on *energeia* that we saw also in Plotinus—from Aristotle: what is a motion or passivity from one viewpoint can be an intelligible activity from another. Appropriately too, Gregory's physiological and mechanical model is daringly concrete.

Gregory next articulates a second model, a computer-like or city-like image of mind thinking, remembering, and perceiving, an image worthy of Augustine's later treatment of memory. How can the mind process so much information without confusion? What kind of entity is mind? He poses and answers the question as follows:

> What is the extent of that inner space into which everything flows together that enters through hearing? Who are the reminder-inscribers of the words that are brought into it? And what kind of receptacle is there for the concepts that are deposited in it through hearing? And how is it, that when many concepts of every kind are pressed in upon

---

[41] *On the Making of Man* 152.17–21: διπλῆ δὲ περὶ τὸ ὄργανον ἡ ἐνέργεια· ἡ μὲν πρὸς ἐργασίαν ἠχῆς, ἡ δὲ πρὸς ὑποδοχὴν τῶν ἔξωθεν νοημάτων. Καὶ οὐκ ἐπιμίγνυται πρὸς τὴν ἑτέραν ἡ ἄλλη, ἀλλὰ παραμένει τῇ ἐνεργείᾳ...

each other, there is no confusion or error as to the respective positions of the contents?

Gregory of Nyssa *On the Making of Man* 152b–c

The mind is, Gregory argues, like some massive city of human subjects that welcomes all comers on both its own and their own terms[42]—some go to market, some to the houses; others to churches, streets, lanes, theaters—each according to his own inclination: "some such city of our mind do I see established in us, which the different entrances through the sense keep filling up, while the mind, distinguishing fairly and examining each of the things that enters, files them properly in their respective places of knowledge" (*On the Making of Man* 152c–d). This is a remarkable passage that both anticipates the *loci* or *topoi* of memory (invented in antiquity) that will become important in the Middle Ages and Renaissance[43] and yet recalls "the city in discourses" that Socrates founds and establishes as "a model in heaven" (*Republic* 591e–592b). Gregory brings this model down from heaven, as it were, and shows us that the kingdom of heaven is not only among us, but also within us—as is also the spirit of philosophy that makes us truly musical. As Socrates says at the end of *Republic* 9: the one who possesses *nous* "will always cultivate the *harmony* of the body for the sake of the *symphony* of his soul;"[44] and Glaukon replies, "Indeed he will, if he is to be truly musical" (τῇ ἀληθείᾳ μουσικός, *Republic* 591d4–5).

To sum up, the groundwork for some of the major conclusions of *On the Making of Man* is already established in chapter 10.

First, psychic localization is necessary to account for both faculty functioning and impairment; if the organ is impaired, for instance, it cannot receive and transmit the melody. At the same time, however, excessive localization prevents us from appreciating the holistic complexity of the mind/soul in those physiological systems and the higher order possibilities inherent even in mechanistic processes (see *On the Making of Man* chapters 11–16).

Second, after sustained treatment of the question of what belongs in the image of God, the passion, creation, resurrection, transmigration of the soul (*On the Making of Man* chapters 17–28), in chapter 29, Gregory's radical thesis that mind/soul and body have an equal beginning in organic development finally emerges. Neither soul nor body is prior to the other. Gregory argues as follows:

---

[42] *On the Making of Man* 152.27–33: ὥσπερ εἴ τις πολύχωρος εἴη πόλις ἐκ διαφόρων εἰσόδων τοὺς πρὸς αὐτὴν συμφοιτῶντας εἰσδεχομένη ... κατὰ τὴν ἰδίαν ἕκαστος γνώμην.

[43] On this, see Yates 1966.

[44] *Republic* 591d1–3: ἀεὶ τὴν ἐν τῷ σώματι ἁρμονίαν τῆς ἐν τῇ ψυχῇ ἕνεκα συμφωνίας ἁρμοττόμενος φανεῖται.

But since the human being is one—being consisting of soul and body—we are to suppose that the origin of [the human being's] structure is one and common (ἀλλ᾽ ἑνὸς ὄντος τοῦ ἀνθρώπου, τοῦ διὰ ψυχῆς τε καὶ σώματος συνεστηκότος, μίαν αὐτοῦ καὶ κοινὴν τῆς συστάσεως τὴν ἀρχὴν ὑποτίθεσθαι) so that he should not turn out to be older and younger than himself, the bodily taking the lead in him and the other turning up later. But we are to say that in the foreknowing power of God (τῇ μὲν προγνωστικῇ τοῦ Θεοῦ δυνάμει), according to the account adopted a little earlier, the entire fullness of humanity pre-subsisted (τῇ μὲν προγνωστικῇ τοῦ Θεοῦ δυνάμει)[45] ... and to this the prophetic writing witnesses, which says that God knows all things before they come to be ... and in the creation of the individual we are not to put one element before the other, neither the soul before the body nor the reverse ... and if the one should pre-subsist and the other come into being afterwards, the power of the demiurging one would be shown to be something *incomplete* (ἀτελής τις ἡ τοῦ δημιουργοῦντος ἀπελεγχθήσεται δύναμις), as not being sufficient for the whole task all at once (κατὰ τὸ ἀθρόον) ...

Gregory of Nyssa On the Making of Man 233d–236a

Gregory's formulation of his whole-formation theory here implicitly (but clearly) refers to Plato and Plotinus, though its whole context and some of its language are Christian (for example, references to the *Plêrôma* and to God's knowing all things before they come to be). One of the founding principles of the *Timaeus* is that the Demiurge looked to the intelligible Living Creature in making this world, not to a partial model: "for nothing that is a likeness of anything *incomplete* could ever turn out beautiful".[46] Similarly, when Plotinus argues in *Ennead* VI 7 that the Demiurge could not have deliberated or reasoned about making the cosmos, but demiurgic activity must be whole and entire before any reasoning—"all at once" is the adjective he uses of the divine Intellect's activity elsewhere (*athroos*)[47]—he says explicitly that if every divine activity must not be *incomplete* (εἰ δεῖ ἑκάστην ἐνέργειαν μὴ ἀτελῆ[48] εἶναι), it is not lawful to suppose that *anything of God is other than whole and all*, then *everything must exist in any thing which is his* (μηδὲ θεμιτὸν θεοῦ ὁτιοῦν ὂν ἄλλο τι νομίζειν ἢ ὅλον τε καὶ πᾶν, δεῖ ἐν ὁτῳοῦν τῶν αὐτοῦ πάντα ἐνυπάρχειν); and so everything must preexist in God as to become unfolded later in time "as if it had been thought out beforehand as

---

[45] Cf. *Enneads* VI 7.1.45–49.
[46] *Timaeus* 30c5: ἀτελεῖ γὰρ ἐοικὸς οὐδέν ποτ᾽ ἂν γένοιτο καλόν.
[47] E.g. *Enneads* III 7.8.50–51, 11.22, 11.55–57; III 8.9.20; V 5.3.19, 7.8; V 8.6.9–10.
[48] See also Aristotle *Physics* 201b16–202a12.

to what comes later; and this means that there will be ... no deficiency" (*Enneads* VI 7.1.45–48). Plotinus then goes on the subsequent chapters of *Enneads* VI 7 to articulate a theory of whole-formation that allows for the priority of soul to body. Gregory here clearly points out that the preexistence of the soul without the preexistence of the body[49] contravenes both Plato's and Plotinus' fundamental principles (that no work or activity of God can be *incomplete*), and he proceeds in the rest of chapters 29 and 30 to work out the unfolding of body and soul together as we actually experience this in seeds, in the growth of limbs, and in the complementary development of organic structure and thought.

Finally, at the end of *On the Making of Man* in the culminating thesis of the work (chapter 30), Gregory concludes with an independent examination of the construction of the body from the medical point of view, thus indicating his approval of, and continuity with, a long tradition rooted in Genesis and later in the *Timaeus'* account of the generation of the human body, on the one hand, and his radical departure from—or Christian completion of—that tradition, on the other, depending on one's point of view:

> For the project was to show that the seminal cause of our constitution is neither an incorporeal soul nor an unsouled body,[50] but that from animated and living bodies it is generated in the first constitution as a living, animate being, and that human nature, like a nurse, receives and tends it with her own proper powers;[51] and it grows in both aspects and makes its growth manifest correspondingly in each part. For straightaway, by means of this mechanistic/artificial and scientific process of formation, it shows the power of soul interwoven[52] in it, appearing rather dimly at first, but subsequently shining more brilliantly with the perfection of the instrument.
>
> Gregory of Nyssa *On the Making of Man* 253b–c

Gregory of Nyssa's harmony-symphony orchestral, computer-city, and whole-formation models for understanding the complexity of mind, soul, and body are the culmination of an entire tradition—thoroughly innovative and original

---

[49] It should be noted that neither Plato nor Plotinus (nor Origen, Gregory, or Evagrius) believed in a literal, i.e. temporal, preexistence of the soul. If the soul is represented in Plato or Plotinus as preexisting body, this is a logical, nontemporal preexistence.

[50] Cf. *Enneads* VI 7.1–7 (which is effectively Plotinus' version of *On the Making of Man*), especially *Enneads* VI 7.5.5–8: οὕτω γὰρ καὶ οἱ ἐν τοῖς σπέρμασι λόγοι· οὔτε γὰρ ἄνευ ψυχῆς οὔτε ψυχαὶ ἁπλῶς. οἱ γὰρ λόγοι οἱ ποιοῦντες οὐκ ἄψυχοι, καὶ θαυμαστὸν οὐδὲν τὰς τοιαύτας οὐσίας λόγους εἶναι.

[51] As opposed to *Enneads* VI 7.7.8–16; cf. IV 3.9—that is, no World Soul, Platonic *Khôra*, or Receptacle.

[52] Compare *diaplakeisa* in Plato *Timaeus* 36e2, and Plotinus *Enneads* I 1.3.19; and for cognates like *sumplekein* in Plato and Plotinus, see Ast 1969:vol. 3 and Sleeman-Pollet 1980.

because they show that the logical conclusion of Platonism, on its own terms, is not the priority of soul over body, but their equality in organic germination and in their ultimate mature development.

3. Evagrius

We have space only for the briefest look at Evagrius—despite his importance and originality.[53] Among many other things (including his interest in medicine like the "other" Cappadocians), Evagrius presents a map of healthy mind/soul-body functioning, a detailed and groundbreaking account of its pathology, and a fascinating meditation in a chapter of one work that suggests our *historical* mind-body identity is intrinsically dependent on others; we are radically and empirically *inter-subjective beings*. Plotinus certainly believes this from the standpoint of Intellect—and so too, Gregory, if in a different way; but Evagrius is the only one I know to place inter-subjectivity explicitly within the construction of our everyday identity.

First, let us look at the healthy mind/soul-body configuration based on the tripartite soul, which Evagrius describes:

> If the rational (λογικῆς) soul is tripartite, according to our wise teacher,[54] when virtue comes to be in the rational part (ἐν τῷ λογιστικῷ), it is called practical intelligence (φρόνησις), understanding (σύνεσις), and wisdom (σοφία), and when it comes to be in the desiring part, it is called temperance (σωφροσύνη), love (ἀγάπη), and control (ἐγκράτεια), and when in the spirited part, courage (ἀνδρεία) and endurance (ὑπομονή); and in the whole soul, justice (δικαιοσύνη).
>
> Evagrius *Praktikos* 89[55]

The rest of the text that we cannot cite here articulates the practical functions of each of the virtues. Evagrius believed, with Origen, in an original community of all minds or "rational beings" (*logikoi*) in God.[56] Because of the Fall, through misuse of freedom and a lessening intensity of contemplation, mind's

---

53 For Evagrius' works, see Dysinger 2005:17–27.

54 Perhaps, Gregory Nazianzus (Sinkewicz 2003:260n90), but see Ramelli 2015:xviii and 106, who argues it is actually Gregory of Nyssa.

55 For a critical edition of the Greek text, with a French translation, see A. Guillaumont and C. Guillaumont 1971. An older English translation with commentary has been done by Bamberger 1981; See also Sinkewicz 2003:91–114. My translation.

56 This must also be true in different ways for Plotinus (see the striking image of Intellect at *Enneads* VI 7.15.26: "a thing all faces, shining with living faces") and Gregory (see his treatment of the fullness of humanity in *On the Making of Man* 16 [PG 44.185b–d; GNO III i.40]).

original unity disintegrates, and mind falls, through a thickening extension of itself into soul, and becomes attached or linked to a body. As the *logikoi* fall, they take on souls and bodies in accordance with the state of mind in them, and so angels live on the level of mind/reason, human beings on an intermediate level between reason, passion/anger, and desire, and daemons, who are most immersed in matter and dominated by desire and anger, on the lowest level. In *Praktikos* 89 above, the healthy tripartite model characterized by a cluster of nine layered virtues is an embodied model, as in Plato's *Republic*, starting at 435b, but it is actually adapted from a passage in Aristotle or Pseudo-Aristotle, *On the Virtues and the Vices* 1249a–b. So the tripartite system maps onto the body; but in Evagrius the structure of reason-spirit-desire, found in the fourth book of the *Republic*, is transposed above into a reason-desire-spirit structure, which is perhaps an indication of the fragility of embodied existence where the natural ally of reason, the spirited power, can become separated from reason by desire— as is suggested by Socrates at *Republic* 553c–d.[57]

Evagrius' articulation of the pathologies of each power of the embodied soul in accordance (for the most part, but not exclusively)[58] with eight "thought tendencies" (*logismoi, noêmata*) is simply fascinating. The eight thought tendencies (pride, vainglory, acedia, anger, sadness, avarice, fornication, gluttony) give rise later to the "seven deadly sins" tradition under Pope Gregory the Great— with "sadness" disappearing from the list.[59] Evagrius, however, does not compile a list but rather charts the subtle ways that the mind/soul—under the influence of (demonic) suggestion—gradually shuts itself down and comes to inhabit the basement of itself. Pride and vainglory attack and shut down our reason; the noonday daemon (*akêdia*) drowns or suffocates the *nous*;[60] anger, partly as a result of confinement, and sadness, because there seems no way back into the fuller mind/soul, confines consciousness even more to material desire: avarice, fornication and gluttony.[61] But this is no simple fall from the less material to the more material, for Evagrius is well aware that vainglory has a vampire-like compulsion for material things and that fornication can be a lot more in the "head" than avarice or gluttony.[62]

Here I have space only for one example of inter-subjectivity in relation to healthy and pathological thought-in-action. In *Thoughts* 25, Evagrius suggests that even in healthy experience the mind is intrinsically de-centered since it

---

[57] For discussion, see Corrigan 2009:88–92.

[58] Dysinger 2005:36, 115–123.

[59] As recent iterations of the *Diagnostic and Statistical Manual of Mental Disorders* (1994) indicate, we still have little idea what to do with the complex phenomenon of sadness.

[60] *Praktikos* 36.

[61] *Praktikos* 10.

[62] On this, and for the role of daemons, see Corrigan 2009:74–101.

is never simply self-sufficient but in need of the other—our neighbor. In the case of determining the veracity of proofs drawn from the contemplation of nature, he says, in most cases "the heart of my reader" is the determining factor, not his own judgment. He then sets out a theory of representation (that looks Aristotelian)[63] and a thought-example: "Whatever may be the form of the object, such is necessarily the image that the mind receives, whence the mental representations of objects are called copies because they preserve the same form as them."[64] The "shape" (*morphê*) of the sensible object is received by the mind as "an image" or *eikôn*, and called "a likeness" or *homoiôma* because it preserves the *morphê*. There is then an intrinsic continuity between sensible "shape" or *morphê* through "likeness" or *homoiôma* to "image" or *eikôn*.

Evagrius then goes on to argue that "in this way [the mind] receives also [the mental representation] of its own organism—for this too is sensible—but with the exception altogether of its own face, for it is incapable of making this shape in itself, because it has never seen it."[65] However quaint this example may be[66] and whatever Evagrius might be thought to have meant by it (no puddles or reflective surfaces in the desert?), the overall thought is striking and innovative. The face, self, or mind is constantly in need of the other for its own constitution. It cannot get outside of itself to see itself as a whole for the whole is always in process of being given reflexively by the other. If perception is a relatively direct transmission, subjectivity is much more complex, for it is situated in an incoherence, a gap that can never be permanently remedied—except in and through God. The subject is always in need of its own face in the face of the other. "Even one's own appearance one cannot see fully or conceive in its totality ... [but] only by others" (Bakhtin 1989:507).[67] Furthermore, the word *eikôn* here is perhaps chosen deliberately, since the mind, so given to itself by the other, is the likeness or image primarily of God, and it is intended at its best to be part of a community of minds in God. "So pay attention to yourself with regard to how the mind puts on the form of its own body, apart from the face, but in turn expresses in

---

[63] Cf. Aristotle, *On Interpretation* 16a; Clement of Alexandria, *Stromata* 8.23.1; Géhin 1998:241n3; Corrigan 2009:116–119.

[64] *Thoughts* 25.11–14: ὁποία γὰρ ἂν εἴη τοῦ πράγματος ἡ μορφή, τοιαύτην ἀνάγκη καὶ τὸν νοῦν δέξασθαι τὴν εἰκόνα· ὅθεν καὶ ὁμοιώματα λέγεται τὰ νοήματα τῶν πραγμάτων τῷ τὴν αὐτὴν ἐκείνοις διασῴζειν μορφήν. Hereafter the translation is my own.

[65] *Thoughts* 25.14–17: οὕτω καὶ τοῦ ἰδίου ὀργάνου—αἰσθητὸν γὰρ καὶ τοῦτο—χωρὶς δὲ πάντως τῆς ὄψεως· ταύτην γὰρ ἐν ἑαυτῷ μορφῶσαι ἀδυνατεῖ, μηδέποτε θεασάμενος.

[66] Evagrius' general view might be characterized as "ghost-in-the-machine" or "instrumentalist," but the purpose of the theorem seems much more concrete, embodied, and practical than these characterizations would suggest.

[67] Bakhtin 1990:105; cf. 41–42.

discursive thinking its neighbor whole since it has previously grasped and seen such a person whole" (*Thoughts* 25.38–41).[68]

What Evagrius wants to emphasize is the inter-subjective responsibility each of us has for our own actions and the importance of immateriality in everything we do—that is, to become fully conscious of what we do and how we do it. From observation of a gap in consciousness, Evagrius can thus establish the "theorem" that mind is intrinsically inter-subjective. And he concludes the chapter with the other end of the scale, citing *Deuteronomy* 15:9: the anchorite needs to pay attention that there not be "a hidden word" in his heart that is "without thought" (ῥῆμα κρυπτὸν ἐν τῇ καρδίᾳ αὐτοῦ ἀνόμημα), since at the time of temptation, in the presence of the daemon, the mind will not grasp and see his neighbor whole, but will seize/plunder/rape *its own shape* (*Thoughts* 25.45–50).[69] Evagrius then concludes chapter 25 with a definition of the unhealthy thought:

> ... a demonic thought is an *image* of the sensible human being put together in discursive thinking, an incomplete image, with which the mind being moved in a passionate way does or says something lawlessly in hiddenness in relation to the *image being formed successively by it.*

Evagrius Thoughts 25.52–56[70]

I have italicized the words above to emphasize the transition from *eikôn*, as in healthy thinking, to *eidôlon*—which here, I think, means a deceptive image in constant process of being reconfigured or reshaped. It is perhaps strange to think of an inhuman element somehow co-inhabiting a thought! Nonetheless, *Thoughts* 25 is striking, for it starts with the same *eikôn* constitutive of healthy thinking (constructed in accordance with the διάνοια), but ends up with an *eidôlon* and suggests that this is a complex event in constant replicative transmission, ultimately caught in a recurring loop that goes nowhere since it has no *telos*. It is an "incomplete" motion, as Aristotle puts it[71] (as Plato, Plotinus,

---

68 *Thoughts* 25.38–41: πλὴν πρόσεχε σεαυτῷ πῶς ἄνευ τοῦ προσώπου τοῦ ἰδίου σώματος ὁ νοῦς ἐνδύεται τὴν μορφήν, τὸν δὲ πλησίον πάλιν ὅλον κατὰ διάνοιαν ἐκτυποῖ, ἐπειδὴ τοιοῦτον ὅλον προλαβὼν καὶ ἑώρακεν.

69 *Thoughts* 25.45–50: ὁ νοῦς κατὰ τὸν καιρὸν τῶν πειρασμῶν, ἐπιστάντος τοῦ δαίμονος, ἁρπάζειν τοῦ σώματος τοῦ ἰδίου τὸ σχῆμα. Cf. Gregory of Nyssa, *Life of Moses* 44.364a–b (GNO VII i.72.12): τὴν ἁρπακτικὴν διάνοιαν and 72.15–17: νεκρὰ ποιεῖν ἐν τῷ ὕδατι, αὐτά τε τὰ πονηρὰ τῆς διανοίας κινήματα καὶ τὰ ἐκ τούτων ἀποτελέσματα, καθάπερ ἐν τῷ μυστηρίῳ τοῦ Πάσχα.

70 *Thoughts* 25.52–56: λογισμὸς γὰρ δαιμονιώδης ἐστὶν εἰκὼν τοῦ αἰσθητοῦ ἀνθρώπου συνισταμένη κατὰ διάνοιαν, ἀτελής, μεθ' ἧς ὁ νοῦς κινούμενος ἐμπαθῶς λέγει τι ἢ πράττει ἀνόμως ἐν τῷ κρυπτῷ πρὸς τὸ μορφούμενον ἐκ διαδοχῆς εἴδωλον ὑπ' αὐτοῦ. Cf. *Reflections* 13 (translation in Sinkewicz 2003).

71 Aristotle, *Physics* 201b16–202a12; 257b8–9; *On the Soul* 417a16; for commentary, see Joachim 1970.

and Gregory too refuse to impute to the Divine, as we saw above). Also, from Deuteronomy, the demonic thought is *anoêma*—"without thought," "not-thought," or as Evagrius says elsewhere, a thought of something not really existent at all;[72] it has no foundation, as it were, and does not reflect the reality of the created mind. It is precisely, in fact, the absence of a real trace—a traceless trace, one might say, since there is a link, but also a gap between *eikôn* and *eidôlon*.

4. Conclusion

Plotinus' view of the mind/soul-body complex may seem abstract and ghostly, but it in fact articulates a cogent three-tiered structure of human agency based on reasonable interpretations of what we refer to in talking about the qualified body, the psycho-somatic compound, and the immaterial mind/soul. At the same time, Plotinus insists on the empirical reality of individual agency and provides a plausible account of the localization of physiological and psycho-somatic capacities in the context of the nonlocalizable immaterial mind/soul. Plotinus, in short, provides a compelling mind-body map that can help to give structure to the thought of so many later figures.

Gregory goes even further and provides (at least) three compelling models of mind-body interaction: he discovers in mind the "conductor" of an orchestral harmony/symphony model, a model of computer-like or city-like complexity, and, above all, a whole-formation model that makes soul and body radically equal in the Divine foreknowing and in historical development—on *Platonic* grounds. Gregory's insights are surely one of the most overlooked achievements in the history of thought.

Finally, in Evagrius' thought there is a similar economy and yet layered flexibility, since the healthy and pathological models of the embodied mind are located in a radically decentered subject. The immaterial but embodied mind is constituted through inter-subjectivity, for it needs the other to fill in its own face. Pathological functioning, by contrast, is a complex event in constant replicative transmission, an incomplete process that can be reflected on multiple levels as local brain stimulation[73] or body affect or, again, as imprinting different functions of the tripartite soul or as threatening the survival even of the mind itself. In addition, since pathological thinking swings away from the created world of inter-subjective experience into a formative loop of its own making,

---

[72] *Thoughts* 19.14–20; *Gnostikos* 42 and 44.7.
[73] See Evagrius, *Prayer* 72 (Sinkewicz 2003:200).

psycho-somatic pathological behavior tends to focus on what is not, and to become, instead of an *eikôn* of something in the created world, a lower deceptive image—an *eidôlon*—that I have characterized here as effectively an absence of real trace.[74]

---

[74] My treatment of Evagrius here is related to Corrigan 2017.

14

Gregory of Nyssa's Purported Criticism of Origen's Purported Doctrine of the Preexistence of Souls

Ilaria L. E. Ramelli

Abstract: Origen of Alexandria (died ca. 255) and Gregory of Nyssa (late fourth century), Origen's most insightful follower, are the most remarkable Christian Platonists. Their doctrines concerning the body, the soul, and their relation have often been misrepresented in scholarship. For instance, the theory of *metensômatôsis* has been attributed to Origen. This is a gross misunderstanding, as many scholars now fortunately realize, but no less serious a mistake is to ascribe to him the doctrine of a preexistence of bare souls, which received a body only as a result of their fall, or the idea of the eternal existence of spiritual beings, thus coeternal with God, which for Origen existed eternally only in God's mind as paradigmatic ideas, but not as substances on their own. A correction of such mistakes is in order not only to rectify our understanding of Origen's own thought, but also for a reassessment of Gregory of Nyssa's relation to Origen's thought on this score.

The relation of Gregory Nyssen's to Origen's thinking about the interaction of bodies and souls and the creation of rational beings, indeed, is regularly misunderstood in terms of a criticism, on the basis of a section of Gregory's *On the Soul and the Resurrection* and another from his *On the Making of Humanity*. These crucial passages are usually interpreted by scholars as refutations of Origen's alleged doctrine of the preexistence of souls, whereas Gregory is depicted as the advocate of the simultaneous creation of the soul and its mortal body. I shall argue that Gregory's criticism was not targeting Origen in the least and that, just as Origen never supported the doctrine of the preexistence of incorporeal souls, neither did Gregory probably maintain that each soul comes into being at the same time as its mortal body. He was all too aware of the so-called perishability axiom.

ORIGEN OF ALEXANDRIA AND Gregory of Nyssa are among the most remarkable Christian Platonists. Their doctrines concerning the body, the soul, and the relation between the two have often been misrepresented. For instance, the theory of *metensômatôsis* has been attributed to Origen. This is a gross misunderstanding, which many scholars now realize. But no less serious a mistake is to ascribe to him the doctrine of the preexistence of disembodied souls according to which the souls become embodied only as a result of their fall. This interpretation is at odds with Origen's view that no creature is completely disembodied since only the Trinity is incorporeal. Another instance is the attribution to Origen of the idea that spiritual beings are coeternal with God, whereas, according to him, they exist only in God's mind as paradigmatic ideas, but not as substances of their own.

The list of scholars who maintain the above views runs long: I will mention only a few by way of example, and it is all the more significant that they are all fine scholars. Monfrinotti juxtaposes Clement's rejection of the idea of the preexistence of disembodied souls to Origen's alleged reception of it and considers Origen's position to be in agreement with the views of Plato and Philo.[1] Plato and (possibly) Philo, however, supported the theory of *metensômatôsis*—albeit only as a mythical and (possibly) an esoteric teaching, respectively[2]—while Origen rejected it. Costache, who has contributed excellent scholarship to Patristics, speaks of "Origen's concept of the initially disembodied human nature, disavowed by both fathers," namely Gregory Nyssen and Maximus the Confessor.[3] Blowers, in an otherwise rich and inspiring monograph, maintains that Gregory Nyssen, Augustine, and Maximus the Confessor have in common "the rejection of Origen's speculation about double creation, in which spiritual creation preexists material or corporeal creation."[4] He claims again that Nyssen "seeks to apply a corrective to the Origenian doctrine

---

[1] Monfrinotti 2014:206.

[2] So Yli-Karjanmaa 2015:216–248. That Philo taught *metensômatôsis* as an esoteric doctrine is a very interesting hypothesis, although debated by scholars; Yli-Karjanmaa appeals to *On Dreams* 1.137–139; *On the cherubim* 114; *Questions and Answers on Genesis and Exodus* 2.40; fr. 7.3 Harris, where he sees Philo speak of reincarnation with approval.

[3] Costache 2013:273.

[4] Blowers 2012:11. See also Blowers 2012:211: Maximus the Confessor "gleaned much from Evagrius' teaching on the *logoi* of providence and judgment minus its Origenist framework." This last passage also bears on the issue of the reassessment of Evagrius' teaching, which is also in order.

of double creation, the idea that the spiritual creation eternally preexisted the materially embodied one,"[5] and takes *On the Making of Humanity* 28 as "Gregory's most explicit criticism of the Origenian doctrine of the preexistence of spiritual beings."[6] He concludes that, for Origen, bodies were assigned to rational creatures only after their fall, as a punishment.[7] Similar assertions can still be found in the scholarship today. They often draw support from fragments *15 and *17a Koetschau of Origen's *On First Principles*, which come from late and unreliable, hostile authors such as Epiphanius or Justinian himself.[8] A correction of such views is in order not only to rectify our understanding of Origen's own thought, but also for a reassessment of Gregory of Nyssa's relation to Origen's position on this subject. My goal in this chapter is to do just this.

Gregory Nyssen's relation to Origen's understanding of the interaction between bodies and souls and the creation of rational beings is regularly misconstrued as a criticism, on the basis of two passages from Gregory's *On the Soul and the Resurrection* and *On the Making of Humanity*. Scholars usually interpret these passages as evidence for Gregory's refutation of Origen's alleged doctrine of the preexistence of souls. Consequently, they depict Gregory as an advocate of the doctrine of the simultaneous creation of the soul and its mortal body. I shall suggest that, just as Origen probably never supported the doctrine of the preexistence of disembodied souls, neither did Gregory likely hold the view that each soul comes into being at the same time as its *mortal* body (he was all too aware of the so-called perishability axiom). Corrigan in his contribution to this volume remarks: "Gregory here clearly points out that the preexistence of the soul without the preexistence of the body contravenes both Plato's and Plotinus' fundamental principles."[9] This is, I suspect, Origen's position as well.

The opposition between Origen and Gregory on this score is fictitious rather than real.[10] Gregory's criticism, I argue, is targeted at others and not at Origen's purported view of the preexistence of souls. Origen's anthropology, however, was misunderstood and misrepresented, as exemplified by the *Letter to the Synod Concerning Origen* and the *Letter to Mennas* by Justinian, who is considered the promoter of the "condemnation of Origen."[11] Here, Justinian, relying on a dossier against Origen's alleged doctrines collected at the Mar Saba monastery in Palestine, attributes to him the doctrine of the preexistence of disembodied

---

[5] Blowers 2012:146.
[6] Blowers 2012:146n40.
[7] Blowers 2012:91.
[8] Among the few exceptions are Tzamalikos 2007, my review with further arguments in *Rivista di filosofia neo-scolastica* 100 (2008:453–458), and Lekkas 2001:124–140.
[9] See p. 270 above.
[10] This is the case in other respects as well. A systematic investigation is underway.
[11] On this point see Ramelli 2013:724–738.

souls and their coeternity with God-*Logos* within the framework of the protolog-
ical theory of the initial monad/henad. This theory portrays the initial monad
as lost due to sin at the fall, but with the expectation to be restored in the end. As
I will briefly point out, according to Origen, however, rational creatures did not
receive a body for the first time as a result of their detachment from God. They
possessed a spiritual, immortal body from the beginning of their creation as
substances, which Origen distinguished from the eternal existence of their Ideas
or paradigmatic *logoi* in the Mind of God (who is Christ-*Logos*). Origen's teaching
about the eternal existence of the Ideas or *logoi* of all things in the *Logos* and
Wisdom of God is misunderstood by the emperor as the theory of the coeternity
of creatures with the divinity. Rather, Origen maintained that the ideal paradigms of rational creatures preexisted eternally in God's *Logos*-Wisdom together
with the *logoi* of all other things—since the Son, as Wisdom containing many
forms, is the intelligible world[12]—but they became substances once created as
independent beings.[13] Rational creatures were created *ex nihilo*.[14] They began
to exist only at a certain point, although not in the time measured by heavenly
bodies. Therefore, they are not coeternal with God, but they preexisted as projects in God's *Logos* and only subsequently were created as substances "out of
nothing," as confirmed by a passage preserved directly in Greek.[15] The Wisdom
of God, Christ, has contained the ideal paradigms of all beings from eternity,
before their creation as independent substances. These do not subsist eternally
as creatures. God alone is eternal.[16]

According to Justinian, Origen maintained that souls are coeternal with
God. They preexisted their bodies, which they received only as a result of their
sin, and will be reincarnated in other bodies. The doctrine of souls' preexistence
to their bodies was already attributed to Origen at the end of the third century,
as Pamphilus attests in *Apology for Origen* 159: "Concerning the soul, they accuse
him of claiming that it was created before the body."[17] To refute this accusation, Pamphilus has no recourse to his usual strategy of quoting excerpts from
Origen's works; he rather remarks that Origen never composed a treatise *On the
Soul*, because the doctrine of the soul is fraught with incertitude, and the apostolic teaching failed to clarify the soul's origin.[18] As I shall indicate, Origen did

---

[12] *Commentary on John* 1.9.11 and 19.22.5.
[13] *On First Principles* 1.4.4–5: *Secundum praefigurationem et praeformationem semper erant in Sapientia ea, quae protinus etiam substantialiter facta sunt.*
[14] *On First Principles* 2.9.2.
[15] *Commentary on John* 1.19.114–115. See Ramelli 2011a.
[16] See Tzamalikos 2006:21–38, with my review in *Rivista di filosofia neo-scolastica* 99 (2007:177–181); Ramelli 2008.
[17] All translations are mine unless otherwise specified.
[18] *Apology for Origen* 8.

not support the preexistence of disembodied souls, but of intelligent, rational creatures (*noes, logika*) endowed with a spiritual body from their creation. We know that Pierius, Origen's follower and Pamphilus' teacher, supported the preexistence of embodied intellects, as, similarly, Origen and Pamphilus did. Pamphilus remarks that only thus it is possible to explain rational creatures' various conditions without holding God responsible for them. Pamphilus, like Rufinus later, clearly realized that Origen's concern was theodicy and the rejection of Gnostic predestinationism. As I have argued elsewhere,[19] the polemic against Gnostic determinism grounded his theory of rational creatures, from protology to eschatology.

Neither the adversaries of Origen, in the time of Pamphilus, nor Justinian personally read Origen.[20] Justinian produced Greek quotations from Origen's *On First Principles*, but these came from the set of excerpts that had been used for centuries in the Origenistic controversy, cut at the same points, extrapolated from their context, altered, misunderstood, and sometimes falsified.[21] Also in Justinian's day, Facundus of Hermiane identified, in 546–548, the doctrines of Origen that were under attack at that time as preexistence and *apokatastasis*: "human souls had preexisted in a blessed life before the bodies, and all those doomed to eternal punishment, along with the devil and his angels, will be restored to the original beatitude."[22] The reason for Justinian's criticism is the consideration of Origen as a Christian Platonist and the supposed irreconcilability of Platonism and Christianity. In the *Letter to the Synod about Origen*, the first thing the emperor says about the Origenist monks is that they followed Pythagoras, Plato, and Origen.[23] Then, he traces back their doctrines of the initial monad and the souls' preexistence and their fall to Pythagoras, Plato, and Plotinus (*Letter to the Synod about Origen* 124). Likewise, in his *Letter to Mennas*, Justinian claims Origen's heresy for being entirely substantiated by Plato's philosophy and, in the whole of his letter, calls Origen's philosophy *muthologêmata* to show that it is a derivation from Greek myths.[24]

Justinian presents Origen's view of the preexistence of disembodied souls as entailing the transmigration of souls even into animal bodies. Indeed, as for

---

[19] Ramelli 2006; 2009a; further 2013:137-215. That the polemic against "Gnostics" and Marcionites occupied Origen until the end of his life and informed his thought (*pace* Heine 2011) is now clearly confirmed also by the recently discovered Munich homilies.

[20] See Ramelli 2014.

[21] *Letter to Mennas* 106–116.

[22] *In Defense of the Three Chapters* (CPL 866), 4.4.13–15; 93–112.

[23] *Letter to the Synod about Origen* 122: Πυθαγόρᾳ καὶ Πλάτωνι καὶ Ὠριγένει τῷ καὶ Ἀδαμαντίῳ καὶ τῇ τούτων δυσσεβείᾳ καὶ πλάνῃ κατακολουθοῦντες.

[24] *Letter to Mennas* 72 A-Z: Τί γὰρ ἕτερον παρὰ τὰ Πλάτωνι εἰρημένα τῷ τὴν Ἑλληνικὴν μανίαν πλατύναντι Ὠριγένης ἐξέθετο.

instance Nautin notes, "preexistence of souls and reincarnations go together."[25] The association of the preexistence of disembodied souls with *metensômatôsis* and *apokatastasis* returns again, for instance, in the *Chronicle of Michael Rabo*,[26] where the followers of Maximus the Confessor, represented as Origenists, are made to say:

> We have received from Origen that all the souls of humans, animals, ... and trees had been angels before falling. When they cooled down from the love for God, they were cast down from heavens and condemned to live in bodies as in prisons ... migrating from one body to another. Later there will be a restoration ... the resurrection is the liberation of souls from bodies.
>
> *Chronicle of Michael Rabo* 4.423–425

But Origen denied reincarnation or *metensômatôsis*, criticizing any transmigration of human souls into bodies that are not their own, be these human, animal, or vegetal. Even in Justinian's distorted quotations, the expression "so to say" (ἵν' οὕτως εἴπω) makes it clear that Origen's references to depraved souls that become "beasts" are metaphorical and do not indicate any transmigration of rational souls into animal bodies. Origen repeatedly rejected *metensômatôsis* as impious and incompatible with the Biblical doctrine of the end of the world.[27] For instance, in a passage preserved both in Greek and in Rufinus' translation of Pamphilus' *Apology*, Origen made it clear that he utterly rejected the transmigration of souls and rather maintained a metaphorical "animalization" of the worst sinners:

> Those who are alien to the Catholic faith think that souls migrate from human bodies into bodies of animals ... On the contrary, we maintain that human wisdom, if it becomes uncultivated and neglected due to much carelessness in life, becomes like an irrational animal (*uelut irrationabile pecus*) due to incompetence or neglectfulness, but not by nature (*per imperitiam uel per neglegentiam, non per naturam*).[28]
>
> Pamphilus, *Apology for Origen* 80

---

[25] Nautin 1974:398: "*préexistence des âmes et réincarnations vont en effet ensemble.*"

[26] Parallel text in the *Chronicle of the Year 1234* 130.

[27] *Against Celsus* 3.75; 4.7; 4.17; 5.29; 8.30; *Commentary on Romans* 5.1.392–406; 5.9.171–176; 6.8.118–131; cf. *Commentary on Matthew* 13.1–2; *Commentary on Matthews in Series* 38; Pamphilus *Apology for Origen* 10; Origen *Commentary on John* 6.11.71; 6.13.78. See Ramelli 2009:251.

[28] *Commentary on Matthew* 11.17 and *Apology for Origen* 80.

Origen rejected even the transmigration of a soul into other human bodies on the grounds that this would entail the eternity of the world. This "pagan" tenet is contradicted by the Bible, but also by the rational argument that it is necessary to put an end to the process of correction:[29]

> The doctrine of the transmigration of souls (*de transmutatione animarum*) is alien to the Church of God, since it neither has been transmitted by the apostles nor is supported in any place in Scriptures ... the transmigration of souls will be absolutely useless if there is no end to correction, nor will ever come a time when the soul will no longer pass into new bodies. But if souls, due to their sins, must always return into ever new, different bodies, what end will there ever come to the world?[30]
>
> Origen *Commentary on Matthew* 13.1 = Pamphilus *Apology for Origen* 182–184

Origen, on the contrary, claims that there will be an end to the world, which will also enable the process of the eventual *apokatastasis*. I have demonstrated elsewhere the importance of the cessation of all time and all aeons for Origen in this connection.[31] After the end of the world, sinners will be punished indeed, but not by transmigration into other bodies (*non ex transmutatione animarum*). The idea of the end of the world as the reason for the rejection of *metensômatôsis* is recurrently emphasized by Origen:

> If indeed, according to the authority of Scripture, the end of the world will come soon and the present corruptible state will change into an incorruptible one, there seems to be no doubt that in the state of the present life it is impossible to return to a body for a second or third time. For, if one admits this, it will necessarily follow that, given the infinite successions of these passages, the world will have no end.[32]
>
> Origen *Commentary on the Song of Songs* 2.5.24

Justinian connected the doctrine of the transmigration of souls to that of their preexistence: "the cause of this absurdity [sc. *metensômatôsis*] is to believe

---

[29] This motif was very dear to Origen because of his doctrine of *apokatastasis*; Ramelli 2013: 137–215 on Origen and 521–548 on the Antiochenes.

[30] Also reported by Pamphilus *Apology for Origen* 182–183.

[31] In "Time and Eternity" in the *Routledge Handbook of Early Christian Thought*. Origen will be closely followed by Gregory Nyssen in this respect. See Ramelli 2010:57–62; on the same line Boersma 2012:575–612.

[32] Likewise, *Commentary on John* 6.86: "If one supports *metensômatôsis*, as a consequence one will have to maintain the incorruptibility of the world."

that souls preexisted."[33] He cited Gregory Nyssen's refutation of the preexistence of souls,[34] deeming Gregory's attack directed against Origen, which—as I shall argue—is not the case. Nyssen too connected *metensômatôsis* with the preexistence of souls in a causal connection, but he was not speaking of Origen,[35] who rejected, as shown above, the doctrine of *metensômatôsis* and very probably did not uphold the preexistence of disembodied souls either.

Justinian concluded that bodies were not created after souls, as a punishment, but bodies and souls were created together (*Letter to Mennas* 84). Now Origen certainly agreed with such a conclusion, since he thought that the fall transformed rational creatures' bodies into mortal or dark bodies, but did not cause their embodiment for the first time. Rational creatures, in Origen's view, were equipped with a bodily vehicle straight from their creation. This was not yet heavy, corruptible, and mortal, but similar to the spiritual body of the resurrection. After their sin, their fine, luminous, and immortal body was transformed into a mortal, molded body in the case of humans, or a "ridiculous" body in the case of demons (*Commentary on John* 1.17.97–98). Also in the *Commentary on John* 20.22.182 and 1.19.114–115, Origen distinguishes between *ktisma* (the foundation of God's Wisdom, the agent of creation), *poiêma* (the creation of intellects, along with their spiritual bodies and the world, not yet diversified), and *plasma*, what was molded as the subsequent transformation of the spiritual bodies into "material" bodies apt to the life of fallen intellects, in a world that became diversified according to the intellects' diversified wills.[36]

The distinction between the creation of the rational being and the molding of the mortal body is also illustrated in another passage preserved directly in Greek: when the divinity created the human being in its image, Origen says that, according to Scripture, God "has created" (*pepoiêke*) it; when God made the human being from the earth, Scripture clarifies that God "molded" (*eplasen*) it. Thus, Origen concludes, the human being "created" (*poioumenon*) by God is not that which "is formed in the womb," but "what is molded from the earth is what is founded in the womb,"[37] that is, the body of humans after their fall. This, and not the body *tout court*, is what Origen associates with death and sin. He deplores the covering of the "image of God" by the "image of the earthy and dead."[38]

Among rational creatures, angels still possess a heavenly, aethereal, and pure body, similar to that of the stars. Their body does not come from the dust

---

[33] *Letter to Mennas* 88–90.

[34] *Letter to Mennas* 92–93; cf. 96.

[35] I shall propose below the most probable alternatives.

[36] Initially all intellects had one and the same will, because they were all oriented towards God-Good, but later each of them oriented its will elsewhere. See Ramelli 2013c.

[37] *Homilies on Jeremiah* 1.10: Τὸ πλασσόμενον ἀπὸ τοῦ χοῦ τῆς γῆς, τοῦτο ἐν κοιλίᾳ κτίζεται.

[38] *Commentary on John* 20.229. See also *Homilies on Genesis* 13.4.

of the earth and their nourishment is spiritual.[39] Caesarius will follow Origen's line: "angels are incorporeal with respect to us (ἀσώματοι καθ' ἡμᾶς), but in themselves they do have bodies, like wind, fire, or air. Indeed, these are fine and immaterial bodies (λεπτὰ καὶ ἄϋλα), free from the density (παχύτης) of our bodies."[40] I cite him as a good example of the relative meaning of "corporeal" and "incorporeal" in Origen and the Origenian tradition.[41] Still late in his life, Origen spoke of two kinds of bodies, "earthly" and "of any other kind," i.e. spiritual.[42]

In Origen's view, the skin tunics with which Adam and Eve were covered after their sin are not the body *per se* (any kind of body), which they already possessed before their fall, but mortality, which was superimposed on their initially immortal body.[43] It is the heavy, corruptible body God gave humans after their first sin.[44] The Biblical skin tunics conceal a "mystery" or veiled truth deeper than that of the soul's fall as expounded by Plato.[45] Plato postulated a disembodied soul that, by losing its wings, becomes embodied. Origen, revisiting Plato, posits rational creatures endowed from their very creation with a subtle body, which increased its density into a heavy and mortal one after their sin. Origen's exegesis is likely to be reflected in Procopius, who reports that, according to "those who allegorize Scripture," these tunics are not the body, because the human being in paradise already had a body, "fine (λεπτομερές) and suitable for life in Paradise." Some "allegorizers" called this initial body "luminous" (αὐγοειδές) and immortal; "they claim that initially the soul used the luminous body as a vehicle, riding on it (ἐποχεῖσθαι), and this body was later clothed in the skin tunics."[46]

Origen's fellow disciple at Ammonius' school in Alexandria, Plotinus, conceived of daemons, intermediary rational beings between humans and deities, as equipped with bodies made of intelligible matter.[47] This might be

---

[39] *On Prayer* 7.23.4 and 27.9–10.
[40] *Questions and Answers* 47.
[41] I am addressing this point in a work on the relative corporeality of angels and in a monograph on Origen in preparation.
[42] *Exhortation to Martyrdom* 3.
[43] *Homilies on Leviticus* 6.2 (Genesis 3:21).
[44] *Fragments on 1 Corinthians* 29.
[45] Plato *Phaedrus* 248c–d; Origen *Against Celsus* 4.40.
[46] *Commentary on Genesis* 3:21 (PG 87.1.221A).
[47] *Enneads* III 5.6–7. I do not enter here the debate on the identity between Origen the Christian Platonist and Origen the Neoplatonist. On the probability of this identity, I refer, among other works, to Ramelli 2009 (received by e.g. Markschies 2012:119, 138; Tzamalikos 2012:288, 486, 505; 2016:2–4, who rejects "the convenient folly about 'two Origens'—which recently has resulted in 'two Ammonii'!— ... this Origen and the Christian one being the selfsame person," and passim; M. S. M. Scott 2012:180; Urbano 2013:71; Martens 2015:599, 619, etc.), 2011, 2017b; in preparation, with further arguments; Tarrant 2017:323-37; Beatrice 2019; S. Clark forthcoming, and many others.

identifiable with the "luminous vehicle" (*augoeides okhêma*) that souls assume in their descent according to Plotinus.[48] Origen too deemed rational creatures equipped with a subtle, luminous body, which may or may not be transformed into heavy and mortal, or into cold and dark, on account of their sin. There is also a textual correspondence: Origen also designated the subtle and spiritual body of rational creatures as both *augoeides* and an *okhêma*. His depiction of the spiritual body-vehicle as *augoeides* is further confirmed by the sixth-century theologian Gobar.[49] His use of *augoeides* in his paraphrase of Origen reveals that Procopius, too, was referring to Origen. What is more, Origen himself, in a passage of undisputed authenticity and preserved in Greek, describes the angels' bodies as "aethereal" (*aitheria*) and "luminous light" (*augoeides phôs*).[50] In a Latin passage of unquestionable authorship he describes "the quality of the spiritual body" as:

> ... such as to constitute a suitable dwelling place, not only for blessed and perfect souls, but also for all creation, once liberated from enslavement to corruption. In comparison with all these bodies that we see both on earth and in heaven, which are molded and not eternal, what is invisible, not handmade, and eternal is by far superior.
>
> Origen *On First Principles* 3.6.4

The present, mortal body will be turned into "finest, purest, and brightest, as the condition and deserts of the rational nature will require" (*On First Principles* 3.6.4). Here, "finest" corresponds to *leptomeres* and "brightest" to *augoeides*, and the description of the spiritual body as a suitable dwelling place for life in Paradise corresponds perfectly to Procopius' passage.

All this confirms that Procopius was speaking of Origen when he referred to the allegorical interpreters of Scripture who postulated a *leptomeres* and *augoeides* body prior to the fall. Such will also be the risen body in the end, after the deposition of the "skin tunic" that was added to the first body-vehicle.[51] Origen dismissed the idea that God, like a tailor, worked with skins, to cut and sew tunics.[52] This confirms Origen's authorship of a fragment quoted by Theodoret, probably from Origen's lost *Commentary on Genesis:*[53] it is "unworthy of God"

---

[48] *Enneads* II 2, III 6, and IV 3. The relation between the daemons' bodies and the souls' luminous vehicles is proposed by Narbonne 2011:46, which I reviewed with further comments on this point in *Bryn Mawr Classical Review*, October 25, 2011.

[49] Photius *Bibliotheca* Codex 232.288a; cf. 287b–291b.

[50] *Commentary on Matthew* 17.30.

[51] *Commentary on the Psalms* 6 in Pamphilus *Apology for Origen* 157.

[52] Epiphanius *Ancoratus* 62.3.

[53] Fr. 121 *Collectio Coisliniana in Genesim* = Origen *Commentary on Genesis* D11 Metzler.

to imagine that God, "like a tailor who works with skins, cut and sewed those tunics." Some—Theodoret details—identified the skin tunics with mortality (*nekrôsis*), which covered Adam and Eve after their fall. This is Origen's view.

Plotinus' disciple, Porphyry, who was also familiar with Origen's thought, displays the same notion of the skin tunic: "We must remove these many garments, both this visible garment of flesh and those inside, which are close to those of skin ... In the Father's temple, that is, this world, is it not prudent to keep pure our last garment, the skin tunic, and thus, with this tunic made pure, live in the Father's temple?"[54] Bernays and Dodds have detected an influence of the Valentinian interpretation of the skin tunics in Genesis 3:21 as fleshy body;[55] in addition to their hypothesis, I would also suspect Origen's influence. Porphyry shares with Origen the idea of a light, invisible body as a vehicle of the soul that can become thicker and visible; this, according to Porphyry, also explains the apparitions of dead persons as visible ghosts.[56] The same explanation is found in Origen's statement that the *augoeides sôma* enables the apparitions of the dead.[57] An inscription dated to the first or the second century from Sabini reads: "the soul always lives, she who provides life and descended from a divine state" and "the body is the tunic of the soul."[58] Obryk admits—rightly, given the brevity and lack of precise textual correspondences—that these expressions "setzen nicht zwangslaüfig eine eingehende Kenntnis der platonischen Schriften voraus."[59] A fragment of Empedocles (fr. 126), mentioned only in passing by Obryk, seems a closer parallel for the second phrase than the Platonic passages that Obryk does discuss.

The doctrine that the soul cannot exist without a body—the opposite of the preexistence of bare souls—is ascribed by Iamblichus, who was acquainted with Origen's ideas, to "the school of Eratosthenes, the Platonist Ptolemy, and other (Platonists)," among whom Origen may be included.[60] These philosophers thought that souls do not receive a body for the first time only when they begin to ensoul the earthly, mortal body, but from the beginning they had "finer" bodies (*leptotera*). This is Origen's position and it is also detected in Plotinus who postulated a *leptoteron* body as a vehicle for the soul,[61] but, unlike Origen, did

[54] *On Abstinence from Killing Animals* 1.31 and 2.46.
[55] Dodds 1963:308.
[56] *On the Cave of the Nymphs* 11; cf. *On Abstinence from Killing Animals* 2.47.
[57] *Against Celsus* 2.60. This explanation is taken up in turn by Gregory Nyssen at *On the Soul and the Resurrection* 88.
[58] Inscription from Sabini E9 Obryk 2012 (IG XIV 2241): ψυχὴ γὰρ ἀείζως, ἥ τὸ ζῆν παρέχει καὶ θεόφιν κατέβη and σῶμα χιτὼν ψυχῆς.
[59] Obryk 2012:137–138.
[60] Proclus *Commentary on the Timaeus* III 234.32–235.9.
[61] *Enneads* III 6.5.

not think that the soul was joined to it from the beginning. Plotinus, like Plato, supported the preexistence of disembodied souls and *metensômatôsis* (expressed by Plato only in myths, as opposed to theoretical discourse), to which Origen opposed *ensômatôsis*.[62] For Plotinus, the soul acquires the light body only during its descent, and later "more earthly (*geôdestera*) bodies," and probably drops off all of these during its reascent.[63] But for Origen, intellectual creatures were provided with a fine body from the beginning and will keep it after the death of the earthly body—which is the same as the risen body as for individual identity—and in the final restoration. Porphyry, who knew both Plotinus and Origen, sided here with Plotinus, thinking that the light body, gathered from the heavenly bodies, is not with the soul from the beginning or forever, but is acquired during the soul's descent[64] and, like the irrational soul, is discarded by the rational soul during its reascent.[65]

The view that the luminous, light body always accompanies the soul—which is also Origen's view—is later represented within Neoplatonism by Iamblichus, Hierocles, and Proclus.[66] Around the time of Origen, both Galen and Alexander of Aphrodisias—both of whom most likely influenced Origen, as I have argued elsewhere[67]—were concerned with the notion of a subtle body as a "vehicle" (*okhêma*) of the soul.[68] Not so distant chronologically, the *Corpus Hermeticum*, too, presents the concept of a subtle, pneumatic body, which functions as the vehicle of the soul.[69] The second-century anonymous author of *On the Life and Poetry of Homer*[70] applies the notion of a subtle, pneumatic body as a vehicle of the soul only to the time subsequent to the death of the mortal body (128). Around the time of Origen, the notion of the luminous, fine body-vehicle was well established. But the question of whether it coexisted with the rational soul from the beginning was debated.

The notion of a luminous, spiritual body as a vehicle of the soul is useful to Origen both to explain the resurrected body and to avoid the idea of the preexistence of disembodied souls. In his view, no creature is completely disembodied

---

[62] Origen's notion of *ensômatôsis* is being analysed fully in a monograph on Origen in preparation.

[63] *Enneads* IV 3.15 and IV 3.24, respectively.

[64] *Sentences* 13.8; *To Gaurus on How Embryos are Ensouled* 11.3.

[65] Proclus *Commentary on the Timaeus* III 234.18–26.

[66] See Finamore 1985:11–27, 167–168, and all of it; Finamore and Dillon 2002; Shaw 2012:91–112; Ramelli 2014a:106–111 and 2015; also Trouillard 1957; Siorvanes 1996:131–133.

[67] For Galen, see Ramelli 2012b:302–350; for Alexander of Aphrodisias, see Ramelli 2014b:237–290.

[68] See chapter 5 above, pp. 49–62, and Ramelli forthcoming (a):chapter 3.

[69] CH X 13.17.

[70] On this work see Ramelli 2004 and 2007:709–820.

and only the Trinity, God the Creator, is incorporeal. Bodies can be separated from rational creatures[71] in theory only:

> If it is absolutely impossible to claim that any other nature besides the Father, the Son, and the Holy Spirit can live without a body, the argument's coherence compels to understand that rational beings were created as the main creation, but the material substance can be separated from them—and can thus appear to be created before or after them—only theoretically and mentally, because they can never have lived, or live, without matter. For only the Trinity can be correctly thought to live without a body ... The material substance, which by nature is capable of being transformed from all into all, when it is dragged to inferior creatures, is formed into a dense and solid body ... but when it serves more perfect and blessed creatures, it shines forth in the splendor of heavenly bodies and adorns with a spiritual body both God's angels and the risen.

Origen On First Principles 2.2.2

This position is reiterated elsewhere, to feature two of the most important examples: "No one is invisible, incorporeal, immutable, beginningless and endless ... but the Father with the Son and the Holy Spirit,"[72] and:

> I cannot understand how so many substances could live and subsist without a body, whereas it is a prerogative of God alone, Father, Son, and Holy Spirit, to live without material substance and any union with corporeal elements. Therefore, one may say that in the end every corporeal substance will be so purified as to be understood as ethereal and endowed with heavenly purity and integrity.

Origen On First Principles 1.6.4

There will be not a destruction of the material substance, but a change of qualities, the transformation of bodies from mortal into spiritual. Origen even deploys a syllogism to argue that no creature can live without a body.[73]

Origen claimed that only the three *arkhai*—the Trinity—are incorporeal. In a similar vein, Porphyry, who knew Origen, maintained that only the three

---

[71] In the case of Origen, *noes* or rational beings are rational creatures in that they are creatures of God, preexisting eternally in God's mind and receiving existence as independent substances when endowed with a spiritual body.

[72] *Homilies on Exodus* 6.5.21–24; cf. *On First Principles* 4.3.15.

[73] *On First Principles* 2.3.2.

arkhai—Plotinus' Triad: One, Intellect, and Soul—are incorporeal.[74] All other beings have bodies: correspondently, gods have ethereal bodies, daemons have aerial bodies, and souls have earthly bodies. Origen is in dialectical relation to, and is debating with, thinkers who—like other "pagan" Neoplatonists and "Gnostics"—posited that rational creatures can live without any body.[75] Origen often claims that rational creatures always need a body: as long as they exist, there has been and there will be matter, for them to make use of the "corporeal garment/tunic" they need as an expression of their freewill and their deserts. This is because they are mutable from their creation onwards: "because of this mutability and convertibility, the rational nature necessarily had to use a corporeal garment of different kind, having this or that quality according to the deserts of rational creatures" (*On First Principles* 4.4.8). Only God, being immutable, does not need a body that changes qualities.

Therefore, rational creatures were endowed with a body from the beginning of their existence, when God created both them and matter, the latter potentially ready for all sorts of transformations (*On First Principles* 4.4.8). Matter was created by God together with rational creatures: "When Scripture states that God created all 'by number and measure', we shall be correct to apply the noun 'number' to rational creatures or minds ... and 'measure' to bodily matter ... These are the things we must believe were created by God in the beginning, before anything else" (*On First Principles* 2.9.1). Bodies were created together with rational creatures, to serve them as vehicles in their movements (according to the instrumental view of the body from the Platonic *Alcibiades I*). God alone does not need any bodily vehicle, being free from alterations.

The existence of material bodies enabled rational creatures to move and diversify their wills. For "there cannot be diversity without bodies."[76] The world became varied when rational creatures began to diversify their wills, departing from the only Good: "the Creator of the universe, receiving all those germs and causes of variety and diversity, according to the diversity of the intellects, that is, rational creatures ... rendered the world varied and diversified."[77] God transformed and diversified the world according to rational creatures' transformations in terms of the choices of their free will. Rational creatures never exist prior to their own bodies and they can be said to exist before the cosmos only in a mystical sense.[78] Origen may allude to their existence in God's *Logos*-Wisdom

---

[74] *To Anebo* 3. On the identification of the three *arkhai* in Origen and in Plotinus/Porphyry and the possible influence of Origen on Porphyry, see Ramelli 2012 and 2015a:155–156.

[75] *On First Principles* 2.3.3: "However, those who believe that rational creatures can live without a body may observe at this point ..."

[76] *On First Principles* 2.1.4.

[77] *On First Principles* 2.9.2.

[78] *Commentary on the Song of Songs* 2.8.4.

before their actual creation as substances. Likewise, the material world was not created only after rational creatures' fall; it was transformed and diversified on account of their sin, but was already there.[79] Indeed, he remarks that the cause, not of the world itself, but of diversity in it, is "the variety and difference of movements and falls of those who have abandoned the initial unity."[80] Before the diversification, the world existed in unity, composed as it was of rational creatures and their immortal bodies. Matter had already been created, for rational creatures to be equipped with their vehicles from the beginning of their existence as substances.

Besides the Latin translation of his *First Principles*, in *Against Celsus* 7.32—a Greek text that reflects Origen's debate with a Middle Platonist—Origen also claims that the soul always needs a body suited to the place/state in which it happens to be, according to its spiritual progress. Souls must always use a body, even after death.[81] That souls have bodies adapted to their spiritual progress is declared by Origen in a number of other passages, e.g.: "A soul that inhabits corporeal places must necessarily make use of such bodies that are suited to the places in which she dwells."[82] Souls can become thicker or finer, depending on their moral choices:

> the soul who sins becomes thicker ... just as sin thickens a soul, so virtue, on the contrary, makes a soul subtle ... the sinner's soul will thicken, and, so to say, will become fleshly ... If a soul thickens to the point of becoming flesh, God's work is to have it consume and to destroy all that which is made of thicker matter and wraps up the soul, so as to erode and erase the fleshly way of thinking, and thus finally recall the soul to the subtle intelligence of the heavenly and invisible things ... We, who have embodied and thickened our own soul ... should exit flesh.

Origen Homily 2 on Psalm 38.8

Since Scripture and the apostolic teaching have left the origin of souls—and their relation to bodies—unclear,[83] Origen declares it necessary to investigate whether the soul is incorporeal, whether it is simple or composed of two, three, or more parts, and whether it is created.[84] Origen refutes both traducianism and

---

[79] Pietras 2009:653–668.

[80] *On First Principles* 2.1.1.

[81] Methodius *On the Resurrection* in Photius *Bibliotheca Codex* 234.301a.

[82] *Commentary on the Psalms* 1 in Pamphilus *Apology for Origen* 141. For a sojourn in heaven, the soul will possess a luminous body; for a sojourn in hell, it will have a body adapted to suffering (*On the Resurrection* 2 in Pamphilus *Apology for Origen* 134; *On First Principles* 2.10.8).

[83] *On First Principles* 1 pref. 5.

[84] *Commentary on the Song of Songs* 2.5.21–22.

the infusion of a soul in a body already formed in the womb. He denies that the soul is created "when the body appears to be molded," because it would be created by necessity, just to animate the body. Here, Origen is obviously speaking of the heavy, mortal body alone.[85] He rejects the creation of the soul after the mortal body as ridiculous, and considers the alternative: "the soul was created long before, and then it must be thought to have assumed a body on account of some cause." This is again the mortal body, not the spiritual body, as is clear from the immediately preceding statement: "every soul in this life is shadowed by the veil of this thick body."[86]

Souls' function is to mediate between intellects and bodies. For Origen, even Christ-*Logos*, who is God's *Logos* and God, like all rational creatures, is endowed with a rational soul, which mediates[87] between God-*Nous* and the human body of Jesus, and between God and the world. Origen describes Christ's soul as "a medium between God and the flesh," that "the *Logos* might become the human being Jesus."[88] This soul was sent by God to receive a human, mortal body from Mary;[89] thus, the incarnate Christ turns out to be "a composite being,"[90] divine and human. This is possible thanks to the mediation of his soul,[91] which provides a link between Christ's divinity and his human body. Christ's soul functions as a mediator between God (God's *Logos*) and the human being Jesus; additionally, since Christ the *Logos* is the Creator, his soul also plays a mediating role between God the Creator and creation itself. Indeed, Christ is said by Origen to be "the mediator between the non-generated nature (*sc.* that of God) and the nature of all generated beings (*sc.* all creatures)."[92] Christ's assumption of humanity, with its mortal body, was voluntary and not the necessary consequence of sin.[93] This soul of Christ is a rational soul, a *logikon*, whose participation in the *Logos* is perfect, whereas the participation of human souls, and even angelic souls, is not. Since this soul is united with the *Logos* in such a perfect way, in a supreme participation with God the Son, they have become one and the same, *hen*.[94] This soul, therefore, is a rational soul so perfect as to be one with the divine *Logos*. All rational creatures, though, are ultimately called to "deification."[95]

---

[85] *Commentary on the Song of Songs* 2.5.23.
[86] *Commentary on the Song of Songs* 2.5.16.
[87] See Ramelli 2011.
[88] *Against Celsus* 2.42.
[89] *Commentary on John* 20.162.
[90] *Against Celsus* 1.66. See Ramelli 2013a.
[91] *On First Principles* 2.6.3.
[92] *Against Celsus* 3.34.
[93] *Against Celsus* 3.14.32.
[94] *Against Celsus* 6.47.
[95] This point is examined in a monograph on Origen in preparation, chapter 2.

Only for the eventual deification did Origen contemplate the possibility that "becoming God" will imply becoming immaterial, like God.[96] But becoming incorporeal in the final deification is one of the two possible alternatives; the other is the preservation of the body, a spiritual body: "even then the corporeal substance will continue to stick to the purest and most perfect spirits, and, transformed into an ethereal state, will shine forth in proportion to the merits and conditions of those who assume it."[97] Origen claims that rational creatures will have and keep a spiritual body in the eventual restoration: "We must believe that all of this corporeal substance of ours will be brought to that state when every being will be restored to be one and the same thing and 'God will be all in all' ... Once all rational souls will have been brought to this condition, then the nature of this body of ours, too, will be brought to the glory of the spiritual body."[98]

Justinian thought that Origen denied the resurrection of the bodies on the grounds of his alleged belief in the preexistence of disembodied souls (*Letter to Mennas* 92). Origen, instead, taught that the risen body will be the same as one's mortal body in its metaphysical substance or form (*eidos*), but with different qualities. In a passage preserved in Greek, surely authentic, in a polemic with a "pagan" Middle Platonist, Origen remarks that Jesus' risen body was the same as his mortal body (in its *eidos*), but with its qualities changed, so as to have no longer the properties of fleshly weakness:

> Matter, the substratum of all qualities (ὑποκειμένην πάσαις ποιότησιν ὕλην), changes its qualities (ἀμείβειν ποιότητας). Therefore, is it not possible that Jesus' flesh, too, has changed its qualities (ἀμείψασαν ποιότητας) and has become such as it was necessary for it to be in order to inhabit the ether and the places even beyond it, without anything more of the fleshly weakness and the characteristics that Celsus called 'too contaminated'?

Origen Against Celsus 3.42

The pre-lapsarian body of rational creatures, too, was similar to Jesus' risen body, and such will human risen bodies be as well, each one keeping its individual continuity with the mortal body.[99] Origen indeed insists again and again that the individual identity will be kept in the passage from one's mortal body

---

[96] *On First Principles* 3.6.1; 2.3.3–5.

[97] *On First Principles* 2.3.7.

[98] *On First Principles* 3.6.6, with references to John 17:21; 1 Corinthians 15:28. On restoration or *apokatastasis*, see Ramelli 2013.

[99] Slaveva-Griffin expressed this difficulty here: if the pre-lapsarian body is similar to Jesus' risen body, how can it keep its individual continuity with the mortal body? Reply: It is similar to Jesus'

to one's risen body. The qualities of the risen body seem to resemble those of the light, immortal body with which rational creatures were initially equipped. What guarantees the continued identity of the body of a rational creature through transformations is an immutable metaphysical form: "each body is endowed with its individual form."[100] The risen body is the same as the mortal body, but with better qualities: "The same metaphysical form (*specimen* [*eidos*]) endures in us from childhood to old age ... and it will remain the same also in the future, though there will be an enormous change into a better and more glorious body ... However, the metaphysical form (*species*) will not be destroyed, although it will turn into more glorious."[101] Indeed, at the resurrection the saints' bodies will be far more glorious than those they had in the present life, "but they will not be other bodies than these."[102] What will be the same in the mortal and in the risen body is for Origen the body's *eidos*, meaning the form as metaphysical principle, in Aristotelian tenor. This view is characteristic of Alexander of Aphrodisias, who was probably known to Origen.[103]

Origen's philosophical notion of the body's *eidos* gave soon rise to misunderstandings. So, it comes as no surprise that Justinian misrepresented Origen's teaching on the resurrection. Just few decades after Origen's death, Methodius understood *eidos*, in his doctrine of the resurrection, as a mere "shape/appearance" (*morphê/skhêma*), not as metaphysical form, whether immanent or transcendent.[104] Thus he offered a mistaken paraphrase of the views of Origen,[105] who, instead, in his treatise *On the Resurrection*, used *eidos* and *logos* to indicate a body's immutable metaphysical form or principle, which remains unaltered at the resurrection and thereby guarantees its individual continuity. This is the same reason for which Origen's theory could not square even with *metensômatôsis*, which provided in turn the ideal foundation for the doctrine of the preexistence of disembodied souls. In the excerpt from Book 2 of Origen's *On the Resurrection* preserved by Pamphilus, *eidos* and *logos* are translated by Rufinus as *ratio*, *ratio substantialis*, and *ratio substantiae*:

> The *logos* (*ratio*) that contains Paul's substance (*substantiam*)—I mean that of Paul's body—endures unaltered ... Now, thanks to that same *logos*

---

body in that it is immortal and incorruptible, not because it assumes the individual characteristics of Jesus' own body or its metaphysical form.

[100] *On First Principles* 2.10.2.

[101] *Commentary on the Psalms 1* in Pamphilus *Apology for Origen* 141.

[102] *Fragments on Luke* fr. 140 on Luke 9:28; cf. Origen *On the Resurrection* 2 in Pamphilus *Apology for Origen* 132.

[103] Arguments for this in Ramelli 2014b, received e.g. by Chiaradonna 2016:334–335, 340.

[104] Methodius *On the Resurrection* in Photius *Bibliotheca Codex* 234.299a–300b.

[105] Argument in a forthcoming work on Origen in preparation.

of the substance (*substantialem rationem*), which endures unaltered, from the dust of the earth the dead are resuscitated from everywhere, because the above-mentioned logos of the corporeal substance (*ratio illa substantiae corporalis*) will have remained in their bodies, which, fallen onto the earth, will be resuscitated by God's will.

Pamphilus Apology for Origen 130

In an excerpt from Origen's *Commentary on Psalms* preserved by Pamphilus and dealing with the preservation of the body's metaphysical form at the resurrection, *eidos* is rendered as *species*.[106] Gregory Nyssen followed Origen—in this as in so many other cases—when claiming that after death the soul keeps a memory of the structure of its body, so as to be able to reconstitute it at the resurrection. Indeed, Origen already maintained that after death the structure or metaphysical form (*eidos*) of the dissolved body, which arguably corresponds to its *logos*, will be retained by the soul.[107] Precisely because Origen thought of rational creatures as always provided with their own body, he included the issue of the risen body and its relation to the earthly body and the soul in his program of investigation into the soul. He will need to explore:

> the question of the essence of the soul, of the principle of its existence, of its joining this earthly body ... whether it is possible that it enters a body for a second time, whether this will happen during the same temporal cycle and the same worldly arrangement, in the same body or in another, and, if it is in the same, whether it will remain identical to itself in its substance, only acquiring different qualities [i.e. Origen's position], or it will change in both its substance and its qualities, and whether the soul will always make use of the same body or it will change.[108]

Origen Commentary on John 6.14.85

Origen's doctrine of *ensômatôsis*, as opposed to "pagan" (and Basilidean) *metensômatôsis*,[109] entailed that the soul will always make use of the same body: the latter will undergo changes in its qualities, but not in its individual identity and substance. The body of each human at resurrection will be turned from psychic into spiritual (that is, no longer serving the soul, but the intellect and

---

[106] *Apology for Origen* 141.

[107] Methodius *On the Resurrection* 3.6.1.

[108] Origen opposes *metensômatôsis* or transcorporation, meaning that a soul enters different bodies, to *ensômatôsis*, incorporation or embodiment, meaning that a soul enters one single body.

[109] Full treatment in a monograph on Origen's philosophical theology, in preparation.

the spirit): "This same body which is called psychic because now it serves the soul (*psukhê*), when the soul, united to God, will become one and the same spirit (*pneuma*) with God,[110] then it too will pass on to the spiritual condition" (*On First Principles* 3.6.6). Origen illustrates the transformation of the mortal body into the risen one by detailing that, as a consequence of death, a transformation occurs, but the substance of the body continues to exist, and by will of its creator at a certain moment will be brought to life again in the same soul and undergo another transformation. Thus, "what first had been earthly flesh will be dissolved by death and reduced to dust and earth, but then it will be taken again out of the earth, and, yet later, according to the deserts of the soul who inhabits it, will progress into the glory of the spiritual body."[111]

Origen, like Gregory Nyssen who was following him, claimed that the risen, spiritual body will be composed of the same four elements as the mortal body. Origen excluded the Aristotelian fifth element, as illustrated not only by a Latin passage, but also by two Greek ones. The passage preserved in Latin is clear: "The Church's faith does not accept the hypothesis of some Greek philosophers that besides this body, which is made of four elements, there exists another, fifth body (*aliud quintum corpus*), which is completely different from this body of ours."[112] In the first Greek passage, Origen refers to, and sides with, the Platonists as those who do not add a fifth element—against the Aristotelians—and maintain that matter always endures, through changes of qualities.[113] This position was embraced by Origen. In the second Greek passage, Origen criticizes Celsus for his doctrine of the transmigration of human souls into animal bodies based on the conviction that the soul alone is God's creature, while bodies have a different nature. He thus observes that Celsus is inconsistent when he declares that the heavenly, aethereal bodies are of a different nature than human and animal bodies—namely, that they are not composed of the same four elements. Origen attacks the Aristotelian doctrine of the fifth element, remarking that it was rejected by both Platonists and Stoics with good reason:

> Celsus will take refuge in Aristotle and the Peripatetics, who maintain that ether is immaterial and represents a fifth nature in addition to the four elements. But both the Platonists and the Stoics refuted this theory with valid arguments. And we (Christian philosophers) too, who are despised by Celsus, will stand against it, requesting him to explain

---

[110] 1 Corinthians 6:17.
[111] 1 Corinthians 15:44; *First Principles* 3.6.5.
[112] *On First Principles* 3.6.6.
[113] *Against Celsus* 4.60.

and interpret the following words of the prophet: 'The skies will be destroyed; You alone will remain.'

Origen *Against Celsus* 4.56

Being composed of the same elements, an aethereal, heavenly body is not different from the body of an animal or any other sublunar bodies, as Origen concludes (*Against Celsus* 4.56). He further investigates the nature of the risen body in *First Principles* 2.10.1–3. At 10.1, he announces he is going to repeat some points of his now lost *On the Resurrection*, because of those who had criticized him in this respect. These may be "Gnostics" who, albeit theorizing *apokatastasis*, denied the resurrection of the body,[114] Christians who misunderstood Origen's doctrine of the resurrection, and "pagan" Neoplatonists who rejected the resurrection of the body as clashing with *metensômatôsis*. The debate between Origen and "Gnostics" (Valentinians) on the resurrection is indeed reflected in the *Dialogue of Adamantius* as well.[115]

As briefly mentioned above, the issue of the soul and its relation to the body was crucial also for "pagan" Neoplatonists, first of all for Plotinus, Origen's fellow disciple. It is well known that Porphyry stalled Plotinus' lectures for three days with questions "about the way in which the soul is in the body."[116] Plotinus never stopped answering. He devoted the treatises that Porphyry collected in the fourth *Ennead* to the soul, its origin, and its union with the body, and criticized Epicurean and Stoic representations of the soul as an aggregate of atoms, without intrinsic unity and stability; he based his argument on the psychology of Plato's *Phaedo* (*Enneads* IV 7.2–4). Porphyry, too—who knew Origen's *On First Principles* and probably his *Commentary on John*—discussed the soul in several works and defended its immortality against the Peripatetic Boethus, but also against Stoic and Epicurean theories.[117] Longinus also devoted a monograph, cited by Eusebius, to the examination of the soul and its preexistence; he too refuted Stoic and Epicurean materialistic notions of the soul.

Gregory of Nyssa did the same in his dialogue *On the Soul and the Resurrection*, which took over Origen's *On the Resurrection* also in the light of Methodius and probably the *Dialogue of Adamantius*, as well as Bardaisan of Edessa—whose anthropology, protology, and eschatology were misunderstood, like Origen's.[118]

---

[114] See Ramelli 2012a:33–45.

[115] See Ramelli 2012–2013; further in Ramelli 2019; a critical edition, commentary and monograph are in preparation.

[116] *Life of Plotinus* 13.10–11.

[117] See his *On the Soul, Against Boethus; To Gaurus on How Embryos are Ensouled*.

[118] Ramelli 2007a, and at least the reviews by Tzamalikos, *Vigiliae Christianae* 62 (2008:515–523); Edwards, *The Journal of Ecclesiastical History* 60 (2009:764–765) and Maspero, *Zeitschrift für antikes Christentum* 15 (2011:592–594). On Gregory's knowledge of at least Bardaisan's work on Fate, on

The misrepresentation of these doctrines of Origen has been facilitated by the Origenistic controversy and the attribution of later radicalized Origenistic theories to Origen himself, but also by virtually all scholars' habit of interpreting Gregory of Nyssa's and Maximus the Confessor's criticism of the doctrine of the preexistence of disembodied souls as a criticism of Origen's theories.[119] This is arguably not the case. After demonstrating elsewhere that Maximus was not attacking Origen,[120] I shall concentrate here on Gregory's criticism and argue that in fact it had different targets. Gregory, probably the most faithful follower of Origen, and one of the most insightful, was aware that Origen never supported the preexistence of disembodied souls. In the passages from Gregory's *On the Soul and the Resurrection* and *On the Creation of the Human Being*, which are usually considered to be criticisms of Origen, Gregory attacks *metensômatôsis* and the preexistence of bare souls, and not Origen's doctrine.

Gregory did not believe in the preexistence of souls to bodies, but very likely neither did Origen. Gregory maintains in *On the Making of Humanity* 28, as well as in *On the Soul and the Resurrection* 121, that a soul does not exist before its body, nor a body before its soul—a view that Origen defended against "pagan" *metensômatôsis*. In both Gregorian texts this discussion is interconnected exactly with a refutation of *metensômatôsis* (*On the Making of Humanity* 28; *On the Soul and the Resurrection* 108), which cannot be a refutation of Origen. In *On the Soul and the Resurrection* 108, the preexistence of souls is ascribed to the same people who supported *metensômatôsis*, and the repeated reference to the loss of the soul's wings points to Plato and Neoplatonism. Far from refuting Origen, Macrina's declaration is in perfect agreement with Origen's ideas:[121]

> we maintain that around the soul there comes to be constituted the same body as before, formed by the harmonic union of the same elements; those people, on the contrary, think that the soul passes on to other bodies, of both rational and irrational beings, and even beings deprived of sense-perception.
>
> Gregory of Nyssen *On the Soul and the Resurrection* 108

---

the misinterpretations of Bardaisan's thought over the centuries, and for a comparison between his thought and Origen's, see Ramelli 2009b:138–142, received by Crone 2012:116–118, Speidel 2012:11–41, and Possekel 2012:515–541.

[119] This habit seems to owe much to Koetschau 1913:102. See pp. 278–284 above.

[120] Ramelli 2013:738–757.

[121] Macrina is the main speaker of the dialogue, playing the role of Socrates in Plato's dialogues. This dialogue by Gregory is a Christian remake of Plato's *Phaedo*: for a nondualistic reading of this dialogue, see Chapter 6 in this volume and Fattal 2016.

The individual identity between the mortal and the risen body, which Macrina supports, was already defended by Origen, as explained above. That both the mortal and the risen body are composed by the same four elements, arranged with different qualities, was also maintained by Origen, as I have pointed out earlier. It seems that the qualities result from the elements' different combinations: if the elements' arrangement changes, the qualities change.

Further, Macrina's reference to the transmigration of human souls into animals and even plants rules out that the target of Gregory's criticism may be Origen. Moreover, in *On the Soul and the Resurrection* 116–117 Gregory describes the soul's fall into a mortal body as a result of the loss of its wings and the concurrence of the soul's own sin and the coupling of two human beings or animals, or even the sowing of a plant by a farmer. This cannot possibly allude to Origen's ideas. The scene of souls that await their incarnation and watch for the birth of baby humans or animals to sneak into their bodies was also ridiculed by Lucretius in *On the Nature of Things* 3.776–781 long beforehand. Gregory may have known his passage, or one can more easily hypothesize an intermediate or a common source. At any rate, the theory, which is already ridiculed by Lucretius, cannot obviously be that of Origen.

What is more, Gregory's reference to those—plural—who have treated the *arkhai* in *On the Making of Humanity* 28 is regularly misunderstood as a specific reference to Origen, but in fact it is a reference to those who deal with protology in general: "Some of those who came before us, who have dealt with the issue of the *arkhai*, thought that souls preexist as a population in a state of their own."[122] Thus, for instance, the discussion *peri arkhôn*, "concerning the principles," in Justin refers to the Stoics and Thales, and has nothing to do with Origen, who lived only after Justin.[123] In Clement, the same treatment *peri arkhôn* refers to Greek philosophers in general: he claims that a mystery concerning the Savior is concealed in the Greeks' theories "in metaphysics and theology."[124] Even if one should take *peri arkhôn* as a title—which is not at all granted—Gregory could well refer to many other works *On First Principles* (*Peri Arkhôn*), such as those by Porphyry or Longinus. Porphyry, who may have been a Christian for a while and surely met Origen and possibly attended his lectures,[125] supported the eternity of the intellect and *metensômatôsis* in his own *Peri Arkhôn*. Porphyry's *First*

---

[122] *On the Making of Humanity* 28: Τοῖς μὲν γὰρ τῶν πρὸ ἡμῶν δοκεῖ, οἷς ὁ περὶ τῶν ἀρχῶν ἐπραγματεύθη λόγος, καθάπερ τινὰ δῆμον ἐν ἰδιαζούσῃ πολιτείᾳ τὰς ψυχὰς προϋφεστάναι λέγειν.

[123] *Apology for Origen* 2.7.8; *Dialogue with Trypho* 7.2. On the genre of περὶ ἀρχῶν in philosophy before and after Origen, see Ramelli 2009.

[124] *Who is the Rich Man Who Will Be Saved?* 26.8; cf. *Stromata* 4.1.2.1; 5.14.140.3.

[125] That he met or frequented Origen is attested by Porphyry himself; that he was initially a Christian is stated by Socrates Scholasticus, see Ramelli 2009.

Principles, like other Middle and Neoplatonic works of this kind, corresponds to Gregory's criticism more closely than Origen's *First Principles*.

Gregory speaks of "some of those before us" (τοῖς μὲν τῶν πρὸ ἡμῶν), and not "one of us" Christians. He means thinkers who supported the transmigration of souls and wrote on the *arkhai*, on protology, and metaphysics: in addition to Plato and other ancient philosophers, he may refer to Plotinus and Porphyry. Both Pythagoras and Empedocles believed in the transmigration of human souls not only into animals, but also into plants. Plato also suggested this in *Timaeus* 91d–92c, but in a mythical form. Plotinus followed Plato in *Enneads* III 4.2, speaking of *metensômatôsis* of humans into animals and plants. He was of course aware that he was commenting on a myth, so his degree of seriousness here is unclear. Moreover, Plotinus discussed the *arkhai* in his *Enneads*,[126] and Porphyry both wrote a *Peri Arkhôn, On First Principles*,[127] and supported *metensômatôsis* and perhaps extended it to animals. Augustine excludes that Porphyry admitted of the transmigration of human souls into animals: "he thought that human souls can fall into humans alone."[128] Aeneas of Gaza attests that Iamblichus and Porphyry rejected a literal reading of Plato's notion of transmigration of human souls into animals, on the grounds that a rational soul cannot become irrational (*Theophrastus* PG 85.893AB). Nemesius *On the Nature of Humanity* 117 Morani (cf. 35 Morani) opposes Iamblichus to Porphyry, ascribing to the former the transmigration of human souls into animal bodies, but not to the latter. But Eusebius, who came earlier and was well acquainted with Porphyry's writings, ascribes to him the opinion that the souls of irrational creatures and those of humans are not different from one another.[129] At least a passage by Porphyry himself seems to posit the transmigration of a human soul into the body of a wolf or a lion.[130] Both Deuse (1983:129–167) and A. Smith (1984) think that Porphyry maintained both a literal and a metaphorical conception of the transmigration of human souls into animal bodies. The metaphorical one seems to me similar to that of Origen, who, however, disavowed the literal one. Later on, Proclus denied that a human soul could be transformed into the soul of an animal, but he

---

[126] Περὶ τῶν τριῶν ἀρχικῶν ὑποστάσεων, *On the Three Hypostases That Are the First Principles*, is the title given by Porphyry—probably under the nonacknowledged inspiration of Origen—to a core section of Plotinus' *Enneads*. See Ramelli 2012; further in a future monograph on Origen's philosophical theology. Every school has its own version of *peri arkhôn*, Origen is not the first one to invent it or to promulgate it; just like Porphyry, he is influenced by his preceding tradition. See Ramelli 2009.

[127] See Ramelli 2009.

[128] *The City of God* X 30: *In solos homines humanas animas praecipitari posse sentiret*. But against this see A. Smith 1984 and Carlier 1998.

[129] Eusebius *Demonstration of the Gospel* I 10.7.

[130] Stobaeus *Anthology* 1.447.19.

admitted that for some time it could be attached to an animal body.[131] According to Olympiodorus, to designate the Platonic doctrine of the transmigration the term *metensômatôsis*, which indicates a change of bodies but a permanence of soul, is to be preferred to *metempsukhôsis*, which rather points to a permanence of body but a change of souls.[132]

Gregory's expression οἱ μὲν τῶν πρὸ ἡμῶν does not refer to Origen, or to any Christian. This is further confirmed by references of the same kind by Christian authors, and Gregory himself, to non-Christians. Origen refers thrice to Philo the Jew in exactly the same terms: "one of those who came before us" (τῶν μὲν πρὸ ἡμῶν ... τις), "some of those who came before us" (*quidam ex his ante nos*), and "some of those who came before us" (τῶν πρὸ ἡμῶν τινες).[133] What is more, Gregory himself elsewhere uses the expression "some of those who came before us" (τῶν πρὸ ἡμῶν τινες) in reference to a non-Christian, Philo, in a passage in which Gregory disagrees with him.[134] Therefore, the phrase οἱ τῶν πρὸ ἡμῶν in *On the Making of Humanity* 28 is likely to indicate non-Christians such as Porphyry, Plotinus, or others, in a passage in which Gregory disagrees with them, rather than indicating Origen as it is generally supposed.

The theory attacked by Gregory in *On the Making of Humanity* 28 that "souls preexisted" (τὰς ψυχὰς προϋφεστάναι) "as a population in a State of their own," and only later received a body as a result of their fall, cannot be that of Origen. It corresponds much better to that of Plato and most "pagan" Neoplatonists, as well as some "Gnostics," and the Manichaeans. The last group are another probable target of Gregory's criticism. Indeed, an attack on Manichaeanism is likely in the parallel passage *On the Soul and the Resurrection* 108 as well, where Gregory rejects *metensômatôsis* because it even forbids eating fruit and vegetables. His criticism of the Manichaean doctrine is explicit later in the text:

> How can what moves derive from the stable nature (of God)? How can the dimensional and composite derive from the simple and non-dimensional nature? ... It is equally absurd to maintain either that the creature comes directly from God's nature, or that all beings have been constituted by some other substance ... because one will introduce a material nature extraneous to the divine substance and made equivalent to the eternity of being, qua ingenerated. *This is exactly what the Manichaeans too have imagined, and some exponents of Greek philosophy*

---

[131] Proclus *Commentary on the Timaeus* III 294.21–295.3.
[132] *Commentary on the Phaedo* 9.6, p. 54 Norvin.
[133] Respectively *Commentary on Matthew* 17.17; *Homily on Numbers* 9.5; *Against Celsus* 7.20.
[134] *Life of Moses* 2.191.

adhered to the same opinions, turning this phantasy/myth into a philosophical doctrine.

Gregory On the Soul and the Resurrection 121–124,
translation and emphasis mine

To the theory of the preexistence of souls, Gregory opposes the doctrine of some who thought that the body exists prior to the soul, which he, like Origen and Pamphilus, abhors because it would make "flesh worthier than the soul." But the preexistence of disembodied souls and the creation of their bodies only afterwards is equally rejected by Gregory as a "myth." This designation suits Gnostic and Manichaean mythology, as well as Plato's myths and their interpretations by "pagan" Neoplatonists.

Indeed, Gregory, far from rejecting Origen's purported preexistence of souls, takes over precisely Origen's own heuristic, zetetic method and arguments to refute this myth. Together with Origen, who rejected it more than once, Gregory refutes the doctrine of the transmigration of a soul through human, animal, and vegetable bodies. The ideas refuted by Gregory in the two passages at stake, including the transmigration of human souls into animal bodies, were repeatedly rejected by Origen himself, as demonstrated earlier. Interestingly, in his *Commentary on Proverbs*, Origen attests that some Christians, too, believed in the transmigration of souls, including the reincarnation of human souls into animals: "It seems to me that the theory according to which souls are transferred from some bodies into others has reached even some of those who apparently believe in Christ ... They thought that a human soul migrates into animal bodies."[135] These Christians might also have been a target of Gregory's criticism in *On the Soul and the Resurrection* and *On the Creation of Humanity*, although the mention of thinkers who have treated the issue of the *arkhai* suggests that he was attacking "pagan" Neoplatonists as well, such as Porphyry or Plotinus, possibly the whole tradition of "pagan" Platonism, Pythagoreanism, and Orphism as the bedrock of the transmigration theory. And, as I have indicated, he also had the Manichaeans in mind. Gregory in *On the Making of Humanity* 28, introducing the whole treatment examined here, states: "Probably, it will not be alien from the focus of our treatment to discuss the issue of the relation between soul and body, which is debated in the churches." Then, he begins to treat the theory of "some of those before us who dealt with the issue of the *arkhai*." Note that it is the mind-body relation that it is said to be debated in the churches, not the specific doctrine that Gregory is going to report afterwards and might be Manichaean and/or 'pagan' Platonist. But even if he related the object of his attack with debates in churches, in case his target

---

[135] Pamphilus *Apology for Origen* 186.

were the Manichaeans, this was an issue certainly discussed in the churches in Gregory's day (and still in Augustine's) and the object of refutations. If the target was Porphyry, he was also discussed in the church: Eusebius refuted him for a Christian audience and others did as well. What is crucial to the present point is that Gregory does not target Origen in his criticism of the preexistence of disembodied souls and their *metensômatôsis*.

In *On the Making of Humanity* 28, Gregory maintains that the soul does not exist before the body, nor the body before the soul:[136] it is pivotal to establish *which* soul and *which* body. In the following chapter (*On the Making of Humanity* 29), he insists that the cause of the constitution of the soul and the body of each human is one and the same. Very probably he means the intellectual soul, i.e. the intellect as the highest faculty of the soul, since Gregory emphasizes the accessorial, adventitious nature of the soul's lower faculties in *On the Soul*. And which body—the mortal body or the fine, incorruptible, spiritual one? Gregory repeats that the totality of humanity began to exist first (*proüphestanai*). What preexisted is humanity, not disembodied souls—Origen would agree. Gregory distinguishes God's plan from the substantial existence of rational creatures, which began at a certain point as a result of God's act of creation. The creation of humanity "at the beginning" further differs from the earthly existence of each human in a given historical time, in which the soul manifests itself gradually along with the growth of the body. Gregory speaks of the development of the faculties of the soul in the child—the same doctrine as Iamblichus, who at the end of the third and the beginning of the fourth century says that this theory had not yet been expressed (indeed, it will be expressed soon by Gregory). In his work *On the Soul*, Iamblichus, after reporting Porphyry's opinion that a baby receives a soul upon its birth, expresses his own as follows:

> Some other opinion might arise, not expressed as yet, that there are very many powers and essential properties of the soul, and that at critical moments, in different ways at different times, when the body that is coming into being is suited to do so, it partakes first of the vegetative life, then of sensation, then of the appetitive life, then of the rational soul, and lastly of the intellectual soul.
>
> Iamblichus On the Soul 31, 381 Wachsmuth,
58.10-21 Finamore–Dillon[137]

In fact, this doctrine of the gradual development of the faculties of the soul was upheld by the Stoics (SVF II 83), though within an immanentistic context.

---

[136] Cf. *On the Soul* 121.
[137] The translation is according to Finamore and Dillon 2002.

Gregory took it over in a transcendent framework, but he never states that the intellectual soul comes into existence at the same time as the *mortal* body.

The soul is defined by Gregory as "created, living, and intellectual substance, which by itself infuses a faculty of life and of apprehension of sense-perceptible objects into an instrumental body equipped with organs of sense-perception, as long as the nature that can receive these faculties subsists," i.e. as long as the mortal body is alive.[138] This definition, which has many parallels in Middle and Neoplatonism,[139] stands if the soul is regarded as created *before/outside time*. This would dissolve the contradiction raised by the perishability axiom, which arises if the body with which the soul is said by Gregory to be originated is understood as the *mortal* body. Gregory, like Basil in his *Hexaëmeron*—to which Gregory offers a continuation—is well aware of that axiom, which was regarded as rooted in Plato.[140] Basil cited it in *Hexaëmeron* 1.3: "the beings that had *a beginning in time* will necessarily have *an end in time* as well."[141] Gregory knew this axiom and, like Origen, applied it to the world: if it is created in time, it will necessarily have an end (*On the Making of Humanity* 23). He even deems the perishability axiom to be grounded in Scripture.[142]

Now, when Gregory states that the soul is created at the same time as the body, if he means the *mortal* body, this would imply that the soul is created in time and thus is not immortal. This, indeed, is Norris's conclusion from Gregory's thesis that the soul is created together with the body: "Nyssen rejects not only the doctrine that the soul is everlasting, but also the view that the individual soul comes into existence apart from its body"—for Norris understands this "body" as mortal.[143] If Gregory indeed meant that the (intellectual) soul is created with the mortal body, this would give rise to a flat contradiction. Gregory, however, does *not* say that the body at stake is the mortal one. I suspect his reticence is intentional, since he was aware of the problem entailed by the perishability axiom and knew Origen's and Pamphilus' position in this respect.

---

[138] *On the Soul* 29B GNO 3/3.15.6–9: Οὐσία γεννητή, οὐσία ζῶσα, νοερά, σώματι ὀργανικῷ καὶ αἰσθητικῷ δύναμιν ζωτικὴν καὶ τῶν αἰσθητῶν ἀντιληπτικὴν δι᾽ ἑαυτῆς ἐνιεῖσα, ἕως ἂν ἡ δεκτικὴ τούτων συνεστήκῃ φύσις. Analysis in Ramelli 2016a. *Gennêtos* was used by Plato *Timaeus* 28b–c, well known to Gregory, to indicate the cosmos, created by the Demiurge outside time.

[139] Alcinous *Handbook of Platonism* 117 Hermann = 49 Whittaker; Plotinus *Enneads* IV 7 on the soul as generated and of intellectual nature, see pp. 260 above and 311 below; the authentic human being coincides with the (rational) soul; Iamblichus *On the Soul* in Stobaeus *Anthology* 1.362 Wachsmuth.

[140] Philoponus *Against Proclus On the Eternity of the World* 17 refers to *Republic* 546a; *Phaedrus* 245d. See also Krausmüller 2009:48 and further arguments in my review of the book in *Bryn Mawr Classical Review*, September 2010.

[141] My translation, as ever, unless otherwise stated.

[142] Wisdom 7:1–18; PG 45.796BC.

[143] Norris 1963:28.

Pamphilus (*Apology for Origen* 168–170) had made extensive use of the perishability axiom precisely in defense of Origen's doctrine of the origin of the *logika*. After observing (166) that in the Church there were different opinions on the origin of the soul, and after rejecting, on the basis of theodicy, that of the simultaneous creation of soul and mortal body (167), he rejects traducianism as well, and invokes the perishability axiom against both theories: the intellectual soul "will necessarily die together with the body, and will necessarily be mortal if it was sown, formed, or born at the same time as the body" (*si simul cum corpore vel seminata vel formata vel nata est*, 168), clearly the mortal body. Souls "will necessarily corrupt along with bodies, if they also have the same origin as bodies and at the same time as bodies, according to their same *logos* or constitutive principle" (*si eandem cum corporibus etiam originem sumunt secundum ipsorum rationem*, 170). Pamphilus obviously means *intellectual* souls, as is clear from the following passage:

> [Origen] admits that all souls are of one and the same substance, both immortal and rational (*et immortales et rationabiles*) ... created by God. But when they were created, all at the same time at the beginning (*olim simul*) or now every time a person is born (*aut nunc per singulos nascentium*), why should we take the risk of adhering to either opinion?
>
> Pamphilus *Apology for Origen* 171

In *Apology for Origen* 172, too, Pamphilus remarks that, since there is no doctrine on the origin of the soul "in the apostolic preaching," as Origen had already underlined, one cannot dub "heretics" those who have different opinions in this respect.[144]

The perishability axiom stands if Gregory meant that the soul is created together with a *spiritual* body, the one the human being had before the fall and will recover at the resurrection, and which became mortal only after the fall. This is suggested also by Gregory's statement in one of his last works:

> In the large house of God, the Apostle says, some vases are made of gold or silver; with this, I think, he meant the *created, intelligent, and incorporeal*[145] substance. Other vases, on the other hand, are of wood or clay— and with this, I think, he means us (i.e. humans), *who have been made earthy and of clay as a consequence of our disobedience*. The sin, committed

---

[144] So also *Apology Sent to Anastasius* 6.

[145] It must always be taken into account that Gregory, like Clement, Origen, and other Christian Platonists, uses the terms "corporeal" and "incorporeal" in a relative way. Specific work is being devoted to this essential point.

by means of a piece of wood, made us *wooden vases, while we formerly were golden vases.* And the use of the vases is different *according to the dignity of their matter.* ... But a certain vase can, by its free will, *become a golden vase, from wooden,* or a silver vase, from clay.

> Gregory *Homily 7 on the Song of Songs,*
> my translation and emphasis

Like Origen, Gregory refers to the passage of rational creatures from one order to another; even the Pauline vases metaphor is the same as that which Origen used in *First Principles* 3.6.6 to differentiate the mortal body from the spiritual, pre-lapsarian (and risen) body. Rational creatures' bodies are transformed according to their moral choices. They all had luminous, spiritual bodies before the fall, but these were transformed into mortal or demonic bodies on account of sin—something that Evagrius too, a disciple of Nyssen, stressed.[146] But after the elimination of sin, these bodies too will be angelic again, as they were in the beginning.

Importantly, this reading is confirmed by Anastasius of Sinai, who attests that both Gregory Nyssen and Nazianzen, whom he calls "divine Gregories," believed that "Adam had a body that was incorruptible, immortal, and more immaterial"; this "was turned by God into a body that is liable to passion and denser."[147] This doctrine is likely to have been misrepresented by Barsanuphius of Gaza, who ascribes the theory of the preexistence of souls to both Nazianzen and Nyssen.[148] Still in the late fifteenth *Homily on the Song of Songs,* Gregory revisits Plato's myth of the fall of the soul's wings, ruling out *metensômatôsis,* as Origen did. After establishing, on the basis of Matthew 23:37, that Scripture teaches that "in the nature of God there are wings," he goes on to consider that the human being was made in the image of God; "therefore, the one who was created according to the image also had the likeness to the Archetype in every respect," referring to the first creation of the human being, before the fall.

> But, according to Scripture, the Archetype of human nature has wings: as a consequence, *our nature, too, was created winged,* so as to have its likeness to God also in its wings ... Wings means power, beatitude, *incorruptibility,* and the like. Thus, the human being, too, *possessed these qualities, as long as it was completely similar to God,* while *subsequently the inclination towards evil deprived us of those wings.* When we left the protection of God's wings, we were *despoiled of our own wings.* For this reason, God's

---

[146] See Ramelli 2015b; further, in-depth treatment in a study on Origen in preparation.
[147] *Sermon II: On the Constitution of Humankind after the Image of God* 3.
[148] *Against the Doctrines of the Origenists* (PG 86.891–902).

grace was revealed and illuminated us, that we could *reject impiety and worldly desires,* and could *put on our wings again* by means of holiness and justice.

Gregory of Nyssa Homily on the Song of Songs 15

A rational creature, *nous* and immortal, incorruptible body, it seems here, existed before the fall and will be recovered at the final resurrection-restoration.

We have thus seen that the relation of Gregory Nyssen's ideas about the interaction of bodies and souls and the creation of rational beings to Origen's ideas on this matter is probably slightly different from how it is generally represented. He is regularly misunderstood as criticizing Origen's supposed doctrine of the preexistence of disembodied souls in *On the Soul and the Resurrection* and *On the Making of Humanity*, whereas Gregory is described as the advocate of the simultaneous creation of the soul and its mortal body. I have suggested that, just as Origen probably never supported the doctrine of the preexistence of disembodied souls, neither did Gregory likely maintain that each soul comes into being at the same time as its *mortal* body. There are many hints to this end, not last Gregory's awareness of the Platonic perishability axiom.

The Soul-Body Relation in Augustine's Early Works

Lenka Karfíková

Abstract: In his early works, which preceded his consecration as a priest in 390, Augustine seems to combine the Platonic idea of human being identical with its soul and the Aristotelian anthropology regarding human being as a composite of soul and body (accessible to him through Varro, Celsus, and Cicero). The chapter traces the problems related to this question including the impassibility of soul as known from Plotinus (*Enneads* III 6). In comparison to the Cassiciacum dialogues (386), where Augustine understood the body more or less as an obstacle to the true purpose of man, which is contemplation, we can see a certain shift in his works in the period between 387 and 390. Augustine appreciates the ambivalence of the relationship between the body and the soul. The body, naturally subordinate to the soul and a true object of its action, became the soul's victim rather than its prison. The right order has been violated by the soul, which wrenched itself free from God's control because of its desire to be autonomous, or its excessive enjoyment of corporeal things.

IN HIS ACCOUNT OF CHRISTIAN morals against the Manichaeans, Augustine presents several possibilities for understanding the union of the body and the soul in a human being, presumably taken over from Varro's lost treatise *On Philosophy*: as a union of two parts in one whole (such as, for example, a two-horse chariot or a centaur); as the soul alone, which uses the body (in the way a rider uses a horse); or, on the contrary, as the body alone, which is used by the soul (in the way a "lamp" is what we call the vessel alone, not necessarily the vessel with a fire, although it is designed for a fire).[1] Unlike in his later work *The City of God*, where—in Varro's footsteps—he opts for the first alternative mentioned above,[2] in this passage of his anti-Manichaean polemic, Augustine deliberately refrains from preferring one over the other.[3] Elsewhere in the same book, however, he says that: "a human being, as he appears to a human being, is a rational soul using a mortal and earthly body."[4] This definition probably corresponds to the metaphor of a rider using a horse[5] in the list given above, and that is why the passage seems to indicate that a human being is the soul alone, even though the soul is somehow related to the body. The phenomenological supplement in Augustine's definition, "a human being, as he appears to a human being" (*homo, ut homini apparet*), defines the role of the vulnerable and mortal body as a medium of the appearance of the soul, and an ambivalent one, as we will see.

In this chapter, I will deal with the issue of the soul-body relationship in Augustine's early works; that is, works that preceded his consecration as a priest in 390. This issue shows nicely that in Augustine's thinking, the influences of Varro, whom Augustine knew from his youth,[6] of Cornelius Celsus, to whom he referred at that time as well,[7] and of the omnipresent Cicero, complement his fascination with the "books of the Platonists" (i.e. "a small number of treatises by Plotinus," as he also calls them)[8] to form a not quite unequivocal conception, in which Neoplatonic elements prevail. It is only gradually, although prominently even in these early years, that biblical motifs begin to assert themselves in Augustine's idea of the relationship between the soul and the body.

---

[1]   *On the Morals of the Catholic Church and on the Morals of the Manichaeans* I 4.6 (CSEL 90.8–9). For a reference to Varro's treatise in the same context, see Augustine *The City of God* XIX 1 (CCSL 48.657).

[2]   See *The City of God* XIX 3 (CCSL 48.662).

[3]   *On the Morals* I 4.6 (CSEL 90.9).

[4]   *On the Morals* I 27.52 (CSEL 90.52): *Homo igitur, ut homini apparet, anima rationalis est mortali atque terreno utens corpore.*

[5]   See also *On Order* II 6.18 (BA 4.2.214–216).

[6]   *On Order* II 20.54 (BA 4.2.324). See also Cipriani 1996:369–400. Varro's anthropology was probably influenced by the Aristotelianism of his teacher Antiochus of Ascalon (on his anthropological ideas, see Pépin 1971:115–126).

[7]   *Soliloquies* I 12.21 (CSEL 89.33). The quotation from Cornelius Celsus given here begins as follows: *Nam quoniam duabus partibus compositi sumus, ex animo scilicet et corpore ...* See also Hagendahl 1967:34 (*test.* 43). Celsus was an encyclopedist, similar to Varro in many respects; according to Quintilian (*Institutes of Oratory* X 1.124), he was influenced by the philosophy of the "Sextians"—a mixture of Neo-Pythagoreanism and Roman Stoicism; see Barwick 1948:119. In another passage, Augustine says that this author collected information about several philosophical schools in the form of a doxographic text (*To Quodvultdeus, On Heresies* praef. 5 [CCSL 46.288]). On this philosopher, see also Wellmann 1900.

[8]   *Confessions* VIII 2.3 (CCSL 27.114), VII 9.13 (CCSL 27.101); *On the Happy Life* 1.4 (BA 4.1.58).

1. Liberation from the Body

Despite Augustine's assurance that a human being is fundamentally both the soul and the body (for example, in his *On the Happy Life* in which he and his relatives and friends were engaged on the day of his thirty-second birthday),[9] his statements in his early works resemble in many respects the Neoplatonic notion of the true self, which is the soul.[10] According to the Neoplatonists, too, the soul looks after the body, but it is to carry out this duty while turned entirely towards the Intellect—incidentally, as it were (this is best exemplified by the World Soul; its care for the body of the universe is, therefore, flawless).[11] The turning of the individual soul to the body that it looks after can be regarded as an unpropitious alternative preventing the soul from turning towards the divine, and as such, it is "a sin" (*hamartia*).[12] Whether the descent of the soul into the body is a consequence of the soul's wrongdoing or rather a duty which it fulfills for the welfare of the body remains an open question for the Neoplatonic authors.[13]

Augustine's dialogue *Against the Academics*, his oldest extant work, even features Platonic metaphors of the body as a "stain" (*corporis labes*)[14] or "a prison" of the soul, and not merely in the sense of "a guard post" (*throura*) from Plato's *Phaedo* (62b4), but literally in the sense of "a dark prison house" (*tenebrosus carcer*) that prevents the soul from learning the truth.[15] Although these remarks are uttered by the young Licentius, with whom Augustine probably does not identify entirely, Augustine explicitly avows his affinity with Platonism (regarding Platonism, revived by Plotinus,[16] not only as a philosophy compatible with Christianity, but also as a way of explicating Christian teachings by means

---

[9] According to *On the Happy Life* 2.7 (CCSL 29.68), a human being consists of a body and a soul and is aware of both, but real beatitude is to be sought in the soul, and a wise man, who has achieved it, is not bothered by the needs of the body; see *On the Happy Life* 4.25 (CCSL 29.78–79).

[10] This tradition is based on the *Alcibiades I* (130c), where Plato's authorship is arguable (but it is in fact a logical implication of Plato's philosophy). See also e.g. Plotinus *Enneads* IV 7.1 and pp. 260 and 304 above. On the issue of what a human being is, see also *Enneads* I 1; on the question of "who we are" (which cannot be answered easily because we are "many things"), cf. *Enneads* I 1.9.7; also VI 4.14.16–26, IV 3.27.2, IV 4.18.10–15, I 1.7.14–17.

[11] Plotinus *Enneads* IV 8.2, IV 3.12.11–14; Porphyry *Sentences* 30.5 Brisson.

[12] Plotinus *Enneads* IV 8.4.12–31; Porphyry *Sentences* 30.11–19 Brisson.

[13] The term *hamartia* is used in this connection by Plotinus (*Enneads* IV 8.5.16). For a different concept, however, cf. *Enneads* III 9.3.1–2 and I 1.12.24–27. On this aporia, see Bréhier 2008:78–82. As Plotinus himself points out (*Enneads* IV 8.1.23–50), not even Plato gives a clear answer to this question: see *Phaedo* 62b3–6 and 67c6–d2; *Phaedrus* 246b6–c6 and 248c5–8; *Cratylus* 400c1–10; *Republic* 514a2–b6, 619d1–7; *Timaeus* 34a8–35a1.

[14] *Against the Academics* I 4.11 (CCSL 29.10); cf. *Phaedo* 66b5–6.

[15] *Against the Academics* I 3.9 (CCSL 29.8); cf. *Cratylus* 400c1–10; *Phaedo* 65a–67b; *Enneads* IV 8.2.42–45.

[16] *Against the Academics* III 18.41 (CCSL 29.59–60).

of reason).[17] He goes on to state that according to these philosophers, wisdom, which in the true sense pertains to God, cannot be achieved in this life, even in one dedicated to philosophy, but only after the soul has been separated from the body, "when you cease to be a human being" (*cum homo esse desieris*).[18]

What we truly are, therefore, is not a temporary union of the soul and the body, but the soul alone. As he makes clear in *On Order*, the soul must withdraw into itself in order for a man to know what he truly is;[19] he who is only concerned with objects of sensory perception is not in the real sense "with himself" (*secum*).[20] Augustine dares to say about his own mother that: "because of her age" (Monica was slightly above fifty at that time) "or because of an admirable balance," her soul has not only freed itself from follies, but it also "extricates itself from the defilement of the body and in many respects has reached itself."[21]

It follows that the philosophical program of knowing oneself must include turning away from the sensible world, as *Ratio* itself explains to Augustine in his *Soliloquies*; later, however, in his *Retractations*, Augustine will rebuke the *Ratio* for such an extreme promotion of Porphyry's maxim.[22] The light of the truth will not illuminate those who remain "imprisoned in this cage" (*in hac cavea inclusis*) until their wings disengage themselves from the "glue" (*viscum*) of sensible things and become free from finding delight in those things.[23] Similarly, Augustine emphasizes in a letter to his correspondent Nebridius that one must turn away from the senses because even though a human being consists of both soul and body, the soul is better mainly because of the part that contains true forms, i.e. *mens* or *intellegentia*.[24]

As we have seen in his earliest works from his holiday in Cassiciacum in 386, Augustine does not understand the concept of a human being as a union of soul and body in terms of a rider using a horse, but rather in terms of a caged bird.[25] The body does not seem to be of any use to the soul at all; it even prevents the soul from gaining knowledge. In his correspondence with Nebridius, Augustine uses the metaphor of a "vehicle" (*vehiculum*), although not for the material body,

---

[17] *Against the Academics* III 20.43 (CCSL 29.61); cf. *Retractations* I 1.4 (CCSL 57.10).

[18] *Against the Academics* III 9.20 (CCSL 29.46); cf. *Enneads* V 8.7.33–35.

[19] *On Order* I 1.3 (BA 4.2.74): ... *homo sibi ipse est incognitus. Qui tamen ut se noscat, magna opus habet consuetudine recedendi a sensibus et animum in se ipsum conligendi atque in se ipso retinendi.*

[20] *On Order* II 2.5 (BA 4.2.174).

[21] *On Order* II 17.45 (BA 4.2.294–296): ... *cuius animum vel aetate vel admirabili temperantia remotissimum ab omnibus nugis et a magna labe corporis emergentem, in se multum surrexisse cognosco.*

[22] *Soliloquies* I 14.24 (CSEL 89.37): ... *penitus esse ista sensibilia fugienda.* Cf. *Retractations* I 4.3 (CCSL 57.15); Porphyry *Letter to Marcella* 8.12, 32.2, 34.2–3; probably also Porphyry *On the Return of the Soul*; Augustine *The City of God* X 29 (CCSL 47.305). See J. J. O'Meara 1969:128–130.

[23] *Soliloquies* I 14.24 (CSEL 89.37). On this metaphor and its Platonic background, see Courcelle 1975:381–393.

[24] *Letters* 3.4 (CSEL 34.1.8).

[25] On the caged bird metaphor, see pp. 116–119 and 138 above.

but for "a body or kind of body" (*veluti perpetuo quodam corpore vel quasi corpore*),[26] which, according to some authors, constantly accompanies the soul and makes it possible for the soul to move from one place to another;[27] it is not clear to Augustine whether such a body exists at all, but his aim is to clarify the fact that it cannot be truly intelligible if it is to be located in a place.[28] Also, it is probably a body consisting of more layers that Licentius hints at in *Against the Academics* when he says that the mind must be released from all "corporeal covers" (*involucra corporis*).[29]

The issue of a soul that does not move, although it moves the body, also appears in Licentius' exposition in *On Order*. Augustine's young disciple seems to employ the expression "sage" (*sapiens*) to refer to the higher soul, constantly turned towards God; in this life, it unites with the body and the lower soul, which possesses, *inter alia*, sensory perception and memory.[30] Augustine himself, from whom Licentius had learned about this teaching,[31] is no longer satisfied with it and tries to explain that a "sage" consists of the whole soul and also of the body (*non solum ex corpore et anima, sed etiam ex anima tota constare sapientem*).[32] This self-revision (or "first retractation"),[33] however, does not entail a rejection of the Neoplatonic anthropology, even though Augustine expresses several reservations in this respect (for example, he cannot believe that the soul, after it has departed the body, forgets everything it learned during its corporeal life).[34]

Augustine's interpretation of the Stoic (and Cicero's) definition of a human being as a "rational mortal animal" (*animal rationale mortale*) as he presents it in *On Order*, is very symptomatic.[35] Both differences in the definition, which distinguish a human being from animals as well as gods, respectively, are regarded

---

[26] *Letters* 13.2 (CSEL 34.1.30). In Porphyry *Sentences* 29 Brisson, we can find references to *pneuma*, which accompanies the soul and is created from individual spheres, but not a "vehicle." The *pneuma*, unknown to Plotinus, was identified in later Neoplatonists with a "pneumatic vehicle"; see Pépin 2005:593. On the gradual crystallization of this notion in the Platonic Academy, see Dillon 2009:349–356 and pp. 53–56 above. On this theme in Augustine, see Bermon 2011:587–595.

[27] *Letters* 13.3 (CSEL 34.1.31): ... *ita nescio quid illud, de quo quaerimus, corpus, quo inniti anima, ut de loco ad locum transeat*.

[28] *Letters* 13.3–4 (CSEL 34.1.31). On the dating of *Letters* 13 to the Cassiciacum period, see Goldbacher 1923:12; Bermon 2011:220–222.

[29] *Against the Academics* I 8.23 (CCSL 29.16): ... *cum ab omnibus involucris corporis mentem quantum potest evolvit et se ipsum in semet ipsum colligit*. On this "striptease of the soul," see Pépin 1954:300–306.

[30] *On Order* II 6.18–19 (BA 4.2.216–220); II 2.6 (BA 4.2.176–178); cf. *Enneads* IV 3.25.35–45.

[31] *On Order* II 2.7 (BA 4.2.178).

[32] *On Order* II 2.6 (BA 4.2.176).

[33] See Guitton 1933:201.

[34] *Soliloquies* II 20.36 (CSEL 89.97–98); cf. *Enneads* IV 3.27, IV 3.32, IV 4.1.

[35] *On Order* II 11.31 (BA 4.2.254–256). Similarly, also *On the Magnitude* 25.47 (CSEL 89.190); cf. Cicero *On Academic Skepticism* II 7.21; Quintilian *Institutes of Oratory* V 10.56.

by Augustine as a reference to the double movement of the soul: its descent to mortal things and its possible "return" (*regressus*) to *ratio*.[36]

The Neoplatonic ideal of turning away from the body and sensuality also corresponds to Augustine's soteriology in his Cassiciacum period, which is concerned less with the salvation of man as a union of soul and body, than with the salvation of the soul from the "burden of the body" and its return into the heavenly home.[37] It will be possible one day to dispose of the body, which is now used for sensory perception and thus distracts the soul from more substantial knowledge; with the body, we will also dispose of all the trouble caused by the body (*multas molestias corporis*). In that way Augustine explains that faith and hope are still necessary in this life, even though perhaps it is possible to know God and thus attain beatitude while this life lasts.[38]

Naturally, Augustine knows that in His kindness to mankind, the supreme God had "the authority of the divine Intellect descend into the human body." The aim of this rescue action was to call the souls not only with a word, but also with an act, so that they could "return to themselves and into their homeland."[39] Similarly to his Neoplatonic predecessors, Augustine describes the union of the soul and the Intellect with a metaphor of wedlock in which philosophical love enables the soul, educated in the liberal arts and beautiful through its virtue, not only to overcome death, but also to enjoy a beatific life.[40]

In Augustine's earliest works, we can thus trace an urgent need to turn away from the body and, in this respect, to liberate oneself, rather than an account of how the soul is united with the body. The duality of this issue is expressed succinctly in one of Porphyry's *Sentences*: "What nature has bound together, that nature may loose, and what soul has bound together, that it itself may loose; but nature has bound body in soul, while soul has bound itself in body. It

---

[36] *On Order* II 11.31 (BA 4.2.256). On the Porphyrian inspiration of this account, see J. J. O'Meara 1958:104; I. Hadot 1984:106. At the same time, however, Doignon (1997:257n151) points out similarities to Cicero (cf. *Cato the Elder on Old Age* 21.77, *An Exhortation to Philosophy* fr. 115 Grilli = 102 Straume-Zimmermann (= Augustine *On the Trinity* XIV 26).

[37] *Against the Academics* II 1.2 (CCSL 29.19): ... *rursus proiecto totius corporis onere recurret in coelum*. On the notion of the expected "return" to heaven (*rediturus in caelum*), see also *Against the Academics* II 9.22 (CCSL 29.30) and *Retractations* I 1.9 (CCSL 57.9–10).

[38] *Soliloquies* I 7.14 (CSEL 89.22–23).

[39] *Against the Academics* III 19.42 (CCSL 29.60): ... *cui* (scil. *intellegibili mundo*) *animas multiformibus erroris tenebris caecatas et altissimis a corpore sordibus oblitas nunquam ista ratio subtilissima revocaret, nisi summus deus populari quadam clementia divini intellectus auctoritatem usque ad ipsum corpus humanum declinaret atque submitteret, cuius non solum praeceptis, sed etiam factis excitatae animae redire in semet ipsas et resipiscere patriam, etiam sine disputationum concertatione potuissent*. On the motif of the homeland of souls, see *Enneads* I 6.8.16–21 (cf. *Iliad* 2.140), but also Ambrose of Milan *Isaac* 8.78 (CSEL 32.1.698). A similar idea can be found in the lines of Philippians 3:20 and Hebrews 11:13–16.

[40] *On Order* I 8.24 (BA 4.2.128); cf. Doucet 1995:231–252.

is nature, therefore, that releases body from soul, but soul releases itself from body" (*Sentences* 8).[41]

Porphyry was intensely interested in not only the Neoplatonic moral and spiritual program of the unbinding of the soul from the body, but also the work of "nature"; i.e. how the soul is united with the body, and how the soul affects the body or is affected by it.[42] Augustine goes on to address these issues shortly after his return to Milan from his holiday in Cassiciacum in his outline *On the Immortality of the Soul* and later on, in Rome, in *On the Magnitude of the Soul*.

2. The Soul Acting upon the Body

In his *On the Immortality of the Soul*—an attempt at proving the immortality of the soul on the basis of its relationship to *ratio*, which, too, is immortal—Augustine first and foremost rejects the notions of the soul as a mere accident (color or shape) or a balance of elements in the body (*temperantia*),[43] or an "inseparable harmony" of the body.[44] The soul may turn away from the body towards thinking,[45] in which it is not aided by the body ("it is enough when the body does not hinder it"),[46] and, therefore, is independent of it. The soul moves the

---

[41] *Sentences* 8 Brisson: ὃ ἔδησεν ἡ φύσις, τοῦτο φύσις λύει, καὶ ὃ ἔδησεν ἡ ψυχή, τοῦτο αὐτὴ λύει· ἔδησε δὲ φύσις μὲν σῶμα ἐν ψυχῇ, ψυχὴ δὲ ἑαυτὴν ἐν σώματι. φύσις μὲν ἄρα λύει σῶμα ἐκ ψυχῆς, ψυχὴ δὲ ἑαυτὴν λύει ἀπὸ σώματος; hereinafter translation is according to Dillon 2005. On the way in which the soul "binds" itself in body, see *Sentences* 7 Brisson: ψυχὴ καταδεῖται πρὸς σῶμα τῇ ἐπιστροφῇ τῇ πρὸς τὰ πάθη τὰ ἀπ' αὐτοῦ καὶ λύεται δὲ πάλιν διὰ τῆς ἀπαθείας ("A soul binds itself to body through directing its attention towards the affections which derive from it, and is freed from it, in turn, through [the achievement of] impassibility." On *Sentences* 7 and 8, see also pp. 139–140 above.

[42] As Porphyry says, he spent three whole days discussing the issue with Plotinus (*Life of Plotinus* 13.10–12), and he himself returned to it several times; see *Miscellaneous Questions* fragments 259–261 Smith, *Sentences* 33.44–59 and 35.19–24 Brisson; see also *To Gaurus on How Embryos are Ensouled* 10.5 (Dorandi 174–176) and 12.1–3 (Dorandi 180–182) for the question of the union of the soul with the embryo. On the problem of the union of the soul with the body, cf. also *Enneads* VI 4.4–8 passim, and IV 3.20–23.

[43] *On the Immortality of the Soul* 10.17 (CSEL 89.118–119). The expression *temperatio* appears in Cicero's account of the opinion of the soul maintained by Pherecrates of Phthia, who also regarded this force as inseparable from the body (*Tusculan Disputations* I 10.21). The notion of the soul as a "mixture" of corporeal elements is challenged by Plotinus as well (cf. *Enneads* IV 7.8⁴).

[44] *On the Immortality of the Soul* 2.2 (CSEL 89.102). The concept of the soul as a harmony of the body was already rejected by Plato (*Phaedo* 86b9–c1), where it is introduced by Simmias, a disciple of the Pythagorean scholar Philolaus (61d6–7), which might be the reason why it was later regarded as a Pythagorean teaching; it was not supported by Aristotle either (*On the Soul* 407b30–33).

[45] *On the Immortality of the Soul* 10.17 (CSEL 89.119); very similarly also *Sentences* 41.13–14 Brisson and *Miscellaneous Questions* fr. 259F.141–147 Smith.

[46] *On the Immortality of the Soul* 1.1 (CSEL 89.102). The idea of the body as an obstacle to thinking, which is independent of the body, can be found in Plato (see *Phaedo* 66b–d); similarly *Enneads* I 8.4, II 9.17.1–10, IV 8.2.42–45.

body without changing itself,[47] and, above all, it gives the body the form on which the body depends in terms of the measure of its being and in its being as such. The soul obtains this form from "eternal reasons"; it is on these reasons that the soul depends in its being and in the measure of its being.[48] It is not bound to the body spatially (*non localiter iungitur*);[49] it is not localized in the body, but it is present in all its parts (*tota singulis partibus simul adest*)[50] because "the whole soul perceives what a certain part of the body suffers (*passionem*) even if not in the whole body."[51] (Like Plotinus, Augustine rejects the Stoic idea of an impulse passed through the body by means of a local transmission, i.e. a series of "messengers."[52]) Despite its ontological superiority and independence, the soul turns towards the body with interest and desire, but it is still capable of keeping some distance ("asking itself" about its relationship to the body).[53] It

[47] *On the Immortality of the Soul* 3.3 (CSEL 89.103–104). Augustine's idea of the soul which does not move itself but moves the body is certainly closer to that of Aristotle than to the Platonic tradition. Aristotle, too, maintained that the soul moves the body (*On the Soul* 407b17–19) without moving itself (*On the Soul* 405b31–406a2, 408b30–31), i.e. is not self-moved, unlike in Plato (*Phaedrus* 245c5–9) or Cicero (*Tusculan Disputations* I 22–23.53).

[48] *On the Immortality of the Soul* 15.24 (CSEL 89.125f). On the role of the soul as a medium between the intelligible and the sensible worlds, see Plato *Timaeus* 34b–37c, *Phaedrus* 230a3–6; Plotinus *Enneads* IV 7.13, IV 8.7.1–8, IV 3.12.30–35; Porphyry *Sentences* 5.1–2 Brisson.

[49] *On the Immortality of the Soul* 15.24 (CSEL 89.125). Augustine probably wants to exclude the Stoic notion of a mixture of the soul and the body in the manner of κρᾶσις δι' ὅλων (cf. SVF II 797) or *mixis* (SVF II 471), a notion that was also challenged by Plotinus (*Enneads* IV 7.8²)—on this issue, see Chiaradonna 2005:127–147. Augustine will later speak about a union of the soul and the body in terms of "a mixture" (*mixtura* or *commixtio*), but not in the manner of two material substances because the immaterial soul maintains its integrity in this union (like light in the air); see *Letters* 137.3.11 (CSEL 44.110). On this passage, which has a close parallel in Nemesius of Emesa *On the Nature of Man* 38–39 Morani and whose source is said to be Porphyry's treatise *Miscellaneous Questions*, see Fortin 1959:111–123. On Porphyry himself, see Dörrie 1959. On Porphyry in Nemesius, see p. 356 below.

[50] *On the Immortality of the Soul* 16.25 (CSEL 89.128); cf. *Enneads* IV 9.1.5–6: ὅλη πανταχοῦ ἐν ἑκάστῳ μέρει. It was probably Plotinus who applied this Parmenidian kind of presence (cf. Plato *Parmenides* 131b1–2) not only to ideas, but also to the soul.

[51] *On the Immortality of the Soul* 16.25 (CSEL 89.128): *Partis enim corporis passionem tota sentit, nec in toto tamen corpore*; cf. *Enneads* IV 2.2.1–10 and 40–42, IV 7.7, VI 4.6.5–19.

[52] *On the Immortality of the Soul* 16.25 (CSEL 89.128). In *Enneads* IV 7.7, Plotinus challenges the Stoic notion of perception as "a transmission" (*diadosis*) of a stimulus from one part of the body through others until it reaches the ruling principle (*to hēgêmonoun*); cf. also Porphyry *Miscellaneous Questions* fr. 261F.18–25 and 42–48 Smith. In his polemic, Augustine does not use the term "transmission," but speaks about a "messenger" (*nuntius*), similarly to Calcidius in his account of Chrysippus; see Calcidius *Commentary on the Timaeus* 220 (Bakhouche 1.446 = SVF 2.879).

[53] *On the Immortality of the Soul* 13.20 (CSEL 89.122): *Nam omnis eius adpetitus ad corpus, aut ut id possideat, est, aut ut vivificet, aut ut quodammodo fabricetur, aut quolibet pacto ei consulat. ... Neque ullum rei huius certius argumentum est quam cum seipsum hinc interrogat animus.* This passage is sometimes interpreted as evidence of Augustine's Aristotle-like anthropology, in which a human being is not merely a rational soul, but a being that consists of a soul and a body and for whom action is as substantial as contemplation; see Cipriani 2007:152.

also casts the body aside in its sleep and deals with images of fantasy derived from previous "sensory perceptions" (*imagines sensibilium*), or with intelligible contents, which are independent of the body.[54]

The most systematic account of the soul can be found in *On the Magnitude of the Soul*, in which Augustine takes it for granted that a human being consists of a body and a soul,[55] and the soul is defined as "a certain substance, participating in *ratio* and suited to the ruling of the body" (*substantia quaedam rationis particeps regendo corpori adcommodata*).[56] Thus, not only the soul's participation in *ratio*, but also its relationship to the body, seems to be of importance.

In order to expound the relationship between the soul and the body, Augustine compares it to that between "a sound" (*sonus*) and its "meaning" (*significatio*), the combination of which creates "a name" (*nomen*). In this way, he not only explains how meaning is transferred from the speaker's mind into that of the hearer—i.e. a certain revelation of one's own thoughts to another person—but he also wants to point out that although a sound can be divided into phones, meaning cannot, and it is not contained spatially in the sound.[57] Some words, nevertheless, can be divided into meaningful units (for example, *Luci-fer*),[58] similarly to some animals that live after they have been cut into parts (here Augustine refers to a centipede's vivisection as he once observed it).[59]

---

[54] *On the Immortality of the Soul* 14.23 (CSEL 89.124–125). Augustine's account of dreaming as a possible access to the intelligible reality is sometimes regarded as evidence of Porphyry's influence; cf. *Miscellaneous Questions* fr. 259F.129–141 Smith. On this issue, see Dörrie 1959: 63–64, 67–68, 204–206; Pépin 1977:240–242. Undoubtedly, it is part of the Platonic tradition of the interpretation of this topic: cf. Plato *Republic* 571c–572a, *Timaeus* 45d–46a; Calcidius *Commentary on the Timaeus* 248–249 and 252–253 (Bakhouche 1.478 and 480–482); similarly also Cicero *Republic* VI 17(17)–18(19), VI 24(26)–26(28), *Cato the Elder on Old Age* 22.81, *On Divination* II 67.139–140, II 62.128, I 57.129, I 30.63; Plotinus *Enneads* IV 7.8[5].9–11; Macrobius *Commentary on the Dream of Scipio* I 1.1–9 (Armisen-Marchetti 1.1–4); cf. also Ambrose of Milan *On the Death of Brother Satyrus* I 73 (CSEL 73.247) and Tertullian *On the Soul* 43.1–12 (CCSL 2.845–848), who collected a whole anthology of ancient teachings on dreaming. On Augustine's theory of dreaming, see Dulaey 1973:176.

[55] *On the Magnitude* 1.2 (CSEL 89.132).

[56] *On the Magnitude* 13.22 (CSEL 89.158). Here Augustine refers to the soul as *animus*, not *anima*, although the latter term prevails in the whole dialogue. Both expressions are also used interchangeably in *On the Immortality of the Soul*; perhaps they rather attest to the Ciceronian and Neoplatonic traditions, respectively, instead of expressing a difference between the rational soul and the soul as such (according to another passage, both meanings are covered by the term *anima*); cf. *On Eighty-Three Various Questions* 7 (CCSL 44a.15). The terminological issue *animus* versus *anima* was discussed in Karfíková 2013:123–125.

[57] *On the Magnitude* 32.66–67 (CSEL 89.213–214).

[58] *On the Magnitude* 32.67 (CSEL 89.215).

[59] *On the Magnitude* 31.62 (CSEL 89.209–210). As Augustine explains, this case differs from a lizard's tail that moves after it has been cut off because the fire and the air, united through the soul with the moist and earthly body, leave and thus cause the deserted body to jolt; see *On the Magnitude* 31.62 (CSEL 89.208f). The latter phenomenon is mentioned by Plotinus as well (cf. *Enneads* IV

In the case of the divided sound, however, the diminution is not spatial, but temporal, even though meaning, unlike sound, is not extended in time either (*significatio non distenta per tempus*).[60] By this analogy, Augustine wants to support the opinion of "the most learned men" who claim that "the soul is not divided by itself, but it can be divided by the body"[61] (though not in the way in which the color is divided in the body, because the color of one part of the body does not depend on another).[62]

In another passage, Augustine refers to the relationship between the body and the soul as *contemperatio* in order to say that because of this "balancing" or "accommodation," the body can perceive even where it is not located (or, more precisely, exactly there), as is the case with the eye.[63] The soul, which is not localized in space, is "there" where its attention is directed (*intendit se*).[64]

In the entire dialogue *On the Magnitude of the Soul*, he addresses Evodius' questions regarding: (1) the origin of the soul (*unde sit*); (2) the quality of the soul (*qualis sit*); (3) its quantity (*quanta sit*); (4) the reason for this embodiment (*cur corpori fuerit data*); (5) its nature when embodied (*cum ad corpus venerit qualis efficiatur*); and (6) its nature after it leaves the body (*qualis cum abscesserit*).[65] A more detailed account, however, is only given about the "quantity" of the soul, which also gave the treatise its title. Some of the questions are hardly answered at all,[66] but their list is of more interest as a catalogue of topics that Augustine

---

4.29.6–7). The life of dissected animals is also discussed by Aristotle (*On the Soul* 409a9–10 and 411b19–27) and Lucretius (*On the Nature of the Things* 3.652–669).

[60] *On the Magnitude* 32.68 (CSEL 89.215–216).

[61] *On the Magnitude* 32.68 (CSEL 89.216): ... *utrum quod a quibusdam doctissimis viris dicitur, ita sese habeat, animam per seipsam nullo modo, sed tamen per corpus posse partiri.* Cf. Plotinus *Enneads* IV 1.1.20–22: εἰς ὅλον γὰρ τὸ σῶμα δοῦσα αὐτὴν καὶ μὴ μερισθεῖσα τῷ ὅλη εἰς ὅλον τῷ ἐν παντὶ εἶναι μεμέρισται (The soul "gives itself to the whole body and is not divided in that it gives itself whole to the whole and is divided in that it is present in every [part]," translation Armstrong 1984:23); similarly also *Enneads* IV 2.1.69–76, VI 4.1.27–29 and 4.26–34; cf. Pépin 1977:245 with n3. Porphyry summarizes this idea in *Sentences* 5.1–2 Brisson: ἡ μὲν ψυχὴ τῆς ἀμερίστου καὶ <τῆς> περὶ τὰ σώματα μεριστῆς οὐσίας μέσον τι ("The soul ... is a certain medium between an impartible essence and an essence which is divisible about corporeal bodies."). These ideas originate in Plato *Timaeus* 35a.

[62] *On the Immortality of the Soul* 16.25 (CSEL 89.128): *secundum partes molis a se distantes.* The color of the cheek need not be modified if the color of the leg changes. Although the color is also just one and whole in all places, it is not living unity: its presence does not bind all the places together. Cf. also *Enneads* IV 2.1.38–41 and 45–50; on this issue, see further Tornau 2005:162–178.

[63] *On the Magnitude* 30.59 (CSEL 89.206).

[64] *On the Magnitude* 33.71 (CSEL 89.219).

[65] *On the Magnitude* 1.1 (CSEL 89.131).

[66] *On the Magnitude* 36.81 (CSEL 89.231).

saw as related to the soul.[67] They also quite distinctly mirror the idea of a soul that is independent of the body to a large degree, although it is meant to rule it.

2.1 On the Origin of the Soul

According to Augustine, the question of the origin of the soul (*unde*) can be addressed in two ways. First, the "homeland" from which the soul comes is God, who created the soul.[68] This Plotinian "homeland," which we encountered in the Cassiciacum dialogues,[69] is a kind of periphrasis for the divine origin of the soul, by which, it should be noted, Augustine means the fact that it was created by God, not that it is identical to God.

However, if, on the other hand, the question *unde* is concerned with, is of what the soul consists (*unde constet*), the only answer Augustine offers is that it is not created from the four primary elements, but has its own simple substance (*simplex quiddam et propriae substantiae*), different from that of God, just as the four elements have theirs.[70] Although the soul forms the body, it is not merely its form, but also a substance in its own right. Both aspects of the question *unde* are linked in Cicero's account of the soul, whose faculties, such as memory and thinking, make it superior to the four primary elements, which is why it must be of divine origin.[71]

2.2 On the Quality of the Soul

The quality of the soul is characterized only briefly. Augustine limits himself here to the human soul, which is described as "similar to God" (*deo similis*).[72] This quality is probably based on the biblical line about the creation of man "in God's image and likeness" (Genesis 1:26); the line was quoted in Augustine's *Soliloquies*,[73] and it will reappear in his first exposition of the book of Genesis[74]

---

[67] There is also a similar list of questions in *On Order* II 5.17 (BA 4.2.210): *Anima vero unde originem ducat quidve hic agat, quantum distet a Deo, quid habeat proprium, quod alternat in utramque naturam, quatenus moriatur et quomodo immortalis probetur.*

[68] *On the Magnitude* 1.2 (CSEL 89.132): *Propriam quandam habitationem animae ac patriam deum ipsum credo esse, a quo creata est.*

[69] See n39 above.

[70] *On the Magnitude* 1.2 (CSEL 89.132–133).

[71] *Tusculan Disputations* 1.27.66.

[72] *On the Magnitude* 2.3 (CSEL 89.133).

[73] *Soliloquies* I 1.4 (CSEL 89.9).

[74] *On Genesis Against the Manichaeans* I 17.28 (BA 50.222). Here Augustine's main point (similar to Origen *Homilies on Genesis* I 13 ([GCS N.F. 17.24–25]) is that likeness to God does not naturally relate to the body, but to the "inner man" (*secundum interiorem hominem*), and it must be sought in "reason and intellect" (*ratio et intellectus*). See also Dulaey 2004:518–523.

and one of his *Eighty-Three Different Questions*.[75] As Augustine has it now, the likeness of the human soul to God consists in its immortality;[76] later (in the anti-Manichaean exposition of the book of Genesis), he will see it in *ratio* and in the intellect.

2.3 On the Quantity of the Soul

As for the "quantity of the soul," Augustine, following the Neoplatonists, says that the soul is not extended spatially (*caret spatio*); it is not localized in any place (*non loco animam contineri*),[77] and, therefore, probably not even in the body it animates.[78] It is not corporeal,[79] and it does not even have the extension of geometric figures, although it is able to bring out extension in its memory[80] or imagine it in its fantasy.[81] Instead, the soul seems to be more like a point that does not have extension (*puncto ... quod ... partibus caret*) from which all geometrical figures are derived, because the soul, despite being without exten-

---

[75] *On Eighty-Three Various Questions* 51.4 (CCSL 44a.81–82). Here Augustine is referring to the opinion of some of his predecessors. Cf. Origen *Homilies on Genesis* I 13 (GCS N.F. 17.26–27)—that the only real "image and likeness" of God is Christ, while men were created "in the image and likeness" (*ad imaginem et similitudinem*) as a kind of image of an image; there also seems to be a possible difference between the "image" as the spiritual component of a human being (*mens, spiritus*) and the "likeness," which pertains to the other components. These distinctions, however, both terminological and factual, are rather reported as other scholars' opinions. On Augustine's teaching of the image of God in a human being, its sources and its development, see McCool 1959:62–81; Somers 1961:105–125; Markus 1964:125–143.

[76] *On the Magnitude* 2.3 (CSEL 89.134). Origen also says that the inner man, created in the image of God, was immortal: *incorruptus atque inmortalis*. Cf. *The Homilies on Genesis* I 13 (GCS N.F. 17.24).

[77] *On the Magnitude* 31.64 (CSEL 89.212). Aristotle rejected the "quantity of the soul" (τὸ λέγειν τὴν ψυχὴν μέγεθος εἶναι) in his polemic against Plato's *Timaeus* (cf. *On the Soul* 407a3); however, the Neoplatonic teaching explicitly rejects the spatial extension as well; see Plotinus *Enneads* VI 4.4–8 et passim, IV 3.20–23; Porphyry *Sentences* 27 and 31 Brisson. Marius Victorinus (*Against Arius* I 32 [CSEL 83, 112–113]) also says that only matter is characterized by quantity, while the soul is defined by its animating force (*vitalis potentia*) and its intellect (*intellegentia*). Similarly, as we will see, Augustine rejects the spatial quantity of the soul; instead, he focuses on its activity, including animation and intellectual ability.

[78] *On the Magnitude* 31.61 (CSEL 89.208): *... non esse animam in corpore viventis animantis*. Augustine mentions this as an elusive, but not nonsensical opinion of the "most learned men" of the past and the present as well; cf. Plotinus *Enneads* IV 3.20.1–27; Porphyry *Sentences* 31 Brisson. The history of this theory and the discussion of Augustine's possible sources are summarized in Pépin 1977:216–225.

[79] *On the Magnitude* 14.23 (CSEL 89.158) and 3.4 (CSEL 89.135). Similarly, in *On Eighty-Three Various Questions* 20 (CCSL 44a.25), Augustine says that only the body is located in a place with three dimensions. As Morano (1974:101–111) points out, it was thanks to Augustine that the idea of the soul as immaterial gained ground in European thinking for a long time, although it was not taken for granted in antiquity.

[80] *On the Magnitude* 5.8 (CSEL 89.140–141).

[81] *On the Magnitude* 14.23 (CSEL 89.158). Augustine and Evodius perform this exercise in *On the Magnitude* 6.10–11.17 (CSEL 89.142–152); cf. also *On the Measure* 14.24 (CSEL 89.160).

sion, controls the limbs and is like an "immobile axis" (*cardo*) around which the bodily movements revolve.[82]

According to Augustine, the nonextended soul moves the body when given a command (*nutus*) by its will, i.e. by its "intention" (*intentio*);[83] this takes place through the "nerves," which serve as ropes (*nervis quasi tormentis utitur*) and whose system (*nervorum machinamentum*) is adjusted to the shape of the body.[84] Although this passage does not rule out the possibility that by the expression *nervi* Augustine refers to sinews (this is how the term *neuron* is used in Plato's *Timaeus* and in one passage in Plotinus),[85] it is quite probable that he does actually mean motor nerves (known since the third century BCE, thanks to Herophilus and Erasistratus—and also mentioned in Plotinus).[86] In his later works, Augustine says that the soul uses the "nerves" to move the individual limbs by means of its will,[87] which is transmitted in the body through the "air infused into the nerves" (*aer, qui nervis infusus est*).[88] This information corresponds to the medical opinions about *pneuma* (*aer* in Augustine), which mediates not only sensory perception in the body, but also motor intentions.[89]

The question about the "quantity" of the soul can also be understood as an inquiry into the capability of the soul (*quantum valeat*).[90] This formulation is reminiscent of Plotinus' amazement at how the soul is "great" without being

---

[82] *On the Magnitude* 14.23 (CSEL 89.159). On the properties of the point, see *On the Magnitude* 11.18–12.19 (CSEL 89.152–154). Similarly, on the soul resembling the center that unites a circle, see *On Order* I 2.3 (BA 4.2.76–78). Plotinus, too, uses the metaphor of a circle, mainly in order to emphasize the common center of all souls (*Enneads* VI 4.5 and VI 9.8). On Augustine's metaphor of an axis or a hinge, see also *On the Magnitude* 17.30 (CSEL 89.167); *On Eighty-Three Various Questions* 8 (CCSL 40a.15).

[83] *On the Magnitude* 22.38 (CSEL 89.178–179); *On the Immortality of the Soul* 3.4 (CSEL 89.105).

[84] *On the Magnitude* 22.38 (CSEL 89.178–179). Here Augustine also explains the role of dryness and moderate temperature for the good mobility of "nerves"; he mentions their atony in sleep and with the "lethargics" in contrast to their agitation with the "frenetics."

[85] *Timaeus* 74a7–b7, 74d2–e1, 75c8–d5, 77d6–e6, 82c7–d5, 84a1–b2, 84e2–7 (unfortunately, this passage is missing in Calcidius' translation); *Enneads* III 2.7.10.

[86] *Enneads* IV 3.23.9–14; perhaps also IV 4.34.32. On the ambiguous usage of the expression *neuron* in Plotinus, see Sleeman and Pollet 1980:676.

[87] *On the Nature and Origin of the Soul* IV 5.6 (BA 22.584).

[88] *On the Literal Meaning of Genesis* VII 19.25 (BA 48.544).

[89] On the medical usage of the Stoic teaching on *pneuma*, see Verbeke 1945:175–220; Solmsen 1968:569–575. Augustine might have drawn his medical knowledge from the famous physician Vindicianus, of whom he speaks in *Confessions* IV 3.5 (CCSL 27.42) and VII 6.8 (CCSL 27.97); see also Bardy 1953:329–331. He could also have used the encyclopedic works by Varro, Celsus, and others; see Marrou 1958:141–143; Agaësse and Solignac 1972:710–714. According to Verbeke (1945:505), Augustine avoids using the term *spiritus* as an equivalent of the Greek *pneuma* for material things; instead, he prefers the equivalents *aer* or *lux*.

[90] *On the Magnitude* 3.4 (CSEL 89.134).

extended spatially or having a bodily mass,[91] and also of the virtues "gener-osity" (*magnanimitas*) and "patience" (*longanimitas*).[92] Augustine does not limit the question to its moral aspect, but proposes seven degrees that may be distinguished in the acting (*actus*) of the soul[93]—presumably inspired by Varro regarding the first three activities, and the Neoplatonic hierarchy of virtues for the last four degrees.[94]

In the first degree (*animatio*), the embodied soul endows the earthly and mortal body with life and unity, ensures the nourishment and its distribution to the individual organs, and maintains the balance of the body and the manner of its being (*congruentia, modus*) in terms of the individual growth and the preser-vation of the species. These tasks of the soul also pertain to plants.[95]

In animals, the second degree is sensory perception (*sensus*) and motion, as well as the rhythm of waking and sleeping. Reproduction involves sexual intercourse and taking care of the offspring. Dealing with corporeal things establishes a habit whose force—i.e. "memory" (*memoria*)—holds even nonpresent things.[96]

The third degree of the soul (*ars*), which is reserved for human beings and enables the development of arts and culture in the broadest sense, is a form of memory not based on the force of habit, but on attention and sign representa-tion (*animadversione atque signis*); moreover, it is not related to the past only, but also to the future. This degree, according to Augustine, also involves the ability to joke and play.[97] Presumably, these are various kinds of an exclusively human

---

[91] *Enneads* IV 2.1.69–70: μέγεθος οὐκ ἔχουσα παντὶ μεγέθει σύνεστι and *Enneads* VI 4.5.1: τὸ μέγα αὐτῆς ... οὐκ ἐν ὄγκῳ.

[92] On *magnanimitas*, cf. Cicero *On Duties* I 152; Aristotle *Nichomachean Ethics* 1123a34–1125a16 (*megalopsukhia*). Augustine does not mention this virtue, but refers to the biblical expression *makrothumia*, which he translates as *longanimitas*. His main point is that it is a metaphorical expression; see *On the Magnitude* 17.30 (CSEL 89.166–167). On the history of these terms in ancient philosophy and Scripture, see Gauthier 1951.

[93] Their summary is given in *On the Magnitude* 35.79 (CSEL 89.228): *... primus actus ... dicatur animatio, secundus sensus, tertius ars, quartus virtus, quintus tranquillitas, sextus ingressio, septimus contemplatio.* A shortened version of the scale is also provided in *On Free Choice of the Will* I 8.18.61–65 (CCSL 29.222–223).

[94] This is the opinion of du Roy 1966:257–260; see also Cipriani 1996:388–396. Other Neoplatonic inspirations are discussed in O'Daly 1987:14–15 and Neil 1999:197–215. On Varro, see Augustine *The City of God* VII 23 (CCSL 47.204); on Neoplatonic degrees of virtues, see Plotinus *Enneads* I 2; Porphyry *Sentences* 32. It is mainly Porphyry who makes a clear distinction between four degrees: (1) the virtues of a citizen; (2) the virtues of those who aspire to contemplation; (3) the virtues of those who have reached contemplation; and (4) the virtues of the Intellect itself (*Sentences* 32 Brisson). Plotinus does not posit the last degree; by the same token, Augustine does not speak about the virtues of God, but about the virtues of the soul with God.

[95] *On the Magnitude* 33.70 (CSEL 89.218).

[96] *On the Magnitude* 33.71 (CSEL 89.218–219).

[97] *On the Magnitude* 33.72 (CSEL 89.220).

ability to detach oneself from one's immediate surroundings, i.e. to deal with the body from a distance (*circa corpus*).⁹⁸

The fourth degree of the soul, which, unlike the previous three, is not concerned with the relationship between the soul and the body, but with the soul itself (*ad seipsam*),⁹⁹ is moral quality (*virtus*) and consideration for others (*nihilque velle alteri quod sibi nolit accidere*), but also an ability to obey the authority and commands of wise men as divine exhortations.¹⁰⁰

The fifth and sixth degrees of the quantity of the soul (i.e. *tranquillitas* and *ingressio*, respectively), involve, according to Augustine, completed purification, which began on the previous level; the soul "happily dwells in itself" (*se ... in se ipsa laetissime tenet*),¹⁰¹ getting ready for the contemplation of the truth.¹⁰² First, the soul dwells in itself (*in se ipsa*), and then goes on to transcend itself towards God (*ad Deum*).¹⁰³

Finally, the seventh and last degree is the contemplation of the truth (*contemplatio*), when the soul "comprehends what truly and supremely is" (*intel-legendi ea, quae vere summeque sunt*).¹⁰⁴ This degree pertains to a soul which, having detached itself from the body, dwells with God (*apud deum*),¹⁰⁵ either after death, or in an exceptional ecstasy.¹⁰⁶

If the question about "quantity" is concerned with the number of souls, Augustine is slightly at a loss: apparently, it is not possible to say either that there is only one soul (because one is happy and the other miserable) or that there are many; it is most probably the case that the soul is one and many at the same time (*unam simul et multas*), although Augustine unfortunately does not elaborate on this (Plotinian) solution.¹⁰⁷

---

98   *On the Magnitude* 35.79 (CSEL 89.228).

99   *On the Magnitude* 35.79 (CSEL 89.228).

100 *On the Magnitude* 33.73 (CSEL 89.220–221).

101 *On the Magnitude* 33.74 (CSEL 89.222).

102 *On the Magnitude* 33.74–76 (CSEL 89.222–223).

103 *On the Magnitude* 35.79 (CSEL 89.228).

104 *On the Magnitude* 33.75 (CSEL 89.222).

105 *On the Magnitude* 35.79 (CSEL 89.228).

106 *On the Magnitude* 33.76 (CSEL 89.223–225). Here Augustine mentions death as a gateway to beatific contemplation and also "great and incommensurable souls" which have been endowed with such vision in this life. See Teske 1994:288–289. O'Connell (1968:168) admits the possibility that it is a constant activity of the soul which—like in Plotinus—remains a permanent part of the Intellect even after its incarnation.

107 *On the Magnitude* 32.69 (CSEL 89.217). Plotinus characterizes the soul as "one and many" (ἓν καὶ πολλά), *Enneads* V 1.8.25–26. On the question as to whether all souls are one, see *Enneads* IV 9 and IV 3.1–8; Porphyry *Sentences* 37.1–35 Brisson. See also O'Daly 1987:60–62.

2.4 On the Reason For the Embodiment of the Soul

In *On the Magnitude*, we do not learn anything about the reason for the embodiment of the soul; it is only later, in book three of his *On Free Choice of the Will*, that Augustine posits several alternatives: either the soul is sent to the body by God, or it descends into it *sponte sua* (apart from two more possibilities of explaining the origin of the individual soul, namely the passing of all souls from one and the creation of each individual soul separately).[108]

Augustine does not seem to have completely identified himself with Evodius' idea of the soul as not only immortal, but even "eternal" (*aeterna*);[109] at the same time, however, he adds that the soul may have "brought with it all liberal arts," which it remembers after incarnation during learning (*reminisci et recordari*).[110] Similarly, in *On Free Choice*, he asks Evodius to consider "whether the soul lived another sort of life before its association with the body and whether it lived wisely."[111] In his correspondence with his Platonizing friend Nebridius, Augustine also probably assumes some kind of existence of the nonembodied soul, which is not yet affected by sensory experience,[112] and is endowed with vision, which it will remember after incarnation in the manner of Platonic *anamnêsis*. Unlike Nebridius, nevertheless, Augustine does not maintain that, together with the recollection of intelligible objects, the soul also brings with it some *a priori* knowledge of sensible contents.[113]

2.5 On the Soul's Nature When Embodied

When embodied, the soul's task is to rule the body and look after it (*agendo atque administrando corpori anima data*),[114] as was the case in the first two degrees of its "quantity." The soul itself is to be subordinated to God, which is why it

---

[108] Cf. *On Free Choice of the Will* III 20.56.188–58.199 (CCSL 29.307–309). Augustine characterizes the four possibilities given here as follows: (1) *una anima facta est, ex qua omnium hominum animae trahuntur nascentium*; (2) *singillatim fiunt in unoquoque nascentium*; (3) *in Dei aliquo secreto iam existentes animae mittuntur ad inspiranda et regenda corpora singulorum quorumque nascentium*; and (4) *alibi animae constitutae non mittuntur a Domino Deo, sed sua sponte ad inhabitanda corpora veniunt*.

[109] *On the Magnitude* 20.34 (CSEL 89.173–174). On the difference between what is eternal (*aeternum*), i.e. immutable, and what is immortal (*immortale*), i.e. living without an end, see *On Eighty-Three Various Questions* 19 (CCSL 44a.24). As for eternity, the soul only participates in it; see *On Eighty-Three Various Questions* 23 (CCSL 44a.27).

[110] *On the Magnitude* 20.34 (CSEL 89.173).

[111] *On Free Choice of the Will* I 12.24.81 (CCSL 29.227): ... *utrum ante consortium huius corporis alia quadam vita vixerit animus et an aliquando sapienter vixerit, magna quaestio est, magnum secretum*.

[112] *Letters* 7.2.3 (CSEL 34.1.14): *anima, priusquam corpore utatur*; *Letters* 7.2.5 (CSEL 34.1.16): *ad animam, priusquam inhaereat sensibus*; *Letters* 7.2.5 (CSEL 34.1.17): *animam ... nondum corpore sentientem*; *Letters* 7.3.7 (CSEL 34.1.18): *eam* (scil. *animam*), *priusquam corpore sensibusque utatur*.

[113] *Letters* 7.2.3 (CSEL 34.1.14).

[114] *On the Magnitude* 36.81 (CSEL 89.230).

was endowed with "free choice" (*liberum arbitrium*).[115] Augustine is especially concerned with this faculty of the soul in his anti-Manichaean investigation of the origin of evil in the will, as it is elaborated in *On Free Choice* the first book of which was written before Augustine's consecration as a priest.[116]

2.6 On the Soul's Nature When Disembodied

When the soul abandons the body, it is either punished for its free choices (by the preservation of its guilt), or rewarded (the reward being God, or, in other words, truth).[117] According to Augustine, the good awaiting the soul in the future also includes the resurrection of the body; this notion, in his opinion, is one in which it is difficult to believe, but can be regarded as a fact as certain as that the sun that sets today will also rise tomorrow.[118] For the time being, this Christian teaching does not play an important role in Augustine's thinking as far as the relationship between the body and soul is concerned.[119]

3. The Body Acting upon the Soul?

The question of whether the body can act upon the soul (and whether the soul is mutable at all) seems to concern Augustine mainly with respect to Plotinus, who, in his treatise on impassibility, explicitly rejects the idea that the incorporeal soul can suffer any change (ἀπαθῆ αὐτὴν καὶ ἄτρεπτον).[120] All changes and movements of the soul, according to him, are only realizations of the natural inclinations of the soul,[121] or they are changes in the body that the soul causes without itself being changed.[122] This idea—although it contradicts Plato's conception,[123] and is not shared by the middle Platonists either[124]—is also, to some degree, advocated by Porphyry.[125]

---

[115] *On the Magnitude* 36.80 (CSEL 89.229).

[116] Cf. *Retractations* I 9.1 (CCSL 57.23).

[117] *On the Magnitude* 36.81 (CSEL 89.231).

[118] *On the Magnitude* 33.76 (CSEL 89.225).

[119] As Miles (1979:131) concludes, apart from the doctrine on incarnation, it was the idea of resurrection that later helped Augustine in his "herculean task" of newly appreciating the body or even making it the "cornerstone" of his theology.

[120] *Enneads* III 6.1.26–27. For the whole exposition, see *Enneads* III 6, "On the Impassibility of Things Without Body"; similarly *Enneads* IV 6.2.1–9.

[121] *Enneads* III 6.2.45–52 and III 3.27–35.

[122] *Enneads* III 6.3.1–26.

[123] *Timaeus* 43c and 86b–87a.

[124] For example, Alcinous posits a "part of the soul subject to affections" (τὸ παθητικὸν τῆς ψυχῆς) apart from the rational one, see *The Handbook of Platonism* 152.14, 156.35–37, 173.12–15, 176.41–43, 177.12–14, 183.39–41, 185.26–30; see also Whittaker 1990:75n11.

[125] *Sentences* 21.3–5 Brisson: φθείρεται δὲ οὐδὲν ἀσώματον ... ὥστε πάσχειν οὐδέν. ("Nothing incorporeal suffers dissolution ... so that none is subject to sensory experience.") See also *Sentences*

In the outline *On the Immortality of the Soul*, Augustine hesitantly admits that the human soul is mutable (*animae mutatio*),[126] and distinguishes two kinds of transformation it undergoes (namely, the changes caused by the body and the changes caused by the soul itself—surprisingly, he has greater doubts concerning the latter group):[127] "The changes of the soul are either due to what the body experiences (*secundum corporis passiones*), or what the soul itself experiences (*secundum suas*)."[128] If the changes originate in the body, they are caused by "age" (*aetates*), "diseases" (*morbi*), "pain" (*dolores*), "labor" (*labores*), "discomforts" (*offensiones*), and "pleasures" (*voluptates*). On the contrary, the following originate in the soul: "desire" (*cupiendo*), "joy" (*laetando*), "fear" (*metuendo*), "grief" (*aegrescendo*), "endeavor" (*studendo*), and "learning" (*discendo*).

In connection with the teaching on *perturbationes*, or *passiones*, Augustine will later explicitly refer to Cicero;[129] there is no known model for his catalogue as a whole, however. The four elementary movements of the soul caused, according to him, by the soul—i.e. desire, pleasure, fear, and grief (ἐπιθυμία, ἡδονή, φόβος, λύπη)—had already appeared in Plato,[130] and Augustine himself takes them for granted.[131] Cicero mentions them in his discussions of Stoicism, where these movements (*pathê* or *perturbationes*) represent an unreasonable relationship to a future good (*libido* = "desire"), a present good (*laetitia* = "joy"), a future evil (*metus* = "fear"), and a present evil (*aegritudo* = "grief").[132] Under the hardships of the body, Cicero presumably subsumes "disease" (*morbus*) and "weakness" (*debilitas*); in another passage, he mentions them, together with the four given above, under the heading of "affects of the spirit or the body."[133]

18.1–8 Brisson.

[126] *On the Immortality of the Soul* 5.7 (CSEL 89.108) and 5.9 (CSEL 89.109–110). In an earlier passage, Augustine advocated the immutable soul; see *On the Immortality of the Soul* 2.2 (CSEL 89.103). This notion was also explicitly renounced in his *Retractations* I 5.2 (CCSL 57.16). Similarly, in *On Free Choice of the Will* II 12.34.135 (CCSL 29.260), Augustine regards the soul as changeable.

[127] See *On the Immortality of the Soul* 5.9 (CSEL 89.110).

[128] *On the Immortality of the Soul* 5.7 (CSEL 89.108). Later, Augustine will regard the expression *passiones*, which comes from Apuleius, as one of the equivalents of the Greek *pathê*. See Apuleius *On the God of Socrates* 12–13; in the context of his polemic against Apuleius, Augustine *The City of God* VIII 17 (CCSL 47.234) and IX 4 (CCSL 47.251): *perturbationes, affectiones vel affectus, passiones*. It literally refers to what the soul suffers and to what it is exposed, i.e. motions, excitements, affectations, or passions.

[129] *On the Immortality of the Soul* 14.5 (CCSL 48.420): *non ex carne tantum afficitur anima, ut cupiat metuat, laetetur aegrescat, verum etiam ex se ipsa his potest motibus agitari.*

[130] See *Republic* 429c9–d1 and 430a6–b1; *Phaedo* 83b6–9.

[131] See *Confessions* X 14.22 (CCSL 27.166): *quattuor esse perturbationes animi, cupiditatem, laetitiam, metum, tristitiam.*

[132] See *Tusculan Disputations* 4.6.11. The rendering of *cupiditas* as the equivalent of *libido* (i.e. ἐπιθυμία, "desire") is not surprising; see e.g. *Tusculan Disputations* 3.11.24 and 4.6.12.

[133] *About the Composition of Arguments* I 25.36: *Affectio est animi aut corporis ex tempore aliqua de causa commutatio, ut laetitia, cupiditas, metus, molestia, morbus, debilitas et alia quae in eodem genere*

However, "pleasure" (*voluptas* as the equivalent of *hêdonê*) appears in Cicero's catalogue as a synonym for "joy" (*laetitia*),[134] not as a *passio* pertaining to the body rather than to the soul, as Augustine would have it.

Augustine does not seem to maintain that, strictly speaking, the body affects the soul, because, in his opinion, that which affects (*efficiens*) is always superior to what it acts upon.[135] Since the body is not superior to the soul, it cannot affect it.

The issues concerning the way the body acts upon the soul are also dealt with, in the analysis of "perception" (*sensus*) in *On the Magnitude*. First, perception is defined along the lines of "what the body experiences does not go unnoticed by the soul" (Plotinus refers to a similar definition as a traditional one).[136] After some consideration, Augustine goes on to add that this experience is "by itself" (*per se ipsam*) known to the soul.[137] That makes sensory perception different from a *judgment* the soul makes on the basis of a sensation (for example, when seeing smoke infers the presence of a fire, which is not the object of perception). Thus, the definition of perception must exclude situations in which the soul knows about what the body experiences through a different "experience" (*passio*) or the soul infers it from something else.[138] For example, the soul knows about the growth of nails, but not because of a sensation, but through observing their length: this *passio* (i.e. nail growth) is not by itself known to the soul, but it is known "by some other means" (*per aliud*).[139] Perception is when something does not go unnoticed by the soul "because of the body" (*per corpus*), not "because of reason" (*per rationem*), for it is the case that animals also have perception—even animals can have "bodily experience known by itself."[140]

This raises the question of what it means that a *passio* of the body is known to the soul "by itself"? Does it presuppose that the body acts upon the soul?

---

reperiuntur.

[134] See *Tusculan Disputations* 3.11.24 and 4.7.14–9.21.

[135] *On Eighty-Three Various Questions* 28 (CCSL 44a.35): *Omne autem efficiens maius est quam id quod efficitur.*

[136] *On the Magnitude* 23.41 (CSEL 89.182): *Nam sensum puto esse non latere animam quod patitur corpus.* Plotinus *Enneads* I 4.2.3–4: τὸ αἰσθάνεσθαι τοῦτο λέγουσι, τὸ τὸ πάθος μὴ λανθάνειν. On Augustine's theory of perception, see Vanni Rovighi 1962:18–32; Gannon 1956:154–180; Miles 1979:9–39; O'Daly 1987:80–102.

[137] *On the Magnitude* 24.45 (CSEL 89.187): *Cum ergo per passionem corporis non latet aliquid animam, non continuo sensus vocatur unus de quinque memoratis, sed cum ipsa passio non latet.* See also *On the Magnitude* 25.48 (CSEL 89.193): *Iam video sic esse definiendum, ut sensus sit 'passio corporis per seipsam non latens animam'.*

[138] *On the Magnitude* 34.46 (CSEL 89.189–190).

[139] *On the Magnitude* 25.48 (CSEL 89.192–193).

[140] *On the Magnitude* 30.58 (CSEL 89.205).

In book six of *On Music* (this book was probably written after Augustine's return to Africa),[141] he explicitly rejects the idea that the soul is affected by the body in the sense of being acted upon by the body as the creator acts upon matter.[142] The soul is not acted upon by the body; on the contrary, the soul acts upon the body (*nec ab isto quidquam illam pati arbitror, sed facere de illo et in illo*). It animates the body with its intention (*intentione facientis*), which sometimes goes smoothly, but sometimes with difficulty. In the latter case, the soul will notice the effort it has to put into it, and because of this "attention" (*attentio*), it will also perceive the hardships of the body and its effort or pain.[143]

In his analysis of an auditory sensation in book six of *On Music*, which is based on Ambrose's iambic verse "God Maker of All Things" (*Deus creator omnium*).[144] Augustine posits several kinds of numerical structures or rhythms (*numeri*) that work together in the sensation: *numeri sonantes* (sounding rhythms); *numeri occursores* in the sensation, which make it possible for the soul to notice the stimulation of the sensor; *numeri recordabiles* stored in the memory; *numeri progressores*, through which the soul affects the body; and *numeri judiciales*, which measure the other ones.[145]

Here he says quite clearly that during perception, the soul is not affected by the body: what the soul "feels" is its own activity[146] in which it somehow "goes to meet" (*ire obviam*) the experiences of the body.[147] By some kind of transmission, the soul affects the sensors, and this is what it experiences during perception;[148] for example, hearing is animated even before the arrival of the voice by some kind of movement (*ante istum sonum vitali motu in silentio corpus aurium vegetabat*), which then collides with the movement of the air coming from the outside.[149] As for the other sensors, the soul also elicits in them something homogenous with the sensations that are to be experienced in order for "the like to connect with

---

[141] The dating of the books of *On Music* is not quite clear: Augustine started to work on them before he was baptized in Milan, but finished them after his return to Africa; see *Retractations* I 6 (CCSL 57.17). Book six of *On Music*, whose content makes it different from the previous, more technical ones, is also mentioned in *Retractations* I 11.1 (CCSL 57.33), which seems to support its being dated later. On this issue, see Jacobsson 2002:x–xxviii.

[142] *On Music* VI 5.8 (BA 7.376).

[143] *On Music* VI 5.9 (BA 7.378–380).

[144] Cf. Ambrose of Milan *God Maker of All Things* (Walpole 1922:46).

[145] *On Music* VI 2.2–5.12 (BA 7.360–386). On the titles of the individual *numeri*, see *On Music* VI 5.16 (BA 7.394); further specification in *On Music* VI 9.24 (BA 7.412–414). See also Wulf 2013:56–76. An analysis of an auditory sensation can be found in Plato *Timaeus* 80a–b, which does not speak about "rhythms," but "movements."

[146] *On Music* VI 5.10 (BA 7.382): *... videtur mihi anima cum sentit in corpore, non ab illo aliquid pati, sed in ejus passionibus attentius agere.*

[147] *On Music* VI 9.24 (BA 7.412).

[148] *On Music* VI 5.11 (BA 7.384): *... motus suos animam, vel actiones, vel operationes, ... non latere cum sentit.*

[149] *On Music* VI 5.11 (BA 7.384).

the like" in the sense of the adequacy of the elements (*temperantia*); in other words, it activates "something luminous in the eyes, something from the purest and finest air in the ears, something from the thick [air] in the nose, something moist in the mouth and something earthly and muddy in touch."[150] Thus, the soul experiences its own activities, not those of the body (*a se ipsa patitur, non a corpore*).[151] The activities, according to Augustine, are some kind of movement, whose speed, however, is not evenly distributed because of the uneven concentration of *pneuma*; this is why the soul cannot feel some experiences of the body, such as the ones in the bones, hair, or nails.[152]

In Augustine's exposition of seeing, the soul emits light through which it sees what is located elsewhere than the seeing eye itself, as if it touches a distant object with a cane (*quasi virga visus*).[153] This theory, derived from Plato's *Timaeus*,[154] is also found in Stoicism, which gives rise to the idea that the *pneuma* permeates the body; this idea was widely accepted in contemporary medicine.[155] In Augustine's account, it is somewhat spiritualized: Augustine (for the time being?) does not maintain that the "cane" is made of material *pneuma*, but stresses the role of the intention of the will, and as we have already seen, he explicitly rejects the Stoic teaching on the material transmission of information.[156]

In many respects, however, Augustine's effort to deny that the body acts upon the soul resembles Plotinus' account of perception. According to the Neoplatonic author, the soul is immutable, and that is why corporeal objects do not affect the soul, but only the sense organs, from which the soul collects information. Perception, then, is a kind of judgment and an activity during which the

---

[150] *On Music* VI 5.10 (BA 7.382): *Sed iste sensus, qui etiam dum nihil sentimus, inest tamen, instrumentum est corporis, quod ea temperatione agitur ab anima, ut in eo sit ad passiones corporis cum attentione agendas paratior, similia similibus ut adjungat, repellatque quod noxium est. Agit porro, ut opinor, luminosum aliquid in oculis, aerium serenissimum et mobilissimum in auribus, caliginosum in naribus, in ore humidum, in tactu terrenum et quasi lutulentum.*

[151] *On Music* VI 5.12 (BA 7.386).

[152] *On Music* VI 5.15 (BA 7.390): *... quia minus libero aere penetrantur, mobili scilicet elemento, quam ut motus ibi possit ab anima fieri tam celer, quam est ille adversus quem fit cum sentire dicitur.* On the term *aer* as the equivalent of the Greek *pneuma*, see p. 321 with n88 and n89, above.

[153] *On the Magnitude* 23.43 (CSEL 89.185).

[154] *Timaeus* 45b–d and 67c–68a. Here the process of seeing is explained in terms of a fusion of the inner fire coming out of the eye and the outer light into some kind of homogenous light beam that transmits the movements of the things from which it refracts back into the soul.

[155] According to the Stoics, "visual *pneuma*" comes out of the "ruling part" (*hêgêmonikon*) of the soul (i.e. from the heart) during seeing; through the pupil, it compresses the air and creates in it some kind of conic visual field, the base of which is the object that is perceived. The pressure that is thus created in the air and that is called *sunentasis*, or *intentio*, is felt with "a cane" (*baktêria*), as it were, and the information about the perceived object is thus secured (see SVF II 863–871). See also Todd 1974:251–261 and Ingenkamp 1971:240–246.

[156] See also Rohmer 1954:493.

soul is not acted upon, but acts (even though it processes information which was obtained "externally").[157]

And yet, in the same book of *On Music*, Augustine also admits that the mortal body, corrupted by the sin of the soul, affects the soul (*facere aliquid in anima corpus potest*) in the sense that the soul feels the experiences of the body (*passionem corporum sentire*). According to this interpretation, the body was totally subjected to the soul in paradise, but the soul lost this control because of the soul's own failure when the soul stopped obeying the Creator.[158] Here again it is the soul that allows the body to affect it instead of making the body subordinate.

In one of his letters to Nebridius, Augustine also admits that the body affects the soul in some way. As he puts it, each movement of the soul brings about a change in the body (*omnem motum animi aliquid facere in corpore*): not only a visible change in its expression or motion caused by, *inter alia*, anger or joy, but perhaps also each thought elicits some kind of visually unrecognizable movement the trace of which is stored in the body (*vestigia sui motus animus figit in corpore*) and may be reactivated later, for example in another thought or in a dream. Similarly, however, the body can affect the soul: as the physicians noticed, an excess of bile makes one angry (*fellis abundantia nos ad iram crebriorem cogat*). Augustine goes on to emphasize, though, that the excess of bile is caused by the irascibility of the soul (*abundantia facta sit irascentibus nobis*), and the influence of the body on the soul thus only mirrors the activity of the soul (*quod suo motu animus fecit in corpore, ad eum rursus commovendum valebit*).[159]

4. The Ambivalence of the Mortal Body

The most detailed explanation of Augustine's teaching on the corrupted relationship between the soul and the body, exemplified by the body acting upon the soul, is given in his first exposition of the book of Genesis (which, by the way, is his very first exegetical work).[160] Here Augustine analyses two accounts of the

---

[157] On the impassibility of the soul, see p. 325 with notes 120–122 above. Plotinus deals with perception in greater detail in *Enneads* I 1.7, II 8, IV 3.23 and 26, IV 4.23, IV 5, IV 6.1–2. See Gordon H. Clark 1942:357–382. Blumenthal 1971:67–79 and 1976:45–51, Emilsson 1988, and Chiaradonna 2011:parts 1–2.

[158] *On Music* VI 4.7 (BA 7.372).

[159] *Letters* 9.3–4 (CSEL 34.1.20–22). Presumably, Augustine refers to the sinister influence of the soul, the consequences of which the soul cannot control any more (*poena peccati*), similarly as in *On Music* VI 5.14 (BA 7.388).

[160] Augustine himself says that he wrote it after his return to Africa (*Retractations* I 10.1 [CCSL 57.29]), but with respect to his other statements it seems probable that he started to work on it in Rome in 388; see Dulaey 2004:15–17. On the biblical text used by Augustine (pre-Jerome *Vetus Latina*, inspired by the Septuagint), see Dulaey 2004:533–535.

creation of man in Genesis 1:26 and 2:7, which, as he himself admits, are not easily reconcilable. He knows that some Christian interpreters (*nonnuli nostri*) relate the creation to God's "image and likeness" (Genesis 1:26) to the "inner man" (*homo interior*), and creation from "the clay of the ground" (*limus terrae*, Genesis 2:7) to the human body.[161] Augustine himself understands the second account in Genesis 2:7 as a more detailed elaboration of the brief statement in Genesis 1:26 (*superius breviter insinuati diligentior retractatio*), and therefore interprets "the clay" (*limus*), a mixture of water and earth, as a union of the soul and the body: water bonds earth and holds it together; similarly, the soul gives unity to the "matter of the body" (*corporis materiam*) and prevents it from decaying.[162]

Breathing "the breath of life" (*spiritus vitae*) in Genesis 2:7 also admits several interpretations: it either suggests the creation of the soul (if, previously, only the body was ready), or perhaps it is only now that the soul, which was still "as if in the mouth of God, that is, in His truth and wisdom," is placed into the body. Or, finally (this is the option Augustine seems to prefer),[163] "the breath of life" may refer to "sensuality" (*sensus*), which adds up to the previous creation of the body and the soul; that is, "man as an animal" (*homo animalis*) is created. According to Augustine, the "spiritual man" (*spiritalis*) is not mentioned yet because God's order has not been issued for a human being to follow and thus become spiritual. "The breath of life" (or *sensus*) is an equipment which pertains to human beings even after their sin, not a spiritual quality proved in their relation to God.[164]

This interpretation indicates that, for Augustine, both biblical accounts refer to the creation of man simultaneously as a body and a soul, with the one in Genesis 2:7 being more detailed. On the other hand, in his interpretation of paradise from Genesis 2:5, when "there was no man," he also mentions the previous existence of the "invisible creature" (*invisibilis creatura*), indicated by

---

[161] *On Genesis Against the Manichaeans* II 7.9 (BA 50.288). Apart from Philo (*On the Creation of the World* 134), this interpretation is also familiar to the Christian interpreters Origen (*The Homilies on Genesis* I 13 [GCS N.F. 17.24]), Hilary of Poitiers (*Tractate on the Psalms* 118.10(Iod).6–8 [CSEL 22.442-443], and 129.5 [CSEL 22.651]), and especially Ambrose of Milan (*On Noah* 24.86 [CSEL 32.1.474-475]), whose influence on Augustine was indisputable and probably also provided to him the knowledge of Origen's exegesis; see Teske 1992:179-185 and Dulaey 2002:276-295. Heidl (1999:597-604) assumes that Augustine read Origen's expositions of Genesis in a translation which is now lost. In the period 388-389, Rufinus' translation of Origen's *Homilies on Genesis* probably did not yet exist, which is why most interpreters argue that Augustine's knowledge of Origen was only secondhand in this period; see Somers 1961:111-117.

[162] *On Genesis Against the Manichaeans* II 7.9 (BA 50.288-290).

[163] Similarly also Hilary of Poitiers *Tractate on the Psalms* 118.10(Iod).8 (CSEL 22.443).

[164] *On Genesis Against the Manichaeans* II 8.10 (BA 50.290-292). Later, Augustine will add that in accordance with the apostle (1 Corinthians 15:45) only the body should be referred to as *animale*, not the whole man; see *Retractations* I 10.3 (CCSL 57.32).

the expression "the green of the field and food" (*viride et pabulum agri*).[165] The soul, which, before its sin, is also characterized as the "invisible creature,"[166] was later "soiled by earthly desires and it was born, as it were, on the earth."[167] However, in this passage, probably inspired (whether directly or indirectly) by Origen's exposition of the book of Genesis, Augustine does not seem to describe the sin of the soul which later fell into the body; instead, he rather anticipates the sin of man, who was created as a union of the body and the soul from the very beginning, as related in Genesis 3.[168] Here, again, it is the soul that sins, and the body, as its instrument, bears the more obvious consequences of this failure.

Even though composed of a soul and a body, man was part of paradise; that is, he led a happy life.[169] The body in paradise (*caro*) did not yet know "carnal concupiscence" (*carnalis concupiscentia*);[170] on the contrary, the body was completely subordinated to the soul because "reason" (*ratio*) ruled its "animal part" (*animalis pars*) and, through this part, it also ruled the body. Augustine finds this harmony in the biblical account of the creation of woman (Genesis 2:18-23)—according to his interpretation, the animal part of the soul (also *appetitus*)—as a help to man, i.e. reason (also *mens interior*).[171] The fact that Adam (reason) named the animals shows what in a human being rules the animals and what is also supposed to rule the animal soul ("woman").[172]

---

[165] *On Genesis Against the Manichaeans* II 4.5 (BA 50.278) and II 6.7 (BA 50.284).

[166] *On Genesis Against the Manichaeans* II 3.5 (BA 50.276): ... *antequam anima peccaret*; also II 6.7 (BA 50.284).

[167] *On Genesis Against the Manichaeans* II 3.5 (BA 50.276): *Terrenis enim cupiditatibus sordidata tamquam super terram nata vel super terram esse recte dicitur.*

[168] Dulaey 2004:61–65 and 512–513. Some interpreters claim that a human being consisting of a soul and a body was only created after the first sin, which is not quite accurate; cf. O'Connell 1968:158 and 162; Rombs 2006:48–50 and 65; more cautiously, also Teske 1991:141–155. It is rather the case that the sin of the soul changes the character of the body, as was later admitted by O'Connell (1993:130–133), who, however, does not regard the original body as a real body because of its invisibility, although we have seen that Augustine himself ascribes to this body "animality" endowed with sensory perception that also persists after the fall. O'Connell (1993:136) even indicates that it was only after the fall of the soul that human beings were individualized. This interpretation can find hardly any support in Augustine's work or, for that matter, in that of Plotinus, who even posited the ideas of particulars (not only individual souls anchored in the Intellect); see *Enneads* V 7. It is not quite justified, either, to attribute to Plotinus an identification of the world soul with the community of all souls before their incarnation as found in Teske 1991:143.

[169] *On Genesis Against the Manichaeans* II 9.12 (BA 50.296).

[170] *On Genesis Against the Manichaeans* II 12.17 (BA 50.312).

[171] *On Genesis Against the Manichaeans* II 11.15 (BA 50.306–308). Origen (in Rufinus' translation) allegorizes the character of man as a "spirit" (*spiritus*) and woman as a "soul" (*anima*); see *The Homilies on Genesis* I 15 (GCS N.F. 17.30–31). Ambrose of Milan *On Paradise* 2.11 (CSEL 32.1.271) and 11.51 (CSEL 32.1.308) interprets the pair as *mens* (or *nous*) and *sensus animi* (or *aisthêsis*) respectively, as with Philo *On the Creation of the World* 165.

[172] *On Genesis Against the Manichaeans* II 11.16–12.16 (BA 50.308–310).

As for the sin of the first men, Augustine says that the serpent (the devil)—
a being originally good, but corrupted by its own will[173]—through the woman
(sensual delectation [*delectatio*]), seduced the man (reason); this description,
according to Augustine, can be applied to all sins.[174] This fall resulted from the
misuse of the fruit of the tree[175] that was "in the middle of paradise" (*in medio
paradisi*, Genesis 2:9), in other words, inside the happy soul as its medial place
(*medietas animae*) between the corporeal domain it rules and God to whom it
is meant to be subordinate.[176] The snake's temptation was based on the soul's
desire to break free from God's dominion, take His place, and not be completely
dependent on Him.[177] The soul thus turned away from God to itself,[178] started
to be ashamed of its simplicity (*simplicitas*), or nudity (transparency), and went
on to cover itself with fig leaves (pretense, Genesis 3:7). This is the origin of
hypocrisy (*hupocrisis*) in which men hide themselves (Genesis 3:8), pretend to
be what they are not (*simulatio*),[179] and speak "from their own" (cf. John 8:44),
i.e. from the property they took as their own.[180] This verbal pretense, symbolized by the veil of fig leaves, is further intensified by God's punishment: instead
of the fig leaves, men are given "tunics of skin" (*tunicae pelliciae*, Genesis 3:21)
made of dead animal skins. These tunics symbolize (in Origen's interpretation
already) the mortal body[181] as a place of even more radical hiddenness and
potential pretense. The original body, subordinated to the soul and absolutely
transparent, has thus changed into an instrument of deceit.[182]

The transition from immortality to mortality, which pertains to animals,[183]
also brings about exhaustion and fragility of the body,[184] labor pains,[185] and

---

[173] *On Genesis Against the Manichaeans* II 14.20 (BA 50.318) and II 28.42 (BA 50.378).

[174] *On Genesis Against the Manichaeans* II 14.20–21 (BA 50.318–322). On the sources of this allegorical
interpretation, see Dulaey 2004:548–549.

[175] *On Genesis Against the Manichaeans* II 15.22 (BA 50.324).

[176] *On Genesis Against the Manichaeans* II 9.12 (BA 50.300). The medial position of the soul is also
mentioned by Plotinus in *Enneads* II 9.2.5–10; III 2.8.9–11 and 4.36–38; IV 8.7.

[177] *On Genesis Against the Manichaeans* II 15.22 (BA 50.324).

[178] *On Genesis Against the Manichaeans* II 16.24 (BA 50.328).

[179] *On Genesis Against the Manichaeans* II 15.23 (BA 50.326). On the sources of this interpretation, see
Dulaey 2004:550–551. Presumably, Augustine knew it from Ambrose *On Paradise* 13.63 and 65
(CSEL 32.1.322–324).

[180] *On Genesis Against the Manichaeans* II 16.24 (BA 50.330).

[181] *On Genesis Against the Manichaeans* II 21.32 (BA 50.350). Cf. Origen *Homilies on Leviticus* 6.2 (SC
286.276–278). It is not clear, however, how Augustine had become acquainted with this interpretation when he was writing *On Genesis Against the Manichaeans* (see Dulaey 2004:551–553).

[182] *On Genesis Against the Manichaeans* II 21.32 (BA 50.348–349).

[183] *On Genesis Against the Manichaeans* II 21.32 (BA 50.350).

[184] *On Genesis Against the Manichaeans* II 7.8 (BA 50.286f): *Dicimus enim tabidum et fragile et morti destinatum corpus humanum post peccatum esse coepisse.*

[185] *On Genesis Against the Manichaeans* II 19.29 (BA 50.338–339).

the body wrenching itself free from the control of reason.[186] For human beings (unlike for animals), however, this "mortality" (*mortalitatis conditio*) is not natural, but is a "punishment" (*supplicium*), and thus a burden;[187] the ground becomes "cursed" (*maledicta*, Genesis 3:17), and the body, instead of serving the soul, "weighs it down" (*aggravat animam*, cf. Wisdom 9:15).[188] The order in man, who stopped obeying God and wanted to rule himself ("to be like God"), got lost because he disrupted the order: he lost control over his body and his previous beatitude and was expelled from paradise.[189] More precisely, "under the weight of his own sins," he fell out of paradise to his appropriate place, as it were; he was not expelled by God, but "released" (*dimisit, non exclusit*, cf. Genesis 3:23).[190]

Still, according to Augustine, the mortal body is not merely an instrument for the punishment of human beings, but it also reveals the truth. Human deception, disguising itself as the truth under the fig leaves, is disclosed as a sham by means of the "tunics of skin": human opaqueness is thus convicted, sealed, and brought to light.[191] Also, the mortality of the body is a painful demonstration of the truth about man, of his origin in the earth, which he tried to hide when he wanted to take God's place. "The cloud of our flesh" (*nubilum carnis*) was eventually adopted by the Son of God as an instrument of human salvation[192]—here Augustine is no longer interpreting the text of Genesis in terms of its "historical" content, but in terms of the "prophetic" one,[193] concerned not with the first Adam, but the second one, i.e. Christ, and his bride—the church.[194]

Also, speech as the first veil of the soul after it started to be ashamed of its transparency is not only an instrument of deception, as Augustine's exposition has it for the fig leaves, but also an instrument of salvation: it is due to the opaqueness of speech, which allows and requires an allegorical exposition.[195]

---

[186] *On Genesis Against the Manichaeans* II 15.22 (BA 50.324).

[187] *On Genesis Against the Manichaeans* II 19.29 (BA 50.340).

[188] *On Genesis Against the Manichaeans* II 20.30 (BA 50.342–343); similarly, II 27.41 (BA 50.348–349): ... *non naturae esse, sed poenae.*

[189] *On Genesis Against the Manichaeans* II 15.22 (BA 50.322–323).

[190] *On Genesis Against the Manichaeans* II 22.34 (BA 50.352). The fall of the soul caused by its weight (οἷον βρίθοντα εἰς αὐτούς) is also mentioned by Plotinus (*Enneads* IV 3.13.30–31), who is familiar with the notion of the soul which succumbed to its arrogant ambition (*hê tolma*) to gain independence (τὸ βουληθῆναι δὲ ἑαυτῶν εἶναι); cf. *Enneads* V 1.1.1–8; also III 7.11.15–17 and 20–23. The similarity of these passages is emphasized by O'Connell 1968:177–182.

[191] *On Genesis Against the Manichaeans* II 21.32 (BA 50.348–350). On the body as the clothing of the soul, see also Plato *Gorgias* 523a–524a. On the ancient tradition of this motif, see Pépin 1954:293.

[192] *On Genesis Against the Manichaeans* II 5.6 (BA 50.280).

[193] *On Genesis Against the Manichaeans* II 2.3 (BA 50.272). On the interpretation *secundum historiam* (or *secundum litteram*) and *secundum prophetiam* (i.e. *figurate, in aenigmate*), see Dulaey 2004:40–58.

[194] *On Genesis Against the Manichaeans* II 24.37 (BA 50.360–364).

[195] *On Genesis Against the Manichaeans* II 4.5 (BA 50.278).

Scripture must use allegories, i.e. say one thing and mean another, because men are not able to understand God's intents directly any more. Moreover, words themselves are signs, and their relationship to the things they designate is far from direct.[196] The "cloud" shrouding the soul, then, is not only the body, but also speech, as Augustine puts it in his exposition of Genesis 2:5. Even this cloud, however, can pour beneficial rain, i.e. impart teaching of the truth.[197] As an "invisible creature," the soul originally did not need such a teaching because it was irrigated by "its own spring, that is, by the truth flowing from its interior" (*de intimis suis manante veritate*).[198] But the fallen soul, entangled in lies and the deception of its own words, can only be saved by God's Word, not human words, although even God's Word is mediated by the words of prophets and apostles.[199]

This exposition of the soul entangled in the deception of words and the body gives a new meaning to the parallel Augustine draws in *On the Magnitude*; that is, the analogy between the soul and the body on the one hand, and words and their meanings on the other. Speech and the body are both the expression and the veil of the soul; they are both the obscuring exterior and the revelation of the exterior in its obscuring function. At the same time, however, it is through these two veils, or "clouds"—i.e. speech and the body—that salvation can approach men.[200]

5. Healing of the Body

In his first systematic exposition of Christian teaching, *On the True Religion*, in which many interpreters see traces of Porphyry's influence, Augustine also deals with the relationship between the soul and the body in a purely theological sense.[201] The sin of the first men is explained here as their turning away from God and 'enjoyment of corporeal things' (*frui corporibus*)—i.e. the forbidden fruit from paradise. By this turn, men cut themselves off from the source of their

---

[196] Augustine deals with this issue in *On the Teacher* 10.29–30 (CCSL 29.188–189). Without signs, only speech itself can be demonstrated; speech itself, however, is a sign.

[197] *On Genesis Against the Manichaeans* II 4.5 (BA 50.276–278). On the way this exposition was influenced by Origen, see Dulaey 2004:540.

[198] *On Genesis Against the Manichaeans* II 4.5 (BA 50.278). The original transparency of the body is also discussed by Plotinus (*Enneads* IV 3.18.20–22). The similarity of these passages to Augustine's exposition is emphasized by O'Connell 1968:163–164.

[199] *On Genesis Against the Manichaeans* II 4.5 (BA 50.276–278).

[200] Buckenmeyer (1971:197–211) tries to find the benefit of the body (and the signs) for the soul in Augustine's earlier works as well, which is a very difficult task.

[201] On the echoes of Porphyry in this work, see Dörrie 1924:64–102; Theiler 1966:160–251; Voss 1963:237–239; du Roy 1966:315n3; on the whole work, see du Roy 1966:309–409; also Desch 1980:263–277.

own being and started to head towards 'nothingness' (*vergit ad nihilum*).[202] The body as such is not a source of evil (that would be an abuse of things which are good in themselves),[203] and it is not pure nothingness either because it is given its form by the giver of all forms, that is, by God (who is "unmade" but also the "most formed of all forms"). Here the soul is called "the life" (*vita*) of the body; life, which, however, also comes from God (this applies to individual animals as well as to the world as a whole, animated, as Augustine maintained at that time, by the world soul).[204] If the soul turns away from God, its life becomes carnal and earthly (*vita carnalis et terrena efficitur*), and the body, whose animation depends on the soul, succumbs to transitoriness and death.[205] Turning towards corporeal things thus brings corruption not only to the soul, but, paradoxically, also to the body, which, on top of that, becomes the soul's punishment (*fit poenalis dilectori suo*), burden, and temptation.[206]

Only a new intervention of the Creator's wisdom through which the soul is endowed with the Holy Spirit and the human being thus made "spiritual" can restore the inverted order: the soul will enjoy God and through the soul, the original stability will be restored to the body (*hoc corpus restituatur pristinae stabilitati*); in other words, the body will be incorruptible. That, however, can only be expected as the eschatological victory over death, i.e. not in this life.[207] Then the body will become "aetheric" (*aetherium*) again, and, therefore, transparent for the thoughts of the soul: it will no longer be the ambivalent medium revealing the soul's obscurity.[208]

In this exposition, the body predominantly appears to be the victim of the soul and its unpropitious free choice.[209] Before the soul's sin, the body was perfect, but then it succumbed to weakness and death (*post peccatum factum est imbecillosum et morti destinatum*). As a sad demonstration of the soul's guilt, the body in its weakness even gives the soul an impetus for salvation.[210] Nevertheless,

---

[202] *On the True Religion* 11.21 (CCSL 32.200). Enjoyment in terms of *frui* is appropriate only when it is related to the goal, i.e. God, not when it is for the sake of the means, as Augustine explains in *On Eighty-Three Various Questions* 30 (CCSL 44a.38–40). That is why such an attempt to "enjoy corporeal things" is inappropriate.

[203] *On the True Religion* 20.39 (CCSL 32.211).

[204] *On the True Religion* 11.21–22 (CCSL 32.200–201). On the soul animating the world, see also *On the Immortality of the Soul* 15.24 (CSEL 89.126).

[205] *On the True Religion* 12.23 (CCSL 32.201–202).

[206] *On the True Religion* 20.40 (CCSL 32.211); see also 21.41 (CCSL 32.212–213).

[207] *On the True Religion* 12.24–25 (CCSL 32.202). Later on, Augustine will specify that the resurrected body will not only be returned to the paradisiacal state, but will be animated by the Spirit, not the soul (cf. 1 Corinthians 15:44–45); see *Retractations* I 13.4 (CCSL 57.37–38); similarly, I 11.3 (CCSL 57.34).

[208] *On Eighty-Three Various Questions* 47 (CCSL 44a.74).

[209] On free choice, see *On the True Religion* 14.27–28 (CCSL 32.204).

[210] *On the True Religion* 15.29 (CCSL 32.205).

the actual "new formation" is given to the soul by divine Wisdom, which brings the soul from its dispersion into plurality back to unity and thus, through the soul, the body is saved and brought back to life as well.[211]

Unlike in the older Cassiciacum works, what we encounter here is not salvation of the soul from the body, but salvation of the soul and the body from their fallen state. In this context, Augustine even mentions the soteriological principle, according to which "it was necessary to receive the very nature which was to be liberated."[212] God's Wisdom (the Son of God) received "the whole man" (*totum hominem suscipere*), body and soul, and moreover, a man born of a woman so that neither sex is excluded.[213] According to Augustine, "carnal men" (*carnalibus*), who perceive through the bodily senses (*corporeisque sensibus deditis*), must be shown not only visibly, but also "in a true man" (*in vero homine*), what the worth of "human nature" (*humana natura*) is in the eyes of God.[214] The body is a medium of salvation because the soul, having fallen into time, needs a "temporal medicine" (*temporalis medicina*) administered through the body (*ipsis carnalibus formis*).[215] On top of that, God's plan of salvation does not only aim at the soul, but through the soul the body is to be saved as well.[216]

As Augustine has it now, in the economy of salvation (*dispensatio temporalis*)[217] the incarnation of divine Wisdom, that is, the acceptance of the "whole man," has a predominantly pedagogical and exemplary meaning.[218] Apart from the sad memento in the form of the mortal body, this is a much stronger stimulus to renew the proper order that had been realized in the man Jesus and in which the body serves the soul and the soul is subjected to God. This order, it must be added, was not established automatically or through force: God invites and persuades men (*suadendo et monendo*),[219] for it was His intention from the very beginning that men should submit to Him of their free will, not out of necessity.[220]

---

[211] *On the True Religion* 12.24–25 (CCSL 32.202–203).

[212] *On the True Religion* 16.30 (CCSL 32.206): *Ipsa enim natura suscipienda erat quae liberanda.*

[213] *On the True Religion* 16.30 (CCSL 32.205–206); similarly, *On Eighty-Three Various Questions* 11 (CCSL 44a.18) on the liberation of both sexes; 14 (CCSL 44a.20) on Christ's real body, which was not a mere phantasm.

[214] *On the True Religion* 16.30 (CCSL 32.205–206).

[215] *On the True Religion* 24.45 (CCSL 32.215–216); also Ambrose of Milan *On the Sacrament of the Incarnation of the Lord* 6.56 (CSEL 79.252–253).

[216] *On the True Religion* 23.44 (CCSL 32.214).

[217] *On the True Religion* 26.48 (CCSL 32.217).

[218] *On the True Religion* 16.32 (CCSL 32.207); similarly, *On Eighty-Three Various Questions* 25 (CCSL 44a.31) and 43–44 (CCSL 44a.64–66) on the exemplary meaning of Christ's life.

[219] *On the True Religion* 16.31 (CCSL 32.206).

[220] *On the True Religion* 14.27 (CCSL 32.204); also *On Eighty-Three Various Questions* 2 (CCSL 44a.11).

6. Conclusion

In comparison to the Cassiciacum dialogues, where Augustine understood the body more or less as an obstacle to the true purpose of man, which is contemplation, we can see a certain shift in his works in the period between 387 and 390. Most of all, he appreciates the ambivalence of the relationship between the body and the soul. The body, naturally subordinate to the soul and a true object of its action, became the soul's victim rather than its prison. The right order has been violated by the soul, which wrenched itself free from God's control because of its desire to be autonomous, or its excessive enjoyment of corporeal things. As we have seen, Augustine presents the triune motif of the soul's desire to be autonomous, its turning away from God, and turning towards corporeal things in different passages with different accents or with different motivations. For all three elements, we can find not only biblical inspiration in Genesis 3 (disobeying God's order, longing to be "like gods," enjoying the fruit of paradise), but also Neoplatonic analogies (here, too, the soul is on the border between the Intellect and the corporeal sphere, and turning towards one means turning away from the other;[221] and here, too, the soul longs to possess its own property, as it were, and that is why it separates itself from the Intellect[222]). In any case, this unpropitious turn also affects the body in the form of its fragility, mortality, and opaqueness, which, in turn, become a burden for the soul. It is not only in its fall into mortality, but also in its renewal that the body depends on the soul. That is the reason why God's rescue mission is predominantly aimed at the soul, but it is through the soul that the body will be saved as well. As the soul's victim, the body is a sad memento; at the same time, however, it is also the place where the "man received from God's Son," that is, Jesus Christ, could manifest the proper order leading to salvation—the subordination of the soul to God and of the body to the soul—in order to appeal to other souls entangled in mortality. It is thanks to his example, says Augustine in *On the Magnitude of the Soul*, that there is no need to copy the image because we, as the painters of our lives, can imitate the model itself, in other words, God's Wisdom, which manifested itself in a human being.[223]

---

[221] Cf. Plotinus *Enneads* I 2.4.12–15, II 9.2, I 4, III 2.4.36–42 and 8.9–11, IV 8.4 and 7.24–26, V 1.1.22–29, and VI 9.7.16–23; Porphyry *Sentences* 30.11–19 Brisson.

[222] Cf. Plotinus *Enneads* III 7.11.15–20. On this motif, which brings Plotinus close to the gnostic idea of the mythical "fall," see Jonas 1962:313–314.

[223] See *On the Magnitude* 33.76 (CSEL 89.225). Presumably, this—not quite clear—parable is directed against the Manichaeans, see McWilliam 1997:172–177, or against Porphyry, see J. J. O'Meara 1987:363, Neil 1999:212, and Catapano 2003:377n256.

"As We Say That the Lover Is Bound by the Beloved Woman"

The Soul–Body Relation According to Nemesius of Emesa

PIER FRANCO BEATRICE

Abstract: The problem of the union of soul with body is one of the main themes of the treatise *On the Nature of Man*, written by Nemesius, bishop of Emesa, circa 600, against pagans and heretics. This chapter analyzes Nemesius' use of philosophical sources, especially Porphyry, and tries to explain how he has managed to apply these arguments to the union of the divine Word with His manhood in the context of the post-Chalcedonian controversies and the developments of Syrian Neoplatonism. Important conclusions concerning salvation are also drawn from his theory of providence and free will, and from his polemics against determinism.

1. Re-dating Nemesius

RECENT DECADES HAVE SEEN A considerable increase in the number of studies devoted to analyzing the treatise of Nemesius *On the Nature of Man*. After the publication of the masterly commentary by Sharples and Van der Eijk (2008), it seems that there is nothing or very little more to add. From now on, one will need to refer to this book for the necessary information on the Nemesian bibliography and on the numerous sources of his thought that have been identified.[1] Yet, despite this, the enigmas of Nemesius' work have not been completely revealed. This is due essentially to the fact that the figure of the author is still wrapped in a thick cloak of mystery, nothing precise is yet known about his personality, about the time in which he lived, and in general about the

---

[1]   Nemesius' text is quoted from this translation, but see also Telfer 1955.

historical and cultural context in which he was active. All the attempts to identify the author with other Nemesii have so far proved totally unsuccessful. The lack of certain details about the man is a serious limit to understanding the text that has come down to us under his name.

The situation is made even more difficult by the fact that an unfortunate series of ambiguities and misunderstandings has ended up producing among scholars a form of agreement, a completely unfounded consensus, that places Nemesius between the end of the fourth and the middle of the fifth centuries, and that therefore leads to a distorted interpretation of the meaning of some of his statements and of the real relationships between his work and the sources from which he may have drawn. The fact that, in the absence of any certain information, Robert Devreesse (1945) prudently ignored the name of Nemesius in drawing up the chronological list of the bishops of Emesa between the fourth and the seventh century, may be considered an important exception, an appreciable sign of the scholar's scientific rigor.[2]

We can therefore no longer avoid the need to overcome this state of deadlock and to find, if possible, some kind of documentation that will enable us to draw up a more precise outline of the man and of his work. A fortunate discovery, which we reported some years ago in the Proceedings of the Ninth Origen Colloquium,[3] seems to offer a key that will allow us to place Nemesius in his time and thus correctly reinterpret some aspects of his work that, until now, have been completely misunderstood. That is the aim we wish to achieve with this chapter.

The first author who had an in-depth knowledge of Nemesius and his treatise is Maximus the Confessor in the seventh century. In previous centuries, the sources are silent. Not only does Maximus draw and reprocess the thoughts of Nemesius on freedom of choice, but he is the first to state the name and ecclesiastical office of one of his favorite authors, Nemesius, Bishop of Emesa. After Maximus, the name of Nemesius and some extracts from his work are quoted in the *Questions and Answers* by Anastasius of Sinai,[4] and by other Byzantine writers (Michael Glykas, Meletius, Nilus Doxopatres),[5] whereas John of Damascus, strange though it may seem, quotes freely from the treatise of Nemesius, without however giving his name.[6]

---

[2] Devreesse 1945:203–205. However, Nasrallah (1971:223–224) takes it for granted that Nemesius was bishop of Emesa at the beginning of the fifth century and that he died before 431.

[3] Beatrice 2009:523–524.

[4] Anastasius of Sinai *Questions and Answers* 18, 24 (PG 89.505c, 89.545b). This is the eleventh-century version published by Gretser (1617), but in the "original collection" (CCSG 59), Nemesius does not appear.

[5] Morani (1981:101–151) provides an exhaustive survey of the indirect tradition.

[6] See Beatrice 2010a:218.

The decisive testimony for our purpose is to be found in the florilegium of twelve patristic dyothelite passages defining the will, published as an appendix to *Short Theological and Polemical Treatises* 26, written by Maximus in reply to the questions asked by the monk Theodore.[7] It is important to note that this florilegium, regardless of the problem of the authenticity of the fragments quoted,[8] is structured according to the chronological order of the authors quoted. In fact, it begins with extracts from works by Irenaeus of Lyons and Clement of Alexandria, continues with extracts from Alexander of Alexandria, Eustathius of Antioch, Athanasius of Alexandria, Gregory of Nyssa, Diadochus of Photike, Anastasius of Antioch, and ends with two extracts from Nemesius, Bishop of Emesa, and two extracts from Maximus the Confessor.[9] Maximus is called "saint," which implies that the final editor of the florilegium could hardly have been Maximus himself!

Be that as it may, this is a chronological span that goes from the end of the second century to the mid-seventh century, and in this list Nemesius is placed after Anastasius, who was the Chalcedonian Patriarch of Antioch in the second half of the sixth century (559–570 and 593–598),[10] and before Maximus the Confessor, who lived between the end of the sixth century and the mid-seventh century (580–662). This undoubtedly means that Nemesius was bishop of Emesa approximately in the years between the end of the sixth and the beginning of the seventh century, that is, at the time of the Emperors Maurice, Phocas, and Heraclius, during the Persian wars, and just before the Arab conquest of Syria. This florilegium provides the irrefutable testimony on the true dating of Nemesius, even though, unfortunately, it is not backed up by any other source. More cannot be done.

2. Nemesius and Syrian Paganism around 600

In any event, this new dating, which places Nemesius two centuries later than the current chronology, is exceptionally important since it sheds some unexpected light on the significance of his work, first of all as regards the relationship with the pagans (*Hellênes*). Twice Nemesius unambiguously reveals that his writing is aimed not only at Christians but also at pagans:

> This directly stops the mouths of those who try to attack the unification of God with man. For the majority of pagans make this an object

---

[7] Maximus the Confessor *Short Theological and Polemical Treatises* 26 (PG 91.276a–280b); Nemesius at PG 91.277c–d.

[8] For discussion, see Jankowiak and Booth 2015:66–67, who, however, wrongly count twenty patristic passages.

[9] See the commentary and French translation by Larchet and Ponsoye 1998:49–50 and 268–271.

[10] Devreesse 1945:118–119.

of derision, saying that it is impossible, implausible and unseemly that the divine should come together with the mortal nature by mixture and unification. But we make use of their own reputable witnesses and shrug off the accusation.

Nemesius *On the Nature of Man* 43 Morani[11]

Here Nemesius is referring in particular to Porphyry, who moved his tongue against Christ (Πορφύριος ὁ κατὰ Χριστοῦ κινήσας τὴν ἑαυτοῦ γλῶσσαν), and takes him as a witness to the Christian truth, since the testimonies of enemies on behalf of the Christians are strong and permit no reply. And again elsewhere Nemesius writes, "But since this discussion is not directed to these (Christians, and possibly Jews) alone, but also to the pagans ..."[12] This means that Nemesius had a declaredly apologetic purpose. But what pagans did he have in mind? Certainly not the pagans who lived between the fourth and the fifth century, but rather those pagans living in the region of Emesa, who during the sixth century had been visited by the Neoplatonist philosopher Damascius, one of the "seven movers," on his return from Persia.[13] Precisely in Emesa, in 538, Damascius composed an epitaph for the young slave girl Zosime, carved on a stele discovered in 1925, "I, Zosime, who was before a slave in body only have now gained freedom for my body too."[14] Damascius, of course, did not pass through Emesa in vain, without leaving notable traces of his authoritative presence, namely followers, disciples, and, above all, books of Neoplatonic philosophy.

It is hard to imagine Nemesius in the role of a bishop who persecuted the pagans, as did Stephen, bishop of the nearby town of Harran who, by order of the Emperor Maurice, unleashed a bloodthirsty hunt of local pagans with the aim of forcing the largest possible number of them to convert. As the Jacobite Patriarch Dionysius of Tel-Mahre reports:

> At this time Maurice commanded Stephen, the bishop of Harran, to initiate a persecution of the pagans there. When this bishop received the order, he began to persecute them. Many became Christians; and as for those who refused, he would cut them in half with a sword and hang their sides along the streets of Harran. The governor of Harran at that time was a man called Acindynus; in name he was a Christian, but

---

[11] Translation in Sharples and Van der Eijk 2008:85.

[12] Nemesius *On the Nature of Man* 120 Morani; translation in Sharples and Van der Eijk 2008:204–205.

[13] On the complex problems connected with the exile of the seven members of the Academy to Persia and their return, see Lane Fox 2005:231–244 and Watts 2005:285–315.

[14] SEG VII 121. The epitaph is attributed to Damascius in the *Palatine Anthology* VII 553, but here Damascius speaks as distinct from the inscription: "Zosime ... has now gained ..." See Ahbel-Rappe 2010:425n31.

in secret a pagan. He was betrayed to the bishop by his scribe, a young person called Honorius and they impaled him on the tell in Harran. Honorius himself replaced him as city-governor.

Dionysius of Tel-Mahre *Chronicle* §5[15]

The attitude of Nemesius, on the other hand, seems comparable to that of the anonymous author of a Syriac work containing a collection of "the prophecies of the pagan philosophers in abbreviated form." This text was composed probably between the end of the sixth and the beginning of the seventh century; that is, in the very period in which we intend to place Nemesius' work, and presents considerable similarities with the *Theosophy*, a Greek anonymous work composed in the early years of the sixth century.[16] The purpose of the above-mentioned collection was to convert the pagans of Harran by means of testimonies drawn from the Greek wisdom of which they professed to be followers:

> Since a person is likely to believe testimonia from his own background rather than anything alien or from outside, we have diligently taken care to introduce, lay before you and show you testimonia from certain wise men and philosophers who belong to the same religion as you ...

Anonymous Work in Syriac[17]

The apologetic method used both by Nemesius and by the Harran compiler aimed to persuade the pagans to abandon the error to which they stubbornly remained attached, not by invoking the authority of the biblical prophecies, which they clearly did not recognize and were not willing to accept, but by making use of the testimonies on the truth of the Christian faith that were to be found in the religious and philosophical texts in which they placed their trust, sometimes even the works of notorious enemies of the Christian religion like Porphyry. And yet their obstinate idolatrous disbelief must at a certain point have appeared totally inexcusable and no longer tolerable in an empire that had by then become completely Christian. One may therefore surmise that the violent persecutory action originated after the failure of this soft "apologetic" approach, if one does not want to believe, instead, that the apologetic discourse was created as an ideological support of the persecution, or afterwards as justification of the persecution that had already been carried out.

Anyway, Nemesius and his Syrian contemporary in Harran use different languages and proof-texts, evidently because they are addressing different

---

[15] Translation by Palmer 1993:114.
[16] See Beatrice 2001.
[17] The translation is according to Brock 1983:227. See also Arzhanov 2019:103–110.

groups. It can be easily seen that the anonymous Harran compiler, who writes only for pagans, reports the sentences of Thules, Orpheus, Hermes Trismegistos, Sophocles, Apollo, the Sibyls, the sentences of Pythagoras, Plato, Plotinus, Amelius, and Porphyry, and especially those of the indigenous prophet Baba, to stimulate the pagans to accept the mysteries of the Christian faith about the Trinity and the Incarnation. On the other hand, Nemesius, who writes for both Christians and pagans, does not resort to purported pagan prophecies of Christianity but displays his learned knowledge of medical and philosophical texts, including those of Galen and Aristotle, to develop his doctrine on the nature, dignity, and freedom of man.

3. Theological Polemics

The new dating proposed here allows us at last to definitively clear away any problematic and necessarily inconclusive speculations on possible connections between Nemesius and Pelagius.[18] The times and places in which they lived were too far apart for any significant comparison to be made. Instead, an attempt to determine Nemesius' ecclesiastical position in Syria in the sixth to seventh centuries appears promising.

At the time of Nemesius, there were three Christian groups: the Nestorians, the Monophysites, and the Neo-Chalcedonians. We are justified in wondering to which of these three groups the bishop of an important metropolitan see like Emesa, which was part of the patriarchate of Antioch, might have belonged.

We can exclude the Nestorians. Nemesius rejects as erroneous the interpretation of certain influential men, according to which the unification of the divine nature with the human nature in Christ is caused by the "good pleasure" (consent or grace) of God, insisting, on the other hand, that, if one may plausibly state that the reception of the body came about by consent, the union without confusion is through God's own nature and not by grace.[19] Among the influential men criticized by Nemesius we must certainly count Theodore of Mopsuestia, who seems to have been the first to introduce the Christological notion of *eudokia*:

---

[18] After Bellarmine's claim that Nemesius *sapit Pelagianismum*, many scholars have thought it necessary to deal with this issue. Among many others, see e.g. Telfer 1955:215–216, Streck 2005:9–17, Sharples and Van der Eijk 2008:7, with further bibliography.

[19] Nemesius, *On the Nature of Man* 44 Morani: οὐκ εὐδοκία τοίνυν ὁ τρόπος τῆς ἑνώσεως ὥς τισι τῶν ἐνδόξων ἀνδρῶν δοκεῖ ἀλλ᾽ ἡ φύσις αἰτία. τὸ μὲν γὰρ ἀναλαβεῖν σῶμα κατ᾽ εὐδοκίαν εἴποι τις ἂν εὐλόγως γεγενῆσθαι τὸ δὲ ἐνούμενον μὴ συγχυθῆναι κατὰ τὴν οἰκείαν τοῦ θεοῦ φύσιν οὐ κατ᾽ εὐδοκίαν γίνεται.

Therefore we do not say that God makes his indwelling either by essence or by activity. What then is left? What account shall we use which seems to preserve the particular mode of indwelling in these matters? It is clear that it is fitting to speak of the indwelling as occurring by 'good pleasure' ... In him (i.e. Christ), on the other hand, we do not say that the indwelling took place in this way ... but 'as in a son.' Being thus well pleased, he indwelt.

Theodore *On the Incarnation* VII[20]

And elsewhere:

The type of unification which is according to 'good pleasure,' preserving the natures unconfounded and undivided, produces one person of both ... for it is in the way that involves consent that the one born from the very womb of the Virgin was united with the Divine Word.

Theodore *Letter to Domnus* VII [21]

For this reason it is customary, indeed correct, to indicate Theodore as the target of Nemesius' criticism,[22] but because of the new dating of Nemesius we must widen the horizon, including among the supporters of this doctrine of the Incarnation rejected by Nemesius also other authoritative "Antiochene" theologians such as Nestorius[23] and Theodoret of Cyrus.[24] Cyril of Alexandria, and other orthodox polemicists, explicitly denounced the doctrine of the Incarnation "by good pleasure" (*kat' eudokian*) as a characteristic error of the Antiochene Christology.[25] In the sixth century, Leontius of Byzantium identified in Nestorius, his teachers, and disciples, the fathers of this impious doctrine which had still many followers in his time.[26] Nemesius is therefore on a line of continuity with the anti-Nestorian criticism developed by the Neo-Chalcedonian Leontius of Byzantium.

We can also exclude the possibility of Nemesius being a Monophysite. The first certainly Monophysite bishop of Emesa was Basil who, around 630, took part, with the Monophysite Patriarch of Antioch Athanasius and ten other

---

[20] PG 66.973a–d, translation in Behr 2011:280–283.
[21] PG 66.1012c–1013a.
[22] Telfer 1955:303n6; Sharples and Van der Eijk 2008:86n414.
[23] Nestorius frr. 201–202. See Loofs 1905:219–220.
[24] Theodoret of Cyrus *Eranistes* II (Greek text in Ettlinger 1975:137–138). Here *eudokia* is found together with *philanthrôpia* and *kharis*. The last word was already used by Diodore of Tarsus (fr. 27), as opposed to *phusis*. See Gahbauer 1984:235–236.
[25] See Beatrice 2009:509–512.
[26] Leontius of Byzantium *Against Nestorians and Eutychians* I (PG 86.1.1300b–1301c).

Monophysite bishops from the region, in the conference of Hierapolis where the attempted theological compromise proposed by the emperor Heraclius was rejected.[27] So there is no reason to doubt that Nemesius, whose treatise is quoted with appreciation in the works of orthodox authors such as Maximus the Confessor, Anastasius of Sinai, and John of Damascus, was a Neo-Chalcedonian bishop.

Above all, the Christological formula of "the union without confusion" of the two natures of Christ points in this direction. Nemesius writes about the union of God the Word with man:

> This kind of mixture or unification (ὁ τρόπος τῆς κράσεως ἢ ἐνώσεως) is more novel. He [God the Word] both is infused and remains altogether unmixed, uncompounded, uncontaminated and unchanged (ἄμικτος καὶ ἀσύγχυτος καὶ ἀδιάφθορος καὶ ἀμετάβλητος) not affected with them [body and soul] but only acting with them ...
>
> Nemesius *On the Nature of Man* 42 Morani[28]

Due to the traditional incorrect dating, scholars have tended to see Nemesius as a significant "forerunner" of the Chalcedonian formula, a milestone on the road that led ancient Christian thought towards the final dogmatic formulation of the council.[29] Quite the contrary, it must be said that not only was Nemesius not a forerunner of Chalcedon, but he adopted and used in his anthropological and Christological discourse a formula that had by then become the tag of identification for the followers of Chalcedonian orthodoxy in the Byzantine church in opposition to the deviations set up by the rival churches of the Nestorians and the Monophysites. The Chalcedonian doctrine of the unconfused union of the two natures represents, in the logic of Nemesius' anthropology, the culminating moment and the definitive illustration of the way in which the union of body and soul should be conceived in the unity of the human being. However, there is a difference between the human example and the divine prototype. Indeed, the further specification that Nemesius introduces when he claims that, in its union with man, the Word remains impassible as it was before the union, unlike the soul, which suffers through sympathy with the body, seems intended to be a precise reply to the *theopaschite* error implicit in the monophysite Christology:

> God the Word, while united with man, remained uncompounded and uncontained, but not in the way the soul is. For the soul, being one

---

[27] Devreesse 1945:102n7.
[28] Translation in Sharples and Van der Eijk 2008:84.
[29] Among many others, see e.g. Gahbauer 1984:424.

of the things which are complex, seems both to be affected with the body in a way through its affinity with it (δοκεῖ καὶ συμπάσχειν πως δι' οἰκειότητα τῷ σώματι), and sometimes to master it, sometimes to be mastered.[30] But God the Word is not in any way Himself altered by this affinity that concerns body and soul, nor does He share in their weakness (οὐδὲ μετέχων τῆς ἐκείνων ἀσθενείας), but by giving them a share in His divinity He becomes one with them while remaining one as He was before the unification.

Nemesius *On the Nature of Man* 42 Morani[31]

The anthropological model and Christological speculation support each other in the unitary development of Nemesius' theological discourse. In this, he again found an important predecessor in Leontius of Byzantium, who drew up this interpretation in his polemical treatise directed simultaneously against the Nestorians and the Eutychians. Before Nemesius, Leontius had already taken a stand against both groups about the correct use of this simile. The Nestorians rejected the comparison since the soul is never without body, whereas the divine Word preexists human nature. Besides, man is made up of imperfect parts, whereas Christ is totally perfect. On the other hand, the Eutychians cherished the simile, but they wrongly considered the human example of the union of soul and body as the perfect image of "the confusion" of the natures in the divine prototype. Leontius accepts the traditional image of man composed of soul and body to give an approximate example of the union of the two natures in Christ, thus showing that the Word is substantially united to the human body and is never seen without it, but the distinction is preserved in the union, as also occurs for man who maintains the distinction of soul and body in the union.[32] It is worth remembering that, besides Leontius and Nemesius, other pro-Chalcedonian theologians thought that the union of the two distinct substances of the body and soul was a paradigm of the hypostatic union of the person of Christ. Suffice it to mention Faustus of Riez[33] and Anastasius of Sinai.[34]

What was dear to the hearts of Leontius and Nemesius was the statement that the hypostatic union must be understood "according to the substance," to contrast both Nestorian Christology, characterized by "the division" of the two

---

[30] A similar concept about the bond of "sympathy" between the soul and the body in Damascius. See Westerink and Combès 1989:273, Van Riel 2010:684–688.

[31] Translation in Sharples and Van der Eijk 2008:84. The same argument in John of Damascus *Against the Jacobites* 57 (Kotter 1981:129–130).

[32] Leontius of Byzantium *Against Nestorians and Eutychians* I (PG 86.1.1280b–1281b).

[33] Faustus of Riez *Letters* 7 (CSEL 21.204). On Faustus' Christology, see Hainthaler 2016:263–275.

[34] Anastasius of Sinai *Guide Along the Right Path* 18–19 (CCSG 8.273–279). See Uthemann 2015:174–181.

natures, and the opposing Monophysite Christology, based, at least in the judg-ment of the Chalcedonian theologians, on the idea of a total "confusion" of the two natures. This worry is what led Nemesius to polemicize also against the Eunomians who were in his eyes guilty of claiming with Aristotle that the sensa-tions are the powers of the body, and that therefore in Christ the divine powers were mixed with the powers of the body, that is the bodily senses, and brought about their unification.[35]

The Chalcedonian doctrine of the "unconfused union" of the two natures represents for Nemesius an important antidote, not only against the Nestorians and the Eunomians, but also against Origen's arbitrary speculations on the ranks of souls, their risings and their descendings, which he considers totally inconsistent with the Scriptures and not in harmony with Christian doctrine.[36] Also the statement that man alone among rational beings possesses the privi-lege of the soul, which is shared neither by daemons nor by angels, to receive pardon on repentance, could be directed against Origen, even though he is not mentioned by name.[37] It seems, therefore, correct to conclude that, contrary to what is currently claimed, Nemesius was informed of the fact that Origen and his followers supported doctrines that deviated from orthodoxy regarding the preexistence of souls and the universal restoration. But he was certainly not referring to the condemnations of 399–400. Much more plausibly he had in mind the condemnations pronounced by Justinian in 543, and by the Council of Constantinople ten years later in 553, at the conclusion of the second Origenist controversy.[38]

In short, it may be said that Nemesius takes his distance both from the theologians of the Antiochene School—Theodore of Mopsuestia, Nestorius, and Theodoret of Cyrus—and from Origen and the Origenists, simply because the doctrines of both these opposing groups had been definitively condemned by the Council of Constantinople of 553.[39] On the other hand, Nemesius' condem-nation of Monophysitism is implicit in his use of the Chalcedonian formula "unconfused union." At this point, the silence on Eutyches becomes insignifi-cant and loses all its weight as an argument for the dating of Nemesius' treatise.

---

[35] Nemesius *On the Nature of Man* 43–44 Morani.

[36] *On the Nature of Man* 44 Morani: τοὺς γὰρ βαθμοὺς τῶν ψυχῶν καὶ τὰς ἀναβάσεις καὶ καταβάσεις, ἃς Ὠριγένης εἰσάγει, μηδὲν προσηκούσας ταῖς θείαις γραφαῖς μηδὲ συναδούσας τοῖς τῶν Χριστιανῶν δόγμασι, καταλειπτέον. For more details, see Beatrice 2009:506–515.

[37] *On the Nature of Man* 9–10 Morani.

[38] On the double condemnation of Origenism in those years, see Price 2009:2.270–286 and Ramelli 2013:724–738.

[39] See the fourteen canons in ACO 4.1.240–244, and Price 2009:2.120–126. Origen is explicitly mentioned in canon eleven.

4. Nemesius and the Syrian Tradition on Psychology and Anthropology

It has often been thought, apparently wrongly, that to understand Nemesius' anthropology it would be useful to make a comparison with his more famous, and much better known, contemporary Gregory of Nyssa, author of two works on an anthropological subject, *On the Making of Man* and *On the Soul and the Resurrection*. This error in perspective was also favored by the fact that the whimsical vicissitudes of the manuscript tradition have sometimes confused the two names. Some manuscripts attribute to Gregory the paternity of sections two and three of *On the Nature of Man*, while others the whole treatise.[40] In fact, besides the chronological distance of two centuries that separates them, one needs to consider above all the diversity of the contexts and of the intentions of the two authors.

It is true that, for both Gregory and Nemesius, man seems to be the supreme being created last because the whole universe came to be on his account,[41] the only being placed on the boundary between, and binding together in himself, the visible, nonrational reality with the intelligible, rational reality, therefore participating in both dimensions—Gregory *meson* and Nemesius *en methoriois*.[42] Nemesius and Gregory also had the same critical attitude towards Origen's doctrine of the soul. Nevertheless, while Gregory criticizes the doctrine of the preexistence of souls, as he found it in Origen's *On First Principles*, because he supports the idea that soul and body are born and develop together,[43] Nemesius criticizes not the idea itself of the preexistence of souls, but Origen's theory of the ascents and descents of souls.[44] Moreover, while acknowledging that man was born in the image and likeness of God (Genesis 1:26–27), that he communes with Christ and is a child of God, Nemesius consciously uses the ancient and widespread philosophical definition of man as "a microcosm" (*mikros kosmos*) that binds together in himself mortal and immortal elements, joins the rational with the irrational, and carries in his own nature the image of the whole creation.[45] On the contrary, Gregory considered this definition pagan and rejected it because, in his opinion, it was incompatible with the biblical and ecclesiastical doctrine that man is the image of the Creator's nature.[46] And while Gregory insists on the

---

[40] On the very complex history of the text, see Morani 1981.

[41] Gregory *On the Making of Man* 2 (PG 44.132d–133b), Nemesius *On the Nature of Man* 4–5, 11 Morani.

[42] *On the Making of Man* 18 (PG 44.181b); *On the Nature of Man* 2, 5, and 6 Morani.

[43] *On the Making of Man* 28–29 (PG 44.229b–240b).

[44] *On the Nature of Man* 44 Morani.

[45] *On the Nature of Man* 15 Morani.

[46] *On the Making of Man* 16 (PG 44.177d–180a).

impossibility of expressing and comprehending the nature of the mysterious bond of the soul-mind with the body,[47] Nemesius does not hesitate, as we shall see in more detail, to tackle the discussion of the topic in section three with the conceptual tools offered by Neoplatonic speculation. Essentially, Nemesius is less conditioned than Gregory by the biblical text because his real interest is not exegetical, but prevalently philosophical and apologetic.[48]

The fact is that Nemesius' anthropology is better understood if it is compared not so much with Gregory as with various documents that reveal the particular attention paid to issues concerning the soul and anthropology in general in the literature of the Syrian region, both in Greek and in Syriac, between the fifth and the ninth century. The following texts may be quoted: "Gregory Thaumaturgus" *To Tatian, On the Soul*, which was later translated from Greek into Syriac,[49] stating for a pagan audience that the soul is an incorporeal and simple substance, immortal and rational; books five–six of the *Cure for Greek Maladies* where Theodoret of Cyrus deals with the nature of man, the soul-body relationship, and the problem of freedom;[50] the dialogue *Theophrastus* by Aeneas of Gaza;[51] the *Treatise On the Composition of Man* by the bishop Ahudemmeh (sixth century),[52] who was also the author of a work entitled *That Man is a Microcosm*; in the seventh century, the *Commentary on the Hexaëmeron* by Jacob of Edessa, in which we find once again, as well as the criticism of Origen's psychology (though without naming him), the analogy between the union "without mixture and confusion" of the soul with the body and the union "without mixture, confusion and change" of God with the human nature in the hypostatic union of Christ;[53] and, in the ninth century, the treatises *On the Soul* by John of Dara and by Moshe bar Kepha in which traces of the use of Nemesius have been found.[54]

Nemesius should be placed chronologically between Ahudemmeh and Jacob of Edessa, and finally we need to acknowledge that, contrary to the general opinion, his was not the "first" treatise on Christian anthropology. This literature

---

[47] *On the Making of Man* 15 (PG 44.177b–c): ἡ δὲ τοῦ νοῦ πρὸς τὸ σωματικὸν κοινωνία ἄφραστόν τε καὶ ἀνεπινόητον τὴν συνάφειαν ἔχει ... ἀλλὰ κατά τινα τρόπον ἀμήχανόν τε καὶ ἀκατανόητον ἐγγίζων ὁ νοῦς τῇ φύσει καὶ προσαπτόμενος καὶ ἐν αὐτῇ καὶ περὶ αὐτὴν θεωρεῖται οὔτε ἐγκαθήμενος οὔτε περιπτυσσόμενος ἀλλὰ ὡς οὐκ ἔστιν εἰπεῖν ἢ νοῆσαι ... See also *On the Making of Man* 12 (PG 44.160d and 161b).

[48] This does not mean, of course, that Nemesius ignores or underestimates the Biblical text; for a list of quotations, see e.g. Vanhamel 1982:97–98.

[49] The Greek text is printed twice, with slight differences, in PG 10.1137a–1145b (Gregory Thaumaturgus) and PG 91.353c–361b (Maximus the Confessor). See Lebreton 1906:73–83.

[50] Critical edition and German translation by Scholten 2015.

[51] See Colonna 1958. English translation and commentary by Dillon and Russell 2012.

[52] See Nau 1905:97–115.

[53] Vaschalde 1932:268–289.

[54] See Reller 1999:253–268, Zonta 1991:223–258 and 2014:113–122.

on the soul of man is developed in an eminently religious context where there is a strong intention to seek some kind of harmony between the Patristic theological tradition and the data supplied by the doxographic tradition of profane philosophy.[55] The important role played by Nemesius in the Syrian tradition of studies on the soul is also demonstrated by the fact that the Nestorian Patriarch Timothy, in his *Letter* 43 of the year 782–783, asks his correspondent Pethion to search out, and send him, the work by a certain "philosopher" called Nemesius (he apparently no longer knew that Nemesius had been a bishop or intentionally avoided to recognize the value of a Chalcedonian bishop) on the structure of man, which begins, "Man is excellently constructed as a rational soul and body ..." Timothy knows that the treatise has roughly five sections and that at the end Nemesius promises to write a treatise on the soul, but this second part is missing.[56] Timothy's interest in Nemesius is easily explained if we consider that he dealt extensively with anthropological themes in his *Letter* 2 to the deacon and court physician Boktišoʻ.[57]

A comparative, in-depth, and systematic study on Nemesius, in the light of all this vast Syriac documentation, has yet to be made, but it promises to considerably enrich our understanding of the man, his work, and his cultural environment. What really matters, for now, is that we have found the path to follow.

5. The Nature of the Soul

In the first section of his treatise, Nemesius discusses the problem of the structure and the collocation of man in the cosmos, resorting to a wide and well-documented doxography. The names of the authors whose opinions Nemesius deems it necessary to quote appear right from the start: Plotinus and Apollinaris of Laodicea claim that man is divided into three parts, i.e. body, soul, and intellect, while other philosophers, such as the Stoics, Aristotle, and Plato, support various other opinions, but all are generally in agreement in stating that the soul is superior to the body.[58] In section two, Nemesius deals directly with the soul.

Nemesius has an easy task denouncing the profound disagreements between the doctrines put forward in the Greek schools of philosophy concerning the nature of the soul. During the discussion, Nemesius criticizes at length and rejects the arguments of the Stoics Cleanthes and Chrysippus supporting the

---

[55] Hugonnard-Roche (2014:17–64) provides an up-to-date bibliographical survey on the Syriac texts. See also Arzhanov 2019:202–220.

[56] *Letter* 43.7. I quote from Brock 1999:237. See also Heimgartner 2012:51–52.

[57] See Braun 1953:21–47.

[58] Sharples and van der Eijk 2008:35–51.

idea that the soul is a body,[59] and the theory of Aristotle who defines the soul as "the first actuality of a natural body which potentially has life" (*entelekheia*).[60] In this context he explicitly declares his agreement with the arguments of Ammonius, "the teacher of Plotinus," and of Numenius, the Pythagorean, in favor of Platonic psychology, which is based on the radical otherness of the soul with respect to the body.[61]

But after having presented the various opinions of the ancients, Nemesius does not ignore the need to also discuss the doctrines of two Christian theologians such as the Neo-Arian Eunomius and Apollinaris.[62] Of the former he accepts the "Platonic" truth of the statement that the soul is an incorporeal substance, but rejects the "Aristotelian" error according to which the soul is created in the body. Of the latter he rejects the traducianist theory according to which the souls are born from souls as the bodies from bodies. Nemesius also criticizes the psychological doctrines of Eunomius and Apollinaris as being erroneous and contradictory, since both end up by denying the immortality of the soul, which was so dear to Nemesius himself. Instead, Nemesius thinks with Plato that the soul is a self-sufficient substance which, thanks to its autonomous movement, carries along that of the bodily organism; it is immortal and preexists the body, as is demonstrated by the indisputably true thesis of the *anamnêsis* found in Plato's *Phaedo*; that is, the theory that acts of learning are acts of recollection.[63]

Nemesius specifies that the soul comes in contact with the body neither by means of continuous creation nor by transmission. If with the Greeks the doctrine of the immortality of the soul is accompanied by the dogma of *metempsukhôsis*, what really matters is that one does not admit the transmigration of the soul from man into the bodies of animals but only into the bodies of other men, as Iamblichus has rightly observed in his monograph *That Transmigrations Do Not Occur From Men into Irrational Animals nor From Irrational Animals Into Men but From Animals to Animals and From Men to Men*.[64] Coming from a Christian bishop, this is a surprising admission that is difficult to explain and may be interpreted in different ways. It is not clear whether Nemesius, following Iamblichus' exegesis of Plato, endorses here the theory of the transmigration from man to man or whether he is simply claiming that human souls and animal souls are intrinsically different.

---

[59] Sharples and van der Eijk 2008:57–59.

[60] Sharples and van der Eijk 2008:52–53 and 64–68. The definition comes from Aristotle *On the Soul* 412a19–b6.

[61] *On the Nature of Man* 17–18 Morani.

[62] *On the Nature of Man* 30–32 Morani; Sharples and van der Eijk 2008:69–71.

[63] *On the Nature of Man* 22–23 Morani, citing *Phaedo* 91e–92e.

[64] *On the Nature of Man* 34–35 Morani 1987, Beatrice 2005:255–260, and Sharples and van der Eijk 2008:73–74.

Be that as it may, it is worth emphasizing that, contrary to what is generally believed, the polemics against Eunomius and Apollinaris cannot be used as an argument to date Nemesius at the end of the fourth century. In fact, it is not necessary to think that Nemesius argues exclusively against his contemporaries, and that therefore the chronology of Eunomius and Apollinaris should be taken as the immediate *terminus post quem* for the work of Nemesius. Since Eunomius and Apollinaris were important theologians, they had followers and were at the center of heated disputes even after their death. Not only did the Council of Constantinople in 553 condemn them along with other formidable heresiarchs such as Arius, Macedonius, Nestorius, Eutyches, and Origen,[65] but their doctrines were well known and were still fought in the seventh century, as is shown by the vast documentation collected by Lietzmann for Apollinaris[66] and by Vaggione for Eunomius.[67] We must read Nemesius' criticism in the light of all these sources and place it in its historical context, which is that of the theological controversies that developed between the sixth and the seventh century, before the outbreak of the monothelite crisis.

Nemesius thus comes to establish that the soul is an incorporeal, intelligible, and immortal substance. Nemesius concludes that, really, the divinely inspired and absolutely reliable teaching of the sacred Scriptures is sufficient proof of the soul's immortality. Instead, for those who do not accept the Christian writings (an allusion to the pagan addressees of his treatise), it suffices to prove that the soul is none of those things that perish and is therefore immortal.[68]

6. The Relationship between Soul and Body

Nemesius' adherence to Neoplatonic anthropology is revealed even more explicitly in section three, where he plans to inquire how the union of the soul with the soulless body comes about—a really puzzling question. The union of the soul with the body is an old issue, widely debated in Greek philosophy, especially since the Stoics had explained the paradox of the interpenetration of soul and body by resorting to the notion of "complete blending" (κρᾶσις δι' ὅλων). According to the Stoics, there is nothing in the body that possesses soul that lacks a share in the soul.[69] The Stoic Hierocles, writing in approximately the first half of the second century, explains that the soul is a body that is wondrously

---

[65] See Price 2009:2.123.
[66] Lietzmann 1904:79–128 and 204–270.
[67] Vaggione 1987:165–185.
[68] *On the Nature of Man* 38 Morani.
[69] See Alexander of Aphrodisias *On Mixture and Increase* 4 Groisard. Long (1996:231) proposes a different translation: "for none of the soul lacks a share in the body which possesses the soul," but the general meaning does not change.

blended and wholly intermingled (συγκέκραται κατὰ πᾶν) with the animal body in a physical process of coextension, most similar to the one which occurs in the case of red-hot iron.[70] The theory of the total blending of the bodies, and therefore also of the corporeal soul and of the animal body, gave rise to many objections from Platonists and Peripatetics. Plutarch ascribes to Arcesilaus the confutation of this Stoic doctrine.[71] Alexander of Aphrodisias deals at length with the issue in *On Mixture and Increase*, criticizing above all Chrysippus,[72] and again in the *Supplement to On the Soul (Mantissa)*, especially in chapters "On the Soul," "That the Soul is Incorporeal," "That the Capacities of the Soul are Many and Not One," and "That it is Impossible for Body to Extend Through Body," insisting in particular on the incorporeal nature of the soul-*entelekheia*.[73]

When Nemesius in turn tackles the question, he cannot avoid becoming involved in such a long and important debate. He considers, and rejects with various arguments, the three types of mixture already pointed out by Chrysippus and criticized by Alexander of Aphrodisias: (1) the soul and the body are unified, change together, and both perish together like the elements; (2) they are beside each other like chorus-men in a dance or pebble by pebble; (3) they are mixed together like wine and water. In short, for Nemesius soul and body are not united, adjacent, or mixed (μήτε ἥνωται μήτε παράκειται μήτε κέκραται). Nemesius also excludes Plato's hypothesis according to which the soul uses the body and puts the body on like a garment resorting to the argument that, since a tunic is not one with its wearer, the soul cannot be one with its garment. All that remains is a fifth solution, the last and the only true one, put forward by Ammonius, "the teacher of Plotinus." According to Nemesius, Ammonius claimed that:

> Intelligible things had such a nature as to be both unified with things capable of receiving them, as are things which perish together with one another, and when unified, to remain unconfused and not perish, like things which are juxtaposed.

> Nemesius *On the Nature of Man* 39 Morani[74]

The philosophical principle on which Nemesius bases his conception of the relationship of the soul with the body is therefore that the soul, being an intelligible and incorruptible reality, is unified with the body while remaining altogether uncompounded with it, thus without undergoing alterations; not only,

---

[70] Hierocles *Elements of Ethics* III 56–IV 22 (Bastianini and Long 1992:318–320). English translation and commentary by Ramelli and Konstan 2009:10–11 and 44–46.

[71] Plutarch *Against the Stoics on Common Conceptions* 1078b.

[72] Alexander *On Mixture and Increase* 3–12. See Groisard 2013.

[73] See Sharples 2008. Also Plotinus (*Enneads* II 7) criticizes the Stoic solution.

[74] Translation in Sharples and Van der Eijk 2008:80.

but, as it is incorporeal, the soul is not circumscribed in space, it controls the body and is not in the body as in a vessel or a wine skin, but rather the body is in the soul.[75] The soul is therefore in a body not as in a place, but as in a relationship to the body, being present just as God is said to be in us. Resorting to an enlightening erotic metaphor, Nemesius continues:

> We say that the soul is bound by the body in its relationship and inclination towards something and disposition, *as we say that the lover is "bound" by the beloved woman*, neither in a bodily sense nor in place but by their relationship.
>
> Nemesius *On the Nature of Man* 41 Morani[76]

Striking similarities between Nemesius and the thought and language used by Porphyry, especially in the *Sentences* 1, 3, 27, 28, 31, 33, and 39 Lamberz, have rightly been reported for some time. This is not surprising if we remember that the "prodigy" of the incorporation of the soul,[77] "that divine and paradoxical mixture,"[78] had a central role in the religious and philosophical thought of Porphyry, who discussed it for three whole days with Plotinus.[79]

But what is even more important is that Nemesius quotes verbatim an excerpt on the unification of soul and body from the second book of Porphyry's *Miscellaneous Investigations*:

> It is not to be denied that a certain substance can be received for the completion of another substance, and can be a part of this substance while retaining its own nature together with completing another substance, and, while becoming one with another, can retain its own unity and moreover, while itself untransmuted, it can transmute those things into which it comes so that they gain its activity by its presence.
>
> Nemesius *On the Nature of Man* 43 Morani[80]

---

[75] Sharples and van der Eijk 2008:81–82.

[76] Translation in Sharples and Van der Eijk 2008:83. Nemesius *On the Nature of Man* 41 Morani: καὶ γὰρ τῇ σχέσει καὶ τῇ πρός τι ῥοπῇ καὶ διαθέσει δεδέσθαι φαμὲν ὑπὸ τοῦ σώματος τὴν ψυχὴν ὡς λέγομεν ὑπὸ τῆς ἐρωμένης δεδέσθαι τὸν ἐραστήν οὐ σωματικῶς οὐδὲ τοπικῶς ἀλλὰ κατὰ σχέσιν.

[77] Porphyry *The Cave of the Nymphs* 14 (Seminar Classics 609 S.U.N.Y. at Buffalo 1969:16).

[78] Porphyry *To Gaurus on How Embryos are Ensouled* 47 Kalbfleisch.

[79] See Porphyry *Life of Plotinus* 13.11.

[80] Translation in Sharples and van der Eijk 2008:85. Slaveva-Griffin (2014:9–42) has pointed out that the "Galenic" *On the Seed*, a text of unknown provenance and which shows similar propensity for merging philosophical and medical themes, also refers to Porphyry as a proponent of the Platonic understanding of soul and body.

This literal quotation presents many problems that are not easily solved. Nemesius explains that these words of Porphyry about "the unification of soul and body" (λέγει δὲ ταῦτα περὶ τῆς ἑνώσεως τῆς ψυχῆς καὶ τοῦ σώματος) are a decisive argument for silencing the pagans who deride the union of God with man as impossible, because they come from an authoritative witness of pagan culture who even spoke against Christ. The testimonies unintentionally given by the adversaries of Christian truth apparently are of a particular value. As we have seen, this is part of the apologetic method of Nemesius. However, on the literary level, this quotation requires further consideration.

We shall start by saying that, in the light of the new chronology that we have established, Nemesius is not the first author to quote the *Miscellaneous Questions*. This work is mentioned for the first time in the fifth century by Proclus, once under the title *Miscellanea*[81] and once under the title *Miscellaneous Problems*.[82] It appears again in the following century among the sources used in the *Answers to Chosroes* by Priscian of Lydia (*Commixtae quaestiones*).[83] Nemesius comes third in chronological order, but his testimony is particularly worthy of note because he is the first to mention the existence of book two. A Byzantine scholium on Basil mentions the existence of book four,[84] and the *Suda* maintains that the work consisted of seven books.[85] But, whatever the nature, structure, and size of the *Miscellaneous Questions*, and whatever the relations of this work to the other works that Porphyry dedicated to problems of psychology, it is nevertheless a work in which the problems of the nature and origin of the soul, of its parts, and its union with the body, must have been treated at the same time and in connection with other related philosophical themes such as the study of geometry and the criticism of Aristotle's theory of the fifth element.[86]

Nemesius, who admits only the four traditional elements, could very likely have read in this work the criticism of Aristotle's theory about the fifth body, athereal and cyclic,[87] but he could also have found here the arguments for rejecting the Aristotelian doctrine of the soul-*entelekheia*, which we know for certain was criticized by Porphyry in his writing on the soul addressed to the Platonist Boethus.[88] Moreover, concerning the intense use of book three

---

[81] Proclus *A Commentary on the First Book of Euclid's Elements* Prologue II 56 Friedlein.

[82] Proclus *Commentary on the Republic* I 233–234 Kroll. On Augustine and Porphyry's *Miscellaneous Questions*, see p. 316n49 above.

[83] Bywater 1886:42.

[84] Pasquali 1910:206–208.

[85] See *Suda* "Porphyry," Adler 1971:IV 178.

[86] For a discussion of the contents of Porphyry's *Miscellaneous Questions,* see Dörrie 1959 and Beatrice 2005:260–280.

[87] *On the Nature of Man* 52 Morani.

[88] See frr. 6 and 8 Mras, in Eusebius *Preparation for the Gospel* XV 11.1.4. I am not convinced by Karamanolis 2006:291–298, who attributes fr. 8 Mras to Atticus. Besides, I also find it difficult to

of Aristotle's *Nicomachean Ethics* in the course of the discussion on voluntary action and choice (*On the Nature of Man* 93–104 Morani), it is hardly conceivable that Nemesius knew and used the four commentaries on Aristotle's treatise by Aspasius, Alexander of Aphrodisias, "Heliodorus," and an anonymous writer relying on Adrastus of Aphrodisias.[89] It is much more likely that he had direct recourse to Porphyry who certainly commented on parts of this work, as several medieval Arabic sources testify.[90]

It therefore seems highly probable that it was Porphyry's *Miscellaneous Questions* that provided Nemesius with information on the doctrines of Numenius and especially Ammonius, "the teacher of Plotinus," whom he evidently held in great regard.[91] Porphyry was notoriously an admirer of Numenius, and of the thought of Ammonius he knew what he had learnt at different times from four of his teachers, who in turn had been disciples of Ammonius himself, namely Origen, Longinus, Antoninus, and Plotinus.

This brings us to the problem, which is indeed complex and of no easy solution, of the doxographic sources that Nemesius may have used in composing his treatise. If for the most ancient philosophers there is no lack of traces of the use of the *Opinions of the Philosophers* of Aëtius, a work explicitly quoted by Theodoret of Cyrus,[92] which was presumably still known in Syria at the time of Nemesius, the variations and additions point to the use of one or more intermediate doxographic sources.[93] This observation becomes worth considering especially as regards the knowledge of Numenius and Ammonius. Porphyry is certainly the best candidate, seeing that Nemesius quotes an excerpt from the *Miscellaneous Questions* word for word. But then one must not forget that

---

accept both the common opinion that Porphyry's treatise was written against the Peripatetic Boethus (first century BCE), and the proposal of Moraux (1973:172–176), who argues that the target was the Stoic Boethus (second century BCE). Nobody seems to have taken into consideration the possibility that the addressee of Porphyry's reply is to be identified with the Platonist Boethus (second century) who shared the literal interpretation of the Platonic doctrine of *metempsukhôsis* with Plotinus, Harpocration, and Numenius (according to Aeneas of Gaza *Theophrastus* [Colonna 1958:12]; see Beatrice 2005:271–272), and wrote two Platonic *lexica* mentioned by Photius *Bibliotheca* 154 and 155.

89 Resemblances and differences between Nemesius and these commentaries have been scrupulously analyzed for the first time by Streck 2005:44–85. See also Söder 2010:259–275.

90 See Karamanolis 2006:306–308.

91 The *Collectio Ammonii scholarum*, published by an otherwise unknown Theodotus, and included by Priscian of Lydia among his sources (Bywater 1886:42), most probably is a collection of the lectures given by Ammonius the son of Hermias (fifth-sixth century), and should not, therefore, be considered as the second source for Nemesius' knowledge of the doctrines of Ammonius, the teacher of Plotinus. On the other hand, the "indisputable growth of the legend of the Christian Ammonius," proposed by Rist (1988:402–415), is bound to remain an ungrounded conjecture.

92 Theodoret of Cyrus *Cure for Greek Maladies* II 95, IV 31, and V 16.

93 See the discussion by Mansfeld and Runia 1997:291–299.

Porphyry was also the author of the *Philosophical History* in four books, from the beginnings to Plato, a work that was well known to Christian apologists such as Eusebius of Caesarea, Cyril of Alexandria, Theodoret of Cyrus, and the author of the *Theosophy*. Nor can one rule out the possibility that Nemesius also used the *Miscellanies* of Origen, thanks to which, as well as with the texts and doctrines of Plato, Aristotle, and Numenius, he could have come in direct contact with the philosophy of the "Hebrews," that is, Philo of Alexandria.[94] But here we must stop, in the absence of explicit documentation.

7. Nemesius and Syrian Neoplatonism

The most delicate issue remains that of the knowledge Nemesius might have had of the *Enneads* of Plotinus, an author so important as to be quoted first by Nemesius at the beginning of the treatise, along with Apollinaris, among the supporters of the body-soul-intellect trichotomy. Nemesius also knows, and twice repeats, that Plotinus was a disciple of Ammonius. Now the question remains: Did Nemesius have direct knowledge of the *Enneads* of Plotinus, or should we believe that he read only the extracts he found in later sources (and, if so, which ones)? The answer to this question, as is evident, does not concern only the philosophical background of Nemesius, but also clearly has implications for our general knowledge of the history of the text of the *Enneads* in late antiquity and, in particular, of its circulation in Syria.

One must not think that Plotinus was known only, as is natural to expect, among the pagan intellectuals who left a trace of their passage in Syria between the fourth and the sixth century, from Iamblichus to Damascius. Equally interested readers of the *Enneads* can also be found among the Christians of Syria and Palestine, starting from a contemporary of Iamblichus, Eusebius of Caesarea, at the beginning of the fourth century.[95] In the fifth century, the name and the work of Plotinus, the disciple of Ammonius, were well known to Theodoret of Cyrus,[96] and to Aeneas of Gaza,[97] and in the following centuries clear and conspicuous traces of the use of Plotinus' work, even without mentioning his name, have been noted in the scholia of John of Scythopolis to the *Pseudo-Dionysian Corpus*,[98]

---

[94] The expression "the Hebrews" (*On the Nature of Man* 6, 11, 53, 68 Morani) most likely refers to Philo. See Sharples and van der Eijk 2008:41n214. Origen's *Miscellanies* still circulated in the sixth century, as is shown by the *Codex Von der Goltz*. On Nemesius' possible use of the *Miscellanies*, see Beatrice 2009:526–531.

[95] Eusebius *Preparation for the Gospel* XI 17 and XV 10 and 22.

[96] Theodoret *Cure for Greek Maladies* VI 60.

[97] Aeneas of Gaza *Theophrastus* (Colonna 1958:45–46).

[98] See Rorem and Lamoreaux 1998:119–137 (in particular the use of *Enneads* I 8).

and in the Syriac version of these same scholia by Phokas of Edessa.[99] It will be remembered that Plotinus is also mentioned in the Syriac collection of prophecies addressed to the pagans of Harran. There are therefore sufficient elements to think that Plotinus' work circulated in Syria both in pagan and Christian circles in those centuries, which makes it easy to explain the presence of the name of Plotinus in the treatise of Nemesius.

Nevertheless, the information provided by Nemesius on the anthropological trichotomy supported by Plotinus can hardly come from a direct reading of the *Enneads*, since Plotinus speaks of human beings as made up simply of body and soul.[100] Henry, too, thought that Nemesius had not read the *Enneads*. We can however easily dismiss his hypothesis, which complicates things further and cannot be proven, that Nemesius was a witness of the "oral" tradition of Plotinus' teaching, quite distinct from the written tradition, for the simple reason that there is a span of at least three centuries between Plotinus and Nemesius.[101] It appears much simpler and more convincing to think that Nemesius may have found Plotinus' opinion reported by some other author, for example Iamblichus or Porphyry. From Porphyry, in particular, he might also have learnt that Plotinus was a disciple of Ammonius. Theodoret, too, knew that Plotinus had been, with Origen, a disciple of Ammonius, but it is not by chance that in his presentation of the philosophical theories about the soul he draws information from the writings of Plutarch, Porphyry, and Aëtius, not Plotinus.[102] He quotes extensively only from *On Providence* (*Enneads* III 2)[103] and from *On the Three Primary Hypostases* (*Enneads* V 1.6–7).[104]

Without going too far afield, Aeneas of Gaza informs us that Plotinus' *Where Does Evil Come From?* (*Enneads* I 8) was quoted and commented on by Porphyry in his treatise entitled *The Oracles of the Chaldeans*, that is, the *Philosophy According to the Oracles*.[105] It seems likely that in the seventh century, Sophronius of Jerusalem had some knowledge of this work or of some parts of it.[106] Aeneas' words, in particular, lead us to believe that it was Porphyry who passed on the knowledge of the work of Plotinus, and that he also conditioned its interpretation. A very similar case is that of the *libri platonicorum* read by Augustine in Milan, which I have elsewhere proposed to identify with the Latin version of Porphyry's *On*

---

[99] See Frank 1987:101–108.

[100] As noted by Sharples and van der Eijk 2008:35n184.

[101] Henry 1938:xiv–xv and xxvii.

[102] Theodoret *Cure for Greek Maladies* V 16.

[103] *Cure for Greek Maladies* VI 59–72.

[104] *Cure for Greek Maladies* II 82–83.

[105] Aeneas *Theophrastus* (Colonna 1958:45).

[106] Sophronius mentions Porphyry's report on sacrifices in *The Miracles of the Saints Cyrus and John* 31 (PG 87.3.3521b–c). See English translation and commentary by Bonner 1942:8–10.

Philosophy According to the Oracles carried out by Marius Victorinus, and in which Augustine found more or less large excerpts from the *Enneads*.[107] It is worth remembering in this context that the *arcanae de animae reditu disputationes*, mentioned by Macrobius, give another important example of the transmission of Plotinus' *Enneads* through Porphyry's work in the Latin West.[108]

Furthermore, as is generally recognized, Porphyry's *Sentences* also contain much material coming from Plotinus, and following this path it is not difficult to arrive at the so-called *Theology of Aristotle*. The Arabic translator attributes this work to Porphyry, but it contains so many extracts from the last three *Enneads* that it is currently, if erroneously, considered a direct, even though disordered, Arabic translation of the *Enneads*. In actual fact, I see no reason to deny that, as is correctly indicated in the title, Porphyry is to be considered the true author of the Greek *Vorlage* of this commentary, which has clearly come down to us incomplete. Resorting to the same method employed in the *Sentences*, here too Porphyry interweaves his own philosophical speculations with extensive quotes from Plotinus, so much so that the result is a real paraphrase of Plotinus' text. The *Sentences* by Porphyry and the anonymous *Theology of Aristotle* are the only known examples of a paraphrase of the *Enneads*, which is why both works should be attributed to one and the same author who can only be Porphyry.[109]

The author of the *Theology of Aristotle* also indicates the true title of his work, *The Philosophy of the Few*, an expression which, once its Porphyrian paternity is acknowledged, can only be understood as the Arabic *interpretatio* of the original Greek title *Philosophy According to the Oracles*.[110] This is no surprise, if we remember that Porphyry's *Philosophical History* has been transmitted in the Syriac and Arabic sources with the title *Chronicle*, possibly through a Syriac translation of the Greek expression *philosophos chronographia* found in the *Chronicle* of the Antiochene John Malalas.[111]

It is not our intent to establish whether the Arabic translation was made directly from the Greek original or whether there may have been an intermediate Syriac translation. This is still a matter of heated debate.[112] As is known, Porphyry was widely translated into Syriac, but a direct translation from Greek into Arabic cannot be excluded.[113] In any event, what appears to be even more interesting for our investigation is that the translator of the *Theology of Aristotle*

[107] Beatrice 1989:248–281.
[108] Macrobius *Commentary on the Dream of Scipio* I 13.16; see Beatrice 2010b:49–50.
[109] See Beatrice 2005:281–285.
[110] *Theology of Aristotle* IV 41–42 (G. Lewis 1959:381). See Beatrice 2010b:45–46 and 2016:133.
[111] Malalas Chronicle 2. 56 (Thurn 2000:40).
[112] See Brock 2007:293–306.
[113] For example, the Patriarch Timothy in *Letter* 43.2 to Pethion (Brock 1999:235–236 and 240–241) claims that he has translated Aristotle's *Topica* from Syriac into Arabic through the agency of

into Arabic was a Syrian Christian of Emesa: *'Abd al-Masîh ibn 'Abdallâh ibn Nâ'ima al-Himsî*. This leads to the supposition that, however paradoxical it may at first appear, the knowledge of the works of Plotinus and Porphyry was preserved and passed down to the Arabs not by the pagans of Harran, but rather by the Christians of Syria and Palestine. In particular, both the Greek bishop Nemesius and the Syrian translator of the *Philosophy of the Few* bear witnesses to the fact that Emesa was an important center of transmission of Neoplatonism from the sixth to the ninth century.

---

the teacher Abû Nûh, but that contemporaneously some others were translating this work from Greek into Arabic.

17

Philosophy, Religion, and Architecture

Genesis and *Apogenesis* in Platonism, the Cult of Mithras, and Roman and Christian Architecture

Robert Hannah

Abstract: From an allegorical interpretation of a passage in Homer's *Odyssey* by Porphyry, we learn that the midsummer solstice was regarded as the point of entry for souls from heaven into this world, a process called *genesis*. Its opposite, *apogenesis*, the return of souls to heaven, occurred at the midwinter solstice. Midway between the solstices lie the equinoxes, which were regarded as the points of cosmic balance, where the lord of *genesis* took his seat to oversee the processes of *genesis* and *apogenesis*.

Porphyry's point of departure is Homer's description (*Odyssey* 13.93–112) of a cave sacred to the nymphs on Odysseus' home island of Ithaka. His interpretation can be traced back to a predecessor, Cronius, a mid-second century Platonist with Pythagorean leanings, and, in turn, to Cronius' associate, Numenius. Evidently, however, the notion that the soul had a celestial route for descent to earth and ascent to the heavens was much older than the second century. For when Porphyry himself instantiates this view of the cosmos through reference to the ritual cave of the adherents of Mithras' cult, a Roman mystery religion with older Near Eastern connections, he also reminds his readers that Plato (*Laws* 896e5–6) "says that there are two openings, one through which souls ascend to the heavens, the other through which they descend to earth" (*On the Cave of the Nymphs* 29).

This chapter investigates the idea of psychical migration in its philosophical, religious, and architectural contexts, particularly by taking it beyond the pagan world and into the Christian. The author has argued elsewhere (Hannah 2009, Hannah and Magli 2011) that outside the ritual caves of the Mithraists, certain imperial Roman buildings also incorporate this worldview, notably the domed structures of the Pantheon, completed by Hadrian in the second century, and before it the second palace of Nero, the *Domus Aurea*, in the first century. Later on in time, Byzantine churches also amalgamate the dome, sunlight, and liturgy in a Christianized version of the pagan idea (Potamianos 2000).

FROM THE THIRD-CENTURY Neoplatonic philosopher, Porphyry, we learn that the midsummer solstice was regarded by Platonic philosophers from the second century and, curiously, by adherents of the cult of Mithras, as the point of entry for souls from heaven into this world, a process called *genesis*. Its opposite, *apogenesis*, the return of souls to heaven, occurred at the midwinter solstice. Midway between the solstices lie the equinoxes, which were regarded as the points of cosmic balance, where the lord of *genesis* took his seat to oversee the processes of *genesis* and *apogenesis*. In this chapter I wish to explore this notion both within and outside Neoplatonism, into the realms of pagan (specifically Mithraic) and Christian thought, and to show how it is instantiated in contemporary public buildings. My hypothesis is that the pivotal times of the solstices were regarded as providing liminal "passageways" between the time-bound, mortal world of the "here and now" and the timeless or perpetual, immortal world of the "hereafter," and that these routes into and out of this world were overseen from the midpoints in the solar cycle, the equinoxes. My proposal, that philosophy might help explicate the architecture, stems from the extended allegorical explanation by Porphyry of a description from Homer's *Odyssey* (13.102–112) of a cave sacred to the nymphs on Odysseus' home island of Ithaka. So let us start with Porphyry.

1. Porphyry on Homer's *Cave of the Nymphs*

The tradition within which Porphyry stands viewed the material world—called the sensible world because of our perception of it through the senses—as an inherently inaccurate representation of reality. Instead, reality was to be perceived through the intellect, and the resultant intelligible world lay beyond this earthly world, in the celestial realm. This view of the cosmos was promoted by the later followers of Plato who have been called Neoplatonists since the nineteenth century: e.g. Plotinus (204–270), Porphyry, his pupil (234–305), Iamblichus, his pupil (245–325) in the third century, and Proclus (412–485) in the fifth century.

The Neoplatonists in particular expressed their philosophy via the literary genre of the commentary, or exegesis, on the original Platonic texts, especially the extended philosophical treatises of the *Timaeus*, the *Laws*, and the *Republic*. The use of this genre is of course well-known in other traditions, notably Judaism and Christianity, both of which owe a significant debt to Platonism and its later followers. Commentary is now better understood as a vehicle for the development of innovative philosophical thought, rather than simply an exposition of previous scholarship with no independent thought, a brush that the Neoplatonists were unfairly tarred with for a long time. These later philosophers certainly eclectically picked and chose their way through earlier philosophical traditions, not only the Platonic but also Aristotelian and Stoic. They certainly sought consciously to enable Plato's and Aristotle's often contradictory statements on metaphysics to mesh together by subtle or creative reinterpretations. But they also used these discussions to present distinctly new ideas which advance earlier Greek thought.

The philosophy of Plotinus has long held sway in the historical development of European metaphysics, from the Italian Renaissance, through the eighteenth century Enlightenment to twentieth century postmodernism. From it we are used to the allegorical reinterpretation of older texts, to the point that one scholar titled his book on the Neoplatonic view of Homer as *Homer the Theologian*.[1] But the end of the twentieth century saw the emergence of interest in the more scientifically oriented (as we would understand the notion of science) philosophy of Proclus, allowing us to gain a more rounded appreciation of this influential school of philosophy beyond its theological aspect.[2]

For the purposes of this examination, I am concerned with a commentary that Porphyry produced on a small section of Homer's epic.[3] In this part of the *Odyssey*, Odysseus has been stranded on the island of the Phaiakians while returning from the war at Troy to his home on the island of Ithaka. At the start of Book 13, the Phaiakians take Odysseus back to Ithaka:

> At the head of the harbour is a long-leafed olive tree, and near it a pleasant, shadowy cave sacred to the nymphs that are called Naiads. Therein are mixing bowls and jars of stone, and there too the bees store honey. And in the cave are long looms of stone, at which the nymphs weave webs of purple dye, a wonder to behold; and therein are also ever-flowing springs. Two doors there are to the cave, one toward the

---

[1] Lamberton 1986.
[2] Martijn 2010 and Pedersen 2012.
[3] All references to Porphyry's *On the Cave of the Nymphs in the Odyssey* are taken from the Arethusa edition: Seminar Classics 609, 1969.

North Wind, by which men go down, but that toward the South Wind is
sacred, nor do men enter thereby; it is the way of the immortals.

Homer *Odyssey* 13.93–112[4]

Porphyry is not the first to seek an explanation of the Homeric description
of the cave on Ithaka.[5] He himself refers to a predecessor, Cronius, a mid-second
century Platonist with Pythagorean leanings, and later talks of others, notably
Numenius, Cronius' associate, who have sought explanations, both factual and
allegorical.[6] Porphyry's approach is largely to retail the explanation of a couple
of his predecessors, starting with Cronius, who provides, through a detailed
series of questions, an extended deconstruction of the passage in the *Odyssey*,
which informs the rest of Porphyry's analysis. On the factual side, Porphyry
uses geographical descriptions of the island of Ithaka to conclude that Homer
was not writing complete fiction (*On the Cave of the Nymphs* 5). On the allegorical
side, by using Neoplatonic conceptions of the world and its elemental structure, the philosopher finds consistency in the use of a cave as a signifier for the
cosmos as a whole, in its sensible and intelligible dimensions. The cave in its
sensible mode, for instance, is characterized as dark, stony, and moist, terms
that we can find in Neoplatonic analyses of the nature of the world (*On the Cave
of the Nymphs* 5–6 and 9). This leads on to his report that Zoroaster first had
the idea of dedicating a natural cave to Mithras, "the creator and father of all,"
as the cave "bore for him the image of the Cosmos which Mithras had created
and the things which the cave contained, by their proportionate arrangement,
provided him with symbols of the elements and climates of the Cosmos" (*On the
Cave of the Nymphs* 6). After Zoroaster, others then followed suit in practice and
in concept, with the Pythagoreans and then Plato also envisaging the cosmos as
a cave (*On the Cave of the Nymphs* 8).

The elemental association of the cave with moisture leads Porphyry to the
important step of also linking the cave with souls and their passage into life.
The powers that preside over waters are nymphs, he says, but more particularly
naiad nymphs, a term also apparently and crucially applied to souls descending
into *genesis*. The ancients, he tells us, "thought that the souls settle by water,
which is divinely inspired, as Numenius says; in support of this he [Numenius]
cites the words of the prophet, 'the spirit of God was borne upon the waters'"
(*On the Cave of the Nymphs* 10), a phrase that we recognize from Genesis 1:2. Such
is the eclectic background that Porphyry, or his source, is drawing upon.

---

[4] All translations are my own, unless otherwise noted.
[5] See especially Lamberton 1986:318–324.
[6] To use Beck's translation of *hetairos* (Beck 2006:86), rather than "pupil" as in the Arethusa edition
1969:23.

Having established that Homer's cave is "consecrated to souls and to ... the nymphs who preside over streams and springs" (*On the Cave of the Nymphs* 13), Porphyry proceeds to explain the features within the cave described by Homer— the stone mixing-bowls and amphorae, in which bees store honey. These also are associated with souls and *genesis* (*On the Cave of the Nymphs* 13–20). Porphyry then returns to the nature of the cave itself, with its two entrances, one facing north and used by mortals, the other south and used by immortals (*On the Cave of the Nymphs* 20). The explanation promoted by Porphyry is that already given by Numenius and his pupil, Cronius:

> The cave being a likeness and symbol of the cosmos, Numenius and his associate Cronius say there are two extremities in heaven, of which nothing is more southerly than the winter one and nothing more northerly than the summer one. The summer one is in Cancer, while the winter one is in Capricorn.
>
> Porphyry *On the Cave of the Nymphs* 21

"Nothing" in this passage must mean "nothing on the apparent solar and planetary path," for it is particularly the sun's apparent path across the sky that interests Porphyry. At Mediterranean latitudes the sun traverses through the year a limited arc along the horizon. The sun will not rise or set outside the arc on the eastern and western horizons between the two solstices, namely the winter solstice in late December when the sun is to the south in Capricorn, and the summer solstice in late June, when it is to the north in Cancer.

Porphyry continues:

> The theologians therefore make these two gates, Cancer and Capricorn, but Plato says they are two openings [as of a cave]. Of these they say Cancer is the gate through which the souls descend, and Capricorn the one through which they ascend. Cancer is northern and enables descent, while Capricorn is southern and enables ascent. The northern belongs to souls descending into generation (εἰς γένεσιν). And the gates of the cave that face to the north are rightly for the descent for men; but the southern are not for the gods, but for those ascending to the gods ...
>
> Porphyry *On the Cave of the Nymphs* 22–23

The points of the midsummer and midwinter solstices are significant because they are the extreme points of the sun's path across the heavens (and with it the moon and planets, who are also divine). These points represent gateways for entry into the sublunary world ("under the moon," the nearest celestial body to the earth), and exit from it.

All this leads Porphyry to conclude that:

> Therefore he [Homer] dedicated the gates neither to the east and west nor to the equinoxes, namely Aries and Libra, but to the south and north and to the gates most southerly to the south and those most northerly to the north, because he dedicated the cave to souls and water nymphs. But for souls these places are fit for generation (γενέσεως) and degeneration (ἀπογενέσεως).
>
> Porphyry *On the Cave of the Nymphs* 24

It is at this point that he refers this vision of the cosmos again to the beliefs of the cult of Mithras:

> Therefore they assigned to Mithras a seat at the equinoxes. For this reason he carries the sword of Aries, the sign of Mars, and rides a bull, as Taurus belongs to Venus. Being creator and lord of generation (γενέσεως) Mithras is appointed over the equinoctial circle, with the north on his right and south on his left, and Cautes is appointed to the south because it is hot, and <Cautopates> to the north because of the cold of the wind.
>
> Porphyry *On the Cave of the Nymphs* 24[7]

From here Porphyry expands at some length on the significance of "north" and "south" (*On the Cave of the Nymphs* 25–29), and on the meaning of the twofold entrance (*On the Cave of the Nymphs* 29–31)—at which point he reminds us that Plato "says that there are two openings, one through which souls ascend to the heavens, the other through which they descend to earth" (*On the Cave of the Nymphs* 29). He finishes with an interpretation of the olive tree near Homer's cave as a symbol of divine wisdom, and of the toils and ultimate victory of both Odysseus and of the soul (*On the Cave of the Nymphs* 31–33). Overall, Porphyry reads Odysseus himself as emblematic of one who "passes through the stages of *genesis* and, in doing so, returns to those beyond every wave who have no knowledge of the sea ..." (*On the Cave of the Nymphs* 34).

Porphyry's references to the cult of Mithras in this treatise have tended to dominate modern scholarship's approach to this short exegesis,[8] and indeed

---

[7] I have retained the readings "Cautes" and "<Cautopates>" from the Arethusa edition 1969. I am aware of only Turcan (2006:762) as expressing doubts about these.

[8] For example, Beck 1984, Ulansey 1989, Turcan 1993, and Beck 2006.

they were a starting point for me some years ago in my search to understand the metaphysical interpretation of the solstitial and equinoctial points in the cult itself, and then more broadly in Roman society.[9] At that time, I was interested in explicating only the iconography of Cautes and Cautopates—the two regular framing figures in the archetypal icon of the cult of Mithras, the so-called tauroctony. These two males are dressed in "Phrygian" form with floppy caps, tunic, and trousers, thus referencing the reputed eastern source of the cult. They each hold a torch, one upraised (Cautes), the other lowered (Cautopates). Apposite to our present discussion is that in these attributes I saw symbols of *genesis* (when the torch is held downwards) and *apogenesis* (when it is held up); that is, of birth into this world (*genesis*) and of birth into the afterlife (*apogenesis*).

To recap: according to Porphyry, in Mithraic belief, the midsummer solstice was regarded as the point of entry for souls from heaven into this world and represented *genesis*. Here the sun was in Cancer in June and at its most northerly, and suited for descent into this world. At the midwinter solstice, on the other hand, there lay the point of reentry to heaven, which was called *apogenesis*, the return from *genesis*. Here the sun was in Capricorn in December and at its most southerly, and suited to ascent into the upper world. In the Mithraic cult, which shares this worldview, the Sun god Mithras oversaw this migration of souls from his seat midway between the solstices, at the equinoxes. The cult's meetings and rituals took place in a cave-like setting, whose form was regarded as a symbol of the cosmos.

2. Platonic Pathways of the Soul

According to one view of Porphyry's essay *On the Cave of the Nymphs*,[10] the reference to the cult of Mithras is a particular instance of a more widespread view among philosophers from the second century that the solstitial points represent gateways for entry into this world and exit from it. The citations by Porphyry to his philosophical forebears, Numenius and Cronius, indicate something of this wider circle. Even before then, however, we have seen that Porphyry was aware of Plato's conception of paired passageways for the soul in the afterlife (*Republic* 614c–d).[11] In his "Myth of Er," Plato envisioned two openings in the earth and another two in the heavens. As the souls of the dead were judged, the just were directed to the opening on the right and traveled upwards through the heavens, while the unjust had to take the route to the left and traveled downwards. A similar conception of two roads, one to the Isles of the Blessed, the

---

[9] Hannah 1996.
[10] Well represented by Turcan 1975, and reiterated at Turcan 2006:762, in a review of Beck 2006.
[11] Not *Laws* 896e5–6 as noted in the Arethusa edition 1969:29.

other to Tartarus, occurs in the *Gorgias* (524a). Under Numenius the openings in the heavens become gateways, one at the tropic of Cancer in mid-summer for souls to descend in *genesis* to the earthly world, and the other at the tropic of Capricorn in mid-winter for souls to ascend back to heaven in *apogenesis* from the earth.[12] Plotinus, under whom Porphyry studied in Rome, could have been the source for the simple antithesis of *genesis* and *apogenesis*, as it appears at *Enneads* III 4.6.12–16.

Numenius, and Porphyry after him, however, hang a great deal more metaphysics onto the binary notion of *genesis* and *apogenesis* than Plotinus appears to have done. Plotinus refers simply to the human soul having the same form before *genesis*—signifying "birth"—and after *apogenesis*—meaning "death." There is no mention of gates or pathways between these two states of being. So we have to ascertain what caused Numenius in particular to attach the gateways of *genesis* and *apogenesis* to the solstitial signs in the zodiac. According to Beck, with whom I am inclined to agree, the answer lies with the Mithraic cult, which in essence predates the philosophy.[13] Somehow the cult's cosmology (or, rather, "bits and pieces of Mithraic practice and theory") entered into Numenius' discourse and subsequently into Porphyry's.

But what seems in Porphyry to be simply a celestial map of routes down from heaven to earth and out again via the tropics at the solstices had originally in Plato's mind eschatological connotations. These connotations were that the judgment handed down to the just gave them the right of reentry to the heavens, while the alternative judgment of the souls of the unjust sent them downwards under the earth to Tartarus. In this sense, Plotinus remains close to Plato, as his notion of *genesis* and *apogenesis* appears in the context of the judgment of the soul after death. There is no obvious sense of this apocalyptic perception in Porphyry when he describes the openings in the heavens for the soul at *On the Cave of the Nymphs* 24, but at the end of his treatise his final description of Odysseus as "one who passes through the stages of *genesis* and, in doing so, returns to those beyond every wave who have no knowledge of the sea ..." (*On the Cave of the Nymphs* 34) might have reminded readers of the description of the same hero at the end of Plato's much earlier and more overtly eschatological "Myth of Er":

> And by chance the soul of Odysseus, happening to draw the last lot of all, came to choose, and from memory of its earlier toils pulled back from ambition and went about for a long time seeking the life of a private, carefree man, and with difficulty found it lying somewhere

---

[12] This belief is also attributed to Numenius later by Proclus, *Commentary on the Republic* II 128.26–129.13. Macrobius also repeats the idea, although he attributes it only to anonymous "natural scientists" (*physici*) in his *Commentary on the Dream of Scipio* I 12.1.

[13] Beck 2006:85–87.

disregarded by the others, and seeing it said that it would have done the same even if it drawn it first, and chose it gladly.

Plato *Republic* 620c–d

Plato's soul of Odysseus stands for the human soul, which has passed through the vicissitudes of life and has come through battered, but victorious and wiser. The same arguably applies to Porphyry's Odysseus. Both writers had an eschatological perspective.

3. Time in Space: Imperial Roman Architecture

To what extent did this conception of the cosmos, with permeable boundaries and balance-points at certain times of the solar year, pervade ancient society beyond the bounds of esoteric philosophy and mystery cult? Here I will argue that it is instantiated also in other cultural monuments, namely imperial Roman buildings. I will explore two such structures, the Octagonal Room in the ("the Golden House"), *Domus Aurea* the second palace of the emperor Nero in Rome, built in 64–68; and the Pantheon in Rome, as it was rebuilt under Hadrian by 128 and survives still today, but which may preserve aspects of the original structure erected by Agrippa under Augustus in 27 BCE. Then I will say something about post-Classical adaptations of these ideas.

3.1 The "Golden House" of Nero

The physical remains of Nero's extensive palace are nowadays largely limited to the domestic wing on the Esquiline Hill.[14] Here Voisin pointed out that the orientation of the wing was not a necessary function of the local topography.[15] Rather, its strict east-west alignment, which is unique in Imperial structures, must have served some further purpose. This purpose is highlighted in the wing's central room, the Octagonal Room, where at particular times of the year, Voisin pointed out, astronomical observations define its dimensions[16] (the latter two of which are of interest here):

Observation 1: The north celestial pole is visible from the interior's perimeter, through the approximately 6m wide oculus of the dome.

Observation 2: The summer solstice's midday sun falls completely on the ground within the room.

Observation 3: The equinoctial midday sun falls directly on to the north door.

---

[14] Fabbrini 1995 and Ball 2003.
[15] Voisin 1987.
[16] See further Hannah, Magli, and Palmieri 2016.

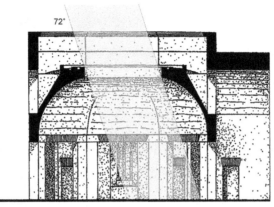

Figure 1. Rome, Nero's "Golden House," the Octagonal Room, N–S section: the fall of the midday sun (at altitude 72° in Rome) at the summer solstice on to the ground within the room (after Hannah and Magli 2011:501 Figure 11).

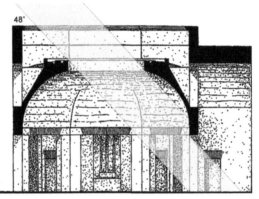

Figure 2. Rome, Nero's "Golden House," the Octagonal Room, N–S section: the fall of the midday sun (at altitude 48° in Rome) at the equinoxes across the threshold of the northern doorway (after Hannah and Magli 2011:501 Figure 12).

Figure 3. Rome, Nero's "Golden House," the Octagonal Room, N–S section: the fall of the midday sun at the equinoxes across the northern doorway's threshold (Voisin 1987:516 Figure 3; reproduced by permission of L'École française de Rome).

The fall of the midday sun in Rome on the summer solstice (Observation 2) is illustrated in Figure 1. The upper rim of the fall of the sun within the room practically coincides with the juncture of the floor and the northern doorway's threshold. So the sun defines the perimeter of the room.

The fall of the midday sun on the equinoxes (Observation 3) is illustrated in Figures 2 and 3. The lower rim of the sun strikes the juncture of the floor and the northern doorway's threshold, while its upper rim coincides with the top of the doorway. The sun thus measures out the dimensions of the openings in the walls of the Room. The doorway leads to the *nymphaeum*, so that earth, water, and sky are bound together.

Nero's association with the sun is well-attested.[17] In the *Domus Aurea* complex alone there was the colossal statue of the Sun, which stood not far from the Octagonal Room[18]—its name is preserved in that of the Colosseum, the amphitheatre that was later built nearby; and in Nero's later portraits in coin and sculpture he wears the radiate crown that was usually associated with the Sun god.[19] The historian Suetonius reports of "the Golden House" itself:

He [Nero] built a house from the Palatine all the way to the Esquiline, which he called the Passageway House at first, but then, when it was destroyed by fire soon afterwards and rebuilt, the Golden House ... The main dining hall was circular; it turned round constantly day and night, like the heavens.

Suetonius *Nero* 31

The temptation to regard the Octagonal Room as this very dining room has had to be tempered in recent years by the discovery of another structure from the palace on the Palatine hill, where a revolving mechanism seems to have been a feature.[20]

The poet Lucan, writing in Nero's time (ca. 60), has the apotheosized emperor joining the heavens and finding his proper seat midway between the northern and southern celestial spheres, where he will ensure stability and balance:

When your watch is over and eventually you seek the stars, your preferred heavenly palace will receive you, with the sky rejoicing, whether it delights you to hold the scepter, or to mount the fiery

[17] L'Orange 1947 and Champlin 2003.
[18] Bergmann 1994 and Albertson 2001.
[19] Hiesinger 1975 and R. R. R. Smith 2000.
[20] Wilson 2011.

chariot of Phoebus and to light the earth that fears nothing, with the sun replaced by a wandering light: it will be ceded to you by every god, and nature will leave to your decision which god you wish to be, where you wish to set your rule of the universe. But may you not choose your seat in the northern sphere, nor where the hot sky of opposite south sinks; from there you will see your Rome with star aslant. If you press one part of the boundless ether, the heavenly axis will feel the weight. Hold the weight of heaven balanced in the middle of the sphere: let all that part of bright ether be empty, and let no clouds block the light from Caesar.

Lucan Civil War 1.45–59

Here we have a sentiment matching that given us by Porphyry of the role played by Mithras in his cult's cosmic vision. There the god Mithras was placed at the equinoctial region of the celestial equator, with the north to his right and the south to his left, overseeing the passage of souls into and out of this world (or out of and into the world of the gods). Here, with Lucan's eyes, we now see the emperor, apotheosized after death, seated somewhere between north and south (where exactly is left unclear), maintaining cosmic balance.

In the Octagonal Room, surmounted by its cave-like dome, the equinoctial sun at noon fully illuminates the northern doorway, which gives entry to a *nymphaeum*—a space sacred to water nymphs. Let us recall again the associations highlighted by Porphyry between water, nymphs, and souls descending into *genesis*:

Therefore he [Homer] dedicated the gates neither to the east and west nor to the equinoxes, namely Aries and Libra, but to the south and north and to the gates most southerly to the south and those most northerly to the north, because he dedicated the cave to souls and water nymphs. But for souls these places are fit for generation (γενέσεως) and degeneration (ἀπογενέσεως).

Porphyry On the Cave of the Nymphs 24

Nero's Octagonal Room therefore presents a convincing case in which architectural elements in a major Roman building were symbolically tied to the sun's passage through the year. That these associations held metaphysical significance for the emperor himself, as a figure overseeing the cosmos and its passage of souls, is then suggested by the contemporary poetic admonition by Lucan to the soon-to-be-apotheosized Nero.

3.2 The Pantheon

From this imperial building we can trace a line of major architectural structures that play with the same design features and, arguably, the same metaphysical concerns. The palace of Domitian on the Palatine in Rome may have used these ideas, but its remains are too scanty or underexamined to be sure.[21] The Pantheon, as completed a generation later under Hadrian in 128, is the outstanding exemplar.

The Pantheon is the best preserved ancient monument in Rome, but its meaning remains obscure. It was originally built by Agrippa around 27 BCE, probably as a circular building more or less open to the sky and oriented to the north. This structure was destroyed by fire under Domitian, then rebuilt from the time of Trajan, and finally completed in its present form under Hadrian circa 128.[22]

The building is composed of a rectangular portico with three lines of columns fronting a rotunda that is designed with a huge hemispherical dome 43.3 meters in diameter and built over a cylinder that has the same diameter and is as high as half of it. Like the Octagonal Room in Nero's palace, the roof is punctured by an *oculus*, this time 8.3 meters wide. It is the only source of

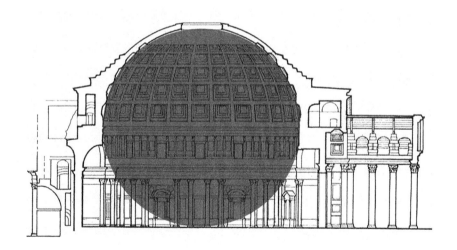

Figure 4. Rome, the Pantheon, N–S section: theoretical occupation of the rotunda by a perfect sphere (after Hannah and Magli 2011:488 Figure 2).

---

[21]   See, however, Hannah 2019 for evidence of the association between Domitian and the sun made by the contemporary poets Martial and Statius, and the potential for a relationship between the building and the sun.

[22]   Hetland 2007.

direct light, since no sunlight can directly enter from the north-facing door throughout the whole year. The dimensions of the rotunda mean that within the main domed section of the building a perfect sphere may be imagined filling the inner space like a gigantic football (Figure 4). In structural terms, however, this perfect space is an illusion, because the interior domed roof is not in fact a hemisphere as it appears to be: seen from the outside, the dome is flattened, its interior having been filled in so as to create the illusion of a hemisphere.

The historian Cassius Dio (53.27.2), writing some 70 years after Hadrian, notes that this emperor used the Pantheon sometimes as an audience hall. He also notes that the building had many statues, including Mars and Venus, and suggests that the name was derived from the building's vaulted roof, which resembles the heavens. Perhaps because of this, the building has usually been interpreted as a temple. Since other functions are certainly implied by Dio, it may be wiser to think of the building as multifunctional center with a religious aspect but more generally used.

For a temple, the orientation of the Pantheon would undoubtedly be very unusual, when compared with Italic, Roman, and Greek temples, as the building is oriented to the north (it is actually skewed 5.5 degrees with respect to true north). An explanation proffered by Nissen a century ago was that the building is in fact the temple mentioned by Pliny the Elder as the only one he knew of that was dedicated to a comet.[23] In this case Pliny identifies the comet as the one that was observed following the assassination of Julius Caesar in 44 BCE, during games that Octavian was celebrating in honor of Venus Genetrix. According to Pliny (*Natural History* 2.93–94), the comet was taken by the ordinary people to be a sign that the soul of Caesar had been received among the immortal gods. Nissen suggested that the Pantheon's odd orientation is then towards that part of the sky in which the comet appeared.

This idea, I think, finds support in light of recent work on comets in the Roman world.[24] Pliny quotes Augustus himself as noting that the comet was visible for seven days in that region of the sky that is visible *sub septentrionibus*; this may mean literally "under the Septentriones," the name given by the Romans to stars in the constellations of both the Great Bear and, on occasion, the Little Bear, which stand on either side of the invisible, north celestial-pole. In their study of this comet of 44 BCE, Ramsey and Licht have argued against such a literal interpretation, at least with regard to the Great Bear, instead preferring a more generalized translation of "in the north," because their calculations of the position of the comet at the time of its appearance make a placement under the Great Bear—i.e. to the northwest—problematic.[25] They do, however, allow

---

[23] Nissen 1873.
[24] Ramsey and Licht 1997.
[25] Ramsey and Licht 1997:86–90.

the phrase *sub septentrionibus* to be a possible reference to the *Little* Bear, as this constellation would lie between north and northeast, and due north at the time of the comet's appearance; the comet itself appeared in this region, which is between the constellations of Cassiopeia, Perseus, and Andromeda. It is in this direction that the Pantheon is oriented.

In the context of the monumentalization of birth and rebirth that we are examining here, this interpretation of the original Pantheon as a memorial to the comet that signaled the apotheosis of Julius Caesar is attractive. This would remain a unique instance in a building's use of a comet and, if it is a temple, an uncommon instance of a nonsolar orientation. It also remains impossible

Figure 5. Spain, Baelo Claudia: plaster cast of a roofed
spherical sundial (photograph by Hannah).

to be more precise about the actual alignment of the comet, or to know how the Romans would have noted it for future reference if they wanted to align a structure like the Pantheon towards its rising point. The issue is complicated by the fact that the view to the point on the horizon, towards which the Pantheon was arguably oriented, was blocked at the north end of the Campus Martius by the Mausoleum of Augustus, the construction of which started probably before circa 31 BCE.[26] So the Pantheon could well have been built simply to face the Mausoleum, which faced back to it. The external similarity of the circular Pantheon to the circular Mausoleum seems a more plausible cause for the Pantheon's slight diversion from true north.

However this may be for the original Pantheon, it is the interior of the building as built under Hadrian that is of more interest here. This interior, with its limited lighting, has caused some—myself included—to compare it to a particular type of sundial, which captures sunlight within a shadowy interior.[27] The type is called the *hemicyclium*, and is known from both literature (e.g. Vitruvius and Faventinus) and from material remains (Figure 5). It consists of a stone block carved out into a hollow hemisphere, with a hole let into its upper surface, through which the sunlight falls on to the south-facing surface inside. A series of reference lines, which typically signify the summer and winter solstices, and the spring and autumn equinoxes (the last as a single line between the other two), are incised on this surface, as in standard sundials.

We can see the same effect of sunlight within the Pantheon as we see in the *hemicyclium*, and here we may focus on the effect at noon at the time of

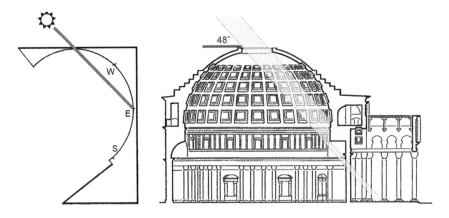

Figure 6. *Hemicyclium* and the Pantheon, N–S sections:
the fall of the midday sun (at altitude 48° in Rome)
at the equinoxes (after Hannah and Magli 2011:493 Figure 4).

---

[26] Haselberger et al. 2002:166.
[27] Hannah 2009a:145–154 and 2009b.

Figure 7. Rome, the Pantheon: the fall of the midday sun
at the equinox on September 23, 2005 on to the juncture of the
cylinder and the dome (photograph by Hannah).

the equinoxes (Figures 6 and 7). At noon, we are halfway through the daylight period; at the equinoxes, we are halfway through the sun's annual cycle from one solstice to another. At this moment, the sun strikes the interior of the Pantheon over the entrance doorway, precisely at the juncture between the base cylinder and the roof's dome, which lies halfway up the height of the building. That this is by design, not coincidence, is suggested by the artificial nature of the hemisphere, and by the accurate correspondence of the midpoints in time and space in a building on so large a scale. The architecture harnesses the noontime sunlight at other moments in the year, most notably at the cusps between one zodiacal month and the next, when the midday sunbeam crosses distinct articulations in the patterned decoration of the floor, vertical wall, and domed ceiling, suggesting a coherent organizing principle in the decorative plan (Figure 8).

That principle is probably a calendrical one, and quite likely a religious one at that.[28] On April 21, on the cusp between the zodiacal "months" of Aries and Taurus, the midday sun shone directly on the threshold of the huge doorway entrance to the Pantheon, so that anyone entering the building at that moment was cast into a spotlight of sunshine (Figures 8 and 9).[29] This day was the festival of the birth of the city of Rome. We can furthermore see that, in the Roman festival calendar, the winter solstice coincided with the festival of the Birthday of the Sun, and that this may have been signaled by the illumination of the second-top row of ceiling coffers at that time (Figure 10). Unfortunately, a similar solar connotation in the calendar seems not to be able to be found for the summer solstice (Figures 11), which occurred at the time of the festival of *Fors Fortuna* (the goddess of good fortune). What relationship, if any, that festival had with the summer solstice is unknown.[30]

But to return to the equinoctial dates: it is worth recalling that, according to Dio (53.27.3), Agrippa had initially intended that the original Pantheon be named after Augustus—presumably as an "*Augusteum*" rather than a more ambiguous but safer "*Caesareum*"—as well as containing a statue of the emperor. This dedication was rejected by Augustus, in keeping with sensitivities at that time regarding any lifetime cult of the emperor within Rome. Nonetheless, as has already been noted above, the divinization of the *deceased* ruler was established at Caesar's death with the help of the appearance of a comet, and a case has been made for regarding the original Pantheon as a temple to that comet. Soon afterwards Roman literature suggests that a particular point of cosmic balance was understood to be assigned to the emperor in the heavens, namely, the autumn equinoctial point, which is situated in Libra at one of the junctures between the celestial equator and the sun's path on the ecliptic. By Nero's time, as we have seen, Lucan (*Civil War* 1.45–59) has set the apotheosized emperor in the heavens on the celestial equator, so as to ensure balance and stability.

---

[28] Hannah and Magli 2011.

[29] *The Universe: Ancient Mysteries Solved—Roman Engineering* 2015.

[30] See Hannah (forthcoming) for suggestions on the relationships between the sun and the festival calendar of the Arval Brethren, who at one time met in the Pantheon.

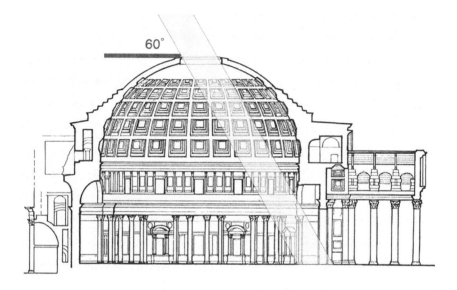

Figure 8. Rome, the Pantheon, N–S section: the fall of the midday sun (at altitude 60° in Rome) on April 21, 2007 (after Hannah and Magli 2011: 495 Figure 7).

Figure 9. Rome, the Pantheon: the fall of the midday sun on to the doorway on April 21, 2007 (photograph by Agostino, after Hannah and Magli 2011:495 Figure 8).

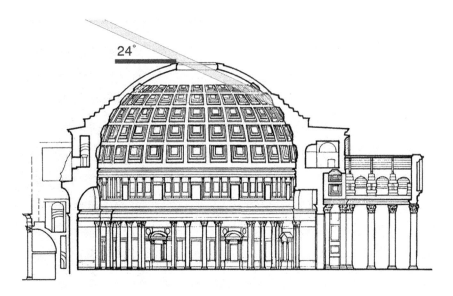

Figure 10. Rome, the Pantheon, N–S section: the fall of the midday sun (at altitude 24° in Rome) at the winter solstice (after Hannah and Magli 2011:494 Figure 6).

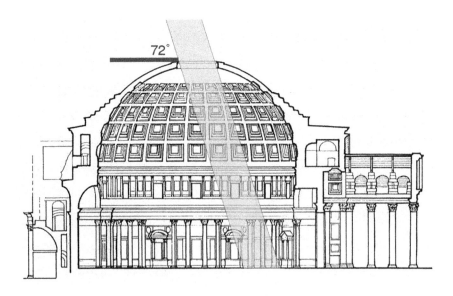

Figure 11. Rome, the Pantheon, N–S section: the fall of the midday sun (at altitude 72° in Rome) at the summer solstice (after Hannah and Magli 2011:496 Figure 9).

In the context of the Pantheon's midday light show through the year, the equinoctial display looks deliberately contrived at midpoints in space and time. Furthermore, it stands midway between the winter solstice's illumination of the row of coffers in the dome (Figure 10) and the summer solstice's illumination of the marble paving in the floor (Figures 11). On both occasions the sunlight strikes a clear point of the pattern in the decorative schemes of roof and floor, promoting again the belief that this is all carefully orchestrated in the overall design and decoration of the building. The full explication of the noontime illumination through the months still awaits us.

4. Christianity

The Christian calendar incorporates reference to the solstices and equinoxes, through the feasts of the conception and birth of Jesus and, by extension, of his forerunner, John the Baptist, born six months earlier. If we follow the treatise *On the Solstices and Equinoxes*, once attributed to John Chrysostom, we start with the conception by Elizabeth of John the Baptist. This is signaled by the annunciation to John's father Zechariah, who is busy in connection with the festivals of Tishri, and it places the conception at the autumnal equinox. Later, at her own annunciation, the mother of Jesus, Mary, is told that Elizabeth is already six months pregnant, so Jesus' conception is set six months after John's and at the spring equinox. The birth of Jesus therefore takes place nine months later at the winter solstice, while his cousin John was born six months earlier at the summer solstice. Confirmation of the calculation was provided by the belief that the date of the death of Jesus, fixed at the time of Passover, coincided with that of his conception.[31]

The story is, of course, more complicated than this, as there were rival dates for the celebration of Jesus' birth—notably January 6 in the eastern churches, the date of the feast of the Epiphany. The fourth century bishop, Epiphanius, correlated this date, as the birth of Jesus, with the pagan Egyptian celebration of the Birth of *Aiôn* (Eternity), the son of *Korê* (the Maiden).[32] Assuming this is the same festival as that referred to by Macrobius in the fifth century, it is related somehow to the winter solstice, despite the date difference. The sun was imagined as a small child and a statue of such was brought out from a shrine (Macrobius *Saturnalia* 1.18.10).

The winter solstice remained a significant event in the Christian consciousness for some time, to judge from an admonition by Pope Leo I in the fifth

[31] Talley 1991:91–99.
[32] Talley 1991:103–107.

century in one of his Nativity sermons, when he attacked the continuing practice of churchgoers on entering Saint Peter's basilica in Rome of turning round
at the top of the entrance steps so as to bow to the rising sun.[33]

Both in the Octagonal Room of the *Domus Aurea* and in the Pantheon, we
saw that architectural space and annual time were explicitly linked into cosmological signposts. In terms of the design of the two structures, the moments of
the equinoxes are especially noteworthy. As we have seen, in Greek and Roman
thought, the equinoxes held a particular significance, not only as an obvious
point of balance in the cosmos, but on a metaphysical level also as a point from
which the souls of individuals could be overseen as they migrated from one
world to another. This was a metaphysical link that later generations would
not lose, as research on the Christian descendants of the Pantheon, the domed
churches of the Byzantine world, indicates that here too the light of the sun was
harnessed so as to illuminate special moments in the liturgy. Here, the binding
of time and eternity is alluded to in the churches at the central moment of the
Eucharist, which was spotlighted by the sun's being channeled through carefully
situated windows (Figure 12).[34] Thus, the time-bound, mortal worshipper was
linked with Christ, the timeless, immortal God-man. In itself, in Constantinople,
it looks likely that the church of Hagia Sophia was deliberately oriented on its

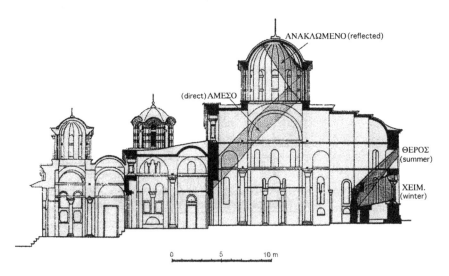

Figure 12. Section through a Byzantine church, showing light reflected onto
the apex of the dome and direct light on the frescoes in the nave and on the
altar (after Potamianos 2000, by permission of the author).

---

[33] Talley 1991:100–101.
[34] Potamianos 1996:2000.

longitudinal axis towards what was calculated in antiquity as the direction of the winter solstice sunrise.[35]

Elsewhere in the western Christian world, we find the practice of orienting churches eastwards in the range of sunrise and particularly towards the place of the equinoctial sunrise. Documentary evidence between the third and seventh centuries and literary evidence through to the twelfth century indicate an expectation that churches would be oriented so that the apse looked east and specifically towards the equinoctial sunrise. A recent study of pre-Romanesque churches (built before 1086) in the Iberian Peninsula has demonstrated a strong relationship with the canonical equinox of March 25, which signals the period of Easter. The eastern orientation points the participants in the liturgy towards the direction where it is expected that Christ will rise again on Judgment Day, while also roughly directing the churches towards Jerusalem.[36] The association with Eastertime itself correlates with the fact that it was traditionally a period when baptism would take place, when new converts would be "reborn" into a new spiritual life.

5. Conclusion

In his allegorical reading of the *Cave of the Nymphs in Homer's Odyssey*, Porphyry mentions the belief in metaphysical "passageways" for the soul at the times of the solstices, and the supervision of the soul's migration on the part of Mithras from his seat on the equinoxes. The belief was instantiated in the esoteric world of the cult of Mithras, but was more widespread, since, for example, Porphyry demonstrates its currency in philosophical circles before his own time. The fact that the cult reified the belief in the form of its cultic Cave suggests that other architectural structures might also demonstrate the adaptation of the belief. Two significant imperial buildings in Rome, where Porphyry taught, seemed worth investigating: Nero's "Golden House" and Hadrian's Pantheon. In both it can be demonstrated that the equinoctial sun played a major part in their design. The solar associations of Nero are well known, and his contemporary, poet Lucan, advises him to take his seat midway between the north and the south to ensure cosmic balance. The Pantheon represents extraordinarily accurate alignment

---

[35] Schibille 2009. That the church is some 2 degrees askew of the actual solstitial sunrise is a function of the difference between antique and modern modes of calculating the amplitude of the sun. The orientation of this church may have been significant on other days. Jabi and Potamianos 2007 have shown that it may represent the azimuth of the sun at the third hour of different days, notably both December 25 (Julian), which is Christmas Day, and the equinox, with the beam of sunlight being filtered through different windows in the apse on each occasion.

[36] González-Garcia and Belmonte 2015. We may note also that this same orientation eastward and towards Jerusalem tended to underpin the depiction of the world in medieval *mappaemundi*.

in space and time, between the equinoctial midday sun and the articulation between cylinder base and domical roof in the rotunda. Whether the building provided a stage for imperial presentations on certain dates of the year remains unknown, but other alignments—with the winter solstice and the Birthday of Rome—suggest a linkage with festivals in the Roman calendar through the year. Similar interrelationships exist in early Christian architecture, in both western and eastern Christendom, with buildings aligned towards the points of sunrise at the equinoxes or the solstices, and associated buildings and liturgy with beliefs in spiritual rebirth.

PART IV

BY WAY OF CONCLUSION

18

Moving Forward

SVETLA SLAVEVA-GRIFFIN

THE PRIMARY GOAL OF this volume, as stated in the beginning, "is to bridge the gap between the two most influential perspectives on the concepts of soul and body in the transformative times of the first six centuries of the Common Era."[1] This gap is bridged by the philosophical and religious pathways that stay on separate and yet convergent courses in explicating the relation between the two pillars of human existence. The two pathways, the book demonstrates, lead to the same goal and employ conceptual and rhetorical methods which are not as opposite as have been often considered.

Lovers of the Soul, Lovers of the Body shows the two pathways in a dialogue with each other, as captured by the two facing peacock images on the book cover. We chose the two fragments of a Roman mosaic from Syria—dated to 400s–500s, courtesy of the J. Paul Getty Museum—in order to recreate the opposing and yet unified dialogue in which the seventeen chapters enter on the pages of the book. One of the images—no matter which—represents the Greco-Roman tradition according to which the peacock is the sacred bird of Hera as the queen of gods and men. With the eyes on its tail reflecting the stars of the celestial vault, this tradition captures the top-down omnipresence of the divine in the physical world, including the downward relation between soul and body.[2] The other image represents the Christian tradition according to which the peacock is a symbol of immortality. With the peacock's nondecaying flesh and annual renewal of plumes, this tradition celebrates the upward notion of the body's resurrection.[3] In both traditions, the peacock's body symbolizes the divine underlying principle of the human body. Like the images, the Greco-Roman and

---

[1] See p. xix above.
[2] Ovid *Metamorphoses* 1.720–723.
[3] Augustine *City of God* XXI 4.

Christian traditions convey the same meaning of the upwardly origin and destination of the body.

The two mosaic images, although in a fragmented state now, are intended to be in a dialogue with each other, as displayed at the Getty Villa, in order to complete the meaning of their composition. Their full aesthetic value transpires only when they are not apart. In fact, the empty space between them is the active intellectual (one might imagine) space of their dialogue in which the one side cannot complete its compositional meaning without the other. Their individual characteristics are identical to the extent that they are interchangeable and, if flipped, they continue the dialogue between them.

We found the same interchangeability in the characteristics of the two pathways to which the individual chapters of the book contribute. This interchangeability has been the most challenging, but also the most rewarding aspect of our editorial work of putting the volume together. Originally, we planned to organize it in two parts, featuring the antithetical divide between the soul and the body, implied by the title of the book. In that organizational model, we found the lack of philosophical and religious borders between the chapters appealing because it emphasized the commonalities rather than the polarities between the two schools of thought each pathway represents.

This thematic organization composed the unifying message we intended the collection to send, but not without challenges. The first challenge was to find clear marks of distinction between chapters on the soul and chapters on the body. Although some chapters dealt predominantly with one or the other, as will be synthesized below, they all engaged with both concepts explicitly and implicitly in an interchangeable way, which supported the rationale of the book, as we designed it, more so than originally expected. The demarcation of this conceptual organization faced the challenge of becoming arbitrary and ultimately disrupting the projected course of dialogue between the two pathways.

This model would have made the two peacock images on the cover of the book face away from each other. It would have also posed the danger of anachronism between the chapters in each part. For example, Zosimos' mechanistic attempt of extracting the soul from the body would precede the Middle Platonic and Hellenistic Jewish views of the soul's superiority to the body. The pathways of the soul and the body, like the two images on the front cover, did not support a strict compartmentalization between "the lovers of the soul" and "the lovers of the body." The conceptual hypermobility of either side naturally lent itself to a diachronic organization.

Perhaps our historically grounded training also led us to the diachronic organization of the chapters in three parts featuring, respectively, the foundational contribution of Plato and Aristotle, and the evolving perspectives on the soul-body relation, in imperial and late ancient "pagan" Platonism on the one hand, and in Hellenistic Jewish and Christian Platonism on the other. With the diachronic progression of the chapters, the outline of the two interchangeable pathways began to emerge. It became clear that we could send from the direction of the two pathways the unifying message of the book stronger with the same intensity and converging results. This organization also brought the benefit of allowing the chapters, as they go along, to establish multiple lines of communications internally, within each part, and externally, with the other part. It opens an indefinite number of dialogues, establishing correspondent lines of communication within and across each pathway.

As result, each chapter contributes its own voice to the polyphony of philosophical and religious perspectives bridging the scholarly divide between them. Some chapters firmly ground their investigation on either the philosophical or religious side of the bridge. Among them are the discussion of Galen's views on the Platonic tenet of the soul's immortality, the grades and modes of ensoulment in Porphyry and Proclus, Zosimos' extraction of the soul from the body, Philo's soteriology, and Origen's and Gregory of Nyssa's understanding of souls' preexistence. These chapters communicate with each other by firmly demarcating the two sides of the bridge. What they also have in common is their shared emphasis on the soul.

Another group of chapters gathers building material that stretches to the other side of the bridge in order to project the path that would bring the two sides together. Among them are the comprehensive treatments of the soul-body views in Plato, Aristotle, the Middle Platonists, Augustine, and Nemesius. These chapters demonstrate the polychromatic gradient scale of the above views, which creates a continuum, not a rift, between the concepts of soul and body on the philosophical and religious pathway. This group is also punctuated by the chapters establishing direct lines of communication about the body between Plotinus and the Gnostics or Plotinus and Origen, and the philosophical and religious confluence in pagan and Christian architecture.

The last group of articles come from both sides of the bridge but meet in the middle arguing for more moderate and at times more tolerant views on either side of the bridge when it comes to the body itself, the Gnostic pessimistic views of the body, the strict antithesis between the philosopher Origen and the theologian Athanasius, and Gregory of Nyssa's and Evagrius' layered flexibility, which keeps soul and body in balance. This last group of chapters makes a strong case for reconsidering the standard nomenclature and developing more nuanced ways of understanding the polychromatic nature of the soul-body relation in late antiquity. This relation builds a suspension bridge where the philosophical and religious pathways meet. This suspension bridge is what we defined, in the beginning of the conclusion, as the intellectual space between the two facing peacock images on the cover of the book.[4]

In some kind of a balance check between what we set the book to do and what it has done, we have selected three messages from different chapters, articulating in their own voice the six principal contributions of the book as outlined on page xx of the Introduction.

The first quotation is the concluding statement of Turner's overview of the Gnostic views of the body in light of their Platonic background in Part I: "Rather than accounting for their common pessimism and optimism in terms of theory of social crisis, however, it seems more promising to view both groups [Gnostics and Platonists] engaging in a common enterprise to apply—and where necessary to reinterpret—ancient traditional wisdom to the even more age-old problem of the situation of the self in the ever-changing world."[5]

In an implicit dialogue with Turner's call for moderating the binary soul-body lenses, the second quotation culminates Remes's summation in Part I that "being in the body is a way of actualizing" the body's particular kind of good: "Embodiment, then, is moderate rather than weak: in and within embodied activities the body contributes to the goals enabled by it. Moderate embodiment fits also well together with the late Neoplatonic idea of the kinds of goodness particular to different entities. The soul's good is according to intellect, while the body has its own kind of good, a good according to nature."[6]

The third quotation, coming from Edwards's summarizing statement in Part II, joins the spirit of reexamination of the two previous quotations by issuing a general call to both sides of the bridge: "There are other fields of intellectual history in which scholars dispense with labels altogether, writing the history of persons rather than parties. We may hope that one day this will not be true only of other fields."[7]

The individual chapters have contributed their own voice to formulating the manifesto, articulated by the three quotations above, for liberating the relation between soul and body and between philosophy and religion from labels and disciplinary compartmentalization. The book fills a gap in the recent scholarship on the soul-body relation in antiquity. It contextualizes this relation in the larger cultural milieu of late antiquity. It offers a real-time dialogue, with primary and secondary sources, between the mutually evolving perspectives on soul and body from the Hellenistic times onward. It relates the soul-body

---

4 See pp. 389–390 above.
5 See p. 109 above.
6 See p. 191 above.
7 See p. 251 above.

relation to the topic of soteriology, which gains prominence in all stripes of Platonisms.

At the end, it charts future directions of research about the relation between philosophy and religion in late antiquity. Dated to the 400s–500s, the two facing peacocks on the front cover are contemporaneous to the two pathways presented in the book. Their compositional dialogue, we hope, will yield fruitful results, as illustrated by Ramelli's proposal for one such integrative line of future research next.

The Study of Late Ancient Philosophy
Philosophy and Religion—"Pagan" and Christian Platonism

Ilaria L. E. Ramelli

T ARRANT HAS RECENTLY remarked that: "the philosophy of late antiquity now stands where Hellenistic philosophy did in the early 1970s. It is, at least for the Anglo-analytic tradition in the history of philosophy, the new unexplored territory."[1] Gerson's edited *Cambridge History of Philosophy in Late Antiquity*[2] also gives due credit to the importance of late antiquity in the history of philosophy and treats imperial and late ancient philosophy as a legitimate successor of "classical" (ancient) philosophy and in full continuity with it. Assessments of this kind are welcome and bode well for the future study of (Christian) patristic, Hellenistic Jewish, and early Islamic philosophy. But a great deal of work still needs to be done for their full integration in the study of ancient philosophy. This integrative approach has informed our undertaking in the book to offer, as noted in the introduction, "a polyphony of perspectives" about the soul-body relation in imperial and late antique philosophy, "pagan" as well as Hellenistic Jewish and patristic philosophy, against the background of "classical" ancient philosophy, especially Plato and Aristotle.[3]

There are clear and compelling reasons, demanding new research. Imperial and late antique philosophy, including Hellenistic Jewish and patristic philosophy, is a growing and extremely promising field of research that still needs a huge deal of investigation at the highest scholarly level. Imperial and late antique philosophy in the present book is contemplated within ancient philosophy and theology/religion. The effort behind this volume is to bridge the divide

---

[1] Tarrant 2007:viii.
[2] Gerson 2010.
[3] See pp. xxii and xxvii above.

between philosophical and theological-religious approaches. The dichotomy between philosophy and theology, which is customary of our post-Kantian perspective, and, which, of course, has its theoretical and historical reasons, does not prove to be helpful for the study of late ancient thought in general, and for the study of the soul-body relation in imperial and late antique thought in particular. This dichotomy has been also recently questioned by T. A. Lewis from the vantage point of philosophy of religion.[4] It is often the case that scholars of ancient philosophy are not exposed to and thereby do not even consider patristic philosophy a part of their field of study, whereas scholars of patristics, early Christianity, and religious studies, in their turn, are not exposed to and thereby are not intimately familiar with ancient and late antique philosophy. Such compartmentalization of competences, ways of thinking, and methods of investigation is one of the main reasons for which this all-important field of research still awaits much serious and painstaking work. An excessive compartmentalization diminishes the opportunity for sophisticated thinking, complex perspectives, and groundbreaking interdisciplinary research and scholarship. This book has modestly aimed to provide one such example.

"Pagan" and Christian Platonists were discussing the very same issues, often offering similar solutions, even if sometimes couched in polemical or apologetic tone. For instance, among these common issues are: theology, protology, metaphysics, the theories of the *Logos*, *logoi*, and Ideas, virtues and vices, *apatheia* and passions, hamartiology, and, prominent among these, the soul-body relation, anthropology, embodiment, soteriology, and eschatology. The last five areas form a closely intertwined set of theories. In most respects, it is difficult to mark binaries between "pagan" and Christian Platonism. Platonism is coterminous with the understanding of *philosophia* and *theologia perennis* in the first six centuries of the first millennium. This is articulated in many forms, including patristic Platonism.

Also, in Classical and Late Antiquity, philosophy was closely related to theology and religion. It was very much engaged in the exegesis of theological traditions. This engagement frequently took the form of allegoresis, that is, allegorical exegesis, from Stoicism to (so-called) Middle- and Neoplatonism, including, again, patristic Platonism. Allegoresis was an integral part of philosophy in the Stoic and Platonic traditions. By indicating how religious traditions expressed philosophical truths, this method elicited the very nature of the relation between religion and philosophy.[5] It is important to keep in mind that, while there is no word for "religion" in Greek, Latin, or Hebrew (and the concept

---

[4] T. A. Lewis 2015.
[5] This pivotal interface is pointed out by Ramelli 2011d, 2013c, and 2014e.

itself is elusive in their respective cultures), there are words for "philosophy" in Greek, which coined it, and also in Latin, and there is a word for "theology" too, coined again in Greek. The latter term referred to the part of philosophy that dealt with the divine, and interpreted religious traditions (expressed in literary, cultic, and iconographic forms) in philosophical terms. It is here that allegoresis comes to the fore on both pathways.

Theology was, indeed, part and parcel of philosophy in antiquity and late antiquity. The study of the divinity was the crowning discipline within philosophy. I have highlighted this point in a number of studies, which are further supported by Fraenkel's demonstration that for "pagan," Jewish, Christian, and Muslim philosophers, philosophy and religion were not really distinct before the Enlightenment.[6] Origen of Alexandria, for instance, the Christian Platonist, who was a theologian and an exegete as a distinctive part of his identity as a philosopher, biblical exegesis and the study of the divinity pertained quintessentially to philosophy. But the same is the case with the ancient religious traditions allegorized by Stoic and "pagan" Platonists. This is true of ancient and late antique philosophers in general, "pagan", Jewish, and Christian (and early Islamic) alike, from Stoic allegorists to Middle and Neoplatonists, Philo, Clement of Alexandria, and Origen himself, down to the early Mediaeval Christian Platonist Eriugena and beyond.

Of course, I do not advocate a confusion of methodologies between contemporary philosophy and theology, or simply a return to pre-Kantian or pre-Cartesian philosophy, or even to ancient and medieval philosophy as a necessary paradigm for doing philosophy academically today. What I advocate is for Hellenistic Jewish and patristic philosophy—particularly patristic Platonism, in which theology/ religion was just as prominent as in pagan Neoplatonism—as well as early Islamic philosophy,[7] to be considered part and parcel of classical and late ancient philosophy and to be studied as such.

Consistently, this volume has aimed at deconstructing the dichotomy between the ancient philosophical and Christian views on the soul-body relation.[8] The topic of the soul-body relation was closely connected to theology in pagan, Jewish, and Christian Platonism alike, through the question of how the soul (and possibly the body) come into existence from the divinity,[9] as well as through the issue of soteriology and—when applicable—eschatology. Asceticism

---

[6] Fraenkel 2012; Ramelli 2009c, 2013d, 2014a, 2015e.

[7] The latter is not represented in the volume for reasons of chronology and space, but it will in later projected works.

[8] See the Introduction, pp. xxi-xxiv above.

[9] I use the singular, thinking of philosophical henotheism (for "pagan" Platonism; Hirsch-Luipold calls it "polylathric monotheism") and monotheism (for Jewish and Christian Platonism).

is also relevant to this line of consideration. Recent research shows that asceticism does not have so much to do with hatred of the body as with justice, as Plato had already indicated, and that motivation runs as a red thread through "pagan," Jewish, and Christian philosophical asceticism, which is ultimately of Pythagorean and Platonic nature.[10] These areas of investigation in late ancient philosophy still deserve a great deal of work in the future, and the present volume strives to represent a step in this direction.

I have suggested elsewhere that Proclus may attest to a Neoplatonic reception of Origen whose exegesis of Plato was held in high regard. Tellingly, Proclus, like Porphyry and Hierocles, treats Origen as a member of the Platonic tradition. His disagreements with Origen's metaphysics take the form of intra-Platonic discussions. Proclus never mentions that Origen was a Christian, although he was most probably aware of this. Instead, he treats him as another Platonist.[11] Just as Porphyry had regarded Origen's "Greek" metaphysics and theology as Platonism to the point of borrowing from him, Proclus is equally able to regard the philosophical side of Origen's (Christian) Platonism, taking it as Platonism *tout court*, as interesting and authoritative.[12]

In turn, Christian Platonists such as Origen, like the Hellenistic Jewish Platonist Philo, took the Bible as their authoritative text, reading it through the lens of Platonism, at the same time valuing and interpreting Plato's dialogues and allegorizing his myths, assimilating them to Scripture's myths.[13] In the Bible, Origen—like Philo before him—found Plato's teachings, thinking that Plato was inspired by Scripture or by the same *Logos* that was manifested in the Bible.[14] Similarly, "pagan" Platonists held as authoritative not only Plato's dialogues, but also religious texts such as the *Chaldean Oracles*, which were no less revelation than the Bible to many "pagan" Platonists. Porphyry, for instance, commented on them according to John Lydus (*Chaldean Oracles* fr. 365 Smith); Iamblichus and Proclus treated the *Chaldean Oracles* as authoritative and interpreted them Platonically.[15] In some cases, as with Numenius and Amelius, "pagan" Platonists commented on the Bible besides commenting on Plato.

---

[10] Arguments in Ramelli 2016b.

[11] For example, *Commentary on the Timaeus* I 31.19–32, I 60.1–12, I 68.12–15, I 76.31–77.9, I 83.19–28, I 86.20–87.6, I 93.8–15, I 162.15–30.

[12] Porphyry *Against the Christians* fr. 39 Harnack = Eusebius *Ecclesiastical History* 6.19.4–8. For example, Porphyry projected conceptual novelty of "hypostasis" as individual substance onto Plotinus' metaphysics and protology, as argued by Ramelli 2012b, received by Karamanolis 2014:307, Martens 2015:611, Havrda 2016:35, etc. Further in a monograph in preparation.

[13] See Ramelli 2008b and 2017.

[14] See, e.g. Ramelli 2008b and 2012c.

[15] Athanassiadi 1999; 2006:31–70; Stroumsa (2016:24) also considers these *Oracles* "a holy text" for Neoplatonism.

Platonism in imperial and late antiquity was not only "pagan," to the exclusion of Christian and Hellenistic Jewish Platonism. Dörrie has famously considered Christianity as "anti-Platonism,"[16] a view criticized by Strutwolf, Ramelli, Boyarin, and Kobusch, among others.[17] Christian Platonism in imperial and late antiquity was part and parcel of the history of Platonism. Fowler has recently noted that "the religious and philosophical issues of the beginning centuries of the Common Era might helpfully be discussed in terms of 'orthodoxy' and 'heresy', and less so in terms of 'pagan' and 'Christian'."[18]

Kobusch, Ramelli, and Fürst have further argued that the Harnackian model of the Hellenization of Christianity implies an incompatibility between Christianity and philosophy.[19] On the contrary, many Christian thinkers represented Christianity as philosophy and construed it through philosophical structures, categories, and arguments. This trend is best illustrated by Origen who clearly states in *Against Celsus* 4.9: "Anyone who constructs *a Christian philosophy* will need *to argue the truth of his doctrines with proofs of all kinds*, taken both from the divine scriptures *and from rational arguments*."[20] In his own terms, Origen revisits Philo's distinction, quoted in the introduction, between "lovers of the soul" and "lovers of the body" to conclude that Christianity without philosophy is only for the "simple-minded masses" (*Against Celsus* 4.9).[21] In light of this heightened conceptual exchange between Christian and non-Christian Platonists,[22] Tarrant's remark that "what it meant to be a Platonist was still far from clear" in early imperial Platonism becomes programmatic for the line of research proposed here.[23]

Platonism in the time of Origen, and in part even later, was not only "pagan" institutional Platonism. There are historical facts that speak against the compartmentalization between non-Christian philosophy and Christian religion and require a more serious consideration than so far given. The school of

[16] Dörrie 1976:508–523.
[17] Strutwolf 2001, Boyarin 2004, Ramelli 2009c, and Kobusch 2014.
[18] R. Fowler 2016:5.
[19] Kobusch 2006:26–33, 152; Fürst 2007; Ramelli 2009c, received by Markschies 2012:119, 138; Tzamalikos 2012:288, 486, 505; M. S. M. Scott 2012:180; Jacobsen 2012; A. P. Johnson 2012; Leppin 2012; González 2014:71; Urbano 2013:71; Karamanolis 2014:286, 307; Proctor 2014:419; Crawford 2015; Martens 2015:599, 619; Digeser 2016:29n2, 31n42; Karamanolis 2016. Specific works on Origen's philosophical theology and on a systematic comparison between Origen and Plotinus are underway.
[20] The translation is according to Chadwick 1953, the emphasis is mine.
[21] See pp. xxii–xxiii above.
[22] Sometimes it is even difficult to categorize a philosopher in either of these groups, e.g. Ammonius Saccas, the early Origen, or the early Porphyry, or later Dionysius. See my work on Origen's philosophical theology in preparation, Chapter 1, for Ammonius and Origen, and Ramelli 2019 on Dionysius.
[23] Tarrant 2010:99d.

Ammonius, like Ammonius himself, was probably both Platonist and Christian. Origen defended philosophers who were also presbyters, such as Heraclas, who was a Platonist and, like Origen and Plotinus, a disciple of Ammonius. Origen himself not only was a Christian Platonist and a presbyter, but also had "pagan" philosophers at his Christian school, where he taught philosophy. He was even admired and respected by Platonists—from Porphyry (and likely Plotinus) to Proclus—as a philosopher. Plotinus had Christian disciples (surely "Gnostics" and probably other Christians) at his "pagan" Platonic school, which—even in its rather informal structure—can be regarded as an institution of Platonism. Before attending Plotinus' lectures, Porphyry seems to have attended Origen's Christian school.[24] Synesius was a disciple of the Neoplatonist Hypatia and attended her "pagan" Platonic school in Alexandria, possibly along with other Christians.[25] Even as a Christian bishop, he continued his adherence to the Platonic tenets and rejected, for example, a literalist understanding of the resurrection—as Origen, Gregory of Nyssa, and Evagrius also did—by insisting on the transformation of the earthly body and on a holistic concept of resurrection, also involving soul and mind.[26] In the West, Marius Victorinus' theology was likewise so deeply informed by Platonic metaphysics as to be criticized as not Christian enough.[27]

Rigid boundaries between "pagan" institutional Platonism and Christianity are difficult to draw. Platonism embraced "pagan" as well as Hellenistic Jewish and Christian Platonism in imperial and late antiquity. Origen, Plotinus, and Porphyry were all negotiating the legacy of Ammonius, namely Neoplatonism. In Tarrant's words, they participated in "internal quarrels about Platonism's true nature."[28] This is very much the core of imperial and late antique philosophy, and this conclusion also applies to the pivotal issue of the soul-body nexus—closely related to theology, anthropology, ethics, and soteriology—as highlighted by the polyphonic nature of the philosophical and religious pathways explored in the book.

---

[24] Ramelli 2009c and Simmons 2015.
[25] Bregman 2010:421.
[26] Synesius *Letters* 105.
[27] See Cooper 2016.
[28] Tarrant 2010:70.

Contributors

PIER FRANCO BEATRICE is Professor in Classics and Religious Studies at the University of Padua and a member of the Advisory Board of the *Journal of Early Christian Studies*, the official journal of the North American Patristics Society. He has extensively published on Porphyry and the Christian writers of Late Antiquity. His publications include *Anonymi Monophysitae Theosophia: An Attempt at Reconstruction* (2001) and *The Transmission of Sin: Augustine and the Pre-Augustinian Sources* (2013). He has also coedited *Chromatius of Aquileia and His Age* (2011) and *Pascha Nostrum Christus. Essays in Honour of R. Cantalamessa* (2016).

LUC BRISSON is Emeritus Director of Research at the National Center for Scientific Research (Paris). He is author of numerous works on Plato and Plotinus, including bibliographies, translations, and commentaries, among which are *Platon, le mots et les mythes* (1982, published in English as *Plato the Myth Maker*, 1999) and *Einführung in die Philosophie des Mythos I* (1996, published in English as *How Philosophers Saved Myths: Allegorical Interpretation and Classical Mythology*, 2004). He has also edited *Platon. Oeuvres completes* (2008) and *Plotin: Traités* 9 volumes, with J.-F. Pradeau (2002–2010).

KEVIN CORRIGAN is Samuel Candler Dobbs Professor of Interdisciplinary Humanities at Emory University. His recent publications include *Evagrius and Gregory: Mind, Soul, and Body in the Fourth Century* (2009), *Reason, Faith, and Otherness in Neoplatonic and Early Christian Thought* (2013), *Plotinus: Ennead VI.8. Translation, Introduction, and Commentary*, with J. D. Turner (2017), *Love, Friendship, Beauty and the Good: Plato, Aristotle, and the Later Tradition* (2018). He has also edited *Religion and Philosophy in the Platonic and Neoplatonic Traditions*, with J. D. Turner and P. Wakefield (2012) and *Gnosticism, Platonism, and the Late Ancient World: Essays in Honour of John D. Turner*, with T. Rasimus (2013).

JOHN DILLON is Emeritus Fellow in Classics and Emeritus Regius Professor of Greek, Trinity College, Dublin. He has written, coauthored and coedited many books, most recent among which are *Iamblichus of Chalchis, The Letters. Edited with Translation and Notes*, with W. Polleichtner (2010), *Aeneas of Gaza, Theophrastus, with Zacharias of Mitylene, Ammonius*, with S. Gertz and D. Russell (2012), *Plato's*

Philebus: Selected Papers from the Eighth Symposium Platonicum, with L. Brisson (2010), *Studies on Plato, Aristotle and Proclus: Collected Essays on Ancient Philosophy of John J. Cleary*, with B. O'Byrne and F. O'Rourke (2013), *Plotinus, Ennead IV 3-4, 29: Problems Concerning the Soul. Translation, with Introduction and Commentary*, with H. J. Blumenthal (2015). His collected papers are gathered in *The Golden Chain* (1990), *The Great Tradition* (1997), and *The Platonic Heritage* (2012).

OLIVIER DUFAULT obtained a PhD in ancient history from the University of California, Santa Barbara and was a postdoctoral scholar at the Institut d'Études Anciennes at Laval University as well as at the Graduate School Distant Worlds at the Ludwig-Maximilians-Universität Munich. He is the author of *Early Greek Alchemy, Patronage and Innovation in Late Antiquity* (2019).

MARK EDWARDS has been Tutor in Theology at Christ Church Oxford and University Lecturer (now Associate Professor) in Patristics at the University of Oxford since 1993. Since 2014 he has held the title Professor of Early Christian Studies. His publications include *Origen against Plato* (2002), *Culture and Philosophy in the Age of Plotinus* (2006), *Catholicity and Heresy in the Early Church* (2009), *Image, Word and God in the Early Christian Centuries* (2012), and *Religions of the Constantinian Empire* (2015).

JOHN F. FINAMORE is Professor of Classics at the University of Iowa, editor of *The International Journal of the Platonic Tradition*, and president of the US section of the International Society for Neoplatonic Studies. He is the author of *Iamblichus and the Theory of the Vehicle of the Soul* (1985), *Iamblichus De Anima: Text, Translation, and Commentary*, with J. M. Dillon (2002). Among his most recent edited volumes are *Platonic Interpretations: Selected Papers from the Sixteenth Annual Conference of the International Society for Neoplatonic Studies*, with E. Perl (2019) and *Studies in Hermias' Commentary on Plato's Phaedrus*, with C. Manolea and S. Wear (2019).

DIMKA GICHEVA-GOCHEVA is Associate Professor in History of Philosophy at Sofia University. She has widely published on ancient philosophy, including *In the Labyrinth of Plato and Aristotle* (1994), *New Essays on Aristotelian Teleology* (1999), *The University: Where to?* (2002), *On Europe and the University* (2005). She has also translated *Aristotle: On the Heavens* (2006, in Bulgarian) and edited *The Political Thought of the European "past"* (2010) and *The Challenge: Aristotle* (2018). Her articles are found in *ΠΟΙΚΙΛΙΑ. A Book on the Classical Greek Thinkers* (2013). Her recent work (second habilitation) is a study of justice and the just in Herodotus, Thucydides, Sophocles, Plato, and Aristotle (2019).

ROBERT HANNAH is Emeritus Professor at the University of Waikato, New Zealand. He was formerly a member of the Department of Classics at the University of Otago, and then Dean of Arts & Social Sciences at the University of Waikato. He is a Fellow of the Society of Antiquaries of London, and a Fellow of the Royal Society of New Zealand. He has written extensively on the use of astronomy in Greek and Roman cultures. His publications include *Greek and Roman Calendars: Constructions of Time in the Classical World* (2005) and *Time in Antiquity* (2009). He is currently working on the monograph *Time, Eternity and the Afterlife in Antiquity and the early Middle Ages*.

AARON P. JOHNSON is Associate Professor in Classics and Humanities at Lee University. He specializes in the intellectual cultures and Greek literature of the later Roman Empire. He is the author of *Ethnicity and Argument in Eusebius' Praeparatio Evangelica* (2006), *Religion and Identity in Porphyry of Tyre* (2013), and *Eusebius* (2014) as well as a number of articles on the thought and literature of the third and fourth centuries. His current work is dedicated to the fifth century Cyril of Alexandria's *Against Julian*.

LENKA KARFÍKOVÁ is Professor of Philosophy at Charles University (Prague). She also collaborates with the Center for Patristic, Medieval and Renaissance Texts at Palacký University in Olomouc. Her research interests focus on Early and Mediaeval Christian authors inspired by the Platonic Tradition. Her publications include *De esse ad pulchrum esse. Schönheit in der Theologie Hugos von St. Viktor* (1998), *Gregory of Nyssa: Contra Eunomium II. An English Version with Supporting Studies* (2007), *Nomina divina: Colloquium Dionysiacum Pragense* (2011), *Grace and the Will according to Augustine* (2012), *Von Augustin zu Abaelard: Studien zum christlichen Denken* (2015), *Gnadenlehre in Schrift und Patristik* (2016), and *Augustine on Recollection between Plato and Plotinus* (*Studia patristica*, 75/1, 2017, 81–102).

CARLOS LÉVY is Emeritus Professor of Roman philosophy and literature at the Sorbonne, Fellow of the Israel Institute of Advanced Studies, and Senior Fellow in the Maimonides Center for Advanced Studies at the Hamburg University. He is the author of numerous authoritative studies, articles, and collections in Hellenistic and Roman philosophy, with frequent excursions to the earlier and later periods of ancient philosophy leading among which are *Cicero Academicus: Recherches sur les Académiques et sur la philosophie cicéronienne* (1992), *Les philosophies hellénistique* (1997), *Philon d'Alexandrie et le langage de la philosophie* (1998), and *Les présocratiques à Rome*, with S. Franchey d'Espèrey (2018).

ILARIA L. E. RAMELLI has been Professor of Roman History, Senior Research Fellow in Ancient Philosophy, Patristic Theology and Hellenic Studies (Durham; Oxford University, Corpus Christi; Sacred Heart University, 2003–present; Princeton), in Religion (Erfurt), Senior Visiting Professor of Greek Thought (Harvard; Boston University), of Church History, Fowler Hamilton Fellow (Oxford, Christ Church), and Full Professor of Theology and Britt endowed Chair (Graduate School of Theology, "Angelicum" University). She is also Professor of Theology (Hon., Durham University), director of international research projects, *Humboldt-Forschungspreis* Senior Fellow at Erfurt MWK, elected Senior Fellow, Bonn University; CEU Institute of Advanced Study and Distinguished Professor of Patristics (Hon., KUL). She authored numerous books, articles, and reviews in leading scholarly journals and series, on ancient philosophy, patristic theology and philosophy, early Christianity, Biblical exegesis, late antiquity, and the relationship between Christianity and classical culture. Her recent books include *Evagrius' Kephalaia Gnostika* (2015), *Social Justice and the Legitimacy of Slavery: The Role of Philosophical Asceticism from Ancient Judaism to Late Antiquity* (2016), *A Larger Hope?* (2019); she also edited *Evagrius between Origen, the Cappadocians, and Neoplatonism* (2017) and *Eriugena's Christian Neoplatonism and its Sources* (2021).

PAULIINA REMES is Professor in theoretical philosophy, especially history of philosophy, in Uppsala University. She is the author of *Plotinus on Self. The Philosophy of the 'We'* (2007) and *Neoplatonism* (2008), and the coeditor, together with S. Slaveva-Griffin, of *The Routledge Handbook of Neoplatonism* (2014). Thematically, her current interests range from ancient methodology, epistemology, and Platonic conversational norms to notions of self, self-knowledge, and agency.

SVETLA SLAVEVA-GRIFFIN is Associate Professor of Classics at Florida State University. She has published widely on topics at the intersection of philosophy, science, and medicine in late antiquity. She is the author of *Plotinus on Number* (2009) and the coeditor, with P. Remes, of *The Routledge Handbook of Neoplatonism* (2014). Her current research interests lie in the presence of the art of medicine in Neoplatonism.

HAROLD TARRANT studied at Cambridge and Durham Universities. He taught at the University of Sydney from 1973 to 1993, after which he was Professor of Classics at the University of Newcastle Australia until 2011; though he has retired to the United Kingdom, he still has honorary positions at both Australian universities. He was a member of the Executive Committee of the International Plato Society (1995–2001), and has written, coauthored and coedited several books relating to Platonism, most recently *Proclus: Commentary on Plato's Timaeus* vol. 1 (2007) and vol. 6 (2017), *The Neoplatonic Socrates*, with D. A. Layne (2014), *The Platonic Alcibiades I: the Dialogue and its Ancient Reception*, with F. Renaud (2015), *Brill's Companion to the Reception of Plato in Antiquity* (2018), and *The Second Alcibiades: a Dialogue on Prayer and on Ignorance* (2020).

JOHN D. TURNER was Cotner Professor of Religious Studies and Charles J. Mach University Professor of Classics and History at the University of Nebraska-Lincoln. He was the author of *Sethian Gnosticism and the Platonic Tradition* (2002), a principal contributor to the English and French language critical editions of seven of the Nag Hammadi texts, *Plotinus: Ennead VI.8. Translation, Introduction, and Commentary*, with K. Corrigan (2017). He also edited *Platonisms: Ancient, Modern, and Postmodern*, with K. Corrigan (2007) and *Plato's Parmenides and Its Heritage* 2 vols, with K. Corrigan (2010). He was honored in the volume *Gnosticism, Platonism, and the Late Ancient World. Essays in Honour of John D. Turner*, edited by K. Corrigan and T. Rasimus (2013).

Bibliography

This is a combined bibliography of the primary and secondary sources in all chapters. Critical editions, commentaries, and translations are listed by the name of their modern authors.

Addey, C. 2014a. "The Daimonion of Socrates: Daimones and Divination in Neoplatonism." In Layne and Tarrant 2014:51–72.

———. 2014b. *Divination and Theurgy in Neoplatonism: Oracles of the Gods.* Burlington, VT.

Adler, A., ed. 1971. *Suidae Lexicon.* Lexicographi Graeci I. Stuttgart.

Agaësse, P., and A. Solignac. 1972. "Notes." *Bibliothèque augustinienne* 48:710–714.

Ahbel-Rappe, S., trans. 2010. *Damascius' Problems and Solutions Concerning First Principles.* American Academy of Religion, Religion in Translation Series. Oxford.

Albertson, F. C. 2001. "Zenodorus's 'Colossus of Nero.'" *Memoirs of the American Academy in Rome* 46:95–118.

Allan, D. J., ed. 1936. *Aristotelis De Caelo libri quattuor.* Oxford.

Anagnostopoulos, G., ed. 2009. *A Companion to Aristotle.* London.

Anatolios, K. 1988. *Athanasius: The Coherence of his Thought.* New York.

Annas, J. 1999. *Platonic Ethics, Old and New.* Ithaca, NY.

Armstrong, A. H. 1966–1988. *Plotinus: Enneads.* 7 vols. Cambridge, MA.

———. ed. 1970. *The Cambridge History of Later Greek and Early Medieval Philosophy.* Cambridge.

———. 1978. "Gnosis and Greek Philosophy." In *Gnosis: Festschrift für Hans Jonas,* ed. B. Aland, 87–124. Göttingen.

Arnoldt, U. 1960. *Die Entelechie: Systematik bei Platon und Aristoteles.* Vienna.

Arnzen, R. 2013. "Proclus on Plato's Timaeus 89e3–90c7." *Arabic Sciences and Philosophy* 23:1–45.

Arzhanov, Y., ed. and trans. 2019. *Syriac Sayings of Greek Philosophers: A Study in Syriac Gnomologia with Edition and Translation.* Corpus Scriptorum Christianorum Orientalium 669–Subsidia Tomus 138. Leuven.

Ast, J. 1969. *Lexicon Platonicum.* 3 vols. New York.

Athanassiadi, P. 1999. "The Chaldaean Oracles." In *Pagan Monotheism in Late Antiquity*, ed. P. Athanassiadi and M. Frede, 149–183. Oxford.

———. 2006. *La lutte pour l'orthodoxie dans le platonisme tardif.* Paris.

Aubenque, P. 1962. *Le problème de l'être chez Aristote. Essai sur la problématique aristotélicienne.* Paris.

Ayache, L. 1997. "Est-il vraiment question d'art médical dans le *Timée?*" In Calvo and Brisson 1997:55–63.

Bahktin, M. 1990. "Author and Hero in Aesthetic Activity." In *Art and Answerability: Early Philosophical Essays by M. M. Bahktin*, ed. and trans. M. Holquist and V. Liapunov, 4–256. Austin, TX.

Ball, L. F. 2003. *The Domus Aurea and the Roman Architectural Revolution.* Cambridge.

Balme, D. 1962. "Development of Biology in Aristotle and Theophrastus: Theory of Spontaneous Generation." *Phronesis* 7:91–104.

———. 1965. *Aristotle's Use of the Teleological Explanation.* London.

———. 1975. "Aristotle's Use of Differentiae in Zoology." In *Articles on Aristotle*, Vol. 1, ed. J. Barnes, M. Schofield, and R. Sorabji, 183–193. London.

———. 1991. *Aristotle: History of Animals: Books 7–10.* Cambridge, MA.

Bamberger, J. E. 1981. *Evagrius Ponticus: The Praktikos; Chapters on Prayer.* Kalamazoo, MI.

Bardy, G. 1953. "Saint Augustin et les médecins." *Année théologique augustinienne* 13:327–346.

Barnes, J., ed. 1984. *The Revised Oxford Translation of Aristotle.* 2 vols. Princeton, NJ.

———. ed. 1995. *The Cambridge Companion to Aristotle.* Cambridge.

Barney, R. 1998. "Socrates Agonistes: The Case of the Cratylus Etymologies." *Oxford Studies in Ancient Philosophy* 16:63–98.

Barney, R., T. Brennan, and C. Brittain, eds. 2012. *Plato and the Divided Self.* Cambridge.

Barry C., W.-P. Funk, P.-H. Poirier, and J. D. Turner, eds. 2000. *Zostrien (NH VIII, 1).* Bibliothèque copte de Nag Hammadi, section "Textes" 24. Québec.

Barwick, K. 1948. "Zu den Schriften des Cornelius Celsus und des alten Cato." *Würzburger Jahrbücher für die Altertumswissenschaft* 3:117–132.

Bastianini, G., and A. A. Long, eds. 1992. "Hierocles." *Corpus dei papiri filosofici greci e latini.* Parte I, *Autori Noti.* 1.2:268–451. Florence.

Bastianini, G., and D. Sedley, eds. 1995. "Anonymous Commentary on Plato's Theaetetus." *Corpus dei papiri filosofici greci e latini*, Parte III: Commentarii 3:227–562. Florence.

Beatrice, P. F. 1989. "Quosdam Platonicorum Libros: The Platonic readings of Augustine in Milan." *Vigiliae Christianae* 43:248–281.

———. ed. 2001. *Anonymi Monophysitae Theosophia: An Attempt at Reconstruction.* Supplements to Vigiliae Christianae 56. Leiden.

———. 2002. "The Word 'Homoousios' from Hellenism to Christianity." *Church History* 71:243–272.

———. 2005. "L'union de l'âme et du corps. Némésius d'Émèse lecteur de Porphyre." In Boudon-Millot and Pouderon 2005:253–285.

———. 2009. "Origen in Nemesius' Treatise *On the Nature of Man*." In *Origeniana Nona: Origen and Religious Practice of His Time*, ed. G. Heidl and R. Somos, 505–532. Bibliotheca Ephemeridum Theologicarum Lovaniensium 228. Leuven.

———. 2010a. "Péché et libération de l'homme chez Jean Damascène." In *Les forces du Bien et du Mal dans les premiers siècles de l'Église*, ed. Y.-M. Blanchard, B. Pouderon, and M. Scopello, 211–236. Théologie historique 118. Paris.

———. 2010b. "Semantic Shifts in Augustine's Use of the Word *Profanus*." In *Les frontières du profane dans l'Antiquité Tardive*, ed. É. Rebillard and C. Sotinel, 37–53. Collection de l'École Française de Rome 428. Rome.

———. 2016. "So Spoke the Gods: Oracles and Philosophy in the So-called Anonymous Commentary on the Parmenides." In *Theologische Orakel in der Spätantike*, ed. H. Seng and S. Sfameni Gasparro, 115–144. Bibliotheca Chaldaica 5. Heidelberg.

———. 2019. "Porphyry at Origen's School at Caesarea." In *Origeniana Duodecima: Origen's Legacy in the Holy Land*, ed. B. Bitton-Ashkelony, A. Kofsky, and L. Perrone, 267–284. Bibliotheca Ephemeridum Theologicarum Lovaniensium 302. Leuven.

Beck, R. 1984. "Mithraism since Franz Cumont." In *Aufstieg und Niedergang der römischen Welt*, ed. H. Temporini, II 17.4: 2002–21.

———. 2005. "Mithras." In *The Oxford Classical Dictionary*, ed. S. Hornblower and A. Spawforth, 991–992. Oxford.

———. 2006. *The Religion of the Mithras Cult in the Roman Empire: Mysteries of the Unconquered Sun*. Oxford.

Behr, J., ed. 2011. *The Case against Diodore and Theodore: Texts and Their Contexts*. Oxford Early Christian Texts. Oxford.

Bekker, I., ed. 1831. *Aristotelis Opera omnia*. Berlin.

Berger, M. 1998. "'Schwer' und 'Leicht' in Platons Timaios." In *Mousopolos Stephanos: Festschrift für Herwig Görgemanns*, ed. M. Baumbach, H. Köhler, and A. M. Ritter, 390–396. Heidelberg.

Bergmann, M. 1993. "Der Koloss Neros: die Domus Aurea und der Mentalitäts-wandel im Rom der früher Kaiserzeit." Trierer Winckelmannsprogramme 13. Mainz.

Bermon, E. 2011. "Lettres 3 à 30." *Bibliothèque Augustinienne* 40/A.

Berthelot, M., and C.-É. Ruelle, eds. 1887–1888. *Collection des anciens alchimistes grecs*. Vol. 3. Paris.

Bertrand, D. 2005. "Origine de l'âme et animation du corps humain." In Boudon-Millot and Pouderon 2005:299–320.

Bidez, J. 1913. *Vie de Porphyre. Le philosophe Néo-platonicien*. Gand and Leipzig.

Blowers, P. 2012. *Drama of the Divine Economy*. Oxford.

Blumenthal, H. J. 1971. *Plotinus' Psychology: His Doctrines of the Embodied Soul*. The Hague.

———. 1976. "Plotinus' Adaptation of Aristotle's Psychology: Sensation, Imagination, and Memory." In *The Significance of Neoplatonism*, ed. R. B. Harris, 41–58. Norfolk. Repr. 1993 in H. J. Blumenthal. *Soul and Intellect: Studies in Plotinus and Later Neoplatonism*. Aldershot.

Bodnár, I. 2005. "Teleology Across Natures." *Rhizai* 2.1:9–30.

Bodnár, I., and P. Pellegrin. 2006. "Aristotle's Physics and Cosmology." In *A Companion to Ancient Philosophy*, ed. M. L. Gill and P. Pellegrin, 270–291. London.

Boersma, H. 2012. "Overcoming Time and Space: Gregory of Nyssa's Anagogical Theology." *Journal of Early Christian Studies* 20:575–612.

Bonitz, H. 1870. *Index Aristotelicus*. Berlin.

Bonner, C. 1942. "A Tarsian Peculiarity (Dio Prus. Or. 33) with an Unnoticed Fragment of Porphyry." *Harvard Theological Review* 35:1–11.

Bos, A. 2003. *The Soul and its Instrumental Body*. Leiden.

Boudon-Millot, V., and B. Pouderon, eds. 2005. *Les Pères de l'Église face à la science médicale de leur temps*. Théologie historique 117. Paris.

Boulos, W. H. K. 2001. "St. Athanasius' Doctrine of Grace in Contra Arianos I." *Studia Patristica* 36:477–481.

Boyadjiev, T., trans. 2005. *Plotin: Enneads*. Sofia.

Boyarin, D. 2004. "By Way of Apology: Dawson, Edwards, Origen." *Studia Philonica Annual* 16:188–217.

Boys-Stones, G. 2017. *Middle Platonist Philosophy 80 BC to AD 250: A Study and Collection of Sources in Translation*. Cambridge.

Boys-Stones, G., and J. H. Haubold, eds. 2010. *Plato and Hesiod*. Oxford.

Brashear, W. 1995. "The Greek Magical Papyri: An Introduction and Survey." *Aufstieg und Niedergang der römische Welt* Part II 18.5:3380–3684.

Braun, O., ed. 1953. *Timothei Patriarchae: Epistulae I*. Corpus Scriptorum Christianorum Orientalium 75, Scriptores Syri 31. Louvain.

Bréhier, É. 1925. *Les idées philosophiques et religieuses de Philon d'Alexandrie*. Paris.

———. 1928. *La Philosophie de Plotin*. Paris. 3rd ed., 2008.

Bregman, J. 2010. "Synesius of Cyrene." In Gerson 2010:1.520–537.

Brentano, F. 1911. *Aristoteles und seine Weltanschauung*. Hamburg.

———. 1975. *On the Several Senses of Being in Aristotle*. Trans. R. George. Berkeley. Orig. pub. 1862 as *Von der mannigfachen Bedeutungen des Seienden nach Aristoteles*. Freiburg.

Brisson, L. 1974. "Du bon usage du dérèglement." In *Divination et rationalité*, ed. J. P. Vernant, 220–248. Paris.

———. 1974. *Le même et l'Autre dans la structure ontologique du "Timée" de Platon*. Paris.

———. 1982. *Platon. Les mots et les mythes*. Paris.

———. trans. 1989. *Platon. PHÈDRE*. Paris.

———. trans. 1992. *Platon. Timée. Critias*. Paris.

———. 1997a. "Le corps animal comme signe de la valeur d'une âme chez Platon." In *L'Animal dans l'Antiquité*, ed. B. Cassin and J.-L. Labarrière, 227–245. Paris.

———. 1997b. "Perception sensible et raison dans le Timée." In Calvo and Brisson 1997:307–316.

———. 1999a. "La réminiscence dans le Ménon (80e–81e) et son arrière-plan religieux." In *Anamnese e Saber*, ed. J. T. Santos, 23–61. Lisbon.

———. 1999b. "Plato's Theory of Sense Perception in the Timaeus: How It Works and What It Means." In *Proceedings of the Colloquium in Ancient Philosophy* 13, ed. J. Cleary and G. Gurtler, 147–176. Lanham.

———. 2000. *Lectures de Platon*. Paris.

———. 2003. "Le corps des dieux." *Les dieux de Platon*. Actes du Colloque de Caen 24–26 janvier 2002, ed. J. Laurent, 11–23. Caen.

———. 2004. "Justifying vegetarianism in Plato's Timaeus (76e–77c)." In *Greek Philosophy in the new Millennium: Essays in honour of Thomas M. Robinson*, ed. L. Rossetti, 313–319. Sankt Augustin.

———. 2005a. "Le Système philosophique de Porphyre dans les Sentences: Physique et Éthique." In Brisson 2005b:1.107–138.

———. ed. 2005b. *Porphyre: Sentences*. 2 vols. Paris.

———. 2005c. "Un modèle géométrique du corps humain chez Platon." In *L'Architecture de la vie: de Platon à la tensegrité*, ed. P. A. d'Alessio and J. Dhombres, Série II, Vol. 9, Fasc. 2, *Sciences et techniques en perspective*. 55–68. Turnhout.

———. 2006. "The Doctrine of the Degrees of Virtues in the Neoplatonists: An Analysis of Porphyry's Sentence 32, its Antecedents, and its Heritage." In *Reading Plato in Antiquity*, ed. H. Tarrant and D. Baltzly, 89–105. London.

———. 2007. "La réminiscence dans le Ménon (81c5–d5)." In *Gorgias-Meno: Selected Papers from the Seventh Symposium Platonicum*, ed. M. Erler and L. Brisson, 199–203. Sankt Augustin.

———. 2008. "Reminiscence in Plato." In *Platonism and Forms of Intelligence*, ed. J. Dillon and M.-É. Zovko, 179–190. Berlin.

———. 2010. "Platon et la cosmologie." *Forme et origine de l'Univers: Regards philosophiques sur la cosmologie*, D. Parrochia and A. Barrau, 179–195. Paris.

———. 2013. "Le Timée de Platon et le traité hippocratique Du régime, sur le mécanisme de la sensation." *Études Platoniciennes* 10. journals.openedition.org/etudesplatoniciennes/367.

Brisson, L., G. Aubry, F. Hudry, et al., eds. and trans. 2012. *Porphyre: Sur la manière dont l'embryon reçoit l'âme*. Paris.

Brisson, L., M.-H. Congourdeau, and J.-L. Solère, eds. 2008. *L'Embryon: Formation, antiquité grecques et latine, traditions hébraïque, chrétienne et islamique*. Paris.

Brisson, L., and J. Marie Flamand. 2005. "Notes sur les Sentences 32." In Brisson 2005b:2.628–642.

Brisson, L., and W. Meyerstein. 1995. *Inventing the Universe: Plato's Timaeus, the Big Bang, and the Problem of Scientific knowledge*. Albany, NY.

Brisson, L., M.-O. Goulet-Cazé, R. Goulet, and D. O'Brien, eds. 1992. *Porphyre. La Vie de Plotin*. Vol. 2. Paris.

Brock, S. 1983. "A Syriac Collection of Prophecies of the Pagan Philosophers." *Orientalia Lovaniensia Periodica* 14:203–246. Repr. 1992. In *Studies in Syriac Christianity: History, Literature, and Theology*. Variorum 7. Aldershot.

———. 1999. "Two Letters of the Patriarch Timothy from the Late Eighth Century on Translations from Greek." *Arabic Sciences and Philosophy* 9:233–246.

———. 2007. "A Syriac Intermediary for The Arabic theology of Aristotle? In Search of a Chimera." In *The Libraries of the Neoplatonists*, ed. C. D'Ancona, 293–306. Philosophia Antiqua 107. Leiden.

Brunschwig, J. 2000. "Metaphysics Λ9: A Short-Lived Thought Experiment?" In *Aristotle's Metaphysics Lambda*, ed. M. Frede and D. Charles, 275–306. Oxford.

Brunschwig, J., and G. E. R. Lloyd, eds. 2003. *A Guide to Greek Thought: Major Figures and Trends*. Cambridge, MA.

Buckenmeyer, R. E. 1971. "Augustine and the Life of Man's Body in the Early Dialogues." *Augustinian Studies* 2:197–211.

Bull, C. 2018. *The Tradition of Hermes Trismegistus*. Leiden.

Burns, D. M. 2015. "μίξεώς τινι τέχνη κρείττονι: Alchemical Metaphor in the Paraphrase of Shem (NHC VII, 1)." *Aries* 15:81–108.

Burnyeat, M. 1990. *The Theaetetus of Plato: With a Translation of Plato's Theaetetus by M. J. Levett*. Indianapolis.

———. 2000. "Plato on Why Mathematics is Good for the Soul." In *Mathematics and Necessity: Essays in the History of Philosophy: Proceedings of the British Academy*, ed. T. Smiley, 103:1–81.

———. 2001. *A Map of Metaphysics Zeta*. Pittsburgh, PA.

———. et al. 1979. *Notes on book Zeta of Aristotle's Metaphysics, Being the record of a Seminar Held in London 1975-1979*. Study Aids Monograph 1. Oxford.

Burnyeat, M., et al. 1984. *Notes on book Eta and Theta of Aristotle's Metaphysics*. Study Aids Monograph 4. Oxford.

Byl, S. 1980. *Recherches sur les grands traités biologiques d'Aristote: Sources ecrites et préjugés*. Brussels.

Bywater, I., ed. 1886. *Prisciani Lydi quae exstant*. Supplementum Aristotelicum I.2. Berlin.

Caluori, D. 2015. *Plotinus on the Soul*. Cambridge.

Calvo, T., and L. Brisson, eds. 1997. *Interpreting the Timaeus-Critias: Proceedings of the IV Symposium Platonicum*. Sankt Augustin.

Camplani, A. 2000. "Procedimenti magico-alchemici e discorso filosofico ermetico." In *Il tardoantico alle soglie del Duemila: diritto, religione, società*, ed. G. Lanata, 73–98. Pisa.

Camplani, A., and M. Zambon. 2002. "Il sacrificio come problema in alcune correnti filosofiche di età imperial." *Annali di storia dell'esegesi* 19:59–99.

Carlier, J. 1998. "L'après-mort selon Porphyre." In *Retour, repentir, et constitution de soi*, ed. A. Charles-Saget. Paris.

Carpenter, A. 2008. "Embodying Intelligence: Animals and Us in Plato's Timaeus." In *Platonism and Forms of Intelligence*, ed. J. Dillon and M.-É. Zovko, 39–57. Berlin.

Casiday, A., and F. W. Norris, eds. 2007. *The Cambridge History of Christianity: Constantine to c. 600*. Vol. 2. Cambridge.

Castelletti, C., ed. 2006. *Porfirio: Sullo Stige*. Testo greco a fronte 99. Milan.

Catapano, G. 2003. *Agostino, Sull' anima: L'immortalità dell'anima. La grandezza dell'anima*. Milan.

Chadwick, H. 1953. *Origen: Contra Celsum*. Cambridge.

Chadwick, J., and W. N. Mann, trans. 1978. *Hippocratic Writings*. London. Repr. 1983.

Champlin, E. 2003. *Nero*. Cambridge, MA.

Charron, R. 2005. "The Apocryphon of John (NHC II, 1) and the Greco-Egyptian Alchemical Literature." *Vigiliae Christinae* 59:438–456.

Charron, R., and L. Painchaud. 2001. "'God is a Dyer': The Background and Significance of a Puzzling Motif in the Coptic Gospel According To Philip (CG II, 3)." *Muséon* 114:41–50.

Cherniss, H. 1930. *The Platonism of Gregory of Nyssa*. Berkeley.

———. 1933. *The Riddle of the Early Academy*. Baltimore.

———. 1944. *Aristotle's Criticism of Plato and the Academy*. New York.

———. 1971. *Aristotle's Criticism of Presocratic Philosophy*. New York.

Chiaradonna, R. 2005. "L'anima e la mistione stoica. Enneads IV,7[2], 8². " In *Studi sull'anima in Plotino.* Elenchos 42: 127–147. Naples.

———. 2007. "Porphyry's Views on the Immanent Incorporeals." In Karamanolis and Sheppard 2007:35–49.

———. 2009a. "Galen and Middle Platonism." In *Galen and the World of Knowledge,* ed. C. Gill, T. Whitmarsh, and J. Wilkins, 243–260. Cambridge.

———. 2009b. *Plotino.* Rome.

———. 2011. "Plotinus' Account of the Cognitive Powers of the Soul: Sense Perception and Discursive Thought." *Topoi.* doi: 10.1007/s11245-011 -9114-7.

———. ed. 2012. *Filosofia tardoantica.* Rome.

———. 2016. "Porphyry and the Aristotelian Tradition." In *Brill's Companion to the Reception of Aristotle in Antiquity,* ed. A. Falcon, 321–340. Leiden.

Chiaradonna, R., and F. Trabattoni, eds. 2009. *Physics and Philosophy of Nature in Greek Neoplatonism.* Leiden.

Chlup, R. 2012. *Proclus: An Introduction.* Cambridge.

Christiansen, M. 2005. "Sentences 29.27–29." In Brisson 2005b:600–601.

Cipriani, N. 1996. "L'influsso di Varrone sul pensiero antropologico e morale nei primi scritti di S. Agostino." *L'Etica cristiana nei secoli III e IV: Eredità e confronti* 369–400. Rome.

———. 2007. "Il tema agostiniano dell'actio-contemplatio nel suo quadro antropologico." *Augustinianum* 47:145–169.

Clark, A. 2008. *Supersizing the Mind: Embodiment, Action, and Cognitive Extension.* New York.

Clark, Gordon H. 1942. "Plotinus' Theory of Sensation." *The Philosophical Review* 51:357–382.

Clark, Gillian H., trans. 2000. *Porphyry: On Abstinence from Killing Animals.* Ithaca, NY.

———. 2007. "Augustine's Porphyry and the Universal Way of Salvation." In Karamanolis and Sheppard 2007:127–140.

———. 2011. "Acerrimus inimicus? Porphyry and the City of God." In *Le Traité de Porphyre contre les chrétiens: Un siècle de recherches, nouvelles questions,* ed. S. Morlet, 395–406. Paris.

Clark, S. Forthcoming. "Plotinus, Eriugena and the Uncreated Image." Lecture at the Oxford Workshop, *Eriugena's Christian Neoplatonism and its Sources in Patristic Philosophy and Ancient Philosophy,* dir. I. L. E. Ramelli, Oxford University, August 2019, *Studia Patristica.*

Cleary, J. J. 1995. *Aristotle and Mathematics: Aporetic Method in Cosmology and Metaphysics.* Leiden.

Cleary, S. A. 2000. "How to Build a Human Body: An Idealist's Guide." In Wright 2000:43–58.

Code, A. 2010. "Aristotle on Plato on Weight." In *One Book: The Whole Universe; Plato's Timaeus Today*, ed. R. D. Mohr and B. M. Sattler) 201–211. Las Vegas, NV.

Colonna, M. E., ed. 1958. *Enea di Gaza. Teofrasto*. Naples.

Colson, F. H., and G. H. Whitaker, trans. 1929. *Philo: On the Creation. Allegorical Interpretation of Genesis 2 and 3*. Cambridge, MA.

Colson, F. H., trans. 1939. *Philo: On the Special Laws, Book 4. On the Virtues. On Rewards and Punishments*. Cambridge, MA.

Cooper, S. A. 2016. "The Platonist Christianity of Marius Victorinus." *Religions* 7:122.

Copleston, F. 1968–1976. *A History of Philosophy*. 3 vols. London.

Corrigan, K. 1996. *Plotinus' Theory of Matter-Evil and the Question of Substance: Plato, Aristotle, and Alexander of Aphrodisias*. Leuven.

———. 2009. *Evagrius and Gregory: Mind, Soul and Body in the 4th Century*. Farnham, UK.

———. 2010. "Simmias' Objection to Socrates in the Phaedo: Harmony, Symphony and Later Platonic/Patristic Responses to the Mind/Soul-Body Question." *International Journal of the Platonic Tradition* 4.2:147–162.

———. 2017. "Trauma Before Trauma: Recognizing, Healing and Transforming the Wounds of Soul-Mind in the Works of Evagrius of Pontus." In *Evagrius Between Origen, the Cappadocians, and Neoplatonism: Papers Presented at the Seventeenth International Conference on Patristic Studies held in Oxford 2015*, Bd. 10 (ed. I. Ramelli, K. Corrigan, M. Tobon). *Studia Patristica* 84:123–136.

Costache, D. 2013. "Living above Gender: Insights from Saint Maximus the Confessor." *Journal of Early Christian Studies* 21:261–290.

Courcelle, P. 1972. "Flugel (Flug) der Seele." *Reallexicon für Antike und Christentum* VIII. Stuttgart.

———. 1975. *Connais-toi toi-même: De Socrate à saint Bernard*. 2:381–393. Paris.

Craik, E. M. 2015. *The 'Hippocratic' Corpus: Content and Context*. London.

Crawford, M. 2015. "Ammonius of Alexandria, Eusebius of Caesarea, and the Origins of Gospels Scholarship." *New Testament Studies* 61:1–29.

Crombie, I. M. 1963. *An Examination of Plato's Doctrines*. Vol. 2. London.

Crone, P. 2012. "Daysanis." In *Encyclopedia of Islam*. 3rd ed, 116–118. Leiden.

Cudworth, R. 1820. *The True Intellectual System of the Universe*. London.

Cunliffe, R. J. 1963. *A Lexicon of the Homeric Dialect*. Norman.

D'Ancona, C. 2005. "Les Sentences de Porphyre entre les Ennéades de Plotin et les Éléments de Théologie de Proclus." In Brisson 2005b:1.139–250.

Daremberg, C., ed. 1848. *Fragments du Commentaire de Galien sur le Timée de Platon.* Paris.

De Haas, F., and J. Mansfeld, eds. 2004. *Aristotle: On Generation and Corruption, Book I.* Symposium Aristotelicum. Oxford.

De Lacy, P. 1978–1984. *Galen: On the Doctrines of Hippocrates and Plato.* 2 vols. Berlin.

Denyer, N., ed. 2001. *Plato: Alcibiades.* Cambridge.

Derchain, P. 1962. "Mythes et dieux lunaires en Égypte." *Sources Orientales V: La Lune, Mythes et Rites.* Paris.

des Places, É., ed. 1973. *Numénius: Fragments.* Paris.

———. 1977. *Atticus: Fragments.* Paris.

Desch, W. 1980. "Aufbau und Gliederung von Augustins Schrift De vera religione." *Vigiliae Christianae* 35:263–277.

Deuse, W. 1983. *Untersuchungen zur mittelplatonischen und neuplatonischen Seelenlehre.* Wiesbaden.

Devreesse, R. 1945. *Le Patriarcat d'Antioche depuis la paix de l'Église jusqu'à la conquête arabe.* Études Palestiniennes et Orientales. Paris.

Dick, D. R. 1970. *Early Greek Astronomy to Aristotle.* Ithaca, NY.

Diehl, E., ed. 1903–1906. *Procli Diadochi In Platonis Timaeum commentaria.* 3 vols. Leipzig.

Digeser, E. DePalma. 2016. "The Usefulness of Borderlands Concepts in Ancient History: The Case of Origen as Monster." In *Globalizing Borderland Studies in Europe and North America*, ed. M. North and J. Lee, 15–32. Lincoln.

Dillon, J. M. 1977. *The Middle Platonists: 80 B.C. to A.D. 220.* Rev. with new afterword, 1996. Ithaca, NY.

———. 1980. "The Descent of the Soul in Middle Platonic and Gnostic Theory." In *The Rediscovery of Gnosticism: Proceedings of the International Conference on Gnosticism at Yale, March 28–31, 1978. Sethian Gnosticism*, ed. B. Layton. Vol. 2. Supplements to Numen 41. Leiden.

———. 1983. "Plotinus, Philo and Origen on the Grades of Virtue." In *Platonismus und Christentum*, ed. H.-D. Blume and F. Mann, 92–105. Münster.

———. 1993. *Alcinous: The Handbook of Platonism.* Oxford.

———. 2003. *The Heirs of Plato: A Study of the Old Academy (347-274 BC).* Oxford.

———. trans. 2005. "English Translation and Notes." In Brisson 2005b:2.795–835. Paris.

———. 2009a. "How Does the Soul Direct the Body, After All? Traces of a Dispute on Mind-Body Relations in the Old Academy." In *Body and Soul in Ancient Philosophy*, ed. D. Frede and B. Reis, 349–356. Berlin.

———. ed. 2009b. *Iamblichi Chalcidensis in Platonis Dialogos Commentariorum Fragmenta.* Westbury, CT.

————. 2013. "Shadows on the Soul: Plotinian Approaches to a Solution to the Mind-Body Problem." In *Plato Revived: Essays on Ancient Platonism in Honour of Dominic J. O'Meara*, ed. F. Karflik and E. Song, 73–84. Berlin.

Dillon, J. M., and H. Blumenthal, trans. 2015. *Plotinus. Ennead IV.3–IV.4.29: Problems Concerning the Soul*. Las Vegas, NV.

Dillon, J., S. Gertz, and D. Russell. 2012. *Aeneas of Gaza. Theophrastus with Zacharias of Mytilene: Ammonius*. Ancient Commentators on Aristotle. Bristol.

Dodds, E. R. 1963. *Proclus: The Elements of Theology*. 2nd ed. Oxford. Repr. 1992.

Doignon, J. 1997. *Bibliothèque Augustinienne* 4/2:257.

Donini, P. L. 1974. *Tre studi sull' aristotelismo nel II secolo d. C.* Turin.

————. 2008. "Psychology." In *The Cambridge Companion to Galen*, ed. R. J. Hankinson, 183–209. Cambridge.

Dörrie, H. 1924. "Das Verhältnis des Neuplatonischen und Christlichen in Augustins de vera religione." *Zeitschrift für neutestamentliche Wissenschaft* 23:64–102.

————. 1959. *Porphyrios' "Symmikta Zetemata": Ihre Stellung in System und Geschichte des Platonismus nebst einem Kommentar zu den Fragmenten*. Munich.

————. 1966. "Die Lehre von der Seele." In *Porphyre*, ed. O. Reverdin, 165–187. Entretiens Hardt 12. Geneva.

————. 1976. *Platonica Minora*. Munich.

Doucet, D. 1995. "L'époux des âmes. Porphyre, Ambroise et Augustin: De bono mortis 14–20; De Ordine I, 8, 24." *Revue des etudes augustiniennes* 41:231–252.

Drijvers, H. W. 1968. "The Origins of Gnosticism as a Religious and Historical Problem." *Nederlands Theologisch Tijdschrift* 22:321–351.

Drobner, H. R. 2008. "Christian Philosophy." In *The Oxford Handbook of Early Christian Studies*, ed. S. Ashbrook Harvey and D. G. Hunter, 673–688. Oxford. Online ed. 2009. doi: 10.1093/oxfordhb/9780199271566.003.0034.

du Roy, O. 1966. *L'intelligence de la foi en la Trinité selon saint Augustin: Genèse de sa théologie trinitaire jusqu'en 391*. Paris.

Duhem, P. 1913. *Le Système du Monde. Histoire des doctrines cosmologiques de Platon à Copernic. Tome I: La cosmologie hellenique*. Paris.

Duke, E. A., W. F. Hicken, et al., eds. 1995. *Platonis Opera*. Vol. 1. Oxford.

Dulaey, M. 1973. *Le rêve dans la vie et la pensée de saint Augustin*. Paris.

————. 2002. "L'apprentissage de l'exégèse biblique par augustin, I." *Revue des etudes augustiniennes* 48:267–295.

————. 2004. "Introduction" and "Notes." *Bibliothèque Augustinienne* 50.

Düring, I. 1961. *Aristotle's Protrepticus and the Sources of its Reconstruction*. Gotheburg.

————. 2005. *Aristoteles: Darstellung und Interpretation seines Denkens*. Heidelberg.

Düring, I., and G. E. L. Owen, eds. 1957. *Aristotle and Plato in the Mid-fourth Century.* Papers of the Symposium Aristotelicum held at Oxford in August 1957. Gothenburg.

Dysinger, L. 2005. *Psalmody and Prayer.* Oxford.

Edwards, M. 1992. "The Vessel of Zosimos of Panopolis." *Zeitschrift für Papirologie und Epigraphik* 90:55–64.

———. 1998. "Did Origen Apply the Word Homoousios to the Son?" *Journal of Theological Studies* 49:658–670.

———. 2002. *Origen against Plato.* Surrey.

———. 2006a. *Culture and Philosophy in the Age of Plotinus.* London.

———. 2006b. "Nicene Theology and the Second God." *Studia Patristica* 40:191–195.

———. 2012. "Further Reflections on Origen's Platonism." *Adamantius* 18:317–324.

Elders, L. 1966. *Aristotle's Cosmology: A Commentary on the De Caelo.* Assen.

———. 1972. *Aristotle's Theology: A Commentary on Book Lambda of the Metaphysics.* Assen.

Emilsson, E. K. 1988. *Plotinus on Sense-Perception: A Philosophical Study.* Cambridge.

———. 2007. *Plotinus on Intellect.* Oxford.

Engels, E.-M. 1982. *Die Teleologie des Lebendigen.* Berlin.

Esposito, A. 1991. "Il sangue nel Timeo di Platone." In *Atti della VI Settimana Sangue e Antropologia* [Roma, 23–28 novembre 1987], *Sangue e antropologia nella teologia,* ed. F. Viattoni, t. 1:443–450. Rome.

Ettlinger, G. H., ed. 1975. *Theodoret of Cyrus. Eranistes.* Oxford.

Eucken, R. 1879. *Geschichte der philosophischen Terminologie.* Hildesheim.

Fabbrini, L. 1995. "Domus Aurea: il Palazzo sull' Esquilino." In *Lexicon Topographicum Urbis Romae,* ed. E. M. Steinby, 2:56–63. Rome.

Fairbanks, A., ed. and trans. 1898. *The First Philosophers of Greece.* London.

Fattal, M. 2016. *Du Bien et de la crise: Platon, Parménide et Paul de Tarse.* Paris.

Festugière, A.-J. 1949–1954. *La révélation d'Hermès Trismégiste.* I. *L'astrologie et les sciences occultes* (1949); II. *Le Dieu cosmique* (1949); III. *Les doctrines de l'âme* (1953); IV. *Le Dieu inconnu et la gnose* (1954). Études bibliques. Paris.

———. ed. 1968. *Commentaire sur le Timée: Traduction et Notes.* Vol. 5. Paris.

———. 1969. "L'ordre de lecture des dialogues de Platon aux Ve/VIe siècles." *Museum Helveticum* 26:281–296.

Festugière, A.-J., and A. D. Nock, eds. 1954. *Corpus hermeticum.* Tome IV: Fragments extraits de Stobée (XXIII–XXIX). Paris.

Finamore, J. F. 1985. *Iamblichus and the Theory of the Vehicle of the Soul.* Chico.

Finamore, J. F., and J. Dillon, trans. 2002. *Iamblichus: De Anima. Text, Translation, and Commentary.* Leiden.

Finamore, J. F., and E. Kutash. 2016. "Proclus on the Psychê: World Soul and the Individual Soul." In *All From One: A Guide to Proclus*, ed. P. d'Hoine and M. Martjin, 122–138. Oxford.

Fine, G. 1986. "Immanence." *Oxford Studies in Ancient Philosophy* 4:71–97.

Fischer-Homberger, E. 1969. "Hysterie und Misogynie, ein Aspect der Hysterie-geschichte." *Gesnerus* 26.1:117–127.

Fleet, B. trans. 2016. *Plotinus. Ennead IV.7: On the Immortality of the Soul*. Las Vegas, NV.

Fleischer, M. 1976. *Hermeneutische Anthropologie: Platon, Aristoteles*. Berlin.

Fletcher, R. 2014. *Apuleius' Platonism: The Impersonation of Philosophy*. Cambridge.

Foerster, W., ed. 1972. *Gnosis: A Selection of Gnostic Texts*. Vol. 1. In *Patristic Evidence*, trans. R. McL. Wilson. Oxford.

Fortin, E. L. 1959. *Christianisme et culture philosophique au cinquième siècle. La querelle de l'âme humaine en Occident*. Paris.

Fortuna, S. 2007. "Galeno e il *Timeo* di Platone (91a)." *Filologia, papirologia, storia-deitesti. Giornate di studio in onore di Antonio Carlini: Udine, 9–10 Dicembre 2005*, 273–288. Pisa.

Fowden, G. 1986. *The Egyptian Hermes*. Princeton, NJ.

Fowler, H. N., trans. 1926. *Plato: Cratylus*. Cambridge, MA.

Fowler, R., ed. and trans. 2016. *Imperial Plato*. Las Vegas, NV.

Fraenkel, C. 2012. *Philosophical Religions from Plato to Spinoza*. Cambridge.

Frank, R. M. 1987. "The /use of the Enneads by John of Scythopolis." *Le Muséon* 100:101–108.

Frankfurter, D. 2000. "The Consequences of Hellenism in Late Antique Egypt: Religious Worlds and Actors." *Archiv für Religionsgeschichte* 2:162–194.

Fraser, K. A. 2004. "Zosimos of Panopolis and the Book of Enoch: Alchemy as Forbidden Knowledge." *Aries* 4:125–147.

———. 2007. "Baptised in Gnôsis: The Spiritual Alchemy of Zosimos of Panopolis." *Dionysius* 25:33–54.

Frede, D. 1992. "Disintegration and Restoration: Pleasure and Pain in Plato's Philebus." In Kraut 1992:425–463.

Frede, M. 1987. "On Galen's Epistemology." In *Essays in Ancient Philosophy* (ed. M. Frede) 65–86. Minneapolis. Repr. 1981.

Frede, M., and M. Patzig, trans. 1988. *Aristoteles: Metaphysik, Buch Z*. 2 vols. Munich.

Frère, J. 1997. "Thumos et kardia (Timée 59c2–70d6)." *Kléos* 1:9–16.

Friedlein, G., ed. 1873. *Procli Diadochi in primum Euclidis Elementorum librum commentarii*. Leipzig.

Funk, W.-P., M. Scopello, P.-H. Poirier, and J. D. Turner, eds. 2004. *L'Allogène (XI,3)*. Bibliothèque copte de Nag Hammadi, section "Textes" 30. Québec.

Bibliography

Fürst, A. 2007. *Christentum als Intellektuellen-Religion. Die Anfänge des Christentums in Alexandria.* Stuttgart.

Furth, M. 1988. *Substance, Form and Psyche: An Aristotelian Metaphysics.* Cambridge.

Gahbauer, F. R. 1984. *Das anthropologische Modell: Ein Beitrag zur Christologie der frühen Kirche bis Chalkedon.* Das östliche Christentum, Neue Folge 35. Würzburg.

Gannon, M. A. I. 1956. "The Active Theory of Sensation in St. Augustine." *The New Scholasticism* 30:154–180.

Gauthier, R.-A. 1951. *Magnanimité: L'idéal de la grandeur dans la philosophie païenne et dans la théologie chrétienne.* Paris.

Géhin, P., C. Guillaumont, and A. Guillaumont, eds. 1998. *Évagre Le Pontique: Sur les pensées.* SC 438. Paris.

Gerson, L. P., ed. 1996. *The Cambridge Companion to Plotinus.* Cambridge.

———. ed. 2010. *The Cambridge History of Philosophy in Late Antiquity.* 2 vols. Cambridge.

———. 2013. *From Plato to Platonism.* Ithaca, NY.

Gigon, O. 1950. *Aristoteles. Vom Himmel. Von der Seele. Von der Dichtkunst.* Zurich.

Gill, C. 2000. "The Body's Fault?: Plato's Timaeus on Psychic Illness." In Wright 2000:59–84.

———. 2006. *The Structured Self in Hellenistic and Roman Thought.* Oxford.

Gill, C., and S. Morton, eds. 2007. *The Passions in Roman Thought and Literature.* Cambridge.

Gill, M. L., and P. Pellegrin, eds. 2006. *A Companion to Ancient Philosophy.* London.

Gilson, É. 1971. *D'Aristote à Darwin et retour. Essai sur quelques constantes de la biophilosophie.* Paris.

———. 1974. *L'être et l'essence.* Paris.

Gioé, A., ed. 2002. *Filosofi medioplatonici del II secolo d.C.: Testimonianze e frammenti.* Naples.

Goldbacher, A., ed. 1923. "Augustinus: Epistulae, Praefatio editoris et indices." *Corpus Scriptorum Christianorum Orientalium* 58.

Gomperz, T. 1969. *A History of Ancient Philosophy.* 4 vols. London.

González, E. 2014. *The Fate of the Dead in Early Third Century North African Christianity.* Tübingen.

González-García, A. C., and J. A. Belmonte. 2015. "The Orientation of Pre-Romanesque Churches in the Iberian Peninsula." *Nexus Network Journal* 17:353–377.

Goold, G. P. 1933. *Aristotle: Metaphysics.* Trans. H. Tredennick. Cambridge, MA.

———. ed. 1942. *Aristotle: Movement of animals. Progression of animals.* Trans. E. S. Forster. Cambridge, MA.

————. ed. 1942. *Aristotle: On the Parts of Animals.* Trans. A. L. Peck. Cambridge, MA.

————. ed. 1965 and 1970. *Aristotle: Historia Animalium.* Trans. A. L. Peck. 2 vols. Cambridge, MA.

Gordon, R. 2012. "Mithras." *Reallexikon für Antike und Christentum* 24:964–1009.

Gosling, J. C. B., and C. C. W. Taylor. 1982. *The Greeks on Pleasure.* Oxford.

Gotthelf, A., ed. 1985. *Aristotle on Nature and Living Things.* Bristol.

Gotthelf, A., and J. G. Lennox, eds. 1987. *Philosophical Issues in Aristotle's Biology.* Cambridge.

Gottschalk, H. B. 1986. "Boethus' Psychology and the Neoplatonists." *Phronesis* 31:243–257.

Goulet-Cazé, M.-O. 1992. "Remarques sur l'edition d'Eustochius." In Brisson 1992:2.71–76.

————. 2005a. "Le Système philosophique de Porphyre dans les Sentences: Métaphysique." In Brisson 2005b:1.31–105.

————. 2005b. "Notes sur les Sentences 27." In Brisson 2005b:2.573–586.

————. 2005c. "Notes sur les Sentences 28." In Brisson 2005b:2.586–590.

Gourinat, J.-B., and J. Barnes, eds. 2009. *Lire les Stoïciens.* Paris.

Graham, D. W. 1987. *Aristotle's Two Systems.* Oxford.

————. ed. and trans. 2010. *The Texts of Early Greek Philosophy, Part 1.* Cambridge.

Grams, L. 2009. "Medical Theory in Plato's Timaeus." *Rhizai* 6.2:161–192.

Gregorić, P. 2007. *Aristotle on the Common Sense.* Oxford.

Griffin, M., trans. 2015. *Olympiodorus: Life of Plato and On Plato First Alcibiades 1–9.* London.

Grillmeier, A. 1975. *Christ in Christian Tradition.* London.

Grimes, S. 2010. "Natural Methods: Examining the Biases of Ancient Alchemists and Those Who Study Them." In *Esotericism, Religion, and Nature,* ed. A. Versluis, C. Fanger, L. Irwin, and M. Phillips, 5–26. Minneapolis, MN.

Groisard, J., ed. 2013. *Alexandre d'Aphrodis: Sur la mixtion et la croissance (De mixtione).* Paris.

Guillaumont, A., and C. Guillaumont, ed. and trans. 1971. *Évagre le Pontique: Traité pratique ou le Moine.* SC 170–171. Paris.

Guitton, J. 1933. *Le temps et l'éternité chez Plotin et Augustin.* Paris.

Guthrie, W. K. C., trans. 1945. *Aristotle: On the Heavens.* Cambridge.

————. 1978. *A History of Greek Philosophy.* Vol. 5. Cambridge.

————. 1983. *A History of Greek Philosophy.* Vol. 6. Cambridge.

Hackforth, R. 1936. "Plato's Theism." *Classical Quarterly* 30:4–9.

Hadot, I. 1984. *Arts libéraux et philosophie dans la pensée antique.* Paris.

Hadot, P. 1987. "La physique comme exercice spirituel ou pessimisme et optimisme chez Marc Aurèle." In *Exercices spirituels et philosophie antique*, ed. P. Hadot, 119–133. Paris.

———. 1995. *Qu'est-ce que la philosophie antique?* Paris.

Hagendahl, H. 1967. *Augustine and the Latin Classics I.* Gothenburg.

Hainthaler, T. 2016. "Faustus, Abbot of Lérins and Bishop of Riez, and His Christology." In *Pascha Nostrum Christus: Essays in Honour of Raniero Cantalamessa*, ed. P. F. Beatrice and B. Pouderon, 263–275. Théologie historique 123. Paris.

Hall, T. S. 1965. "The Biology of the Timaeus in Historical Perspective." *Arion* 4:109–122.

Halleux, R. 1981. *Alchimistes grecs, vol. 1: Papyrus de Leyde. Papyrus de Stockholm. Fragments de recettes.* Paris.

Hallum, B. 2008. *Zosimus Arabus. The Reception of Zosimos of Panopolis in the Arabic/Islamic World.* London.

Hamilton, E., and H. Cairns, eds. 1989. *The Collected Dialogues of Plato Including the Letters.* Princeton, NJ.

Hamlyn, D. W. 1968. *Aristotle: De anima. Books II and III* (With a Report on Recent Work by Christopher Schields). Oxford.

Hammond, M., trans. 2006. *Marcus Aurelius: Meditations.* London.

Hankinson, R. J. 1991. "Galen's Anatomy of the Soul." *Phronesis* 36:197–233.

———. 1992. "Galen's Philosophical Eclecticism." *Aufstieg und Niedergang der römischen Welt* II 36:5.3505–3522.

———. 2006. "Body and Soul in Galen." In *Common to Body and Soul*, ed. R. A. H. King, 232–258. Berlin.

Hannah, R. 1996. "The Image of Cautes and Cautopates in the Mithraic Tauroctony Icon." In *Religion in the Ancient World: New Themes and Approaches*, ed. M. Dillon), 177–192. Amsterdam.

———. 2009a. "The Pantheon as a Timekeeper." *British Sundial Society Bulletin* 21.4:2–5.

———. 2009b. *Time in Antiquity.* London.

———. 2019. "The Orchestration of Time in Ancient and Medieval Buildings." In *Archaeoastronomy in the Roman World*, ed. G. Magli, A. C. Gonzalez-García, J. A. Belmonte, E. Antonello, 37–56. New York.

Hannah, R., and G. Magli. 2011. "The Role of the Sun in the Pantheon Design and Meaning." *Numen* 58:486–513.

Hannah, R., G. Magli, and A. Palmieri. 2016. "Nero's 'Solar' Kingship and the Architecture of Domus Aurea." *Numen* 63:511–524.

Hanson, R. P. C. 1988. *The Search for the Christian Doctrine of God.* Edinburgh.

Happ, H. 1971. *Hyle. Studien zum aristotelischen Materie-Begriff.* Berlin.

Hartmann, N. 1941. *Zur Lehre vom Eidos bei Platon und Aristoteles.* Berlin.

Haselberger, L., et al. 2002. *Mapping Augustan Rome.* Journal of Roman Archaeology. Supplementary Series 50. Portsmouth, RI.

Havrda, M. 2016. *The So-Called Eighth Stromateus by Clement of Alexandria: Early Christian Reception of Greek Scientific Methodology.* Leiden.

Heidegger, M. 1967. "Vom Wesen und Begriff der Φύσις: Aristoteles Physik, B, I." In *Wegmarken,* vol. 9 (ed. 2, 239–301) Frankfurt.

Heidl, G. 1999. "Did the Young Augustine Read Origen's Homily on Paradise?" In *Origeniana Septima. Origenes in den Auseinandersetzungen des 4. Jahrhunderts,* ed. W. A. Bienert and U. Kühneweg, 597–604. Leuven.

Heimgartner, M., ed. 2012. *Die Briefe 42-58 des Ostsyrischen Patriarchen Timotheos I.* Corpus Scriptorum Christianorum Orientalium 645, Scriptores Syri 249. Leuven.

Heine, R. 2011. *Origen: Scholarship in the Service of the Church.* Oxford.

Helleman-Elgersma, W. 1980. *Soul-Sisters: A Commentary on Enneads IV 3 (27), 1-8 of Plotinus.* Amsterdam.

Hengestermann, C. 2011. "The Neoplatonism of Origen in the First Two Books of the Commentary on John." In *Origeniana Decima,* ed. S. Kaczmarek, H. Pietras, and A. Dziadowiec, 75–91. Leuven.

Henry, P. 1938. *Les États du Texte de Plotin.* Museum Lessianum, Section Philosophique 20. Paris.

Henry, P., and H.-R. Schwyzer, eds. 1964–1983. *Plotini Opera.* 3 vols. Oxford.

Hermann, C. F., ed. 1883. *Platonis Dialogi secundum Thrasylli Tetralogias.* 6 vols. Leipzig.

Hetland, L. M. 2007. "Dating the Pantheon." *Journal of Roman Archaeology* 20:95–112.

Hiesinger, U. 1975. "The Portraits of Nero." *American Journal of Archaeology* 79:113–124.

Hilhorst, A., and T. Silverstein, eds. 1997. *Apocalypse of Paul.* Geneva.

Himmelfarb, M. 1983. *Tours of Hell.* Oxford.

———. 1993. *Ascent to Heaven in Jewish and Christian Apocalypses.* Oxford.

Holmes, B. 2010. *The Symptom and the Subject: The Emergence of the Physical Body in Ancient Greece.* Princeton, NJ.

Hugonnard-Roche, H. 2014. "La question de l'âme dans la tradition philosophique syriaque (VIe-IXe siècle)." *Studia graeco-arabica* 4:17–64.

Hunt, G. R. 1996. "Manufacture and Use of Hook-tools by New Caledonian Crows." *Nature* 379:249–251.

Ierodiakonou, K. 1997. "Quatre couleurs: blanc, noir, brillant et rouge (Timée 67c4-68d7)." *Deucalion* 15:267–286.

———. 2005. "Plato's Theory of Colours in the Timaeus." *Rhizai* 2:219–233.

Ildefonse, F. 1992. "Perception et discours dans l'Ancien stoicisme." *Philosophie et langage* 14.2:31–45.

Ingenkamp, H. G. 1971. "Zur stoischen Lehre vom Sehen." *Rheinisches Museum* 114:240–246.

Ioppolo, A. 1990. "Presentation and Assent: A Physical and Cognitive Problem in Stoicism." *Classical Quarterly* 40:433–449.

Irwin, T. 1995. *Plato's Ethics.* New York.

Iskandar, A. Z. 1976. "An Attempted Reconstruction of the Late Alexandrian Medical Curriculum." *Medical History* 20.3:235–258.

Jabi, W., and I. Potamianos. 2007. "Geometry, Light, and Cosmology in the Church of Hagia Sophia." *International Journal of Architectural Computing* 5(2):303–319.

Jackson, H. M. 1990. "The Seer Nikotheos and his Lost Apocalypse in the Light of Sethian Apocalypses from Nag Hammadi and the Apocalypse of Elchasai." *Novum Testamentum* 32:250–277.

Jacobsen, A.-C. 2012. "Conversion to Christian Philosophy—the case of Origen's School in Caesarea." *Zeitschrift für Antikes Christentum* 16:145–157.

Jacobsson, M. 2002. *Aurelius Augustinus: De musica liber VI. A Critical Edition with a Translation and an Introduction.* Stockholm.

Jaeger, W. 1913. "Das Pneuma im Lykeion." *Hermes* 48:29–74.

———. 1923. *Aristoteles: Grundlegung einer Geschichte seiner Entwicklung.* Berlin.

———. 1934. *Aristotle: Fundamentals of the History of his Development.* Oxford.

———. 1964. *Die Theologie der frühen Griechischen Denker.* Stuttgart.

Jankowiak, M., and P. Booth. 2015. "A New Date-List of the Works of Maximus the Confessor." In *The Oxford Handbook of Maximus the Confessor*, ed. P. Allen and B. Neil, 19–83. Oxford.

Jannone, A., ed. 1995. *Aristote: De l'âme.* Trans. E. Barbotin. Paris.

Joachim, H. H. 1922. *Aristotle: De generatione et corruptione.* Oxford.

———. 1970. *Aristotle: The Nicomachean Ethics.* Oxford.

Johansen, T. K. 2012. *The Powers of Aristotle's Soul.* Oxford.

Johnson, A. P. 2012. "Philosophy, Hellenicity, Law: Porphyry on Origen, Again." *Journal of Hellenic Studies* 132:55–69.

———. 2013. *Religion and Identity in Porphyry of Tyre: The Limits of Hellenism in Late Antiquity.* Cambridge.

———. Forthcoming. "Personal Knowledge in Porphyry's Thought: The Epistemological Role of Experience."

Johnson, E. 1906. *The Argument of Aristotle's Metaphysics.* New York.

Jonas, H. 1934–1954. *Gnosis und spätantiker Geist.* Vol. 1: *Die mythologische Gnosis.* Vol. 2: *Von der Mythologie zur mystischen Philosophie.* Forschungen zur religion und Literatur des Alten und Neuen Testaments n.F. 33. Göttingen.

———. 1962. "Plotin über Ewigkeit und Zeit. Interpretation von Enneads III 7." In *Politische Ordnung und menschliche Existenz*, ed. A. Dempf, H. Arendt, and F. Engel-Janosi. Munich.

Jouanna, J., ed. and trans. 1975. *Hippocrate: La nature de l'homme.* Corpus Medicorum Graecorum I 1, 3. Berlin.

———. 2007. "La théorie de la sensation, de la pensée et de l'âme dans le traité hippocratique Du régime: Ses rapports avec Empédocle et le *Timée* de Platon." *Aion* 29:9–38.

Joubaud, C. 1991. *Le corps humain dans la philosophie platonicienne: Étude à partir du Timée, Bibliothèque d'Histoire de la Philosophie.* Paris.

Jowett, B. 1989. "Cratylus." In Hamilton and Cairns 1989:421–474. Princeton, NJ.

Kalbfleisch, K., ed. 1895. *Die neuplatonische, fälschlich dem Galen zugeschriebene Schrift Πρὸς Γαῦρον περὶ τοῦ πῶς ἐμψυχοῦνται τὰ ἔμβρυα.* Berlin.

Kalligas, P. 2014. *The Enneads of Plotinus: A Commentary.* Vol. 1. Princeton, NJ.

Kannengiesser, C. 2006. "The Dating of Athanasius' Double Apology and Three Treatises against the Arians." *Zeitschrift für Antike Christentum* 10:19–33.

Karamanolis, G. E. 2006. *Plato and Aristotle in Agreement? Platonists on Aristotle from Antiochus to Porphyry.* Oxford.

———. 2007. "Porphyry's Notion of Empsychia." In Karamanolis and Sheppard 2007:91–109.

———. 2014. *The Philosophy of Early Christianity.* London.

———. 2016. "Early Christian Philosophers on Aristotle." In *The Brill Companion to Aristotle's Reception*, ed. A. Falcon, 460–479. Leiden.

Karamanolis, G., and A. Sheppard, eds. 2007. *Studies on Porphyry.* London.

Karfik, F. 2004. *Die Beseelung des Kosmos. Untersuchungen zur Kosmologie, Seelenlehre und Theologie in Platons Phaidon und Timaios.* Munich.

———. 2005. "What the Mortal Parts of the Soul Really Are?" *Rhizai* 2.2:197–218.

Karfíková, L. 2013. "Das Verhältnis von Seele und Ratio in Augustins Abhandlung De immortalitate animae." In *Plato Revived: Essays on Ancient Platonism in Honour of Dominic J. O'Meara*, ed. F. Karfík and E. Song, 117–137. Berlin.

Karin, A. 1996. "Porphyrios als Helfer in griechischen Nöten. Brief an Markella Kap. 4." In *Worte, Bilder, Töne. Studien zur Antike und Antikerezeption*, ed. R. Faber and B. Seidensticker, 201–210. Würzburg.

Kirk, G. S., J. E. Raven, and M. Schofield. 2006. *The Presocratic Philosophers.* 2nd ed. Cambridge.

Kissling, R. C. 1922. "The OCHÊMA-PNEUMA of the Neo-Platonists and the De insomniis of Synesius of Cyrene." *American Journal of Philology* 43:318–330.

Knipe, S. 2011. "Sacrifice and Self-Transformation in the Alchemical Writings of Zosimus of Panopolis." In *Unclassical Traditions, Vol. 2: Perspectives from*

East and West in Late Antiquity, ed. C. Kelly, R. Flower, and M. S. Williams, 59–69. Cambridge.

Kobusch, T. 2006. *Christliche Philosophie*. Darmstadt.

———. 2014. Review of *Athen und Jerusalem*, by W. Schröder. *Göttingische Gelehrte Anzeigen* 266.3–4:132–150.

Koetschau, P. 1913. *Origenes: Gegen Celsus*. Leipzig.

———. 1913. *Origenes Werke*. Vol. 5: *De Principiis*. Leipzig.

Kotter, B., ed. 1981. *Die Schriften des Johannes von Damaskos*. Vol. 4: *Liber de haeresibus. Opera polemica*. Patristische Texte und Studien 22. Berlin.

Krämer, H.-J. 1968. "Grundbegriffe akademischer Dialektik in den biologischen Schriften von Aristoteles und Teophrast." *Rheinisches Museum* 111:293–333.

Krausmüller, D. 2009. "Faith and Reason in Late Antiquity." In *The Afterlife of the Platonic Soul*, ed. M. Elkaisy-Friemuth and J. Dillon, 47–76. Leiden.

Kraut, R., ed. 1992. *The Cambridge Companion to Plato*. Cambridge.

Krell, D. F. 1975. "Female Parts in the Timaeus." *Arion* 2:400–421.

Kroll, G., ed. 1899. *Procli Diadochi in Platonis Rem Publicam Commentarii*. Vol. 1. Leipzig.

Krulak, T. 2016. "Defining Competition in Neoplatonism." In *Religious Competition in the Greco-Roman World*, ed. N. Desrosiers and L. Vuong, 79–84. Atlanta, GA.

Kühn, C. G., ed. 1822. *Galeni Quod Animi Mores Corporis Temperamenta Sequuntur*. In *Claudii Galeni Opera Omnia*. Vol. 4. Leipzig.

———. ed. 1823. *Galeni De placitis Hippocratis et Platonis*. In *Claudii Galeni Opera Omnia*. Vol. 5. Leipzig.

Kühn, W. 2005. "Notes sur les Sentences 8." In Brisson 2005b:2.396–397.

Kukkonen, T., and P. Remes, eds. 2016. "Divine Word and Divine Work: Late Platonism and Religion." *Numen* 63:139–146.

Kullmann, W. 1974. *Wissenschaft und Methode: Interpretationen zur aristotelischen Theorie der Naturwissenschaft*. Berlin.

———. 1998. *Aristoteles und die moderne Wissenschaft*. Stuttgart.

L'Orange, H. P. 1947. *Apotheosis in Ancient Portraiture*. Oslo.

Labrune, M. 1992. "États d'âme. Le corps dans la philosophie de Platon." In *Le corps*, ed. J.-C. Goddard and M. Labrune, 27–47. Paris.

Lakmann, M.-L. 1994. *Der Platoniker Tauros in der Darstellung des Aulus Gellius*. Leiden.

Lamberton, R. 1986. *Homer the Theologian: Neoplatonist Allegorical Reading and the Growth of the Epic Tradition*. Berkeley.

Lamberz, E., ed. 1975. *Porphyrii Sententiae ad Intelligibilia ducentes*. Bibliotheca Scriptorum Graecorum et Romanorum Teubneriana. Leipzig.

Lane Fox, R. 2005. "Appendix: Harran, the Sabians and the Late Platonist 'Movers'." In *The Philosopher and Society in Late Antiquity: Essays in Honour of Peter Brown*, ed. A. Smith, 231–244. Swansea.

Larchet, J.-C., and E. Ponsoye, eds. 1998. *Saint Maxime le Confesseur: Opuscules Théologiques et Polémiques*. Paris.

Lautner, P. 2005. "The Timaeus on Sounds and Hearing with Some Implications for Plato's General Account of Sense-Perception." *Rhizai* 2:235–253.

———. 2011. "Plato's Account of the Diseases of the Soul in Timaeus 86b1–87b9." *Apeiron* 44:22–39.

Lavaud, L. 2007. *Plotin: Traités 38–41*. Paris.

Layne, D. A., and H. Tarrant, eds. 2014. *The Neoplatonic Socrates*. Philadelphia, PA.

Lebreton, J. 1906. "Le traité de l'âme de Saint Grégoire le Thaumaturge." *Bulletin de Littérature ecclésiastique* 8:73–83.

Leemans, A. D. 1937. *Studie over den wijsgeer Numenius van Apamea: met uitgave der fragmenten*. Bruxelles.

Lefèvre, C. 1971. "Quinta natura et psychologie aristotélicienne." *Revue philosophique de Louvain* 69:5–43.

———. 1972. *Sur l'évolution d'Aristote en psychologie*. Leuven.

Lehmann, K. 1945. "The Dome of Heaven." *The Art Bulletin* 27:1–27.

Leithard, P. J. 2011. *Athanasius*. Ada.

Lekkas, G. 2001. *Liberté et progrès chez Origène*. Turnhout.

Leppin, H. 2012. "Christianisierungen im Römischen Reich: Überlegungen zum Begriff und zur Phasenbildung." *Zeitschrift für Antikes Christentum* 16:247–278.

Letrouit, J. 1995. "Chronologie des alchimistes grecs." In *Alchimie: Art, histoire et mythe*, ed. D. Kahn and S. Matton, 11–93. Paris.

Leunissen, M. 2010. *Explanation and Teleology in Aristotle's Science of Nature*. Cambridge.

Lévy, C. 2005. "Deux problemes doxographiques chez Philon d'Alexandrie." In *Philosophy and Doxography in the Imperial Age*, ed. A. Brancacci, 79–102. Florence.

———. 2006. "Philon d'Alexandrie et les passions." In *Réceptions antiques: lecture, transmission, appropriation intellectuelle*, ed. L. Ciccolini, C. Guérin, et al., 27–41. Paris.

———. 2008. "La conversion du scepticisme chez Philon d'Alexandrie." In *Philo of Alexandria and Post-Aristotelian Philosophy*, ed. F. Alesse, 103–120. Leiden.

———. 2010. "Breaking the Stoic Language: Philo's Attitude towards Assent (sunkatathesis) and Comprehension (katalêpsis)." *Henoch* 32:33–44.

Lewis, G. 1959. *Plotiniana Arabica*. Plotini Opera. Vol. 2, ed. P. Henry and H.-R. Schwyzer. Paris-Bruxelles.

Lewis, T. A. 2015. *Why Philosophy Matters for the Study of Religion & Vice Versa.* Oxford.

Lietzmann, H. 1904. *Apollinaris von Laodicea und seine Schule. Texte und Untersuchungen.* Tübingen.

Linguiti, A. 2014. "Physics and Metaphysics." In Remes and Slaveva-Griffin 2014:343–355.

Litwa, D. 2014. "The Deification of Moses in Philo of Alexandria." *Studia Philonica Annual* 26.1–27.

Lloyd, A. C. 1990. *The Anatomy of Neoplatonism.* Oxford.

Lloyd, G. E. R. 1968. *Aristotle: The Growth and Structure of his Thought.* Cambridge.

———. 1988. "Scholarship, Authority and Argument in Galen's Quod Animi Mores." In *Le opere psicologiche di Galeno. Atti del terzo Colloquio Galenico internazionale, Pavia, 10-12 settembre 1986,* ed. P. Manuli and M. Vegetti, 125–143. Naples.

Lloyd, G. E. R., and G. E. L. Owen, eds. 1978. *Aristotle on Mind and the Senses.* Proceedings of the 7th Symposium Aristotelicum. Cambridge.

Lo Presti, P. 2015. *Norms in Social Interaction: Semantic, Epistemic, and Dynamic.* Lund.

Long, A. A. 1982. "Soul and Body in Stoicism." *Phronesis* 27:34–57. Repr. 1996. In A. A. Long, *Stoic Studies,* 224–249. Cambridge.

Loofs, F. ed. 1905. *Nestoriana: Die Fragmente des Nestorius.* Halle.

Lulofs, H., and J. Drosaart, eds. 1965. *Aristotelis De Generatione Animalium.* Oxford.

Mahé, J.-P. 2009. "Science occultes et exercices spirituels." In *Gnose et philosophie. Études en hommage à Pierre Hadot,* ed. J.-M. Narbonne and P.-H. Poirier, 75–86. Quebec City.

Mahoney, T. A. 2005. "Moral Virtue and Assimilation to God in Plato's Timaeus." *Oxford Studies in Ancient Philosophy* 28:77–91.

Manetti, G. 1993. *Theories of the Sign in Classical Antiquity.* Trans. C. Richardson. Bloomington, IN.

Männlein-Robert, I. 2001. *Longin. Philologe und Philosoph: Eine Interpretation der erhaltenen Zeugnisse.* Munich.

Mansfeld, J. 1990. "Doxography and Dialectic: the 'Sitz im Leben' of the Placita." *Aufstieg und Niedergang der römischen Welt* II, 36, 4, 3056–3229.

Mansfeld, J., and D. T. Runia. 1997. *Aëtiana. The Method and Intellectual Context of a Doxographer.* Vol. 1: *The Sources.* Philosophia Antiqua 73. Leiden.

Mansion, S., ed. 1961. *Aristote et les problèmes de méthode.* Proceedings of the 2nd Symposium Aristotelicum. Leuven.

Manuli, P., and M. Vegetti. 1977. *Cuore, sangue e cervello: Biologia e antropologia nel pensiero antico.* Milan.

Maritain, J. 1940. *Science and Wisdom.* London.

———. 1961. *On the Use of Philosophy*. Princeton, NJ.

Markov, M. 1979. *Aristotle: On the Soul*. Sofia.

Markschies, C. 2012. *Hellenisierung des Christentums: Sinn und Unsinn einer historischen Deutungskategorie*. Leipzig.

Markus, R. A. 1964. "'Imago' and 'Similitudo' in Augustine." *Revue de études augustiniennes* 10:125–143.

Marmodoro, A., and B. Prince, eds. 2015. *Causation and Creation in Classical and Late Antiquity*. Cambridge.

Marrou, H.-I. 1958. *Saint Augustin et la fin de la culture antique*. 4th ed. Paris 1958.

———. 1982. *A History of Education in Antiquity*. Trans. G. Lamb. Madison, WI.

Martelli, M., ed. 2013. *The Four Books of Pseudo-Democritus*. Wakefield.

———. 2014a. "L'alchimie en syriaque et l'œuvre de Zosime." In *Les sciences en syriaque*, ed. É. Villey, 191–214. Paris.

———. 2014b. "The Alchemical Art of Dyeing: The Fourfold Division of Alchemy and the Enochian Tradition." In *Laboratories of Art*, ed. S. Dupré, 1–22. Cham.

———. 2017. "Alchemy, Medicine and Religion: Zosimus of Panopolis and the Egyptian Priests." *Religion in the Roman Empire* 3:202–220.

Martens, P. W. 2015. "Embodiment, Heresy, and the Hellenization of Christianity: The Descent of the Soul in Plato and Origen." *Harvard Theological Review* 108.04:594–620.

Martijn, M. 2010. *Proclus on Nature: Philosophy of Nature and its Methods in Proclus' Commentary on Plato's Timaeus*. Leiden.

Martinich, A. P. 1996. *The Philosophy of Language*. 3rd ed. New York.

Marx-Wolf, H. 2016. *Spiritual Taxonomies and Ritual Authority: Platonists, Priests, and Gnostics in the Third Century C.E.* Philadelphia, PA.

McCool, G. A. 1959. "The Ambrosian Origin of St. Augustine's Theology of the Image of God in Man." *Theological Studies* 20:62–81.

McWilliam, J. 1997. "'Not Painted from Another Picture': Augustine, *De quantitate animae* 33,76." *Studia Patristica* 33:172–177.

Meijering, E. J. 1968. *Platonism and Orthodoxy in Athanasius: Synthesis or Antithesis?* Leiden.

———. 2010. "Athanasius on God in Creation and Revelation." *Church History and Religious Culture* 90:175–197.

Mercati, G. 1901. "Note di letteratura biblica e cristiana antica." *Studi e testi* 5. Rome.

Mertens, M., ed. 1995. *Alchimistes grecs*. Vol. 4.2: *Zosime de Panopolis. Mémoires authentiques*. Paris.

———. 2002. "Alchemy, Hermetism and Gnosticism at Panopolis c. 300 A.D.: The Evidence of Zosimus." In *Perspectives on Panopolis: an Egyptian Town from*

Alexander the Great to the Arab Conquest, ed. A. Egberts, B. P. Muhs, and J. van der Vliet, 165–175. Leiden.

Meyer, M., ed. 2007. *The Nag Hammadi Scriptures. The International Edition.* New York.

———. 2008. *The Nag Hammadi Scriptures. The Revised and Updated Translation of Sacred Gnostic Texts.* New York.

Miles, M. R. 1979. *Augustine on the Body.* Missoula, MT.

Miller, H. W. 1962. "The Aetiology of Disease in Plato's Timaeus." *Transactions of the American Philological Association* 93:175–187.

Mitchell, C. W. 1921. *S. Ephraim's Prose Refutations of Mani, Marcion, and Bardaisan* II. London.

Monfrinotti, M. 2014. *Creatore e Creazione. Il pensiero di Clemente Alessandrino.* Rome.

Morani, M. 1981. *La tradizione manoscritta del "De Natura Hominis" di Nemesio.* Milano.

———. ed. 1987. *Nemesii Emeseni De Natura Hominis.* Bibliotheca Scriptorum Graecorum et Romanorum Teubneriana. Leipzig.

Morano, D. V. 1974. "Augustine's Linguistic Success in De Quantitate Animae." *Augustinian Studies* 5:101–111.

Moraux, P. 1965. *Aristote: Du ciel.* Paris.

———. 1973. *Der Aristotelismus bei den Griechen von Andronikos bis Alexander von Aphrodisias.* Peripatoi 5. Berlin.

Mortley, R. 2013. *Plotinus, Self and the World.* Cambridge.

Mouzala, M. G. 2014. "Olympiodorus and Damascius on the Philosopher's Practice of Dying in Plato's Phaedo." *Peitho: Examina Antiqua* 1:177–198.

Moyer, I. S. 2011. *Egypt and the Limits of Hellenism.* Cambridge.

Mras, K., and É. des Places, eds. 1982–1983. *Die Praeparatio Evangelica.* GCS, *Eusebius Werke VIII.1–2.* 2nd ed. Berlin.

Nails, D. 2002. *The People of Plato: A Prosopography of Plato and Other Socratics.* Indianapolis, IN.

Narbonne, J.-M. 1993. *Plotin: Les deux matières [Ennèade II 4 (12)].* Paris.

———. 2011. *Plotinus in Dialogue with the Gnostics.* Studies in Platonism, Neoplatonism, and the Platonic Tradition 11. Leiden.

Nasrallah, J. 1971. "Saints et évêques d' Émèse (Homs)." *Proche Orient Chrétien* 21:213–234.

Natali, C. 2003. "Antropologia, politica e la struttura del Timeo." In *Plato Physicus: Cosmologia e antropologia nel Timeo*, ed. C. Natali and S. Maso, 225–241. Amsterdam.

Nau, F., ed. 1905. "Traité d' Ahoudemmeh sur la composition de l'homme." *Histoires d'Ahoudemmeh et de Marouta, métropolitains jacobites de Tagrit et de l'Orient (VIe et VIIe siècles) suivis du traité d'Ahoudemmeh sur l'homme: Textes syriaques inédits publiés, traduits et annotés*, 97–115. Paris. Repr. Nau, F. 1982. PO, Vol. 3. fasc. 1, n° 11, Turnhout.

Nautin, P. 1974. "Les fragments de Basilide sur la souffrance et leur interpretation par Clément d'Alexandrie et Origène." In *Mélanges d'histoire des religions offerts à H.Ch. Puech*. Paris.

Neil, B. 1999. "Neo-Platonic Influence on Augustine's Conception of the Ascent of the Soul in De Quantitate Animae." In *Prayer and Spirituality in the Early Church*, ed. P. Allen, et al., 2:197–215. Brisbane.

Nesselrath, H.-G., ed. 2010. *Plutarch: On the Diamonion of Socrates*. Tübingen.

Nicholson, O. 1995. "The End of Mithraism." *Antiquity* 69:358–362.

Nissen, H. 1873. "Über Tempel-orientierung." *Rheinisches Museum* 28:513–557.

Nock, A. D. 1964. *Early Gentile Christianity and its Hellenistic Background*. New York.

Norris, R. 1963. *Manhood in Christ: A Study in the Christology of Theodore of Mopsuestia*. Oxford.

Norvin, W., ed. 1987. *Olympiodori Philosophi in Platonis Phaedonem Commentaria*. Hildesheim.

Nussbaum, M., and A. O. Rorty, eds. 1995. *Essays on Aristotle's De Anima*. Oxford.

Nutton, V., ed. 1981. *Galen: Problems and Prospects*. London.

———. 2004. *Ancient Medicine*. London.

Nuyens, F. 1948. *L'évolution de la psychologie d'Aristote*. Leuven. Orig. pub. 1939 as *Ontwikkelingsmomenten in de zielkunde van Aristoteles*. Amsterdam.

O'Brien, D. 1997. "La définition du son dans le Timée de Platon." In *Studies and the Platonic Tradition: Essays Presented to John Whittaker*, ed. M. Joyal, 59–64. Aldershot.

O'Brien, M. 2002. *Apuleius' Debt to Plato in the Metamorphoses*. Lewiston, NY.

O'Brien Wicker, K. 1987. *Porphyry the Philosopher: To Marcella*. Atlanta, GA.

O'Connell, R. J. 1968. *St. Augustine's Early Theory of Man, A.D. 386–391*, Cambridge.

———. 1993. "The De Genesi contra Manichaeos and the Origin of the Soul." *Revue des êtudes augustiniennes* 39:129–141.

O'Daly, G. 1987. *Augustine's Philosophy of Mind*. London.

O'Meara, D. 1985. "Plotinus on How Soul Acts on Body." In *Platonic Investigations: Studies in Philosophy and the History of Philosophy*, ed. D. J. O'Meara, 13:247–262. Washington.

———. 2003. *Platonopolis: Platonic Political Philosophy in Late Antiquity*. Oxford.

———. 2010. "Plotinus." In Gerson 2010:1.301–324.

O'Meara, J. J. 1958. "Augustine and Neo-Platonism." *Recherches augustiniennes* 1:91–111.

———. 1969. "Porphyry's Philosophy from Oracles in Eusebius's *Praeparatio Evangelica* and Augustine's Dialogues of Cassiciacum." *Recherches augustiniennes* 6:103–139.

———. 1987. "Parting from Porphyry." *Congresso internazionale su S. Agostino nel XVI centenario della conversione, Roma, 15–20 settembre 1986* 2:357–369. Rome.

O'Neill, W., trans. 2011. *Proclus: Commentary on the First Alcibiades.* Text edited by L. G. Westerink. Platonic Texts and Translations, vol. 6. Dilton Marsh, Westbury.

Obryk, M. 2012. *Unsterblichkeitsglaube in den griechischen Versinschriften.* Berlin.

Owens, J. 1978. *The Doctrine of Being in the Aristotelian "Metaphysics."* 3rd ed. Toronto.

Paganardi, A. 1990. "L'éros sunousías del Timeo: Un' eccentricità nello schema psicologico tripartito di Platone." *Discorsi* 10:305–319.

Page, T. E., ed. 1942. *Aristotle: Generation of Animals.* Trans. A. L. Peck. Cambridge.

Palmer, A., trans. 1993. *The Seventh Century in the West-Syrian Chronicles.* Including two seventh-century Syriac apocalyptic texts introduced, translated and annotated by S. Brock, with added annotation and an historical introduction by R. Hoyland. Translated Texts for Historians 15. Liverpool.

Pasnau, R. 1999. *Thomas Aquinas: A Commentary on Aristotle's De Anima.* New Haven, CT.

Pasquali, G. 1910. "Doxographica aus Basiliusscholien." *Nachrichten d. K. Gesellschaft der Wissenschaften zu Göttingen. Philologisch-historische Klasse,* 194–228. Repr. 1986. In *Scritti filologici. I. Letteratura greca,* 539–574. Florence.

Peck, A. L. 1953. *The Connate Pneuma: An Essential Factor in Aristotle's Solution to the Problems of Reproduction and Sensation.* Oxford.

Pedersen, S. 2012. *Regularly Irregular Motion in Proclus' Celestial Physics.* PhD diss., University of Otago.

Pellegrin, P. 1986. *Aristotle's Classification of Animals. Biology and the Conceptual Unity of the Aristotelian Corpus.* Trans. A. Preus. Berkeley.

———. 2009. *Le vocabulaire d'Aristote.* Paris.

Pépin, J. 1954. "Saint Augustin et le symbolisme néoplatonicien de la vêture." *Augustinus Magister* 1:293–306. Paris.

———. 1971. *Idées grecques sur l'homme et sur Dieu.* Paris.

———. 1977. *Ex Platonicorum persona. Études sur les lectures philosophiques de saint Augustin.* Amsterdam.

———. 2005. "Notes sur les Sentences 29." In Brisson 2005a:2.590–606.

Perkins, J. 1995. *The Suffering Self: Pain and Narrative Representation in the Early Christian Era.* London.

Pettersen, A. 1990. "The Arian Context of Athanasius of Alexandria's Tomus ad Antiochenos." *Journal of Ecclesiastical History* 41:183–198.

Petty, R. 2012. *Fragments of Numenius of Apamea.* Westbury.

Pietras, H. 2009. "L'inizio del mondo materiale e l'elezione divina in Origene." In *Origeniana Nona* , ed. G. Heidl and R. Somos, 653–668. Leuven.

Pohlenz, M. 1929. *Plutarchi Moralia*, vol. 3, Leipzig.

Polansky, R. 2007. *Aristotle's De Anima.* Cambridge.

Popov, P. S. 1976. *Aristotle: On the Soul.* Moscow.

Pormann, P. E. 2010. "Medical Education in Late Antiquity from Alexandria to Montpellier." In *Hippocrates and Medical Education*, ed. M. Horstmanshoff, 419–441. Leiden.

Possekel, U. 2012. "Bardaisan and Origen on Fate and the Power of the Stars." *Journal of Early Christian Studies* 20:515–541.

Potamianos, I. 1996. *Light into Architecture: Evocative Aspects of Natural Light as Related to Liturgy in Byzantine Churches.* PhD diss., University of Michigan.

———. 2000. *To phôs stê Vyzantinê ekklêsia.* Thessalonike.

Preisendanz, K. 1928 and 1931. *Papyri Graecae Magicae.* Vol. 2. Stuttgart.

Price, R. 2009. *The Acts of the Council of Constantinople of 553 with Related Texts on the Three Chapters Controversy.* 2 vols. Translated Texts for Historians 51. Liverpool.

Prieur, J.-M. 2005. "Aèce selon l'histoire ecclésiastique de Philostorge." *Revue d' histoire et de philosophie religieuse* 85:529–552.

Prinzivalli, E. 2010. "Origen." In Gerson 2010:1.283–297.

Proctor, T. 2014. "Daemonic Trickery, Platonic Mimicry: Traces of Christian Daemonological Discourse in Porphyry's De Abstinentia." *Vigiliae Christianae* 68:416–449.

Quinn, F. X. 1964. "Theory of Spontaneous Generation According To the Ancients." *Classical Bulletin* 40.2.

Quispel, G. 2008. *Gnostica, Judaica, Catholica.* Leiden.

Ramelli, I. L. E. 2004. *Allegoria.* Vol. 1: *L'età classica.* Milan.

———. 2006. "La coerenza della soteriologia origeniana: dalla polemica contro il determinismo gnostico all'universale restaurazione escatologica." In *Pagani e cristiani alla ricerca della salvezza*, ed. V. Grossi, 661–688. Rome.

———. 2007a. *Allegoristi dell'età classica: Opere e frammenti.* Milan.

———. 2007b. *Gregorio di Nissa Sull'anima e la resurrezione.* Milan.

———. 2008a. "Origene ed il lessico dell'eternità." *Adamantius* 14:100–129.

———. 2008b. "Philosophical Allegoresis of Scripture in Philo and its Legacy in Gregory of Nyssa." *Studia Philonica Annual* 20:55–99.

———. 2009a. *Bardaisan of Edessa: A Reassessment of the Evidence and a New Interpretation; Also in the Light of Origen and the Original Fragments from Porphyry.* Piscataway, NJ.

———. 2009b. "Origen, Bardaisan, and the Origin of Universal Salvation." *Harvard Theological Review* 102:135–168.

———. 2009c. "Origen, Patristic Philosophy, and Christian Platonism: Re-thinking the Christianisation of Hellenism." *Vigiliae Christianae* 63:217–263.

———. 2010. "Αἰώνιος and Αἰών in Origen and Gregory of Nyssa." *Studia Patristica* 47:57–62.

———. 2011a. "Atticus and Origen on the Soul of God the Creator: From the 'Pagan' to the Christian Side of Middle Platonism." *Jahrbuch für Religionsphilosophie* 10:13–35.

———. 2011b. "Cristo-Logos in Origene." In *Dal Logos dei Greci e dei Romani al Logos di Dio* (ed. R. Radice and A. Valvo) 295–317. Milan.

———. 2011c. "Origen the Christian Middle/Neoplatonist." *Journal of Early Christian History* 1:98–130.

———. 2011d. "The Philosophical Stance of Allegory in Stoicism and its Reception in Platonism, 'Pagan' and Christian." *International Journal of the Classical Tradition* 18:335–371.

———. 2012–2013. "The Dialogue of Adamantius: A Document of Origen's Thought? Part One." *Studia Patristica* 52:71–98.

———. 2012–2013. "The Dialogue of Adamantius: A Document of Origen's Thought? Part Two." *Studia Patristica* 56.4:227–273.

———. 2012a. "Apokatastasis in Coptic Gnostic Texts from Nag Hammadi and Clement's and Origen's Apokatastasis: Toward an Assessment of the Origin of the Doctrine of Universal Restoration." *Journal of Coptic Studies* 14:33–45.

———. 2012b. "Origen, Greek Philosophy, and the Birth of the Trinitarian Meaning of Hypostasis." *Harvard Theological Review* 105.3:302–350.

———. 2012c. "Philo as Origen's Declared Model: Allegorical and Historical Exegesis of Scripture." *Studies in Christian-Jewish Relations* 7:1–17.

———. 2013a. "Gesù Cristo come entità mostruosa e ibrida in rappresentazioni pagane e cristiane tra II e III secolo." In *Monstra: Costruzione e percezione delle entità ibride e mostruose nelle culture del Mediterraneo antico* (ed. I. Baglioni) 2:239–250. Rome.

———. 2013b. *The Christian Doctrine of Apokatastasis: A Critical Assessment from the New Testament to Eriugena.* Supplements to Vigiliae Christianae 120. Leiden.

———. 2013c. "The Philosophical Role of Allegoresis as a Mediator between φυσική and θεολογία." *Jahrbuch für Religionsphilosophie* 12:9–26.

———. 2013d. "Harmony between ἀρχή and τέλος in Patristic Platonism." *International Journal of the Platonic Tradition* 7.1:1–49.

———. 2014a. "Alexander of Aphrodisias: A Source of Origen's Philosophy?" *Philosophie Antique* 14:237–290.

———. 2014b. "Decadence Denounced in the Controversy over Origen: Giving Up Direct Reading of Sources and Counteractions." In *Décadence: "Decline and Fall" or "Other Antiquity"?*, ed. T. Fuhrer and M. Formisano, 263–283. Heidelberg.

———. 2014c. "Iamblichus, De Anima 38 (66,12–15 Finamore-Dillon): A Resolving Conjecture?" *Rheinisches Museum* 157:106–111.

———. 2014d. "The Divine as Inaccessible Object of Knowledge in Ancient Platonism: A Common Philosophical Pattern across Religious Traditions." *Journal of the History of Ideas* 75.2:167–188.

———. 2014e. "Valuing Antiquity in Antiquity by Means of Allegoresis." In *Valuing the Past in the Greco-Roman World. Penn-Leiden Colloquium on Ancient Values VII*, ed. J. Ker and C. Pieper, 485–507. Leiden.

———. 2015a. "Ethos and Logos: A Second-Century Apologetical Debate between 'Pagan' and Christian Philosophers." *Vigiliae Christianae* 69.2:123–156.

———. 2015b. *Evagrius' Kephalaia Gnostika: A New Translation of the Unreformed Text from the Syriac*. Atlanta, GA.

———. 2015c. *Evagrius's Kephalaia Gnostika: Monographic Essay, New Readings from the Ms., Translation, and Commentary*. Leiden.

———. 2015d. "Proclus and Christian Neoplatonism: A Case Study." In *The Ways of Byzantine Philosophy*, ed. Mikonja Knežević, 37–70. Alhambra, CA.

———. 2015e. "The Relevance of Patristic Exegesis to Contemporary Biblical Hermeneutics." *Religion and Theology* 22:100–132.

———. 2016a. "Patristic Philosophy: A Critical Study." *International Journal of the Platonic Tradition* 10:95–108.

———. 2016b. *Social Justice and the Legitimacy of Slavery: The Role of Philosophical Asceticism from Ancient Judaism to Late Antiquity*. Oxford.

———. 2017a. "Gregory Nyssen's and Evagrius's Biographical and Theological Relations: Origen's Heritage and Neoplatonism." In *Evagrius Between Origen, the Cappadocians, and Neoplatonism: Papers Presented at the Seventeenth International Conference on Patristic Studies Held in Oxford 2015*, ed. I. L. E. Ramelli, K. Corrigan, and M. Tobon, 165–231. Bd. 10. Studia Patristica 84. Leuven.

———. 2017b. "Origen and the Platonic Tradition." In *Plato and Christ: Platonism in Early Christian Theology*, ed. J. Warren Smith, 8.2:21. doi: 10.3390/rel8020021.

———. 2017c. "Origen to Evagrius." In *A Companion to the Reception of Plato in Antiquity* (ed. H. Tarrant, et al.) 271–291. Leiden.

———. 2019. "The Dialogue of Adamantius: Preparing the Critical Edition and a Reappraisal." *Rheinisches Museum* 62:1–25.

———. Forthcoming (a). "The Logos/Nous One-Many between 'Pagan' and Christian Platonism." Lecture, British Patristics Conference, Cardiff University, 5–7 September 2018. *Studia Patristica*.

———. Forthcoming (b). "Origen, Evagrios, and Dionysios." In *The Oxford Handbook to Dionysius the Areopagite*, ed. M. Edwards, D. Pallis, and G. Steiris, Oxford.

———. In preparation. *Origen of Alexandria's Philosophical Theology: A Chapter in the History of Platonism.*

Ramelli, I., and D. Konstan, eds. 2009. *Hierocles the Stoic: Elements of Ethics, Fragments, and Excerpts.* SBL Writings from the Greco-Roman World 28. Atlanta.

Ramirez Corria, F. 1964. "Platon y la historia del zoospermo." *Finlay* 3:19–24.

Ramsey, J. T., and A. Lewis Licht. 1997. *The Comet of 44 B.C. and Caesar's Funeral Games.* Atlanta.

Rankin, H. D. 1963. "On ΑΔΙΑΠΛΑΣΤΑ ΖΩΙΑ (Plato, *Timaeus* 91d3)." *Philologus* 107:138–145.

Rapp, C. 2012. *Aristoteles. Zur Einführung.* Hamburg.

Rasimus, T. 2009. *Paradise Reconsidered in Gnostic Mythmaking: Rethinking Sethianism in Light of the Ophite Evidence.* Nag Hammadi and Manichaean Studies 68. Leiden.

Reeve, C. D. C., trans. 1997. "Cratylus." In *Plato: Complete Work*, ed. J. M. Cooper and D. S. Hutchinson. Indianapolis.

Reitzenstein, R., ed. 1904. *Poimandres.* Leipzig.

Reller, J. 1999. "Iwannis von Dara, Mose Bar Kepha und Bar Hebräus über die Seele, traditionsgeschichtlich untersucht." In *After Bardaisan: Studies on Continuity and Change in Syriac Christianity in Honour of Professor Han J. W. Drijvers*, ed. G. J. Reinink and A. C. Klugkist, 253–268. Orientalia Lovaniensia Analecta 89. Leuven.

Remes, P. 2006. "Plotinus' Ethics of Disinterested Interest." *Journal of the History of Philosophy* 44:1–23.

———. 2007. *Plotinus on Self: The Philosophy of the 'We.'* Cambridge.

———. 2013. "Reason to Care: The Object and Structure of Self-Knowledge in *Alcibiades I*." *Apeiron* 46:270–301.

Remes, P., and S. Slaveva-Griffin, eds. 2014. *The Routledge Handbook of Neoplatonism.* London.

Renaud, F. 2014. "The Elenctic Strategies of Socrates: The Alcibiades I and the Commentary of Olympiodorus." In Layne and Tarrant 2014:118–126.

Renaud, F., and H. Tarrant. 2015. *The Platonic Alcibiades I: The Dialogue and its Ancient Reception*. Cambridge.

Respici, L. 2000. *Uomini capovolti: Le piante nel pensiero dei Greci*. Biblioteca di Cultura Moderna 1152. Bari.

Reydams-Schils, G. 1999. *Demiurge and Providence: Stoic and Platonist Readings of Plato's Timaeus*. Turnhout.

Riley, M. W. 2005. *Plato's Cratylus: Argument, Form, and Structure*. Amsterdam.

Rist, J. M. 1988. "Pseudo-Ammonius and the Soul/Body Problem in Some Platonic Texts of Late Antiquity." *American Journal of Philology* 109:402–415.

Ritner, R. K. 1993. *The Mechanics of Ancient Egyptian Magical Practice*. Chicago.

Robinson, J. M., and R. Smith, eds. 1988. *The Nag Hammadi Library in English*. New York. 3rd revised edition. Leiden. Orig. pub. 1978.

Rohmer, J. 1954. "L'intentionnalité des sensations chez Augustin." *Augustinus Magister* 1:491–498. Paris.

Rolfes, E. 1923. *Die Philosophie des Aristoteles als Naturerklaerung und Weltanschauung*. Leipzig.

Rolke, K. H. 1975. *Bildhafte Vergleiche bei den Stoikern*. Hildescheim.

Rombs, R. J. 2006. *Saint Augustine & the Fall of the Soul: Beyond O'Connell & His Critics*. Washington, DC.

Romeri, L. 2002. *Philosophes entre mots et mets: Plutarque, Lucien et Athénée autour de la table de Platon*. Grenoble.

———. 2005. "L'akolasia est en nous (Platon, Tim. 72e): deux solutions à l'intempérance humaine; Platon et Plutarque." *Kentron* 21:225–240.

Rorem, P., and J. C. Lamoreaux. 1998. *John of Scythopolis and the Dionysian Corpus*. Oxford.

Rosenmeyer, T. G. 1998. "Name-Setting and Name-Using: Elements of Foundationalism in Plato's Cratylus." *Ancient Philosophy* 18:41–60.

Ross, W. D., ed. 1936. *Aristotle's Physics*. Oxford.

———. ed. 1950. *Aristotelis Physica*. Oxford.

———. ed. 1955. *Aristotelis Fragmenta Selecta*. Oxford.

———. ed. 1961. *Aristotelis De Anima*. Oxford.

Rotondaro, S. 1997. "Il pathos della ragione e i sogni: Timeo 70d7–72b5." In Calvo and Brisson 1997:275–280.

Routila, L. 1969. *Die aristotelische Idee der ersten Philosophie. Untersuchungen zur ontotheologischen Verfassung der Metaphysik des Aristoteles*. Amsterdam.

Runia, D. T. 2001. *Philo of Alexandria: On the Creation of the Cosmos According To Moses*. Leiden.

Russell, D. 2005. *Plato on Pleasure and the Good Life*. Oxford.

Rutten, C. 1956. "La Doctrine des Deux Actes dans la Philosophie de Plotin." *Revue Philosophique* 146:100–106.

Ryle, G. 1949. *The Concept of Mind.* Chicago. Repr. 2002.

Scarry, E. 1985. *The Body in Pain: The Making and Unmaking of the World.* Oxford.

Schaff, P., and H. Wallace. 2007. *Nicene and Post-Nicene Fathers.* Second Series, Vol. 5. New York.

Scheffel, W. 1976. *Aspekte der Platonischen Kosmologie.* Leiden.

Schenke, H.-M. 1981. "The Phenomenon and Significance of Sethian Gnosticism." In *The Rediscovery of Gnosticism.* Vol. 2. *Sethian Gnosticism,* ed. B. Layton, Studies in the History of Religions 41. Leiden.

Schibille, N. 2009. "Astronomical and Optical Principles in the Architecture of Hagia Sophia in Constantinople." *Science in Context* 22.1:27–46.

Schmitz, H. 1985. *Die Ideenlehre des Aristoteles.* 3 vols. Bonn.

Scholten, C. 2015. *Theodoret: De Graecarum Affectionum Curatione. Heilung der griechischen Krankheiten.* Supplements to Vigiliae Christianae 126. Leiden.

Schröder, H. O., ed. 1934. *Galeni In Platonis Timaeum Commentaria Fragmenta.* Corpus Medicorum Graecorum Suppl. I. Leipzig.

Schüssler, I. 1982. *Aristoteles, Philosophie und Wissenschaft.* Frankfurt.

Schwyzer, H.-R. 1974. "Plotinisches und Unplotinisches in den *APHORMAI* des Porphyrios." In *Plotino e il Neoplatonismo in Oriente e in Occidente,* Atti del Convegno di Roma promosso dall' Academia Nazionale dei Lincei, 221–252. Rome.

Scolnicov, S. 1997. "Freedom and Education in Plato's Timaeus." In Calvo and Brisson 1997:363–374.

Scott, M. S. M. 2012. *Journey Back to God: Origen on the Problem of Evil.* Oxford.

Scott, W. B. 1936. *Hermetica* 4:9–27. Oxford.

Scribano, S. 2007. "Spunti e riflessioni in margine alla concezione platonica della riproduzione umana: Per un commento a Tim. 90e6-91d5." In *La sapienza di Timeo: Riflessioni in margine al Timeo di Platone* (ed. L. M. Napolitano Valditara) 379–402. Milan.

Sedley, D. 1997. "'Becoming Like God' in the Timaeus and Aristotle." In Calvo and Brisson 1997:327–339.

———. 1998. "The Etymologies in Plato's Cratylus." *Journal of Hellenic Studies* 118:140–154.

———. 2010. "Hesiod's Theogony and Plato's Timaeus." In *Plato and Hesiod,* ed. G. R. Boys-Stones and J. H. Haubold, 246–259. Oxford.

Seel, G. 1982. *Die Aristotelische Modaltheorie.* Berlin.

Segal, A. 1980. "Heavenly Ascent in Hellenistic Judaism, Early Christianity and their Environment." *Aufstieg und Niedergang der römische Welt.* Part II 23.2:1332–1394.

Seminar Classics 609, trans., 1969. *Porphyry. The Cave of the Nymphs in the Odyssey*. Arethusa Monographs 1. Buffalo, NY.

Sharples, R. W. 2008. *Alexander Aphrodisiensis: De Anima Libri Mantissa*. Peripatoi 21. Berlin.

Sharples, R. W., and P. J. van der Eijk, trans. 2008. *Nemesius: On the Nature of Man*. Translated Texts for Historians 49. Liverpool.

Shaw, G. 2012. "The Role of Aesthesis in Theurgy." In *Iamblichus and the Foundations of Late Platonism*, ed. E. Afonasin, J. Dillon, J. Finamore, 91–112. Leiden.

Sheppard, A. 2007. "Porphyry's Views on Phantasia." In Karamanolis and Sheppard, 2007:71–76. London.

Shields, C., ed. 2003. *The Blackwell Guide to Ancient Philosophy*. London.

Simmons, M. B. 2009. "Porphyry's Universalism: A Tripartite Soteriology and Eusebius' Response." *Harvard Theological Review* 102:169–192.

———. 2015. *Universal Salvation in Late Antiquity: Porphyry of Tyre and the Pagan-Christian Debate*. Oxford.

Singer, P. N., ed. 2013. *Galen: Psychological Writings*. Cambridge.

Sinkewicz, R. 2003. *Evagrius of Pontus. The Greek Ascetic Corpus*. Oxford Early Christian Studies Series. New York.

Siorvanes, L. 1996. *Proclus: Neo-Platonic Philosophy and Science*. New Haven, CT.

Sisko, J. E. 2006. "Cognitive Circuitry in the Pseudo-Hippocratic Peri Diaites and Plato's Timaeus." *Hermathena* 180:5–17.

Skemp, J. B. 1947. "Plants in Plato's Timaeus." *Classical Quarterly* 41:53–60.

Slaveva-Griffin, S. 2009. *Plotinus on Number*. Oxford.

———. 2010. "Medicine in the Life and Works of Plotinus." *Papers of the Langford Latin Seminar* 14:93–117.

———. 2014. "Plotinian Motifs in the Pseudo-Galenic De Spermate." In *Neoplatonic Questions*, ed. J. M. Zamora Calvo, 9–42. Berlin.

———. 2018. "Herakles' Thirteenth Labor." In *At the Crossroads of Graeco-Roman History, Culture, and Religion: Papers in Memory of Carin M. C. Green*, ed. S. W. Bell and L. L. Holland, 1–17. Oxford.

Sleeman, J. H., and G. Pollet, eds. 1980. *Lexicon Plotinianum*. Leiden.

Smith, A. 1974. *Porphyry's Place in the Neoplatonic Tradition*. The Hague.

———. 1984. "Did Porphyry Reject the Transmigration of Souls into Animals?" *Rheinisches Museum* 127:277–284.

———. ed. 1993. *Porphyrii Philosophi Fragmenta*. Stuttgart.

———. 1996. "Dunamis in Plotinus and Porphyry." In *Dunamis nel Neoplatonismo*, F. Romano and R. L. Cardullo, 63–77. Florence.

———. 2004. *Philosophy in Late Antiquity*. London.

Smith, M. A. 1931. *The Works of Aristotle: De Anima*. Oxford.

Smith, R. R. R. 2000. "Nero and the Sun-god: Divine Accessories and Political Symbols in Roman Imperial Images." *Journal of Roman Archaeology* 13:532–542.

Smith, W. D. 1979. *The Hippocratic Tradition*. Ithaca, NY.

Smyth, H. W. 1984. *Greek Grammar*. Cambridge, MA.

Söder, J. 2010. "Die Selbstmächtigkeit des Menschen: Nemesios von Emesa über das freie Entscheidungsvermögen." In *Wille und Handlung in der Philosophie der Kaiserzeit und Spätantike*, ed. J. Müller and R. Hofmeister Pich, 259–275. Beiträge zur Altertumskunde 287. Berlin.

Solmsen, F. 1957. "The Vital Heat, the Inborn Pneuma and the Aether." *Journal of Hellenic Studies* 77.1:119–123.

———. 1968a. "Greek Philosophy and the Discovery of the Nerves." *Kleine Schriften*. Vol. 1:536–582. Hildesheim.

———. 1968b. *Kleine Schriften* 1. Hildesheim.

Somers, H. 1961. "Image de Dieu. Les sources de l'exégèse augustinienne." *Revue des études augusiniennes* 7:105–125.

Song, E. 2013. "Ashamed of Being in the Body? Plotinus versus Porphyry." In *Plato Revived: Essays on Ancient Platonism in Honour of Dominic J. O'Meara*, ed. F. Karfík and E. Song, Berlin.

Sorabji, R. 1980. *Necessity, Cause and Blame: Perspectives on Aristotle's Theory*. London.

———. 2005. *The Philosophy of the Commentators 200–600 AD: A Sourcebook*. Volume 1: *Psychology (with Ethics and Religion)*. Ithaca, NY.

Spaemann, R., and R. Low. 1981. *Die Frage Wozu? Geschichte und Wiederentdeckung des teleologischen Denkens*. Munich.

Speidel, M. 2012. "Making Use of History Beyond the Euphrates." In *Mara bar Serapion in Context*, ed. A. Merz and T. Tieleman, 11–41. Leiden.

Speliopoulos, L. 1997. "La physiologie de la vision dans le Timée de Platon." *Deucalion* 15:247–266.

Sperling, G. 1999. *Das Pantheon in Rom: Abbild und Mass des Kosmos*. Munich.

Stavrianeas, S. 2008. "Spontaneous Generation in Aristotle's Biology." *Rhizai* 5.2:303–338.

Stead, G. C. 1964. "The Platonism of Arius." *Journal of Theological Studies* 15:16–31.

Stenzel, J. 1931. *Metaphysik des Altertums*. Munich.

Sterling, G. E. 1993. "Platonizing Moses: Philo and Middle Platonism." *Studia Philonica Annual* 5:96–111.

Stocks, J. L. 1922. *Aristotle: De Caelo*. Oxford.

Stolzenberg, D. 1999. "Unpropitious Tinctures: Alchemy, Astrology & Gnosis According To Zosimos of Panopolis." *Archives internationales d' histoire des sciences* 142:3–31.

Streck, M. 2005. *Das schönste Gut: Der menschliche Wille bei Nemesius von Emesa und Gregor von Nyssa.* Forschungen zur Kirchen—und Dogmengeschichte 88. Göttingen.

Stroumsa, G. 2005. *La fin du sacrifice.* Paris.

———. 2016. *The Scriptural Universe of Ancient Christianity.* Cambridge, MA.

Struck, P. 2003. "Viscera and the Divine: Dreams as the Divinatory Bridge Between the Corporeal and the Incorporeal." In *Prayer, Magic, and the Stars in the Ancient and Late Antique World*, ed. S. B. Noegel, J. T. Walker, and B. Wheeler, 125–136. University Park, PA.

Strutwolf, H. 2001. "Interpretatio Graeca. Selbstverständnis und Polemik im Konflikt der Weltanschauungen des 4. Und 5. Jahrhunderts." In *Christen und Nichtchristen in Spätantike, Neuzeit, und Gegenwart*, ed. W. Kinzing and M. Vinzent, 23–40. Mandelbach.

Talley, T. J. 1991. *The Origins of the Liturgical Year.* New York.

Tanaseanu-Döbler, I. 2009. "'Nur der Weise ist Priester': Rituale und Ritualkritik bei Porphyrios." In *Religion und Kritik in der Antike*, ed. I. Tanaseanu-Döbler and U. Berner, 113–116. Münster.

Tarán, L. 1975. "Academica: Plato, Philip of Opus, and the Pseudo-Platonic Epinomis." *Memoirs of the American Philosophical Society* 107. Philadelphia, PA.

Tarrant, H. 1993. *Thrasyllan Platonism.* Ithaca, NY.

———. 2007. *Proclus' Commentary on Plato's Timaeus.* Cambridge.

———. 2010. "Platonism before Plotinus." In *The Cambridge History of Philosophy in Late Antiquity* (ed. L. Gerson) 1:66–97. Cambridge.

———. 2014. "Platonist Curricula and their Influence." In *The Routledge Handbook of Neoplatonism*, ed. P. Remes and S. Slaveva-Griffin, 15–29. London.

———. 2017. "Plotinus, Origenes, and Ammonius on the King." In *Religio-Philosophical Discourses Within the Greco-Roman, Jewish and Early Christian World*, ed. A. K. Petersen and G. van Kooten, 323–337. Leiden.

Taylor, R. 1979. "Persons and Bodies." *American Philosophical Quarterly* 16:67–72.

Telfer, W. 1955. *Cyril of Jerusalem and Nemesius of Emesa.* The Library of Christian Classics 4. London.

TeSelle, E. 1974. "Porphyry and Augustine." *Augustinian Studies* 5:131–133.

Teske, R. J. 1991. "St. Augustine's View of the Original Human Condition in the De Genesi Contra Manichaeos." *Augustinian Studies* 22:141–155.

———. 1992. "Origen and St. Augustine's First Commentaries on Genesis." In *Origeniana Quinta*, ed. R. J. Daly, 179–185. Louvain.

———. 1994. "St. Augustine and the Vision of God." In *Augustine: Mystic and Mystagogue*, ed. F. Van Fleteren, et al., 287–308. New York.

The Universe: Ancient Mysteries Solved—Roman Engineering. 2015. The History Channel.

Theiler, W. 1965. *Zur Geschichte der teleologischen Naturbetrachtung bis auf Aristoteles.* 2nd ed. Berlin.

———. 1966a. *Forschungen zum Neuplatonismus.* Berlin. Orig. pub. 1993 as *Porphyrios und Augustin.* Halle.

———. 1966b. "Gott und Seele in kaiserzeitlichen Denken." *Forschungen zum Neuplatonismus.* Berlin.

———. 1973. *Aristoteles: Über die Seele.* Berlin.

Thomassen, E. 2006. *The Spiritual Seed: The Church of the Valentinians.* Nag Hammadi and Manichaean Studies 60. Leiden.

Thomson, R. W. 1973. *Athanasius: Contra Gentes and De Incarnatione.* Oxford.

Thurn, I., ed. 2000. *Ioannis Malalae Chronographia.* Corpus Fontium Historiae Byzantinae 35. Berlin.

Tipton, J. A. 2013. *Philosophical Biology in Aristotle's Parts of Animals.* Studies in History and Philosophy of Science 26. Cham.

Todd, R. B. 1974. "Συνέντασις and the Stoic Theory of Perception." *Grazer Beiträge* 2:251–261.

Tornau, C. 2005. "Plotinus' Criticism of Aristotelian Entelechism in Enn. IV,7[2],8^5,25–50." In *Studi sull'anima in Plotino.* Elenchus 42:149–178. Naples.

Tredennick, H. 1989. "Phaedo." In Hamilton and Cairns 1989:40–98. Princeton, NJ.

Trouillard, J. 1957. "Réflexions sur l'ὄχημα dans les Éléments de théologie de Proclus." *Revue des études grecques* 70:102–107.

Turbayne, C. 1976. "Plato's 'Fantastic' Appendix: The Procreation Model of the Timaeus." *Paideia* 5:125–140.

Turcan, R. 1975. *Mithras Platonicus: Recherches sur l'hellénisation philosophique de Mithra.* Leiden.

———. 1993. *Mithra et le Mithriacisme.* Paris.

Turner, J. D. 1980. "The Gnostic Threefold Path to Enlightenment: The Ascent of Mind and the Descent of Wisdom." *Novum Testamentum* 22.

———. 2001. *Sethian Gnosticism and the Platonic Tradition.* Bibliothèque copte de Nag Hammadi, section Études 6. Québec.

———. 2007. "The Book of Thomas and the Platonic Jesus." In *L'évangile selon Thomas et les textes de Nag Hammadi: Québec du 29-31 mai 2003*, ed. L. Painchaud and P.-H. Poirier, Bibliothèque copte de Nag Hammadi section Études 8. Québec.

Tzamalikos, P. 1991. *The Concept of Time in Origen.* New York.

———. 2006. *Origen: Cosmology and Ontology of Time.* Leiden.

———. 2007. *Origen: Philosophy of History and Eschatology.* Leiden.

———. 2012. *The Real Cassian Revisited*. Leiden.

Ulansey, D. 1989. *The Origins of the Mithraic Mysteries: Cosmology and Salvation in the Ancient World*. New York.

Urbano, A. 2013. *The Philosophical Life: Biography and the Crafting of Intellectual Identity in Late Antiquity*. Washington, DC.

Uthemann, K.-H., 2015. *Anastasios Sinaites: Byzantinisches Christentum in den ersten Jahrzehnten unter arabischer Herrschaft*. Arbeiten zur Kirchengeschichte 125/1–2. Berlin.

Vaggione, R. P., ed. 1987. *Eunomius: The Extant Works*. Oxford.

van den Berg, R. M. 2008. *Proclus' Commentary on the Cratylus in Context*. Leiden.

Van Den Kerchove, A. 2012. *La voie d'Hermès*. Leiden.

van Riel, G. 2010. "Damascius." In Gerson 2010:2.667–696.

van Riel, G., and P. Destrée, eds. 2009. *Ancient Perspectives on Aristotle's De Anima*. Leuven.

Vanhamel, W. 1982. "Némésius d' Émèse." *Dictionnaire de spiritualité* 11:92–99.

Vanni Rovighi, S. 1962. "La fenomenologia della sensazione in Sant' Agostino." *Rivista di filosofia neo-scolastica* 54:18–32.

Vaschalde, A. 1932. *Iacobi Edesseni Hexaemeron seu in opus creationis libri septem*. Corpus Scriptorum Christianorum Orientalium 97, Scriptores Syri 56. Leuven.

Verbeke, G. 1945. *L'évolution de la doctrine du pneuma du stoïcisme à S. Augustin: Étude philosophique*. Paris.

Vermaseren, M. J., ed. 1956. *Corpus inscriptionum et monumentorum religionis Mithriacae*. The Hague.

Viltanioti, I. F. 2017. "Divine Powers and Cult Statues in Porphyry of Tyre." In *Divine Powers in Late Antiquity*, ed. A. Marmodoro and I. F. Viltanioti, 61–73. Oxford.

Vlastos, G. 1981. "Plato's Supposed Theory of Irregular Atomic Figures." In *Platonic Studies*, 2nd ed., ed. G. Vlastos, 366–373. Princeton, NJ.

———. 1995. *Studies in Greek Philosophy*. Vol. 2: *Socrates, Plato, and their Tradition*. Ed. D. W. Graham. Princeton, NJ.

Voisin, J-L. 1987. "Exoriente Sole (Suétone, Ner. 6). D'Alexandrie à la Domus Aurea." In *L'Urbs: Espace urbain et histoire (1er siècle av. J.-C. – IIIe siècle ap. J.-C.)* . Publications de l'École Française de Rome 98:509–543. Rome.

Volk, K. 2004. "'Heavenly Steps': Manilius 4.119–121 and Its Background." In *Heavenly Realms and Earthly Realities in Late Antique Religions*, ed. R. Boustan and A. Yoshiko Reed, 34–46. Cambridge.

von Arnim, H. F. 1887. "Quelle der Überlieferung über Ammonius Sakkas." *Rheinisches Museum* 42:276–285.

———. 1931. *Die Entstehung der Gotteslehre des Aristoteles*. Vienna.

von Balthasar, H. U. 1939a. "Die Hiera des Evagrius." *Zeitschrift für katholische Theologie* 63:86–106 and 181–206.

———. 1939b. "Metaphysik und Mysik des Evagrius Pontikus." *Zeitschrift für Askese und Mystik* 14:31–47.

von Lieven, A. 2000. *Der Himmel über Esna*. Wiesbaden.

Voss, B. R. 1963. "Spuren von Porphyrios 'De regressu animae' bei Augustin 'De vera religione.'" *Museum Helveticum* 20:237–239.

Wallis, R. E., trans. 1869. *The Writings of Cyprian, Bishop of Carthage*. Vol. 2. Edinburgh.

Walpole, A. S., ed. 1922. *Early Latin Hymns: With Introduction and Notes*. Cambridge. Repr. 1966. Hildesheim.

Walsh, P. G., trans. 1995. *Apuleius: The Golden Ass*. Oxford.

Watts, E. 2005. "Where to Live the Philosophical Life in the Sixth Century? Damascius, Simplicius, and the Return from Persia." *Greek, Roman, and Byzantine Studies* 45:285–315.

———. 2006. *City and School in Late Antique Athens and Alexandria*. Berkeley.

Wehrli, F., ed. 1969. *Herakleides Pontikos: Die Schule des Aristoteles*. Vol. 7, 2nd ed. Basel.

Wellmann, M. 1900. "Cornelius Celsus." *Paulys Realencyclopädie* IV.7:1273–1276.

Wendland, P., ed. 1962. *Philonis Alexandrinis Opera Quae Supersunt*. 2 vols. Berlin.

Westerink, L. G., ed. 1956. *Olympiodorus: Commentary of the First Alcibiades of Plato, Critical Text and Indices*. Amsterdam.

Westerink, L. G., and J. Combès, eds. 1989. *Damascius: Traité des premiers principes*. Vol. 2. *De la Triade et de l'Unifié*. Paris.

Whittaker, J., ed. 1996. "The Terminology of the Rational Soul in the Writings of Philo of Alexandria." *Studia Philonica Annual* 8:1–20.

Whittaker, J., and P. Louis, eds. and trans. 1990. *Alcinoos: Enseignement des doctrines de Platon*. Paris.

Wijsenbeek-Wijler, H. 1978. *Aristotle's Concept of Soul, Sleep and Dreams*. Amsterdam.

Wilberding, J. 2011. *Porphyry: To Gaurus On How Embryos are Ensouled and On What is in Our Power*. London.

———. 2014. "Neoplatonism and Medicine." In Remes and Slaveva-Griffin 2014:356–371.

Wildberg, C. 2008. "Olympiodorus." In *The Stanford Encyclopedia of Philosophy* (ed. E. N. Zalta) plato.stanford.edu/archives/fall2008/entries/olympiodorus.

Wiles, M. F. 1962. "In Defense of Arius." *Journal of Theological Studies* 13:339–347.

Williams, N. P. 1927. *The Ideas of the Fall and Original Sin*. Oxford.

Williams, R. 2003. *Wound of Knowledge: Christian Spirituality from the New Testament to St. John of the Cross*. Cambridge.

Wilson, R. J. A. 2011. "Neue Forschungen an der Domus Aurea." *Antike Welt* 5:6.

Winston, D., trans. 1981. *Philo of Alexandria: The Contemplative Life, the Giants, and Selections.* Mahwah.

Wright, M. R., ed. 2000. *Reason and Necessity: Essays on Plato's Timaeus.* London.

Wulf, S. 2013. *Zeit der Musik: Vom Hören der Wahrheit in Augustinus' De Musica.* München.

Yates, F. A. 1966. *The Art of Memory.* Chicago.

Yli-Karjanmaa, S. 2015. *Reincarnation in Philo of Alexandria.* Atlanta, GA.

Young, F. M. 2006. "Monotheism and Christology." In *The Cambridge History of Christianity: Origins to Constantine,* ed. M. M. Mitchell and F. M. Young, 452–469. Cambridge.

Zachhuber, J. 2000. *Human Nature in Gregory of Nyssa.* Leiden.

Zago, M. 2010. *Tebe magica et alchemica.* Padova.

Zambon, M. 2002. *Porphyre et le moyen-platonisme.* Paris.

Zeyl, D. J., trans. 2000. *Plato: Timaeus.* Indianapolis.

Zonta, M. 1991. "Nemesiana Syriaca: New Fragments from the Missing Syriac Version of the *De Natura Hominis.*" *Journal of Semitic Studies* 36.2:223–258.

———. 2014. "Iwânnīs of Dârâ's Treatise on the Soul and Its Sources: A New Contribution to the History of Syriac Psychology around 800 AD." In *De l'Antiquité Tardive au Moyen Âge: Études de logique aristotélicienne et de philosophie grecque, syriaque, arabe et latine offertes à Henri Hugonnard-Roche,* ed. E. Coda and C. Martini Bonadeo, 113–122. Études musulmanes 44. Paris.

Index of Passages Cited

General Index

accident, 315

act(ing), activity (*energeia, actus*), 6, 168, 178, 181, 261, 263, 329–330; Demiurge's, 224, 269; of first cause, 42; individual soul's, 16–18, 55, 60; Intellect's, 269; intellectual, 20, 22, 89, 143; intelligible, 267

action, 15, 52–53, 183–186, 190, 223, 263, 338

actuality, 36–37, 44, 52, 92, 255, 258–259, 352

Aeneas of Gaza, 300, 350, 358, 359

Aeons, aeonic, 92, 97, 98, 102, 104, 105, 283

aether (*aithêr*), 27–28, 51–52, 53

Aëtius of Antioch, 196

Aëtius, philosopher, 357, 359

affections (*pathê*), 34, 48, 70, 83–84, 116, 123–125, 164, 186, 258–259, 326; absence of (*apatheia*), 140, 396. *See also* perception

agent, 31, 85, 118, 172–174, 181, 183, 191, 239, 256, 263, 266

Ahudemmeh, 350

air: in the body, 10, 12, 39, 321, 328–329; as cause of illness, 12; as a living environment, 6, 17, 19, 20, 22, 82; as a primary element, 4, 8–9, 11, 14, 27, 73, 160, 162

Albinus (Platonist), 56, 68, 74, 86

Alcinous, 70–89

alchemy, 193–196, 213–214

Alcmaeon of Croton, 34

Alexander of Aphrodisias, 255, 288, 294, 354, 357

allegory (*allêgorêsis*), allegorizers, 56, 206, 210, 227, 285, 396

Ammonius Saccas, 352, 354, 357–359, 399, 400

Anastasius of Antioch, 341

Anastasius of Sinai, 306, 340, 346–347

angels. *See* daemons

animal(s), 6, 17–19, 20–22, 35, 39, 42–43, 83, 93, 94–95, 145, 176, 177–182, 226, 257, 284, 299–300, 313, 317, 322, 327, 333–334, 336; activities, 180–181; and anatomical experiments, 60; bodies, 296–297, 300–302, 352, 354; as living being (*to zôion*), 4, 71, 116, 121, 178; man (*homo animalis, appetitus*), 331; mortal rational (*animal rationale mortale*), 313; part (*animalis pars*), 332; and reproduction, 30–31; sacrifices, 141; world/kingdom, species, 3, 28–29, 31–32, 73. *See also* metensô-matôsis

animatio, 322

Anonymous Work in Syriac, 343

anthropogony, 91

John of Dara, 350
John of Scythopolis, 358
John Lydus, 398
John Malalas, 360
John Philoponus, 51, 74
John, the Baptist, 383
Justin, 242
Justinian, 279, 280, 283, 293, 348
knowledge, 124–127, 211–213, 227; a
    priori, 324; about the body, 129;
    intellectual, 4, 18; inward, 242;
    objects of, 84, 157; possession of,
    37; process of, 222–223; self-, 86,
    93, 94–95, 97, 109, 175, 179, 183,
    189
Leontius of Byzantium, 345, 347
life (*vita*): *passim;* appetitive, 303;
    ascetic, 92; beatific, 314; breath
    of, 331; concept/principle of,
    xxviii, 29–30, 36–46; human/
    mortal, 13, 71, 76–77, 83–85, 89,
    99, 140, 145; immaterial, 195;
    intellectual, 79, 165; moral, 156;
    of the gods, 80; philosopher's,
    xxiii–xxiv, 143; political/civic,
    173, 183, 186, 189; rational/
    irrational, 14, 159, 164, 166–168;
    return to, 211, 213; Spirit of, 106;
    spiritual, 385
liver, 14, 56, 57, 60, 262, 263, 265
living being(s) (*to zôion, ta zôia*),
    xxviii, 3, 4–7, 11, 20–23, 34, 116,
    123, 181–184, 223; perfect, 27;
    scale of, 18, 22; types of, 22, 43
localised (*localiter*), 316
logismos, 223–228
logos, ratio, 294–295, 305, 396; enmat-
    tered, 255–256, 261; God's, 290,
    292, 398; intellect, 239; Son as,
    238, 246, 280, 292
Lucan, 373–374, 380, 385
Lucian of Samosata, 198, 199
Macrina, 299

Macrobius, 360, 383
Manichaeanism/Manichaeans,
    301–303, 309
marrow. *See* bone
Maximus of Tyre, 67
Maximus the Confessor, 278, 282, 298,
    340–341, 346
meaning (*significatio*), 317–318
medial place (*medietas*), 333
medicine, 13, 15, 57, 86, 127, 129, 188,
    263, 271, 329; temporal, 337
memory (*memoria*), 267–268, 313,
    322; from an earlier existence,
    79; faculty of, 78, 141, 144–152,
    319; of higher objects, 16. *See also*
    recollection
metallurgy, 163
metaphor, 179, 210, 219–222, 228,
    229, 230, 306, 310, 312, 314,
    355; chariot, 6, 56, 70, 228, 230;
    puppet, 219; of soul, 219–222,
    228–229, 230, 310, 312, 314
metensômatôsis, 20–23, 277–278,
    282–284, 288, 294–306
Methodius, 294, 297
Michael Glykas, 340
Michael Rabo, 282
mind (*mens*), 224, 312, 332; active 260;
    -body relation, 302; body-soul-,
    xxix–xxx, 50, 253–257, 263–275;
    divine, 92, 93, 221; God's, 278,
    280; human, 221, 226; individual,
    78, 227; release/autonomy from
    corporeality, 222, 313; self within
    the self, 85; soul-, 260, 262, 350;
    as spring, 220
Mithraic cult, mystery, 364, 369–370,
    374
Mithras, 364, 366–369, 385
Moderatus of Gades, 68
moisture, wetness, 8, 85, 138, 151,
    152, 162, 164, 264, 366
Monophysite(s), 345–346, 348

psychology, *passim*; Aristotelian, 34;
   Christian, xxix; memory, corporeality, 144–152; (Neo)Platonic/
   Platonist, xxiii–xxiv, xxix, 54,
   111, 115, 352; and ritual, 141–144;
   religious, xxv, 217; Stoic, 134, 221,
   231. *See also* soul
punishment (*kolasis, supplicium*), 95,
   113–114, 146–147, 212–213, 279,
   281, 333–334, 336
purification, xxiii, 87, 143, 150, 184,
   185, 323
Pythagorean/Pythagoreanism, 52, 77,
   363, 366, 398
qualities, 6, 33, 173, 176, 178, 185,
   259, 289; of bodies 165, 255, 256,
   293–295, 299; of human nature,
   306; of the natural/physical
   world, 27, 36, 94, 256; of souls 156
quantity, 6, 12, 33, 318; of soul,
   320–323, 324
rational: Creator-God, 77; crea-
   tures/beings, 223, 271, 279–281,
   284–286, 289–295, 298, 303,
   306–307, 313, 348; discourse, 176;
   faculty, activities, ability, 85, 172
   179–181; power, 18, 22, 264; principles (*logoi*), 99, 149. *See also* soul
reascent, 288
reason (*logos, ratio*), 70, 77, 165, 188,
   227, 265, 272, 327, 332
reasoning (*logismos*), 223–228
rebirth. *See metensômatôsis*
receptacle, 76, 103, 267
recollection (*anamnêsis*), 79, 140, 144,
   324, 352. *See also* memory
redemption, 88–89, 98, 247
reincarnation. *See metensômatôsis*
reproduction. *See* generation
resurrection, 100, 247, 264, 282, 284,
   293–295, 297, 307, 325, 389, 400;
   of Christ, 246

retribution, 8, 17, 20–21, 23
return (*apogenesis, regressus*), 83, 94,
   98, 142, 165, 211, 213, 283, 314,
   363–364
rhythms (*numeri*), 328
ritual, 141–144, 363–364
sacrifice, 141, 144, 146, 204, 208, 210.
   See also ritual
sage (*sophos, sapiens*), 226, 313
salvation, 65, 86–89, 93, 95, 98–101,
   107, 109, 142, 213, 246, 249, 314,
   334, 336–337, 338
sameness: circle of, 7
Savior, 95, 97–98, 100, 104, 197, 245,
   299
seed (*sperma*): atoms as, 34; biolog-
   ical/physiological, 10–11, 96, 104,
   151; of Seth, 104; spiritual, 98;
   universal, 96
seeing (*visus*), 329
"self," 65, 73–74, 85–86, 94, 95, 107,
   112, 115, 120–121, 148, 173, 175,
   187–188, 195, 214, 258, 273, 311
self-control, -knowledge (*sôphrosunê*),
   86, 93, 94, 97, 109, 175, 183–184,
   189, 191
Seneca, 221
sensations (*aisthêseis*), 15, 39, 83, 164,
   328, 348
serpent(s), snake, 32, 204, 228, 229,
   333; flesh of, 210
Severus, 49, 60–62, 68
sexual organs, 11–12, 20
signs (*sêmata, signa*), 19, 23, 113, 127,
   130, 199, 335; solstitial, 370
Simplicius, 96
sin, failure, guilt (*hamartia, peccatum*),
   16, 85, 91, 98, 145, 239, 249, 264,
   280, 284–286, 291, 292, 305–306,
   311, 325, 330, 331–332, 333, 335,
   336
sinew(s), 8, 12, 53, 180, 321